World Archaeology

Volume 1 No 1
June 1969

This issue

Recent work and new approaches

World Archaeology

Volume 1 No 1 June 1969

Published thrice yearly by the proprietors
Routledge & Kegan Paul Ltd
68–74 Carter Lane, London EC4

Printed in Great Britain by
The Camelot Press Ltd, London and Southampton

Contents

page
iv Editorial note

1 Studies of early culture in East Africa
Glynn Ll. Isaac

29 Problems in Indian archaeology, and methods and techniques adopted to tackle them
H. D. Sankalia

41 Recent work in West Africa: new light on the Nok Culture
Bernard Fagg

51 The origins of western and eastern Slav towns
Witold Hensel

61 The Centre for Medieval Archaeological Research, University of Caen
Michel de Bouard

68 Some problems and methods in statistical archaeology
David G. Kendall

77 Some techniques for the evaluation of archaeological magnetometer surveys
Irwin Scollar

90 Searching for structure within multivariate archaeological data
F. R. Hodson

106 A rectangular Early La Tène Marnian house at Chassemy (Aisne)
Ralph M. Rowlett, Elsebet S.-J. Rowlett, Michel Boureux

Editorial Note

World Archaeology is a new journal, international in range and in scholarship. Deliberately flexible in approach, and admitting no restriction of period or of place, the journal aims to synthesize the best contemporary thought on matters of common interest to archaeologists the world over. It is the voice, essentially, of a fresh generation of professional archaeologists. But its appeal is as much to the wide, interested public for which archaeology has become something more than a passing enthusiasm, something less than a deliberate vocation.

While no work of outstanding importance will be refused a place in the journal, *World Archaeology* is designedly a journal of debate, not of record. Individual issues will be planned, for the most part, about a central theme. They will treat, in the numbers already projected, problems of chronology and technique, methodology and culture. They will reflect a broad range of opinions, drawing widely on the experience of different disciplines and on the practice of varying schools.

The first issue of the new journal appears under the broad heading 'Recent Work and New Approaches'. It treats, as its successors will do, topics of general interest in the company of specialist comment and report. New work on the archaeology of Africa is viewed in analytical outline by Glynn Isaac and Bernard Fagg. Professor Hensel, on the Polish evidence, presents an archaeological interpretation of urban origins in Eastern Europe. Recently developed methods of research, currently in use in India and in France, are described by Professors Sankalia and de Bouard. A statistical approach to sequence-dating is presented by Professor Kendall, and computer techniques in archaeological survey and data evaluation are discussed by Irwin Scollar and Roy Hodson. Dr Rowlett's important paper on his excavations at Chassemy, in France, publishes for the first time the plan of an Early La Tène Marnian house, still unparalleled elsewhere.

There have been delays, for which neither the contributors nor the present publishers are in any way to blame, in the production of this first issue of the journal. Nevertheless, it may be seen as an appropriate beginning to a series the editors believe to be of major importance to the study and understanding of archaeology as an international discipline. As such, they present it to the public.

Studies of early culture in East Africa

Glynn Ll. Isaac

The past two decades have witnessed a rising interest in prehistoric archaeology. The application of enlarged funds, rigorously conducted excavation, and imaginative new research methods, have greatly enhanced our knowledge of many segments of prehistory; in particular the understanding of two formative movements in cultural evolution has been advanced beyond all recognition. These are first, the earliest stages of tool-making in the Old World, and secondly, the antecedents of food production by agriculture in both the Old and the New Worlds. For the first time, archaeological observations of 'fossilized' cultural and behavioural patterns are replacing speculation. In both cases, the sequence of stages now appears very different from what had become widely accepted versions.

This paper reviews aspects of various investigations into early culture, which have recently been carried out in Eastern Africa. It covers material published in a series of scattered reports; but the synthesis has been made possible by the author's participation in field-work during the years 1961–5. Visits to important sites, discussions with such senior colleagues as Mrs M. D. Leakey, L. S. B. Leakey, R. L. Hay, W. W. Bishop and J. D. Clark have contributed greatly to the development of the views expressed here.

The new kinds of investigations which are enlarging our understanding of Early and Middle Pleistocene culture can conveniently be divided into the following categories:

1 Geophysical measurements of the time-scale.
2 Cross-disciplinary reconstruction of palaeo-environments and the palaeogeographic setting of archaeological evidence.
3 Exposure by excavation of patterned associations of artefacts on individual camps or activity sites.
4 Analysis of the features of sets of artefacts, each made by one group of hominids during a short period of time.

If this list strikes scholars of the European Neolithic, Bronze and Iron Ages as 'old hat', perusal of all but the most recent literature concerned with the 'Lower Palaeolithic' will rapidly show how very scarce such information had previously been. The foregoing list provides a sequence of headings for the review.

TABLE I

Geophysical data available as a basis for the chronology of the 'Lower Palaeolithic' in East Africa

Estimate of age in millions of years	Geophysical method	Material and provenance	Association with cultural entities
0·06	C^{14} date	Wood and charcoal, Kalambo Falls Floor[1]	In an Upper Acheulian occurrence
0·7	Correlation with Palaeomagnetic Reversal Chronology	Date of changeover from the Mutuyama Reversal Epoch to the Bruhnes Normal Epoch.[2] This change occurs within the Humbu Formation	*Underlies* two Lower Acheulian occurrences within the Humbu Formation[3]
1·57–1·66	Potassium argon date	Tuffs of Marker Bed A within Bed I Olduvai Gorge[4]	Interstratified with Oldowan occurrences
1·70–1·76	Potassium argon	Ignimbrite (*Nué ardente*) in Bed I Olduvai[5]	Interstratified with Oldowan occurrences
2·03–0·28	Fission track date	Ignimbrite (*Nué ardente*) in Bed I Olduvai[6]	Interstratified with Oldowan occurrences
1·92	Fission track date	Basalt within Bed I, Olduvai[7]	Stratified below the lowest known Oldowan occurrence
1·85–1·91		Tuffs within Bed I, Olduvai a few feet below the Basalt[8]	Stratified below the lowest known Oldowan occurrence

[1] Vogel and Waterbolk 1967.
[2] Cox *et al.* 1967.
[3] Isaac 1967.
[4] Runs 1045, 1050, 1062, Curtis and Evernden 1965.
[5] Runs 1043, 1053, 1057, 1058, 1179, Curtis and Evernden 1965.
[6] Fleischer *et al.* 1965.
[7] Run 1100, Curtis and Evernden 1965.
[8] Runs 1080, 1088, Curtis and Evernden 1965.

1 The time-scale

The present state of knowledge of the chronometry of the Pleistocene in East Africa, is summarized in table 1. Table 2 shows a tentative correlation of the most reliable dates with some rock stratigraphic units, fossils, and cultural stratigraphic entities. The most securely dated strata in regional sequence are three volcanic horizons in Olduvai, Bed I, dated by a series of potassium-argon measurements, which form a concordant sequence ranging from approximately 1·9 million years to 1·6 million potassium-argon years (Evernden and Curtis 1965; Hay 1967a). Since the order of magnitude of these dates has been corroborated by correlation with palaeomagnetic reversal chronology (Cox, Dalrymple and Doell 1967), longstanding archaeological scepticism about them can perhaps be relaxed. Bed I does *not* coincide with the base of the Pleistocene if, following most readings of the recommendations of the International Geological Congress of 1948, this includes the Villafranchian and equivalents.

However, the base of the Pleistocene was in fact defined in terms of rock-stratigraphic units in one regional sequence; namely the strata assigned to the Callabrian stage in its type area (Italy). Direct chronometric determinations of the age of the Callabrian formations have not yet been achieved. Correlation of micropalaeontological data and geomagnetic polarity chronology led Glass *et al.* (1967) to suggest an age of 2 million years from the Plio-Pleistocene boundary in Callabria and elsewhere. Since potassium-argon age determinations by Curtis (1967) indicate a time span extending from *c.* 3·5 million years to 1·8 million years ago for the Villafranchian, such an arrangement would necessitate placing most of the Villafranchian back into Pliocene. Other workers (e.g. Flint 1965; Savage and Curtis, in press) prefer to use the first evidences of glaciation as the basis for drawing the Plio-Pleistocene boundary. K/Ar dates for early glaciations in various parts of the world approximate to 2·7 million years (e.g. Curry 1966; Mathews and Curtis 1966; Opdyke *et al.* 1966).

Terminal occurrences of 'Lower Palaeolithic' industries in Eastern Africa have been dated only at Kalambo Falls, where Upper Acheulian artefact assemblages are associated with carbon just young enough to permit of C^{14} age determinations. A series of dates for the Acheulian and overlying horizons indicates a minimum age of *c.* 60,000 C^{14} years for the end of Acheulian occupation at that locality (Gr. N 4896 Vògel and Waterbolk 1967; Howell and Clark 1963).

Between the Olduvai Bed I dates and the Kalambo dates there lies an interval of 1·6 million years, for which chronometric data is much less satisfactory. One item of dating evidence comes from a long sedimentary sequence in the basin of Lake Natron, which lies about thirty miles to the north-west of Olduvai Gorge (plate 1) (Isaac 1965, 1967a). Here a sequence of sediments and lavas appears to span the last switchover of the polarity of the earth's magnetic field. This event is well dated by potassium-argon determinations in other parts of the world, and is placed at *c.* 0·7 million years by Cox, Dalrymple and Doell (1967). The Humbu Formation of the Peninj Group overlies the Hajaro lava which has this reversed palaeomagnetic polarity. There appears to have been no major time-lag between lava and overlying tuffaceous sediments. The Humbu Formation yielded an australopithecine mandible (*Australopithecus* cf. *boisei*) and vertebrate fossils which are provisionally correlated with those of the upper part of Bed II Olduvai. A

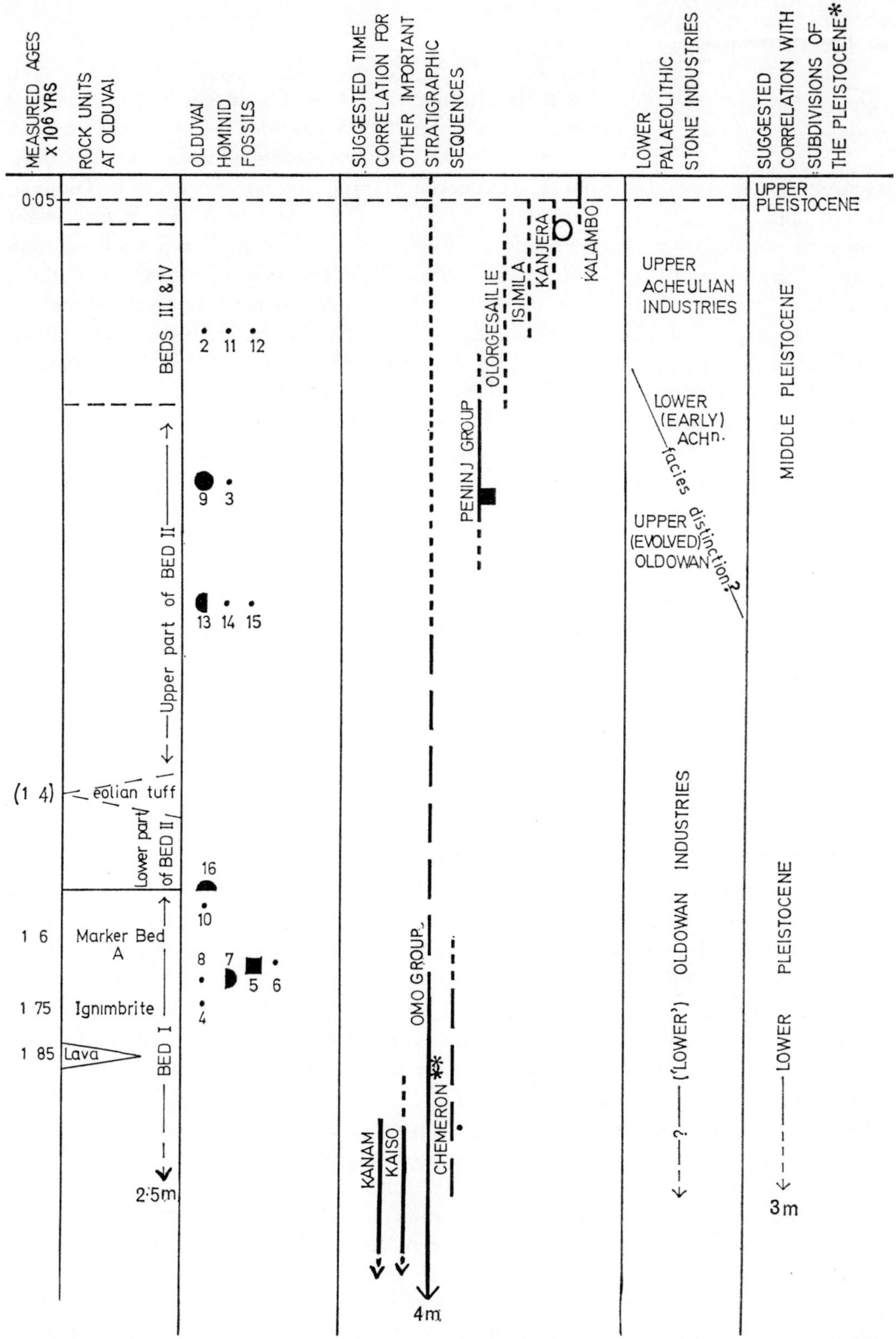
MEASURED AGES X 10⁶ YRS
ROCK UNITS AT OLDUVAI
OLDUVAI HOMINID FOSSILS
SUGGESTED TIME CORRELATION FOR OTHER IMPORTANT STRATIGRAPHIC SEQUENCES
LOWER PALAEOLITHIC STONE INDUSTRIES
SUGGESTED CORRELATION WITH SUBDIVISIONS OF THE PLEISTOCENE*
0·05
(1 4)
1 6
1 75
1 85
BEDS III &IV
Upper part of BED II
eolian tuff
Lower part of BED II
Marker Bed A
Ignimbrite
Lava
BED I
2·5m
2 11 12
9 3
13 14 15
16
10
8 7 5 6
4
KALAMBO
KANJERA
ISIMILA
OLORGESAILIE
PENINJ GROUP
OMO GROUP
CHEMERON **
KAISO
KANAM
4m
UPPER ACHEULIAN INDUSTRIES
LOWER (EARLY) ACHⁿ.
facies distinction?
UPPER (EVOLVED) OLDOWAN
('LOWER') OLDOWAN INDUSTRIES
UPPER PLEISTOCENE
MIDDLE PLEISTOCENE
LOWER PLEISTOCENE
3m

TABLE 2 (opposite)

Aspects of chronology, rock stratigraphy, hominid stratigraphy and cultural stratigraphy in East Africa

Tentative and conjectural placements of boundaries or correlated columns are indicated by dotted lines.

Key to the symbols designating fossil hominids

(i) Forms, the classification of which is widely agreed

■ *Australopithecus* (*Zinjanthropus*) *boisei*

● *Homo* (*Pithecanthropus*) *erectus*

○ *Homo cf. sapiens*

(ii) Debated classifications

◖ *Homo habilis*/*Homo erectus*

◓ *Homo habilis*/*Australopithecus*/'proto-Pithecanthropine'

◗ *Homo habilis*/*Australopithecus* sp. (cf. *africanus*)

(iii) Small fragments

* Subdivisions after INQUA 1932 (cf. Zeuner 1959) modified by the inclusion of the Villafranchian and equivalents, as recommended by Section H of the 18th International Geological Congress 1948)

** For general review of fossiliferous formations in East Africa see Cooke 1958; for Chemeron Beds, see Martyn 1967.

Lower Acheulian assemblage from slightly higher in the Formation adds strength to the correlation. At a level between the stratum containing the mandible and the strata containing the Acheulian occurrences, and at a height of 60 ft above the reversed lava, there is locally an interbedded lava flow with normal polarity.[1] This stratigraphic evidence indicates that the magnetic polarity change of 0·7 million years ago occurred during deposition of the Humbu Formation, and by extension, during the deposition of the upper part of Bed II at Olduvai.

A potassium-argon date for the upper part of Bed II has been widely quoted. This was first reported in Leakey, Evernden and Curtis (1961) as 0·36 million years, and was later amended to 0·5 million years (Evernden and Curtis 1965, run 405, 405a). Although this result is reasonable in terms of stratigraphic 'dead reckoning', the position of the source horizon in the sequence is uncertain. The horizon could not be relocated, and the date should consequently be discarded (R. L. Hay 1967b: 226). Dates of about 1 million years for the top of Bed I (Leakey *et al.* 1961) were based on contaminated specimens from mis-correlated horizons (Hay 1963; Evernden and Curtis 1965). Hay (pers. comm.)

[1] Potassium-argon determinations on the samples of the highly vesicular (reversed) Hajaro lava proved impossible, and a single run on the lava with normal polarity gave a result quoted as 1·4–1·6 (G. H. Curtis 1967.). This date was considered anomalous in relation to geomagnetic reversal chronology. Subsequent discovery of numerous minor polarity events renders the estimate more acceptable.

estimates by extrapolation of sedimentation rates, dates of 2·5 million years for the base of Bed I, below the basalt member, and 1·5 for the top of Bed I (Marker Bed). By the same method, the eolian tuff of Bed II appears to be *c.* 1·4 million years old.

There are no chronometric data for Lower and Middle Pleistocene strata in other parts of Africa. Palaeontological evidence indicates that the earliest Transvaal australopithecine breccias, Sterkfontein (type site), Makapansgat and Taungs, may well be as old as, *or older than* Bed I at Olduvai (Cooke 1963; Ewer 1967). New faunal data from Olduvai may necessitate alteration of this correlation, but no compelling evidence for revision has yet been presented.

The Moroccan and North African sequences can be related to the East African sequence only through the correlation of mammalian fossils and artefacts. The earliest artefacts found in Morocco (e.g. from Tardiguet-er-Rahla) are dated as 'Middle Villafranchian' (Biberson 1961). However, a complex of bio-stratigraphic, rock stratigraphic and climatic evidence is involved and the artefacts may not be older than those of Olduvai Bed I, which are rated by similar concatenations of evidence as 'Upper Villafranchian'.

Geophysical chronometry has enlarged the previously accepted estimates of Pleistocene time to such an extent that it is necessary to consider whether previously accepted views of the nature of early cultural evolution remain acceptable. This point is further discussed in section 4, which deals with 'stages' in the archaeological record.

2 Palaeogeography and environment

East Africa is an important source of evidence for the earliest phases of human culture for several reasons:

1 The region lay within the geographic range of incipient hominid forms.
2 During Early and Middle Pleistocene times, numerous sedimentary sequences were deposited in and around the Rift Valleys. The contents of many of these deposits are now being exposed by erosion (plate 1).
3 Many areas within the sedimentary basins were favourable to hominid occupation.
4 Because volcanoes were active, sites were intermittently preserved by burial under ash falls or alluvial deposits of tuff.
5 Extensive and determined searches have been made in the region. These have largely been led by L. S. B. Leakey, or inspired by his successes.

It is argued by some that East Africa has yielded crucial evidence because it was the site of hominid and human origins (Ardrey 1961; L. S. B. Leakey 1961a: 1–3). Although this may be so, the hypothesis rests solely on the absence of comparable fossils and artefacts from other regions. This lack of evidence might equally well be due to non-preservation of fossils or to default of appropriate searches for them. For the present, it seems best to view East Africa as part of an early hominid bio-geographic province of unknown extent, which included Lake Chad (Coppens 1967), Morocco, probably included South Africa, and possibly included South East Asia (Robinson 1963; Simons and Pilbeam

1965). While we are in no position to chart the bio-geography of early hominid evolution, the known distribution of Middle and early Upper Pleistocene stone industries does suggest that the most heavily vegetated regions of Africa – the Congo Basin and the Guinea Coast of West Africa – were not occupied until much later (J. D. Clark 1965: 833).

The evidence from Olduvai Gorge occupies a central place and the elegantly conceived environmental and geographical reconstructions achieved by the intensive stratigraphic and mineralogical research of R. L. Hay, have a correspondingly important position (Hay 1963, 1965, 1966, 1967 a & b). This work, in conjunction with the geophysical measurements of Curtis and Evernden, has shown that the sediments exposed in the gorge represent a quasi-continuous sequence extending from a time prior to 2 million potassium-argon years up to a point in the Middle Pleistocene as yet undated (table 2). During this entire period, the regional climate (precipitation/evaporation balance) as judged by water salinity and certain highly specific mineral alteration reactions, appears to have oscillated only within the arid and semi-arid range of conditions.

The eolian tuff in Bed II at Olduvai provides a convenient dividing line between bio-stratigraphic and culture-stratigraphic divisions within the formation, and it is believed to represent an episode of increased aridity (M. D. Leakey 1967: 418). However, the magnitude of the climatic event cannot be evaluated since volcanic eruption could have been a factor in initiating the eolian deposition. The Peninj group of sedimentary formations in the adjoining Natron basin corroborate this evidence for general stability of conditions (Isaac 1965: 127, 1967a: 242). Research in the Albert Rift has also demonstrated a long-term stability of sedimentation conditions extending from Miocene to Middle Pleistocene times. These sediments lack specific indicators of climate, such as the diagnostic mineralogy of the Olduvai and Natron sediments, but the implications are similar (Bishop 1965: 306).

Suppositions concerning a widespread and prolonged 'Pliocene drought' in Africa have entered literature concerning human evolution (e.g. Ardrey 1961: 257–82; Fox 1967: 419). There is *no* substantial geological evidence to support such an interpretation, and stratigraphic sequences in both the Western and Eastern Rifts of East Africa now provide specific evidence to the contrary.

Recent studies of late Pleistocene and Holocene pollen cores (van Zinderen Bakker 1967; D. A. Livingstone 1967) indicate that *some* temperature fluctuations on African highlands correspond with *some* glacial episodes of high latitudes. Sequences of lake level fluctuations correspond less exactly. However, temperature is of less critical importance in tropical regions than in temperate zones, and, because advance and retreat of large ice sheets were not involved, oscillations in temperature may have been rapidly expressed ecologically. Hence the climatic history of Africa is likely to prove an exceedingly long and complex series of relatively *low amplitude* oscillations. Until we obtain detailed pollen record, changes during the Early and Middle Pleistocene may remain unresolved, and palaeoanthropologists may be wise to treat climatic variation as an undifferentiated factor in the complex ecological setting of cultural evolution. Hominid adaptation by inter-related genetic and cultural changes could have been a response to competition and stress produced by subtle shifts in biological balances, rather than by major bio-geographic changes induced by climatic variation.

Work on the palaeo-environmental setting of the Transvaal australopithecines has yielded a more exact climatic history than is available in East Africa (Brain 1958). However, even in this case the scale of environmental oscillation is well within the range of conditions to which a primate species such as *Papio ursinus* is adapted.

Available data including the distribution of fossils make it appear that savannah and open grassland was the ecological setting for early cultural developments, but African savannahs are extremely diverse in their biology, climate and physiography. We are wholly ignorant of the extent to which geographical or chronological variation amongst them or within them has influenced hominid evolution. This remains to be investigated.

3 Occupation sites and activities

It is widely known that actual patterned 'camp' sites dating from as far back as 1·75 million years have been exposed by excavation and studied in great detail (e.g. L. S. B. Leakey 1960, 1961b, 1963b; M. D. Leakey 1967). During the past decade, the excavation of a few such sites has provided a tiny sample of information from scattered points in the vast time-space continuum of the 'Lower Palaeolithic'.[1]

Published data for all these sites are restricted to preliminary reports, so that generalizations are premature. However, certain issues have been brought into focus.

Until the post-war reorientation of palaeolithic prehistory, scholars had tended to concern themselves narrowly with artefacts. This was especially true for Lower and Middle Pleistocene studies. Early Pleistocene archaeology was envisaged as the task of discerning gradual elaboration of design and increase in technical mastery. At the most, it appeared that the course of 'fossilized' traditions could be plotted as they shifted in space and developed through time. These objectives remain as the taxonomic and culture-chronologic framework of Pleistocene prehistory, but it now appears that more ambitious reconstructions can be based on a firm foundation of fact, *if* suitable sites are diligently sought and carefully excavated. There seems no reason why archaeologists should not reconstruct by prolonged and painstaking research, some basic features of early Pleistocene life such as:

1 The number of persons forming social groups.
2 Patterns of movement and settlement.
3 Aspects of diet and economic activity.
4 Probable extent of territorial range.
5 Aspects of the patterning of inter-group contacts and differentiation (i.e. micro-cultural taxonomy).

In the paragraphs following, some attempt is made to justify these claims by example. Other suggestions are made of avenues as yet wholly unexplored, but which seem worthy of investigation.

[1] For example, Kalambo Falls, Zambia (Howell and Clark 1963). Isimila, Tanzania (Howell *et al.* 1962). Olduvai, Tanzania (M. D. Leakey 1967). Olorgesailie, Kenya (L. S. B. Leakey 1952; Isaac 1966). Torralba, Spain (Howell 1966; Butzer 1965). Vertesszöllös, Hungary (Kretzoi and Vertes 1965). Latamne, Syria (J. D. Clark 1966b). Ubeidiya, Israel (Stekelis 1966).

The size of prehistoric groups and the nature of settlement patterns is deduced as a matter of common practice from the plans of villages and from the contained evidence for duration of occupation. Some attempts have been made to work out quantitative relationships between size and population (e.g. Cook and Heizer 1965). Cautious extension of such inferences back into the Pleistocene may be possible, though special problems do arise.

Very few single occupation camp-sites have yet been excavated over sufficient extent to permit estimates of the size of residence groups. One such as FLK I ('Zinjanthropus Site') at Olduvai (M. D. Leakey 1966a, 1967). The occupation had taken place on a single clearly defined clay (?palaeosol) horizon. An area of *c.* 3,000 sq ft was exposed by excavation, and its contents mapped. These consisted of bone debris, artefacts and manuports.[1] A pattern of differential distributions and differential densities was discerned. A central zone, about 21 ft × 15 ft, was characterized by a high density of material, including numerous flakes and bone splinters; further out was a diffuse scatter with higher relative proportions of 'heavy duty' tools: large choppers, polyhedrons, core scrapers, etc., and manuports. Uncomminuted bone material was also more common peripherally, with allegedly marrow-free bones such as scapulae, mandibles and pelvic bones preponderating. Such a pattern may eventually enable us to suggest limits for the size of the resident group. Probably common sense is as good a basis as any for an estimate, but by way of control, the data of Cook and Heizer (1965: 70–1) or R. Lee (pers. comm.) can be cited. Lee's figures for the relationship of site size to group size amongst the Kung bushmen ranges from about 60 sq ft per person to 200 sq ft, with the best estimate being about 140 sq ft per person. Lee's figures were based on the areas in which windbreaks stood; measurement of refuse strewn areas would surely have been larger. If one suspends criticism for the sake of illustration, and does the arithmetic, the estimate of site population for FLK I would be less than twenty, and probably less than ten. Alternatively, if one admitted the possibility that the central zone was analogous to a house, in terms of the space requirements of individuals occupying it, one could use the data of Cook and Heizer. A median value of 25 sq ft per person per house is obtained from the table of records for California Indians (Cook and Heizer 1965: 70–1). The central zone would, on the basis of this relationship, accommodate ten to twelve individuals. These figures may or may not prove to be valid estimates but they accord with common sense. They are cited here to stress the importance of comparative data from ethnography for archaeology.

A small number of apparently complete Acheulian camp sites at Olorgesailie have been reported by Isaac (1966, 1968). These range in average diameter from 6 to 20 m., and consist of high concentrations of artefacts, manuports and sometimes bone refuse (e.g. plates 2 & 3). The margins of the sites were found to be sharply defined and this was tentatively ascribed to the action of a limiting barrier such as a thornbranch barricade. Alternatively, favourable circumstances for the occupation might have been sharply limited by the edges of a shaded area or the limits of a sandy patch of ground. Subsequently, the author has become aware of a natural agency other than human occupation,

[1] *Manuports* is a term proposed to designate introduced but unmodified stones (M. D. Leakey 1966a).

which might have effected the concentrations. The 'kinematic wave' effect (Leopold *et al.* 1966; Isaac 1967b) may well have resulted in the concentration of stones originally deposited by men along a stretch of stream bed. If this alternative hypothesis proves correct, the group size estimates cited by Isaac (1968) are without basis. Whether the concentrations are undisturbed camps or secondary aggregates of originally separate occupation accumulations, they each show marked stylistic idiosyncrasy of artefact morphology, and imply recurrent occupation of the same locality over a span of time, perhaps less than a generation, by the same hunting band. In one case (see caption of plate 3 and below) there is evidence for a specific economic activity, the hunting of baboons, perhaps at regular seasonal intervals.

Some information is accumulating regarding the choice of topographic location and substratum for 'Lower Palaeolithic' camp sites. The Oldowan sites of Beds I and II at Olduvai were located on the flats adjacent to the salt lake in areas traversed by the streams of fresh water coming off the slopes of Ngorongoro and Lemagrut. The known Acheulian sites were situated on better-drained ground in the vicinity of stream beds and stream conglomerates (R. L. Hay 1967a). Similarly at Natron, Olorgesailie and Latamne, occupation seems to have been located in the sandy beds of shallow seasonal streams.[1] The predilection of Acheulian hunters for sand and gravel-bar camp-sites may account for the prodigious quantities of handaxes recovered from some quite small gravel pits in Europe. It is more likely that man was the concentrating agency, than that fluviatile forces aggregated initially dispersed pieces.

In contrast to the localized concentrations of occupation material cited as examples, other sites yield widespread diffuse occurrences presumably derived from sporadic usage of a generalized area. Thin scatters of this kind covering areas up to 150 × 120 m. are known at Olorgesailie. The Torralba and Ambrona Acheulian sites appear to be samples from a fairly wide area of alluvial flats which were a locale for the killing and butchering of elephants (Howell 1965, 1966) and which came to be dotted with broken up carcasses and discarded artefacts.

It is widely assumed that some species of early men were primarily hunters. Since bone remains fossilize more readily than plant remains, this view tends to be perpetuated. Studies of surviving 'hunters' such as the Bushmen or Hadza (R. Lee 1968; J. Woodburn 1968) indicate that while meat is crucial in diet and has great prestige value, it generally accounts for much less of the food intake than gathered vegetable foods. The 'Lower Palaeolithic' situation may well have been similar; remains of edible plants were recovered from the Kalambo Acheulian floors (Howell and Clark 1963: 488).

The fact that small and juvenile animals are preponderant on the FLK I ('Zinjanthropus') floor, has received wide attention (L. S. B. Leakey 1963a; Cole 1963: 118). More recent work has shown that faunal remains ranging from rodents to proboscideans may be associated with Oldowan industries (M. D. Leakey 1967: 428).

It has recently been suggested that Acheulian hunters helped bring about the extinction of about twenty-six genera of large mammals, believed to have disappeared during

[1] Geological circumstances at each of these sites preclude the possibility that these are entirely mechanical aggregates derived from wide scatter of artefacts made by different bands over a long time-span.

the Middle Pleistocene (Martin 1966, 1967). The samples of African Pleistocene fauna are not yet sufficiently numerous in relation to the vast extent of time and space involved for the hypothesis to be verified or refuted. Martin has not dealt adequately with all the taxonomic or stratigraphic issues involved in measuring changes in the rate of extinction (L. S. B. Leakey 1966a, 1967). Yet, whatever the outcome of this controversy, there are excellent examples of effective and specialized hunting by Acheulian groups – notably the dismembered *Pelorovis* herd at Olduvai BK II (L. S. B. Leakey 1957), the remains of more than fifty giant baboons at Olorgesailie DE/89 B (see plates 2 & 3), and the large number of *Elephas antiquus* carcasses at Torralba and Ambrona (Howell 1966). More generalized hunting practices are suggested by the variety of species found at sites such as Ternifine, Sidi Zin and some Olduvai examples. Many other Acheulian camps lack or virtually lack bone remains; this is in some cases due to conditions of preservation; as for instance at Kalambo Falls and Isimila (Howell and Clark 1963). Elsewhere, for example Olorgesailie or Latamne, the reason may be either initial lack *or* subsequent dispersal by scavengers (Isaac 1967b, 1968; Clark 1966a).

Hunting methods remain largely a matter for conjecture; nor do we know the extent to which scavenging was important. The robust baboons represented at the Olorgesailie site (plate 3) may have been trapped by surrounding their roost at night, just as the Hadza, a hunting tribe in Tanzania did until recently (J. Woodburn 1968). The Torralba and Ambrona sites have evidence of widespread burning, which may have been used for drives (Howell 1965).

Fire is not documented in Lower or Middle Palaeolithic sites in Africa (Oakley 1956), but the absence of traces of fire from many 'Middle Stone Age' open sites, by contrast with the abundance of ash and charcoal in cave sites, raises the doubt that charcoal may not have been preserved. Microscopic particles of charcoal were identified in Olorgesailie sediments but were not directly associated with occupation sites (D. Livingstone, pers. comm.).

Despite the shortcomings of the available evidence concerning social organization and economic activities, the data will already support some conclusions concerning fundamental aspects of behaviour. The observed, localized concentrations of traces of occupation strongly imply that some Lower and Middle Pleistocene hominids were operating from well defined, if intermittently shifting *base camps*. The profusion of bone at some of these sites indicates not only the importance of *hunting* (and/or scavenging), but also of *food sharing*. These are behaviour patterns that are distinctive to man, and either absent or very much less well developed in all other primates. Initially this kind of behaviour was evidently practised by hominid forms having brains which were only a little larger than those of the modern apes, though we know nothing of functional differences which may have existed despite the limitations of brain volume. The observed area of some sites and the quantities of material in them also make it clear that some 'bands' in the Lower and Middle Pleistocene were considerably larger than 'nuclear family' groups. Reconstructions of stages in the evolution of human social behaviour from the evidence of comparative studies of modern primates (including man) need to accommodate these archaeological findings.

4 Artefacts and palaeo-anthropology

Despite the importance of the features of occupation sites for palaeo-anthropology, stone artefacts remain the 'skeleton' of fossilized culture. These are, in effect, the only element of the evidence which recur in all sites, and which can therefore serve as a basis for the recognition of cultures and traditions. However, there is need for a radical reorganization of thinking about the kind of inferences and classifications which can be made from available samples of Early and Middle Pleistocene artefacts. Some of the issues are discussed below, along with comments on 'stages' in cultural evolution in East Africa.

A significant hindrance to interpretation is the almost complete ignorance of the function of Lower Palaeolithic artefacts. Without a knowledge of function we will remain severely limited in our understanding of observed variation in the morphology of 'types' and in the 'typologically' defined contents of assemblages. There are several ways in which a better understanding may be achieved, though little has yet been done. First, an expanded corpus of associations between artefact types and traces of activities such as butchering, or pounding vegetable material, may help elucidate the problem. Secondly, edge damage and micro-wear may provide useful evidence (Semenov 1964; Keller 1966; Clark *in* Howell 1965). Finally, it is conceivable that chromatographic techniques of analysis which have been developed for identifying infinitesimally minute traces of organic substances in ancient sediments, may detect traces of diagnostic organic molecules on the edges of carefully excavated, uncontaminated specimens.

During earlier years of archaeology, the common models for the classification of prehistoric culture were ladderlike sequences of named entities, culminating in the elaborate scheme of De Mortillet (in Daniel 1950: 103–5). This century has witnessed steady diminution in the importance of such conceptual frameworks for most segments of prehistory. However, in palaeolithic studies they persist. The sequences have been extensively fragmented into partially independent, regional columns, but their essential character is often apparent in the serial numbers which are given to the subdivisions. Often, some kind of logically attractive continuous thread is claimed to run evenly through the series: e.g. Somme Acheulian I–IV, Moroccan Pebble Culture 1–4 and Acheulian 1–8, East African Acheulian 1–10. The results of excavations of site complexes such as those of Olduvai, Isimila or Olorgesailie (M. D. Leakey 1967; Howell *et al.* 1962; Isaac, unpublished) strongly suggest that in many cases, the differences *between* the contents of contemporary or near-contemporary sites can be as great or greater than the differences formerly used to define cultural-stage entities in a sequence (fig. 1). Clearly then, a valid stage can only be recognized when numbers of stratigraphically correlated *assemblages* are available, and can be shown to share features which differentiate them from similarly defined earlier and later stages. Single site assemblages, however large, are an insufficient sample. A recent discussion of procedures appropriate to defining cultural and stratigraphic entities is contained in Bishop and Clark (1967).

It appears to the writer that if criteria of the kind indicated above are applied to the information available, only three, or possibly four, culture-stratigraphic entities can be recognized in the 'Earlier Stone Age' (='Lower Palaeolithic') of East Africa. These are as follows:

Upper Acheulian (=late Acheulian of Howell and Clark 1963)
Lower Acheulian (=early or lower Acheulian of M. D. Leakey 1967)
'Developed Oldowan' (M. D. Leakey 1967). This entity may be in part a facies of the Lower Acheulian.
Oldowan (M. D. Leakey 1966a, 1967)

Only industries of Oldowan aspect (see M. D. Leakey 1966a for a clear definition) have been recovered from Bed I at Olduvai, and in the portion of Bed II below the eolian tuff. With the possible exception of a few specimens from Kanam (Leakey 1935) and Kanyatsi (de Heinzelin 1961) Oldowan sites have not been found in any other well-dated context in East Africa.[1] Elsewhere, the author regards only the Moroccan sites (Biberson 1961), Ain Hanech (Balout 1955), Tunisia, and perhaps the Grotte du Vallonet, Southern France (de Lumley 1963) as *proven* Lower Pleistocene (='Villafranchian equivalent') occurrences of artefacts. Other sites such as those of the Saoura (Alimen and Chavaillon 1962), the Angola coast (J. D. Clark 1966a) or Kota Tampan, Malaya (Walker and Sieveking 1962) all depend on geomorphology and uncertain stratigraphic extrapolations for their dating. In view of the expanded time span estimated for the duration of the Pleistocene, such extrapolations have become especially hazardous.

In the portion of Olduvai Bed II above the eolian tuff, assemblages of purely Oldowan aspect occur, but are demonstrably contemporaneous with assemblages containing Acheulian elements. These industries have been designated 'developed Oldowan' by M. D. Leakey (1967). The archaeological situation is complex, and is discussed below.

In archaeological literature Oldowan industries are commonly characterized as being dominated by 'pebble choppers'. However, M. D. Leakey (1966a) has shown that choppers make up only a small fraction of the total industry: *c.* 6%. Of the secondarily trimmed tools, the various types of choppers and allied forms such as polyhedrals and discoids make up approximately 70%, with a site variation range of *c.* 40–75%. The balance of the retouched tools include a variety of surprisingly delicate and well-made scrapers on flakes, and large cores or chunks. Burin-like forms also occur in small numbers, and range from delicate pieces to larger, cruder tools.

The careful work of M. D. Leakey indicates that during the vast time span of the Oldowan, radical transformation of the typology and morphology of stone tools did *not* occur. However, despite the conservatism, two significant tool forms not represented in the earliest assemblages appear in sites at the top of Bed I, and continue on into industries above the eolian tuff in Bed II. These are the *proto-biface*, a form morphologically intermediate between a chopper and a handaxe; and the *spheroid*, a subspherical stone or core with its ridges pounded by battering (M. D. Leakey 1966a, 1967). The known duration of the Oldowan at Olduvai is of the order of *half a million years* (*see* table 1), and the small extent of detectable 'progress' in stone craft during that time requires review of interpretations which involve ideas of slow and inexorable cultural growth. Accounts of pre-handaxe technological development have frequently defined stages in

[1] A stone artefact assemblage of Oldowan aspect but of recent age has been reported by M. D. Leakey (1966b). This makes clear the need for secure dating evidence before any site is accepted as a useful record of pre-Acheulian culture

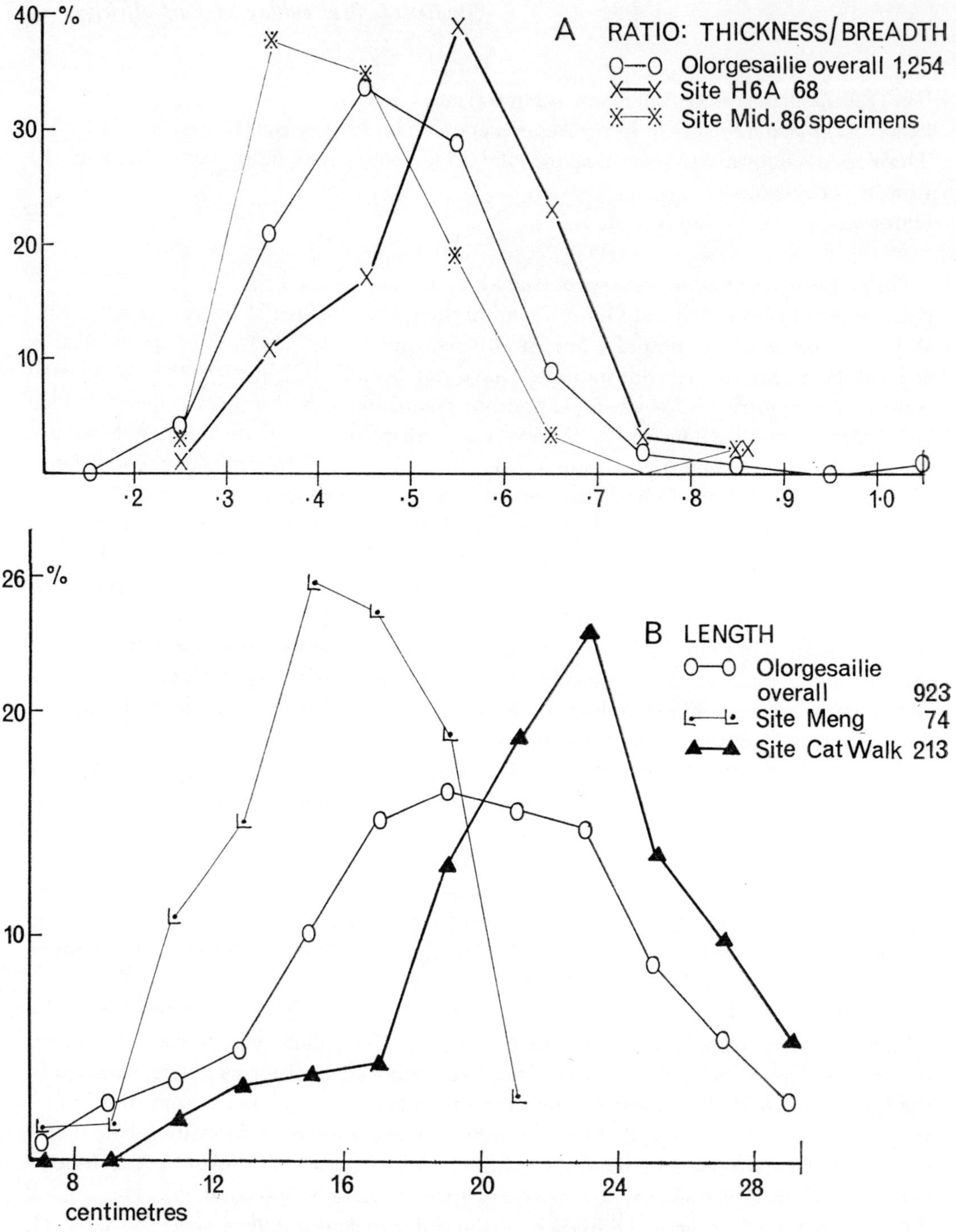

Figure 1 Frequency distribution illustrating the extent of idiosyncratic divergence between penecontemporaneous sites in Member 7 of the Olorgesailie Formation:

A All 'bifacial tools': distribution of the thickness/breadth ratio for two selected site samples and the overall aggregate of nine site samples. (Mann-Witney non-parametric analysis of variance test $p. < 0{\cdot}001$)

B Handaxes: distribution of length in two selected site samples. (Analysis of variance Snedecors F. text $p. < 0{\cdot}001$)

which at first only a few trimming flakes were struck in one direction, followed by other stages involving increasing numbers of directions (Lowe 1952; Biberson 1961). In the light of the Olduvai evidence such interpretations seem improbable.

The cultural situation in the portion of Bed II above the eolian tuff is of critical importance because the transition between Oldowan and Acheulian occurs within this segment of the stratigraphic sequence. In the first monograph on the archaeological material from Olduvai (Leakey 1951) the transition was described as a gradual transformation of the morphology of choppers into crude handaxes which characterized the Chellean stages of the Chelles-Acheuls. The development of new forms was accompanied by the persistence of decreasing proportions of archaic forms. More detailed work by Dr and Mrs Leakey has led them to revise their views (M. D. Leakey 1967). It now appears that, while the Oldowan assemblages of upper Bed I and lower Bed II show some shift in an Acheulian direction (see above), the first true handaxes appear in assemblages which are unmistakably Acheulian. So abrupt does the change appear, that cultural intrusion has been suggested as a possible explanation (M. D. Leakey 1967). The first assemblages with handaxes at Olduvai occur above the eolian tuff, and because many of the forms are simple but delicate, and because cleavers are present, the Leakeys (1967) have abandoned the term 'Chellean' in favour of 'early Acheulian'. A closely analogous sequence of events has been described from the Moroccan littoral (Biberson 1961: 189–92).

In Morocco a long sequence of 'pebble culture' assemblages showed only minor changes including the incorporation of handaxe-like forms. Then in Layer M, Sidi Abderahman, with apparent abruptness, a simple but complete Acheulian assemblage succeeded an 'evolved pebble culture' assemblage. In this case also, the handaxe industry was so different from the conventional notion of an intermediate stage that Biberson has abandoned the 'Clacto-Abbevillian' label formerly given to it, and has termed it 'Acheulian I'. In Morocco the subsequent sequence is seen by means of a series of single sites at relatively widely spaced horizons, whereas at Olduvai a sequence with numbers of spatially distinct, pene-contemporaneous sites has been studied. In both cases there is a persistence of Oldowan forms after the appearance of Acheulian forms, but at Olduvai the persistence of almost complete Oldowan assemblages has been demonstrated (M. D. Leakey 1967). Mrs Leakey is able to recognize three categories of assemblage in the upper part of Bed II: 'early Acheulian' industries, 'developed Oldowan' and a compound category 'Acheulian-developed Oldowan'.[1] The developed Oldowan differs from the Oldowan by the continuance of the trend towards increased numbers of proto-bifaces, spheroids and possibly scrapers. The Acheulian tools, for which only one site inventory is published, are characterized by a high proportion of handaxes, about 50%, and spheroids, about 17%.[2] Data are available for two examples of the compound entity, which is like the developed Oldowan save only that a comparative small number of tools, 11–30%, are handaxes. These have a tendency to be small and misshapen by comparison with Acheulian specimens.

[1] M. D. Leakey (pers. comm.) proposes to term the two latter: 'developed Oldowan A and B', respectively.

[2] These percentages are adjusted from the data of M. D. Leakey (1967) by the elimination of utilized and battered pieces from the tool count.

Mrs Leakey tentatively advances one possible explanation for this situation, namely, that the Acheulian industry represents a cultural advance over the Oldowan, which was intrusive to the immediate region, initially coexisting with groups preserving Oldowan traditions. It seems possible that some of these groups may have imitated the new forms, or acquired discarded specimens, thus effecting the 'hybrid' assemblages.

Other possible explanations need to be considered. It appears possible that 'thresholds' exist in stone technology, so that certain techniques are either present or absent and intermediate expressions are virtually non-existent. The tools and debitage of two assemblages may differ markedly as a consequence of application or non-application of only *one* specific technique: a possible example of this is the removal of blades with a punch. All African Acheulian industries of confirmed early Middle Pleistocene date involve the manufacture of tools from large flakes (i.e. greater than 10 cm.); whereas no series of flakes of this size have been reported from any Oldowan assemblage. When present in Acheulian industries such flakes often do not appear to be the tail-end of a frequency distribution with a mode under 10 cm. They may appear as a separate modality (fig. 2). It is suggested that the striking of large flakes involved the 'formulation' of a set of deliberate techniques quite separate from those used in the flaking practised throughout the time span of the Oldowan. Large flakes removed forcefully tend to be side-struck flakes with a form not remote from that of a handaxe or cleaver, so that minimal retouch is required to convert them into rough examples of these tools. The aspect of an Oldowan tool kit could be radically and abruptly altered simply by the invention or acquisition of this new practice. It is possible to imagine that in some circumstances the innovant tool forms were required and in others not, thereby providing a possible explanation for variations in the frequency of the new forms. Frequency of tools made on flakes may also have been affected by the size of raw material in the vicinity of the sites. The striking of large flakes requires large blocks or boulders and in a largely stoneless environment such as the surrounds of Lake Olduvai, the proximity of large cobbles may have been an influential factor in causing differences between sites.

The range of variation reported for Olduvai in the proportion of bifaces to other tools (0–54%) does not exceed the range observed in other partially Acheulian site complexes (0–95% at Olorgesailie, 20·5–77·5% at Isimila). In both situations there is a choice between hypotheses involving 'activity variants' or 'parallel phyla of culture'. The dilemma has not yet been decisively resolved.

Assemblages including handaxes made on large flakes had certainly appeared in East Africa by 700,000 years ago (Humbu Formation, table 1). They may be appreciably older since R. L. Hay (pers. comm.) has estimated that the earliest Acheulian occurrences in Bed II at Olduvai (e.g. EF–HR) are close to being 1·4 million years old. Acheulian industries persisted in East Central Africa until approximately 60,000 B.P. (Kalambo Falls, J. D. Clark 1965; Vogel and Waterbolk 1967). Despite the enormous extent of time involved, it is only possible at present to recognize two culture-stratigraphic subdivisions with any certainty (table 2). The tools of Lower Acheulian industries are characterized by simpler workmanship and minimal, bold retouch indicative of stone hammer technique (plate 4). Upper Acheulian industries commonly include refined tool forms with large numbers of the shallow invasive trimming scars, typical of the cylinder hammer technique. The number of trimming scars and the ratio of thickness to breadth

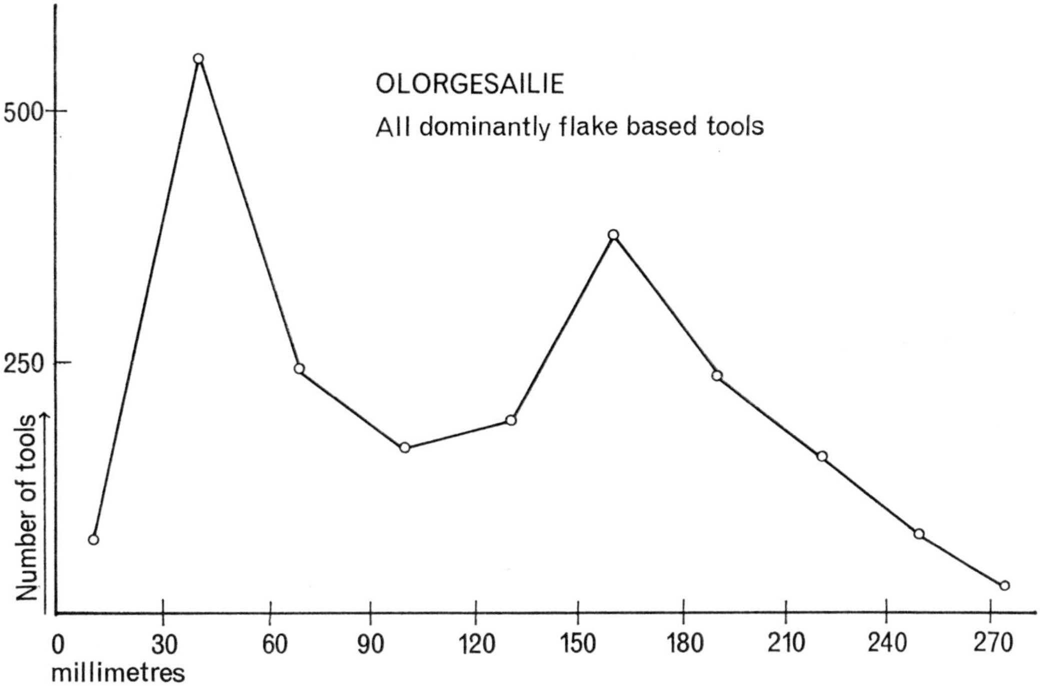

Figure 2 Olorgesailie Acheulian: the frequency distribution of length for a sample formed of all tool categories of which most constituent items are based on flakes. It is suggested that the bimodal pattern may result from the fact of a deliberate and distinct technique for striking large flakes

promise to be useful quantitative discriminants between the two subdivisions (fig. 3). The Lower Acheulian only partially corresponds with what was formerly called 'Chellean', as cleavers and delicate minimally retouched handaxes may be present instead of, or in addition to, the heavy pick-like forms described by L. S. B. Leakey (1951: 42–72).

Occurrences of 'early' Middle Pleistocene Acheulian industries are more widespread than confirmed Oldowan occurrences; however, they are still exceedingly rare. The Sterkfontein extension, Kliplaatdrif (Mason 1962), Olduvai (M. D. Leakey 1967), Peninj (Isaac 1967a), the Casablanca sites (Biberson 1961) and Ternifine (Balout 1955) occurrences can be regarded as the only important African sites the stratigraphic relations of which have been satisfactorily determined. The majority of 'Chellean' plots contributed by some workers to the recently published *Atlas of African Prehistory* (Clark 1967) quite possibly represent no more than sporadic finds of crude rolled Upper Acheulian pieces in poorly dated gravels.

The 'typological' diversity of large and small tools in the Upper Acheulian has received considerable attention recently and need not be discussed in detail here (see Kleindienst 1961, 1962; Howell and Clark 1963). A list of types proposed by Kleindienst (1962) is now in widespread use in sub-Saharan Africa (e.g. Howell *et al.* 1962; J. D. Clark 1964; Keller 1966). The use of such a scheme helps to standardize descriptions of assemblages, but it also obscures many important features of the industries. Recent

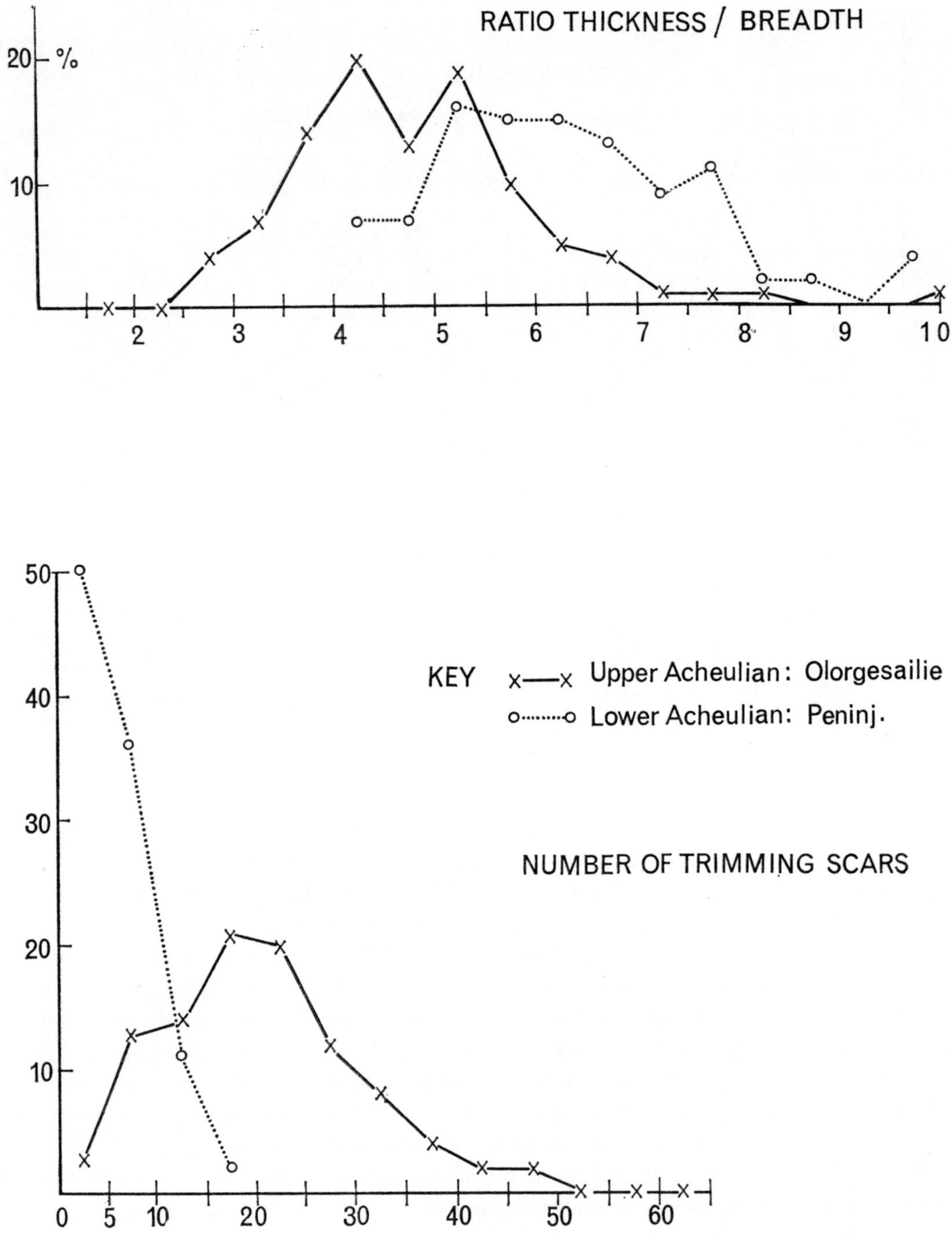

Figure 3 Measurements of the attributes 'relative thickness' (thickness/breadth ratio) and number of trimming scars may provide useful quantitative discriminants in distinguishing Lower and Upper Acheulian assemblages. Samples of bifacial tools from Olorgesailie and Peninj provide examples of each

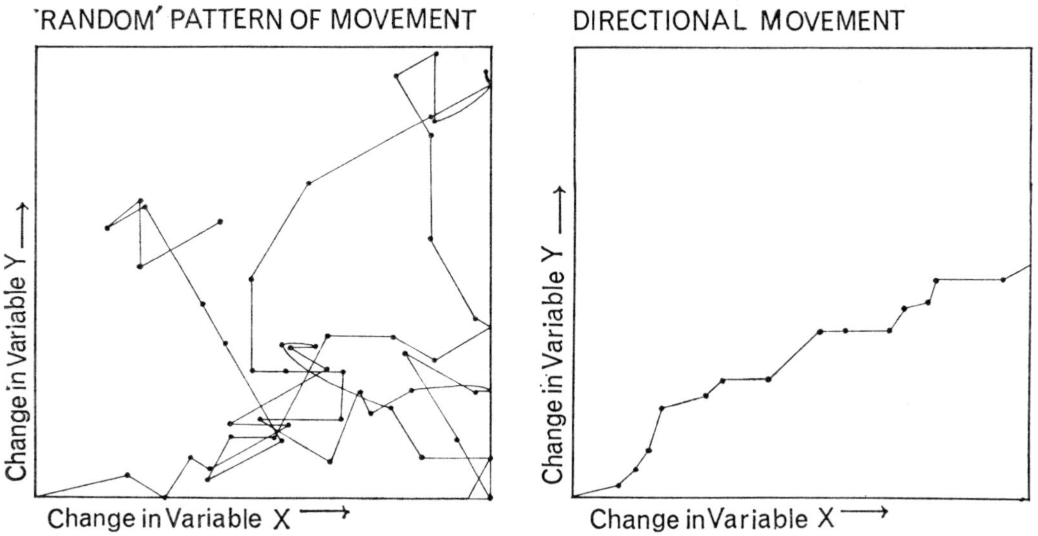

Figure 4 A diagram contrasting 'random walk' movement (*left*) with directional, progressive movement (*right*)

quantitative morphological studies of the Olorgesailie artefacts strongly suggest that the types are arbitrary segments of complex multi-attribute modalities with large variances. The development of quantitative attribute analyses may well provide a more meaningful basis for comparing assemblages than the comparison of 'type' inventories.

Quantitative studies have shown that Acheulian assemblages vary greatly even within such comparatively small space–time limits as the Isimila or Olorgesailie site complexes (Kleindienst 1961; Isaac, unpublished). They vary both in regard to their contents as expressed in percentage inventories, and in regard to the morphology of items falling in a single class. Statistical tests on the Olorgesailie material show that variation of both kinds is far greater than could be expected as a result of sample variation in relation to common population values. Variation in the frequency of types has been interpreted as related to differences of activity on briefly occupied sites (Clark 1959; Posnansky 1959; Kleindienst 1961: 44). This is a reasonable if untested hypothesis. However, the morphological, stylistic differences between the contents of two near contemporaneous camp sites has much more the aspect of micro-cultural variation. Conceivably individual craftsmen or hunting-bands had marked stylistic idiosyncrasies. The implications of such an hypothesis if it can be sustained are considerable. Perhaps under ideal circumstances, patterns of variation may be observed in sufficient detail to allow inference concerning demography and inter-group relationships (see Binford 1963). However, there are implications also for the macro-taxonomy of culture. Variation of the kind envisaged is liable to have been partially *stochastic*: that is, individual traditions may have oscillated at random within certain limits, giving innumerable minor, but real variants of artefact assemblages (fig. 1). 'Random walk' variation was probably superimposed on directional trends which may have been continual and gradual, or erratic and intermittent (fig. 4). The practical upshot of this view of Lower Palaeolithic cultural variation is that large samples of cultural 'fossils' will be needed to define culture-stratigraphic or culture-geographic entities. The size of individual site samples beyond a minimum of, for example, forty or fifty large tools[1] is less important than the number of sites used as the basis of definition. Given a time continuum of almost a million years, and a space continuum of more than a whole continent, the difficulties of obtaining suitable representative samples for contiguous regions during numerous restricted segments of time will generally be slender. Pleistocene prehistorians may do well to be content with large but firmly established industrial divisions and to divert their attention from attempts at elaborate seriation to the reconstruction of behaviour patterns.

5 Early culture and human palaeontology

The importance of East Africa as a source of evidence concerning early culture is greatly enhanced by the association of the cultural evidence with hominid fossils (see table 2), forming an evolutionary series the length of which has no parallel in any other region. The taxonomy and phyletic relations of these fossils is currently the subject of some dispute. However, the fact of controversy over the classification of some of the fossils is possibly an indication of their intermediate evolutionary position between hitherto clearly separated taxa.

At least two varieties of fossil hominids are known to have been contemporary with 'Oldowan' (*sensu stricto*) industries. One variety (*Zinjanthropus*) is widely accepted as a robust australopithecine. The remaining Bed I and lower Bed II fossils are comparatively gracile, and are variously assigned to *Australopithecus sp.* (cf. *africanus*) (Robinson 1965) to *Homo habilis* (Leakey, Tobias and Napier 1964) *or* by L. S. B. Leakey (1966b) to *Homo habilis* and a 'proto-pithecanthropine' (table 2). The gracile form is widely regarded as the principal tool maker (e.g. Tobias 1965; M. D. Leakey 1967). Whatever the outcome of the taxonomic controversy it is clear that the forms from Bed I and the base of Bed II generally had smaller brains than hominids assigned to *Homo erectus*. Post-cranial bones from Bed I show that some of the hominids, probably the gracile forms, had feet in a moderately advanced stage of adaptation to bipedal gait (Napier 1967). Hand bones show a combination of advanced modification for manipulation (Napier 1962), and strong muscular features more characteristic of pongid hands (Tuttle 1967).

In the portion of Bed II above the eolian tuff, Lower Acheulian industries and the surviving industries of Oldowan type occur in the same stratigraphic zone as a definite specimen of *Homo erectus* (Olduvai hominid 9, Tobias 1965; L. S. B. Leakey 1966b), and a form provisionally assigned to *Homo habilis* (Olduvai hominid 13, Leakey *et al.* 1964) but stated to have strong affinities with *H. erectus* (Tobias and Von Koeningswald 1965).

Field studies of chimpanzees (Goodall 1964) have indicated that simple tool-making and using is of wider occurrence than had previously been supposed. However, chimpanzees are not known to be economically *dependent* on tool use, whereas it appears from the morphology of the partly carnivorous Bed I hominids, which lacked large canines and claws, that these forms probably *did* depend on tool use.

[1] The variance of many morphological parameters for the Olorgesailie site samples is such that satisfactory statistical significance is commonly attained with samples of this size when they are compared with each other.

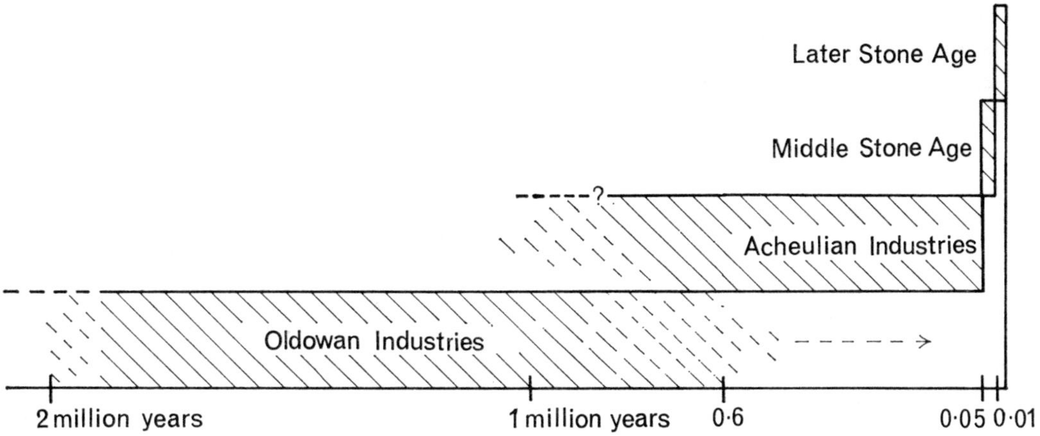

Figure 5 Diagrammatic representation of a pattern of increasing rate of change in African prehistory:
The currently recognized major technological divisions are represented as arbitrary units on the vertical axis, while time is represented on the horizontal axis. The development in stone-craft within each of the first two divisions was very small in relation to the vast duration of time involved. Middle Stone Age is partially equivalent to Middle Palaeolithic in terms of technique and range of forms, Later Stone Age to Upper Palaeolithic and Mesolithic

6 Stages in cultural development

The archaeological evidence gathered up to the present gives limited testimony concerning the stages by which important human behaviour patterns have developed, only specific events in the evolution of artefact design and technology being well documented. As has been indicated, the record suggests prolonged phases of relative stability with stochastic variation, and a very limited amount of gradual 'progressive' change (fig. 5). The Oldowan and Acheulian entities appear to have been separated by a comparatively rapid change dependent on a single technical step which by its very nature could not have been taken gradually. Though not discussed here, both the Early Pleistocene inception of stone tool-making and the Upper Pleistocene transition out of the Acheulian may have involved analogous rapid innovation in technological conventions.

It is not wise to view any comparatively static material culture tradition lasting as long as a million years, or half a million years, as representing simply transitional states in the continuous evolution of technology. Clearly these tool kits were for long periods of time in equilibrium with a level of behavioural adaptation which was equally in adjustment with its ecological setting (cf. Lancaster 1968).

Certain aspects of tools may be particularly important as symbols of the mental capabilities of their makers. Variation in the elaboration of stone tool designs in prehistoric and recent Australia was *not* always closely related to the design standards of other artefacts dependent on stone tools for their manufacture. Poorly differentiated stone tool kits comprising simple 'choppers' and flake tools continued to be made throughout Middle and Later Pleistocene times in many regions (Africa, M. D. Leakey 1966b;

South-east Asia, Movius 1948; Australia, Mulvaney and Joyce 1965) Consequently it must be remembered that technology does *not* provide an unequivocable index of 'competence'. However, during this long time interval, the maximum level of stone artefact complexity did rise in various regions during successive time periods. These maximum levels may prove valid indicators of the general state of hominid craft-competence during each major period. Recent publications have emphasized the great morphological diversity of early stone industries, but one suspects that this diversity is in part due to *lack of standardization*; whereas the morphological diversity of some Upper Palaeolithic industries is due to the existence of more *numerous discrete designs* which were closely standardized in mental conception and technical execution. As yet we have no techniques measuring precisely the complex multivariate phenomena, 'standardization'. Such methods are an important requirement.

There is evidence (Lancaster, pers. comm.) for believing that the psychological mechanisms which permit the formulation of, and execution of, a design are related to mechanisms governing the ability to communicate with words. Studies of tool standardization may conceivably be the only indication we can ever get of Pleistocene levels of competence in communication.

The evidence of Lower and Middle Pleistocene occupation sites does not yet furnish us with any basis for recognizing stages in development of social groupings, or in such aspects of economic attainment as hunting prowess and success. All that is clear is that at the outset of the archaeological record in Olduvai Bed I, some basic aspects of behaviour were already more human than pongid. The early hominids were apparently dependent on tools, were operating from temporarily fixed home bases, were hunting and were bringing food back to camp to share (cf. Washburn 1965). A behavioural change of comparable magnitude is not documented again in prehistory until the development of farming. The antecedents of these crucial adaptive shifts in the direction of human behaviour must lie beyond the known record. By the application of archaeological methods to palaeontological excavations in Tertiary deposits, this phase may yet prove amenable to investigation; and the attempt has begun at sites such as Fort Ternan in Kenya (Leakey 1962, 1967b).

ADDENDUM Since this review was written, significant new discoveries have been made in various parts of the Eastern Rift Valley. Most notable have been the finds of the international expedition to the Omo delta and adjoining regions at the northern end of Lake Rudolf. Three parties were lead by C. Arambourg (France), F. C. Howell (USA) and R. E. Leakey (Kenya). Other important discoveries have been made by a research team from Bedford College, London, organized by B. King and W. W. Bishop. The new information from these field researches primarily advances knowledge of the period prior to the oldest sites at Olduvai Gorge. Since this review has been concerned with the archaeological record that begins approximately 2 million years ago, in Bed I, Olduvai, it would not be essential to attempt to incorporate the new data even were they published and available for citation. Meanwhile, suffice it to say that the researches hold out hope that studies of the traces of hominid behaviour can be extended back into the Pliocene, and that the results of such studies, when available, must influence our understanding of the Lower and Middle Pleistocene record.

Acknowledgement

Participation in current research into the prehistoric archaeology of East Africa was initiated during employment by the National Parks of Kenya (1961–2) and the National Museum Centre for Prehistory and Palaeontology (1963–5). Dr and Mrs Leakey encouraged the writer in his research and shared information about many aspects of their own work with him. Part of the work reported here was done with the assistance of grants from the Wenner-Gren Foundation, Boise Fund, British Academy, and the British Institute of History and Archaeology in East Africa. J. Desmond Clark, R. J. Clarke, R. L. Hay, M. D. and L. S. B. Leakey, R. R. Rodden and S. L. Washburn have helped in revision of the draft manuscript for this paper. I am especially indebted to my wife for help throughout the research work and in the preparation of the manuscript and the figures.

20.x.67
(revised November 1968)

Department of Anthropology
University of California
Berkeley

References

Alimen, M. and Chavaillon, J. 1962. Position stratigraphique et évolution de la Pebble Culture au Sahara nord occidental. *Actes du IVe Congrès Panafricain de Préhistoire et de l'étude du Quaternaire. Annales – Séries IN–8° – Sciences Humaines*, No. 40. Museé Royale de l'Afrique Centrale, Tervuren, Belgique. 3–22.

Ardrey, R. 1961. *African Genesis.* Collins, London.

Balout, L. 1955. *Préhistoire de l'Afrique du Nord.* Arts et Métiers Graphiques, Paris. 1–535.

Biberson, P. 1961. Le Paléolithique Inférieur du Maroc Atlantique. *Publications du Service des Antiquités du Maroc.* 17.

Binford, L. R. 1963. 'Red ochre' caches from the Michigan area: a possible case of cultural drift. *South Western Journal of Anthropology.* 19:89–107.

Bishop, W. W. 1965. Quaternary geology and geomorphology in the Albertine Rift Valley, Uganda. In *International studies on the Quaternary*, eds H. E. Wright Jnr and D. G. Frey, Geological Society of America, Special Paper 84.

Bishop, W. W. and Clark, J. D. eds. 1967. *Background to evolution in Africa.* University of Chicago Press, Chicago.

Brain, C. K. 1958. The Transvaal Ape-Man bearing deposits. *Transvaal Museum Memoir*, No. 11:1–131.

Butzer, K. W. 1964. *Environment and archaeology.* Methuen, London.

Butzer, K. W. 1965. Acheulian occupation sites at Torralba and Ambrona, Spain: their geology. *Science.* 150:1718–22.

Clark, J. D. 1959. Further excavations at Broken Hill, Northern Rhodesia. *Journal of the Royal Anthropological Institute.* 89:201–32.

Clark, J. D. 1964. The influence of environment in inducing culture change at the Kalambo Falls Prehistoric Sites. *South African Archaeological Bulletin.* 19:93–101.

Clark, J. D. 1965. The later Pleistocene cultures of Africa. *Science.* 150:833–47.

Clark, J. D. 1966a. The distribution of Prehistoric Culture in Angola. *Museo do Dundo, Diamang, Publicacoes Culturais,* No. 73.

Clark, J. D. 1966b. Acheulian occupation sites in the Middle East and Africa: a study in cultural variability. In *Recent Studies in paleoanthropology,* eds J. D. Clark and F. C. Howell. American Anthropologist Special Publication. 68:2:2:202–29.

Clark, J. D., compiler. 1967. *The Atlas of African prehistory.* University of Chicago Press, Chicago and London.

Cole, S. 1963. *The prehistory of East Africa.* Macmillan, New York.

Cook, S. F. and Heizer, R. F. 1965. The quantitative approach to the relationship between population and settlement size. *Reports of the University of California.* Archaeological Survey. 64:1–97.

Cooke, H. B. S. 1958. Observations relating to Quaternary environments in East and Southern Africa. *Alex I. Du Toit Memorial Lecture No. 5. Geological Society of South Africa,* annexure to vol. LX:1–73.

Cooke, H. B. S. 1963. Pleistocene mammal faunas of Africa with particular reference to Southern Africa. In *African ecology and human evolution,* eds F. C. Howell and F. Bourlière. 65–116.

Coppens, Y. 1967. Les faunes de vertèbres quaternaires du Tchad. In *Background to evolution in Africa,* eds W. W. Bishop and J. D. Clark. University of Chicago Press. Chicago and London. 89–98.

Cox, A., Dalrymple, G. B. and Doell, R. R. 1967. Reversals of the earth's magnetic field. *Scientific American.* 216:44–54.

Curry, R. R. 1966. Glaciation about 3,000,000 years ago in the Sierra Nevada. *Science.* 154: 770–1.

Curtis, G. H. 1967. Notes on some Miocene and Pleistocene Potassium Argon results. In *Background to evolution in Africa,* eds W. W. Bishop and J. D. Clark. University of Chicago Press. Chicago and London. 365–9.

Daniel, G. E. 1950. *A hundred years of archaeology.* Duckworth, London.

Day, M. H. and Napier, J. R. 1964. Fossil foot bones. *Nature.* 201:967–70.

Evernden, J. F. and Curtis, G. H. 1965. Potassium Argon dating of Late Cenozoic rocks in East Africa and Italy. *Current Anthropology.* 6:343–85.

Evernden, J. F., Savage, D. E., Curtis, G. H. and James, G. T. 1964. Potassium Argon dates and the Cenozoic mammalian chronology of North America. *American Journal of Science.* 262:145–98.

Ewer, R. F. 1967. The fossil hyaenids of Africa – a reappraisal. In *Background to evolution in Africa,* eds W. W. Bishop and J. D. Clark. University of Chicago Press. Chicago. 109–24.

Fleischer, R. L., Leakey, L. S. B., Price, P. B. and Walker, R. M. 1965. Fission Track dating of Bed I, Olduvai Gorge. *Science.* 148:72–4.

Flint, R. F. 1965. The Plio-Pleistocene boundary. In *International studies on the Quaternary*, eds H. E. Wright Jnr and D. G. Frey, Geological Society of America, Special Paper 84:497–533.

Fox. R. 1967. In the beginning: aspects of hominid behavioural evolution. *Man.* 2:3:415–33.

Glass, B., Ericson, D. B., Heezen, B. C., Opdyke, N. D. and Glass, J. A. 1967. Geomagnetic reversals and Pleistocene chronology. *Nature.* 216:437–42.

Goodall, J. M. 1964. Tool-using and aimed throwing in a community of free living chimpanzees. *Nature.* 201:1264–6.

Hay, R. L. 1963. Stratigraphy of Beds I through IV, Olduvai Gorge, Tanganyika. *Science.* 139:829–33.

Hay, R. L. 1965. *Current Anthropology.* 6:4:381. Comment on Dr Leakey's comment.

Hay, R. L. 1966. Zeolites and zeolitic reactions in sedimentary rocks. *Geological Society of America*, Special Paper 85, p. 130.

Hay, R. L. 1967a. Hominid-bearing deposits of Olduvai Gorge. In *Time and stratigraphy in the evolution of Man*, a symposium sponsored by the Division of Earth Sciences, National Academy of Sciences, National Research Council, Washington D.C.

Hay, R. L. 1967b. Revised stratigraphy of Olduvai Gorge. In *Background to evolution in Africa*, eds W. W. Bishop and J. D. Clark. University of Chicago Press. Chicago and London. 221–8.

Heinzelin, J. de 1961. Le Paléolithique aux abords d'Ishango. *Institut des Parcs Nationaux du Congo et du Ruanda-Urundi*, Fascicule 6.

Howell, F. C. 1965. *Early Man.* Time Inc. New York.

Howell, F. C. 1966. Observations on the earlier phases of the European Lower Palaeolithic. In *Recent studies in paleoanthropology*, eds J. D. Clark and F. C. Howell. American Anthropologist special publication. Vol. 68, 2, 2:88–201.

Howell, F. C. and Clark, J. D. 1963. Acheulian hunter-gatherers of sub-Saharan Africa. In *African ecology and human evolution*, eds F. C. Howell and F. Bourlière. Aldine, Chicago. 458–533.

Howell, F. C., Cole, G. H. and Kleindienst, M. R. 1962. Isimila, an Acheulian occupation site in the Iringa Highlands. *Actes du IVe. Congrès Panafrican de Préhistoire et de l'étude du Quaternaire. Annales – series IN–8° – Sciences Humaines*, No. 40. Museé Royale de l'Afrique Centrale. Tervuren. Belgique. 43–80.

Isaac, G. Ll. 1965. The Stratigraphy of the Peninj Beds and the provenance of the Natron Australopithecine mandible. *Quaternaria.* VII:101–30.

Isaac, G. Ll. 1966. New evidence from Olorgesailie relating to the character of Acheulian occupation sites. In *Actas del V Congreso Panafricano de Prehistoria y de estudio del Cuaternario*, ed. L. D. Cuscoy. Publicaciones del Museo Arqueologico Santa Cruz de Tenerife, 6. Vol. II: 135–45.

Isaac, G. Ll. 1967a. The stratigraphy of the Peninj Group – early Middle Pleistocene formations west of Lake Natron, Tanzania. In *Background to African evolution*, eds W. W. Bishop and J. D. Clark. University of Chicago Press. Chicago. 229–57.

Isaac, G. Ll. 1967b. Towards the interpretation of occupation debris – some experiments and observations. *Kroeber Anthropological Society Papers.* 37:31–57.

Isaac, G. Ll. 1968. Traces of Pleistocene hunters: an East African example. In *Man the hunter*, eds I. Devore and R. Lee. Aldine, Chicago. 253–61.

Keller, C. M. 1966. *Archaeology of Montagu Cave.* Unpublished dissertation submitted in partial satisfaction of the requirements for the Ph.D. degree, University of California, Berkeley.

Keller, C. M. 1966. The development of edge damage patterns on stone tools. *Man.* 1:4: 501–11.

Kleindienst, M. R. 1961. Variability within the Late Acheulian assemblage in East Africa. *South African Archaeological Bulletin.* 16:35–52.

Kleindienst, M. R. 1962. Components of the East African Acheulian assemblage: an analytic approach. *Actes du IVe. Congrès Panafricain de Préhistoire et de l'étude du Quaternaire. Section III. Annales – Séries IN–8° – Sciences Humaines,* No. 40. Musée Royale de l'Afrique Centrale, Tervuren, Belgique. 81:111.

Kretzoi, M. and Vertes, L. 1965. Upper Biharian (Inter Mindel) Pebble industry occupation site in western Hungary. *Current Anthropology.* 6:74–87.

Lancaster, J. 1968. On the evolution of tool-using behaviour. *American Anthropologist.* 70:56–66.

Leakey, L. S. B. 1935. *The stone age races of Kenya.* Oxford.

Leakey, L. S. B. 1951. *Olduvai Gorge. A report on the evolution of the handaxe culture in Beds I–IV.* Cambridge University Press, Cambridge.

Leakey, L. S. B. 1952. The Olorgesailie Prehistoric Site. In *Proceedings of the first Pan-African Congress on Prehistory,* 1947, eds L. S. B. Leakey and S. Cole. Blackwell, Oxford.

Leakey, L. S. B. 1957. Preliminary report on a Chellean I living site at Bk ii, Olduvai Gorge, Tanganyika Territory. *Proceedings of the Third Pan-African Congress on Prehistory, Livingstone 1955.* Chatto and Windus, London. 217–18.

Leakey, L. S. B. 1960. Finding the world's earliest man. *National Geographic Magazine.* 118: 420–35.

Leakey, L. S. B. 1961a. *The progress and evolution of Man in Africa.* Oxford.

Leakey, L. S. B. 1961b. Exploring 1,750,000 years into Man's past. *National Geographic Magazine* 120:564–89.

Leakey, L. S. B. 1962. A new Lower Pliocene fossil from Kenya. *Annals and Magazine of Natural History.* Series 13, IV: 689–96.

Leakey, L. S. B. 1963a. Very early East African Hominidae and their ecological setting. In *African ecology and human evolution,* eds F. C. Howell and F. Bourlière. Aldine, Chicago. 448–57.

Leakey, L. S. B. 1963b. Adventures in the search for Man. *National Geographic Magazine.* 123:132–52.

Leakey, L. S. B. 1966a. *Nature.* 212:1615–16. Reply to P. S. Martin 1966.

Leakey, L. S. B. 1966b. *Homo habilis, Homo erectus* and the Australopithecines. *Nature.* 209: 1279–81.

Leakey, L. S. B. 1967a. *Nature.* 215:213. Comments on Martin 1967.

Leakey, L. S. B. 1967b. An Early Miocene member of Hominidae. *Nature.* 213:155–63.

Leakey, L. S. B., Evernden, J. F. and Curtis, G. H. 1961. Age of Bed I, Olduvai Gorge, Tanganyika. *Nature.* 191:478–9.

Leakey, L. S. B., Tobias, P. V. and Napier, J. R. 1964. A new species of the genus *Homo* from Olduvai Gorge. *Nature.* 202:7–9.

Leakey, M. D. 1966a. A review of the Oldowan culture from Olduvai Gorge, Tanzania. *Nature.* 210:462–6.

Leakey, M. D. 1966b. Primitive artefacts from Kanopoi Valley. *Nature.* 212:577–81.

Leakey, M. D. 1967. Preliminary summary of the cultural material from Beds I and II, Olduvai Gorge, Tanzania. In *Background to evolution in Africa*, eds W. W. Bishop and J. D. Clark, Chicago University Press. Chicago. 417–42.

Lee. R. B. 1968. What hunters do for a living, or how to make out on scarce resources. In *Man the hunter*, eds I. Devore and R. Lee. Aldine, Chicago. 30–48.

Leopold, L. B., Emett, W. W. and Myrick, R. M. 1966. Channel and hillslope processes in a semi-arid area New Mexico. *Geological Survey professional paper* 352-G. Washington. 193–253.

Livingstone, D. A. 1967. Postglacial vegetation of the Ruwenzori Mountains in Equatorial Africa. *Ecological Monographs.* 37:25–52.

Lowe, C. van Riet. 1952. The Pleistocene geology and prehistory of Uganda. Part II: Prehistory. *Geological Survey of Uganda*, Memoir VI.

Lumley, H. de. 1963. Découverte d'outils préhistoriques d'âge villafranchien dans la grotte du Vallonet (Roquebrune-Cap-Martin, Alpes-Maritimes). *Comptes Rendus, Académie des Sciences, Paris.* 256:4261–2.

Martin, P. S. 1966. African and Pleistocene overkill. *Nature.* 212:339–42.

Martin, P. S. 1967. Overkill at Olduvai Gorge. *Nature.* 215:212–13.

Martyn, J. 1967. Pleistocene deposits and new fossil localities in Kenya. *Nature.* 215:476–79.

Mason, R. 1962. *Prehistory of the Transvaal.* Witwatersrand University Press, Johannesburg.

Mathews, W. H. and Curtis, G. H. 1966. Date of the Plio-Pleistocene boundary in New Zealand. *Nature.* 212:979–80.

Movius, H. L. 1948. The Lower Palaeolithic Cultures of Southern and Eastern Asia. *Transactions of the American Philosophical Society.* 38:329–419.

Mulvaney, D. J. and Joyce, E. B. 1965. Archaeological and geomorphological investigations on Mt Moffat Station, Queensland, Australia. *Proceedings of the Prehistoric Society.* 31:147–212.

Napier, J. 1962. Fossil hand bones from Olduvai Gorge. *Nature.* 196:409–11.

Napier, J. 1967. The antiquity of human walking. *Scientific American.* 216:4:56–67.

Oakley, K. P. 1956. The earliest fire makers. *Antiquity.* 30:102–7.

Opdyke, N. D., Glass, B., Hayes, J. D. and Foster, J. 1966. A paleomagnetic study of Antarctic deep sea cores. *Science.* 154:349–57.

Posnansky, M. 1959. The Hope Fountain Site at Olorgesailie, Kenya Colony. *South African Archaeological Bulletin.* 16:83–9.

Robinson, J. T. 1963. Adaptive radiation in the Australopithecines and the origin of Man. In *African ecology and human evolution,* eds F. C. Howell and F. Bourlière. Aldine, Chicago.

Robinson, J. T. 1965. *Homo habilis* and the Australopithecines. *Nature.* 205:121–4.

Savage, D. E. and Curtis, G. H. in press. The Villafranchian stage-age and its radiometric dating. Typescript of a paper for publication in the *Proceedings of the Society of Economic Palaeontologists and Mineralogists,* Research Committee Symposium on radiometric dating and palaeontological correlation, held in Los Angeles, April 1967.

Semenov, S. A. 1964. *Prehistoric Technology.* Cory, Adams and MacKay, London.

Simons, E. L. and Pilbeam, D. R. 1965. Preliminary revision of the Dryopithecinae (Pongidae, Anthropoidea) *Folia Primatologia.* 3:81–152.

Stekelis, M. 1966. *Archaeological excavations at 'Ubeidiya, 1960–63.* The Israel Academy of Sciences and Humanities, Jerusalem.

Tobias, P. V. and Koenigswald, G. H. R. von. 1964. A comparison between the Olduvai Hominines and those of Java and some implications for Hominid phylogeny. *Nature.* 204:515–18.

Tobias, P. V. 1965. New discoveries in Tanganyika: their bearing on Hominid evolution. *Current Anthropology.* 6, No. 4.

Tuttle, R. H. 1967. Knuckle walking and the evolution of hominoid hands. *American Journal of Physical Anthropology.* 26:171–206.

Vogel, J. C. and Waterbolk, H. T. 1967. Groningen Radio Carbon dates VII. *Radio Carbon.* 9:145.

Walker, D. and Sieveking, A de G. 1962. The palaeolithic industry of Kota Tampan, Perak, Malaya. *Proceedings of the Prehistoric Society, New Series.* XXVIII:103–39.

Washburn, S. L. 1965. An ape's eye-view of human evolution. In *The Origin of Man,* ed. P. L. Devore, a symposium sponsored by the Wenner-Gren Foundation for Anthropological Research, Inc.

Woodburn, J. 1968. An introduction to Hadza ecology. In *Man the hunter,* eds I. Devore and R. Lee. Aldine, Chicago. 49–55.

Zeuner, F. E. 1959. *The Pleistocene Period. Its Climate, chronology and faunal successions.* 2nd edn, Hutchinson, London.

Zinderen Bakker, E. M. van. 1967. Upper Pleistocene and Holocene stratigraphy and ecology on the basis of vegetation changes in sub-Saharan Africa. In *Background to evolution in Africa,* eds W. W. Bishop and J. D. Clark. University of Chicago Press, Chicago. 125–46.

Problems in Indian archaeology, and methods and techniques adopted to tackle them

H. D. Sankalia

Archaeology in India has a multiple role to play. Not only has it to unravel or reveal the country's long prehistoric past, which lies mostly unknown, and wherever known uninterpreted, but it has also to be a handmaid of, and corrective to, a past with a long tradition of unwritten literature. This literature, known as Vedic and Puranic, continued to be handed down orally even in early historic times. Some of it, particularly the bardic (Puranic and epic), naturally got inflated. Thirdly, archaeology has to show how far the pre- and protohistoric cultures can be related to the preliterates who continue to survive in many parts of India.

The Deccan College Research Institute, since its inception, has had two main aims. First, to reconstruct the past with the help of archaeology in all its aspects, including inscriptions. Second, to link history with prehistory through protohistory.

I

Before 1939 scholars made some attempt to study the Purāṇas and epics. Dynastic lists as well as accounts of culture – customs, manners, dress, ornaments, and such aspects of material and spiritual culture – had been prepared. These accounts relied heavily on internal evidence only. To this extent, these works were uncritical. For it was forgotten or never realized that this literature, except the Vedic, was often interpolated, and so the epics and Purāṇas did not refer to one particular culture or age, but to several cultures or ages.

Some more objective standard was necessary to measure or judge the accounts – particularly the span and time factor of events, objects and personalities mentioned in the Purāṇas. Critical editions of various old texts were not enough. What was needed was hypercriticism.

Archaeology though not so well developed some thirty years ago was the only discipline which could supply this norm. The *Vāyu Purāṇa* was then believed to be the oldest Purāṇa according to internal evidence. This Purāṇa was selected for such a critical treatment. Its contents were minutely analysed, card-indexed, and then regrouped into various topics. These were then compared on the one hand with well-dated archaeological objects, such as coins and sculptures, and on the other with equally well-marked stages of literature. It was thus possible to stratify the *Vāyu Purāṇa* with the help of archaeology (Patil 1946: 14).

(i) The Archaic Survivals, which are coeval with the similar material found in the Vedic Literature, 500 B.C., may be safely considered to be the lowest time-limit of this material.
(ii) The Ancient Material of the Purāṇa aligning itself with the early Dharmasutras, the early Buddhist and Jain canonical literature, the *Arthaśāstra* of Kauṭilya, the *Manu Smṛiti*, and the earlier portions of the Great Epic *Mahābhārata*. Broadly speaking, the beginning of the Christian era may be supposed to be the lowest chronological terminus of the material.
(iii) The Accretions or the mass of material that has been incorporated into the body of the text. Most of this material falls in line with the Smṛiti works, the later portions of the Great Epic, etc. It should be noted that this material does not generally cross the chronological line demarcated by the date A.D. 500.

It might also be mentioned that before undertaking this work the lower limit of the various incidents mentioned in the Purāṇas was fixed by classifying the contents of the Gupta inscriptions, which happen to be well dated individually and collectively (Patil 1940: 148–65).

The *Mahābhārata*, one of our two great epics, was similarly approached. Out of its numerous aspects, only those referring to the description of gods and goddesses (iconography) were selected for study. This work, entitled *Iconographical Elements in the Mahābhārata* (Chapekar 1958: 232), takes us very much further than the critical text of the epic prepared by the Bhandarkar Oriental Institute at Poona. Chapekar was able to demarcate three strata or phases in the *Mahābhārata*.

The pre-epic phase is mostly derived from the Vedic and the post-Vedic literature; the first phase covering the early period of the *Mahābhārata* composition may be brought down to 300 B.C., and the second immediately follows it and sometimes may overlap it; the third begins approximately in the first century A.D. and may extend to the Gupta-Chālukyan period. (*c.* A.D. 300–700).

When ancient places or sites referred to in the Purāṇas and epics are scientifically excavated it becomes possible to say on the strength of the stratigraphical data when certain events in the Purāṇas could have taken place. In fact we are able to visualize how and when the stories in this bardic literature got inflated from time to time. Thus our excavations at Dwarka and Tripuri, though on a limited scale, not only proved the antiquity of the former site, but showed that the traditions about its submergence in the sea were well founded, though not so old as popularly believed (Sankalia 1964a, 1966a). The second excavation showed how the city of Tripuri was founded in the Early Iron Age in the sixth to seventh century B.C., how it became Shaiva in the third to fourth century A.D., displacing Buddhism and Jainism and how these incidents were represented in purely Shaiva Purāṇas in the seventh to eight century (Sankalia 1966b).

Likewise, the account of the foundation of Takshaśilā and Pushkalāvatī given in the *Rāmāyaṇa* refers *not* to the earliest foundation of these cities as believed by Wheeler (1962: 15), but to the towns laid out later in chessboard pattern by the Indo-Greeks in the first to second century B.C. (Dani 1967: 25). To this extent the *Rāmāyaṇa* account is late. Here again archaeology affords striking proof of the traditional view and the textual critics who had maintained that the Bālakāṇḍa of the *Rāmāyaṇa* was composed later.

Inscriptions engraved in the 2,000-year-old Brāhmī script and its later variants on stone and copper plates also serve as important evidence. Hitherto these records have been primarily used to reconstruct dynastic histories and to throw light on a few aspects of culture, such as religious tendencies and economic conditions. But they were rarely used for reconstructing the ancient territorial and administrative units or for understanding the composition and growth of ethnic elements in the ancient Indian society. Since many of these inscriptions are land grants to Brāhmaṇas and are dated in the then current calendars, these records provide an invaluable source for such socio-political or administrative studies.

Realizing the importance of these inscriptions, the Deccan College has during the last twenty-five years worked out the territorial units in Gujarat, Maharashtra, Northern Mysore, Madhya Pradesh, parts of Uttar Pradesh, Rajasthan and Madras, ranging over a period of 1,600 years (*c.* 300 B.C.–A.D. 1300). So far the studies on Gujarat are published (Sankalia 1949), those on Maharashtra and Madhya Pradesh are partly so (Sankalia 1967b). Large wall maps (12 ft × 8 ft) in the archaeological museum of the college also depict these reconstructed units against the physiographic background of Gujarat, Maharashtra and Mysore. These studies further provide good data for understanding the composition of the Brāhmaṇas and other classes of society, as well as for understanding the changing customs of naming a child owing to the impact of new cultural forces. For it should be remembered that in India personal names were significant and were indeed a good index to a person's caste as well as religion. Inscriptional names are again of great linguistic significance (Sankalia 1965b).

2

In the field of pure archaeology the aim has been more and more precision in the methods of acquiring the data as well as their interpretation. This may be illustrated by a few examples.

During the last twenty-five years, mainly on the initiative of Deccan College, relics of the Early Stone Age have been found almost everywhere in Central and Western India and Orissa, whereas systematic collections have been made from several districts of Andhra and Mysore (Sankalia 1962–3). These surveys have left little doubt of the wide distribution of the earliest food-gathering people who used, among other stone tools, handaxes and cleavers. Uncertainty exists, however, regarding the formation of the deposits in which these tools were found, and hence about the age of the tools and about the environment in which Early Man lived.

For an understanding of these problems it may be recalled that as far as the Himalayan foot-hills and the Potwar plateau of Western Panjab are concerned, we know from the work of the Yale–Cambridge expedition that the Stone Age tool-bearing periglacial or non-glacial deposits can be directly linked up with the glacier and inter-glacial deposits of the lower Himalayas. These studies have not only dated the various lithic industries on sound geological principles but have also well established the changing environment of North-west India during the pleistocene. As opposed to this, in Peninsular India the artefacts normally occur in a coarse gravel that rests on the basal rock or clay and is capped by a thick deposit of silty sand. The Narmada has three such gravel and silt

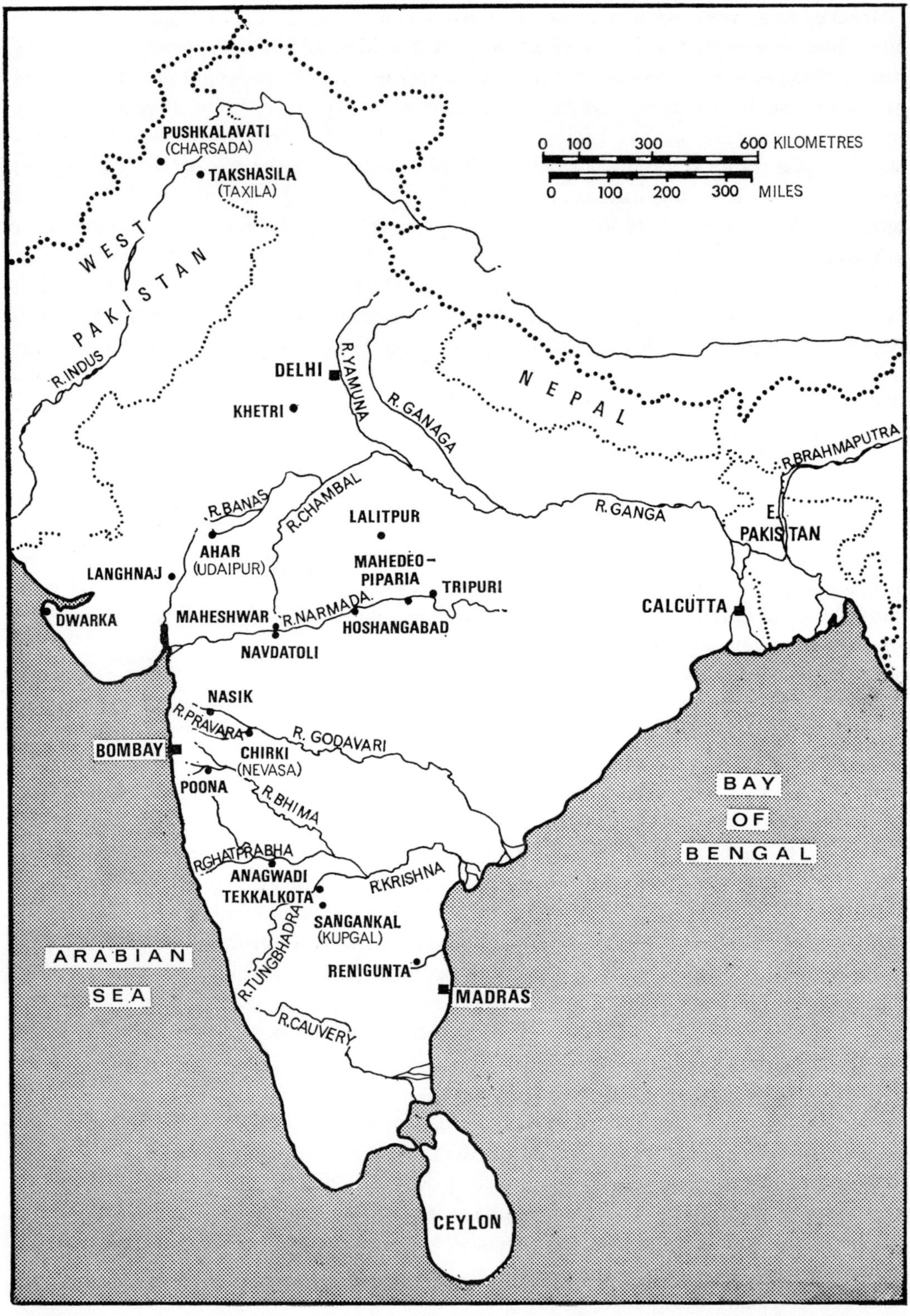

Figure 6 A sketch map of archaeological sites and natural features in India and Pakistan

deposits, while the other rivers have only two, the later ones usually exhibiting finer gravel and a different coloured silt. As a rule the artefacts are found in the gravels and rarely, if at all, in the overlying silt.

As a result of the observations at Nevasa (Sankalia 1956), it was ascertained that the finer middle gravels yielded a stone industry different from that found in the basal and in the top loose gravels. These industries were initially designated as Series I, Series II, and Series III respectively, and are now assigned to Early, Middle and Late Stone Ages. Geologists and prehistorians (De Terra and Paterson 1939: 300, Paterson and Drummond 1962: 17 and Zeuner 1950: 11 and 1963: 14) attribute the deposition of the coarse gravels to a wet climate followed by a drier phase, first causing erosion and later aggradation. Two, three, or four such cycles of wet and dry climates were thus postulated. Our systematic surveys of the Narmada and other rivers in Madhya Pradesh (Joshi *et al.* 1965), the Banas and its tributaries in Rajasthan (Misra 1967), the Goadvari and Pravara (Corvinus-Karve and Rajaguru 1967), the Krishna (Pappu 1966), Mula-Mutha (Mujumdar and Rajaguru 1966a: 131) in Maharashtra, and the Rallakalva (Murty 1966) in Andhra have, however, shown that such deposits can be traced up to or within a few miles of the source of almost all the peninsular rivers.

We have therefore begun to question the simple theory of erosion and aggradation due to a wet and dry climatic cycle. While eustatic causes might be responsible for aggradation and erosion in the lower reaches, as for instance in the Narmada (Wainright 1964), what brought about such uniform formation of deposits in the middle and upper reaches of the peninsular rivers? To understand these problems my colleague Shri S. N. Rajaguru has undertaken a geomorphological study of the Mula-Mutha, whereas Dr Corvinus-Karve has been entrusted with a similar study of the Godavari-Pravara, and a joint expedition of the Archaeological Survey of India and the Deccan College has been working on the Narmada.

From the morphometric analysis of gravels of the Mula-Mutha, Rajaguru has been able to throw some light on the depositional environments of the gravels during the late pleistocene, and his analysis of the associated soils and silts will help elucidate the problem of fluvial sedimentation in the past. Both Rajaguru and Corvinus Karve after their preliminary geological studies in the Godavari-Krishna valleys in Maharashtra have come to one important conclusion: that this part of India, so far supposed to be tectonically stable, had experienced tectonic disturbances of a moderate nature throughout the pleistocene. The main focus of such activities was in the Godavari basin, because of which a heavier sedimentation has occurred in the Godavari as compared to the Krishna. They are now trying to find out the exact role played by the pleistocene climatic changes in the history of these rivers.

Similar detailed studies have been planned around Maheshwar (Madhya Pradesh) where, unlike Hoshangabad-Narsingahpur, the stratigraphy is clearer. Preliminary petrological study of the gravel components in the pleistocene alluvium of the Narmada at Maheshwar has shown that the river in the upper pleistocene times had a much wider channel, about twice the present channel, and the pleistocene deposits are more of alluvial origin than the colluvial ones.

Associated with an understanding of the formation of these early gravel deposits is the assessment of the nature and age of the contained stone industry. So far the collections

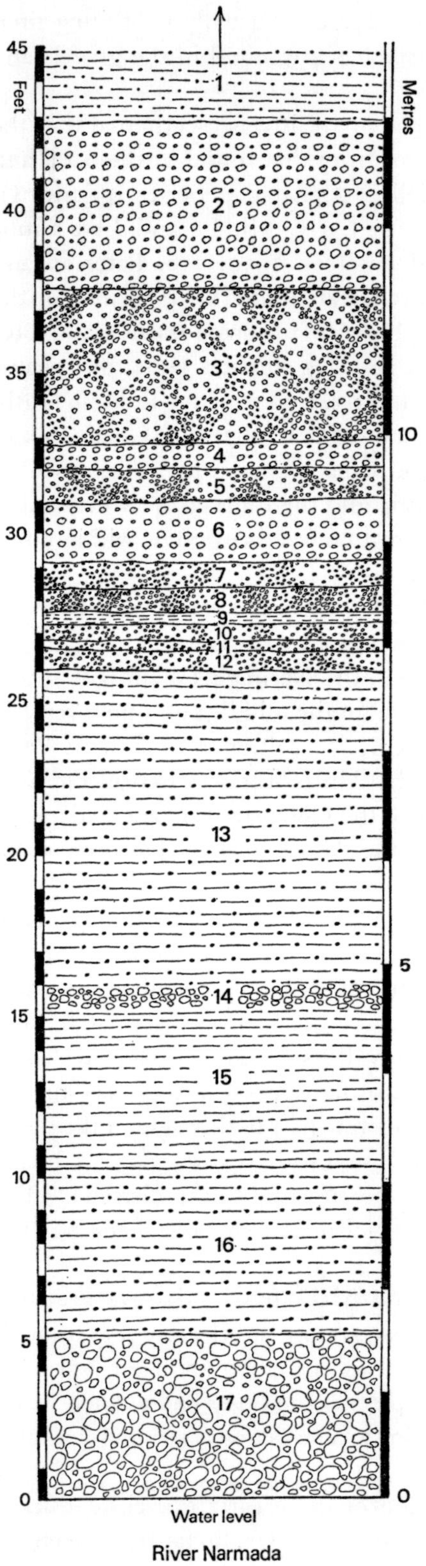

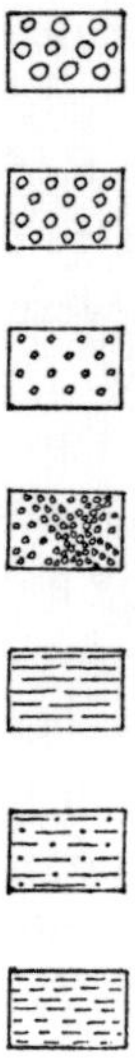

1 Yellow brown sandy silt
2 Pebbly sandy gravel
3 Cross-bedded sandy gravel
4 Pebbly sandy gravel
5 Cross-bedded sandy gravel
6 Pebbly sandy gravel
7 Cross-bedded sand with sticky yellowish tinge
8 Cross-bedded sand with reddish tinge
9 Yellow clay
10 Light grey coloured cross-bedded sand
11 Cross-bedded sand with reddish tinge
12 Grey coloured cross-bedded sand
13 Red brown silty sand
14 Pebbly gravel lense
15 Yellow brown silty clay
16 Yellow brown silty sand
17 Boulder conglomerate (Early and Middle Stone Age tools with a fragmentary bone of *Bos namadicus Falc.*)

Figure 7 The section at Mahadeo Piparia on the Narmada (district Narsimhapur, M.P.). Section of the excavated trench facing north of artefacts have been small and haphazard, hence incapable of statistical treatment. Various theories are therefore current. First, at Mahadeo Piparia on the Narmada one witnesses a development of the handaxe-cleaver industry from a true Oldowan-type pebble industry (Khatri 1966: 98). Secondly, it has been shown that the handaxe industry itself shows two phases – earlier Abbevillian and later Acheulian (De Terra and Paterson 1939: 322; Sen and Ghosh 1963: 16).

We tested these theories by excavating at Mahadeo Piparia, and the result has been most unexpected (Supekar 1965 and 1967). Though the 110 ft cliff is composed of horizontally bedded layers and there is no apparent sign of any disturbance, still the pebbly or bouldery gravel, at a depth of 15 ft from the talus surface, showed a mixture of three different lithic industries: pebble tools and large flakes; ovates, handaxes and cleavers, and between 22 and 80% of tools that are today classed as Middle Stone Age (fig. 7). Thus Supekar's small but careful excavation on the Narmada is indeed an eye-opener. Not only is there no pure-Oldowan or Mahadevian pebble tool industry in the basal gravel, but there is also a combination of pebble tool, advanced handaxe and the Middle Stone Age industries. Thus, surface observations and so-called *in situ* collections from river gravels are suspect.

Our other quest has been the search for the home of Early Man, and particularly for his skeletal remains. The first step is to discover primary sites, sites where man would live even temporarily and make tools from the easily available raw material. Of three such sites, Lalitpur in Madhya Pradesh discovered by Singh (Singh 1965), Anagwadi in Mysore discovered by Pappu (Pappu 1966), and Chirki-Nevasa discovered by Corvinus-Karve, the evidence from the last has been most convincing. Here within an area of 20 ft × 15 ft, 700 tools all in mint condition, made from local coarse reddish basalt as well as dyke basalt, have been found as they were made and left by their makers, along with the debris (Corvinus-Karve 1967 and plate 5). Only a part of this 'camp' has been exposed, and it is hoped that further work in another season will lay bare the remains of man himself.

Another regional survey, by Dr M. L. K. Murty (1966) around Renigunta in Andhra Pradesh, revealed the existence of a blade and burin industry comparable in many respects to the Upper Palaeolithic of Europe. Further intensive work has yielded some 600 tools, all stratigraphically and typologically belonging to a period between the Middle and Late Stone Ages (plate 6). Excavations have therefore been planned at the site which, it is hoped, will give some other evidence about the blade-and-burin culture.

While the large Nevasa collection is under study, Dr Misra (1967) and Dr Pappu (1966) have given us an up-to-date statistical account of the Early, Middle, and Late Stone Age industries found in the Berach basin in South-west Rajasthan and the Krishna basin in Karnatak or Northern Mysore respectively. Dr Misra has employed Chi Square and '*t*' tests to measure inter-industry and inter-culture variability in terms of the frequencies and measurements of various tool types in the Early, Middle, and Late Stone Ages in the Berach basin in South Rajasthan. The use of statistical methods on a bigger scale, will, it is hoped, help in a better understanding of the dynamics of culture change during the Stone Age.

Our excavations at traditionally historic and prehistoric (protohistoric) sites like Nasik, Nevasa, Maheshwar, and Ahar (Udaipur) have not only shown that all these sites are old (of course, probably not so old as the orthodox scholars and laymen believed them to be), but that every one of them represents a distinct group of cultures which flourished in Maharashtra, Madhya Pradesh and Rajasthan between *c.* 1800–1700 B.C. and 1000 B.C. These excavations, preceded and followed by planned explorations, have helped fill on the one hand the gap between the Early Historic and protohistoric, and on the other hand between the prehistoric (Late Stone Age) and the protohistoric. We are now engaged in finding out the identity of the authors of these prehistoric cultures. Out of the several possibilities two or three are most likely, as suggested by the clues offered by a few distinctive pottery shapes (Allchin 1961) and designs as well as shapes (Sankalia 1964b), and by the study of human skeletal remains (Ehrhardt and Kennedy 1965; Kennedy and Malhotra 1966; Nagaraja Rao and Malhotra 1965). The first is that these Chalcolithic cultures were in part at least, if not wholly, brought about by the migration of food-producing communities or their wares, or by the diffusion of ideas from Western Asia. The other theory is that the aboriginal inhabitants of Mysore and Maharashtra (and also Madhya Pradesh and Rajasthan?) were self-supporting pastoral-cum-food-producing people, each producing a specialized type of pottery, but otherwise not much different economically and perhaps racially. These people, who do not seem to be racially much different from the Bhils and other aboriginals or preliterates, were probably driven out to the hills and forests by the later Sanskrit-speaking peoples.

To substantiate these theories, much more evidence is necessary than is available at present. It is also essential to carry out archaeo-ethnographic studies of the preliterates who still live in or around the excavated sites. To achieve the first objective we excavated horizontally Navdatoli, a site opposite Maheshwar, then Ahar, Tekkalkota and Sangankal, the last two in the heart of the Polished Stone Axe cultures. Later Miss Nagar studied the Bhils and others residing around Ahar (Nagar 1966) and Malhotra studied the Boyas (not published). The most positive gain has been the understanding of the Neolithic way of life in Andhra-Mysore (Sankalia 1964c) and the Chalcolithic and Copper Age settlement pattern in Madhya Pradesh and Rajasthan (Sankalia 1967a: 262; Sankalia, Deo and Ansari 1967–8). On these firm bases we shall be able to proceed.

Another problem that was (and is still) occupying the mind of scholars in India was whether there was a hiatus between the Chalcolithic and the Early Historic cultures or between the former and the preceding Stone Age culture. Wheeler's (1948) work at Brahmagiri showed that there was an overlap between the Polished Stone Age and the Megalithic culture. However, our excavations at Nevasa (Sankalia *et al.* 1960) District Ahmednagar revealed the existence of a weathered soil horizon between the Chalcolithic and the Early Historic. This observation was later supported by the late Professor Zeuner when a much larger area at Nevasa was exposed for inspection.

The only way to confirm these observations was to analyse chemically the entire excavated profile by taking samples at every 10 cm. This was done by our archaeological chemist Dr G. G. Mujumdar. His analysis has shown that the weathered layer is a true natural soil developed on the debris of the Chalcolithic habitation. As the formation of such a soil requires an uninterrupted period of at least some hundreds of years, it also proves a definite time gap between the Chalcolithic and the Sātavāhana culture at Nevasa. Further, the comparison of this weathered layer with the virgin black soil occurring at the base of the Chalcolithic habitation, indicates a deterioration in the climate.

Having proved the hiatus at Nevasa, Dr Mujumdar has now enlarged his field, and soil samples from several Chalcolithic–Neolithic sites in Maharashtra and Madhya Pradesh and Mysore have been studied. He has made a comparative study of the black (fossil or buried) soils on which the Chalcolithic–Neolithic people came and settled and the modern soils occurring in these areas. This study has enabled him to postulate better conditions, both as regards climate and vegetation, prevailing in the Chalcolithic–Neolithic period. These fossil soils were found to be richer and more fertile than their modern counterparts and were suited for a better growth of cereals (grasses), which can be taken as an indirect evidence of food-production. These conditions must have subsequently deteriorated to yield the modern soils and vegetation.

Similarly Mujumdar and Rajaguru's study of the weathered or buried soil layer in an ashmound at Kupgal, District Bellary, Mysore has shown the existence of a wet climatic phase between the occupation of the Neolithic, or the ashmound, people and the earlier stone-using people (Mujumdar and Rajaguru 1966b).

The microlithic site at Langhnaj, first dug by the writer in 1941–2 and subsequently worked on for several seasons (Sankalia 1965a), did not yield any datable artefacts from the lower layers, with which were associated many of the human skeletons, animal bones and microliths. Nor is it possible to place this entire complex in a true stratigraphical context, because no more than two layers are visible to the naked eye and the one detected by the late Professor Zeuner (namely, a buried soil layer indicating a humid climatic phase within the main arid phase), is of no practical value. For unless we 'see' the layer, it cannot be dug out. As a last resort, in the absence of charcoal, it was decided to obtain a relative date of the entire 6 ft deposit by analysing the fluorine, nitrogen and uranium content of bones found at various levels. Currently Dr K. P. Oakley is engaged on this work, while the few charred bones have been sent to the Tata Institute of Fundamental Research for C^{14} dating.

Our large-scale horizontal excavations of the Chalcolithic site at Navdatoli on the Narmada in Madhya Pradesh had yielded some 23,000 chalcedony blades and cores, after rejecting 7,000 pieces on the site. This vast collection contains cores in various forms, parallel-sided blades (used and unused), parallel-sided blades with one end slightly curved and pointed and hence hereafter described as 'penknife' blades, serrated blades, a few trapezes, lunates and awls. While excellent statistical accounts could be prepared on this material, it was thought desirable further to ascertain the uses of the various types of artefacts by performing various functions such as cutting wood, vegetables, stalks of grains and shaving; also to relate the artefacts to the excavated remains of each structure, and then to ascertain whether the latter was for human habitation or storage. Further, by plotting the tool types stratigraphically as well as horizontally – as far as practicable relating to the exposed structures – it has become possible to find out the needs of each house in its period. Such a detailed plotting revealed that the lunates, though very few, were required by every house at each of the four phases ranging from 1500 B.C. to 1200 B.C. Nor were these mere survivals from the preceding Late Stone Age period. To answer the problem what the lunates and trapezes were required for and why their number was so small compared to the parallel-sided blades (55%), an examination of the edges of all the blades (including lunates and trapezes) was undertaken. This showed that unlike the parallel-sided and penknife blades, very few lunates had their edges used. It was therefore inferred that the lunates and trapezes served as barbs of harpoons and arrow-heads in fishing and hunting. Unlike the parallel-sided blades, which were used in the home, these would normally be lost once an arrow was shot and hence irretrievable. Their number would thus get smaller and smaller, while that of the parallel-sided blade would remain constant. This and similar inferences enabled us to say something more positive on the socio-economic condition of the inhabitants of Navdatoli from a study of the blade industry alone (Sankalia 1967: 262–8). Pottery and other finds from horizontal excavations could be similarly studied. Instead of having a large pottery section, there should be one devoted to every 'house' of each phase or period. We would thus know how many vessels, and of what type, each house required, and from that the probable size of the family might be inferred. Such a study for a site like Navdatoli would be extremely rewarding.

Our knowledge of metal technology is still very imperfect. When, therefore, in our excavations at Ahar, Udaipur, Rajasthan copper slag as well as copper tools were found, a systematic examination of the entire problem was undertaken. Samples of copper ore from Khetri, Rajasthan, as well as portions of a copper axe and sheet from Period I, Phase b, of the Ahar excavation, were spectrographically and chemically studied by Dr K. K. Hegde of the M.S. University of Baroda (Sankalia, Deo and Ansari 1967–8). These studies enabled us to say that Ahar was a copper-smelting area. This fact, coupled with the total absence of lithic blade industry from the site, further indicates that copper smelting was probably a major economic activity of the inhabitants. Hegde's study also tells us that the copper axes were cast in a crude unventilated sand, or earthy, mould and were left in a cast condition.

In archaeology of the historic periods, among several problems the one that has not been systematically tackled is the one which relates to the early temples, their style of architecture and the images which decorate their walls. For the last fifty years the latter have been used for preparing general corpuses on iconography, and identifications have been attempted very often with the help of texts of a much later period. This is anachronistic to say the least. However, the wider problem is whether the temple and the attendant images follow any particular text or school or whether the latter were written afterwards and embodied in the existing style of architecture and iconography. A group of well-dated temples belonging to a well-defined geographical area was selected for intensive analysis, and the results were compared with the texts believed to have been composed in the period. This study has shown that from the iconographic point of view, the correspondence is rather limited. However this is just the beginning, and a further probe is now in progress regarding another group of temples (Mankodi 1966).

30. ix. 67

Deccan College
Poona

References

Allchin, F. R. 1961. *Utnoor Excavations.* Hyderabad.

Chapekar, B. N. 1958. *Iconographical Elements in the Mahābhārata, Poona.* Ph.D. thesis, Poona University.

Corvinus-Karve, G. 1967. *German News Weekly.* 9.25.6.

Corvinus-Karve, Rajguru, S. N. and Mujumdar, G. C. 1967. *Some Observations on the Pleistocene Geology of Western Maharashtra, India.*

Dani, Ahmad Hasan. 1967. Shaikhan Dheri Excavations. *Ancient Pakistan.* 2 (1965–6):25.

De Terra, H. and Paterson, T. T. 1939. *Studies on the Ice Age in India and Associated Human Cultures.* Washington.

Ehrhardt, S. and Kennedy, K. A. R. 1965. *Excavations at Langhnaj 1944–63, Part III. The Human Remains.* Poona.

Joshi, R. V., Rajguru, S. N. and Sankalia, H. D. 1965. In *Indian Archaeology – A Review.* 1964–5.

Kennedy, K. A. R. and Malhotra, K. C. 1966. *Human Skeletal Remains from Chalcolithic and Indo-Roman Levels from Nevasa: An Anthropometric and Comparative Analysis.* Poona.

Khatri, A. P. 1966. Origin and Evolution of Handaxe Culture in the Narmada Valley (Central India). In *Studies in Prehistory,* eds D. Sen and A. K. Ghosh, Calcutta.

Mankodi, K. L. 1966. *The Hindu Iconography of the South Deccan.* Ph.D. thesis, Poona University.

Misra, V. N. 1967. *Pre- and Protohistory of the Berach Basin, South Rajasthan.* Poona.

Mujumdar, G. G. and Rajuru, S. N. 1966a. Environments as reflected in the River Deposits around Poona. In *Studies in Prehistory,* eds D. Sen and A. K. Ghosh, Calcutta.

Mujumdar, G. G. and Rajguru, S. N. 1966b. *Ashmound Excavations at Kupgal.* Poona.

Murty, M. L. K. 1966. *The Stone Age Cultures of the Chittoor District.* Ph.D. thesis, Poona University.

Nagar, (Miss) Malti. 1966. *The Ahar Culture: An Archaeological and Ethnographic Study.* Ph.D. thesis, Poona University.

Nagarajarao, M. S. and Malhotra, K. C. 1965. *The Stone Age Hill Dwellers of Tekkalakota.* Poona.

Pappu, R. S. 1966. *Pleistocene Studies in the Upper Krishna Basin.* Ph.D. thesis, Poona University.

Paterson, T. T. and Drummond, H. J. H. 1962. *The Palaeolithic of Pakistan.* Karachi.

Patil, D. R. 1940. Gupta Inscriptions and Puranic Tradition. *Bulletin of the Deccan College Research Institute.* 2:148–65.

Patil, D. R. 1946. *Cultural History from the Vayu Purāṇa.* Poona.

Sankalia, H. D. 1949. *Historical Geography and Cultural Ethnography of Gujarat.* Poona.

Sankalia, H. D. 1956. Animal Fossils and Palaeolithic Industries from the Pravara at Nevasa, District Ahmednagar. *Ancient India.* 12:35–52.

Sankalia, H. D. 1962–3. *Prehistory and Protohistory of India and Pakistan.* Bombay.

Sankalia, H. D. 1964a. Archaeology and Tradition. *Indica.* 1:3–17.

Sankalia, H. D. 1964b. New Light on the Indo-Iranian or Western Asiatic relations between India and Western Asia between 1700 B.C. and 1200 B.C. *Artibus Asiae.* 26:312–32.

Sankalia, H. D. 1964c. Stone Age Hill Dwellers of South India. *Indica.* 1:129–40.

Sankalia, H. D. 1965a. *Excavations at Langhnaj, Part I Archaeology.* Poona.

Sankalia, H. D. 1965b. India's Language. *Bhavan's Journal.* August 15:128–33.

Sankalia, H. D. 1966a. Recent Excavations and Past Legends of India. *Conspectus.* 2:29–36.

Sankalia, H. D. 1966b. Dwarka in Literature and Archaeology. In Ansari, Z. D. and Mate, M. S. *Excavations at Dwarka,* Poona.

Sankalia, H. D. 1967a. The Socio-economic Significance of the Lithic Blade Industry of Navdatoli, Madhya Pradesh, India. *Current Anthropology,* 8:262–8.

Sankalia, H. D. 1967b. Historical Geography from Inscriptions. In *Review of Indological Research in the last 75 years,* eds P. J. Chinmulgund and V. V. Mirashi, Poona.

Sankalia, H. D., Deo, S. B. and Ansari, Z. D. 1967–8. *Ahar: The Ancient Tambavati (Copper Age City) at Udaipur.* Poona.

Sen, D. and Ghosh, A. K. 1963. Lithic Culture Complex in the Pleistocene Sequence of the Narmada Valley, Central India. *Rivista Di Scienze Preistoriche.* 18:Fasc. 1–4:3–23.

Singh, Rameshwar. 1965. *Palaeolithic Industries of Northern Bundelkhand.* Ph.D. thesis, Poona University.

Supekar, S. G. 1965. In *Indian Archaeology – A Review.* 1962–3:11.

Supekar, S. G. 1967. *Pleistocene Geology and Prehistoric Archaeology of the Central Narmada Basin with special reference to Narsinghpur District.* Ph.D. thesis, Poona University.

Wainright, G. J. 1964. *The Pleistocene Deposits of the Lower Narmada River.* Baroda.

Wheeler, R. E. M. 1948. Brahmagiri and Chandravalli 1947: Megalithic and other Cultures in the Chitaldurg District, Mysore State. *Ancient India,* 4:180–310.

Wheeler, R. E. M. 1962. *Chārsada: A Metropolis of the North-West Frontier.* Oxford.

Zeuner, F. E. 1950. *Stone Age and Pleistocene Chronology in Gujarat.* Poona.

Zeuner, F. E. 1963. *Environment of Early Man with Special Reference to the Tropical Regions.* Baroda.

Recent work in West Africa: new light on the Nok Culture

Bernard Fagg

A survey of recent developments (excluding for present purposes any reference to protohistoric researches on the medieval empires) in West African archaeology may seem to be premature, especially since so much of the accumulated field-work of recent years is only just approaching detailed publication; but some account of recent trends and opportunities in the West African field will be offered in this paper. This will be followed by a description of current work on the Nok Culture, where much of the perishable material culture, normally lacking in the archaeological record of early African Iron Age sites, can be inferred from a study of its remarkable terracotta figures.

West Africa is taken to extend from the southern fringes of the Sahara desert (15° N) to the Bight of Benin, from Cape Verde to Lake Chad and the Cameroons mountains. Mangrove swamps on the coast yield to high rain forest and secondary forest further inland; the Guinea, Sudan and Sahel savannas succeed each other, merging into semi-desert conditions on the borders of the Sahara. These regions are sensitive to change, especially in the areas of the Sudan and Sahel savannas. A chronological framework related to environmental fluctuations is necessary to appreciate the success or failure of man's efforts at adjustment to changing ecological conditions.

Karl Butzer (1965) has estimated that the latitudinal shifts of semi-desert and grassland belts of the North and South Sahara, prior to the development of agriculture and urban settlement, varied from 50 to 150 miles and at those periods produced a contraction of the axis of the Sahara. Within those regions aeolian activity and phases of desiccation within the Holocene, in particular during the post-Neolithic, have unfortunately either totally obliterated the evidence required or rendered it extremely difficult to obtain.

A case could be made for rating the radiocarbon method of dating late Pleistocene and Recent deposits as the most valuable tool yet available to students of West African archaeology as well as to specialists in palynology, geology, and kindred disciplines. Sites widely scattered throughout West Africa can now be bracketed within the limits of this technique and thus diachronic as well as spatial variations in patterns of settlements, technologies and material culture can be discerned, in addition to the environmental fluctuations.

The preliminary nature of many of the archaeological investigations is particularly evident in the Palaeolithic period, where debris of those early hunters and gatherers is still being gathered by archaeologists. Surface surveys continue to yield numerous

Acheulian tools (Davies 1967), but there are not as yet any known sites which could produce stratigraphical sequences comparable to those at Olduvai or Kalambo Falls, though such sequences most probably exist in the Chad sediments, never likely to be exposed by erosion. The radiocarbon date of >39,000 for the Acheulian horizon at Nok, which was determined in 1957 (Y–142–8) (Barendsen *et al.* 1957: 908), could now profitably be submitted for re-determination by the enrichment process. The preponderance of handaxes over other tool types at Nok, and an analysis of their form, led Robert Soper to attribute a late date to this assemblage, when compared with sites on and north of the Jos Plateau (Soper 1965).

The interrelationships of microlithic sites are equally difficult to determine, but radiocarbon dates from Iwo Eleru, a rock shelter some fifteen miles from Akure in W. Nigera (Shaw 1967), and Rop, a rock shelter in the hills of the Jos Plateau in N. Nigeria (Fagg 1944 and 1965), 9250±200 B.C. and 25±120 B.C. respectively, suggest the survival of a technological tradition from the Late Stone Age to the Iron Age. The latter date is not inconsistent with the most recent dates published for the microlithic implements in the Tassili n'Ajjer (Davies 1967), and is also broadly contemporary with an iron smelting and smithing tradition in Nigeria and an iron using community at Ntereso, Ghana (Davies 1967).

The Sahara itself has produced evidence for Neolithic habitation both where depicted in rock paintings and petroglyphs and through the survival of such artefacts as polished stone implements, microlithic tools and weapons, bone harpoons, fish hooks and pottery. Frequently the culture layers are covered with aeolian sand, as at Tibersat-n-Elias 5 which has yielded the earliest radiocarbon date yet obtained for pastoralism in the Sahara: 5450±300 B.C. (Gif 290). This site lies within the Tassili n'Ajjer series and further radiocarbon dates within the fourth millennium B.C. have been collated by Fagan in the *Journal of African History* (1967). Jebbaren II has radiocarbon determinations of 3520±300 B.C. (Sa 66) and 3420±300 B.C. (Mc 14), associated with the bovine phase of the Saharan rock art. Sefar (3070±300 B.C.), in the same massif, has a Mediterranean flora, as has Meniet (also with a carbon date of the fourth millennium B.C.), which has in addition produced bone fish hooks and sherds decorated by the 'rockering' technique (Davies 1967). A similar technique has appeared on sherds from Ntereso and Taruga. Despite the Saharan results, the early phases of the West African Neolithic have not as yet been isolated, although it is clear that the Chad region, in particular, would yield much useful information through excavation (Lebeuf 1964).

Ntereso, situated on a scarp above the White Volta, contains a Neolithic horizon with radiocarbon dates in the second millennium B.C. (Sr 52, 61, 81). A provisional account of the site and finds has been provided by Davies (1967). The Neolithic artefacts include finely impressed ware, sherds with red paint, Saharan arrowheads, bone harpoons, fish-hooks and miniature celts. Some objects are paralleled by the Kintampo Neolithic. Apart from Ntereso, Neolithic sites in Ghana have not yet been dated.

It would be difficult to overrate the importance of the Chad basin in West African prehistory, with its communications east to the Nile and north to the Mediterranean littoral. Th. Monod (1963) summarized the geological, faunal and palynological studies, mainly undertaken by the French. In North East Chad, eight major sites have produced evidence for the presence of several groups of Pleistocene fauna, one of which was Villafranchian. Hominid remains are represented by a fragment of an eroded cranium which was uncovered at Yayo by Y. Coppens, and was tentatively described as that of an Australopithecine. Unfortunately, in none of those sites were there any associated industries, and so the Palaeolithic succession here as in much of West Africa is still a matter for speculation.

For the Neolithic and Iron Age of the Chad Region the most important single development has been the excavation by Graham Connah in the 'firki' lands (Connah 1967; Grove and Pullan 1963), some thirty miles south of Lake Chad, of a large tell site some 10·6 m. high. Daima lies in the approaches to the Lake Chad–Mandara Mountains Corridor, through which contacts between West Africa and the Nile valley would be sure to pass. The succession covers a period of uninterrupted occupation at least from the fifth century B.C. to the tenth century A.D. as determined by radiocarbon analysis. Furthermore, using smoking pipes as a type fossil, occupation would appear to have lasted until the seventeenth or eighteenth centuries A.D.

The lowest levels at Daima contain the remains of occupation by Neolithic pastoralists using polished stone axes, bone harpoons and good pottery. At about the beginning of the Christian era iron began to be introduced, a fact of very considerable interest in view of the latest dates for iron smelting and smithing at Taruga (see below). Near the top of the sequence the remains of a round house built of puddled earth was identified and not far below was the exciting discovery of a potsherd pavement laid out with sherds set on edge with a herring-bone pattern like those at Ile-Ife, in many other parts of Yorubaland and at Benin City. Crouched or flexed burials within the settlement area remained the normal method of inhumation throughout the occupation of the settlement.

A programme of analysis by emission spectroscopy in the Research Laboratory for Archaeology and the History of Art at Oxford is a development of the greatest interest to the study of all the various copper-alloy metal-casting traditions (Igbo Ukwu, Ife, Benin, Lower Niger Bronze Industry, Jebba-Tada-Giragi, Daima, Dawu (Ghana), etc.)

For Thurstan Shaw's Igbo Ukwu 'bronzes' it was found that all objects with more than 92% copper content were worked by smithing and chasing. All with less than 92% were cast by the *cire perdue* method. Zinc was found to be almost entirely absent from the Igbo Ukwu series in contrast with the later cultures, especially those of Ife and Benin. Tin bronze accounted for forty of the cast specimens submitted for analysis, and lead bronze a further four specimens (Shaw 1965, 1966).

Analyses of the Ife 'bronzes' (Willet 1964) have demonstrated that they were all cast in heavily leaded brass, with the exception of five which were cast in copper. The composition of the brass may, however, not be due to purposeful alloying but to the smelting of naturally mixed ores, which produces orichalcum, with a similar zinc content to modern gilding metal with which the Ife brasses can be most closely correlated. Mines reputed to contain orichalcum ores occur in certain parts of the Southern Sahara, from which supplies of metal were known to have been sent to Nigeria during the Middle Ages (Barker 1965). True bronzes are probably a comparatively late introduction by the seaborne trade from Europe.

A full programme of metallurgical and metallographic analysis of West African bronzes is bound to yield the most valuable results (Shaw 1966).

A simultaneous programme of thermoluminescent dating of the clay cores of West African cast metal objects (many of which have sufficient of the core adhering to the interior surface to provide samples for analysis, though not so often unfortunately in the case of the Benin plaques where removal of the clay core was comparatively easy) could revolutionize our knowledge of the relative chronology of non-ferrous metal-working in West Africa, with all its implications for archaeological and historical studies. A sample of the core of the Udo head recently acquired by the Pitt Rivers Museum, Oxford, has been submitted for testing by thermoluminescence to the Oxford University Research Laboratory for Archaeology and the History of Art, and a preliminary report confirms that it has reasonable thermoluminescent properties and will be suitable for testing when the present programme of quantitative testing on pottery is complete.

The future of the thermoluminescent technique for African studies has an importance which it would be hard to exaggerate, since pottery forms the bulk of all surviving material culture found in archaeological sites from the neolithic to the present day.

Perhaps the largest and most continuous archaeological salvage operation yet carried out in West Africa is that of watching the exploitation of the Plateau Minesfield of Nigeria, where tin, columbite and other valuable minerals are extracted from alluvial deposits, many of which are of Pleistocene and Recent age. The economically workable deposits are scattered over an area considerably in excess of 10,000 square miles, and have produced artefacts of Palaeolithic, Neolithic and Iron Age date. Between 20 and 30 million cubic yards of earth are turned over annually, much of which is mechanically handled. But even in mechanized mines valuable finds can be made, especially if the supervisory staff are interested and sufficiently observant. Almost without exception the discoveries made in mining deposits could not otherwise have been made since, 1. there are hardly ever any surface indications of buried archaeological remains, and 2. the overburden of soil would be far too expensive to remove. Conversely, since the presence of metalliferous ores is unlikely often to be related to traces of early occupation, this is some indication of how much will remain undiscovered and virtually undiscoverable over enormous areas of West Africa.

Of discoveries made during mining operations by far the most spectacular is that of an early Iron Age population whose material remains have come to be known as the *Nok Culture* after the Jaba village of Nok where they were first found. Nok lies at the foot of the Western escarpment of a group of granite hills situated in the centre of the Nassarawa Tableland (also known as the Kafanchan Plateau), which is an outlier of the Central Plateau system of Nigeria, where the main deposits of ore were formed.

The Nok Culture was first recognized in 1944 and in the twenty years which followed a large assortment of specimens were recovered from over thirty sites in an area south and west of the Jos Plateau whose long axis exceeded 300 miles. The main possibility of defining the cultural identity of the material lay in the presence of a very characteristic style of pottery sculpture (plate 7), the best of which is of such high artistic quality as to stimulate the greatest interest among historians of African art. The horizon in the sequence of stratified alluvial deposits in which this sculpture was normally to be found, particularly in the neighbourhood of Nok itself, was in or just above the basal gravels which were as a rule covered by buried sands and clays. If these could be dated, they would provide a very convenient *terminus ante quem* for the terracotta figurines. There were difficulties in accepting any of the radiocarbon dates of carbonized wood specimens from the basal gravels, because of the possibility that these could have been derived by sludging in from earlier deposits. The radiocarbon date of A.D. 200 $\pm$ 80 (Y 474) (Barendsen *et al.* 1957; Fagg 1965) for the clay deposit, a feature common to many of the sites, did not conflict with the very tentative conclusion, arrived at before the development of the radiocarbon method: that the basal gravels were likely to date from the second half of the first millennium B.C.

The identification of associated finds is of course unreliable under alluvial conditions, where some of the material may have been derived from earlier deposits by local re-sorting, which need not cause serious abrasion, e.g., to polished stone axes. Early efforts to isolate the material culture apparently related to the pottery figurines seemed to suggest a transitional phase between the Neolithic and the very beginning of the Iron Age.

It was not, however, until late in 1960 that a site was found which seemed to offer the prospect of isolating good associated evidence *in situ*, though this was not the first time that specimens were found in undisturbed near-surface sites. Two headless terracotta figurines (fig. 8) had been found by miners in the course of prospecting for tin and tantalite in a remote valley named Taruga near the village of Takushara about thirty-four miles south-east of Abuja. A preliminary examination of the deposit in which the figurines

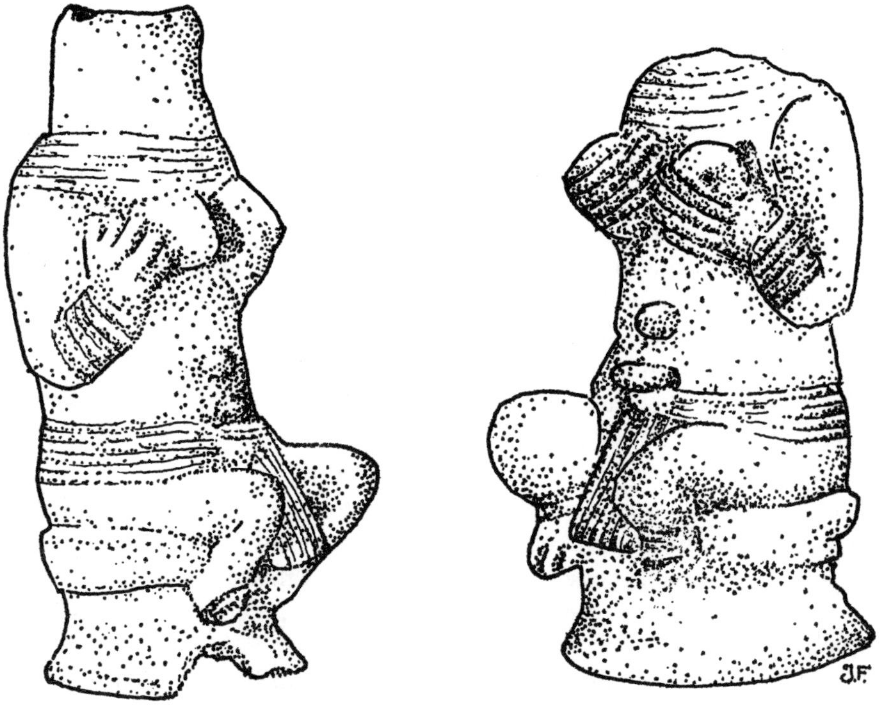

Figure 8 Two headless terracotta figurines found in 1960 at the Taruga site by miners prospecting for tin ($\frac{1}{4}$)

had been found confirmed that they were lying in undisturbed soil, and arrangements were made for a preliminary excavation at the beginning of January 1961.

Taruga is situated approximately in the centre of the Southern Guinea Zone and lies in a group of hills which are cut through by the Takushara River, as it flows westwards towards the Gurara River, a tributary of the Niger. The hills stand a few hundred feet above the gently undulating plain of the Benue Valley, and are covered by typical savannah woodland with some rain forest timber species populating the more densely wooded valleys, with the stream occasionally cutting through steep gorges.

The valley itself contains a relatively flat terrace of about three acres in extent, raised a few feet above the two small streams which flow northwards to join the Takushara river, about 40 ft below the site. A thin covering of superficial deposits provides an attractive surface for occupation, though most recent and modern villages in the area tend to be situated on higher ground with a better field of view and a healthier and more agreeable climate.

The trial excavations undertaken during a period of eight days provided abundant evidence of occupation, with a strong presumption that smelting operations had been carried on in the valley (plate 8). Finds included objects of wrought iron, a quantity of iron slag, fragments of tuyère, large quantities of domestic pottery, a number of figurine fragments (plate 9), red ochre, quartz hammerstones, worn-out querns and small concentrations of charcoal. A sample, carefully collected from layer three, 16 in. in depth, in the densest occupation layer, later provided a radiocarbon determination of 280 ± 120 B.C. (Fagg 1965).

Apart from the terracotta figurines, the most interesting finds are undoubtedly the pottery graters (Fagg 1967), shallow, flat-bottomed dishes, deeply scored inside with a diced pattern to produce a sharply abrasive surface, in all probability used in food preparation. Some are decorated with rim-top grooves and almost all have an elaborately decorated undersurface, both inside and outside the foot-ring, which itself is often decorated, exhibiting a concern for embellishment which surely indicates that they were meant to be seen when not in use.

Charred deposits inside some of the pots which had the appearance of charred food remains were found on examination to be organic, but without sufficient cellular structure surviving for identification.

The confirmation of an early date for Taruga with its Nok style figurines was made doubly interesting by the prospect of finding positive evidence of iron-smelting in sub-Saharan Africa at such a remote period. The first opportunity to return to the site and undertake further excavations came in the 1965–6 dry season.

As a preliminary to excavation, a proton magnetometer survey was carried out in an effort to locate furnaces. In spite of some doubts about the likely efficacy of such equipment so close to the geomagnetic equator, the results of the survey, the first recorded use of the proton magnetometer under tropical conditions, were outstandingly successful (Tite 1966).

Sixty-one magnetic anomalies were located, the majority of which were in the flat central area, which probably indicates the limits of actual occupation. Since it was, initially at least, impossible to predict from the readings what type of feature was indicated, since reverse anomalies and not normal anomalies (as in Europe) are more sig-

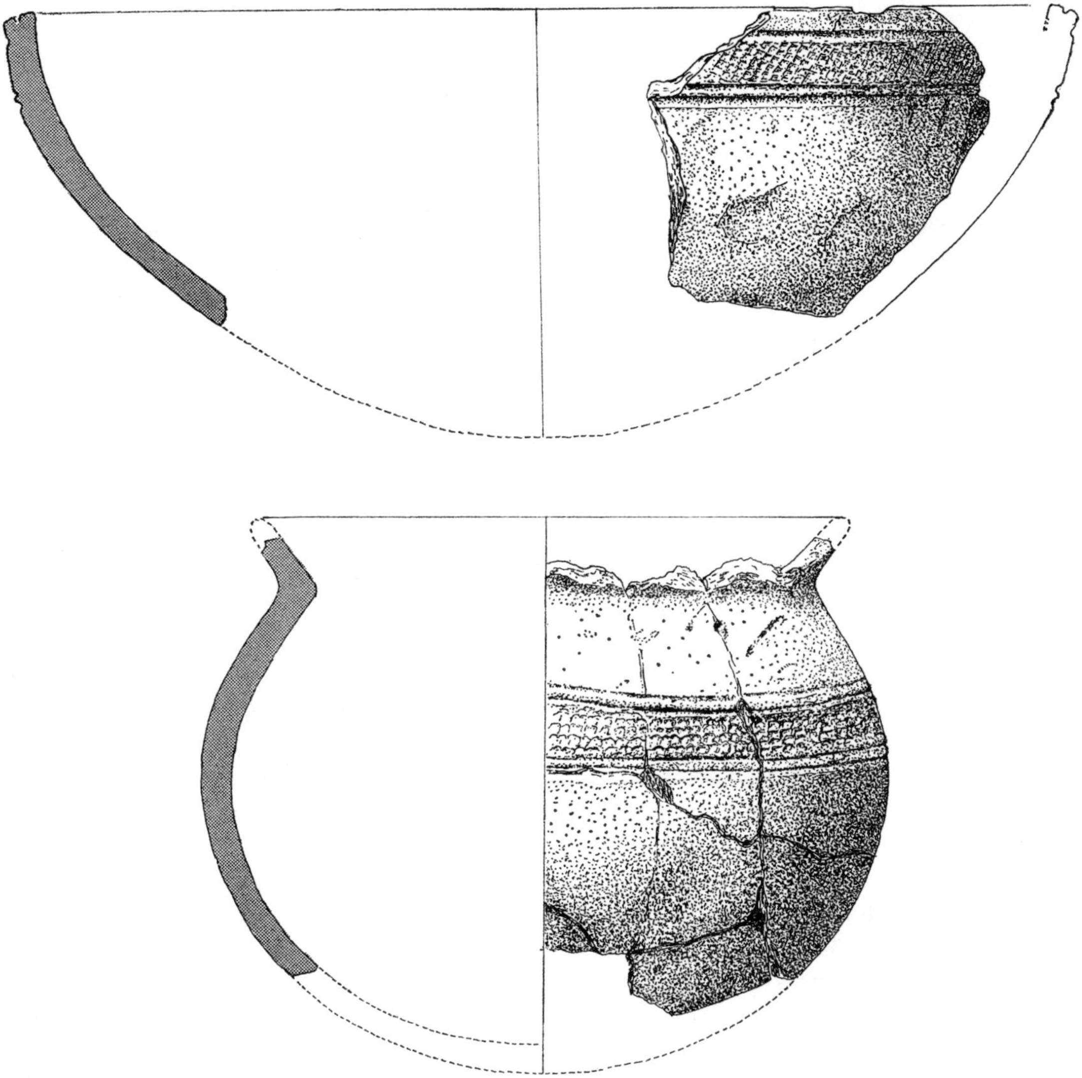

Figure 9 (*a*) Bowl with rim-top groove from the Taruga occupation site. Diameter 28 cm. (½) (*b*) Globular pot from occupation level at Taruga of type now used for cooking relish. Maximum diameter 18 cm. (½)

nificant so near to the geomagnetic equator, the partial excavation of all the anomalies was carried out. Twenty anomalies revealed concentrations of slag and of these nine contained *in situ* the structure of furnace walls and bases (plate 10). It is certainly possible that remains of others may be found beneath the slag in some of the other eleven. One other furnace was located at a point which the magnetometer did not reach. Of these ten furnaces, one has been partially excavated.

The figurine fragments recovered during the 1965–6 season have made possible the reconstruction of a substantial part of a large human figure (plate 11), consisting of an almost complete arm, bent at the elbow, from the right shoulder to the right hand, depicted as a fist clenching an object which cannot be identified. There are also a few fragments of the left shoulder which indicate an identical treatment. These fragments represent part of what must have been an extremely powerful piece of sculpture, and, presuming that it represents a standing figure, it was probably about 80 cm. high.

Fragments of domestic pottery are by far the most numerous of all the artefacts excavated at Taruga and can be divided into two main types (fig. 9): (*a*) bowls or shallow basins, without lips, and (*b*) globular pots with everted lips. The former have diameters ranging from 26 to 36 cm., while the latter vary between 14 and 22 cm. The globular pots resemble modern cooking pots used for soup, or, more accurately, relish. The two types described above account for the vast majority of the potsherds excavated. Decoration includes comb-reeding, channelling, rouletting, curvilinear incisions, cross-hatching and impressed circles.

An indication of the density of the pottery in the site is given by the results of the 1961 excavations, when about 31 cu. yd. of deposit were excavated. These yielded a total weight of 110 kgm. of sherds. Neither the distribution pattern of the furnaces nor the evidence of the pottery give sufficient indication of the precise function of the site. It remains to be determined therefore whether the site represents anything more than an industrial site for seasonal occupation.

The first of a series of radiocarbon determinations on charcoal samples from the second season's work has produced a date of 440 ± 140 B.C. (I–2960). This comes from a horizon 24 cm. below the base of the collecting zone for the earlier determination, thus providing satisfactory confirmation. A piece of iron slag was recovered in association with this charcoal sample.

The total absence of polished stone axes at Taruga and the identity of the style of the figurines with those found at the type-site at Nok does not support for Taruga the tentative conclusion drawn from the evidence of the alluvial deposits at Nok (Fagg 1959) that the cultural context was transitional between the Neolithic and the Iron Age. At another site, Katsina Ala, there was clear evidence that a stone axe or adze had been in active use after three of the superb terracotta heads had been broken from their figures. These three heads were embedded in a mass of lateritic soil in what was thought likely to have been a shrine in a former sacred grove. Trapped inside, in a manner which showed that it must have fallen there, was a thin stone spall, completely fresh where it must have split off the functional end of a stone axe. In this connection it is worth mentioning that there are unconfirmed reports that the Birom, for example, may not cut trees or branch wood in sacred groves except with a stone axe.

Until the presence of neolithic elements can be established beyond doubt elsewhere in the excavation of an undisturbed site, the Nok Culture will now have to be regarded as belonging to the Iron Age.

ADDENDUM During the third season's excavations (December 1967 to January 1968) charcoal was excavated from below the continuous slag layer in one of the furnaces, and the analysis of this sample by Isotopes Incorporated has yielded the following date for what must have been the last firing of this furnace.

Laboratory no.	I 3400
Age in years	2250 B.P. ± 100
B.C. date	300 B.C.

This sample provides satisfactory corroboration for the two previously determined dates for this, the only Nok Culture occupation site yet excavated.

The discovery of much more figurine material has tended to support our hypothesis that the continued absence of any specifically Neolithic elements in the material culture makes it seem likely that the figurines relate to the practice of iron-smelting and that the Nok Culture can now be accepted as exclusively an Iron Age phenomenon.

12. xii. 68

Pitt Rivers Museum
Oxford

References

Barendsen, G. W., Deevey, E. S. and Gralenski, L. J. 1957. Yale Natural Radiocarbon Measurements III. *Science* (1 November 1957). 126:908–19.

Barker, H. 1965. Examination of the Ife Bronze Heads. *Man.* 65:10:23–4.

Butzer, K. 1965. Physical Conditions in Eastern Europe, Western Asia and Egypt before the period of Agricultural and Urban Settlement. *Cambridge Ancient History.* Revised Edition, fascicle: Vol. I, Chapter 2. Cambridge.

Connah, G. 1967. 'Classic' Excavation in North-East Nigeria. *Illustrated London News*, 14 October 1967 (Archaeological Section No. 2276), 42–4.

Davies, O. 1967. *West Africa before the Europeans.* London.

Fagan, B. M. 1967. Radiocarbon Dates for Sub-Saharan Africa: V. *Journal of African History.* 8:3:513–27.

Fagg, B. E. B. 1944. Preliminary Report on a Microlithic Industry at Rop Rock Shelter, Northern Nigeria. *Proceedings of the Prehistoric Society.* N.S. 10:68–9.

Fagg, B. E. B. 1959. The Nok Culture in Prehistory. *Journal of the Historical Society of Nigeria.* 1:4:288–93.

Fagg, B. E. B. 1965. Carbon Dates for Nigeria. *Man.* 65:8:22–3.

Fagg, B. E. B. 1967. Nok Pottery. *South African Archaeological Bulletin.* 22 (I):85:34–5.

Grove, A. T. and Pullan, R. A. 1963. Some Aspects of the Pleistocene Paleogeography of the Chad Basin. In *African Ecology and Human Evolution*, eds F. C. Howell and F. Bourlière, Aldine Publishing Co., Chicago. (Viking Fund Publications in Anthropology, No. 36.)

Lebeuf, J–P. 1964. *The Historian in Tropical Africa.* Oxford.

Monod, Th. 1963. The Late Tertiary and Pleistocene in the Sahara and adjacent Southerly Regions. In *African Ecology and Human Evolution*, eds F. C. Howell and F. Bourlière, Aldine Publishing Co., Chicago. (Viking Fund Publications in Anthropology, No. 36.)

Shaw, T. 1965. Spectrographic Analyses of the Igbo and other Nigerian Bronzes. *Archaeometry*. 8:86–95.

Shaw, T. 1966. Spectrographic Analyses of the Igbo and other Nigerian Bronzes: Postscript. *Archaeometry*. 9:148–50.

Shaw, T. 1967. Radiocarbon Dates from Nigeria (Research Note). *Journal of the Historical Society of Nigeria*. 3:4:743–51.

Soper, R. 1965. The Stone Age in Northern Nigeria. *Journal of the Historical Society of Nigeria*. 3:2:175–94.

Tite, M. S. 1966. Magnetic Prospecting near to the Geomagnetic Equator. *Archaeometry*. 9:24–31.

Willet, F. 1964. Spectrographic Analysis of Nigerian Bronzes. *Archaeometry*. 7:81–3.

The origins of western and eastern Slav towns

Witold Hensel

One of the most controversial problems exercising historians in the period between the two world wars was the origin of the towns of Central and Eastern Europe, especially those of Poland and Ruthenia.[1] Research into this question continued for many years to be exclusively the domain of historians, to be joined towards the end of the nineteenth century and the beginning of the twentieth by historians of law. For some time these last managed to impose their opinions on many of the current investigators. Starting from the assumptions of their own discipline, they claimed that the initial birth of towns in the region under discussion might be determined by establishing the date of the assigning of so-called 'town rights' to well-defined centres. Thus, for example, in Polish conditions this moment might in many cases have been the date of the investing of a rural settlement centre with the code known as the Magdeburg Law. The conclusion followed that the origins of the Polish towns could date back no further than the middle of the thirteenth century, resulting from German colonization, and first inhabited chiefly by settlers attracted to Poland from Germany by Polish sovereigns. This legal and dogmatic opinion concerning the origin of medieval towns was already opposed as early as 1893 by J. Flach, to be followed early in the 'twenties of our century by K. Tymieniecki. Among western scholars the eminent Belgian historian H. Pirenne expressed a similar view regarding the Slav towns. But the scarcity of written sources concerning the Slav towns in the period before the thirteenth century made a wider discussion of their beginnings impossible.

Only with the development of archaeological research, growing considerably in the 'thirties of this century and particularly intensified during the last twenty years, could a new outlook on this exceedingly interesting problem become possible, opening new perspectives both in the history of early medieval Europe in general and in the development of Poland and the eastern Slavs in particular. Excavations carried out on many sites in

[1] For a comprehensive bibliography of the subject, see Hensel *Archeologia o poczatkach miast słowianskich* (Archaeology and the origins of Slav towns), Wrocław-Warszawa-Kraków, 1963. See also the same author's *Méthodes et perspectives de recherches sur les centres ruraux et urbains chez les Slaves (VIIème–XIIIème siècle)*, Warszawa, 1963 (Académie Polonaise des Sciences, Centre Scientifique à Paris, Conférences, fasc. 36); 'Les origines des villes slaves occidentales et orientales', *Atti del VI Congresso Internazionale delle Scienze Preistoriche e Protoistoriche*, vol. I, *Relazioni generali*, pp. 233–62, Roma, 1962; *Die Slawen im frühen Mittelalter*, pp. 293 ff., Berlin, 1965 and *Anfänge der Städte bei den Ost- und Westslaven*, Bautzen, 1967.

Poland, Czechoslovakia and the Soviet Union have provided such quantities of new material that we can now attempt to outline a general theory of the genesis of towns in these nations, accepting a definition of the town as a settlement possessing the following characteristics: 1. a separate economy, 2. consistent space structure, 3. a defensive character, 4. a distinct position in the country's military and administrative system, and 5. an existence in law. Certainly, all these features are typical of the full medieval towns of Central and Western Europe. But they were not necessarily present in the earlier period within which occurred the formation of the towns and their initial struggles for legal freedom. On a general view, this took place early in the medieval period, and for the purposes of this article the period may be defined as the centuries between the end of the sixth century and the middle of the thirteenth. Legal standards were indeed formed only during those centuries, and if legal distinction alone were in question, it would be impossible to consider any given centre as a town throughout the Middle Ages. But a basic distinguishing factor for the earlier years must be the economic standing of a centre, and we might then accept as the essential feature of urbanism the nature of the employment of the population, for it was this that had a character distinctly different from that of the neighbouring rural communities. Space does not permit a wider discussion of such questions, or the quoting of particular instances. But I wish to make it clear that my basic criterion here will be whether there existed in a given centre a population engaged in activities of a handicraft or trading character, or whether its occupations were essentially rural. It should be stressed also that some farming duties performed by craftsmen are not necessarily the distinguishing marks of a rural centre; nor should a village housing a handful of craftsmen, or a periodic fair, inevitably be rated as urban.

On the basis of the material now available, we can state that the period when the towns displayed *all* the characteristics of our first definition was preceded within the Slav nations, as in the West, by the presence of earlier forms. Among these might be distinguished the two varieties defined by the present writer as 'incipient towns' and 'towns endowed with local rights'.

(*a*) I consider 'incipient towns' to be those centres distinguishable by the employment of their inhabitants in occupations other than agriculture. Such people might group in open settlements around a castle or within its enclosure, subject to the prince's justice exercised in his court. They would comprise merchants, craftsmen, and also a population still largely employed on the land. This, therefore, is a settlement transitional between a rural and an urban type, and it is frequently difficult, given the inadequacy of the sources, to distinguish between a conventional village and an incipient town. Particularly is this a problem at the moment, for systematic excavations are beginning to yield objects earlier than the tenth century: earlier, that is, than the period at which most such centres had become incipient towns. Sites that are only partially excavated are naturally most difficult to classify.

Good examples of secure incipient towns in Poland are the remains of settlements already revealed in the lowest, and therefore the earliest, culture layers at Gniezno, Poznań, Opole, Wrocław and Wolin. Among these, Gniezno, Poznań and Wrocław possess a common feature in that the settlement concentration lies near a strongly fortified castle. In each case the settlement clearly consisted of loosely scattered buildings displaying many rural characteristics. But their nature as incipient towns is established by finds indicating on the one hand the occupations of craftsmen and on the other the presence of trade. Gniezno, Wrocław and Wolin together display the largest number of characteristics of such incipient towns. Gniezno, previously an open settlement, had been fortified several times during the ninth century in a very primitive fashion, and the settlements at Opole and Wolin might possibly be considered with it. At Opole one opinion holds that the whole settlement was surrounded by a common rampart, including within it the administrative centre, but that the latter was enclosed by another rampart of its own (fig. 10). Another view, perhaps less likely to be correct, is that there was no distinct area reserved for the seat of administration within the stronghold. As for Wolin, it is not yet possible to say whether the incipient town centred originally on the castle, or whether it grew up at a place where trade with arrivals from foreign parts could most conveniently be effected.

Figure 10 Opole, partly reconstructed plan of the early medieval town and later castle

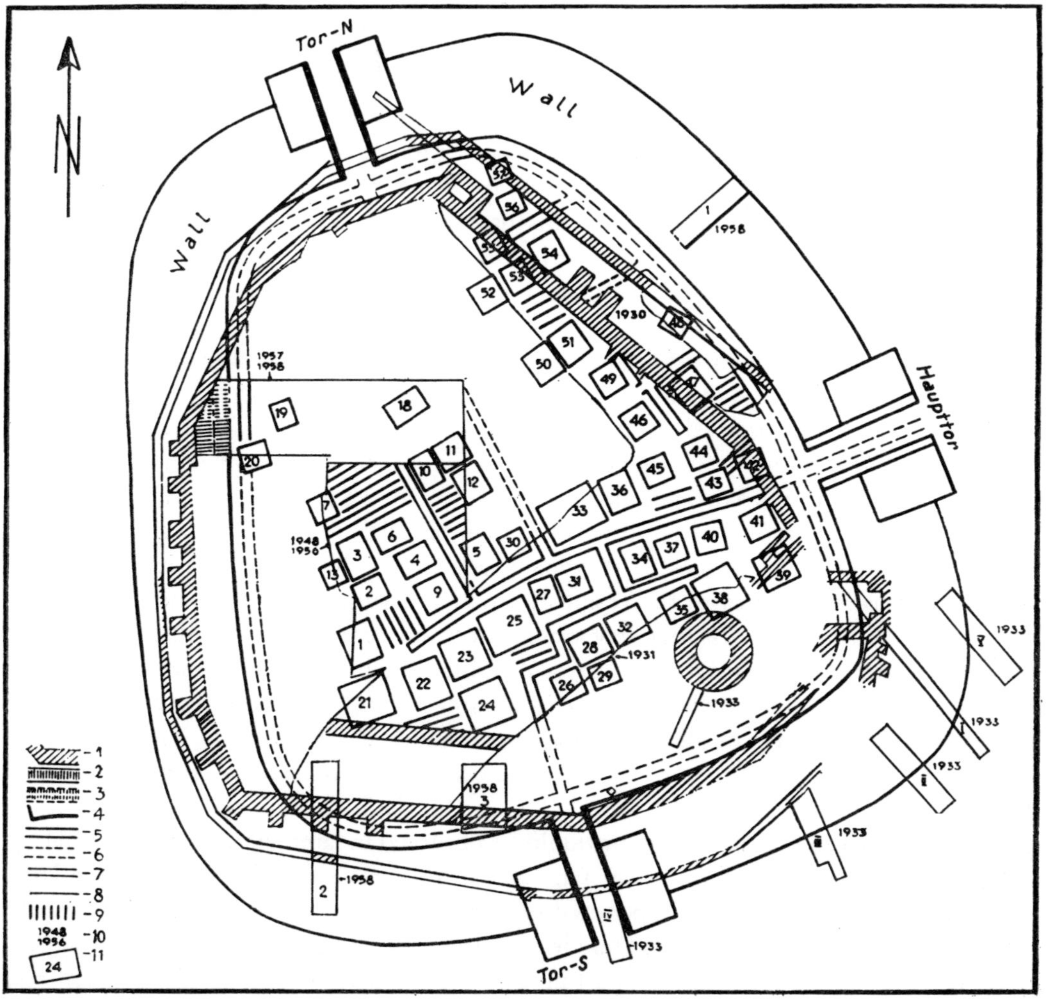

In Czechoslovakia incipient towns appear to have originated earlier than their equivalents in Poland. Certainly their development was more intensive in the regions of Moravia and Slovakia, as also in the area of Bohemia proper at the end of the ninth and the beginning of the tenth centuries. Little more can be said today of the groups of western Slavs, but it seems that the sites situated between the Elbe and the Oder may yet hold many surprises. In particular, the hypothesis that incipient towns may have existed here from at the latest the ninth century seems quite probable. And recent research carried out by scholars in the German Democratic Republic has established the falsity of any suggestion that large parts of these territories (the Sorabic lands) were culturally backward as compared with Bohemia, or that the development of the north-west Slavonic regions lagged behind that of Poland in the tenth century. As for the eastern Slavs, our knowledge of the growth of incipient towns is as yet equally slight, though the example of Kiev establishes that in those regions also such towns might form around a princely castle.

Nevertheless, it would certainly be wrong to believe that *all* incipient towns began life around a fortified stronghold. The practice of Slavonic nations in establishing towns in later ages would suggest the utmost caution in accepting such a view. But there is no doubt that the origin of many towns within fortified strongholds owed its inspiration to the initiative of the authorities, recognizing the advantages of a community centred on the castle, manned by busy craftsmen and traders and sheltered from enemy attack. Certainly it is no accident that the Slavonic words 'gród' and 'gorod' are used not merely to designate a ruler's fortified stronghold, but are also applied to a town. And the modest amount of data so far gathered indicates that the dominant form of incipient town occurred first for the most part in the period when the Slavonic nations began to shape their small and still very unsteady states.

(*b*) Just as the working out of higher social, political and economic forms displays certain differences in point of time between the western and the eastern Slavonic nations, so the same may be observed in the rise of towns 'endowed with local rights'. Their rapid formation was due to the role of a class of feudal masters deeply concerned in the process, as well as to the existence already of the centres we have described as 'incipient' towns. It would be an over-simplification to maintain that towns with local rights grew by a direct evolutionary process from their predecessors. Rather should it be said that their birth was in many cases the result of a new pressure to meet the needs of larger social and political units. In this way whereas certain centres which had the aspect of incipient towns subsequently assumed local rights, others failed and were deserted, or returned to the status of a village. At the same time a number of new towns grew out of the virgin soil to meet the needs of an expanding economy.

It might further be said that towns with local rights, related to larger and richer political entities, displayed in the period immediately following the tenth century a greater regularity of distribution than would be observed in later ages. This was certainly linked with changes in the system of fairs and in the provision of supplies to the local regions. Such towns were not dependent on far-reaching trade, but were economically associated with a local hinterland. Only in the larger centres was distant trade to play an important role, and these took their part in what was virtually a network of urban centres, covering the country and absent only in the forested regions and the marshes. The average distance separating the larger centres might have been as much as between fifty and eighty kilometres; medium-sized centres could have been found at about half that distance, and the smallest must have been very much nearer to each other than that. Such a pattern may be claimed for Poland, Bohemia, and Kiev Ruthenia, but we as yet lack the necessary data with regard to the lands on the left bank of the Oder.

While allowing for certain exceptions (e.g. the question of Wolin), we can now say that the chronology of the formation of early towns falls within the following pattern: they appeared first in the territory of Great Moravia, then among Sorabic tribes, next in the Vistula state, among north-western Slavs (though this requires further examination), in Ruthenia, Bohemia, and finally among the middle and northern Polish tribes. It would be impossible here to discuss even briefly the many varieties of early towns within all these Slavonic groups. I shall therefore mention only some Great Moravian towns, some others in Ruthenia, and a few in Poland.

Among such centres, the towns with local rights in Great Moravia show the features of development at its most primitive, a quality which follows from the time and conditions of their formation. Mikulčice, situated near Hodomin and excavated by J. Poulik of Brno, is the only one of them to have been adequately examined. Here an early urban centre had developed from about the eighth century on the site of an older settlement. It had grown in the ninth century into a large settlement complex with an area of about 100 ha. Its entire plan has not yet been worked out, but it may be supposed that the centre comprised both a single large fortification covering some 6 ha. and several smaller strongholds to which clung vast suburban settlements inhabited by warriors, craftsmen, merchants and peasants. Four stone religious buildings, of several periods, have been found within the large fortification; a fourth stone building seems to have had a lay purpose. The remains of plaster and ornamented stone indicate the rich decoration of the interior of the fortress, and there are signs to suggest that materials re-used from ancient buildings on the site had been employed in its construction. There is no certainty as yet as to the setting from which these buildings derived. Presumably the local rulers were inspired by the German clergy, by Byzantine example (following on the activity of Cyril and Methodius), and also by some Dalmation influence. Many precious objects have been found in graves near the churches, of which ten are now known, and it would seem that the majority of the gold and silver specimens discovered are of local manufacture. A number of handicrafts were practised here, including iron-smelting, smithing, carpentry, and many crafts connected with the working of horn, fibre, leather, wood, iron and clay. Traces of trading activity were also discerned. But in spite of the large area covered by the early town at Mikulčice, a preliminary estimate allows us to presume a population of not more than 2,000, perhaps of less. It was therefore a centre similar in scale to the majority of towns in Central and some areas of Western Europe in the eleventh and twelfth centuries.

Whilst in Moravia there had already been towns of an early type which would disappear with the Magyar invasion of 907 and the fall of Great Moravia, only incipient towns could be said to have existed in Bohemia (e.g. Stara Kouřim, Levy Hradec, Libice). Only in the second quarter of the tenth century did early towns appear in this territory. Among these, Prague has been the most exhaustively examined archaeologically, although the history of this centre still holds many mysteries for us. We do not know, for example, the nature of the mutual relationship of Hradčin to Vyšehrad. They were probably two distinct fortified centres, and it was around these that early urban settlements began to grow, uniting to form medieval Prague. But recent research has suggested that the most active centre was formed near Hradčin, and archaeological and other data indicate an origin at the latest in the second quarter of the tenth century. Much the same story is told by the written sources. The relation of an Arabian traveller of Jewish origin, Ibrahim Ibn Jacob, who stopped in Prague *c.* 965–6, allows us to state that Prague at that time was a steadily growing centre with active craftsmen and regular fairs, supplying both local and distant markets. As one of the largest centres of international trade in Central Europe, Prague acted as an important link in the trade between East and West, its increasing wealth being reflected in the growing number of its stone buildings. There are several important phases earlier than the thirteenth century which may be distinguished in the history of Prague. The town's development was notable in the second half of the tenth century, and there were further advances in the second quarter of the eleventh century and in the twelfth, when stone buildings were raised by the burghers themselves and when a stone bridge was built to span the river, the first of its kind in Central Europe. At the peak of its development, to judge by the area covered, Prague must have held over 10,000 citizens, whereas other urban centres were then very much smaller, with populations not exceeding an average of a few hundred people.

In the Polish lands, towns endowed with local rights appeared first in West Pomerania and Little Poland (Kraków), where they existed already in the ninth century. Their greatest period of development fell, however, in the years between the second half of the tenth and the twelfth century, and they were to go into a widespread decline only after the thirteenth century, surviving in individual cases longer than that (e.g. at Gdańsk until the middle of the fourteenth century, as also at some of the Mazovian centres). Recent excavations have shown that the majority of Polish towns reached their peak in the twelfth century, particularly in the second half of the century. Two types of town, distinguished by differences of spacial design, have been identified as a result of recent

Figure 11 Gniezno, reconstruction of suburbium rampart, tenth to eleventh century

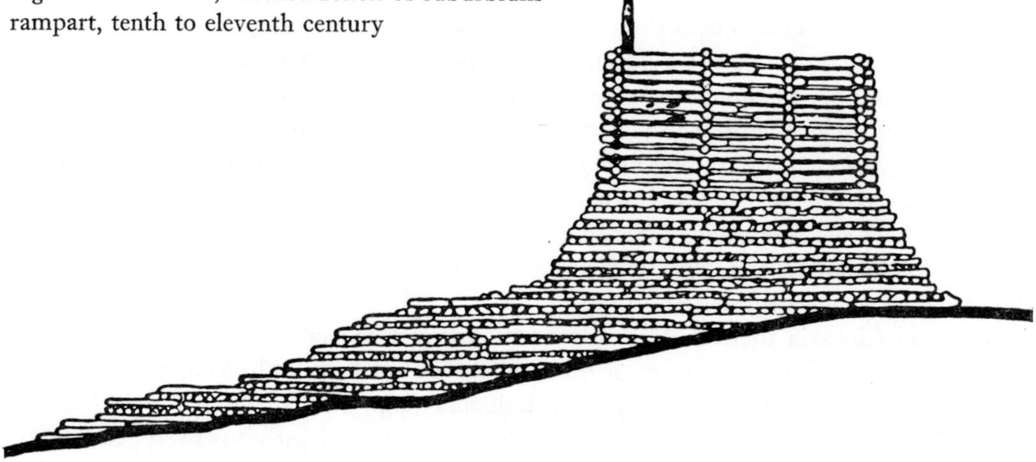

excavation. One type is characterized by concentrated buildings, the other by scattered. In the first, a town consisted of a castle, of buildings closely surrounding it, and of a suburban settlement beyond (plate 12). In the second, suburban dwellings were set at a certain distance from the stronghold. Towns with concentrated buildings were the most frequent in Poland. The majority covered an area of not more than 5–7 ha., even in their best periods, and some settlements were even smaller (e.g. Opole). Towns covering an area of several score hectares were very rare, only Kraków and Wolin achieving such distinction. Not many towns could boast of 10,000 inhabitants, even at their peak, and those with 3,000–5,000 inhabitants were counted among the largest (e.g. Gniezno, Poznán, Wrocław). As in Bohemia, towns with local rights for the most part could number no more than several hundred citizens. Their buildings were mostly of wood, though churches and palaces were often built of stone. Streets were laid with wooden logs, and approaches were guarded by strong ramparts of timber-and-earth construction, less frequently of stone-and-timber (fig. 11). Studies of the craft products from such towns have shown that it may be possible in some cases to distinguish between methods of manufacture of contemporary urban and rural products, for the latter seem to have been more conservative, showing few technical innovations. Both inland and foreign trade have left many marks on the towns, and there is evidence of an active 'middle-man' or service trade in the presence, for example, of butchers' stalls, an intermediary stage between producer on the one hand and consumer on the other. An important characteristic of the towns was the stability of land use over a long period, the same sort of employment persisting on individual house plots despite recurring disasters such as fires. On such evidence, we can suggest that there were quarters, or streets, in the towns reserved to certain types of craftsmen, and may postulate some degree of central control such as certainly existed in later settlements. Legal distinctions, more readily identifiable in the documents, undoubtedly characterized urban life at the time. The citizens of Płock, for example, obtained rights in 1237 which absolved them from military service, 'eo iure fruantur quo et milites Masovienses'. And such institutions as the 'ius forense' and 'libertas fori' early became their privilege.

At about the same time as in Poland, towns with local rights began to develop in a similar way in Ruthenia. Their beginnings go back as far as the tenth century, and their heyday fell within the second half of the twelfth and the first half of the thirteenth centuries. There are many examples to establish that the larger centres in Ruthenia at that time outgrew the corresponding Polish settlements in number of inhabitants, size of site, and wealth. But here again the majority of the towns with local rights rarely had more than a few hundred inhabitants. Of the urban centres studied, two forms have emerged most clearly. One of these might be described as excentric: that is, the suburbs kept to one side only of the stronghold (e.g. early Kiev, Czernihow, and Stara Rjazan). The other type was concentric in plan, with the stronghold situated in the middle of radiating suburbs on all sides (e.g. Novgorod and Moscow). At Kiev the rate of growth was spectacular, for whereas at the beginning of the tenth century it had covered only a few hectares, a century later it had extended to several hundred hectares, with many thousands of inhabitants. At the same time both the number and the quality of the characteristic brick buildings increased considerably. It was in the first half of the eleventh century that the splendid church of St Sophia was built, and the famous Golden Gate was

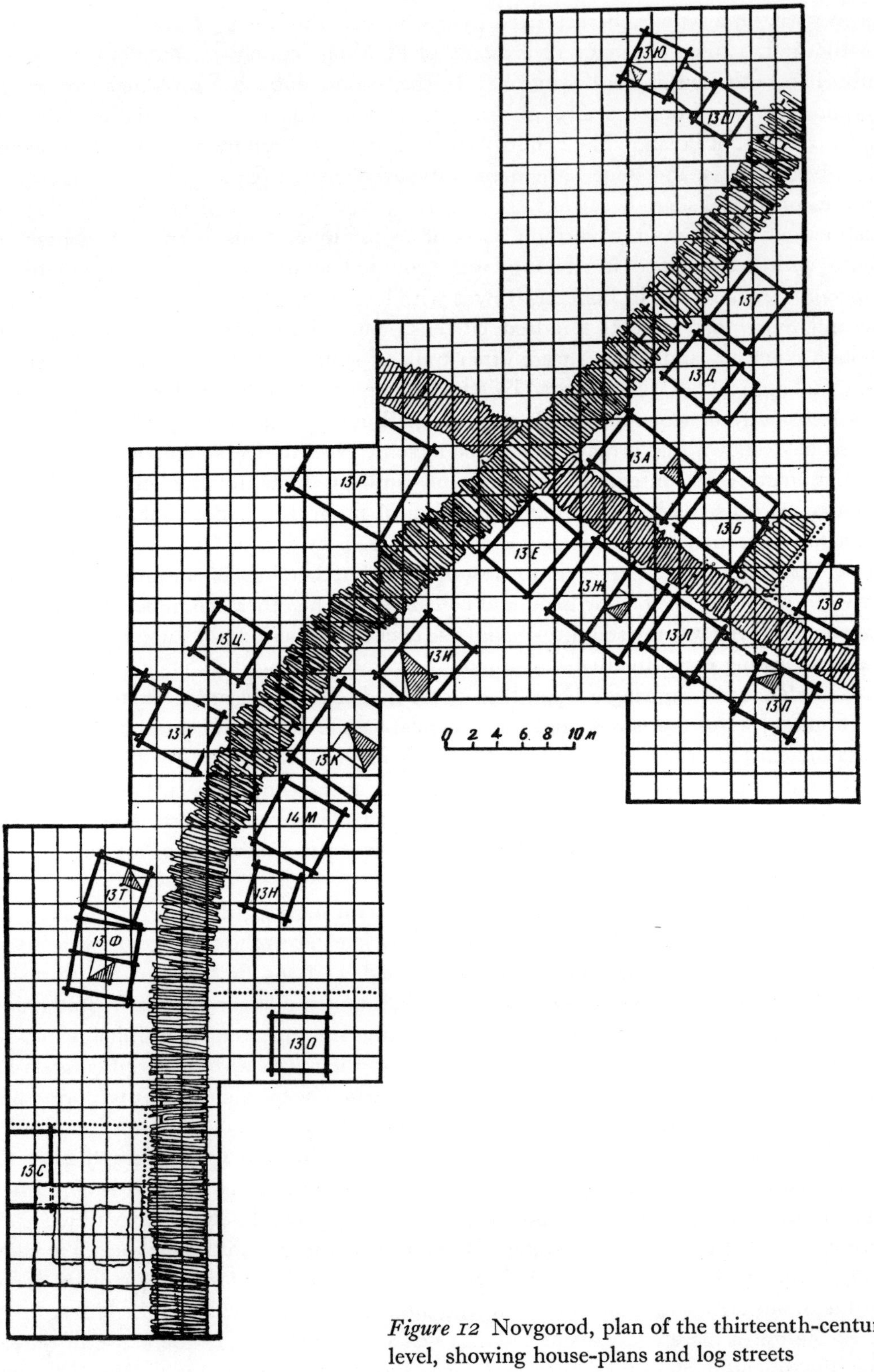

Figure 12 Novgorod, plan of the thirteenth-century level, showing house-plans and log streets

erected in brick at about the same date. Wooden houses, still predominating, were sometimes dug half into the earth, and the ramparts remained of timber construction, though the gates were built of brick. Careful researches have shown that international trade routes linking East and West converged on Kiev from as early as the second half of the ninth century, becoming particularly active in the three centuries which followed. Byzantine influence, quickly predominating, followed the introduction of Christianity from the year 988, and craftsmen coming from various Byzantine provinces appear to have been willing to settle at Kiev. A number of craftsmen's workshops, among them the atelier of a goldsmith, have recently been discovered in the town. But it was a period of recurring disasters, for a plague in 1092 brought about the death of some 7,000 of Kiev's inhabitants, and the Mongol conquest in the mid-thirteenth century checked for many years the development of a town once called the Constantinople of the Slavs.

The city of Novgorod the Great, following the recent campaign of excavations one of the most important archaeological sites in Europe, was established near Lake Ilmen in the tenth century. Through the eleventh and twelfth centuries if covered a smaller area than Kiev, some 200 hectares, and was less densely populated, but it remained wealthy throughout the period and was particularly notable for its elaborate system of log-paved streets, a technique which persisted from the eleventh century until the close of the Middle Ages (plate 13 and fig. 12). Its buildings were of wood and showed no signs of having been sunk in the ground, as at Kiev. Some houses, the property of wealthy citizens, were richly ornamented on their exteriors and might be supported by carved wooden columns. A characteristic feature of the town was the separation between quarters. The merchants lived in a quarter of their own, and craftsmen practised their trade in particular streets, each known for its own speciality. Analyses of various kinds have established that the craftsmen of Novgorod had achieved a high level of technical skill in their time. The town was supplied with sewers and with pipelines, and the discovery of birch-bark documents, many of great interest and including commercial correspondence, has established the high degree of literacy enjoyed by the Novgorod citizenry. Educational activity, explaining such literacy, is witnessed by scholars' slates bearing the alphabet, and by the lively, if primitive, drawings of the children.

In general, therefore, the towns of the western and eastern Slavs may be said to have developed along the same lines as those of Western Europe. The differences, such as they are, are of time, details of space-planning, and dimensions. Undoubtedly the influence of various cultural centres would have played a part in promoting such differences in the towns. But these were matters of architectural detail and equipment rather than important general transformations. In the formative years of the tenth century, it is clear, although cultural currents from differing directions acted upon the western and eastern Slavs, these currents had little effect on the basic structure of their towns, nor did they cause any fundamental differences to occur among them. A similar rhythm of change characterized them all, and influences may have run as much from the East to the West as vice-versa. It was a trend not to be broken until, at the earliest, the middle years of the thirteenth century.

Finally it seems appropriate to say that although many problems concerning urban origins in these lands have been resolved as the result of intensive excavation, many questions remain unanswered, demanding further investigation in the future. Insufficient research in Western Europe has made it impossible to elucidate many of the problems depending on analogies and differences between contemporary societies, and it would be to the advantage of both if extensive research in the field of urban archaeology were now undertaken in the West. A successful comparative method may be applied only if a uniform base exists. But this, for the moment, is lacking.

12.xii.67 *University of Warsaw*

The Centre for Medieval Archaeological Research, University of Caen

Michel de Bouard

In France and some other European countries, the archaeology of historical times long consisted exclusively of the search for ancient monuments or artistic objects, this search being considered as an end in itself. This concept still holds good to a greater or lesser degree. Excavation, then, means digging to try to discover such remains; if they are found, they are studied for their own sakes, so as to highlight their artistic value or uniqueness. Often, indeed, the word 'archaeology' is used to mean the history of art. It is true that this confusion dates from long ago, and this is discussed by Professor S. J. de Laet in his book *Archaeology and its problems*. 'In the Renaissance and Humanistic eras,' he writes, 'most scholars and cultured men were filled with a sometimes extreme enthusiasm for all that concerned Greece and Ancient Rome; and so, in the sphere of archaeological records, they were solely interested in works of art and buildings that had an unquestionable aesthetic character, and they studied them solely from this point of view. Archaeology, in their eyes, was identical with the history of the art of Classical Antiquity' (1954: 8). This confusion continued in the seventeenth and eighteenth centuries. When in the nineteenth century the Middle Ages in their turn excited the curiosity of scholars, their interests were the same. The French Archaeological Society, founded by Arcisse de Caumont, was in fact a History of Art Society. Even in French Universities today the word 'archaeology' is frequently used incorrectly to mean the teaching and diplomas related to the history of art. A few years ago a Swedish observer could write: 'The connection with research in art history is the distinguishing mark of French medieval archaeology' (Cinthio 1962–3: 187). In fact, although since the beginning of the nineteenth century France has produced some eminent historians of medieval art – often called 'archaeologists' – none of them has created for the exploration of the history of the Middle Ages a discipline and methods of research comparable with those perfected in the last 150 years by the prehistorians. These medieval historians have unquestionably perfected ways of interpreting texts; they have often even raised new questions about medieval history. But to illuminate many facets of this history, we still need what we still lack – that is, archaeological study in the full sense of the word, the information that an archaeology worthy of its name can find in the soil, the material remains of vanished civilizations, even the most humble and most lacking in artistic value. We know so little of the actual material civilization of the Middle Ages, of its rural dwellings and centres. Documentary records hardly mention these until the very last centuries of the Middle Ages (wills, lists of goods drawn up after deaths, and so on);

literary sources, when they mention them, give conventional or stylized pictures that are equally useless, for the same reason. Only carefully carried out excavations, then, can throw light on this domain that is so little known.

The University of Caen Centre for Medieval Archaeological Research aims at meeting this need. Three fundamental points govern its activities.

(*a*) Stratigraphical excavation methods must be used to explore the sites occupied in the Middle Ages. Excavations carried out in the time of Arcisse de Caumont and since then have too often consisted in digging down into the ground so as to lay bare architectural remains; stone, a noble material, was uncovered, and the earth that covered it, considered as a base material not worth examining, was rejected. But this earth is in itself an invaluable record. Hosts of men of whom there is no trace in written documents or in architectural works have left in the soil the lowly traces of their dwellings and occupations. It is as though the earth were the book in which their history is written. Before the invention of writing there was no other, and it still has considerable importance for our knowledge of historical times. This soil, a source of history, should be treated with the same respect as documentary records are. Even more so, for archaeological soil is a record that requires far more care than any other. The inexperienced historian who reads a medieval charter inaccurately, or comments inaccurately on it, is not committing an irreparable error; another more experienced historian will follow him and correct his mistakes. But with the soil it is different; it can only be dug once. If it has been clumsily disturbed, it has then lost all value as a historical record. As has been said, archaeology is the only one of history's auxiliary sciences that cannot use its sources without destroying them.

(*b*) The research methods and techniques perfected for other ends by physicists, geophysicists, chemists and botanists must be adapted to the needs of medieval archaeology.

(*c*) Nowadays no archaeological excavation of any importance can be carried out by a lone searcher; the intervention of well organized teams and the collaboration of different laboratories are necessary.

It would be dangerous to consider archaeology as a subject quite distinct from, and independent of, history. As Marc Bloch wrote: 'Il n'y a qu'une science des hommes dans le temps.' Medieval archaeology, in particular, must remain an auxiliary science of history. It is desirable that the medieval archaeologist should be at the same time a competent historian; if he is not, it is absolutely indispensable for him to work in close collaboration with a historian. The information obtained from archaeological excavations carried out on medieval sites is not usually the only record existing concerning these sites or concerning the problems connected with these excavations. To be correctly interpreted, the information must be seen in a more general setting, which is often known through written records or narrative sources. If this setting is not known, there is even a risk of the excavation being carried out badly, because it will not be directed on the right lines.

This is why the study of medieval archaeology at the University of Caen is carried out within the history department. First and second year students (*premier cycle*) can choose the option 'medieval archaeology' from among the auxiliary sciences of history. They are then given a general introduction to some aspects of this subject. In their senior years (*second cycle*) students studying for a history degree can choose to prepare a certificate in medieval archaeology, which is on a par with the certificates in political, religious, economic or social history of the Middle Ages. Students preparing for a master's degree (*maîtrise*) can also write a thesis on medieval archaeology, and obtain a certificate entitled 'Techniques and methods in archaeological research': often the thesis is a report on an excavation carried out by the student. Finally, doctoral theses (*doctorat de troisième cycle*) presented at the Faculté des Lettres et Sciences Humaines of Caen can also deal with medieval archaeology.

Different courses of study prepare the students for these various degrees. In particular, candidates preparing the master's degree (*maîtrise*) are given a thorough grounding in the techniques and methods used in medieval archaeological excavation. A first series of lectures deals with excavation preparations. Students are trained in bibliographical research. They are also shown the help that the medieval archaeologist can receive from records: this help is peculiar to medieval archaeology. Definite and precise examples show that the written record and the archaeological record may be contradictory, and students are taught how to interpret this contradiction. They are also taught the usefulness of a toponymical and micro-toponymical study of the site to be excavated; besides this, students are encouraged to follow the course in historical toponymy given at the University. Several lectures are devoted to the geological and pedological study of the soil which should always be carried out carefully before excavations are undertaken. These lectures are completed by practical work sessions carried out on the sites. The students also learn, of course, the art of interpreting aerial photographs, and even the technique of taking them. Finally, several lessons are devoted to the methods of surveying the soil that the archaeologist can use: and in particular to electric surveying and magnetic surveying; in this case, again, practical exercises are carried out on the site, using Geohm (Gossen) and Tellohm (Nash & Thompson) resistivity meters, and the Elsec proton magnetometer. These methods of locating buried elements are extremely useful in medieval archaeology, where it is often impossible completely to excavate very extensive sites. For example, these instruments make it unnecessary totally to lay bare a filled-in ditch that has become invisible round a motte and bailey type fortification or round a ringwork. A limited excavation exposing two or three metres is sufficient; then, as the depth of the ditch is known, the complete lie can be discovered easily by making lineal borings perpendicular to its direction.

Another series of lectures deals with the actual carrying out of the stratigraphical excavation: cleaning, drawing of the remains appearing on the surface, preparation and drawing of the stratigraphical sections, exact localization of the objects found, drawing up of provisional index-cards for these objects, and so on. . . . Finally, students are given a working knowledge of the scientific techniques and methods that can be used in studying the objects, samples of soils or of various materials collected during the excavation. It is important for the medieval archaeologist to know what can be expected from these methods. The dating of organic matter by measuring the C^{14} rate of disintegration, for example, is usually too inexact to satisfy the medievalist, whereas it gives considerable help to the prehistoric archaeologist. In the same way, palynology does not yet seem capable of providing indications for the historic period that are comparable with those given for more remote times. On the other hand, the medieval archaeologist can expect a great deal from certain other methods of dating, and notably from dendrochronology or the measure of remanent magnetism.

There is one hour per week of anthropology taken with archaeology teaching; students are taught to recognize the different parts of a skeleton, their most characteristic morphological peculiarities, and those that can be considered as ethnic criteria; they are shown how to collect and transport poorly conserved bones.

Practical instruction is given on the sites or in the laboratory. Besides the practical work sessions that accompany and complete the courses, students can take part in excavations that are undertaken all year round by the Centre. This is where they really grow familiar with archaeological research, its difficulties, surprises and hazards. Fairly often these excavations are undertaken unexpectedly, when a chance discovery that must be exploited rapidly has been made during road or building works that can only be held up for a very short time. This is what is sometimes called 'salvage archaeology' (*archéologie de sauvetage*), which is more and more resorted to because of the growing number of big work schemes using very powerful excavators. The digging operations carried out under these conditions are very particular; they need very special knowledge, ability and methods, none of which can be invented on the spot.

The research work undertaken by the Centre is inseparable from its teaching work. The more advanced students, that is, those preparing the master's degree (*maîtrise*) and the doctorate, take an active part in this work. For several years the research programme as regards excavation has dealt mainly with the seigneurial dwellings in the earliest feudal times. Several ringworks of earth and wood have been explored; others are now being explored. Excavations have also been undertaken on motte and bailey type fortifications in Normandy and Anjou. At the same time, a vast bibliographical inquiry is being carried out to collect all the studies that have been published since the beginning of the nineteenth century on the mottes existing in France. These publications are very numerous; some of them, even among the oldest, are not without value; they have also the merit of sometimes mentioning remains that have since been destroyed.

Chance discoveries often lead the research workers of the Centre for Medieval Archaeological Research to excavate cemeteries dating from the Early Middle Ages. These excavations, carried out with the precision that is now indispensable, have already furnished a fairly abundant material. The Centre has undertaken the typological and chronological classification of the burial finds made in Normandy since the beginning of the nineteenth century, dating from the Merovingian and Carolingian eras, and published or conserved in museums.

The laboratory of the Centre works specially on medieval ceramics. In dealing with excavations of medieval sites, ceramics are the chief 'guiding fossil'. When the pottery is decorated, it is usually possible to date it exactly enough after external examination. But generally the ceramics found are ordinary pottery; on certain sites there is no other. Ordinary, non-decorated pottery sometimes has the same forms and the same general appearance over long periods. It is true that archaeologists try to make out variations that might be characteristic of different eras, but this undertaking is difficult and hazardous. So many inexact affirmations have been published in this sphere, and fairly widely accepted too, that what is needed is to start again from scratch, make a clean sweep of most of the datings suggested so far, and seek for new standards, whose date is certain, from which a new and sounder chronology of medieval ceramics can be built up. Taking into account the extreme dispersion of ceramic production in the Middle Ages, which gave rise to numerous and differing regional types, it would be preferable to draw up a chronological scale for each region. To do this, the surest method, one that is open to any careful archaeologist, is to localize very exactly the stratigraphical situation of each fragment collected. In this way at least a relative chronology is obtained, which can be changed into an exact chronology if one of these levels can be dated precisely by the presence of a coin, the traces of a fire mentioned in a text, and so on.

But it is also possible, by internal laboratory analysis of the pottery, to try to discover physical or chemical criteria that may be characteristic of the ceramics of one era or of one region. Research into the phenomena of thermoluminescence is not yet, especially in France, advanced enough to hope for a standard method of dating ceramics in the near future. For the moment, therefore, the laboratory of the Centre restricts itself to making the greatest possible number of observations on fragments of pottery whose date is fairly exactly known. Two index-cards are drawn up for each fragment. On the first are written the results of the chemical analysis that makes it possible to proportion the main components: silica, alumina, and iron, manganese, titanium and lime oxides. The proportion of alkalines is determined by a flame photometer. Accidents due to a possible reducing firing are controlled by an electric kiln; if a greyish or blackish colouring of the paste is due to a lack of oxygen during firing, it will disappear when the fragment is placed in the electric kiln with the correct ventilation. The first card also shows a dilatometric graph obtained with the Chevenard dilatometer. This curve shows the amount of quartz contained in the fragment of pottery, and above all the temperature at which it was fired. Finally, the same card has a microphotograph of a thin lamina taken from the potsherd under study. In this microphotograph a granulometric counting can be made, and the siliceous particles that may have been added to the clay as a scouring agent can easily be told from those that were part and parcel of the clay in the soil from which it was extracted: the former have much sharper angles.

On a second index-card are entered the results of the examinations made with the spectograph. This instrument is very useful for seeking for rare elements in the composition of the paste of the pottery. It is also used for studying the glazes, or slip paintings, that cover decorated pottery, the chemical composition of which may be characteristic of one region or of one era.

Finally, the Centre for Medieval Archaeological Research has recently created a dendrochronology laboratory that has begun collecting samples of wood taken from trees recently felled, or from old beams. Some of these beams come from cider presses and bear an exact date (usually towards the middle of the eighteenth century): others form part of timber framing whose approximate date is known. As there is a considerable analogy between the climate of Normandy and that of the South of England, the dendrochronological graphs drawn up by British research workers, and notably by Dr Schove, can give a useful starting point for Norman dendrochronological research.

For highly specialized research (C^{14}, remanent magnetism), the Centre obtains the collaboration of other laboratories; in particular, it works regularly with Professor

Thellier who visits the Norman excavations fairly frequently so as to take samples of fired clay to measure the remanent magnetism.

Studies of the morphology, decoration, physical or chemical characteristics of medieval ceramics have produced an abundant documentation. Each fragment collected during the excavations by the Centre for Medieval Archaeological Research has a card on which are noted its inventory number, a dimensioned drawing and a description. Similar index-cards are drawn up for the pieces of pottery kept in various museums, or found and published by different archaeologists. Besides, as stated above, two laboratory cards are drawn up for each of the fragments considered as being most typical.

The complete exploitation of such a mass of documents necessarily entails the adoption of a filing and sorting system that will make it possible to find quickly and easily all the fragments having a given characteristic or a given combination of several characteristics. Such a system has been established by Mr J. Cl. Gardin, director of the Centre for Documentary Analysis for Archaeology (National Centre for Scientific Research) with a view to the study of protohistoric ceramics of the Near and Middle East (Gardin 1962). The basic principles of the Gardin method can be used for the study of medieval ceramics. Each piece is divided into several parts: for example, the base, the body, the neck, the rim; each of these parts is minutely described by conventional signs such as the letters of the alphabet, numbers, arithmetic signs; using the same method, the characteristics of the decorations of the piece of pottery are also described, as also all the elements discovered by laboratory examination: chemical composition, firing temperature, porosity, hardness, and so on. For each of these elements, dimensional or quantitative categories are determined, each of which is designated by a sign.

Each of these signs, thus designating a feature that is characteristic from the morphological or decorative point of view, or from an internal structure point of view, has a corresponding punched card, with, at the top, the uncoded definition of this sign. The position of the punch holes on the card represent the inventory numbers in the card-index catalogue of the different fragments having the characteristic designated by the sign in question. To find those pieces of pottery having in common a certain number of characteristics, all that has to be done is to take the punched cards relating to these characteristics, and, with an appropriate instrument, pile them up before a light. The position of those punch-holes where the ray of light goes through all the cards shows the registered numbers of the pieces of pottery having the characteristics in question. With these punched cards it is of course possible to carry out more complex operations; but at the moment a mere sorting operation seems sufficient to facilitate comparative studies.

The code for the analysis of medieval pottery worked out by the Centre for Medieval Archaeological Research is a simple adaptation of Mr Gardin's; it was drawn up with his constant collaboration. A limited number of copies were roneotyped in 1966; the text, revised and augmented, is to be printed in a new edition.

Thus, for the preparation and carrying out of archaeological excavations, and for the study of the objects and samples collected during these excavations, the Caen Centre endeavours to use the different techniques and methods known at the present time; the experiments undertaken aim at adapting them to the sometimes rather special needs of medieval archaeology.

An attempt of this sort does not always meet with approbation. The influence of old ideas is still strong in France, chiefly in the regional societies that recruit above all amateurs who have little experience and are sometimes even actuated by a prejudice in favour of the work methods of the last century. It is certain that they are mistaken, for no real progress will be made without the constant co-operation of archaeologists and scientists. This co-operation is not sufficient if the archaeologist, fixed in his traditional sphere, merely solicits from time to time the opinion of a physicist, a chemist, or a naturalist who is himself confined to his own sphere. Experience proves that occasional collaboration is seldom fruitful; often, indeed, the scientific colleague consulted by the archaeologist will not understand the precise meaning of the question asked him, because this question will be put in terms he is not used to and that do not seem scientific to him; it may even cause him some amusement. So it is indispensable for scientists to work full time within the centres of archaeological research, and even to take part in excavations. This is the only way they will understand the meaning, scope and interests of the analyses they are asked for.

This cohabitation of historian-archaeologists, physicists, chemists, and naturalists in one and the same research team does indeed bring difficulties because of the present division of subjects into water-tight compartments still so marked in many countries. But archaeology is not the only science of man that suffers from this partitioning; linguistics, amongst others, is in the same situation; in the last quarter of a century it has completely modified its work methods, and has greatly profited by doing so. It seems certain that those frontiers, so difficult to cross, that used to separate the domains of different subjects, are now disappearing. New subjects are springing up that will be on the border-line of what are called the 'sciences of man' and the exact or applied sciences.

Yet archaeology does remain essentially a science of man; this is particularly true of medieval archaeology which cannot do without the help of its written sources. The use of scientific methods, however indispensable it may be, is but one part in the activity of the medieval archaeologist, who must be first and foremost a historian, well versed in all the complexity of human vicissitudes, both individual and social.

30.xii.67

Centre for Medieval Archaeological Research
University of Caen

References

Bouard, M. de. 1963. Le centre de recherches archéologiques médiévales de l'Université de Caen. *Revue Historique*. 427.

Bouard, M. de. 1968. L'archéologie médiévale en France. *Rotterdam papers*. 7.

Cinthio, E. 1962–3. Medieval archaeology as a research subject. *Meddelanden fran Lunds Universitets Historika Museum*. 186.

Gardin, J. C. 1962a. *Projet de code pour l'analyse des formes de poteries*. Paris (roneo).

Gardin, J. C. 1962b. Cartes perforées et ordinateurs au service de l'archéologie. *La Nature*. 449.

Laet, S. J. de 1954. *L'archéologie et ses problèmes*. Bruxelles.

Leenhardt, M. 1965. L'utilisation des cartes perforées dans le classement et l'étude de la céramique médiévale. *Annales de Normandie*. 479.

Some problems and methods in statistical archaeology

David G. Kendall

1. Statistical archaeology, like so many branches of applied mathematics, was not invented by mathematicians. It may be thought reasonable to ascribe its invention to Flinders Petrie (1899), for it was he who first formulated and put into practice the principles of what he called *sequence-dating* (more often now called *seriation*). Petrie was confronted with some 900 pre-dynastic Egyptian graves containing representatives of about 800 varieties of pottery, and he was sufficiently in advance of his time to grasp the important principle that the 'incidence matrix' of 'graves-versus-varieties' contains a vast amount of information concerning both the sequential ordering of the graves in time, and the ordinal intervals during which the different varieties of pottery flourished.

By the *incidence matrix*, A, we here understand the array:

$$\{a_{ij}: i=1, 2, \ldots, g; j=1, 2, \ldots, v\}$$

having g rows and v columns, where g is the number of graves and v is the number of varieties of pottery; the entry a_{ij} in the i th row and j th column is then to be set equal to 1 if the j th variety of pottery is represented among the contents of the i th grave, and otherwise it is to be set equal to 0. The assertion that 'A contains information about the true temporal order' derives from the basic archaeological principle that two graves which lie close together in the true temporal order will be more likely to have similar contents than would be the case for two graves which lie further apart in the true temporal order. This principle in its turn derives from the *assumption* that each variety of pottery can be ascribed to a definite segment of the true temporal order, which commences with its innovation and concludes with its obsolescence. It is clear that the assumption will sometimes be an unjustified one, for example when archaistic tendencies are suspected.

Perhaps before proceeding further we should take the opportunity of noting that for 'grave' one can substitute any other form of archaeological deposit (*provided that this is associated with a definite event in time*), and that for 'variety of pottery' one can substitute the presence or absence of some stylistic feature in objects occurring generally throughout the 'cemetery'.

If some or all of the graves contain only a small number of pots then it cannot safely be assumed that temporally adjacent graves will necessarily have varieties of pottery in common, but even in such apparently unfavourable circumstances the matrix A can

Plate 1 An aerial view of a portion of the Gregory Rift Valley to the west of Lake Natron. In the foreground are exposures of the Peninj Group of sediments which elsewhere have yielded a Middle Pleistocene fauna, an australopithecine mandible and a Lower Acheulian assemblage, as well as a lava which can be dated. The sediments were deposited in a shallow rift valley and renewed faulting has dislocated them (see fault scarp middle right) so that erosion has exposed their contents. In the background is the active volcano Oldoinyo Lengai, which has grown since the Middle Pleistocene. Since the Miocene, vents erupting alkaline volcanics have contributed to the favourable conditions for the preservation of fossils in East Africa. In the background is the volcanic barrier which formed the eastern margin of the Olduvai lake basin
Photo. G. Ll. Isaac

Plate 2 This excavation at Olorgesailie, Kenya, exposed a localized concentration of Acheulian artefacts, manuports and bone debris. The material rests on the sandy floor of what was a shallow seasonal runnel. The impressive accumulation can certainly be attributed to localized activities of a group of Acheulian hunters, though natural agencies may have increased the concentration (see text). The occurrence contained more than a ton of stone, including at least 500 handaxes and cleavers *Photo. G. Ll. Isaac*

Plate 3 A vertical view of part of the concentration shown in Plate 2. The occupation debris lay in profusion on and in a 2–4 in. sand lens. Amongst the handaxes and other stones lay the extensively comminuted remains of at least fifty baboons of an extinct, gigantic (robust) baboon *Sinopithecus sp.* It appears that this site was the location for the particular activity of baboon hunting. A baboon femur and an ulna can be seen in this plate *Photo. G. Ll. Isaac*

Plate 4 (below) The two faces of a Lower Acheulian handaxe from the Humbu Formation of the Peninj Group. The tool is formed from a large flake modified by removal of a minimum of thick secondary trimming flakes *Photo. G. Ll. Isaac*

Plate 5 An occupation floor of Early Man, trench VII at Chirki-on-Prava, District Ahmadnagar, Maharashtra

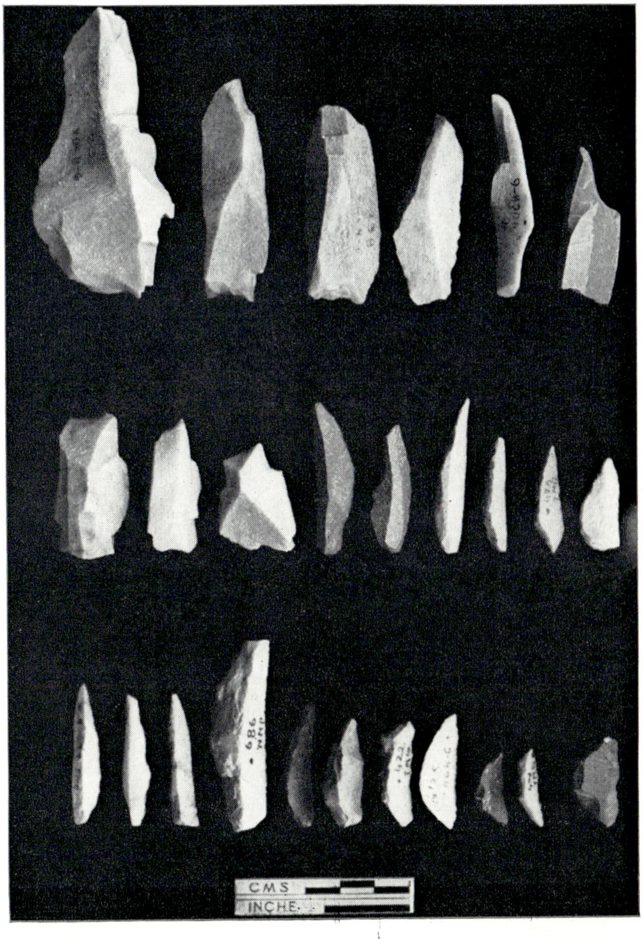

Plate 6 Burins, gravette-like point and lunates, from a site near Renigunta, District Chittoor, A.P.

Plate 7 Terracotta head from a tin mine in the Nok Hills, *c.* 20 cm.

Plate 8 (above) View of part of the Taruga site in February 1966, showing find spot of fragments of a large figure. Among the trees in the middle distance are three of the smelting furnaces

Plate 9 Fragmentary terracotta figurine in Nok style, shown wearing a cap, from the 1961 excavation at Taruga (from a disturbed area)

Plate 10 (above) The top of remains of a shaft furnace discovered by proton magnetometer survey at Taruga, 1966

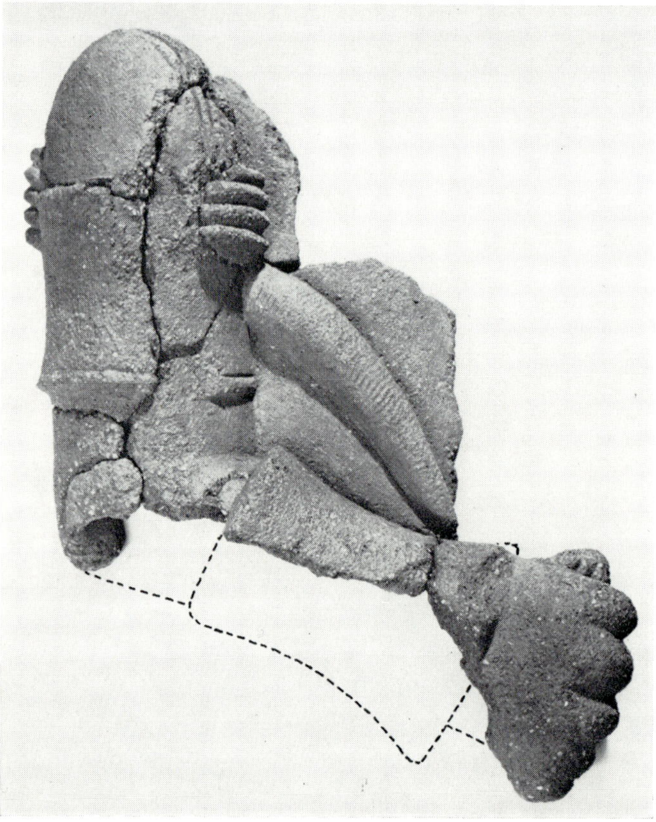

Plate 11 Elaborately decorated right arm of terracotta figure estimated to have been at least 80 cm. high. Excavated at Taruga in 1966

Plate 12 Kruszvica, an air-photograph of the site showing the former extent of I the castle; II and III, the suburbs

Plate 13 Novgorod, street junction at the thirteenth-century level

Plate 14 The site from above (Scollar)

contain chronologically relevant information. Thus if we form the new (square) matrix $V = A^T A$ whose (i, j)th component is:

$$v_{ij} = \sum_{\alpha=1}^{g} a_{\alpha i} a_{\alpha j},$$

then v_{ij} is equal to the number of graves in which the i th and j th varieties are both represented, and it is obvious that V (which is determined when A is given) links the varieties together in a chronologically significant way, for if the temporal ranges of two varieties overlap then they are likely to appear together in a number of graves roughly proportional to the extent of the overlap. Similarly we can form the matrix $V^2 = V \times V$ whose (i, j)th component is

$$v_{ij}^{(2)} = \sum_{\beta=1}^{v} v_{i\beta} v_{\beta j};$$

this enumerates (with suitable weighting) the varieties β which co-exist with the varieties i and j. These considerations bring out the fact that A, through V and its powers V^2, $V^3, \ldots$, may contain far more information about the chronology of the varieties than is apparent on the surface.

On the other hand, if we form the matrix product of A and its transpose A^T in the reverse order we obtain a different (square) matrix $G = AA^T$ whose (i, j)th component is

$$g_{ij} = \sum_{\beta=1}^{v} a_{i\beta} a_{j\beta};$$

this is equal to the number of varieties which are held in common by the graves i and j. The square matrix G contains as many rows (and columns) as there are graves, whereas the square matrix V contained as many rows (and columns) as there were varieties. G and its powers $G^2, G^3, \ldots$ (which are determined when A is given) contain information about the chronology of the graves, and often this information will lie hidden deep within the structure of the original matrix A, and be far from obvious there.

Anyone who knows too much about matrix algebra may be misled at this point into thinking that there is a symmetrical 'duality' between graves and varieties, based on the familiar algebraic row-column duality. It is necessary to warn the reader against falling into this trap. It is *not true* that we can freely interchange the words 'grave' and 'variety'. To do so uncritically can be very dangerous, and the reader will perhaps be most readily persuaded of the truth of this if we point out that a grave occurs at a definite *point* of time, whereas a variety flourishes throughout a definite *period* of time. Thus, when dealing with graves, we are simply interested in whether one grave is earlier or later than another. When dealing with varieties such a question is *meaningless*; we have to ask, of two varieties, whether the range of one precedes, follows, overlaps, includes, or falls entirely within the range of the other, and this essential difference must never be lost sight of. We shall return to this point later.

We are now led to formulate two quite distinct questions:

A(I) Does A contain *enough* information to enable us *in principle* to establish a chronology?

A(II) (If the answer to A(I) is 'yes'.) How can this information be extracted?

To these we might have prefixed the question:

A(O) Were we correct in thinking that the incidence matrix A was derived from chronologically seriated material?

Often the archaeologist will be content to take the affirmative answer to A(O) for granted, but this should not blind us to the fact that it is an askable question.

With regard to A(I) a number of general comments can usefully be made. First, even when A leads to a temporal sequence, it cannot possibly tell us which end of the sequence is the earlier one. We shall always have to label the ends 'late' and 'early' by bringing in external evidence of quite a different kind; thus we might appeal to carbon dates (which might at any rate succeed in distinguishing the two extremities of the sequence), or we might be able to match the varieties of pottery occurring in graves at one extremity of the sequence with varieties already known and assigned to a period believed to have followed those under investigation. Next, we shall not expect to be led to a *unique* temporal sequence; the evidence may well fail to distinguish one order from another obtained by applying a number of nearest-neighbour interchanges – nor would we usually wish to distinguish such orders. Another point is that we can only expect to get information about the *sequential* order; we are not in a position to set up a time-*scale*. (This was of course the reason which lay behind Flinders Petrie's use of the term 'sequence-dating'.)

Thus, when at A(I) we ask whether A supplies enough information for it to serve as the basis of a seriation procedure, we always have in mind the essential limitations of any such process. It may, however, happen that the variety-ranges are so short that the graves are hardly 'linked' at all, or so long that all graves are 'linked' indifferently, or there may be so little pottery that the graves are 'linked' in batches but not as an integral whole. In these circumstances A(I) would qualify for a negative answer, and obviously A(I) should be answered before any attempt is made to set up a chronology. It is my belief that one should be able to answer question A(I) on the basis of the number of rows, the number of columns, the number of 1's and the number of 0's, and perhaps one or two other statistics concerning their distribution within A. But I do not yet know how to do it, and wish only to draw attention to this as an important unsolved problem in Information Theory.

2. Let us now have another look at question (I) in relation to a similar but quite distinct problem which is mathematical and not archaeological, and for which an elaborate mathematical theory is now available. We *can*, and will, formulate it in archaeological language; it is convenient to do this, both because the reader will probably then find it easiest to visualize, and also because the similarities and differences between the two problems will then stand out the better. The fact that they are two different problems must, however, be insisted upon.

We obtain the new problem when we add the *assumption* that *each grave contains representatives of every variety of pottery extant at the time of the interment*. Of course in the archaeological problem this assumption will normally be an absurd one. Consider, however, what its consequences would be for the form of the matrix A. Suppose that the rows of A (that is, the graves) are rearranged in the correct temporal order, then this must now have the effect of *bunching together the 1's in each separate column*. We shall need a name for an incidence matrix whose 1's are so bunched, and it seems to me appropriate to call it a *Petrie matrix*. (Notice that, in this definition, rows and columns play a different role – another instance of the irrelevance of the 'row-column-duality'.)

We can now re-phrase questions (O–II) as follows:

M(O) Is the incidence matrix A such that by at least one method of permuting the rows we can bring it into the Petrie form?

M(I) (If the answer to M(O) is 'yes'.) Is the number of different row-permutations giving the Petrie form to A small enough to make it sensible for us to try to set up a chronology?

M(II) (If the answer to M(I) is 'yes'.) How can we extract the information which A contains about the chronology; i.e. how can we construct a row-permutation which will 'petrify' A?

For the mathematical problem, the answer to question M(O) has been given by D. R. Fulkerson and O. A. Gross (1965). (It is interesting to notice that the motivation for their work was provided by certain questions concerning the genetics of micro-organisms, a nice example, therefore, of the unity of learning.) Their main result (from our present point of view) can be expressed as follows.

If two incidence matrices A_1 and A_2 have the same number of rows and the same number of columns, and if their V-matrices are the same, then A_2 can be row-permuted into the Petrie form if and only if this is possible for A_1.

Thus the question, whether A is a row-permutation of some Petrie matrix, can in principle be answered if we know the square matrix V derived from A, and further reference to A is unnecessary. We may express this by saying that *V contains all the information relevant to question* M(O)

Fulkerson and Gross go on to give a graph-theoretic algorithm enabling one to identify row-permutations of Petrie matrices, using only V. We shall not describe their algorithm here, principally because question (O) is not of primary interest (though of *some* interest) in the archaeological problem. We note however that an *algebraic* characterization of those V-matrices which belong to petrifiable matrices A has not yet been given, so that here is another unsolved problem deserving attention.

We now turn to questions M(I) and M(II) for the mathematical problem. These have been 'answered' in recent work by the writer; we shall summarize it only briefly here. The main result is as follows.

Suppose that V is such that A is petrifiable. Then the row-permutations which petrify A are exactly those which, when applied to the rows and columns of G simultaneously, give to that square matrix the Robinson form.

Thus, once we have decided (e.g. on the basis of the Fulkerson-Gross test, using V) that A is the row-permutation of some Petrie matrix, then the task of throwing A into Petrie form can be accomplished using G alone, further reference to A being unnecessary.

We may express this by saying that G *contains all the information required in constructing a sorting algorithm.* (We shall base our proposed new solution to the archaeological problem on this basic fact alone.)

Notice that the result just cited bears on question M(I) as well as on question M(II), because of the assertion that the petrifying permutations are *exactly* those which (when applied row- and columnwise) have a certain effect on G. It follows that A admits too many petrifying permutations (so that the chronology cannot be recaptured) exactly when G admits too great a symmetry (too many row-and-column operations give G the Robinson form).

At this point it is necessary to say when a square matrix G is said to have the *Robinson form.* By definition, this shall be *when its components never decrease as one progresses along a row towards the main diagonal, and never increase as one continues to progress along that row beyond the main diagonal.* Such matrices play a role in Robinson's quite different discussion (1951) of a quite different problem of seriation, and this is why the proposed terminology seems to me appropriate.

Now let us observe that the 'answers' just given to questions M(O–II) lead one in practice to certain difficulties which become acute as soon as the number of graves is at all large. Shuffling the rows and columns of G is an awkward business in any case, and becomes prohibitively difficult for large numbers of graves unless automatic computation facilities are used. Even then we shall be in trouble if there are more than say eight or nine graves because of the fantastically rapid rate of growth of the factorial function, which means that one has to scan through an enormous number of possible permutations. Accordingly, even in this mathematical problem, a direct attack (implying a scrutiny of all possible row-and-column permutations of G) will often be quite impracticable, and therefore one is driven to look for simpler 'heuristic' procedures, the efficacy of which will be a matter of faith rather than knowledge. Such a procedure will shortly be introduced, but it will be convenient to present it in the context of the archaeological problem (for which it was in fact designed).

3. We have methods which in theory will resolve the mathematical problems M(O–II), although, as has just been explained, they will not often be practicable. In any case we cannot expect them to work, even 'in theory', in the archaeological problem, because there the basic assumption (that a grave contains *all* varieties of pottery extant at the time) will not be satisfied. It will of course be of considerable interest to see how far the exact solution to the mathematical problem retains some approximate validity when the basic assumption is at any rate approximately verified (i.e. when each grave contains *most* of the varieties of pottery extant at the time). This matter awaits investigation, and will not be touched upon further here. Instead we shall propose an entirely new approach to seriation which affords simultaneously, (*a*) an alternative (but heuristic) solution to the mathematical problem, and (*b*) a procedure which might just as well be hoped to prove useful in the archaeological problem. It must be emphasized that the proposal is intended as a *suggestion*, and that its success is in no sense guaranteed. The importance of the theory developed so far is that it has put us in a position in which the suggestion becomes a natural one – it might very well never have been advanced without the theoretical build-up which preceded it, but there is no logical connection between the two.

We start from the basic facts that:

(i) G is a square matrix with symmetric ($g_{ij}=g_{ji}$) components, all of which are non-negative, and
(ii) in the mathematical problem at least, whenever the matrix A does happen to be row-sortable into Petrie form, then all the information relevant to the construction of a sorting permutation is contained in G.

Now let us think of G as a *similarity-matrix for graves*, that is, we shall regard g_{ij} as a direct measure of how like (temporally) the i th grave is to the j th grave. Notice that we do *not* assume that there is any metric structure implied in G, e.g. we do *not* suppose that there exists some measure of 'distance' such that d_{ij} decreases as g_{ij} increases. Nevertheless, we could try to construct a distance-function for pairs of graves in such a way that this inverse relationship is approximately verified – which is another way of saying that we could take the similarity-matrix G as the starting point of a Shepard–Kruskal multi-dimensional scaling procedure. For the details of this procedure see Kruskal (1964); here we shall only sketch the general idea behind it. This is, to represent each grave 'i' as a point P_i located in say k-dimensional space, while endeavouring to do this in such a way that *as far as possible*

$$\mathrm{dist}(P_i, P_j) < \mathrm{dist}\,(P_{i'}, P_{j'}) \textit{ if and only if } g_{ij} > g_{i'j'}. \qquad (*)$$

Unless k is very large indeed it will be impossible to satisfy all the desired inequalities, and the smaller k becomes, the less completely will the inter-point distances be anti-ranked with the inter-grave similarities. Thus, for a small k (and $k=1$ and 2 are the important cases) the requirement (*) can be only very roughly fulfilled. The Shepard–Kruskal program computes the 'error' in achieving this task and then shifts the points (P_i) in such a way as to reduce it, observes the consequences, makes another small shift, and so on. In a great variety of circumstances it has been found empirically that when some sort of metric model 'lies' in a rather vague sense behind the data then the k-dimensional scaling of it, for suitable k, tends to bring this out. In the present example we are assuming that there is a chronological seriation behind the data, and that G contains information bearing on that. It is therefore natural to use G as a similarity-matrix to initiate a one-dimensional scaling ($k=1$). At the same time it must be emphasized that the MDSCAL program contains a number of arbitrary structural elements, as well as an arbitrary initial position from which to start the iterations, so that its use should be accompanied by a healthy scepticism and all the common sense available. It is often useful, and in my opinion vital, even when a 1-dimensional model is being sought, to look at the 2-dimensional solution. The use of several different initial positions, and the separate analysis of sub-samples of the data, provide one with valuable checks of the extent to which the final outcome can be regarded as meaningful.

Full scale experiments with real data will be reported on elsewhere, and here we shall merely illustrate the method by showing it at work on a very simple instance of the mathematical problem. Here is an incidence matrix A which as a matter of fact can (in exactly two ways) be row-permuted into Petrie form.

$g=1$)	1	0	0	1	1	0
2)	0	0	1	0	0	1
3)	1	1	1	1	0	1
4)	0	0	0	0	1	0
5)	1	1	1	1	1	0
6)	1	0	0	0	1	0

This A was in fact used by Fulkerson and Gross to illustrate the use of their graph-theoretic algorithm. The similarity-matrix $G=AA^T$ is:

3	0	2	1	3	2
0	2	2	0	1	0
2	2	5	0	4	1
1	0	0	1	1	1
3	1	4	1	5	2
2	0	1	1	2	2

The MDSCAL program when supplied with this similarity-matrix constructed the following model for the graves.

Grave (i)	1	2	3	4	5	6
P_i	+0·28	−1·62	−0·73	+1·50	−0·14	+0·70

Now let us rearrange the graves so that they acquire the natural order of the representing points (P_i). We get the order:

2 3 5 1 6 4

(or its reverse) – that is, two of the 720 possible permutations on six objects are thus selected (there are *two* because, as explained previously, we can reverse the order without affecting the problem in any way). Thus the MDSCAL program has selected one out of 360 possible arrangements, and as it happens in this particular case just *one* of these 360 possibilities corresponds to a row-permutation which gives to A the Petrie form. We therefore re-arrange the rows of A to see if the 1's are bunched together. The result is:

2)	0	0	1	0	0	1
3)	1	1	1	1	0	1
5)	1	1	1	1	1	0
1)	1	0	0	1	1	0
6)	1	0	0	0	1	0
4)	0	0	0	0	1	0

and so here our method has proved to be successful.

I hasten to add that this may have been good luck. The final 'stress' measurement in the MDSCAL program was high, even after 500 iterations. However, one might allow oneself to feel mildly encouraged.

The reader might find it interesting to look at the G-matrix corresponding to the sorted A. It is

2	2	1	0	0	0
2	5	4	2	1	0
1	4	5	3	2	1
0	2	3	3	2	1
0	1	2	2	2	1
0	0	1	1	1	1

This is, of course, a Robinson matrix.

4. The reader will probably find it instructive to start with the original G-matrix and see how long it takes him, by means of row-and-column permutations, to throw G into Robinson form. The difficulties here are the confusing geometrical situation and also the large number of possible permutations (360 are relevant), which of course rapidly becomes very much larger when the number of graves is increased (several million, with ten graves). The same difficulties arise in Robinson's methods (1951) for dealing with his seriation problem. He was concerned with the seriation of deposits, and instead of an incidence matrix A giving in its (i, j)th component the presence (1) or absence (0) of the j th variety in the i th grave, he had a matrix B giving in its (i, j)th component the percentage composition of the i th deposit which was attributed to the 'object' j. From B a similarity-matrix was constructed, and then Robinson's idea was simultaneously to permute the rows and columns of the similarity-matrix until it assumed what we have called the Robinson form (as nearly as could be managed).

The special difficulties which arise with Robinson's technique when the number of deposits is large has recently been studied by F. Hole and Mary Shaw (1967), who devised a means for sampling from the whole range of possible permutations.

5. Petrie's own solution to the sequence-dating problem hinged on what I have called the Concentration Principle (1963), namely that in the best rearrangement the temporal range of each separate variety will be minimized. Of course in practice we cannot expect to minimize more than one thing at a time, and thus in order to use the Concentration Principle we must somehow combine the ranges of all the varieties and then minimize this consolidated range-index. For Petrie himself this seems to have been a matter for scholarly compromise combined with stylistic insight. I have discussed elsewhere (1963) the extent to which one can crystallize the Concentration Principle into a rational objective tool. Once this is done, one is left with a variant of the problem mentioned in the previous section – how is one to scan through all the millions of permutations in order to find the one which 'concentrates' to the maximum degree? It seems likely that the work by Hole and Shaw will make it worth our while to take up the Concentration Principle type of solution once again.

6. Even with the MDSCAL/$G=AA^T$ approach there are difficulties of scale, but they are less severe. It may even be the case that this approach works best with grave-numbers which would be too large for any other method – say ten or more – and numbers

up to 50 or even 100 might be accommodated. Beyond this, difficulties of time and storage would arise, and it would be necessary to break up the full set of graves into interpenetrating blocks of graves, and to treat each block separately, fitting together the seriations thus obtained in a subsequent operation.

7. Why can one not apply the MDSCAL approach also to V, since that too is a similarity matrix? If this could be done, one would expect the output to throw some light on whether the material was or was not seriated, in view of the Fulkerson–Gross theorem. The difficulty is that what is needed here is not MDSCAL at all, but a different sort of program which has the object of converting a similarity-matrix into a model comprised of segments (D_i) on the line, or of disks (D_i) in the plane, in such a way that v_{ij} is the larger, the more D_i and D_j overlap. No such program exists as yet.

8. As this paper goes to press the results of applying the MDSCAL/$G = AA^T$ method to a set of genuine data have become available. It is agreeable to be able to report that this completely automatic procedure gave a seriation for sixty graves closely concordant with that previously worked out by Dr F. R. Hodson on the basis of *all* the information available from the excavation. Experience with this example has given fresh insight into the best method of employing the MDSCAL/$G = AA^T$ method, and this will be presented on another occasion.

8.i.68 (revised August 1968)

Statistical Laboratory
University of Cambridge

References

Fulkerson, D. R. and Gross, O. A. 1965. Incidence matrices and interval graphs. *Pacific J. Math.* 15:835–55.

Hole, F. and Shaw, M. 1967. Computer analysis of chronological seriation. *Rice Univ. Studies.* 53, no. 3:1–166.

Kendall, D. G. 1963. A statistical approach to Flinders Petrie's sequence dating. *Bull. Int. Statist. Inst.* 40:657–80.

Kendall, D. G. 1969. Incidence matrices, interval graphs, and seriation in archaeology. *Pacific J. Math.*

Kruskal, J. B. 1964. Multidimensional scaling. *Psychometrika.* 29:1–27, 28–42.

Petrie, W. M. Flinders. 1899. Sequences in prehistoric remains. *J. Anthrop. Inst.* 29:295–301.

Robinson, W. S. 1951. A method for chronologically ordering archaeological deposits. *American Antiquity.* 16:293–301.

Some techniques for the evaluation of archaeological magnetometer surveys

Irwin Scollar

In the ten years or so since proton magnetometers were introduced for survey of buried sites (Aitken 1958), there has been surprisingly little published in the way of positive results. Perhaps, in part, this is due to the way in which the magnetometer has sometimes been used – for specific problems in connection with particular excavations. The results are then little worthier of publication than the details of the preliminary surveying grid, for example. In other instances, it may be suspected that the magnetic results obtained either did not correspond to the subsequently excavated features, or the readings produced an uninterpretable pattern. There are probably a number of reasons for the latter. A fair number of soils are so utterly devoid of the necessary magnetic contrast as to be unsurveyable (Scollar 1965). Others are magnetic enough (Leborgne 1955, 1960, 1965) but small variations in the natural topography, depth of plough layer, or near surface geological irregularities produce magnetic readings which obscure those due to the sought-after archaeological features. One task of an evaluation routine is to attempt to improve the interpretation by compensating as far as possible for these two sources of trouble.

Although it is customary, in geological practice, to present the results of a magnetic survey in terms of contours of equal magnetic intensity, this approach is not necessarily the best when dealing with the shallow anomalies of regular geometric shape characteristic of an archaeological site. The eye finds it difficult to recognize such regularities in this type of presentation. Hence the practitioners of archaeological magnetometry soon turned to a presentation which produced a plan more nearly like a half-tone picture, built up either of symbols or dots, the progressive blackening of which indicated greater or lesser values of the local magnetic field. In such a picture, the eye easily picks up regular features even where the anomalies are very slight.

It is intuitively obvious that, when using the symbol or dot mode of presentation, an overall greying can readily happen where deep-lying disturbances of geological origin modify the field over a wide area. This problem is especially acute when the survey deals with areas of the order of several hectares. Such greying can obscure the sought features in some parts of the final picture. Furthermore, at the other end of the scale of anomaly size, it can be readily appreciated that small surface disturbances, bits of surface iron, or local irregularities, tend to produce spots of local blackening which spoil the appearance of the picture. If sufficient in number, these contribute a kind of 'noise' not unlike that seen on a television screen when the received signal is too low or when a car's

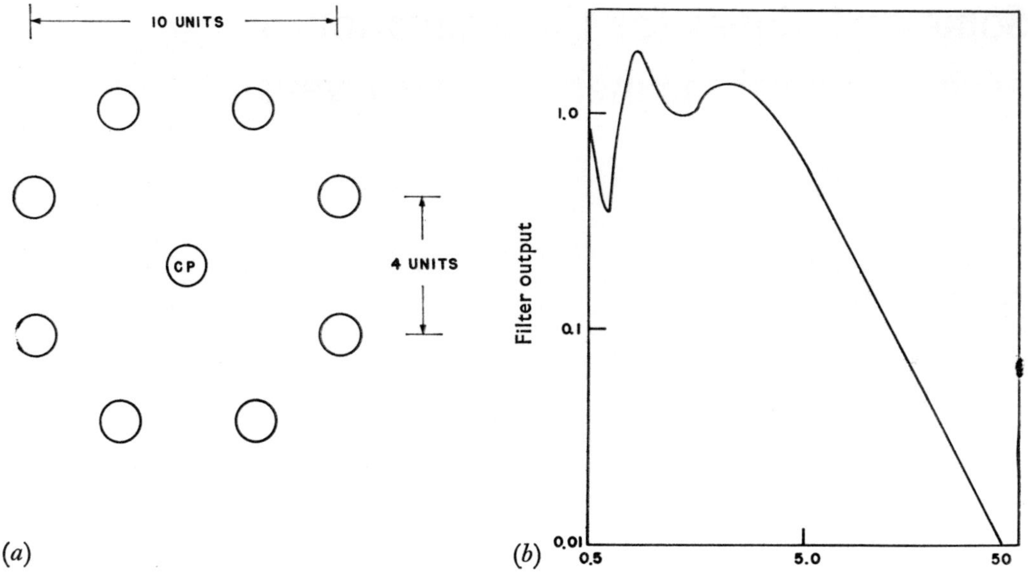

Figure 13

ignition interferes with reception. In fact, trouble due to deep-lying causes and that due to immediate surface disturbance can both be considered a kind of 'noise' which differ from the sought-after archaeological 'signal' from which they differ in size. The deep-lying disturbances affect things over a wide area and can be said to be of long wavelength (or low frequency), while the surface disturbances bother small areas and are hence of short wavelength (or high frequency). The archaeological 'signals' are somewhere between the two, Furthermore, they tend to have regular patterns, whereas the natural disturbances are randomly distributed, in the ideal case.

Now it has been shown (Dean 1958; Fraser *et al.* 1966; Kertz 1966; Mesko 1965, 1966; Scollar 1959) that it is possible to treat the numerical data obtained in a magnetic survey in such a way as to filter out the anomalies of a desired size and to discriminate against the undesired ones. In the simplest instance, this is done by means of a template as shown in fig. 13a. This is moved progressively from one value to the next over the entire magnetic map. The average of the peripheral values appearing in a circle around the central value is subtracted from it and the difference recorded on a separate sheet of paper in the position of the central value. It can be seen that, if a value departs only a little from the average around it, this corresponds to a very slight warping of the magnetic field, an effect which can only be produced by an anomaly either at a considerable depth, of great extent, or one which is very weak. Over an area, the larger the departures of the central points, the nearer to the surface and the stronger the causative feature must be. The actual effect of the template of fig. 13a on various sizes can be calculated (Scollar 1959) and the results are shown in fig. 13b. The ordinate represents the degree of response with unity being equivalent to passing the central point unchanged; the abcissa shows size. It is evident that a simple template of this type discriminates strongly against lengths which exceed the radius of the circle of peripheral values. It passes the shorter lengths (higher frequencies) and thus is said to have a high-pass characteristic.

If, instead of subtracting peripheral values, the average were added, the effect of any single value which departed much from the average would be reduced. Since small surface disturbances have the property of affecting only a few close values, averaging and adding will discriminate against them. In principle, the mathematical analysis of the averaging procedure with addition leads to a response curve which is opposite in tendency to that shown in fig. 13b, with increasing response being obtained for increasing size (or low frequencies). This is then described as a low-pass characteristic. A judicious combination of peripheral circles with weighted averages of various sign can give almost any desired filtering characteristic with respect to size. This is known as a band-pass digital filter (Fraser *et al.* 1966).

It would be possible to illustrate these matters on data obtained from an archaeological site but, because a good assortment of anomaly size is not always at hand, it is more instructive to look at the results obtained on an artificial site, simulated in a computer. This site is made up somewhat like a television test pattern so as to contain features of varying size, shape and orientation. Fig. 14 shows the raw data which is fed to the computer. The 'site' contains readings which are given two values only. In truth, this is very remote indeed from the way magnetic readings vary in practice. A more precise type of simplified anomaly (Linington 1964, 1966) could have been used but, for the present discussion, the data of fig. 14 will be adequate.

Because the computer's line printer does not have an equal ratio between letter spaces and those between lines, the 'site' is apparently elongated vertically. The central square (equal numbers of values on all sides) becomes a rectangle. The horizontal lines are overly thick. To correct for this, an interpolation procedure is used which restores the

Figure 14

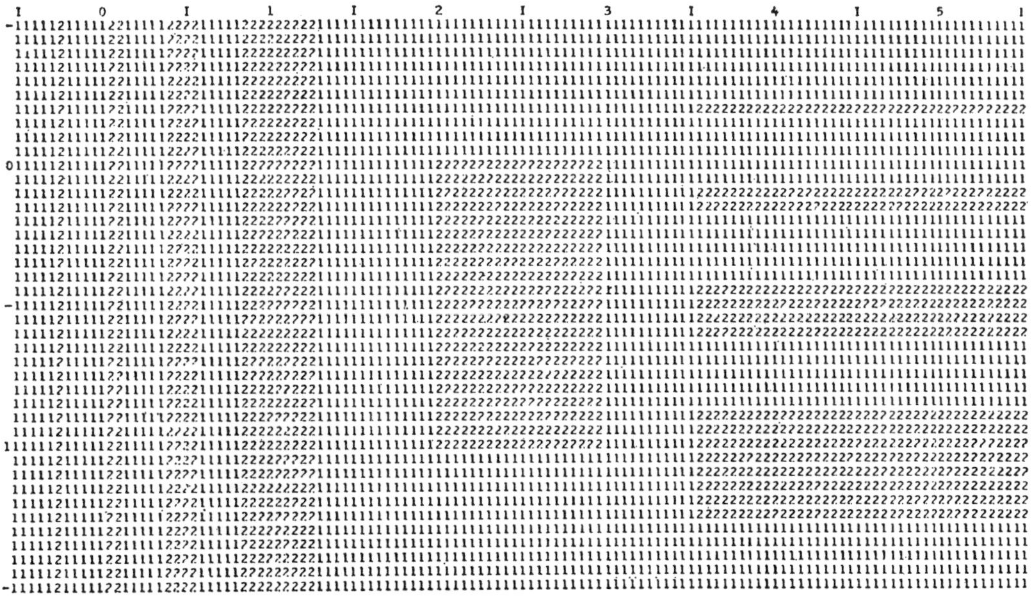

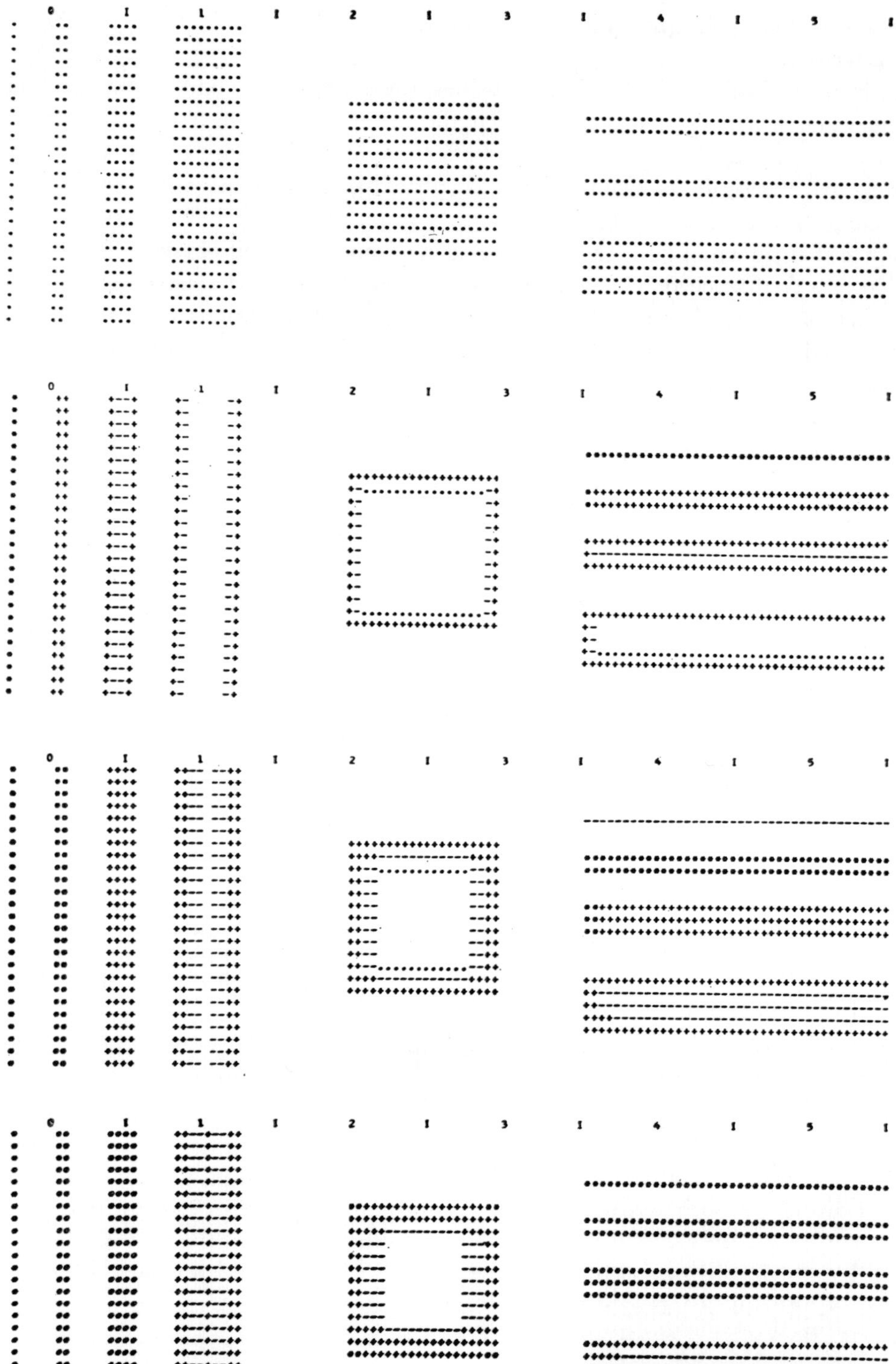

Figure 15

geometry to the correct proportions. Unfortunately, the interpolation will tend to discriminate a bit against weak thin horizontals, whereas verticals of the same intensity pass without error. Furthermore, the numbers are replaced by symbols so that increased symbol area (effective blackening when seen in photographic reduction) represents higher values according to a fixed scheme. Since only two values are present, by subtracting 1, the picture of the raw data appears with one symbol only as shown in fig. 15a.

If we pass data of this type through a low-pass filter, the only result will be to wipe out the thinner lines. The effects of high-pass filters of various radii are shown in fig. 15b, c and d. The filter of shortest radius passes the thinnest lines but blots out all but the edges of the thickest and takes out the centre of the square. As the radius increases, more of the thicker lines survive. For clarity and to prevent loss of data, all values were multiplied by ten before passing through the filter. Hence symbols other than that used in the raw data appear.

Now we pass our original data again through the computer, this time multiplying each 1 or 2 by a random number whose limits are set rather arbitrarily at five times the initial value at a given point. In this way fluctuations not unlike the 'noise' encountered due to minor surface irregularities are obtained, with a 'signal' to 'noise' ratio of two to one. The features, as shown in fig. 16a are now only faintly discernible. If an averaging or low-pass filter is then used, there is a considerable improvement in the regularity of the picture, since the random numbers tend to average out, restoring the initial values. This is shown in fig. 16b. If a high-pass filter alone were used, as shown in fig. 16c, the situation would be made worse instead of better. Using the low-pass followed by the high-pass gives the results shown in figure 16d, where the original outlines are readily visible. Hence, it can be seen that, using a high-pass filter alone on field data will discriminate against large deep-lying disturbances but will also bring up the general surface noise. The combination of low and high-pass characteristics in a band-pass filter produces the best result.

Now, it often happens that very sharp changes appear at localized points in a survey due, for example, to surface iron. We will simulate this in our artificial site by adding a few wild values at odd points as shown in fig. 17a. If we pass data of this type through a high-pass filter, as shown in fig. 17b, the filter will 'ring', that is, not only will the high central point be passed, but also the peripheral points will be affected when they in turn are considered as central points if the high value is included in the average. Thus the anomaly due to the surface iron is made even more intense and is somewhat spread out. Using a low-pass filter, as shown in fig. 17c helps little, for the high value will affect the average at a number of neighbouring points, spreading out the disturbance over a wider area, with reduced intensity. To deal with this problem, an average of values is taken somewhat away from a central point. If the central point departs absolutely (without regard to sign) by more than a pre-set multiple from the absolute value of the average, we replace the central point by the peripheral average. Fig. 17d shows the result of passing the data of fig. 17a through such an operation and then through the same high-pass filter as used in fig. 17b. It can be seen that almost no trace of disturbance remains. The order of digital treatment is then first, point source noise removal, low-pass filtering, and then high-pass filtering. The last two can be combined in a band-pass filter, if desired.

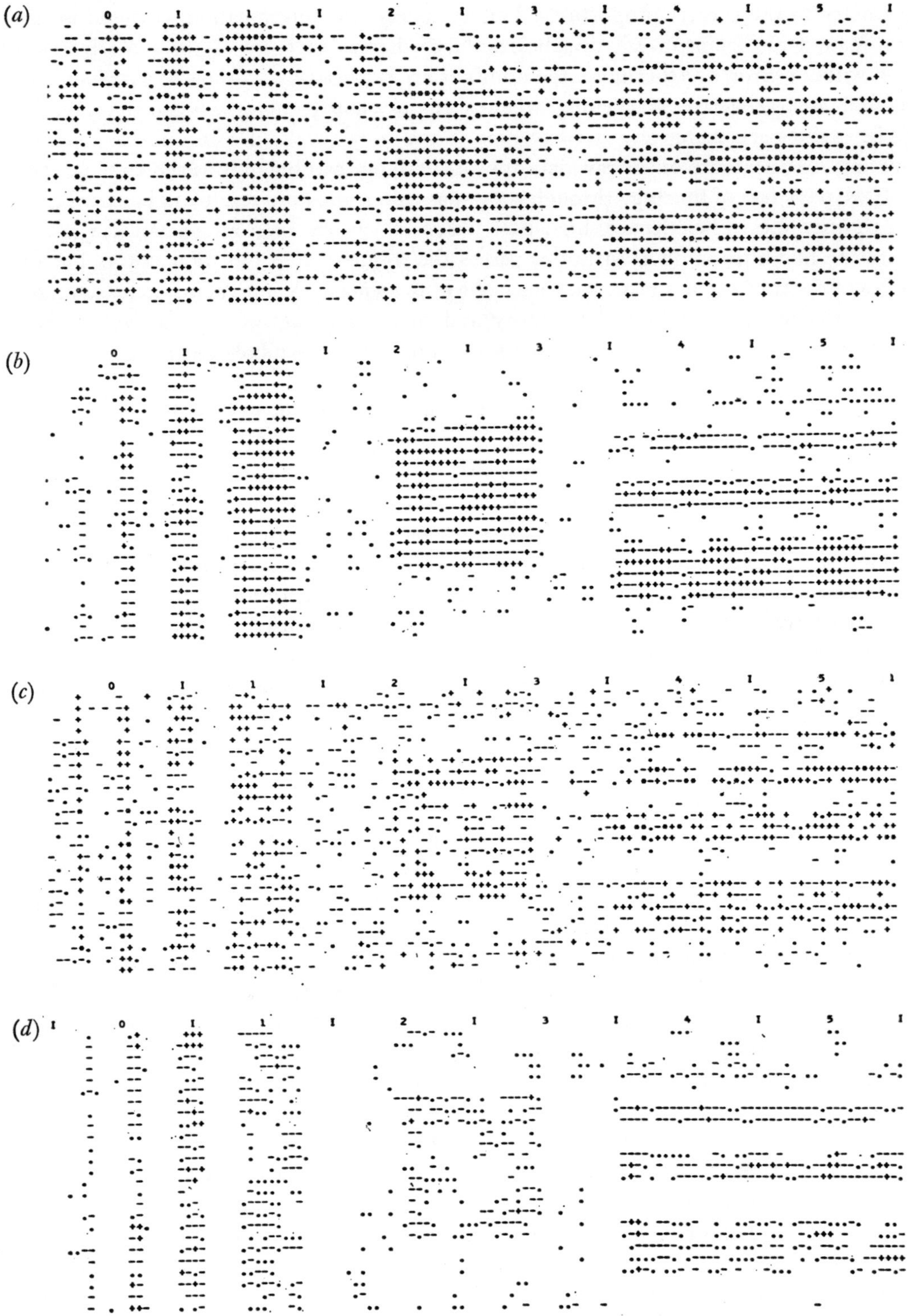

Figure 16

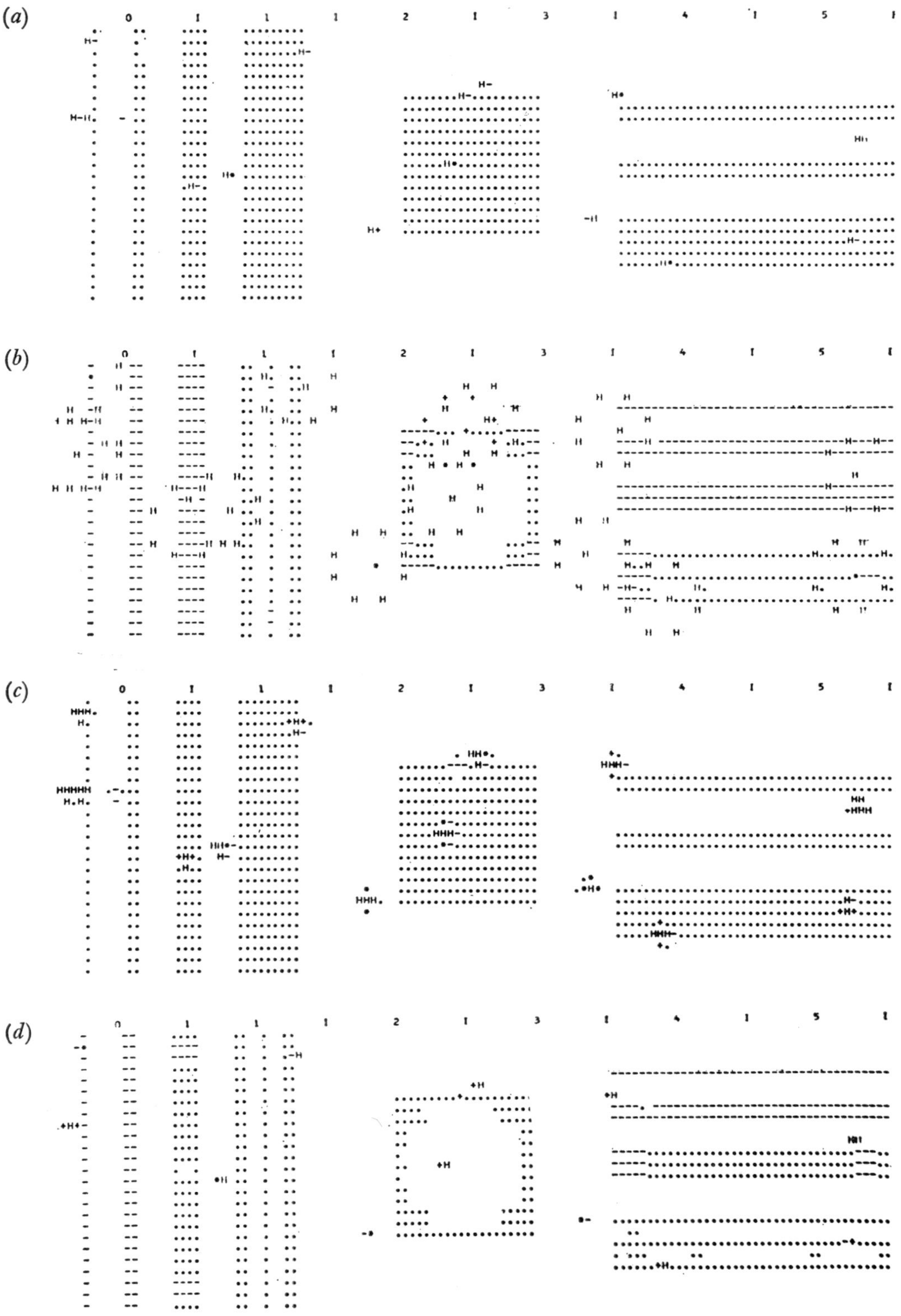

Figure 17

(*a*)

(*b*)

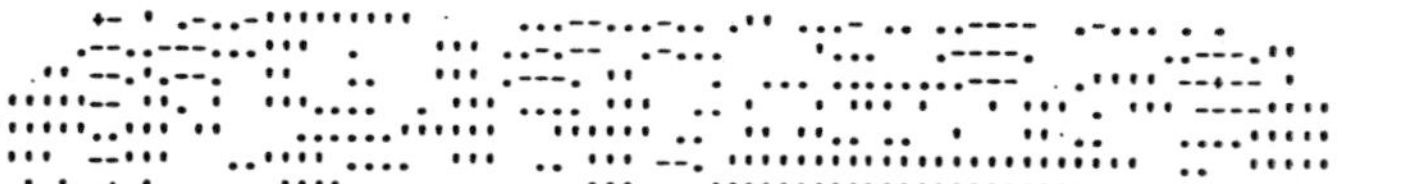

Figure 18

(a)

(b)

(c)

Figure 19

It is now possible to turn to actual data obtained on an archaeological site to see the effect of some subsidiary techniques. Fig. 18a shows the printer output, geometrically corrected, for the raw magnetic data from a small Roman fort in the Rhineland. The area surveyed is roughly a hectare, with measurements made every metre at a height of 60 cm. above the ground using the differential magnetometer described elsewhere (Scollar 1965). Values were measured with respect to a zero level established high over undisturbed terrain outside the site area. Negative values are indicated in the print-out by apostrophes. If this data is filtered, using the sequence described in the previous paragraph, the result, as shown in fig. 18b is not impressively better than the raw data. However, if the negative values are eliminated, even the raw data, as shown in fig. 19a improves in appearance. In this case a discriminator level at zero is established and only values exceeding this level are passed. Two other levels are shown in figs. 19b and c. In fig. 20a–c the discriminator has been used on the filtered data. The optimum value of discriminator level can be readily picked out. If the data had been obtained from an absolute magnetometer, this type of operation would have been essential.

In addition to discriminator control, other simple data changes are possible. The input data can be multiplied by a percentage. This allows one to scale down the blackening on sites which have very strong anomalies to manageable proportions or, alternatively, to enlarge those on sites with weak disturbances. This latter is possible only to the extent permitted by the soil noise. Multiplication after data treatment controls the blackening of the final output and is also useful. A discriminator level can be set before data treatment in some cases and finally a constant can be added to all the data from a given job (see Scollar and Krückeberg 1966) so as to allow one to connect up surveys made over very large areas in a number of sections. In such cases it is not always possible to find reference points which are identical for all parts of the site. Secular variation of the earth's field affects absolute (but not differential) readings taken years apart on a large site and this can be compensated for with the added constant. This is especially important if data is to be filtered through the limits of adjacent survey sections, or artificial anomalies will be produced where the sections join up.

A limit, both upper and lower must be set to the maximum degree of blackening permitted. There are two ways of doing this. One, the simpler, is to agree that all values which exceed a limit will be replaced by that limit. This is very easy. The other is to take some mathematical function of the values which itself tends to approach rapidly a maximum. In practice, the square root or logarithm, being available on the library tape in most computers, are easier to use. The square root gives fairly uniform compression, whereas the logarithm tends to pass smaller variations and compress the larger ones more.

It is evident that if all of the data treatment methods discussed are applied, then the job cannot be done by hand in a reasonable time when the site is large. Therefore, a computer is a necessity. If one is lucky, the computer will have an auxiliary device known as a plotter. This is a magnetic-tape-driven drawing table, capable of producing graphs with high precision and printing a choice of symbols on the surface of a large sheet of paper. Instead of using the printer symbols shown up to now, the plotter can be used to make uniform dots whose number corresponds to the value which results at each point after all calculations have been made. The individual dots can be displaced slightly

(a)

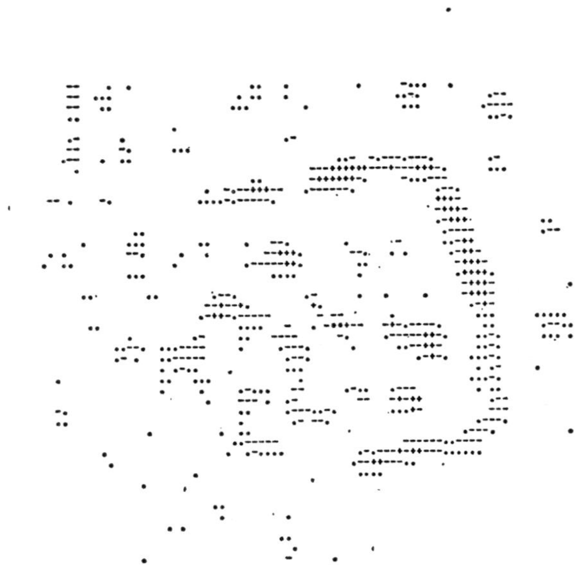

(b)

(c)

Figure 20

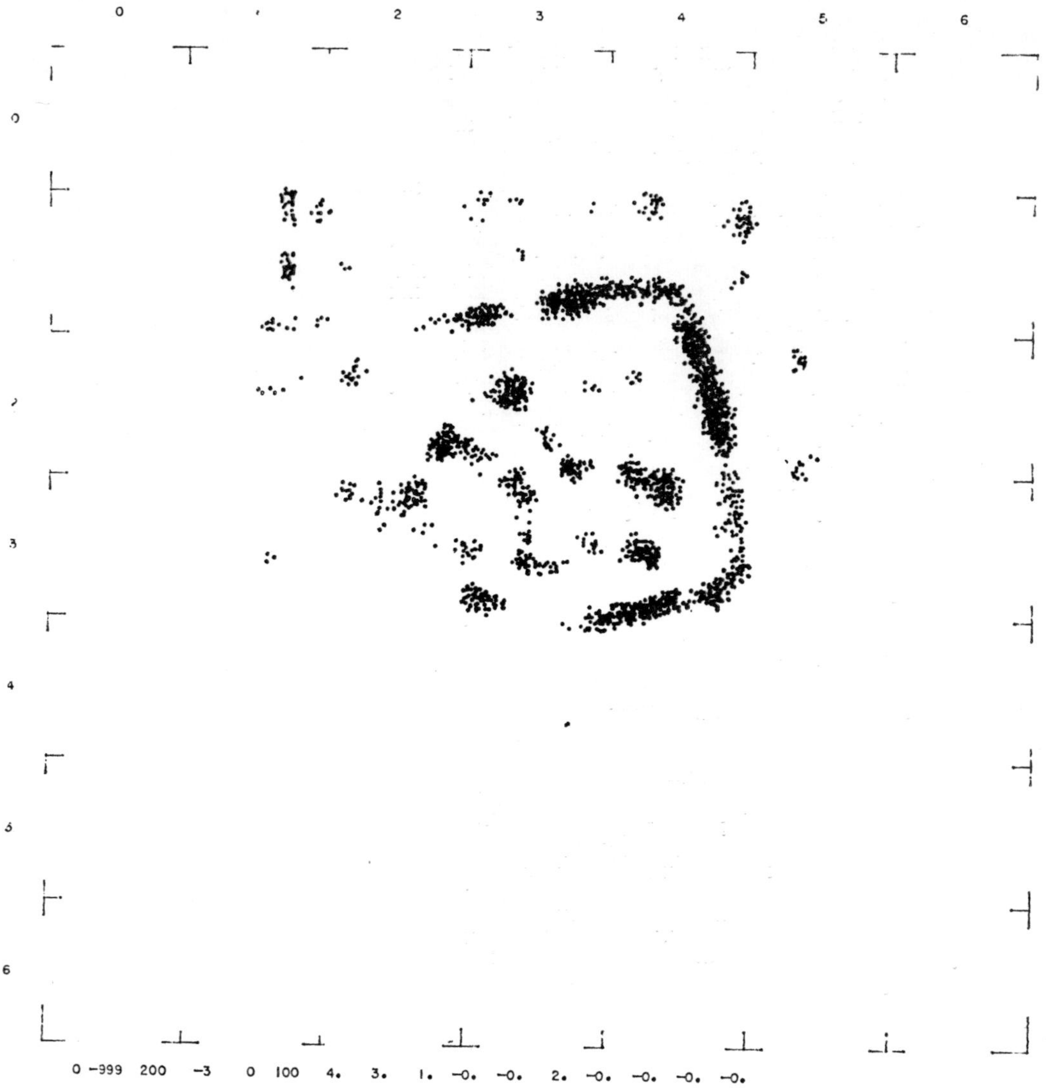

Figure 21

off centre by adding a small random number to each of the central co-ordinates. This produces a very pleasing picture, such as shown for the data of fig. 20 in fig. 21. Grid lines have automatically been drawn corresponding to the actual 20 m. grid used during the magnetic survey in the same computer run. The result resembled closely that obtained on a photograph of the same site (plate 14).

In this brief survey of some evaluation methods, only a few of the simplest techniques have been touched upon. Once, however, the data is in the computer – getting it in and out is rather tricky – then still more sophisticated techniques can be used to search for the faint anomalies in disturbed soils which are of interest to us. Some of these techniques, making use of advances in modern statistics are, at the time of writing, still under development. It is hoped to be able to report on them in the not too distant future.

22.x.67

Labor für Feld Archäologie
Rheinisches Landesmuseum
Bonn

References

Aitken, M. J. 1958. *Archaeometry*. 1:24.

Dean, W. C. 1958. *Geophysics*. 23:97–127.

Fraser, D. C., Fuller, B. D. and Ward, S. H. 1966. *Geophysics*. 31:1066–77.

Kertz, W. 1966. *Gerlands Beiträge zur Geophysik*. 75:1–33.

Le Borgne, E. 1955. *Annales de Géophysique*. 11:399–419.

Le Borgne, E. 1960. *Annales de Géophysique*. 16:159–96.

Le Borgne, E. 1965. *Archaeo-Physika*. I:1–21.

Linington, R. E. 1964. *Archaeometry*. 7:3–13.

Linington, R. E. 1966. *Archaeometry*. 9:51–60.

Mesko, C. A. 1965. *Geophysical Prospecting*. 13:475–88.

Mesko, C. A. 1966. *Geophysics*. 31:606–17.

Scollar, I. 1959. *Bonner Jahrbücher*. 159:309–13.

Scollar, I. 1965. *Archaeo-Physika*. I:21–92.

Scollar, I. and Krückeberg, F. 1966. *Archaeometry*. 9:61–70.

Searching for structure within multivariate archaeological data

F. R. Hodson

In the interests of objectivity and clarity, archaeologists are turning more to a quantitative representation of their data, and tables, histograms and graphs are now commonplace in the more serious archaeological publications. However, presentation of the data is merely a first stage: objectivity is no doubt honoured, but unless some further treatment of the data is possible, clarity may be missed. This is especially true where the quantified data refer to more than two interacting aspects of the same material, such as the features of a set of pots or the trace-elements in a bronze axe. A direct two-dimensional plot, or even a whole series of these, cannot accommodate this kind of multivariate information.

Fortunately, the high-speed computer has made feasible the analysis of multi-dimensional data in ways that were completely impracticable a dozen years ago. It is uncertain at the moment which procedures will ultimately prove to be of most use to archaeologists but, in very general terms, we are looking for methods that will simplify complex data and will reveal structure latent in it.

In order to test some likely procedures of this kind, I have taken three contrasting sets of multivariate archaeological data and have analysed them by available numerical methods. The aim at the moment is to search for useful techniques rather than useful results; however, some of the results themselves already seem of interest.

It is hoped to publish a full account of these experiments shortly as a monograph. This paper is a brief progress report, originally prepared for a meeting of the Biometric Society (British Region) on *Statistical Methods in Archaeology*, held on 7 December 1967. The aim of the paper was to show to statisticians the kind of multivariate data with which the archaeologist is faced, and to suggest to archaeologists procedures that are beoming available to help them.

The three sets of data chosen for experimental analysis are:

1 A series of bronze brooches of the pre-Roman Iron Age in Western Europe. They are taken to represent the general problem of a group of inter-related objects that is difficult to classify by intuitive methods alone (they could be pots or axes just as easily). The material is not directly in quantitative form but may be described in such a way that proportions and attributes are given as continuous or dichotomous variables.
2 A series of fifty well-known Upper Palaeolithic assemblages (basically Aurignacian and Gravettian) from South-western France and Central Europe. The assemblages have

been published, mainly by de Sonneville-Bordes, with the number of tools of standardized types that they contain. Here the problem is to see the wood for the trees: to simplify and find structure behind the mass of detail.

3 A relatively small sample (100) of European copper and bronze objects from the large number that have been analysed for their trace elements. Here the problem is to find groups of objects with similar metal content. Difficulties in measuring the very small quantities of some metals present, and differences between one part of an object and another, make this a particularly intractable set of data.

Some experiments with the first set, the brooches, have already been published and will not be mentioned further in this paper except to repeat that two procedures – Average-Link Cluster Analysis and Multi-dimensional Scaling – showed promising results (Hodson, Sneath and Doran 1966).

Fifty Upper Palaeolithic assemblages of stone tools

The data (See list No. 1)

Fifty assemblages were chosen to represent a basic theme: the first stages of Upper Palaeolithic development in France. This subject has been thoroughly and expertly studied by French prehistorians (de Sonneville-Bordes 1966), and much of the raw material has been published in quantitative form according to a taxonomic system devised and practised mainly by de Sonneville-Bordes. Although most of the assemblages come from the classic sites in the Dordogne and neighbouring areas, a few related assemblages from Central Europe were chosen for comparison (Nos 45–50). The poorest assemblage (No. 1) contained only 127 relevant stone tools, but most contained far more than this – No. 16 over 4,000.

Bordes and de Sonneville-Bordes present palaeolithic levels according to the percentage they contain of a standardized set of stone tool 'types'. The relevant list of Upper Palaeolithic types will be found in Perrot and de Sonneville-Bordes (1954, 1955, 1956a and b). This basic list comprises ninety-two types but several of these are regularly amalgamated by the Bordes in presenting their material and these amalgamations have been followed here (i.e. types 1–2, 5–6, 11–12, 13–14, 17–19, 20–2, 23–4, 27–8, 29–30, 34–7, 38–9, 46–7, 48–51, 56–7, 58–9, 60–3, 65–6, 67–8 and 69–72). Miscellaneous tools (type 92) were omitted from this experiment for obvious reasons. However, microliths (types 79–91) present a more difficult problem: the proportion of these tiny blades recovered at any site must depend largely on the technique of excavation. If they are included, the percentage representation of all the other types would then be weighted according to this external factor, and since the sites under consideration were excavated by different archaeologists at different times, it seemed safer to exclude microliths from this preliminary exercise.

Type 52 was so poorly represented that it was combined with 48–51.

These modifications, then, leave forty-six tool categories, and this was the number of variables used in the analyses.

This is not the place, nor am I qualified, to discuss this type list. A taxonomy based on numerical procedures (cf. Sackett 1966) would be of great value, but so far no such taxonomy exists. Fortunately, it is possible to have some idea of the value of this taxonomy by comparing results from its treatment of stone tools with independent evidence. In this case, some of the sites have produced a very characteristic type of bone tool – split-based, bone points. A rough check on results is provided by the performance of these sites (marked on the diagrams with an asterisk).

The analyses and their results

The Bordes study their material in two chief ways: first, by plotting as a graph the cumulative percentage frequency of tools from any one level. Since the types are always listed on the abscissa in the same order, it is possible to have some idea of the nature of a total assemblage by the shape of its curve. More than one assemblage, but hardly more than five, may be plotted together on the same diagram and their relationship is judged visually by the similarity or otherwise of their curves. Second, to summarize the nature of any assemblage, compound indices are created by amalgamating single types into broad categories – all end-scrapers, all burins, etc.

It seems worth trying to extract as much information as possible from this kind of data, and two additional procedures have been suggested: Factor Analysis by Binford and Binford (1966) and Multidimensional Scaling by Doran and Hodson (1966). This particular set of data has so far been analysed by two forms of cluster analysis, Multidimensional Scaling, Principal Components and a version of Factor Analysis (Varimax Rotation of the first few normalized Principal Components). Results from just two of these procedures will be summarized here: Average-Link Cluster Analysis and Principal Components Analysis.

After percentages for the modified tool-list had been re-computed, the first step was to replace the percentage values by their arcsine square-root equivalent. This is an accepted transformation to improve the characteristics of binomial and similar kinds of data (Bartlett 1947: 45).

Average-Link Cluster Analysis

From a previous study (Hodson, Sneath and Doran 1966) it seemed that this method should prove helpful in establishing archaeological taxonomies. It operates on a matrix of similarity (or distance) coefficients which must be computed between each pair of units (in this case assemblages). The measure of association used was Euclidean distance as in a previous study of Mousterian material (Doran and Hodson 1966). This is calculated by the formula:

$$d_{ij}=(\sum_k[x_{ik}-x_{jk}]^2)^{\frac{1}{2}}$$

where i and j are assemblages and x_{ik} is the transformed value of the percentage of the kth tool-type in assemblage i. An Algol program, written by Dr Shadaksharrapa, carried out an analysis of these distances by the Unweighted-Pair-Group-Method (Sokal and

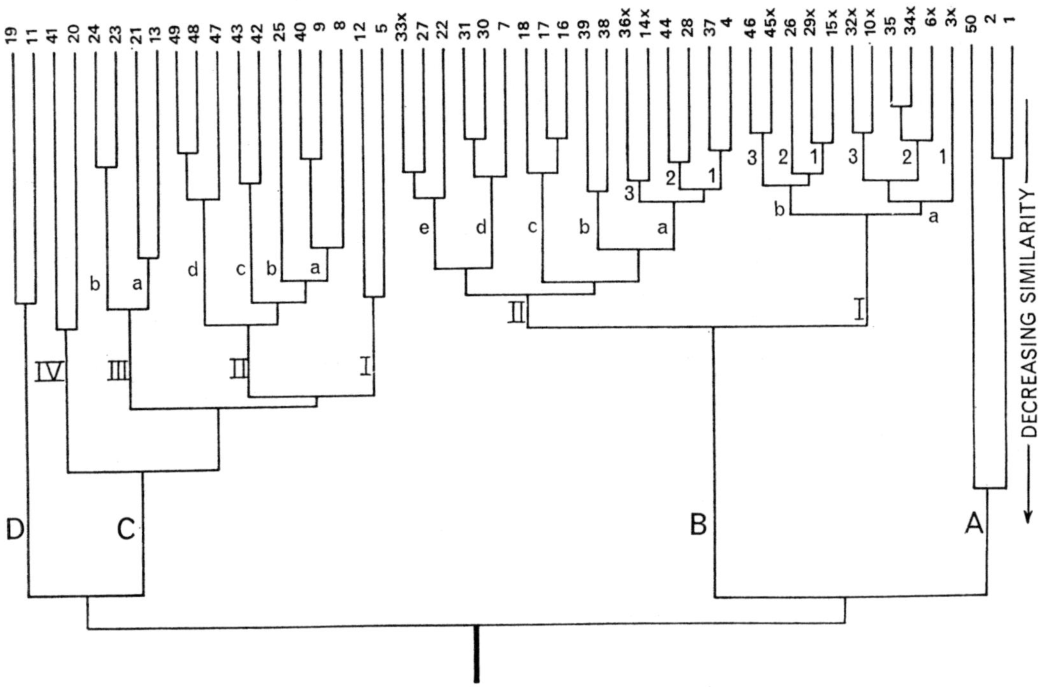

Figure 22 Average-link Cluster Analysis of fifty Upper Palaeolithic assemblages (see list 1). Asterisks mark assemblages with split-based, bone points

Sneath 1963: 189). Fig. 22 is taken from the output of this program and data, run on the SRC Chilton Atlas computer.

Starting from single assemblages at the top, this diagram shows progressively larger groups forming as the distance criterion is relaxed. Some major groups have been labelled for convenience, and levels with split-based bone points are marked by an asterisk. The structure suggested is of two main groups (B and C) with sub-groups, and of two small main groups (A and D).

Principal Components Analysis

This is an accepted procedure in multivariate statistics and is described in textbooks on that subject (e.g. Morrison 1967). Briefly, in non-mathematical terms, it attempts to summarize the data by setting up a series of major reference axes. The first new axis accounts for the maximum possible variance in the sample, the second for the maximum remaining variance and so on. Each successive axis is independent of the others and is located by weighted combinations of all the variables concerned. One end result of the analysis is to produce a sort of scatter diagram locating the subjects of the analysis (here the assemblages) on axes that are defined not by single variables, as with a conventional scatter diagram, but by significant combinations of the variables. These axes or components may prove to be interpretable as independent, underlying features of the data.

A Principal Components Analysis operates via a matrix of relationships between

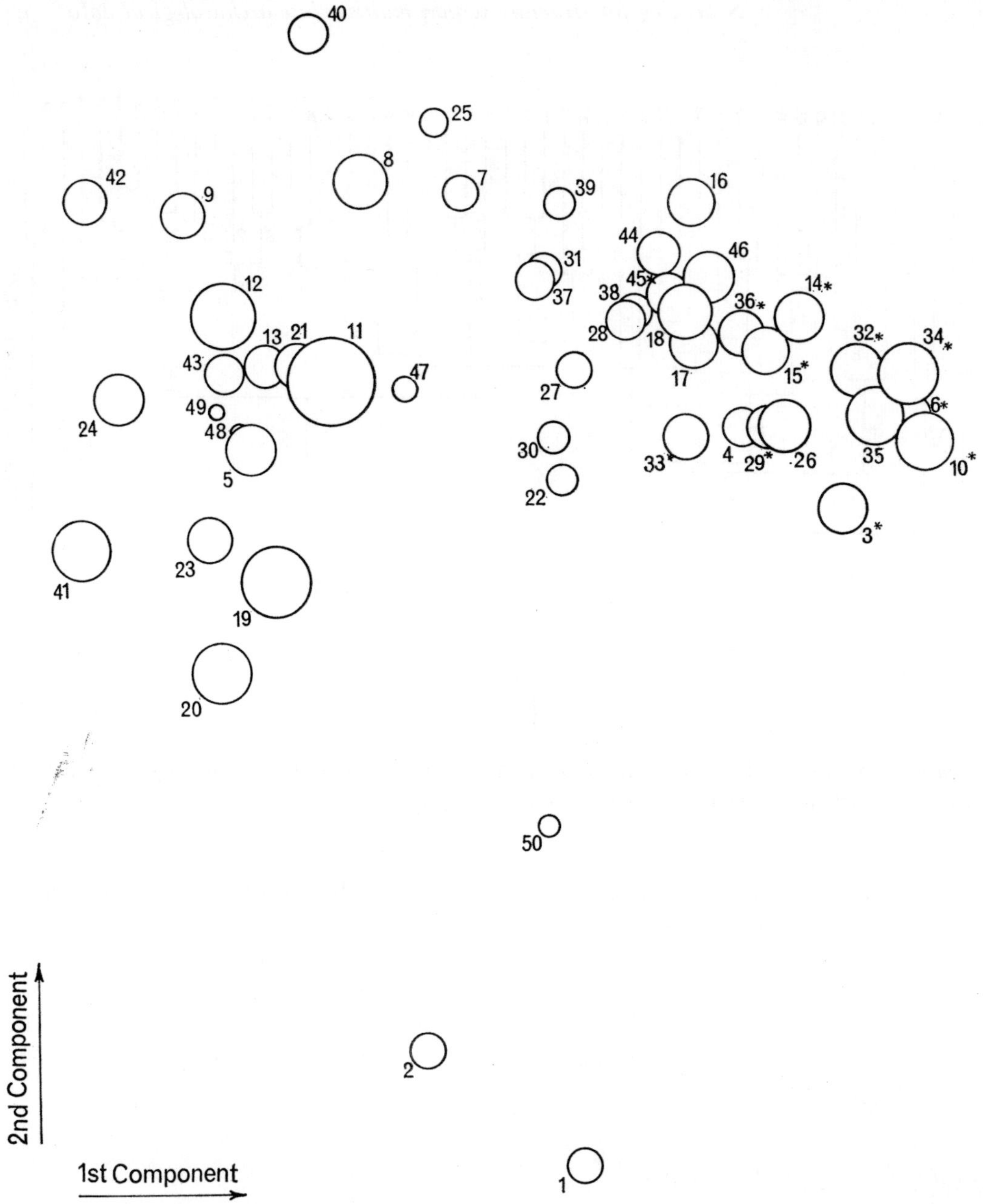

Figure 23 Principal Components Analysis of fifty Upper Palaeolithic assemblages (see list 1). Position of assemblages relative to the first three components (the third suggested by the size of symbols). Asterisks mark assemblages with split-based, bone points

variables – most usually via a matrix of correlation coefficients. Such a correlation matrix for the forty-six tool categories was calculated by the SRC Chilton Atlas computer and the Principal Components were extracted by an available library routine. Locations of the assemblages relative to the first few of these axes were also computed. Results for the first three components are plotted on fig. 23, the third dimension being indicated by the size of the symbols.

The first principal component accounts for approximately 20% of the total variance, the second for 12½%, the third for 9½% – approximately 42% for the three together. The tool types most highly correlated with these axes are given below in descending order of importance (loadings or coefficients of ·50 and over only are given):

1st component

(*a*) Positive (i.e. towards the right of fig. 23):
Carinated and nosed scrapers, end-scrapers on retouched blades, blades with Aurignacian retouch and double end-scrapers (types 11–14, 5–6, 67–8, 3).

(*b*) Negative (i.e. towards the left of fig. 23):
Gravette and related blades and other backed blades, truncated blades, almost all angle and dihedric burins both single and multiple but not *burins dièdres d'angle*, *burins d'angle sur cassure* and *burins transversaux* (types 48–52, 56–9, 40, 41–2, 31, 53, 44, 27–8).

2nd component

(*a*) Positive (i.e. towards the top of fig. 23):
Multiple tools incorporating end-scrapers, again some dihedric and angle burins, double end-scrapers (types 17–19, 27–8, 31, 34–7, 41, 3).

(*b*) Negative (i.e. towards the bottom of fig. 23):
Audi and Chatelperron knives, *racloirs*, *raclettes*, denticulated and notched pieces (types 45–7, 77–8, 74–5).

3rd component

(*a*) Positive (i.e. larger circles):
Font-Robert points and 'bossed' backed blades (types 55, 53).

(*b*) Negative (i.e. smaller circles):
Some burins not included with component 1, i.e. *burins dièdres d'angle* and *burins d'angle sur cassure* (types 29–30).

When projected on to these axes in fig. 23 the assemblages fall into a pattern of three outliers (1, 2 and 50) and two main groups.

Discussion of the Palaeolithic results

A rough check on the procedures is given by their treatment of assemblages with split-based, bone points (marked with asterisks on the diagrams). These are fairly well grouped on both diagrams, and so at least some measure of success is assured for the different steps in both analyses starting from the Bordes type-list and the attribution of tools to it.

Fig. 22 will be discussed first. Of the main stems, B and C clearly correspond with Aurignacian and Gravettian of the accepted classification. The two Chatelperronian levels (1 and 2) and site 50 are separated from the rest as stem A. A little more surprising is the separation of stem D: 11 and 19 (Font-Robert levels at Vachons II and La Ferrassie). This perhaps emphasizes the exceptional nature of these two levels relative to the other Gravettian assemblages.

To move to the sub-groups: B I and B II correspond at first sight with 'Typical' and 'Evolved' Aurignacian, but the structure of B II is complex: B IIa, for example, contains sites that de Sonneville-Bordes has assigned, on good grounds, to both facies. B IIc groups together the evolving 'Aurignacian II, III and IV' levels at La Ferrassie; it is interesting that these are put into a taxonomic group of their own. B IIe includes 22, the famous, very late 'Aurignacian V' level from Laugerie Haute West, with Cellier II and the upper level at Caminade West. Cellier II is, unfortunately, a rather composite level (de Sonneville-Bordes 1960: 87) and the presence of split-based, bone points should not be taken too seriously in this instance.

Of the Gravettian assemblages: C III includes the 'Perigordian VI' assemblages at Laugerie Haute, plus level 5 at Vachons II; C IV 'Perigordian V_2' levels with truncated elements; C II a whole series: C IId Dolní Věstonice levels, C IIc Noailles burin levels, C IIb the single 'Proto-Magdalenian' level. C IIa and C I do not seem to correspond so clearly with an accepted grouping.

It is interesting that the two sets of 'control assemblages' from Central Europe, Vogelherd (45–6) and Dolní Věstonice (47–9) are distinguished as sub-groups but relatively high up the dendogram.

Despite justifiable criticism of average-link as a specific method of clustering (Jardine, Jardine and Sibson 1967), the general potentiality of numerical clustering methods is, I think, clear from this example.

The Principal Components Analysis contrasts with the cluster analysis by presenting information about the variables (tool types) as well as the assemblages. It is not always easy to interpret the weighted combinations of variables that are suggested by a P.C. Analysis: the first component often represents a general 'size' factor of some sort, but succeeding components may not be directly interpretable. One variant of Factor Analysis, Multiple Factor solution with rotation of axes (Harman 1960), attempts to modify the pattern suggested by Principal Components, so that variables are more obviously correlated with new, rotated axes. However, the unrotated solution that is presented here does seem directly interpretable, at least as far as the first three components are concerned.

The variables most highly correlated with the first component suggest a factor opposing generalized Aurignacian (positive) with generalized Gravettian (negative). This is no doubt the main, basic dimension concerned with this set of data. Variables highly correlated with component 2 show it to be contrasting Chatelperronian – or, perhaps, earlier Mousterian traditions – (negative), with more usual Upper Palaeolithic phenomena like dihedric and angle burins. Component 3 seems to be concerned with types that occur at few sites but in relatively large numbers where they do occur. One aspect is clearly 'Font-Robert'.

Fig. 23, which projects the individual assemblages on to these three axes, gives an impression of their interrelationships (similar sites will tend to be close together), but also gives information about individual sites when considered from these three main aspects of tool combinations.

The general configuration of fig. 23 repeats, from a different point of view, some of the main features of fig. 22: the Chatelperronian levels 1 and 2, and site 50 are well separated from both the main groups. The latter (at the top of the diagram) clearly correspond with Aurignacian to the right and Gravettian to the left. The central European sites are again located within the two main groups: the Dolní Věstonice levels, however (47–9), occupy an extreme position on the third axis.

This kind of presentation could be useful to archaeologists if they are attempting to make general hypotheses about their material. Is the Chatelperronian in France really to be grouped with the Gravettian as Perigordian? How distinct are sites in the Dordogne from sites in Central Europe when judged by their stone tools? A diagram like this should certainly help us to make judgements on such issues.

One hundred copper and bronze tools analysed for their metal content

The data

By now, several thousand prehistoric copper and bronze implements from Europe have been examined spectrographically for their major and trace-elements. The resulting information gives an immediate insight into important features of prehistoric technology, such as the alloying of copper with tin, arsenic or lead.

However, it seems reasonable to hope for other types of information from elements that are discovered in much smaller proportions: perhaps the location of ore-sources or specific metal-working traditions. Unfortunately, for this less obvious information to be utlized, the analyses have to be classified, and at once the difficulty of detecting a number of clusters within interacting, multivariate data has to be faced.

Although it is not easy to suggest likely methods for dealing with this classification problem a direct way to assess any results is available: it seems a reasonable hypothesis that metal tools related by their metal content should on the whole come from a similar source (whether an ore source or a workshop source or a combination of both); further, any such source should have a definite geographical centre; consequently, if clusters of objects that are defined uniquely from the evidence of metal content show a clear geographical distribution, the method of producing clusters must be working to a certain extent.

The most ambitious attempt to detect groups within the total range of analyses has been made by a group centred on Stuttgart (Junghans *et al.* 1960). Their basic approach has been criticized more recently by Waterbolk and Butler (1965) at Groningen, in an article that provides an excellent introduction to this whole subject. The Groningen solution is to abandon attempts to define clusters from a wide range of analyses and, instead, to use outside archaeological evidence as an initial indication of groups. While this may provide one useful approach, it may be doubted whether the more direct and objective attitude of the Stuttgart school has yet had a fair trial.

The Groningen criticism is mainly based on specific inconsistencies and unsatisfactory results; the Stuttgart method of grouping (Klein 1953) is in general accepted as valid, and is in fact closely related to the method used at Groningen to define subgroups of finds from hypothetically uniform archaeological complexes that turn out not to produce uniform metal analyses.

It is quite possible, nevertheless, that inadequacies in the Stuttgart results do stem from the statistical method of analysis employed, and not from the basic approach, which the Groningen authors have characterized as 'beginning by ignoring all archaeological grouping of the analyses, and throwing them all into one pot, with the hope that mathematical means will bring them out of the pot again in a logical order' (Waterbolk and Butler 1965: 230). If clusters do exist, there is no reason why this approach should not find them, provided a suitable multivariate technique is employed. The method used at Stuttgart to define groups was in fact essentially 'univariate', dividing and subdividing the total sample successively according to the amount of single elements present.

Since so much effort has been put into obtaining these spectrographic data, it seems worth trying out some suitable, available multivariate procedures. As Walterbolk and Butler summarize it, 'our problem is therefore the arranging of the metal analyses in groups of uniform composition' (1965: 230). A suitable form of cluster analysis should achieve this end, and the results of one such attempt will be presented here.

I was greatly helped in this experiment by R. J. Hartzig, who took this problem as the subject of his thesis in connection with a postgraduate Diploma in Statistics in the Department of Pure Mathematics and Mathematical Statistics of Cambridge University. He selected and prepared the raw data from relevant publications and suggested the transformation of values that will later be described.

One hundred analyses were chosen, from the Stuttgart series, ninety published by Junghans *et al.* (1960) and ten by Schubert and Schubert (1967). The sample numbers given with list 2 refer to these publications. The analyses were chosen from find spots throughout Europe so that it would be simple to see if suggested clusters showed a clear geographical significance. The ten Budapest analyses (90–9) were included as likely examples of a single 'source'. They are from the same hoard, Alsónémedi, and from visual inspection appeared to have a very uniform metal content. If these ten samples were not clustered together by the taxonomic procedure, it could hardly be taken too seriously. Similarly pairs of analyses from the same objects, 1 and 2, and 18 and 19, should provide a rough idea of scale for similarity estimations.

Analyses from Stuttgart are given as follows (the examples are for Nos 1 and 91 of this sample):

Analysis No.	Sn	Pb	As	Sb	Ag	Ni	Bi	Au	Zn	Co	Fe
1	0	0	1·67	1·65	0·44	0	0·1	0	0	0	trace
91	~7	0	0·41	0·72	~0·01	0·27	0	0	0	0	++

These figures are percentages, the unquoted remainder in all cases being copper.

The analysis and its results

One immediate difficulty is apparent from the examples just quoted: although a definite value is usually given, the nature of the laboratory technique automatically entails a few doubtful and approximate values. For this preliminary attempt where the general method only is of most interest, an arbitrary *ad hoc* solution was adopted: symbols like '+' and 'Trace' were represented by what seemed to be a reasonable figure for the elements concerned (0·1 for tin, 0·005 for lead and arsenic, 0·001 for bismuth, 0·002 for gold).

Approximate values were taken at the figure given. Question marks occur rarely, mainly for gold, and were translated as 0·001. Certainly, better solutions than these could be devised.

Euclidean distance seemed appropriate, again, as a basic measure of relationship between samples, but since the variance of the several elements differed so much (roughly in proportion with the mean), and since the distribution of the percentage values are skew (being bounded by zero), some transformation of the raw percentages was required. Hartzig therefore suggested taking D_{ij}, the estimated difference between two samples as

$$D_{ij} = \left(\sum_{k} s_{ij}{}^{k}\right)^{\frac{1}{2}}$$

where $$s_{ij}{}^{k} = \frac{(x_i{}^{k} - x_j{}^{k})^2}{(x_i{}^{k})^2 + (x_j{}^{k})^2}$$

x_i being the value of the k th element in the i th object. Hartzig's program computed distances between each pair of samples according to this formula on the Cambridge University Titan computer. The resulting matrix of distances was then clustered by the program mentioned above in connection with the Palaeolithic analyses. The Algol program was again run on the SRC Chilton Atlas.

The result is presented as fig. 24. The structure of the dendrogram is by no means

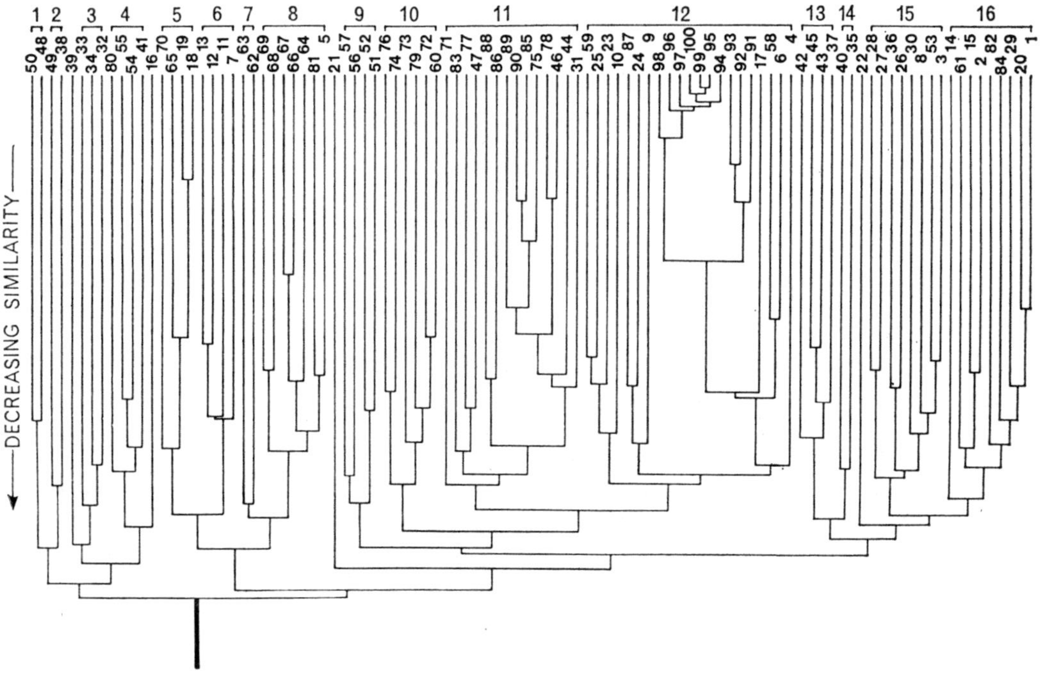

Figure 24 Average-link Cluster Analysis of 100 metal objects spectrographically examined for their trace elements (see list 2). The suggested sixteen 'groups' are defined at a distance level of 2·20

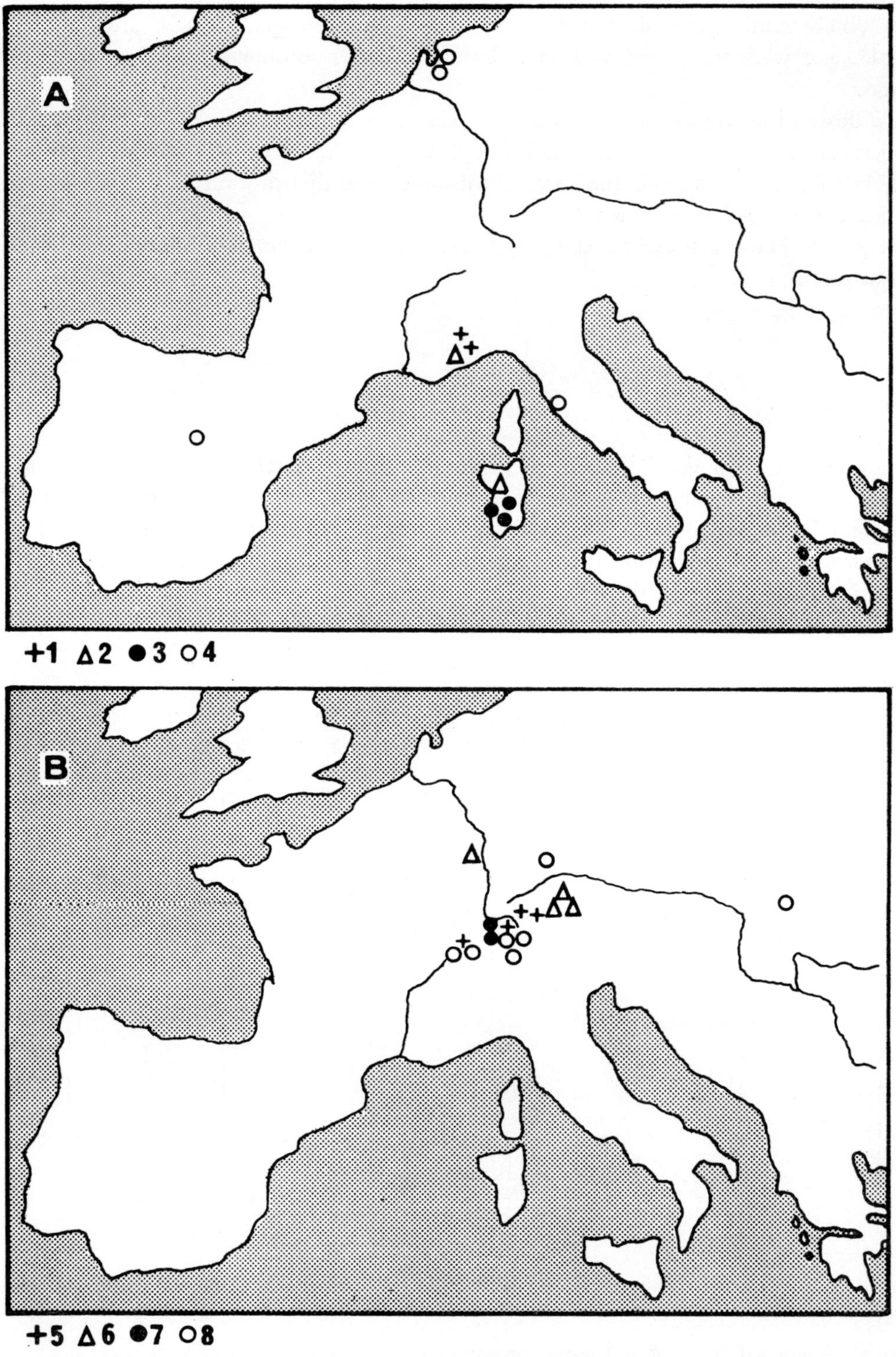

Figure 25 Distributions of hypothetical groups suggested by the Average-link Cluster Analysis (see fig. 24)

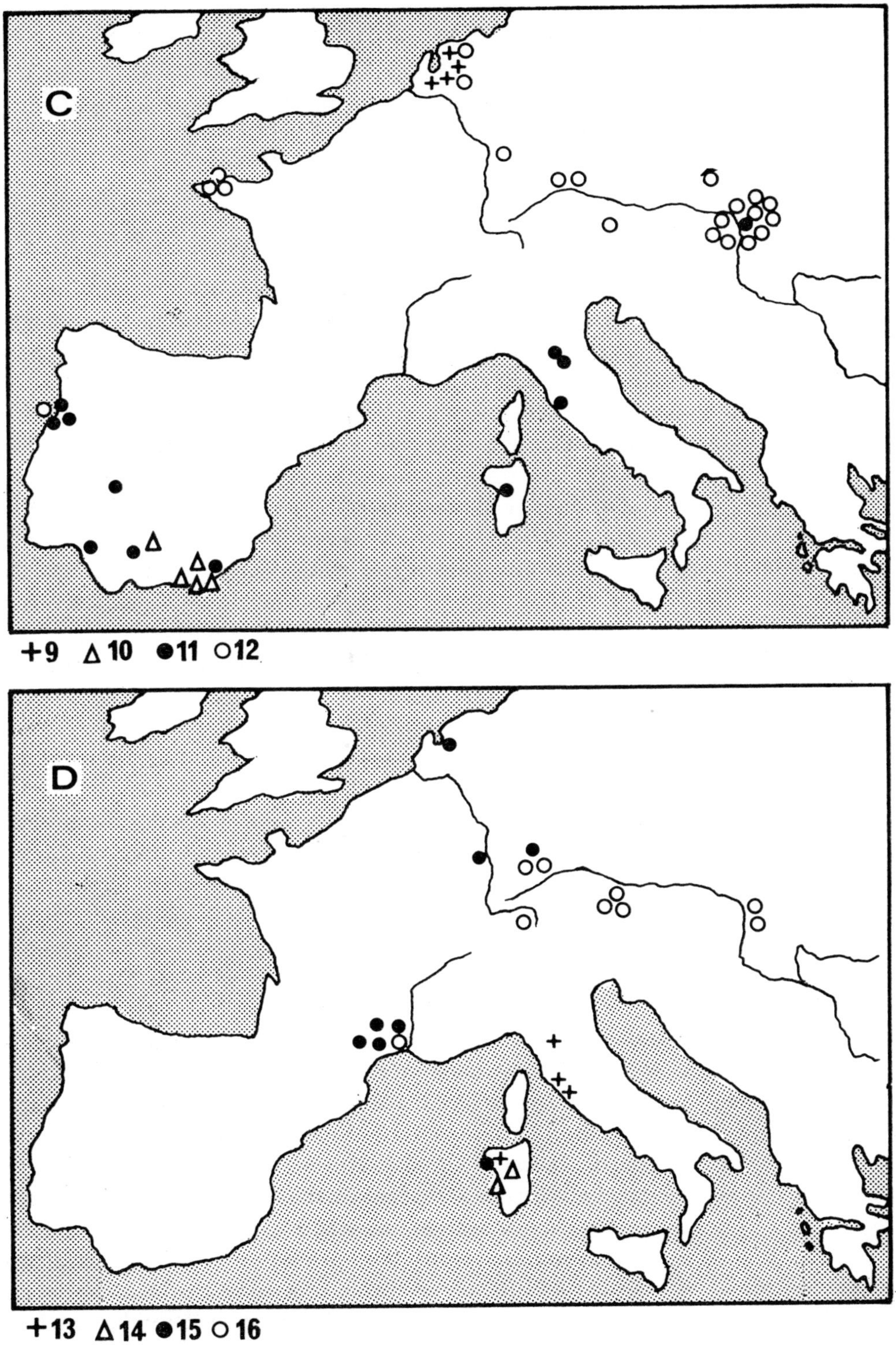

Figure 26 Distributions of hypothetical groups suggested by the Average-link Cluster Analysis (see fig. 24)

simple, and hypothetical source groups could be defined at any distance level. Provisionally, a series of sixteen groups, defined at level 2·20, have been chosen for discussion, and labelled. Their geographical distributions are plotted very roughly on figs 25 and 26. For convenience, these groups are treated under four headings, A, B, C and D, that roughly correspond with structure suggested lower down the dendrogram.

Discussion of the results

The hypothetical source-group from Alsónémedi, Nos 91–100, is clearly grouped and separated from the other analyses as are the two analyses 18–19 from the one axe. 1 and 2, again taken from one axe, are not as clearly isolated as this, but are put in the same subgroup, 16. This not entirely satisfactory result may be due partly to the treatment of a '?' symbol for gold in No. 2. It was taken to imply 'present in very small quantity' for this initial attempt, but treatment as a missing value would obviously be more satisfactory, and would present no problem to a programmer for future experiments.

However, judged by these three immediate checks, the analysis seems to have performed surprisingly well.

The geographical distribution of sub-groups is also encouraging (figs 25 and 26). Of the sixteen main sub-groups suggested by the dendrogram, only 4 and 15 seem really unsatisfactory, and, of course, are not necessarily so. It is worth emphasizing that these groups have been taken well down the dendrogram, i.e. with a relatively large distance criterion. Groups may be defined at any level and it would be expected that the stricter the distance criterion, the more significant the groups.

The results will not be discussed in detail but the general outcome seems clear. Although the Groningen school has criticized the 'all into one pot' approach, in this experiment a mathematical means does seem to have brought analyses out of the pot in a logical order. There seems no reason why, after refinement, this general approach should not yield acceptable, objective results, to compare with conclusions drawn from other possible approaches.

General conclusions

I do not wish to play down the experimental nature of all these results. As already mentioned, the method of clustering demonstrated (average-link) may not be the best for this kind of material. Certainly, this procedure could not in its present form throw any very large number of subjects into a pot at one time (about 200 would be the limit) in the hope of bringing them out in logical order. But, after all, the whole approach is in its infancy. An improved method of clustering that could at the same time cope with a large number of subjects, would be of real value to archaeologists.

For a more general summarization of the structure behind multivariate data, Principal Components is an accepted and readily available procedure that can cope with large numbers of units. It has the advantage of providing information about the variables of the study as well as the subjects, but the kind of simplification it produces, while helpful in giving a general view, will not readily suggest a detailed taxonomy. The most fruitful approach seems to be to look at the data in as many different ways as possible, since each new viewpoint may bring out hidden details of real significance.

It is important to emphasize that none of these methods in itself 'interprets' the material. What they are intended to achieve is an objectively controlled re-presentation of data so that interpretation becomes more straightforward.

Acknowledgements

This work was carried out during tenure of an 'Atlas Senior Research Fellowship in Computer Applications in the Arts and Sciences' offered jointly by the SRC Chilton Atlas Computer Laboratory and Churchill College, Cambridge. I would like to thank the staff of these institutions for their help during this period. I would also like to thank Professor D. G. Kendall and members of the Statistical Laboratory in the Department of Pure Mathematics and Mathematical Statistics at Cambridge University for the facilities and co-operation they have given me during tenure of this award.

The Average-Link Cluster Analysis program, written by G. Shadaksharrapa, was made available by Dr P. H. A. Sneath of the Microbial Systematics Research Unit in the University of Leicester.

15.xii.67

Institute of Archaeology
London

List 1

Upper Palaeolithic Assemblages (figs 22 and 23)

(1)–(5)	La Chèvre (Dordogne) levels 1, 2, 3, 4b, 5i
(6)–(13)	Les Vachons (Charente), Shelter I levels 1, 2, 3, 4; Shelter II levels 3, 4, 5
(14)	Lartet (Dordogne)
(15)–(20)	La Ferrassie (Dordogne), Grand-Abri levels F, H¹, H′, H″, J, K
(21)–(25)	Laugerie Haute (Dordogne), West, levels B, D; East, levels B, B′, F
(26)–(31)	Caminade (Dordogne), West, lower and upper levels; East, levels G, F, D2 inf., D2 sup.
(32)–(33)	Cellier (Dordogne) levels A, C
(34)–(35)	Castanet (Dordogne) levels A, C
(36)	Les Cottés (Vienne) level E
(37)	Fontenioux (Vienne) level D
(38)–(39)	Chanlat (Corrèze) lower and upper levels
(40)	Roque St-Christophe (Dordogne) level A
(41)–(42)	Laraux (Vienne) levels 5, 3
(43)	Gavaudun (Lot-et-Garonne)
(44)	Bassaler-Nord (Corrèze) level 7
(45)–(46)	Vogelherd (Württemberg) levels 5, 4
(47)–(49)	Dolní Věstonice (Moravia) lower level, 'Objects' 1 and 2
(50)	Býci Skála (Moravia)

Data taken from de Sonneville-Bordes 1960, 1965; Arambourou and Jude 1964; Bouyssonie and de Sonneville-Bordes 1956; Klima 1963; Valoch 1966.

List 2

Metal analyses (fig. 24)

Serial numbers as Junghans *et al.* 1960

(1) 111
(2) 113
(3) 151
(4) 155
(5) 157
(6) 178
(7) 190
(8) 191
(9) 302
(10) 305
(11) 139
(12) 140
(13) 141
(14) 186
(15) 187
(16) 221
(17) 223
(18) 252
(19) 254
(20) 263
(21) 496
(22) 498
(23) 500
(24) 501
(25) 502
(26) 503
(27) 504
(28) 505
(29) 536
(30) 537
(31) 549
(32) 550
(33) 553
(34) 554
(35) 557
(36) 558
(37) 559
(38) 560
(39) 501
(40) 565
(41) 609
(42) 611
(43) 612
(44) 616
(45) 617
(46) 618
(47) 619
(48) 669
(49) 671
(50) 672
(51) 677
(52) 678
(53) 679
(54) 680
(55) 683
(56) 685
(57) 687
(58) 683
(59) 689
(60) 691
(61) 786
(62) 787
(63) 789
(64) 791
(65) 793
(66) 794
(67) 795
(68) 796
(69) 797
(70) 798
(71) 810
(72) 815
(73) 816
(74) 818
(75) 819
(76) 820
(77) 822
(78) 827
(79) 829
(80) 832
(81) 835
(82) 840
(83) 841
(84) 842
(85) 851
(86) 693
(87) 853
(88) 854
(89) 855
(90) 857

Serial numbers as Schubert and Schubert 1967

(91) 1
(92) 2
(93) 3
(94) 4
(95) 5
(96) 6
(97) 7
(98) 8
(99) 9
(100) 10

References

Arambourou, R. and Jude, P. E. 1964. *Le Gisement de la Chèvre*, Périgueux.

Bartlett, M. S. 1947. The use of transformations. *Biometrics*. 39.

Binford, L. R. and Binford S. R. 1966. A preliminary analysis of functional variability in the Mousterian of Levallois facies. *American Anthropologist*. 238.

Bouyssonnie, J. and Sonneville-Bordes, D. de. 1956. L'abri No. 2 des Vachons. *Cong. Préhist. France*. 271.

Doran, J. E. and Hodson, F. R. 1966. A digital computer analysis of palaeolithic flint assemblages. *Nature*. 688.

Harman, H. H. 1960. *Modern Factor Analysis*. Chicago.

Hodson, F. R., Sneath, P. H. A. and Doran, J. E. 1966. Some experiments in the numerical analysis of archaeological data. *Biometrika*. 311.

Jardine, C. J., Jardine, N. and Sibson, R. 1967. The Structure and Construction of Taxonomic Hierarchies. *Mathematical Biosciences*. 173.

Junghans, S., Sangmeister, E. and Schröder, M. 1960. *Metallanalysen kupferzeitlicher und frühbronzezeitlicher Bodenfunde aus Europa* (SAM I). Berlin.

Klein, H. 1954. Statistischer Auswertung der Analysenergebnisse. *34, Bericht der Römisch-Germanischen Kommission*. 103.

Klima, B. 1963. *Dolní Věstonice*. Prague.

Morrison, D. F. 1967. *Multivariate Statistical Methods*. New York.

Sackett, J. R. 1966. Quantitative analysis of Upper Paleolithic stone tools. *American Anthropologist*. 356.

Schubert, F. and Schubert, E. 1967. Spektralanalytische Untersuchungen. In Moszolics, A. *Bronzefunde des Karpatenbeckens*. Budapest.

Sokal, R. R. and Sneath, P. H. A. 1963. *Numerical Taxonomy*. San Francisco and London.

Sonneville-Bordes, D. de. 1960. *Le Paléolithique Supérieur en Périgord*. Bordeaux.

Sonneville-Bordes, D. de. 1965. Observations statistiques sur L'Aurignacien du Vogelherd. *Fundberichte aus Schwaben*. 69.

Sonneville-Bordes, D. de. 1966. L'évolution du Paléolithique supérieur en Europe occidentale et sa signification. *Bull. Soc. Préhist. Français*. 3.

Sonneville-Bordes, D. de and Perrot, J. 1954, 1955, 1956a and b. Lexique typologique du Paléolithique Supérieur. *Bull. Soc. Préhist. Français*. 327, 76, 4–8, 547.

Valoch, K. 1966. Die Quartzitindustrie aus der Býci skála-Höhle in Mähren. *Quartär*. 51.

Waterbolk, H. T. and Butler, J. J. 1965. Comments on the use of metallurgical analysis in prehistoric studies. *Helenium*. 227.

A rectangular Early La Tène Marnian house at Chassemy (Aisne)

Ralph M. and Elsebet S.-J. Rowlett and Michel Boureux
with contributions by Jon Friedlander, Willem van Zeist, and Maria Hopf

The La Tène Iron Age Culture of northern Champagne, France, has hitherto been known almost exclusively from cemeteries – there being at least 118 reported for the La Tène Ia phase alone – with hardly anything known from habitations. This state of research inevitably gives a distorted picture of Marnian life and has severely limited the kinds of inferences that could be made, including the testing of hypotheses concerning Marnian migrations.

A Marnian village site has been revealed at Chassemy (Aisne) 'Le Saule Baillot' as a consequence of sandpit exploitation. Because of the immediate danger to some house remains by these operations, the authors, under the supervision of Circumscription Director Professor Ernest Will, excavated the house described here, and the junior author tested some others during the summer of 1964. This research, conducted under the auspices of the American School of Prehistoric Research, was supported by grants from the US National Academy of Science and the Department of Anthropology and Peabody Museum of Harvard University.

This site is located 12 km. east of Soissons (Aisne) in the commune of Chassemy and is only 0·5 km. from the long-known cemetery of Chassemy 'La Fosse Chapelet' (fig. 27) containing burials dating from Hallstatt IIb through La Tène II (Calland 1869; Fleury 1877; Moreau 1888; Hubert 1902; Piette 1925) including a chariot burial, still incompletely published, said to date from La Tène Ia (Bretz-Mahler and Joffroy 1959: 29). Both 'Le Saule Baillot' and 'La Fosse Chapelet' lie in beds of the Vesle River just before it flows into the Aisne. The houses at 'Le Saule Baillot' had been silted over by the Vesle, and then were preserved more or less intact. Before sandpit operations the place had been protected by forest, but there had been some disturbance of the village area by recent military entrenchments, probably made during World War I. Other occupational remains were found between 'Le Saule Baillot' and the cemetery. As in the Marne, no evidence for fortifications was detected.

The cemetery remains clearly relate to the Marne–Aisne group of the Marne Culture, affiliating with other famous sites of the Aisne such as Caranda, Ciry-Salsogne, Armentières, Fère-en-Tardenois, and Trugny and celebrated sites in the Marne Department at Les Jogasses and Mont Gravet (Rowlett 1967). House 9, reported here, dates to the La Tène Ia phase of the Marne Culture on the basis of both typological analysis and radio-carbon age determination, as discussed below.

The houses were built on a moderately fine chalky brown loam deposited by the Vesle

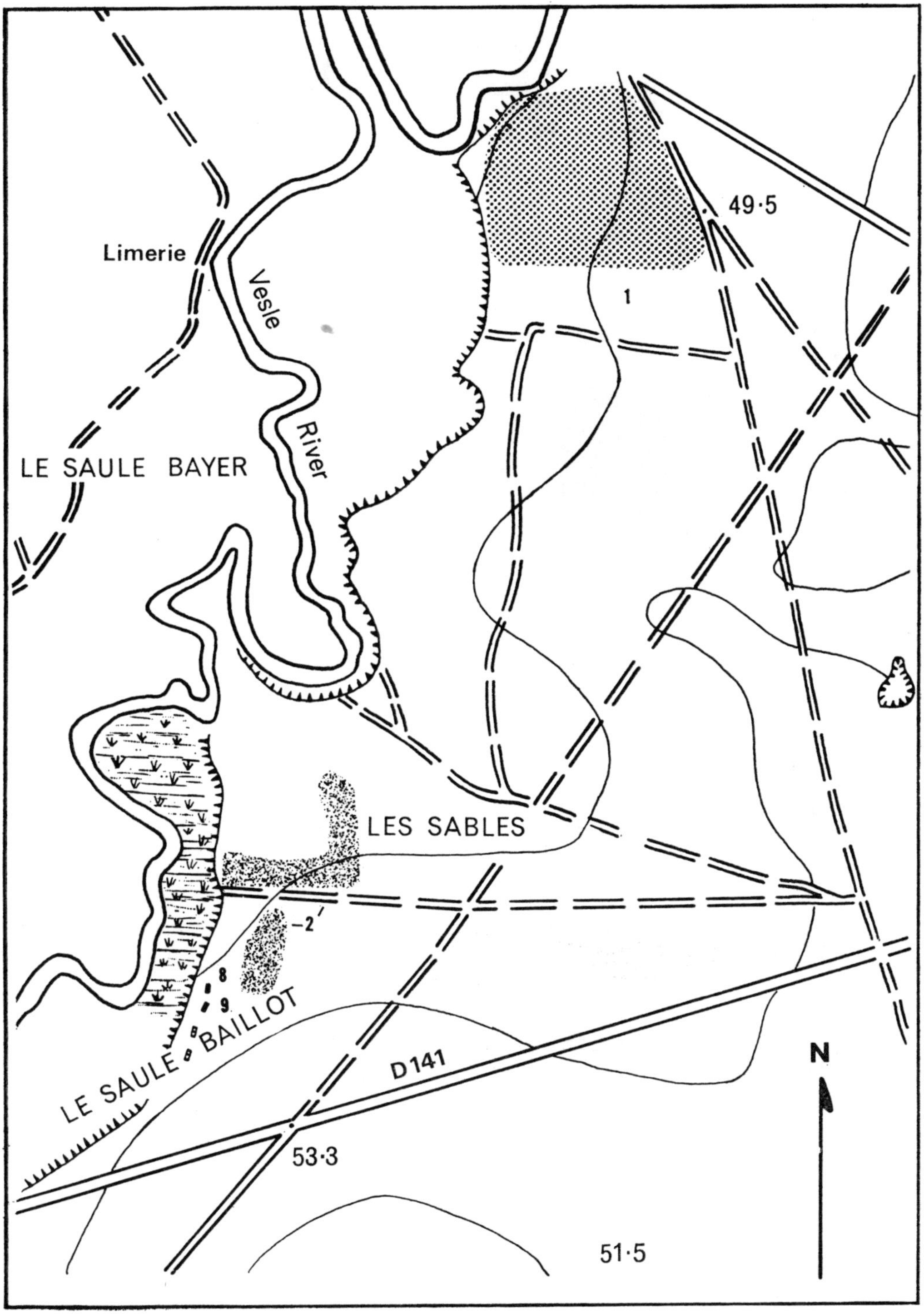

Figure 27 Map of village and cemetery at Chassemy (Aisne): 1, location of cemetery, 2, part of settlement area, 8–9, house sites. Scale: 1/10,000. Adapted from map 'Soissons Nos 7–8' of the Institut Geographique National (France)

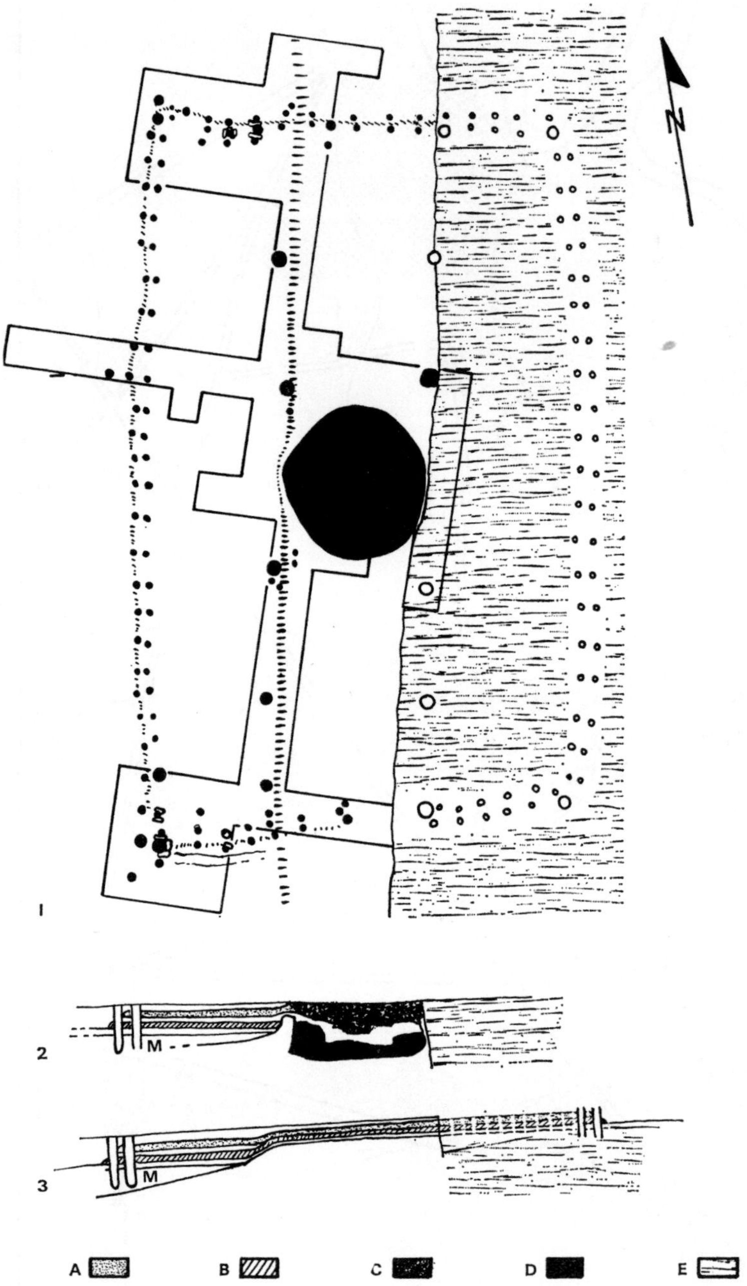

Figure 28 Chassemy House 9: 1, plan of the House, reconstructed assuming bilateral symmetry. The trenches show where all superficial cultural and natural layers were dug away down to the blue marl to double-check excavation procedures. 2, cross-section of house through fireplace. 3, cross-section of house at point indicated on plan, as reconstructed assuming bilateral symmetry. A: Top Floor. B: Bottom Floor. C: Top Hearth. D: Bottom Hearth. E: part removed by sandpit exploration. M: blue marl. Scale: 1/100

in post-Pleistocene times. House 9 remains the best preserved one, although gravel pit operation had split the house longitudinally, taking away the entire eastern one-third before the site came to the attention of prehistorians. For this reason, the house width can only be estimated at *c.* 6·20 m, if one assumes bilateral symmetry. The length may be measured directly, amounting to 9·75 m. (fig. 28:1).

Postmoulds reveal the outline of the walls, centered around the typically Marnian deeply-dug firepit in the center. The walls' main structure consists of moderately large posts, leaving 10–25 cm. diameter holes. Inside the house structure itself were two parallel rows of roof-support postmolds, of about the same sizes and about 1·2 to 1·6 m. apart, except that the posts nearest the fireplaces were 2·8 m. distant from each other. The location of the door is uncertain, although it appears to have been in the south end, hypothetically utilizing one of the roof posts as part of the door frame.

There was no evidence for any interior partitioning between the interior roof support posts, but evidence for the outer wall filling up the intervals between the main bearing posts consists of a series of paired rows of smaller posts 6–10 cm. in diameter. Such posts as these apparently carried the wickerwork for wattle and daub plastering. Although the house at Chassemy had not burned, and therefore none of the wall daub was baked, clumps of clay were occasionally found along the walls, and along the southern end lay a light colored yellow streak of clay which had been washed from the wall of the house by weather (fig. 28:1). The double row of wall curtain posts are by no means unusual, being found in contemporary terp buildings in the Netherlands (van Giffen 1936) and also in southern Scandinavia (Becker 1966). The double row of wall curtain posts sometimes had 'extra' holes, apparently from renovations further evidenced in floor and fireplace deposits.

The floors of the houses were quite simply constructed, consisting merely of the faintest trace of clay, hardly more than 3 cm. thick, put down to stabilize the sand-loam surface initially. After the house had been inhabited for a considerable amount of time, either a human agency or a natural one – flooding – had renovated the floor of the house by depositing a layer about 5–8 cm. thick of somewhat sandier, and browner, loam over the bone and sherd strewn surface of the Bottom Floor, whereupon a new floor, the Top Floor, was built upon the new layer (fig. 28:2–3). This Intermediate Loam between the two floors did contain a little debris, filtering down from the Top Floor and working up from the Bottom Floor, but was much less rich in finds than the two floors themselves. While the Bottom Floor's surface lay intact wherever any part of the house still remained, in a few spots the bulldozer blade had nipped into the surface of the Top Floor.

The centrally located fireplace was in a somewhat asymmetric hole, about 2·03–2·07 m. in diameter. Like that of more summarily studied Marnian houses at Mairy, Poix, and Sarry, the pit was dug surprisingly deeply, reaching a depth of 86 cm., and was somewhat undercut. Even more than the walls and the floor, the firepit exhibited unmistakable traces of remodeling. When the Top Floor had been built, the bottom deposits of the firepit had been sealed off from the upper ones by a layer of grey marly clay, apparently from local deposits of marl or '*tardenois*', which gives the country its name (fig. 28:2). This remodeling keeps the fireplace from being too deep with respect to the now raised floor.

When the house was originally established, the spot chosen was at the edge of an ancient bank of the Vesle River, where formerly a sort of lake or marsh had created marly lacustrine deposits, just to the west below the bank. The bank itself is covered with loess deposits, evidently of Wurmian age, in the top of which were found a few Upper Palaeolithic tools suggesting an Aurignacian industry. Although now the superficial alluvial deposits of the Vesle make the ground surface above the site level, when the firepit of House 9 was dug the last traces of the ancient bank were still visible and the entire row of houses (fig. 27) was built in alignment with the bank. In House 9 the eastern 4·20 m. were about 15–20 cm. higher than the western portion of it (fig. 28: 2–3). Thus in effect a kind of split-level house was created, with one part of the floor higher than the other. Such an arrangement (which was very perplexing when first encountered in excavation) facilitated operations around the fireplace, for when the housewife stood on the lower half, some of the need to stoop low was obviated. Bankettes have been found by Garnier (1961) in a La Tène II village at La Fertè-Gaucher 'le Haut-de-Champaugrain' (Seine-et-Marne) in Champagne Briard, where every house had two, one along each wall.

While some artefacts, potsherds, and bones lay upon and within the floors, the greatest concentration of these materials occurred in the fireplace. There also, particularly in the uppermost level, were numerous pieces of semi-cooked daub, clearly showing the impressions of the wooden sticks against which they had been placed. Only in the firepit did such finds occur. It seems unlikely that this is daub from the walls, as it would have been senseless to have thrown old daub in the firepit, only to have to scoop it out again. Since some of these remains show the traces of more than one piece of wood, they cannot be clay nozzles of bellows either. American archeologist Raymond Wood remarks that very similar daubs are found in the fireplaces of Euroamerican frontier log cabins, where the clay lining of a wooden stick chimney has fallen down. From this parallel, it seems possible that wooden chimneys were used to carry away the smoke in the Chassemy house. The Euroamerican frontier cabins do stem from the Old World, having been introduced by Swedish settlers, and represent a tradition once widespread in barbaric Iron Age Europe, as many Roman bas-reliefs testify.

Artefacts

In addition to the charcoal, ash, artefacts, baked clay remnants, and burnt and unburnt bones, the fireplace, as well as the floor, contained numerous potsherds and other artefacts of stone, ceramics, iron, and one lump of non-ferrous metal.

The excavations yielded a total of 1,653 sherds, including those found outside the house and those which had worked their way down beneath the Bottom Floor. Only 10·2% of these sherds are of the rather well-made dark burnished ware which appears typically in Marne Culture burials. In addition to this expected pottery, there occur also several other wares not normally found in Marnian burials.

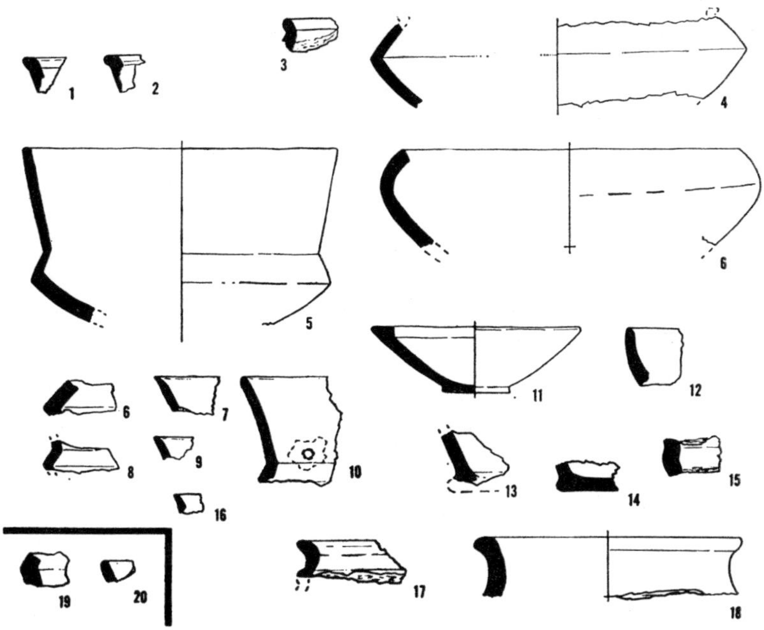

Figure 29 Marnian I Ware. 1–16: handmade from Top Floor. 17–18: wheel-made from Top Floor. 19–20: handmade from Bottom Floor. Scale: 1/4

Pottery wares

GROUP I *Marnian ware of rather fine quality, known from graves also.*

Marnian I (fig. 29) Matrix: almost pure clay with temper of finely ground up chalk, limestone and old pottery, alone or mixed.

Baking: hard enough to enable the ware to ring at the touch.

Coloring: in order of frequency, black on black (7–8 on a 1–9 scale), brown outside with black inside and orange-yellow outside with orange-red inside, various shades.

Surface: clay slip applied and burnished to a high sheen; striations of narrow-edged burnishing tool.

Marnian II (fig. 30) Matrix: basically like Marnian I, but matrix and temper coarser.

Coloring: as on Marnian I except that brown here is more purple and a rare type of yellow (2–3) with orange inside is present.

Surface treatment: clay slip has higher sand content, high sheen less frequent than in Marnian I.

GROUP II *Rather well-made sandy pottery, rarely seen in burials.*

Sandy Marnian (fig. 31: 1–8, 17–24) Matrix: high percentage of silicium-sand makes the ware 'cindery' and requires less temper, which is chalk and old pottery.

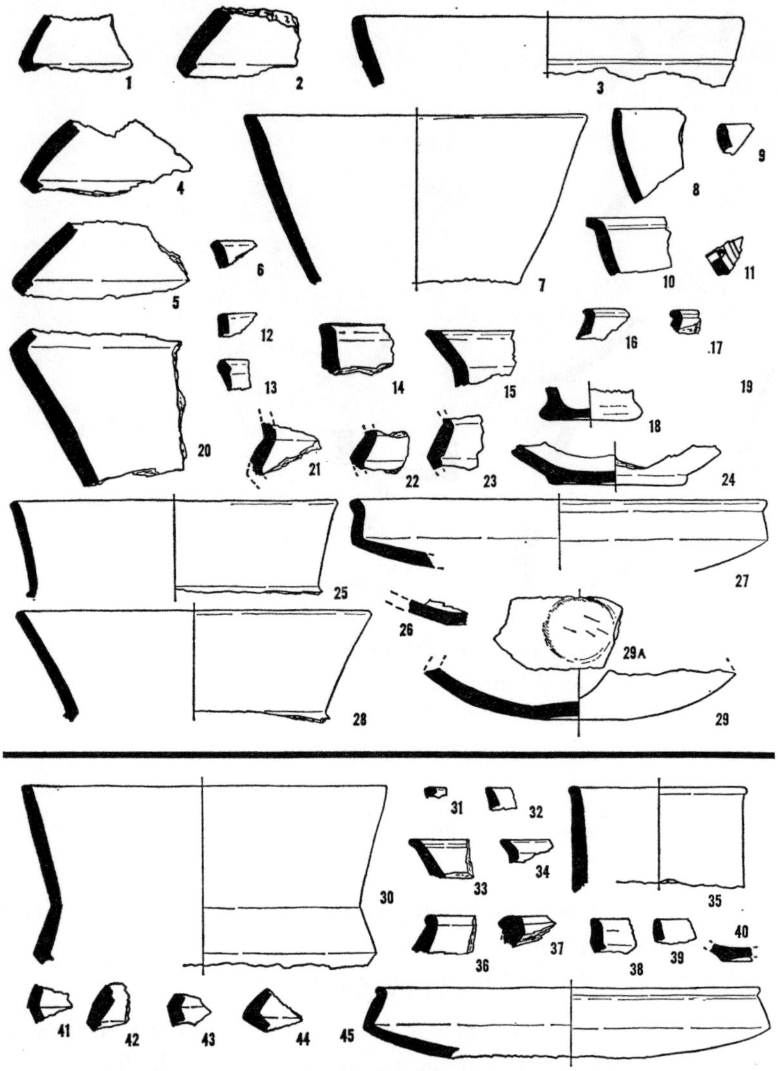

Figure 30 Marnian II Ware. 1–29: Top Floor. 30–45: Bottom Floor. Scale 1/4

Baking: Hard, but, possibly due to the sand content, it does not ring to the touch.

Coloring: in order of frequency, purple-brown with black inside (both 7–8), brown on brown (6–8), and light browns and oranges.

Surface treatment: slip is applied but due to sand content or thin application, burnishing not very successful.

Sandy Ware (fig. 31:12–16, 29–30) Matrix: high sand content of a fusible type so break-edges are flaky; small amounts of chalk and pottery temper.

Baking: uneven within the group from medium hard to moderate, less baked cores often slightly darker than surfaces.

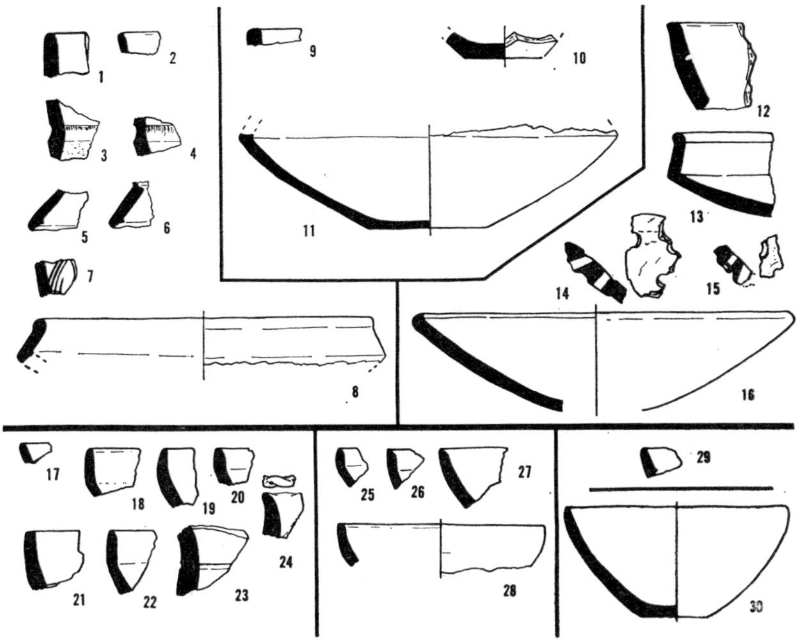

Figure 31 Sand-tempered Wares. 1–16: Top Floor. 1–8: Sandy Marnian. 9–11: Petit-Saint-Jean Ware. 12–16: Sandy Ware. 17–29: Bottom Floor. 17–24: Sandy Marnian. 25–28: Petit-Saint-Jean Ware. 29: Sandy Ware. 30: Sandy Ware from House 8. Scale: 1/4

Coloring: always alike on both surfaces, in order of frequency – purple-brown (7–9), beige-browns, reds, and rare true yellow.

Surface treatment: not *de rigueur*, when used, consists of a slip of the thinned matrix or true clay slip; in the latter case burnishing can approach Marnian greasy texture.

Petit-Saint-Jean (fig. 31:9–11, 25–8) Matrix: high percentage of glimmering sand (quartz?) with equally much pulverized chalk and pottery.

Baking: fair, always producing vertical lines between core and surfaces, breakage often occurring along these lines and the ware crumbles at touch, once broken.

Coloring: serves to distinguish Petit-Saint-Jean ware I from II. I always red-brown surfaces with black cores (7–8). II always monocolored in brown-grays and beige (2–6). Physical differences between the two include more chalk temper and greater thinness in I and more crumbliness for II.

GROUP III *Crude pottery, probably household wares, almost totally unknown from burials.*

Domestic I (fig. 32) Matrix: two merging groups represented, one rather pure clay, one more sandy. Temper sizes correspond with angular, larger pieces in the sandy group, the material for both groups being chalk, limestone, fine gravel, including red and yellow ochre, and pottery.

Baking: correspondingly running from fair to very bad for the sandy group, further making this group's breakage-edges the more crumbly.

Coloring: dull browns of varying darkness with frequent fire-spots for both groups.

Surface treatment: in the clay group the outside is either lightly burnished on a thick clay-slip or well smoothed with a round-ended tool or fingers applied directly on the surface, while the inside is always smooth. The sandy group has a totally untreated outside and smooth inside.

Further difference between the two groups is indicated by the sandy groups' appearing always as less-than-normal sized open bowls and lipped pots.

Domestic II (fig. 33) Matrix: rather pure clay, but temper in such mass that the ware becomes very coarse, as the angular large pieces of the tempering materials include charcoal, chalk, lime, pottery and ochre.

Baking: generally bad, but some sherds can have one rather well-baked side.

Coloring: most sherds have one side brown-gray (3–6) while the other side is gray or yellowish-white (never more than 4) depending on the slip applied.

Figure 32 Domestic I Ware. 1–24: Top Floor. 25–43: Bottom Floor. Scale: 1/4

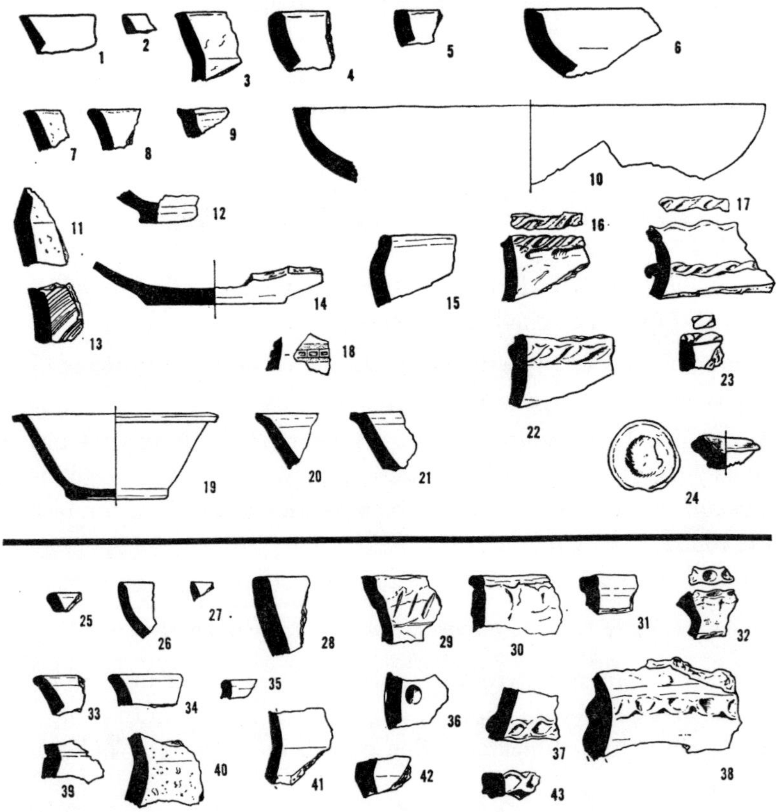

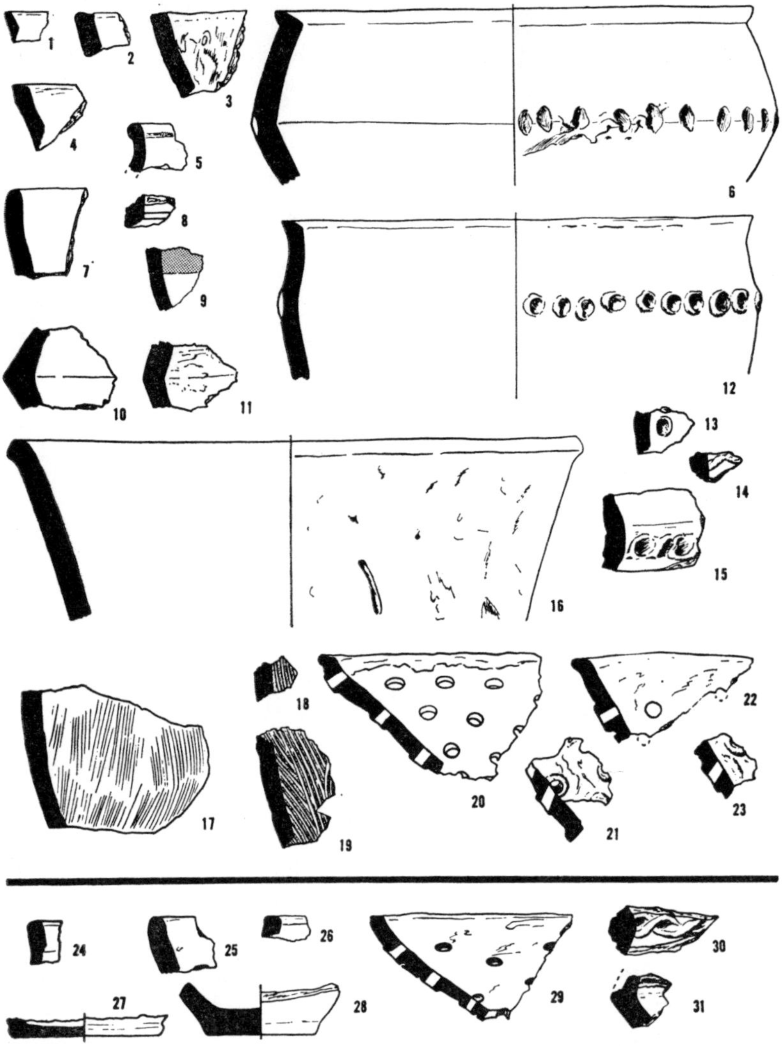

Figure 33 Domestic II Ware. 1–23: Top Floor. 24–31: Bottom Floor. Scale: 1/4

Surface treatment: the slip can be either pure clay and then burnished to almost Marnian greasy touch or a thinner sandy slip with well-smoothed or tooled appearance, the other unslipped side of the sherds is generally less smooth.

This ware is seen in medium sized pots and in several sieves.

Domestic III (fig. 34) Matrix: very coarse with up to 50% of the mass being large angular pieces of temper such as chalk, gravel, pottery and lumps of seemingly unbaked pure clay sometimes forming a solid band between the surfaces.

Baking: While a large part of the total ware is moderately well baked, the extremes range from well-fired to poorly baked.

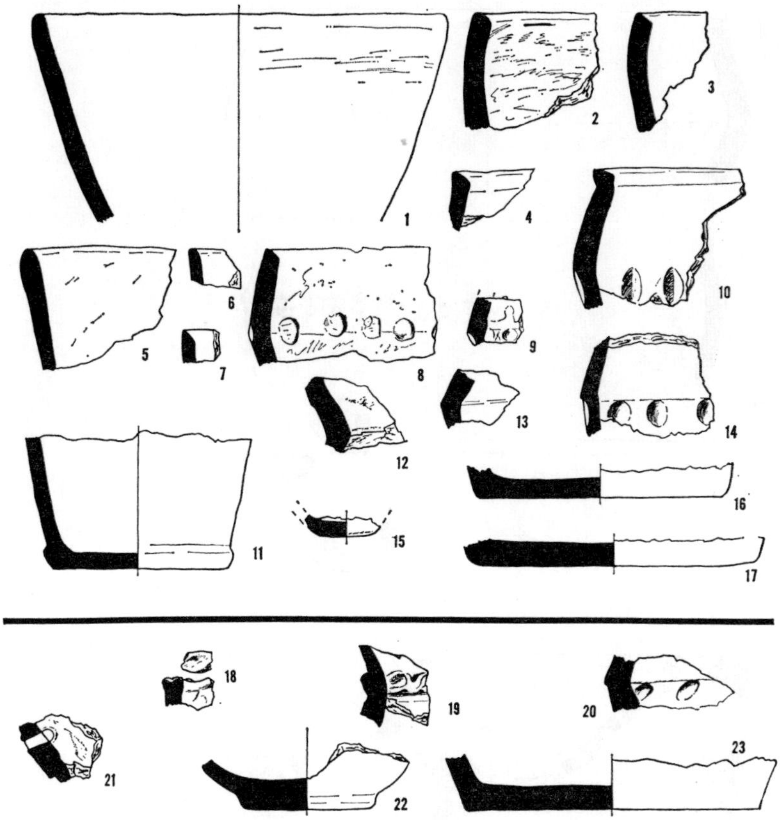

Figure 34 Domestic III Ware. 1–17: Top Floor. 18–23: Bottom Floor. Scale 1/4

Coloring: Generally the whole group is brown (5–7), the well-fired group having more reddish-beige outsides and red fire-spots on the brown insides, while the badly burned group shows black cores with true red-brown (4–6) outsides, spotted by the white temper, and dark brown insides.

Surface treatment: the well-baked group has the outside deliberately roughened by combing, finger-streaking or rubbing with grass or cloth, while the inside is at times almost slickly smoothed. The badly burned group has sometimes a thin wash applied but never more than lightly smoothed surfaces.

Painted Domestic (fig. 33:9) Only one sherd of this ware was found but its paint and fabric distinguish it as a separate type.

Matrix: Sandy with much temper of large to very large lumps of chalk, which shows through on both surfaces.

Baking: Very hard.

Coloring: Thick orange-red paint, inside slipped with mauve-brown.

Surface treatment: Smooth on both sides.

Shell Tempered Ware (fig. 35:3–4, 10–16) Matrix: rather sandy with much, often layered, temper of ground-up mussel shells, visible on both surfaces.

Baking: bad to mediocre, which with the unbinding quality of the temper makes the ware fragile when once broken.

Coloring: the outside is red to red-brown, the inside slipped in mauve-brown.

Surface treatment: both sides are smooth, no tooling visible.

GROUP IV *Rare types of moderate quality, unknown from burials.*

Brick Red Ware (fig. 35:5–8, 17–19) Matrix: almost pure clay with temper of finely ground pottery and red ochre. Break-edges are grainy.

Baking: medium to good.

Coloring: monocolored, ranging from orange-red (3) to crimson (5) with the largest amount being true brick red (4).

Surface treatment: both sides are well smoothed.

This ware resembles that found at Verneuil-en-Halatte (Oise), but it lacks the flint chip temper of the latter (Durvin 1963).

Pink Hard Ware (fig. 35:20) Matrix: sandy with high content of temper of chalk and silicium-gravel, visible on both surfaces.

Figure 35 Minor Wares. 1–9, 20–1: Top Floor. 1–2: Red Polished Ware; 3–4: Shell Tempered Ware; 5–8: Brick Red; 9: Mediterranean sherd; 20: Pink Hard; 21: Pure Clay. 10–19, 22–23: Bottom Floor. 10–16: Shell Tempered Ware; 17–19: Brick Red; 22: Stone Ware; 23: Pure Clay. Scale: 1/4

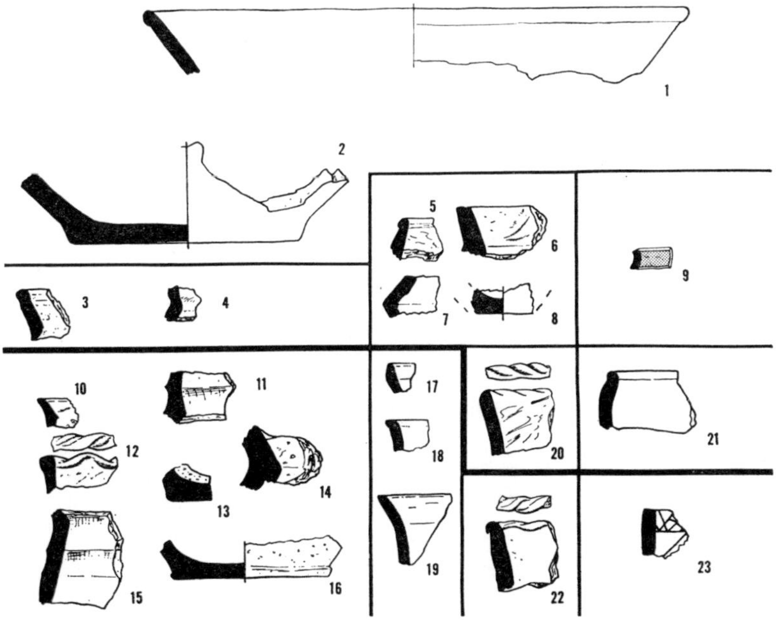

Baking: very hard, yet surfaces tend to erode leaving a pitted appearance.

Coloring: true pink-mauve on the outside, light purple-brown inside, often with somewhat darker core.

Surface treatment: smooth surfaces, never burnished or tooled.

Red Polished Ware (fig. 35:1–2) Matrix: very coarse with small pebbles of chalk, shell and pottery causing angular fractures.

Baking: medium to good.

Coloring: outer surfaces are red to red-brown, the inner always darker, at times black (8).

Surface treatment: well polished or burnished outside, while inside consistently is so gritty that deliberate application of sand could be postulated.

Pure Clay Ware (fig. 35:21, 23) Matrix: pure clay with temper, when visible at all, of tiny lumps of harder clay.

Baking: so soft that, were it not for the purity of the matrix, it could be thought to be unbaked or abnormally baked pieces of other wares.

Coloring: monocolored throughout in light brown-grays.

Surface treatment: smooth on both sides.

Stone Ware (fig. 35:22) Matrix: pure clay, but tightly compacted compared with the Pure Clay Ware. Powdery fine sand either naturally occurs in this clay or was added as temper, as no other tempering material was visible.

Baking: extremely hard.

Coloring: basically gray, as all cores show, but surfaces vary from a warm pure gray to mellow-golden hue, at times seen on the same sherd, as if caused by uneven air-allowance during baking.

Surface treatment: always smoothed without traces of tooling, but with gritty texture caused by the fine sand.

Ceramic forms

Even if no intact vessels of any of these wares were recovered, a few are virtually complete, while the shape of several others may be reconstituted. Almost all of these pots are hand-made – there being only three wheel-made sherds, of which two are from different rims (fig. 29:17–18), representing the first known wheel-made piriform pots in the Marne-Aisne Group territory during the early phases of La Tène. About eighteen different forms can be noted: all rims, detectable forms and decorated shreds are illustrated (figs. 29–35).

Tri-conic carinated vases (Form A) Eight from the Top; one from the Bottom (fig. 30:30). The nearly complete tri-conic vase (fig. 29:5) from the Top Hearth is black where not burned, but the pieces of it recovered from the center of the fireplace had oxidized yellow.

Sharply carinated sherds (ex. fig. 30:42–4) Thirteen in the Top and seven from the Bottom.

Tall bi-conic ceramic situlae (Form B) Five from the Top (ex. fig. 33:6) and one (fig. 30:36) from the Bottom.

Compressed bi-conic vessels (Form b) (fig. 31:11) One from the Top level.

Compressed bi-conic plates (Form b_1) Four from the Top (fig. 30:27 and 29) and one from the Bottom of this archetypal Marnian form.

Cylindrical cist (Form C) There is at least one example (fig. 30:35) of this form, particularly common in the Marne–Aisne Group. It is difficult to determine from sherds whether other cases of the cylindrical or conical cists are represented or whether they may simply be neck sherds of other kinds of vases.

Small conical vessel (Form c) Five examples in the Top (fig. 32:19) and one in the Bottom. Rare, but not unknown, from graves.

Small footed dish (Form c) This small dish with internal ledge rim and ring foot found in the Top Hearth (fig. 29:11) represents a rare but persistent Marnian form.

Low conical platters (Form c) One occurs in the Top (fig. 31:16). The strainers all have essentially this same form; there are six from the Top (figs 31:14–15; 33:20–3) and two from the Bottom.

Tall rounded ceramic situlae (Form B^0) Five from the Top and two from the Bottom (fig. 32:36, 42).

Low rounded rimless bowls (Form b^0) About five from the Top (fig. 29:6); apparently none from the Bottom Floor.

Small rounded bowl (Form b^0) Once of Marnian Ware in the Top (fig. 29:12) and ten times in the Bottom, of which nine are in some version of sandy ware (fig. 31:25–8). These little bowls are found chiefly in the floor area and could have been lamps. The almost intact example from House 8 (fig. 31:30) exemplifies the complete form of this type.

An unusual form not found at all in the Marnian Ware, and therefore as yet without a standard designation, is associated almost exclusively with Domestic Ware. Here there is a sudden flaring of the short neck from the upper shoulder. Often there is an impressed cordon at the neck-shoulder junction. Four such sherds come from the Top (figs 32:3, 17, 22; 33:15) while the Bottom produced five (figs 32:32, 38; 33:30; 34:19) including one in brick-red ware (fig. 35:19).

The Domestic Ware 'button' (fig. 32:24) looks like the top mounted handle for conical lids from La Chaussée (Marne) 215.

Rims

Just as there are certain shapes found among Domestic sherds unknown in Marnian Ware, so there are special rims for this fabric, although sometimes the rims are of the more usual forms met in funerary pottery. The most striking of the special rims are those with turbinated impressions, on top of a rim thickened inside and out, so that it looks like the profile of a pre-molar tooth in cross section (fig. 34:18). A version of decorated rim with a series of juxtaposed pits is also known in Domestic Ware from the Bottom (fig. 32:32). This occupation has also produced a plain version of this tooth-like rim in Domestic Ware (fig. 32:31). Likewise, the turbination appears on a simple pointed rim in the lower occupation on Sandy Marnian and Stone Ware (figs 31:24; 35:22) and in the Top Level on the Domestic and Pink Hard Ware (figs 32:23; 35:20).

Domestic Ware from the Top Level is also strongly associated with a kind of flanged rim with a depression in the middle of it, forming a sort of groove on the lip of the vase (fig. 32:9). One example of this shows up on a Marnian Ware sherd from the late occupation and on a Brick Red sherd in the Bottom (figs 29:1; 35:18).

Other rims have less specific associations, although bead rims characteristically appear on bi-conic plates and ceramic situlae. Otherwise, the Marnian ware seems to be suited with simple lips and rims. Sandy Ware, particularly in the lower levels, does tend to associate with a characteristic rim that slopes backward sharply on the interior of the vase (fig. 31:20, 22, 26–8). This rim seems to go also with the special shape of small rounded bowl, often made in Sandy Ware, which seldom appears in burials.

Decoration

The decorated sherds from House 9 exhibit new types of ceramic ornamentation for the early Marne Culture. This new decoration associates above all with Domestic Ware. Indeed, of all the decorated sherds, by far the largest proportion (29 of 40) are of Domestic Ware. These newer motifs on this ware include circular pits along the shoulder (1 each from Top and Bottom, figs 32:36; 34:9); ovoid pits (fig. 34:8, 14); pointed elliptical pits (figs 33:6; 34: 10, 20); hatch marks (fig. 32:29); and a series of punctated circular pits with raised exterior margins appears on Domestic Ware ceramic situlae from the Top level (fig. 33:12–13). This type of decoration, of course, sometimes covers the entire lower body on Marnian ceramic situlae put in burials.

Such punctations with relief margins also occur on applied cordons on Top Level Domestic Ware sherds (fig. 33:15), while a somewhat similar cordon with impressed circles is known on three rather different Domestic Ware sherds from the lower levels (figs 32:38, 43; 34:19). Turbinated cordons, somewhat like turbinated rims, occur on two Domestic Ware sherds in each level (figs 32:17, 37; 33:14, 30). Another Domestic Ware sherd from the lower hearth has a series of little V-shaped grooves just below the slightly everted rim lip (fig. 32:30).

The Marnian Ware, which is not as extensively decorated in north-western Champagne as in the east (Bretz-Mahler 1961: 10), presents us with examples of linear decoration only. A sherd from the Top levels has a narrow incised line (fig. 30:3), as does Sandy Marnian and Domestic Ware sherds from the Bottom (figs 31:23; 32:39), while double incised lines are on this ware in the Top (fig. 33:8). Six examples of comb-marked ware occur in this occupation level, one in Marnian Ware (figs 30:11; 31:7; 32:13; 33:17–19). Combing is not an Hallstatt IIb characteristic in Champagne.

Wide, 4–5 mm. rills, rare but not totally unknown on Marne Culture grave pottery, are found doubly only on two Shell-Tempered sherds from the Bottom Levels (fig. 35:11, 15) and singly on Sandy Marnian in the Top (fig. 31:3–4). Other forms of incised decoration are much more specialized. One Bottom Floor Pure Clay sherd has a complex finely incised design at the rim (fig. 35:23), while smoothed cordons occur only on the Top Floor's black wheel-made vases. Also found in the Top Floor is a sherd with rectangular stamping (fig. 32:18). Unknown from the Marne Culture itself, this sherd must be an import from either the Hunsrück-Eifel or Armorican Iron Age Cultures. The latter seems more likely to have produced this square stamping, as at Bagatelle (Revelière 1894: Pl. I, 4–6). Possibly such pottery was acquired along with tin and marine shells from Armorica.

Painting is relatively rare on the northern pottery of the Marne-Aisne Group; the only locally made painted sherd at House 9 is a Domestic sherd with a wide band painted in the thick paint, which fades badly in the ground, extensively used by all Marnians. The original color seems to have been orange (fig. 33:9). With the painted vessels should be mentioned a sherd of extremely fine, thin, white ware with a vermilion outer (?) slip (fig. 35:9). This one appears to be a Mediterranean-produced vase imported into Chassemy.

Two pots from the top floor show attempts at repairing earlier cracks before the final breakage. One carinated vase still carries resin on the inside to plug the neatly drilled hole through which some organic ligament must have been passed to bind the crack together (fig. 29:10). A repair hole for a comb-marked sherd shows that even the less carefully made wares were frugally husbanded (fig. 30:11).

Other artefacts

Four spindle whorls constitute another class of ceramic artefacts. The only one that seems to come from the Bottom Floor level (fig. 36:9) is a broken medium dark orange-brown biconical whorl with a rather grainy texture coming from a sand temper. The whorl is nicely smoothed and finished, but being somewhat heavy, it had sunk to the bottom of the lower floor.

The second biconic whorl had also sunk to the bottom of the Top Floor into the top of the Intermediate Layer (fig. 36:3). This broken, tan whorl is also sand-tempered but otherwise made of fine clay and nicely finished. Another spindle whorl came from the Top Floor, near the edge of the fireplace. This black one (fig. 36:1) has a conical form, chalk temper, and finest 'Marnian' finish. Equally well made of 'Marnian' quality is the conical light tan whorl (fig. 36:2) actually found in the Top Hearth. These two conical spindle whorls are of the more usual types found sometimes in La Tène Ia graves of the Marne Culture. In fact, Chassemy cemetery grave 25 (Hubert 1902: 185) produced a very similar one, as did the nearby cemeteries at Caranda grave 16 and Sablonnières 865. Another ceramic piece from the very top of the Top Hearth seems to be an andiron (fig. 36:6).

The eighteen metal finds yield much less information. The fragmentary knife handle still has part of its on-riveted antler handle (fig. 36:5) recovered from the side of the Top Hearth. A curved piece of wire of *c.* 4 mm. section, found cemented with rust against a burnt bone on the Bottom Hearth, appears to be the foot of a La Tène Ia fibula, the allure matching perfectly a bronze one from nearby Ciry-Salsogne grave 47 (fig. 36:15) (Hubert 1902: 193). A small iron bit also from the Bottom Hearth is more enigmatic (fig. 36:16). A hollow iron piece with U-section resembles a shield rim reinforcement, but the curvature is inappropriate (fig. 36:14). From just below the Bottom Floor comes an elongate hollow iron stud, while a more circular one was in the Bottom Hearth (fig. 36:10, 12). In the marl layer used for renovating the fireplace were about ten studs (of which only two were preservable) (fig. 36:11, 13), seemingly fastened formerly to an organic

Figure 36 Ceramic, Shell, and Iron Artefacts. Top Floor. 1–3: spindle whorls; 4: cut shell; 5: iron and antler knife handle; 6: ceramic andiron; 7: iron cocarde with clay core; 8: lump of bronze or copper. Bottom Floor. 9: spindle whorl; 10–13: iron studs; 14: iron 'gutter'; 15: iron fibula foot (?); 16: iron disc. Scale: 1/2

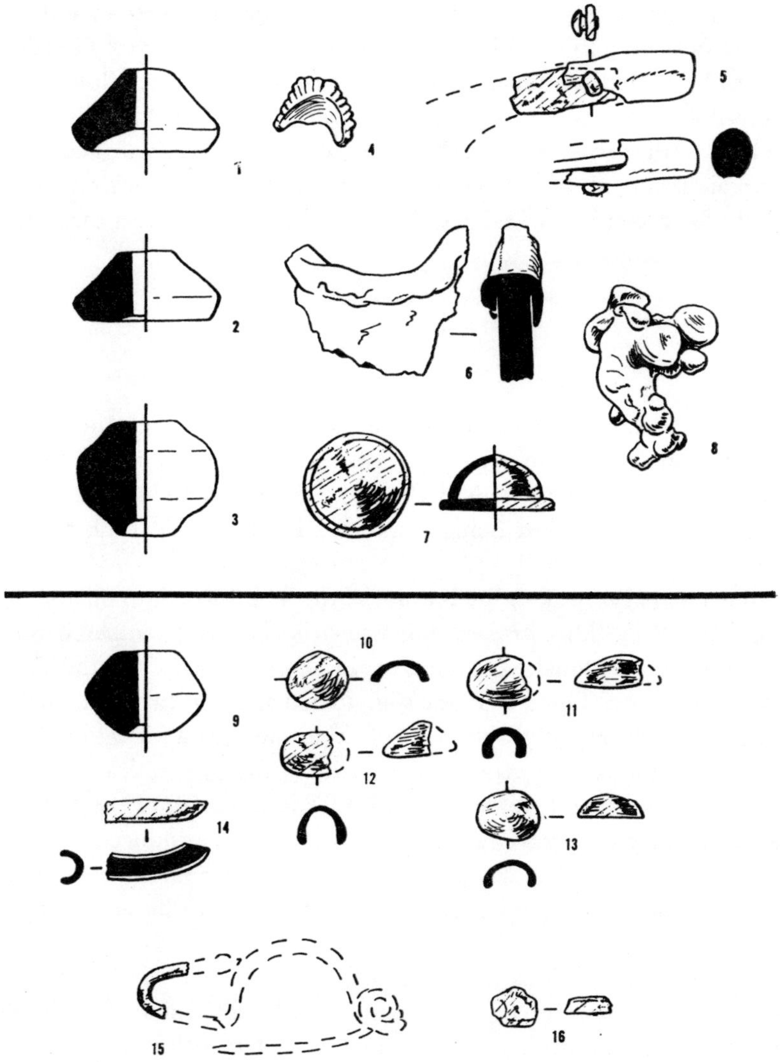

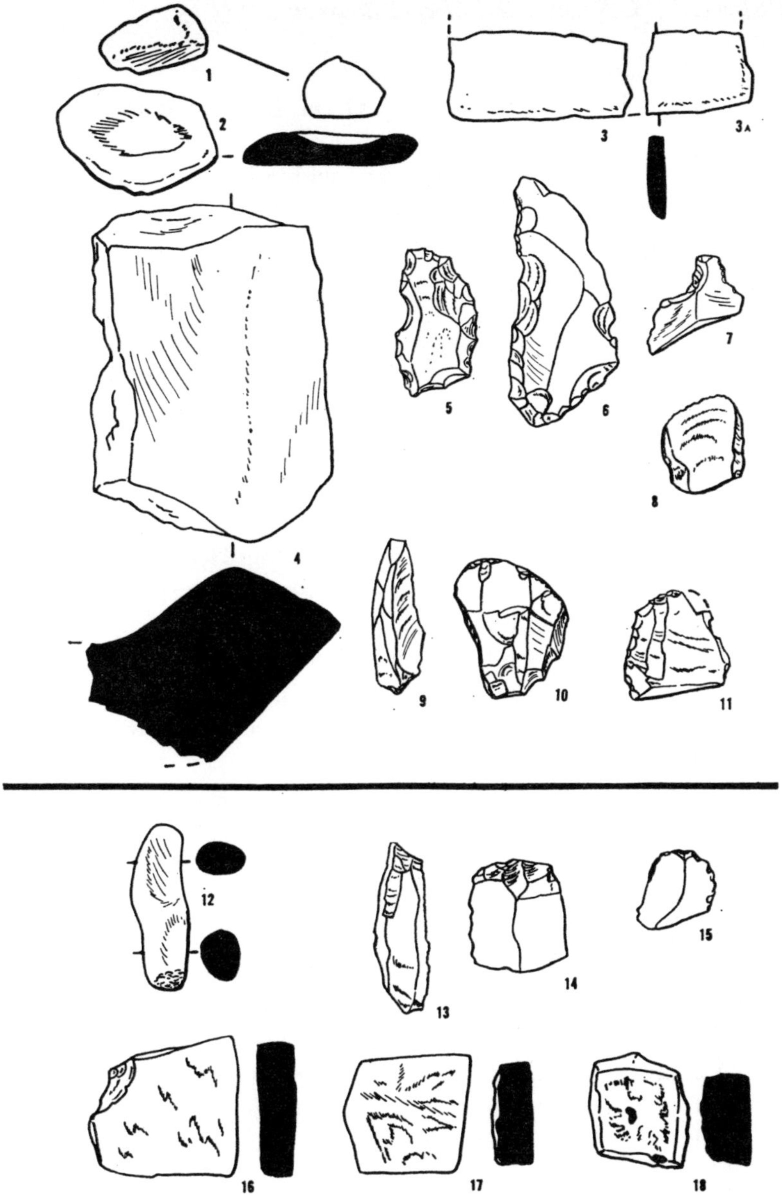

Figure 37 Stone Tools. Top Floor. 1: yellow ochre found sitting upon 2, a small mortar; 3–3A: whetstone; 4: fragment of quern; 5–11: flint tools. Bottom Floor. 12: pestle; 13–15: flint tools; 16–18: three of four ground and polished flint game pieces. Scale: 1/2

band. Such studs of bronze and iron occasionally are encountered in La Tène Ia graves in Champagne; for example, at Écury-sur-Coole (Marne) in a chariot burial (Thiérot 1931: 46).

From the Top Hearth itself comes a domed iron cocarde (fig. 36:7). Made of very thin metal, a clay core helped to keep the dome from being crushed. This cocarde resembles somewhat an iron one in chariot burial 7 in the Les Jogasses La Tène cemetery.

The only other metal object found is an amorphous piece of previously melted non-ferrous metal found in the Top Floor (fig. 36:8). Green in color, it appears to be copper or bronze.

Most of the nineteen stone artefacts are of flint, flaked with a blade-producing technique. Seven appear to be like rather roughly chipped endscrapers, while another looks like a sidescraper (fig. 37:6), but even it has an eccentrically placed endscraper-like edge. Two others are simply unretouched blades with worn edges revealing utilization (fig. 37:9, 13). These scraper-like tools found in the fireplace may best be interpreted as strike-a-lights. Both blades, one in the Top Floor, the other in the Bottom Floor, came from the living area. One endscraper-like tool, with retouched perimeter, was also found in the Top Floor (fig. 37:5) while the piece which most closely resembles an endscraper was also found on the Bottom Floor and may actually have been used for leather-working rather than as a strike-a-light (fig. 37:14).

In the top level was found a broken whetstone of compact sandstone, slate-gray in color (fig. 37:3–3A). A small cylindrical shaped stone in the Bottom Hearth has a heavily battered and abraded end, as if it had been used as a small pestle (fig. 37:12).

At the end of the hearth, but in the Top Floor, sat a curious little stone mortar of pale blue sandstone which would have been useful in conjunction with the small pestle. The basin of this little mortar shows much wear, apparently last having been used for grinding yellow ochre for pigment, conceivably for pot-paint, as a lump of yellow ochre still rested in the central depression (fig. 37:1–2).

A kind of grinding stone, utilized for heavier duty as evidenced by a broken part of a large quern of gray-blue limestone (fig. 37:4), lay at the edge of the Top Hearth opposite the small ochre grinder.

Perhaps the most novel stone artefacts are four small pieces of thin tabular blue flint, about 8–10 mm. thick, with sides polished to form a rectangle about 25–39 mm. per side. The two surfaces have had the weathered oxidized cortex scraped down to the rough unweathered flint surface. Three of these pieces were found in the Bottom Hearth, one in the Bottom Floor. Only three are illustrated (fig. 37:16–18) because the first encountered was not recognized by the excavator as an artefact but rejected as a rare pseudo-morph before the others began to appear, confirming their true nature. Such objects appear to have been game-stones used during the earlier part of the occupation of the house.

Chronology

Since the Domestic Ware and other artefacts not commonly found in Marnian graves are so clearly associated with fine quality Marnian Ware in the house at Chassemy 9, the correct and precise dating of the remains provides us with an entirely new inventory of artefacts in the Marnian repertoire. The well-known Marnian Ware provides us with the best means of fitting the house and its goods into the known Iron Age chronology of Champagne.

Fortunately, some of the clearest dating evidence comes from the very base of the Bottom Hearth. Here rested a biconic plate of La Tène Ia/Ib type, while an archetypal sharply carinated vase of La Tène Ia/Ib lay right within it (fig. 30:30, 45). The Radiocarbon sample GXO 393 was taken from a compact body of fine charcoal lying right on the bottom of the plate and, in effect, within the body of the carinated vase. The straight-walled cist (fig. 30:35) not only confirms this Early La Tène dating, but indicates specifically the La Tène Ia phase. The small rounded bowl, such as fig. 31:28, of which the rims are especially frequent in the lower occupation, is actually found with Hallstatt IIb fibulae at Les Jogasses (Marne) H82, but is known in La Tène Ia contexts in the Aisne at Caranda 2159, Fère-en-Tardenois H2, and Sablonnières H36 (Hubert 1906: 321, 346).

The Bottom Hearth and Floor finds suggest a La Tène Ia date for the beginnings of the house. While the iron piece which is apparently the bent part of a fibula foot (fig. 36:15) seems to be of La Tène Ia type, it is too fragmentary to provide more than corroborative evidence. The radiocarbon date provides more information. Although the date for GXO 393, 590±60 B.C. seems a bit early at the 67% confidence level, at the 95% confidence level the date ranges from 710–470 B.C. Since a date earlier than 500 B.C. is precluded by the very late Hallstatt IIb Vix princess burial, dated by Greek Attic vases (Joffroy 1960: 120–3), found at the Champagne-Burgundian borderland, obviously the Bottom Hearth began sometime between 500–470 B.C. Since the Bottom Hearth contains pottery of well-established La Tène types, it becomes eminently likely that La Tène Ia started before 470 B.C.

The Top Floor and Hearth contain many of the same horizon markers as does the Bottom level – the small rounded dish, found in the uppermost part of the Top Hearth (fig. 29:11), is of a type known in Hallstatt IIb with fibulae at Les Jogasses H34 and H82 (Favet 1936), but these have high, rounded insteps in the vases' feet. The one from the Top Hearth has a flat base and low ring foot similar to those found with La Tène Ia fibulae at Limé 2 (Aisne), Mont Gravet 3 (Bretz-Mahler and Brisson 1958: fig. 68), Grandes Loges 45, and Poix 23. The one from the latter grave has exactly the same rim form as the one from Chassemy.

Furthermore, also in the upper part of the Top Hearth was found the Marnian triconic vase with the same low, narrow shoulder and high flaring neck proportions so characteristic of the Hallstatt IIb phase in northern Champagne (fig. 29:5). The appearance of this form in a La Tène context is not totally unknown in the north-western sector of the Marne Culture. Footless vases, as the one here probably is, of this form occur at least three times at Sablonnières, once at Trugny, twice at Caranda, including grave 2460 with a late La Tène Ia fibula. This Jogassian-like bowl clearly shows that the Top Levels, undoubtedly later than the stratigraphically lower Bottom Floor and Hearth, were also occupied before the La Tène Ia chronological phase had completely run its course. The absence of clear La Tène Ib indicators suggests that the house was abandoned before the beginning of any of the later styles.

A radiocarbon sample from the Top Hearth, GXO 624 was submitted, but gave the unexpectedly high date of 7320±125 B.C. Apparently of charcoal, the sample evidently contained parts of a burned lignite bracelet or amber, both of which do occur in La Tène Ia contexts and either of which could have distorted the age of the sample.

TABLE I

Distribution of each ware per level

	Marnian I	Marnian II	Sandy Marnian	Petit-Saint-Jean	Sandy	Domestic I	Domestic II	Domestic III	Shell Tempered	Brick Red	Pink Hard	Red Polished	Pure Clay	Stone	*Total*
Numbers															
Top Levels	44	78	57	43	79	126	235	248	26	48	5	5	46	0	1,040
Bottom Levels	10	38	54	30	41	92	136	129	38	19	5	0	16	4	612
Percentages															
Top Levels	4·2	7·5	5·5	4·1	7·6	12·1	22·6	23·8	2·5	4·6	0·5	0·5	4·4	0·0	
Bottom Levels	1·6	6·2	8·8	4·9	6·7	15·0	22·2	21·0	6·2	3·1	0·8	0·0	2·6	0·7	

Although the horizon markers indicate that both floors at House 9 were established during La Tène Ia, the relative proportions of the ceramic wares at each level (table 1), when submitted to a X^2 test, are statistically significantly different at the 0·001 probability level. The customs chiefly responsible for this difference are the greater reliance on Sandy Marnian, apparently in place of Marnian I, and Shell Tempered Wares during the ocupation of the Bottom levels. There was also in each level a species of rounded bowl not present in the other. Without other studies at such close range, it would be difficult to say if this difference is caused by stylistic changes during the course of La Tène Ia or by the house's being managed by different housewives at each occupation.

Biota

In addition to artefacts, the fireplace was filled with bones in varying stages of carbonization and a few were strewn about the floors. A total of 405 bones were distributed with 30 from the Top Floor and 315 in the Top Hearth, while 33 were associated with the Bottom Floor and 27 were found in the Bottom Hearth. While most of the bones probably came from animals consumed for food, some of the shells were marine ones that must have had other uses. Most of the marine shells from the Top Hearth were found rather close together, and indeed one shell had been cut and worked. Likewise, an articulated eagle wing, found at the very base of the Bottom Hearth, is considered likely to have been a broom or a fan for stirring the fire – or at least placed in the hearth ceremonially – and not part of the food resources. The great disparity in the number of bones in the Top Hearth as compared with the Bottom Hearth is explained by the fact that many bones occurred right at the top of the hearth, left there perhaps as the house was abandoned, while the bones in the Bottom Hearth, with fires going repeatedly, would long since have been greatly calcined.

The almost equal number of bones found in the floor area of each occupation shows that the occupants at each level must have been eating about the same amount of meat. Further, many of the more carbonized bones of the Bottom Hearth were put in the radiocarbon samples, although no bone which was potentially identifiable as to genus was included. The number of bones identifiable was severely limited by butchering practices, since the average length of osteological remains, even for long bones, was only about 5 cm. Stew must have been an important part of the House 9 menu. As it was, only seventy-four individual items of the faunal remains could be identified as to genus or species.

Chassemy House F9 mammal identifications

by Jon Friedlander

Among the mammal bones have been identified sheep/goat, pig, dog, cattle, deer, bison and hare.

Ovicaprids There are twenty-two bones of sheep or goat. One metapodal and two phalanges seem immature, although a right mandible and first phalanx are unusually small for apparently mature animals. All of the small and immature specimens are from the Top Hearth.

Pig (*Sus scrofa*) There are nine identifiable pig bones, all adult.

Dog (*Canis familiaris*) Eight bones are identified as dog, with two vertebrae showing definite signs of decarnization, evidence that the dog actually constituted a food resource. Only one dog bone, a canine tooth from the lower Bottom Floor, has been identified from the lower levels.

Cattle (*Bos taurus*) Six specimen are cattle. One left scapula fragment from the Bottom Floor is immature, while a Top Hearth left mandibular ramus is small for an adult. These bovine bones actually resemble more closely those of present-day *Bos indicus* than they do those of modern domestic Euroamerican cattle.

Bison (*Bison bonasus*) This identification is secure, as it is based upon two second molars, one from the Bottom Hearth and one from the Bottom Floor, so there can be no question of the confusion of Bos and Bison remains (Olsen 1960).

Cervids While a lumbar vertebra from the Bottom Hearth certainly seems to be from a red deer (*Cervus elaphus*), three specimens of antler from the Top Floor and Hearth are less certain, although the smoothness of these pieces suggest also red deer rather than roe.

Hare (*Lepus sp.*) Hare is represented by one innominate bone carbonized in the lower hearth.

Although the number of identifiable remains from the mammal sample are exceedingly limited, it does reveal interesting tendencies. By far the largest proportion of bones, even from the domesticated species, are those of mature animals, which tend to be somewhat smaller than their modern counterparts. This is especially true of the cattle. The slaughtering age thus tended to be high. The dog bones show clear signs of butchering – including the seventh cervical vertebra, as this would be a most inconvenient place to cut if one merely wanted to kill a dog by beheading it. Lastly, the presence of *Bison*, *Cervus elaphus* and *Lepus* indicates that these people hunted in addition to their herding.

Amphibians

Dr S. M. McDowell, of the Harvard Museum of Comparative Zoology, identified one small bone from the Top Hearth as being the radial-ulna of a frog (*Rana*). Frogs as a Marnian foodstuff have previously been known from those in one biconic jar in the Châlons-sur-Marne chariot burial.

Avians

Dr R. A. Paynter Jr, of the Harvard Museum of Comparative Zoology, kindly identified the three articulated avian bones as being the wing of an eagle (*Aquila*).

Molluscs

Dr W. J. Clench, of the Harvard Museum of Comparative Zoology, has kindly examined the molluscan specimens, identifying the following:

Margaritifera margaritifera Linné Freshwater clams are evidenced by ten shells, seven from the Top Hearth and three from the Bottom Floor and Hearth. Undoubtedly gathered from the Vesle, these clams probably would have been acquired for eating.

Veneridae This marine genus is represented by five examples from the Top Floor (two) and Hearth (three) and one from the Bottom Floor.

Cardium One was found in the Bottom Hearth, another on the Top Floor.

Ostreida This marine shell found in the Top Hearth had obviously been trimmed into an artefact (fig. 36:4).

Additional fragments of eleven marine shells were found in the top levels.

Except for the marine shells, the faunal remains from the house pertain mostly to foodstuffs. Surprisingly enough, although the chalky loam preserved bone rather well, no fish bones were found even if the frog and shellfish show that riverine resources were not ignored. Nevertheless, faunal remains show a rather large number of undomesticated species (16 of 64–25%). While the sample of identifiable bones is admittedly quite small, this figure is not inconsistent with other Marnian evidence. The food remains in Marnian graves of the East Group of the Marne Culture in eastern Champagne have about 25% of wild foodstuffs, although these may have been special foods for the funerary repast. These figures also compare well with 22% wild forms at the Hallstatt site of Saint-Romain (Côte-d'Or) (Josien 1955) and 26% wild in a small Middle and Late La Tène site from near Budapest (Bökönyi 1959: 70–1), although as a rule late La Tène sites have negligible proportions of undomesticated animal remains.

Something of a trend toward less reliance on wild animal foodstuffs may be seen during the course of the occupation of House 9. While the highest levels have 81·6% (40 of 49) domestic species represented, the lowest level has only 53·2% (8 of 15) domestic forms relating to foodstuffs, not counting the eagle wing. Although the sample is very small, a 'Fisher's Exact Test' shows only a 0·04 probability that this distribution occurred by chance. There is no appreciable difference between the two levels in the frequency of *Ovis*, *Bos* and freshwater shellfish, but the later reliance on pig and dog is interestingly more pronounced. While the figures are too small to be conclusive, they possibly suggest that during La Tène Ia there was a marked shift towards domestic food resources, indicative of either a considerable population increase, as inferred from cemetery remains, and/or more productive agriculture during the fifth century. Or do these differences reflect no more than the occupational specialties of the man of the house?

The faunal evidence, particularly the emphasis on sheep as the leading domestic animal, evidently a venerable tradition in Champagne, ties in well with the pollen analysis.

Palynological study of Chassemy (Aisne) House 9 samples

by Willem van Zeist

TABLE 2
Chassemy Pollen Sample, old ground level of house

	Numbers	Percentage
Alnus (alder)	335	67·5
Corylus (hazel)	8	1·6
Tilia (lime)	3	0·6
Ulmus (elm)	1	0·2
Pinus (pine)	2	0·4
Quercus (oak)	2	0·4
Gramineae (grasses)	97	19·5
Cyperaceae (sedge family)	12	2·4
Cerealia (cereals)	1	0·2
Calluna (heather)	4	0·8
Tubuliflorae Compositae (composite family)	6	1·2
Liguliflorae Compositae (composite family)	4	0·8
Polygonum persicaria type (persicaria)	2	0·4
Umbelliferae (parsley family)	1	0·2
Succisa pratensis (devil's-bit scabious)	2	0·4
Chenopodiaceae (goosefoot family)	2	0·4
Cruciferae (mustard family)	1	0·2
Plantago lanceolata (ribwort plantain)	1	0·2
Pteridium (bracken)	5	1·0
indeterminatae	8	1·6
pollen sum	497	

Of the two samples, only the upper one corresponding with the Bottom Floor of the house proved to be suitable for pollen analysis. The lower sample was virtually bare of pollen. That is reassuring from a palynological point of view. It implies that the soil does not contain any appreciable amounts of secondary pollen and that the pollen in the upper sample must for the greater part have been derived from the vegetation in the vicinity of the site.

Table 2 shows the absolute numbers as well as percentages of the total pollen sum. The pollen preservation was rather poor, which may be responsible for the absence of more fragile pollen types.

The interpretation of one pollen spectrum without other data for comparison is always precarious. It is striking that among the tree pollen that of *Alnus* is by far dominant, demonstrating that alder must have been pretty abundant in the river valley. The remarkably low pollen values for upland trees would suggest a considerable clearance of the forest on the higher soils. On the other hand, one would have expected higher values for cereals and particularly for various weeds in case of large-scale farming activities. High grass percentages could point to predominant cattle breeding instead of agriculture, but in that case one would expect relatively high values for plantain, sorrel and a few other plant species.

While the pollen spectrum confirming a wet fifth-century climate gives meager information as to the crops grown, macrofloral evidence, in the guise of eighteen carbonized plant seeds, all except one from the Top Hearth, provides supplementary information.

Carbonized plant remains from Chassemy (Aisne)

by Maria Hopf

Of eighteen specimens from Chassemy, sixteen at least were identifiable to family with some certainty, despite their rather damaged condition.

Cereals

Wheat (three specimens from the Top Hearth).

No. 3 *Triticum aestivum* L.s.l. – common wheat. The very abraded broad grain has rather low back, flattish, somewhat concave front, with narrow crease of which the outer margins are bordered by sharp edges. Size: 5 × 3·5 × 2·5 mm.

No. 5 *Triticum dicoccum* Schübl. – emmer. Slender grain with high back and flat front; the crease is narrow and the embryo broken out. Size: 4·50 × 2·50 × 2·25 mm.

No. 16 *Triticum* cf. *monococcum* L. – probably Einkorn. A strongly corroded, slim grain with rounded ventral, narrowing side, and high back. Size: 4·50 × 2·25 × 2·25 mm.

Barley (three specimens).

No. 4 *Hordeum vulgare* L. of var. *nudum* – naked barley. A spherical short grain with lower half damaged. The narrow crease goes all the way to the tip end; the smooth back lacks palea impressions. Size: 3 × 2·5 mm.

No. 9 *Hordeum vulgare* L. *polystichum* var. *nudum* – naked barley. Left side grain of a triple set as seen from the front side. The asymmetrically formed grain has its back smoothly rounded and the upper one-third of the medially placed crease is somewhat disturbed. Size: 4·75 × 2·50 × 2·25 mm.

No. 15 *Hordeum vulgare* L. var. *nudum* – naked barley. A large grain of naked barley, only slightly damaged on the base and the tip. Size: 3·50 × 2·50 × 2 mm.

Pod fruits

Beans (three specimens, No. 13 from the Bottom Hearth).

No. 6a Half of a seed of the pea-bean family without the seed shell. The edge of the single cotyledon shows damage at one place. The diameter is 3 mm. To judge from the size it could be cf. *Vicia spec.* – broadbean – but unfortunately all definite marks as to species are lacking.

No. 12 Fragment of a legume seed. This seed has not separated into two cotyledon parts, but as the separating line between the seed leaves is partly recognizable inside as well as outside and a remnant of the seed-shell is preserved, the height of the palisade and supporting cells can be determined as being 40–48 μ and 15–20 μ respectively. The low height of both cell-layers indicates some type of bean seed (bean weed?). A closer classification is not possible, however, due to the smallness of the fragment. The diameter is about 4 mm.

No. 13 Piece of a legume seed – *Vicia spec.* Half of a cotyledon is left; the seed shell has come off, but on the inside the contours of the seedling are clearly distinguishable. The diameter is about 2·50 mm. The epidermis cells are no longer distinguishable on the rounded outer side but those of the inner side are all arranged in the same manner. On the basis of this fact and the entire shape, one can assume that one is dealing with a type of bean – *Vicia spec.*

Peas (one specimen).

No. 16 *Legume* – cf. *Pisum spec.* Two fragments of a legume seed not broken along the line separating the two cotyledons, but the seed shell is missing for the most part. On the outer, rounded side of the seed leaf epidermis the cells are oriented in differing directions, so it is possibly a pea – cf. *Pisum spec.*

Uncertainly classified pod fruits.

No. 2 Half seed, slick walls, inside hollow; 3·2 × 3 × 1·5 mm. large; the short remains of a narrow, blunt hilum is preserved. Radicle and seedknob are lacking. The radicle seems not to have been protuberant. The palisade cells in the seed shell are 50 μ, the supporting cells 25 μ high, falling therefore within the range of the lentil. However, since the now hollowed-out seed leaf has been altered so much from its original form, nothing definite can be said about its generic relationships.

No. 6b Seed-half which originally was not broken in the cotyledon area, but which later fell apart into two quarters in the seed-leaf area. The diameter of 3·50 mm. measures somewhat larger than the No. 6a seed-half, but nevertheless probably belongs to the same general size category.

No. 7 Fragment of a seed of the pea-bean family? Originally the seed must have measured *c.* 4·5–3 mm. in diameter and 4 mm. in height, but the preserved part is so small and without distinctive marks that a closer definition as to genus is impossible.

No. 8 Fragment of a seed of the pea-bean family. It consists of half a seed-leaf of which the shell, the hilum, micropyle and radicle are lacking. Carbonization and dehydration seem to have been very strong, apparently ripping out the inside, leaving the baked starch-holding magazine tissue exposed. Size: (2·50) × 3·50 mm.

Nuts

Oak (one specimen).

No. 10 Fruitcup of an oak – *Quercus spec.* This acorn is either a very young fruit, or – more probably – an undeveloped, stunted fruit, as is often found on stalks bearing other fully ripe fruits. The circular cup still encloses most of the acorn. Only the uppermost part with the pistil remnant lies free. The broad, blunt scales of the cup are located alternatively in 7 or 8 circles; the base is rubbed off, so that the stalk junction is not positively recognizable any longer. The size is about 3·75 × 4 mm.; it is not possible to make an assignment to a certain type of oak.

Indeterminate (two specimens)

No. 1 Fragment 3 × 3 mm. large, separated in two seed-leaves, not further definable.

No. 11 Fragments of a round seed – indeterminate.

Of the sixteen specimens presented from Chassemy which could be indentified with some certainty, there are 37.5% cereals and 50% pod fruits. As they are all small and greatly damaged, and since the pod fruits could possibly belong to weeds and the acorn was not fully ripened and thus unusable, one might suppose that these finds from the fireplace are unwanted culls. Although the sizes of the grains, as far as they could be determined, average rather below those finds from different phases of the Iron Age from southern France, the grains compare well with some carbonized ones included in a Marnian burial (and therefore certainly not offal) of early La Tène (but uncertain sub-phase) date from near Châlons-sur-Marne (Marne).

	Pech Maho (Aude) (6th–3rd cent.)	Cayla/Mailhac (Aude) (3rd cent.)	Chassemy (5th cent.)	Marne Department (5th–3rd cent.)
	mm.	mm.	mm.	mm.
T. dicoccum	5·3 × 2·2 × 2·1	—	4·5 × 2·5 × 2·3	4·5 × 2·25 × 1·75
T. aestivum	5·6 × 2·6 × 2·5	4·9 × 3·2 × 2·7	5 × 3·5 × 2·5	—
Hordeum				
slim	6·3 × 2·7 × 2·5	6·2 × 2·9 × 2·3	—	—
thick	5·5 × 2·9 × 2·8	6·1 × 3·7 × 2·8	4·13 × 2·5 × 2·2	4·75 × 2·5 × 3·5

The barley from the south French finds is husked barley; although the husks are worn off, the grains of this kind are usually longer than those of the naked barley. Even taking this into consideration, the three barley grains from Chassemy are exceptionally small and damaged.

Acorns have been found in many habitation areas from all prehistoric periods; obviously they, in addition to hazel nuts, were gathered for nutrition. The undeveloped acorn from Chassemy is possibly the remainder of an acorn cluster of which the other fully matured fruits have been used.

It cannot be definitely stated if there may be lentils or peas among the burned legume specimens. The greater number of the pod fruits might appear to belong to the weedy members of the bean family, as they have short hila similar to *Vicia ervilia* or *Lathyrus aphaca*. Despite this apparent resemblance, however, this identification seems unlikely, as the former grows on calcium-poor soil, while the latter, albeit calcium neutral, prefers dry locations. The soil at Chassemy, derived from limestones and chalks, is calcium rich, and the location, wet today, must have been even more so in the fifth century B.C., to judge from the alder in the pollen sample.

The plant remains described above provide only an incomplete picture of the crops grown at Chassemy. The mean normal grain size should probably be above the evaluations presented here.

To judge from the pollen count, the fields seem to have been rather far from House 9, understandably in as much as the village at Chassemy was of some size and the house was near the swamps and the river, with other houses between it and the most likely place for fields. Charred hazel nut hulls were found in another house by the junior author, and the acorn from House 9 provides further evidence of food gathering. The considerable evidence for hunting and gathering in Champagne shows that some of the La Tène peoples utilized wild resources almost as extensively as did the contemporary northern peoples (Helbaek 1951).

Activities

The twenty marine shells found in the Top Floor and Hearth as well as the two from the Bottom Floor and Hearth indicate something more than food resources. Too far from the Atlantic for the Iron Age transport of fresh marine shell fish, the shells must have been desired for themselves. The appearance of these marine shells concurs well with the sherd of stamped pottery of apparent Armorican connections. Certainly the Marnians had to get tin from somewhere and the Armorican sources would have been moderately close. That a molten piece of metal was found in this house with other Atlantic indications may not be sheer coincidence. The concentration of these exotica in Top levels in association with a greater dependence on domestic meat sources suggests that the top householder was something of a tradesman or artisan; the man of the Bottom Floor spent more time hunting.

The piece of metal was found on the north-west side of the fireplace, although the numerous finds of vessels and food remains make it clear that the house was a dwelling-place. To judge from the fragments of a grinding stone at the south-east corner of the fireplace, milling took place there. The spindle whorls all concentrate on the south-west side of the fireplace, whether from the Top or Bottom Floor. Away from the fireplace there are fewer finds indicative of particular activities, implying that the fireplace provided a source of light. The rarity of finds on the raised portion of the floor suggests that it was kept cleaner than the lower level; perhaps this higher, chalkier – therefore warmer – portion of the house provided the basis for a sleeping platform. House-keeping in general seems to have been moderately neat, there being a tendency for sherds to concentrate along the walls, in the corners, and to a lesser extent, at the foot of the raised floor.

According to Naroll's (1962) formula, based upon a worldwide ethnographic sample, that the number of inhabitants of a dwelling house equals roughly one-tenth of the floor area in square meters, since the House 9 area is 54·6 sq. m. (9·75 m. × 5·6 m.), one estimates that about 5–6 individuals could comfortably have lived here. This would be about the size of a nuclear family, with two active adults, 2–3 offspring, and perhaps an older adult relative. The presence of the Mediterranean sherd, the wheel-made vases, and the Atlantic contacts suggest that the people who lived in the modest House 9 were yeomen, for burial evidence shows that this class did possess such fineries.

28.xi.67

Department of Anthropology
University of Missouri

References

Becker, C. J. 1966. To landsbyer fra tidlig jernalder i Vestjylland. *Nationalmuseets Arbejdsmark.* 39–50.

Bökönyi, S. 1959. Die frühalluviale Wirbeltierfauna Ungarns (vom Neolithicum bis zur La Tène-Zeit). *Acta Archaeologica.* 11:39–102.

Bretz-Mahler, Denise. 1961. Musée d'Épernay. Catalogue de la céramique des cimetières de l'époque de la Tène I. *Mémoires de la Société d'Agriculture, Commerce, Sciences et Arts du Départment de la Marne.* 75:7–60.

Bretz-Mahler, Denise, et Joffroy, René. 1959. Les tombes à char dans l'est de la France. *Gallia.* 1:5–36.

Calland. 1869. Une station de l'âge du bronze dans la vallée de l'Aisne. *Revue Archéologique.* 20:131–4.

Durvin, Pierre. 1963. Les sépultures du second Age du Fer à Verneuil-en-Halatte (Oise). *Celticum, supplément à Ogam-Tradition Celtique.* 6:103–12.

Favret, l'abbé P. M. 1936. Les nécropoles des Jogasses à Chouilly (Marne). *Préhistoire.* 5:24–119.

Fleury, Ed. 1877. *Antiquités et monuments du départment de la Aisne.* I. Paris.

Garnier, Marcel. 1961. Fouilles du 'Haut de Champaugrain', Commune de La Ferté-Gaucher (Seine-et-Marne). *Bulletin de la Société Archéologique Champenoise.* 54:11–16.

Giffen, A. E. van. 1936. Der Warf in Ezinge, Provinz Groningen, Holland, und seine westgermanischen Häuser. *Germania.* 20:40–7.

Helbaek, Hans. 1951. Ukrudtsfrø som naeringsmiddel i førromersk jernalder. *Kuml.* 65-75.

Hubert, Henri. 1902. La Collection Moreau au Musée de Saint-Germain. *Revue Archéologique.* 8:167–206.

La Collection Moreau au Musée de Saint-Germain. *Revue Archéologique.* 8:337–71.

Joffroy, René. 1960. *L'Oppidum de Vix et la civilisation hallstattienne finale dans l'est de la France.* Dijon.

Josien, Thérèse. 1955. La Faune de la Station de Saint-Romain (Côte-d'Or). *Bulletin de la Société Préhistorique Française*. 52:177–85.

Moreau, Frederic. 1889. *La Collection Caranda. Les Fouilles.* III. Saint-Quentin.

Naroll, Raoul. 1962. Floor Area and Settlement Population. *American Antiquity*. 27:587–9.

Olsen, Stanley J. 1960. Post-Cranial Skeletal Characters of Bison and Bos. *Papers of the Peabody Museum, Harvard University*. 35, No. 4.

Piette, E. 1925. Note sur les sépultures Préhistoriques découvertes à Chassemy (Aisne), vallée de la Vesle. (Rapport de M. Ed. Piette, à Craonne-1870). *Bulletin de la Société Archéologique Champenoise*. 19:48–53, 119–24.

Revelière. 1894. Note sur un couteau gaulois, trouvé à Quiberon. *Bulletin de la Société Polymathique du Morbihan*. 157–66.

Rowlett, Ralph M. 1967. *The East Group of the Marne Culture at the Debut of the La Tène Iron Age*. Ph.D. Thesis. Department of Anthropology, Harvard University. Cambridge, Mass.

Thiérot, M.A. 1931. Fond de cabane de l'époque hallstattienne, cimetières celtiques, tombe gallo-romaine des 'Côtes-en-Marne', à Écury-sur-Coole. *Bulletin de la Société Archéologique Champenoise*. 24:38–56, 75.

We would like to call attention to the following article, which has appeared since our study has gone to press:

1967. Fonds de cabanes de l'âge du bronze final et du premier âge du fer en Champagne. *Revue Archéologique de l'Est et Centre-Est*. 18:7–51.

Contributors

Glynn Ll. Isaac is an Assistant Professor in the Department of Anthropology, Berkeley, University of California. He was formerly at the National Museum Centre for Prehistory and Palaeontology, Nairobi, Kenya.

H. D. Sankalia is Professor of Archaeology at Deccan College, Poona, and is the author of many books and papers on the prehistory of the Indian sub-continent.

Bernard Fagg is Curator of the Pitt Rivers Museum in the University of Oxford. He was formerly Director of Antiquities, Federation of Nigeria.

Witold Hensel is Professor of Archaeology at Warsaw University and Director of the Institute for the History of Material Culture, Polish Academy of Sciences.

Michel de Bouard is Dean of the Faculty of Arts at the University of Caen, and is Director of the Centre for Medieval Archaeological Research at that university.

David G. Kendall, who is a Fellow of the Royal Society, is Professor of Pure Mathematics and Mathematical Statistics at the University of Cambridge and a Fellow of Churchill College.

Irwin Scollar is conducting advanced research at the Laboratory for Field Archaeology, Rheinisches Landesmuseum, Bonn.

F. R. Hodson lectures in prehistory at the Institute of Archaeology, London. He has recently held the S.R.C. Atlas Senior Research Fellowship in Computer Applications in the Arts and Sciences at Churchill College, Cambridge.

Ralph M. Rowlett is an Assistant Professor in the Department of Anthropology, University of Missouri.

Abstracts

Isaac, G. Ll.

Studies of early culture in East Africa

The author reviews and comments upon the more important recent investigations into the earliest prehistory of Eastern Africa, with particular reference to the following fields of study: geo-physical measurements of the time-scale; palaeo-environmental and palaeo-geographical evidence; excavation of individual camp or occupation sites; analysis of the features of unified short-period sets of artefacts; human palaeontology and the different varieties of fossil hominids which are associated with the cultural evidence.

Sankalia, H. D.

A few problems in Indian archaeology, prehistoric and historic, and methods and techniques adopted to tackle them

The article states briefly some of the more important problems in prehistoric, protohistoric and historic archaeology in India, and the efforts made at Deccan College to understand them by systematic exploration, excavation and the application of the latest scientific methods.

Fagg, B.

Recent work in West Africa: new light on the Nok Culture

The author begins with a brief account of important recent work in West Africa, ranging from the Palaeolithic period to the Iron Age. The area covered extends from the southern fringes of the Sahara to the Bight of Benin, and from Cape Verde to Lake Chad and the Cameroons Mountains. The second part of the paper includes a description of finds from the excavations at Taruga. A radiocarbon date in the fifth century B.C. has recently been obtained at this site, but the Culture must now be regarded as fully Iron Age. Some examples of the typical Nok terracotta figures are illustrated.

Hensel, W.

The origins of western and eastern Slav towns

Archaeology has contributed important new data to the history of early medieval towns in Eastern Europe. The author draws a distinction between 'incipient towns' and 'towns endowed

with local rights', establishing that urban life in Slavonic lands began as early as the eighth century. Important excavations at Mikulčice, Kiev and Novgorod are quoted.

Bouard, M. de

The Centre for Medieval Archaeological Research, University of Caen

The scientific study of the archaeology of the historic period in France is as yet a relatively new discipline. The Centre for Medieval Archaeological Research at Caen has developed fresh techniques both for teaching and research in this field. These techniques are discussed, with reference in particular to systems of recording and analysis as applied to medieval ceramics.

Kendall, D. G.

Some problems and methods in statistical archaeology

The problem of sequence-dating (seriation) in archaeology is compared and contrasted with the mathematical problem of sorting the rows of a row-permuted Petrie matrix. The mathematical problem has been studied by Fulkerson and Gross and by the author, and to a certain extent may be considered solved. It is suggested here that the theory of Petrie matrices opens up the possibility of an entirely new approach to sequence-dating. This involves constructing a similarity-matrix in a specific way from the initial data (given in the form of an incidence matrix) and then applying the technique of multi-dimensional scaling. The resulting procedure resembles that of Robinson in one respect, but is differently based and makes use of quite different techniques. To illustrate the method, the results of applying it to a very simple example are shown. Large-scale experiments with real data are planned: a final evaluation of the method must await their completion. One such experiment, based on data supplied by F. R. Hodson, has yielded very encouraging results.

Scollar, I.

Some techniques for the evaluation of archaeological magnetometer surveys

Details of digital filtering techniques for magnetic measurements made on archaeological sites are disclosed. These permit the removal of some of the sources of disturbance which make otherwise useful data difficult to interpret. Several other methods for improving the appearance of data via simple arithmetic operations are also discussed. For full data treatment, a computer is a necessity.

Hodson, F. R.

Searching for structure within multivariate archaeological data

The high-speed computer has made feasible procedures for studying complex data that were impracticable a dozen years ago. To find which likely procedures are of most use to archaeologists, experimental analyses have been carried out. Some preliminary results on two well-known sets of material are presented: first, Upper Palaeolithic assemblages of stone tools published quantitatively by de Sonneville-Bordes and others. The sites chosen, broadly Aurignacian and Gravettian, include La Chèvre, Les Vachons, La Ferrassie, Laugerie Haute, Vogelherd and

Dolni Věstonice. Results from two structure-seeking methods are described: Average-Link Cluster Analysis provides a detailed taxonomy; Principal Components Analysis is able to suggest a more general pattern of relationships. Second, some prehistoric copper and bronze objects, spectrographically examined (by the 'Stuttgart School') for their metal content. An Average-Link Cluster Analysis, while not entirely satisfactory, defines several groups with a demonstrable significance.

Rowlett, R. M. et al.

A rectangular Early La Tène Marnian house at Chassemy (Aisne)

House 9 was only one of a number at the rather large village at Chassemy 'Le Saule Baillot' near the Marnian cemetery at 'La Fosse Chapelet'. This rectangular house was first built and occupied very early in the La Tène Ia phase. Although renovated once, it was abandoned before the close of La Tène Ia, perhaps because it was too close to the Vesle River at the peak of the sub-Atlantic climatic era. On the house floors and in the deep-dug fireplace were found previously unknown Marnian cultural elements such as crude household wares, flint game-stones, strike-a-lights, and eagle-wing fans (?), which are practically never found in graves. Biological remains confirm the funereal evidence that wild food resources were extensively utilized, although the post-renovation occupation depended more upon domestic animals. The bulk of the exotic contacts came also from this later occupation, perhaps indicating a difference in the vocational interests of the inhabitants.

Notes to Contributors

Manuscripts should not normally exceed 5,000 words in length. They should be typed on good quality quarto paper (i.e. approx. 10 in. × 8 in., or 26 cm. × 21 cm.), using double spacing throughout. Two copies of the manuscript should be submitted, the author retaining another. Manuscripts and other correspondence should be addressed to the Executive Editor – Dr Colin Platt, Faculty of Arts, The University, Southampton, England.

Referencing should follow the modern scientific convention. Footnotes, wherever possible, should be avoided. Bibliographical references, to be included in the text, should list the author's last name, date of publication, and number of page, e.g. (Clark 1952: 211). Where an author's name has been cited already in the text, reference need only be made to the date of publication and page, e.g. (1952: 211). Extended references should be listed alphabetically at the end of the paper, e.g.

Bouard, M. de 1965. La mesure de la résistivité électrique des sols en archéologie. *Annales de Normandie.* 15:461–77.

Clark, J. G. D. 1952. *Prehistoric Europe: the economic basis.* London.

Wace, A. J. B. 1958. Aegean Prehistory: a Review. *Antiquity.* 32:30–44.

Wheeler, R. E. M. 1943. *Maiden Castle.* Oxford.

Text figures, site plans and distribution maps should be drawn on strong paper, white card, or good quality tracing film. They should measure approximately twice the intended final size (i.e. a published full-page illustration may not exceed 8 in. × $5\frac{5}{16}$ in., or 20·5 cm. × 15·5 cm.) Plates should be printed on glossy paper and should be mounted on thin card. Figures, maps and plates should be titled and numbered.

Each contribution should be accompanied by a brief abstract (100–150 words) summarizing its contents. Abstracts of the papers printed are included at the end of each issue, together with a short note on individual contributors, which should also be supplied.

It is important that authors should submit accurate, well-prepared copy, ready for the printer. Re-drawing of maps or figures cannot be undertaken by the editors, who may return sub-standard work to contributors for re-presentation in an improved form. Galley proofs of all articles will be sent to authors, who are reminded that these are intended for checking, not re-writing. Failure to return proofs by the required date may lead to the executive editor sending his own corrected proofs to the printer without further reference to the author.

Twenty free offprints will be supplied to authors on publication of a paper. Additional offprints may be purchased at cost price, and should be ordered not later than on the return of corrected proofs.

World Archaeology

Volume 1 No 2
October 1969

This issue: Techniques of chronology and excavation

Three issues a year, February, June and October
Single copies £1 5s
Annual subscription £3 3s ($8.00) post free

Orders to the publishers:
Routledge & Kegan Paul Ltd
Reading Road, Henley-on-Thames, Oxon

World Archaeology

Volume 1 No 2 October 1969

Published thrice yearly by the proprietors
Routledge & Kegan Paul Ltd
68–74 Carter Lane, London EC4

Printed in Great Britain by
The Camelot Press Ltd, London and Southampton

Issues of *World Archaeology* now in preparation cover the themes 'Analysis' (January 1970), 'Early Man' (May 1970), 'Urban Archaeology' (September 1970), and 'Subsistence' (January 1971). Further issues are planned for the future on the themes 'Technological Innovation', 'Social Structures', 'Art and Design', and 'Cultural Survival'.

The editors welcome suggestions for contributions to any of the projected issues, and would be glad at all times to consider important new work for immediate publication, whether or not it coincides with an announced theme.

It is not current editorial policy to publish reviews as a regular feature of the journal. Review articles will cover recent literature in particular fields, and a list of books received will be printed from time to time.

Contents

page

143 Some problems in chronology
Homer L. Thomas and Robert W. Ehrich

157 Potential of thermoluminescence in supplementing radiocarbon dating
Elizabeth K. Ralph and Mark C. Han

170 Land and freshwater Mollusca in archaeology: chronological aspects
J. G. Evans

184 Archaeology with a short, isolated time-scale: New Zealand
Wilfred Shawcross

200 Medieval British and Irish coins as dating evidence for the archaeologist
Michael Dolley

208 Metres, areas and robbing
Martin Biddle and Birthe Kjølbye-Biddle

220 Some aspects of the excavation of timber buildings
Philip Barker

---

236 Building in ancient India
M. S. Mate

247 The myth of the mother-goddess
Andrew Fleming

262 Ethnography and archaeological interpretation of funerary remains
Peter J. Ucko

Some problems in chronology

Homer L. Thomas *and* Robert W. Ehrich

Since one of the chief purposes of archaeology is to recover cultural history, questions of time relationship are critical. The following discussion attempts to focus on what we consider to be some vital aspects of the matter. Part 1 concentrates on direct historical applications with substantive examples, while Part 2 concerns itself more with methodological approaches.

I

Recent preoccupation with new scientific methods of archaeological dating has tended to divert interest from the fundamental historical and archaeological concepts which are the primary basis for any chronological outline of cultural development. Despite the tremendous impact of these new techniques, there persist everywhere chronological systems based upon the hypotheses of evolutionary stages inherent in the succession of Stone, Bronze, and Iron Ages. In Scandinavia, for example, the concept of a three-phase Neolithic is still current, and the Middle Neolithic has been subdivided into five and, most recently, six sub-phases to accommodate the copious new field evidence. Even the concept of a Middle Neolithic period becomes increasingly awkward to use because we now realize that this was not a unitary cultural period, but one of great cultural diversity characterized by the Megalithic, Single Grave, and Pitted Ware cultures (Becker 1961: 585–93). This type of chronological problem, clear-cut in Scandinavia, becomes extremely complex in central and eastern Europe, where local chronological systems must correlate with widespread regional ones such as the Starčevo–Körös–Criş culture or the later (Copper Age) Tiszapolgar culture, both masking themselves under different names in different countries.

The conflict among general, regional, local, or national chronological systems is even more evident in Bronze and Iron Age times. Those of Reinecke, Holste, Müller-Karpe and others, devised for central Europe, do not correlate well with those of other areas. Moreover, their emphasis on typology often tends to divide continuous cultural development into a series of static stages which, although sometimes justifiable on economic and technological as well as on typological grounds, often become isolated and divorced from any conception of culture as a human creation. This approach stems in part from the widespread post-World War I reaction against the historical, and more specifically the evolutionary and Kulturkreis, views of human development. This anti-historicalism, shared by the social sciences and particularly by anthropology, was reinforced by the rejection of the nationalistic excesses which characterized so much of archaeological thought immediately before World War II.

Archaeological chronologies, to be useful in the interpretation of human culture, must be constructed upon cultural rather than typological or technological successions, however much such stages may reflect specific cultures. Thus the determination of cultural succession, first within local areas and then over broader areas, becomes the prime task. This has become increasingly evident during the past twenty-five years in chronologies such as those of F. Holste (1953) for the Bronze Age in southern Germany and of E. Lomborg for the early Bronze Age in southern Scandinavia (1959: 51–146). The validity of these chronologies, and of many others, turns upon the interpretation of successions at a particular site or upon assemblages from a specific find group. Once the validity of the site assemblage or succession has been established, the geographic range of a culture may be fixed by a comparative study of assemblages found at various sites. In north-western and northern Europe, where stratified evidence is less available although present on a limited basis for cultures such as Windmill Hill and Funnel Beaker, the cultural succession can now be controlled by either palynological or geochronological evidence.

Until recently the complicated sequence and relative chronology of Palaeolithic and Mesolithic cultures could be determined only by associated faunal and geological evidence. In the early 1950s, Madame Denise de Sonneville-Bordes and her husband developed a quantitative method for typologically analyzing the cultures of the Upper Palaeolithic period in France (1959: 19–34; de Sonneville-Bordes and Perrot 1953: 232 ff.). This system provides a firm basis for the correlation of site assemblages and can be extended from the Upper Palaeolithic culture to Epi-Palaeolithic cultures such as the Azilian, but does not seem to be applicable to subsequent Mesolithic cultures.

Another system of typological analysis with a firm quantitative basis, advanced by A. Bohmers for the Late Palaeolithic and the Mesolithic (1956: 1–38; 1960: 15–58), also involves different typological groupings, one adapted to the Late Palaeolithic and subsequent Epi-Palaeolithic and another to the Mesolithic. Bohmers objects to the accumulation diagrams of the Bordes because only four cultures can be represented on one diagram and because the exact quantities of component types recorded on their diagrams are not clear. He has developed a system that seems to work very well with material from north-western Europe but, since its fixed categories do not include types that were current in the lands bordering the Mediterranean Basin, its usefulness is limited. Max Escalon de Fonton and Henry de Lumley have adapted the Bordes system for southern France by adding types current in complexes such as the Romanellian and Montadian, and by allowing for later Mesolithic types characteristic of the Sauveterrian and Tardenoisian cultures (1956: 379–92; 504–17). In a search for a more universal implication, Georges Laplace-Jauretche has proposed a system of typological analysis designed to embrace the full range of flint types of Palaeolithic, Mesolithic, and Neolithic times (1957: 133–64).

The systems of the Bordes and of Escalon de Fonton indicate that an ordering of site assemblages and consequently of cultures can be effected in limited areas such as the Dordogne and the Midi, while the work of Bohmers, which is more abstract, suggests that a few significant types can establish cultural relationships over a much larger geographical area. When the conclusions from such statistical analyses are supported by stratified evidence buttressed by related evidence for geological or palynological succession, we can assume that there is a firm basis for an archaeological chronology for these periods.

Unfortunately the quantitative method has not been, and probably cannot be, extended to all areas for the assemblages of the Late Neolithic and particularly the Bronze and Iron Ages. Cultures such as the Corded Ware, Globular Amphorae, and Bell Beaker do not possess a sufficient range of types to warrant detailed statistical analysis, if one excludes minor variations of pottery forms and decoration. This is well illustrated by the success of the relatively simple typological ordering of the Beaker culture of the Netherlands (J. D. van der Waals and W. Glasbergen 1955: 5–46), as compared with the unfortunate failure of the attempt to develop by matrix analysis a chronology of the Beaker culture in the British Isles (D. L. Clarke 1962: 371–82).

The more opulently furnished Bronze Age Burials and the rich urnfield cemeteries of the Late Bronze Age (*e.g.* the urnfield at Kelheim, Lower Bavaria) which can be phased on the basis of horizontal stratigraphy (Müller-Karpe 1959: 161–70), as well as the hoards and isolated finds which play such a major role in determining the chronology of the Bronze Age and Iron Age of Europe north of the Alps, never have the range of material that is available from stratified settlements. The crucial importance of settlement finds for the ordering of chronology has long been shown by the excavations at Tószeg, which have been important for the chronology of the Bronze Age in the Middle Danubian Basin (Banner, Bona, Márton 1957: 1–140; Mozsolics 1952: 35–69). Since the interpretation of typological sequences will always be in part subjective, it is not surprising to find differing chronologies advanced for the Hallstatt and La Tène periods by Reinecke, Kossack, Dechelette, Wiedmer, and Viollier (Dehn and Frey 1962: 197–208). However, chronologies based upon typology and controlled by the use of horizontal stratigraphy for cemetery finds can be successful, as is shown not only by Müller-Karpe's work on the Late Bronze Age (1959) but by that of Hodson on the Iron Age (1964: 123–41).

Radiocarbon dating has brought about a drastic reordering of prehistoric chronology. Often, however, the new high chronologies, which have been based almost entirely upon C^{14} dates, have made little use of older evidence for a high dating which has been available since the 1920s. In 1939 V. G. Childe clearly defined the choices between a high and low chronology for Europe, and indicated the necessity of basing theories of culture development upon an absolute chronology (1939: 10–26). He demonstrated that any absolute dating before 3000 B.C. depended upon one's attitude toward the roles of diffusion, time-lag, cultural lag, and independent invention in culture development. Such divergent absolute chronologies as those of Milojčić (1949) and Pittioni (1949: 99–105) resulted from their differing attitudes toward these concepts in their interpretation of the prehistory of Europe.

A comprehensive view of cultural development and therefore of chronological systems has been complicated by many factors. There has been a marked trend toward regional, national, and even local specialization, fully justified by the tremendous expansion of archaeological field-work since the days of Montelius. Furthermore, the decay of Classical and Biblical studies as the foundation of Western education and the rise of a generation of prehistorians trained in the sciences and social sciences have tended to isolate archaeologists in the European field from Classical and Oriental studies. This separation has been further accentuated by the rejection of all consideration of racial and linguistic evidence in the study of European prehistory. It has obviously become increasingly difficult to relate the development of prehistoric Europe, conceived as a series of stages defined in terms of material culture, to the historical development of the Near East, Greece, and Italy. Events with both linguistic and archaeological significance, such as the invasions of the Indo-Iranians and of the Greeks, have major implications for the archaeological chronology of the Late Neolithic and the Bronze Age in Europe.

A prehistory of Europe that would account for its culture history, not only in its internal development but also in its relationships with the Aegean and the Near East, must rest on a sound absolute chronology. Until the discovery of the radiocarbon method of dating, there were two conflicting views of absolute chronology. The low chronology is based on a concept of European development by cultural diffusion from the Near East, but rests upon a considerable time lag *en route*; the high chronology requires a rapid diffusion from the Near East. Although data for archaeological connections could support either view, most archaeologists felt that the weight of evidence favored the low chronology.

Since about 1950 radiocarbon dates have seemed to support the high chronology. At the same time, archaeological work after World War II has brought to light new field evidence which can be better understood if a high chronology is used. This in turn suggests that new emphasis must be placed upon evidence that has always supported a high chronology for European development, palynological material, partly datable by geochronological criteria.

The development of most cultures in north-western, northern, central, and eastern Europe before 3000 B.C. can be fixed in relative and, in part, in absolute terms by association with floral material; it can be phased by pollen analysis and dated by varves and related geochronological phenomena. It is now possible to construct a chronometric sequence for the late Palaeolithic and Mesolithic and to estimate the dates of early Neolithic cultures almost as satisfactorily by these means as by radiocarbon dating, which indeed fully supports them. For the British Isles, the Netherlands, Germany, and the Scandinavian countries, the past twenty years have witnessed the correlation of the succession of climatic phases: Oldest Dryas, Bølling, Older Dryas, Allerød, Younger Dryas, Pre-Boreal, Boreal, and Atlantic (Godwin 1961: 287–320). Varve chronology makes it possible to fix the absolute date of the Boreal and preceding climatic phases, but only provides a basis for estimating, in terms of the successive beach lines of the Yoldia, Ancylus, and Litorina phases of the Baltic, the dates of the Atlantic and Sub-Boreal climatic periods.

Thus, varve dating provides a firm basis for the absolute chronology of only the Mesolithic, and only an estimated *terminus post quem* for the Neolithic, which began in Europe after the Atlantic phase was well established. Before the discovery of radiocarbon dating, however, the beginning of the Neolithic in Europe was estimated by the connections of the *Bandkeramik* culture through the Vinča culture with the Painted Ware cultures of Thessaly or the Near East. Dates estimated from the depth of accumulation of the settlement mounds of the Near Eastern Painted Ware cultures permitted the *Bandkeramik* of central Europe to be dated as early as the fifth millennium B.C. (Pittioni 1949). Although a high chronology was possible in Near Eastern terms, many archaeologists were fascinated by the concept of cultural lag and accepted V. G. Childe's hypothesis of a Vardar–Morava route for the diffusion of the Neolithic into Europe. These concepts, together with the relating of the Starčevo culture to the Sesklo-Dimini succession in Thessaly and a low Near Eastern historical chronology which put the beginning of the Early Helladic *c.* 2700 B.C., seemed to justify placing the *Bandkeramik* culture in the third millennium B.C. (Childe 1948: 86–92).

In the early 1950s, although radiocarbon dates suggested that a shift to a high chronology was necessary, there was little hard archaeological evidence to contravene the assumptions underlying a low one and it was not easy to make the change until the publication of the recent discoveries made in Thessaly and south-eastern Europe. In Thessaly, the discovery of three phases of an Early Neolithic preceding the Sesklo culture offered much better connections than Sesklo for the Starčevo culture, and thus destroyed the synchronism that had long provided the main basis for the low chronology (Milojčić 1959: 7–10). The evidence from Karanovo and several equally early Neolithic sites along the Lower Danube Valley not only permitted the abandonment of the Vardar–Morava route for the diffusion of the Neolithic into Europe, but also allowed for the correlation of the Starčevo and subsequent Painted Ware cultures with the Painted Ware cultures of the Near East (Georgiev 1961: 45–100; Milojčić 1958: 409–17; Garašanin and Nestor 1966: 23–4). However, a few archaeologists such as Milojčić and Garašanin still doubt the validity of C^{14} dating and seek to justify their low chronologies by recent discoveries such as Tărtăria.

Today both archaeological discoveries and C^{14} dates have led to a high chronology for Europe. This is now supported by an aceramic horizon in south-western Asia and the Aegean area dated to the late eighth and the seventh millennium, and by an early pottery Neolithic horizon extending from the Near East through the Aegean into south-eastern Europe, which requires that the diffusion of the first Neolithic across central Europe (the *Bandkeramik* culture) and of the Cardial Neolithic through the western Mediterranean Basin be placed in the fifth millennium. Thus those Neolithic cultures such as Chiozza, Egolzwil, Chassey, and Windmill Hill, found in Italy, Switzerland, France, and the British Isles respectively, and the diffusion of the Funnel Beaker culture across the North European plain into southern Scandinavia must all be placed in the later fourth millennium, a dating supported not only by C^{14} dates but also by their relative chronological position between the earlier *Bandkeramik* and the subsequent cultures of the later Neolithic.

The later Neolithic cultures of Europe have long been dated by traits which have connections in historically dated contexts in Egypt and south-west Asia. Some late Neolithic cultures, such as the Corded Ware, are generally associated with the Indo-European peoples whose movements can be related to the historically-documented Hittites and Indo-Iranians of south-western Asia and, more recently, the now historically-documented Greeks of the Aegean. Unfortunately the considerable disagreement among Egyptologists and Orientalists is of great importance for both Aegean and European chronology. A difference of 270 years between Hayes' date of 3100 (1962: 4–5) and Stock's date of 2830 B.C. (1949: 103) for the beginning of the First Dynasty of Egypt permits the beginning of the Early Bronze Age of the Aegean as early as 3100/3000 (Weinberg 1965: 302–4) or as late as 2500 B.C. (Hood 1961: 196). For Europe this difference is of great significance for the dating of all later Neolithic cultures. C^{14} dates for the Lagozza, Bell Beaker, Corded Ware, and the Scandinavian Middle Neolithic cultures, as well as for material from historically-dated contexts in Egypt and south-western Asia, tend to support the choice of a higher chronology (Thomas 1967). A high historical chronology for Egypt and Mesopotamia, and consequently for the Aegean, would permit the dating of the destruction horizon marking the end of Early Helladic II in Greece, and Troy II and Early Bronze II in Anatolia at *c.* 2300 B.C. (Weinberg 1965: 304–5; Caskey 1964: 15–20). This would be in harmony with C^{14} dates for the Corded Ware culture of central Europe if we assume that this culture correlates with the expansion out of the steppe that has long explained the movement of new peoples into the Aegean and Anatolia (Thomas, to be published with papers of the Third Indo-European Conference).

The next point of disagreement over the historical chronology of Egypt and Mesopotamia centers upon the dating of events of the Second Intermediate period and the reign of Hammurabi. This issue is of great significance, since it will determine the date of the beginning of the Empire in Egypt (Hayes 1962: 17–21; Rowton 1962: 61–3). A high date for the Eighteenth Dynasty would allow the beginning of the Mycenaean Age to be as early as 1580, while a low Egyptian date would place it as late as 1525 B.C. (Wace 1949: 10; Åstrom 1961-2: 148). Although this difference is not great, it can become significant when dates for the Early Bronze Age of central Europe are extrapolated on the basis of connections found in the Shaft Graves of Mycenae. It was this difference that led Childe at one point to place the beginning of Bronze Age A2 at 1500 B.C., while many Central European archaeologists, following the lead of Paul Reinecke, place it in the seventeenth century B.C., a dating now supported by the discovery of Tomb Circle B at Mycenae, which goes back into late Middle Helladic times (Childe 1948: 177–95; 1957: 342).

It is minor differences such as this which explain differences in the absolute dating not only of the Early Bronze but also of the Middle and Late Bronze Ages of Europe. Certainly the choice of date for the beginning of the Late Bronze Age, Hallstatt A, depends upon whether one accepts Furumark's date of 1230/1225 (1944: 260–2) or Stubbing's date of 1180 (1962: 76) for the beginning of the Late Helladic III C period. Differences in the choice of historical dates as a basis for archaeological dating continue throughout the Late Bronze and into the Iron Age, explaining in part the differing chronologies that have arisen for the Hallstatt and La Tène periods.

The construction of archaeological chronologies, not only in the Near East and Aegean but in Europe as well, must, then, be conceived in historical terms. It should be emphasized that in the choice between a high or low historical chronology there can be no picking and choosing as one moves from period to period or area to area in order to buttress a projected theory of regional development. Furthermore, the choice of historical chronology not only must harmonize with the facts of archaeological relationship and connection but also must be supported by an historical interpretation of relationships between the Aegean and the Orient, as well as of those events which are inferred for Europe. Local archaeological connections and sequences, so often the basis for our chronologies, must be related to each other if we are to understand cultural development in human terms. Establishing a chronology, therefore, is not simply a matter of juggling sequences based upon typological or other succession, but is a product of historical synthesis of those sequences and must meet the tests of criticism which have long characterized human thought.

2

When pursuing synchronic relationships and diachronic sequences, many archaeologists tend to forget that their fundamental operational assumptions can be upset by failure to consider the following:

(1) That the entire structure of archaeological interpretation rests first on the classification of data, and that classification itself is a subjective process that involves the selection of criteria which the classifier thinks significant.

(2) That the validity of time and cultural relationships, as adduced from similarities in recovered data, must depend upon the complexity of likenesses.

(3) That in a series of apparently contemporaneous sites some difference in time caused by population spread or cultural diffusion, either in a given direction or spreading outward from a center, may be suspected.

(4) That unless an adequate sample comes from a field setting of established association, the presence of material characteristic of earlier strata is frequently due to disturbance by later occupants of the site, or to the bringing in of earth from earlier neighboring sites for construction or other purposes.

(5) That although there may be, and usually are, stylistic differences associated with different time periods, such sequences must be stratigraphically established, and not simply asserted from *a priori* assumptions of what should have come first in the matter of style or technology.

(6) That differences in style may represent contemporary regional or village variants, or even be the idiosyncratic products of individuals.

(7) That types, as usually recognized, are a part of the traditional subjective classificatory process, are not particularly sacrosanct, and are subject to reclassification in other ways, particularly by factor analysis and the relationship of attributes, in addition to the usual intuitive and aesthetic association by general form.

(8) That although the stratification of a single site may yield numerous phase variations and cultural successions, initially at least, these are applicable to that site only. In other words, different cultures may appear in sequence in a single site but may represent successive occupations by contemporary peoples with differing cultures or culture variants (*e.g.* Tószeg, see Ehrich 1965: 434–5).

(9) That the isolation of minor phases at a single site reflects the cultural vicissitudes of that particular community and may not be applicable over a wide area.

(10) That behind archaeological cultural complexes were people, and that in analyzing his data the archaeologist must take into account the dynamics of living and of cultural

variation and change and must not shuffle and reshuffle them by abstract formalized pattern.

(11) That patterns of detailed archaeological similarity are of little value unless they can be interpreted as common traditions that define ethnic groups or broader populations, shared cultural origins, or specific contacts between communities or regions.

Limitations of space have restricted these comments to an incomplete list of *caveats* as reminders that chronological interpretations, both diachronic and synchronic, even when based on sequence and on complex formal relationships, rest on methodological assumptions of the individual investigator. These are often unstated, often unrecognized, and operationally frequently lead him far astray. No discussion is here possible of the various field situations that may cause serious difficulty in chronological interpretation.

Relative dating of archaeological complexes is, of course, a method of establishing crude synchronic associations. When a network of such relationships can be anchored to a known historical event or a fixed date, a whole network of cultures and culture sequences takes its rightful place in culture history. When the ladder of history is lacking, intermediate steps may involve the correlation of cultural complexes with such phenomena as variations in climate and vegetation, eustatic movements of shore lines, formation of glacial terraces, rates of stream erosion, and the like. The movement here is toward an evaluation of elapsed time.

In addition to the fixed dates of recorded history, whether accurate or not, such as the Egyptian King Lists, a few techniques are now developed far enough to have become widely used, and others are being explored. In this paper there is little purpose in reiterating all of the technical uncertainties with which investigators are now grappling. The recent emergence of relative dating by assessing the degree of hydration in obsidian finds its methodological counterpart in fluorine dating of Pleistocene deposits, in that no fixed scheme is possible because of the strong impact of local environmental conditions, climatic on the one hand and the mineral content of ground water on the other. However, separate rates of hydration are being established for homogeneous climatic zones, and the method is cheap and fast for establishing relative chronological patterns within these zones (Michels 1967). Since the chief scale of calibration must depend upon radiocarbon dates, the technique, except where dendrochronological systems may be valid, can yield no greater accuracy than the clusters of radiocarbon dates against which it will be calibrated.

When we come to fixed dates, the most reliable, despite the fact that they are limited in their direct applicability by their restricted geographical extent, are the systems of dendrochronology and varve counting. Although these use completely different phenomena, they are methodologically akin in that they serve to assess annual climatic variations by the measurement of thickness, and in that patterns of annual variation in sequence are matched from deposit to deposit or from tree to tree to build up a log, or overlapping sequence, to give fixed dates. The current use of the Sequoia and the Bristlecone Pine sequences, now extending back to *c.* 6000 B.C., to calibrate radiocarbon dating techniques is providing evidence of variation in the amount of radiocarbon formation. Adequate corrections will be forthcoming and, from the standpoint of this paper, need cause us little concern, for any such adjustment, provided that the degree of uniformity of radioactivity in the earth's blanket at any one time can be substantiated, will be uniform and across the board. Quitta (1967: 269) does raise the very pertinent question as to how far one can transfer C^{14} corrections from California bristlecone pine to European deciduous trees which grew in different climatic conditions. He definitely considers any conversion of European Neolithic dates, which would seriously disorganize current interpretations, to be premature at this time. We agree.

To what extent variations in the amount of solar energy striking the earth's surface can be correlated with radiocarbon formation is a question that has recently been reopened by support for the Milankovitch hypothesis in new data (Broecker *et al.* 1968). Whether this can be brought down to within the range of radiocarbon dating is something of a question, particularly since the astronomical dates of that system, when applied to the Upper Palaeolithic and Mesolithic periods, were much too old both with regard to estimated dates and to later radiocarbon analysis (*e.g.* dates in Zeuner 1958: 292 as compared with Late and Terminal Mousterian and Early Aurignacian in *Radiocarbon* 9, 1967: 109 ff.).

We are faced here with the common situation that the more recent the period involved the greater is the required accuracy, for otherwise the range of potential error inherent in any of these systems is likely to be greater than that arrived at by estimated, comparative, or relative dating.

Of all the systems of chronometric dating where specific historical information, such as coinage, is lacking, dendrochronology seems the most precise where it is applicable, but is of limited utility because of its geographic restrictions. Although it helps to serve the calibration of radiocarbon dating for the past 8,000 years or so, it is radiocarbon dating that has emerged as the technique currently in use. If the developing method of dating pottery by thermoluminescence can be made more accurate, it would have certain advantages over natural radiocarbon dating for those periods and cultures in which pottery-making flourished (Ralph and Han, below). In like vein, dating by archaeomagnetism may also have a limited utility. It should be stressed, however, that both of these latter techniques still show a wider degree of potential error than does the radiocarbon method and, to compound uncertainty, both are being calibrated primarily by radiocarbon dates than which they can be no more accurate, at least as yet.

As is generally known, a radiocarbon determination is based upon the measured degree of the dissipation of radioactivity that has taken place in a given sample according to a fixed rate established for C^{14}. Since this is a random process in so far as the actual particle disintegrations are concerned, the total pattern of what takes place in the sample being studied is subject to treatment according to the statistics of chance variation and the bell curve of chance distribution. The variables here are the number of carbon atoms involved in the mass, the number of disintegrations taking place in a given period of time, and the length of time of the count with regard to potential time variation. Radiocarbon dates are customarily given with a median date and a standard error expressed as a $\pm$ figure. As has been frequently pointed out (Ralph and Michael 1967; Satterthwaite and Ralph 1960: 177 f.; Stuckenrath 1965: 278–9), this standard error is a purely statistical measure of probable variations within the count itself. Furthermore, the range of the standard error indicates merely that the odds are only 2 to 1 that the true date of the sample falls within those limits. A doubling of the standard error raises the odds to 22 to 1. The standard error of the half-life of radiocarbon may or may not be included in the determination as quoted (see, for example, the introductory statements of the various articles in *Radiocarbon* 8 [1966] and 9 [1967]).

Despite the numerous possibilities of other errors, one major difficulty encountered by archaeologists in making proper use of radiocarbon determinations seems to be a psychological one. The need and desire for fixed dates leads them to forget that the cited date is a mean figure of no special validity. Although the standard error is customarily cited, it is usually thought of as a secondary figure of relatively little significance. Most of us were traumatized by the multiplication tables when we were in the third grade and, even in the face of our subsequent greater intellectual sophistication, we still have an emotional tendency to react to specific figures as definite, and to think of them in that way. Occasionally radiocarbon dates may be plotted with range bars or graphically (Bandi 1963: 89; 1965: 227; Satterthwaite and Ralph 1960: 169, 176; Stuckenrath 1965; Quitta 1967: 65), but it would be far better to write the dates as ranges defined by the minima and maxima of their standard errors. The median date, if desired, could be included as a middle figure in a sequence of three dates. As it is, we think of and utilize the median date in our comparisons and *we do not think in terms of potential range of possibility, which is what the figures actually give us.*

A second feature with regard to the standard error is its proper role in the comparison of median dates that seem to fall close to each other. Ignoring all other possibilities of inaccuracy, such as the archaeological validity of the samples by field association, contamination, and the like, and assuming that both dates are equally valid with regard to the samples themselves and to the process of analysis, one asks whether the difference between the two mean dates is statistically valid and requires explanation, or whether it is invalid and more apparent than real because of overlapping in the range of potential error based on the nature of the process. Traditionally this has been done by simple inspection and, if the standard errors overlap, the difference is taken to be invalid. If a single standard error, or even a double one, embraces both means, the difference between them can certainly be disregarded as having no statistical significance. However, to evaluate the statistical significance of mean differences, the use of the critical ratio may sometimes be of value. If d = the difference between two radiocarbon dates as normally given, and MSE_1 = the standard error of the first date and MSE_2 = the standard error of the second date, then $[d/\sqrt{(MSE_1^2+MSE_2^2)}]$ equals the difference divided by its own standard error. If the resulting critical ratio should be less than 2, the difference would not be statistically valid; if greater than 2, some further explanation would be needed (Satterthwaite and Ralph 1960: 174–5). The simple averaging of discordant runs from the same sample or from the same level, as well as the simple inspection for standard error overlap, glozes over irregularities and may result in a distorted and misleading picture that is based on misinterpretation and false accuracy.

Any individual determination may, of course, be wildly out of line because of misattribution to context, contamination of one sort or another, or chance variation from a standard norm. There can also be possible errors arising from such circumstances as a sample of charcoal coming from a tree that had been long dead before it was burned, or it may have come from inactive heartwood that was the only surviving remnant of a large and old tree, thus giving not only a mean date but an entire standard error that could easily fall a century or two earlier than the archaeological context in which it appeared.

There has rightly been much insistence that clusters of dates are necessary and that any single reading is suspect. In spite of these cautions, where for one reason or another only single dates are available, most archaeologists have a tendency to accept them wholeheartedly if they confirm pre-existing assessments, or to find some excuse to throw them out if they do not fit.

In the light of all the other inaccuracies, actual and potential, what may seem to be a matter of relatively minor importance may really be of much greater significance in the light of compounding error. Although the final detailed determinations have not as yet been established, there is general agreement that 5,730±30 years is much more accurate for the half-life of C^{14} than the previously used figure of 5,568±40 (*Radiocarbon* 5: editorial; Ralph and Han, below; Stuckenrath 1965: 278; Thomas 1967: 11). Despite the general recognition that the new figure is much closer to reality, it is still customary to publish dates based on the older figure, using 1950 as the reference year. As each year goes by, the gap between the year of determination and the reference year increases, and it is already approximately half the standard error of the half-life and of many of the readings. Further, as Stuckenrath points out, since the difference between the two figures is only 3%, the discrepancy in dating amounts to only 100 years in three millennia. However, around 2000 B.C. a difference of a hundred years can be quite significant when applied to the archaeological interpretation of Egyptian, Middle Eastern, and Aegean chronology.

From the standpoint of the physicist or of the geologist who deals with long spans of time and who is almost completely dependent upon radiocarbon determinations as a check on his rough estimates, the error of 3% is insignificant and he can afford to wait until the final adjustments, which in themselves will still be approximations, are arrived at by general agreement.

In the meantime the archaeologist is faced with the problem of arriving at dates requiring a much higher degree of accuracy in a more recent time-scale and in congruence with other data, such as those provided by relative chronologies and the historical record. In this sense it is essential to eliminate as many inaccuracies as possible, and it seems completely unrealistic not to use a more accurate, if still imperfect, figure for puristic reasons. So long as one indicates clearly which half-life he is using, the newer one seems preferable to the old and fits the evidence much more satisfactorily. It was with these considerations in mind that the contributors to *Chronologies in Old World Archaeology* (Ehrich 1965) converted their dates to the newer readings. In spite of disparaging comments on our having done this (Braidwood 1966: 1567; 1967: 174), we are cheerfully unrepentant and still believe that one should use the best tools available.

Apart from the specific historical record and the rather limited uses of tree-ring analysis, radiocarbon determination is not only the most accurate and most widely used means of archaeological dating that we have, it is also being used to calibrate the emerging techniques employing thermoluminescence and archaeomagnetism which, so far at least, can yield results no more accurate than the systems against which they are finally calibrated. Taking into consideration the range implicit in the statistical standard error and the numerous uncertainties which plague each sample and its reading, radiocarbon dating must be viewed as a coarse-meshed screen, most useful the further back one goes in time and in those instances where the chronological information, both sequential and relative, is inadequate or totally lacking. Where the information is relatively full, such as during the later Iron Age, to say nothing of the Classical Greek, Roman, and Medieval periods, the margin of error is usually great enough to render radiocarbon dating virtually meaningless. Before using it, one should know the limits of his question and the nature of the potential answer.

Note: Grateful acknowledgement is made to Elizabeth K. Ralph and Robert Stuckenrath of the University of Pennsylvania for most helpful technical reference materials and discussion.

10.iv.1968

University of Missouri
and
Brooklyn College
City University of New York

References

Åstrom, P. 1961–2. Remarks on Middle Minoan Chronology. *Krētika Chronika.* 15–16:137–50.

Bandi, H.-G. *et al.* 1963. Birsmatten-Basisgrotte: eine mittelsteinzeitliche Fundstelle im unteren Birstal. *Acta Bernensia.* I.

Bandi, H.-G. 1966. C^{14} Dates from Mesolithic Sites in Central Europe. *Proceedings of the Sixth International Conference on Radiocarbon and Tritium Dating.* Washington. 225–31.

Banner, J., Bona, I. and Márton, L. 1957. Die Ausgrabungen von L. Márton in Tószeg. *Acta Archaeologica.* X:1–140.

Becker, Carl J. 1961. Probleme der neolithischen Kulturen in Nordeuropa vom Anfang der Trichterbecherkultur bis zum Aufreeten der Schnurkeramiker. *L'Europe à la fin de l'âge de la pierre.* Prague. 585–94.

Bohmers, A. 1956. Statistics and Graphs in the Study of Flint Assemblages. *Palaeohistoria.* V:1–38.

Bohmers, A. 1960. Statistiques et graphiques dans l'étude des industries Lithiques préhistoriques. *Palaeohistoria.* VIII:15–58.

Bordes, Francois. 1950. Principes d'une methode d'étude des techniques de débitage et de la typologie du Paléolithique ancien et moyen. *L'Anthropologie.* LIV:19–34.

Bourdier, Fr. and Lumley, H. de. 1956. Magdalénien et Romanello-Azilien en Dauphiné. *Bulletin du Musée d'Anthropologie préhistorique de Monaco.* III:123–76.

Braidwood, R. J. 1966. Review of *Prehistoric Societies* by Grahame Clark and Stuart Piggott, in *American Anthropologist.* 68, 6:1566–8.

Braidwood, R. J. 1967. *Prehistoric Men* (7th edn). Glenview, Illinois.

Broecker, Wallace S., Thurber, David L., Goddard, John, Ku, Teh-lung, Matthews, R. K. and Mesolella, Kenneth. 1968. Milankovitch Hypothesis Supported by Precise Dating on Coral Reefs and Deep Sea Sediments. *Science.* 159, 3812:297–300.

Caskey, J. L. 1964. Greece, Crete, and the Aegean Islands in the Early Bronze Age. *Cambridge Ancient History* (2nd edn). I, chap. XXVIa:3–44.

Childe, V. G. 1939. The Orient and Europe. *American Journal of Archaeology*. XLIII:10–26.

Childe, V. G. 1948. The Final Bronze Age in the Near East and in Temperate Europe. *Proceedings of the Prehistoric Society*. XIV:177–95.

Childe, V. G. 1948. *The Dawn of European Civilization* (4th edn). London.

Childe, V. G. 1957. *Ibid.* (6th edn). London.

Clarke, D. L. 1962. Matrix Analysis and Archaeology with particular reference to British Beaker Pottery. *Proceedings of the Prehistoric Society*. XXVIII:371–82.

Dehn, W. and Frey, O.-H. 1962. Die absolute Chronologie der Hallstatt und Frühlatenezeit Mitteleuropas auf Grund des Südimports. *Relazioni Generali. Atti del VI Congresso Internazionale delle Scienze Preistoriche e Protostoriche.* I:197–208.

Ehrich, R. W. ed. 1965. *Chronologies in Old World Archaeology*. Chicago.

Escalon de Fonton, Max and Lumley, Henry de. 1956. Les industries Romanello-Aziliennes. *Bulletin de la Société Préhistorique Française*. LIII:504–17.

Escalon de Fonton, Max and Lumley, Henry de. 1956. Quelques civilisations de la méditerranée septentrionale et leurs intercurrences. *Ibid.* 379–92.

Furumark, A. 1944. The Mycenaean III C Pottery and Its Relationship to Cypriote Fabrics. *Opuscula Archaeologica.* III:194–265.

Garašanin, M. and Nestor, I. 1966. Les peuples de l'Europe du Sud-Est à l'époque préromaine. *Rapport pour la seance pleniere, Ier Congrès international des Études Balkaniques et sud-est Européennes*. Sofia. 20–35.

Georgiev, G. I. 1961. Kulturgruppen der Jungstein- und der Kupferzeit in der Ebene von Thrazien (Südbulgarien). *L'Europe à la fin de l'âge de la pierre*. Prague. 45–100.

Godwin, H. 1961. Radiocarbon dating and Quaternary history in Britain, The Croonian Lecture. *Proceedings of the Royal Society*, Series B. 153:287–320.

Hayes, W. C. 1962. Chronology I, Egypt – To End of Twentieth Dynasty. *Cambridge Ancient History* (2nd edn). I, chap. VI: 3–23.

Hodson, F. R. 1964. La Tène Chronology, Continental and British. *Bulletin of the Institute of Archaeology, University of London.* 4:123–41.

Holste, F. 1953. *Die Bronzezeit in Süd- und Westdeutschland* (*Handbuch der Urgeschichte Deutschlands I*). Berlin.

Hood, M. S. F. 1961. The Home of the Heroes. In *The Dawn of Civilization*, ed. S. Piggott. 195–228.

Laplace-Jauretche, C. 1957. Typologie analytique. Application d'une nouvelle méthode d'étude des formes et des structures aux industries à lames et lamelles. *Quaternaria*. IV:133–64.

Lomborg, Ebbe. 1959. Donauländische Kulturbeziehungen und die relative Chronologie der Frühen Nordischen Bronzezeit. *Acta Archaeologia*. XXX:51–146.

Michels, J. W. 1967. Archaeology and Dating by Hydration of Obsidian. *Science.* 158, 3798: 211–14.

Milojčić, V. 1949. *Chronologie der Jüngeren Steinzeit Mittelund Südosteuropas.* Berlin.

Milojčić, V. 1958. Zur Anwendbarkeit der C^{14}-Datierung in der Vorgeschichtesforschung II. *Germania.* XXXVI:409–17.

Milojčić, V. 1959. Ergebnisse der deutschen Ausgrabungen in Thessalien (1953–8). *Jahrbuch des römisch-germanischen Zentralmuseums Mainz.* VI:1–56.

Mozsolics, A. 1952. Die Ausgrabungen in Tószeg im Jahre 1948. *Acta Archaeologica.* II:35–69.

Müller-Karpe, H. 1959. *Beiträge zur Chronologie der Urnenfelderzeit nördlich und südlich der Alpen.* (*Römisch Germanische Forschungen* 22.) Berlin. 161–70.

Pittioni, R. 1949. *Die Urgeschichtlichen Grundlagen der europäischen Kultur.* Vienna.

Quitta, Hans. 1967. The C^{14} Chronology of the Central and SE European Neolithic. *Antiquity.* XLI, 164:263–70.

Radiocarbon 1963, 1967, 1968. Vols 5, 8, 9. Published by the *American Journal of Science.* New Haven.

Ralph, Elizabeth K. and Michael, Henry N. 1967. Problems of the Radiocarbon Calendar. *Archaeometry.* X:3–11.

Satterthwaite, L. and Ralph, Elizabeth. 1960. New Radiocarbon Dates and the Maya Correlation Problem. *American Antiquity.* 26, 2:165–84.

Sonneville-Bordes, D. de and Perrot, J. 1953. Essai d'adaptation des méthodes statistiques au Paléolithique Supérieur. Premier results. *B.S.P.F.* L:232 ff.

Stock, H. 1949. Der Erste Zwischenzeit Ägyptens, Studia Aegyptica II. *Analecta Orientalia.* XXXI.

Stubbings, F. H. 1962. Chronology, The Aegean Bronze Age. *Cambridge Ancient History* (2nd edn). I, chap. VI:69–77.

Stuckenrath, Robert Jr. 1965. On the Care and Feeding of Radiocarbon Dates. *Archaeology.* 18, 4:277–81.

Thomas, H. L. 1967. *Near Eastern, Mediterranean and European Chronology.* (*Studies in Mediterranean Archaeology* XVII.) Lund.

Thomas, H. L. In press. New Evidence for Dating the Indo-European Dispersal in Europe. To be published with the *Papers of the Third Indo-European Conference.*

Van der Waals, J. D. and Glasbergen, W. 1955. Beaker Types and Their Distribution in the Netherlands. *Palaeohistoria.* IV:5–46.

Wace, A. J. B. 1949. *Mycenae.* Princeton.

Weinberg, S. S. 1965. The Relative Chronology of the Aegean in the Stone and Early Bronze Ages. In *Chronologies in Old World Archaeology*, ed. R. W. Ehrich. Chicago. 285–320.

Zeuner, F. E. 1958. *Dating the Past: an introduction to geochronology* (4th edn). London.

Potential of thermoluminescence in supplementing radiocarbon dating

Elizabeth K. Ralph *and* Mark C. Han

1 Introduction

There is no question of the importance of radiocarbon dating nor of its tremendous contribution to archaeology and geochronology. For dating in certain periods, however, one may point out a few weaknesses.

From the measurements of samples of known age, it has now been established that there have been minor fluctuations in the inventory of C^{14} in past times. These and their possible causes have been published and are the subject of many discussions. The most pronounced fluctuation is the long-term one which has been noted in the first millennium B.C. and continues back in time to the present limit of dendrochronologically-dated samples, to the fifth millennium B.C. The results, obtained in our laboratory, of dating tree-ring-dated sequoias and bristlecone pines are shown in fig. 1. (The data for some of these samples are published in Ralph *et al.* 1965: 179–86.) One sees that there are significant discrepancies in B.C. eras between 'radiocarbon years' and true ages, and that the magnitude of these may be as much as 500 years.

In addition to this long-period deviation from steady-state C^{14} inventories, however, there appear to be some shorter-term fluctuations. Among the most firmly determined of these are those which occur in the period of A.D. 1700 to 1500. As one may see in figs 1 and 2, these are of sufficient magnitude to cause ambiguity for dating, and the discrepancy may be as large as 200 years. This and the next consideration may be seen more clearly in the regression curve (fig. 2).[1] Prior to A.D. 1300 the short-term fluctuations, if statistically significant, are much smaller, but on the *average*, from A.D. 1300 to the beginning of the Christian era, C^{14} dates tend to be slightly earlier than known ages. The difference happens to be about 3% in 'before present' ages which is equal to the difference between ages calculated with the Libby 5,568 half-life (1955: 36) and the new value of 5,730 (Godwin 1962: 984). Whether or not this is a coincidence or whether it reflects the uncertainty in the true value of the half-life cannot be resolved by natural radiocarbon dating alone, since this measurement is dependent also upon the constancy of the C^{14} inventory. At the moment, we can say that for the time span of A.D. 1300 to the beginning of the Christian era, C^{14} ages calculated with the 5,568 half-life are in better agreement with known ages, but that C^{14} dates earlier than this should be calculated with the 5,730 half-life value.

One of the most serious handicaps of radiocarbon dating is the fact that the sample to

1 We are indebted to R. Stuckenrath, Radiocarbon Laboratory, University of Pennsylvania, for his contribution in the preparation of the regression curve.

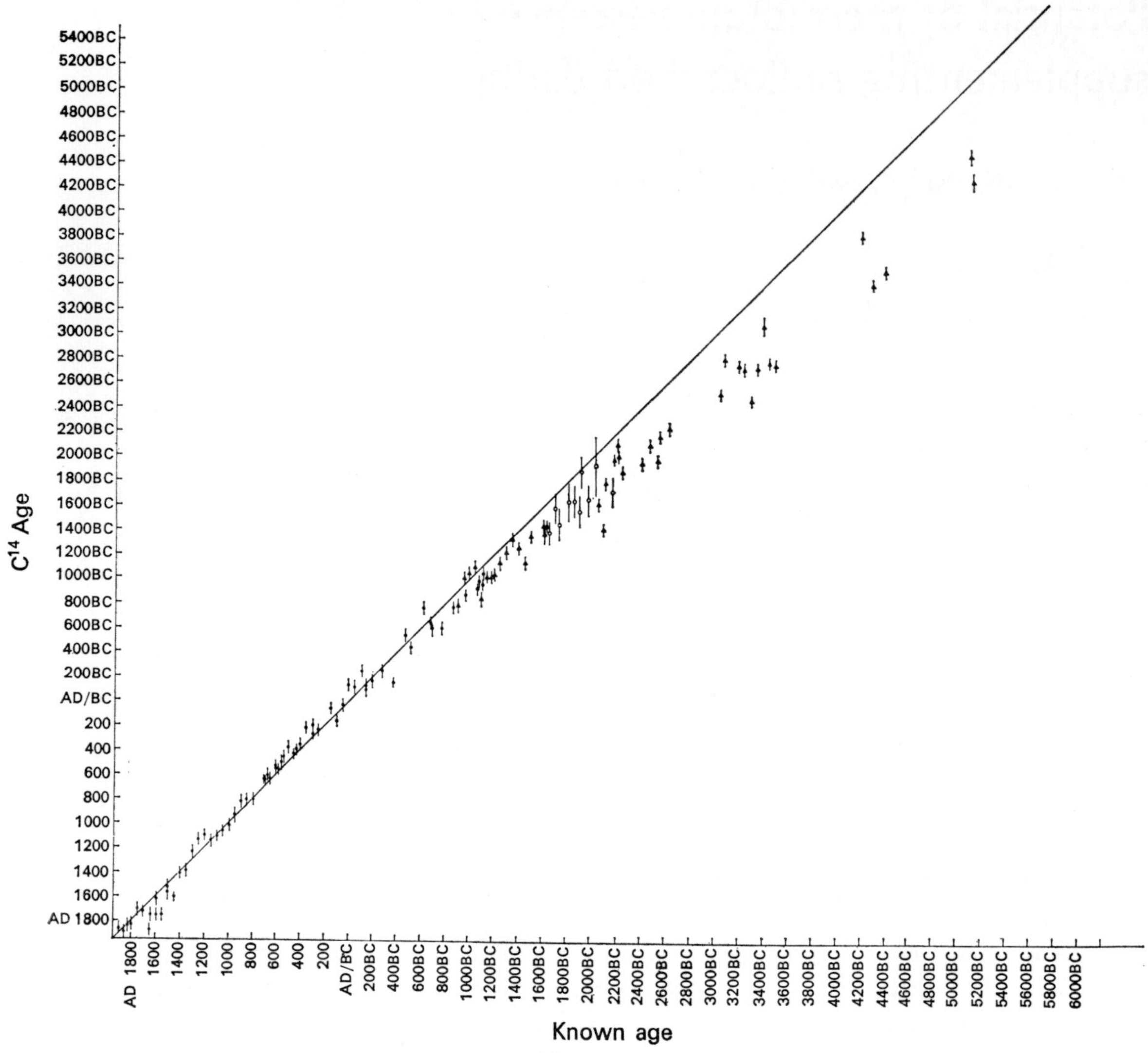

Figure 1 Radiocarbon dates for tree-ring samples of known age (University of Pennsylvania Radiocarbon Laboratory)

be dated is usually related to the occupation level and its artefacts by association only. The accuracy of this association is dependent upon the skill and attention of the excavator. An error in vertical or horizontal stratigraphic interpretation can cause a significant error in the precise relationship of associated materials. Here thermoluminescence has one obvious advantage – artefacts themselves are datable.

Another fortunate circumstance for the application of thermoluminescence is that pottery was used universally throughout the ages back to about 7000 B.C. A minor point which might be mentioned too is that pottery is fragile so that there is less likelihood that the sample to be dated was used for many centuries prior to its final deposition. In con-

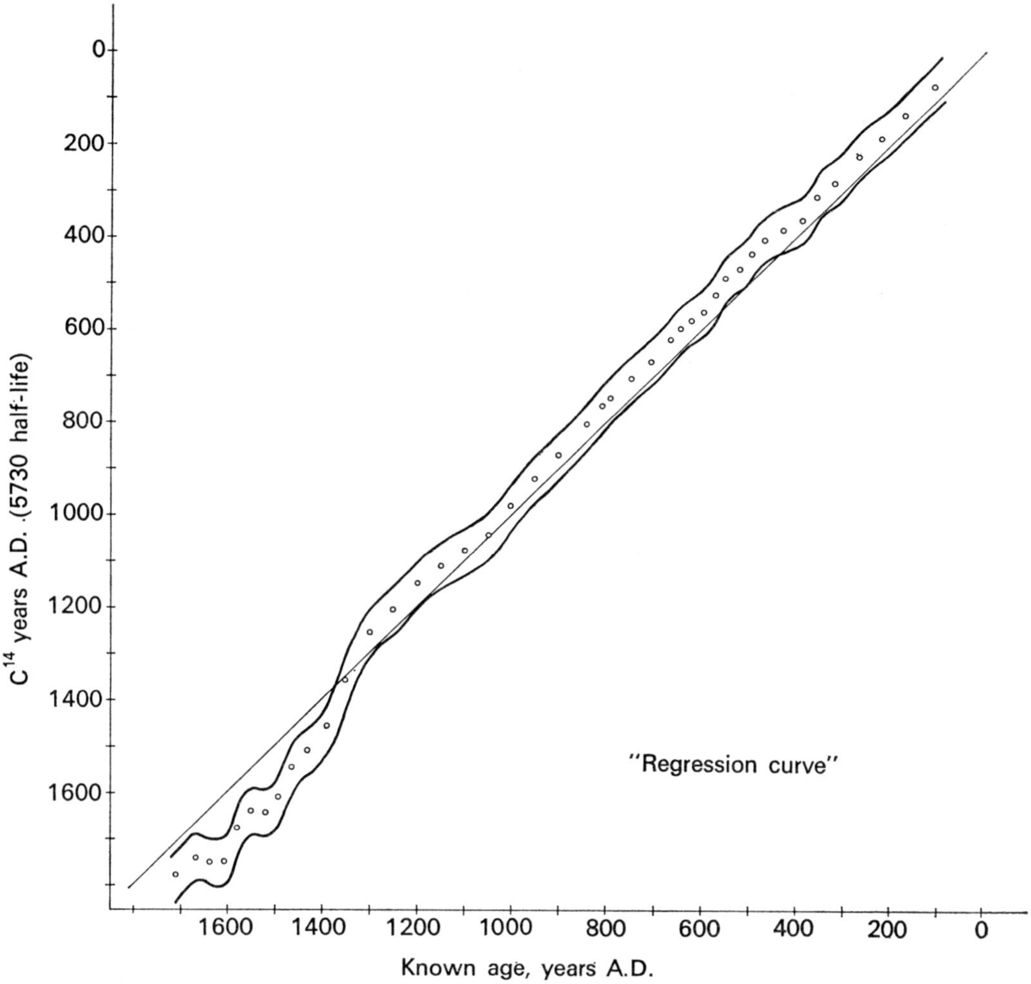

Figure 2 Regression-smoothed plot of radiocarbon dates for tree-ring samples of known age (University of Pennsylvania Radiocarbon Laboratory). The results for the Christian era only are shown in this figure

trast, in C^{14} dating, when it is possible to date the artefact itself, it is usually a piece of a large beam of a structure, plank of a ship, or similar material. Not only is there danger that the beam may have been re-used, but it may have been originally a very large beam from which the outer growth layers, the ones contemporaneous with the time of construction, have disappeared.

Thermoluminescence dating, now in its infancy, has also inherent weaknesses and difficulties. Its potential is based upon the fact that it provides an entirely independent means of dating, and that it is applicable to pottery and other fired ceramics – the objects found most commonly by archaeologists.

2 Development and principles of the method

The suggestion that thermoluminescence might provide a means of dating pottery was made by Farrington Daniels (1953: 349) and also by F. G. Houtermans (1957: 283) some years ago. The technique was investigated further by George Kennedy (1960: 147) and is now being engaged in actively at the Museum Applied Science Center for Archaeology (MASCA), University Museum, University of Pennsylvania (Ralph and Han 1968: 379); the Research Laboratory for Archaeology and the History of Art, Oxford University (Aitken 1968: 369); the Institute of Geophysics and Planetary Physics, University of California at Los Angeles; and also at the Departments of Anthropology and Physics, University of Wisconsin (Mazess and Zimmerman 1966: 347).

Thermoluminescence in pottery is due to the fact that radiations from the traces of radioactive elements in pottery bombard the other constituents of the clays and raise electrons to metastable levels. When the pottery is heated, such as in firing, enough additional energy is supplied to enable each electron to fall back to its stable position and to emit a photon of light. On being reheated, the amount of thermoluminescence observed is, therefore, representative of the accumulated radiation damage and hence of the time elapsed since the original firing of the pottery. Once an object has been heated to a temperature of 400°–500° C and its electrons have emitted their thermoluminescent light, no further light may be obtained by reheating after a relatively short time. Consequently, recently fired ceramic ware or freshly cooled lava, all of which have all electrons in stable states, should show no thermoluminescence.

If all potsherds contained the same inherent radioactivities and were equally susceptible to radiation damage, then the amount of light emitted by a sample upon reheating would provide an age determination. The longer ago the sherd was fired, the greater would be the amount of light emission. Naturally, the situation is not this simple because the compositions of clays and other earth materials are extremely variable. For age determination, therefore, one must include other factors.

First of all, the amount of metastable electron accumulation is dependent upon the rate of radioactive bombardment. This, in turn, is complicated by the fact that various types of radioactivities are involved. In clays the predominant radioactive elements are normally uranium, thorium, and potassium. Each of the first two emit three different types of particles in their decay series: namely, alphas, betas, and gammas, while potassium-40 emits betas only. The first question is: Which particles are most effective in creating radiation damage in clays? On the basis of various experiments, we now assume that alphas are the most effective in creating so-called traps or holes where metastable electrons may lodge, but that these traps may subsequently be filled by the lighter betas, gammas, and other particles. This is somewhat fortuitous because for these very low-level natural radioactivities, the rate of alpha disintegration is easiest to measure, and for uranium and thorium the total rate of disintegration is proportional to the alpha rate. To determine the effect of the potassium-40 contribution, potassium contents of sixteen different potsherds were measured. The results showed little variation in the potassium-40 contents. The average was 2% in sherds from Hasanlu, Iran, and Torre Mordillo, above the plain of Sybaris, Italy. A correction factor based upon these small variations did not improve the correspondence of these samples with their known ages.

In regard to the rate of bombardment, there are other possible complications due to the environment of the sample. There is the question of the contribution from radioactivities in the soil in which the sample has been buried. If we continue to assume, however, that alpha particles are essential in producing the radiation damage, this would be only a surface effect since the range of alphas in clays is very short. If a sample has not been buried very deeply, there is the possibility of a contribution from exposure to cosmic rays. Fortunately, on the basis of our experiments made so far neither of these factors seems to make a significant contribution. On this general subject of radioactivity, experiments, with somewhat contrary results, have been performed by M. J. Aitken and colleagues at Oxford University (Tite 1966: 161).

The third important factor for age determination is the susceptibility of the pottery to radiation damage. This is dependent upon its composition and texture. Experiments have indicated that quartz is the component of clays which is most susceptible to radiation damage, and also that an excess of iron compounds tends to reduce the susceptibility (Fleming 1966: 172). Because of the finite ranges of some types of radioactive particles (especially alphas) the natural grain size of the pottery influences also its susceptibility to radiation damage.

Fortunately, it is not necessary to perform tedious quantitative analyses and separations of each sample because its susceptibility to inherent radioactive bombardment may be determined by the application of an artificial dose. At Oxford and in our laboratory,

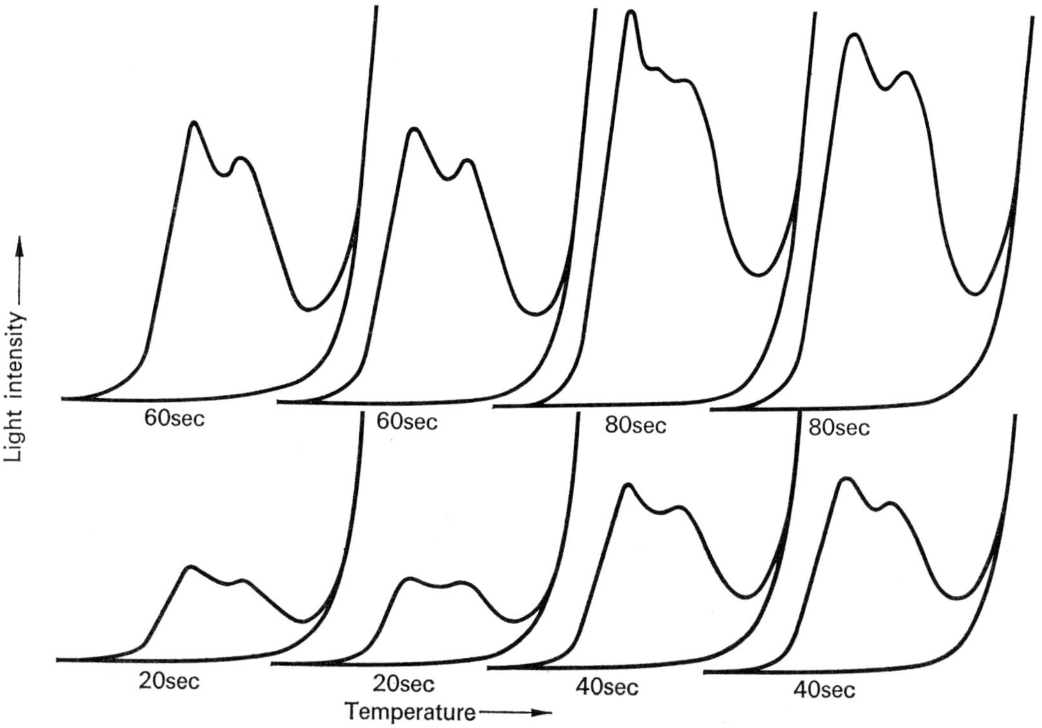

Figure 3 Artificial glow curves obtained after irradiation with X-rays for different lengths of time

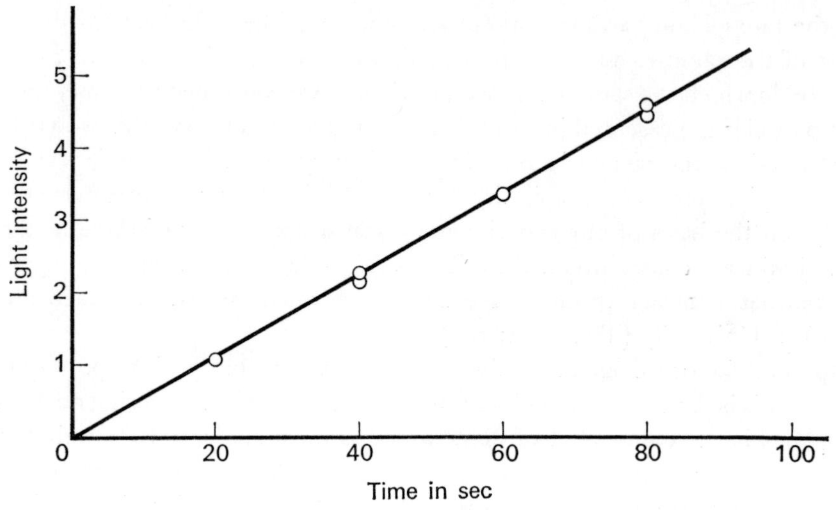

Figure 4 Plot of *A-TL* (Maximum light output at 320° C) versus time of irradiation

experiments with various types and magnitudes of artificial doses have been carried out (Tite 1966: 156; Ralph and Han 1966: 245). At MASCA most of our experiments have been performed with X-rays. The results show that the amount of light intensity emitted is directly proportional to the dose received. Figs 3 and 4 show the results of a pottery sample irradiated with X-rays for different lengths of time. If one subjects all samples to a fixed dose of X-rays, then one can see that the ratio of natural thermoluminescence to artificial thermoluminescence is an indication of the radiation damage caused by the natural process accumulated through time. Therefore, the specific thermoluminescence of a given sample is directly proportional to its archaeological age, as indicated in equation 1.

$$\text{Age} = k\frac{(N\text{-}TL)}{(\alpha)(A\text{-}TL)} \qquad \text{eq. 1}$$

Where,

N-TL = Natural thermoluminescence.

α = Relative radioactive content in pottery, determined by counting the rate of alpha disintegration.

A-TL = Artificial thermoluminescence, or the susceptibility of pottery to radiation damage measured in terms of the thermoluminescence induced by subjecting the sample to a fixed dose of radiation.

k = Proportionality constant.

A few other uncertainties should be mentioned before proceeding to the experimental results. One is the possibility of the loss or decay of metastable electrons, especially from near the surface during the passage of time. This is a serious consideration for geological dating, but for the much shorter archaeological time-scales, it does not appear to be a complicating factor. Another thought is the effect of the differing transparencies of clays upon the detection of the photons emitted when heated. Fortunately, the correction factor applied from the artificial irradiation tends also to correct for this variation. Thirdly, one must consider the effect of grinding the pieces of pottery which is a necessary preliminary in the dating process. Experiments with pre-baked samples indicate that negligible thermoluminescence is induced by our system of grinding.

Our first concern has been to assemble apparatus sufficiently sensitive and reliable to make a quantity of measurements. After initial feasibility experiments with borrowed equipment, the program has been supported by, and appropriate components have been purchased with, funds from the National Science Foundation.

3 Experimental procedure

Samples of pottery are received usually in the form of fragments and are catalogued and washed. The grinding of each sample is done in the following fashion – approximately 10 to 15 grams (a minimum of 3 grams is required) of clean potsherds are crushed to a size below 30 mesh (less than 600 microns) and are then placed in a small ball mill and ground to less than 200 mesh (or 75 microns).

A portion of the ground sample is used to measure its relative radioactivity. Since we have assumed that the major radiation damage is caused by α-bombardment *or* is proportional to it, we have, therefore, constructed special low-background zinc sulphide screens and associated components for this low level detection of α-particles. The α-emissions are counted in infinitely thick layers with the result that comparative values only are obtained.

For detection of the thermoluminescent photons emitted upon heating, our preliminary experiments indicated that rapid heating rates of thin layers of powdered potsherds were essential. Since the accumulation of metastable electrons is very small, high sensitivity is required to detect the light output which happens to be mostly in the visible range.

The apparatus for detection of the thermoluminescence is shown in fig. 5. Samples are mounted on a 3 by 3 inch square of heavy duty aluminium foil by means of the silk screen technique. This is done by mixing a portion of the ground sample with a carrier, silicone oil,[1] which is both chemically and thermally stable up to 600° C, and which helps to produce a thin uniform layer on the foil. (By chance, the silicone oil inhibits any possible effect due to the exposure of the finely ground potsherd to daylight.) The size of the sample deposited on the foil is ¾ of an inch in diameter and it is approximately 0·005 in. thick. (This diameter was dictated by the area that can be heated uniformly by our particular furnace.) The foil on which the powdered pottery is mounted is pressed into the sample holder with the sample facing upward, and the back side of the foil is coated with a layer of graphite to obtain maximum heat absorption. The holder is then placed on the furnace, and it is heated linearly in a nitrogen atmosphere by means of a programmed control system from a starting temperature of 70° up to 450° C. Two thermocouples are located in direct contact under the back side of the foil, one for the purpose of recording the temperature, and the other for the feedback to the control system. The light emitted

[1] A type of silicone oil which we have found suitable is Duxe Silicone (500 centistokes) made by Duxe Products, Cincinnati, Ohio.

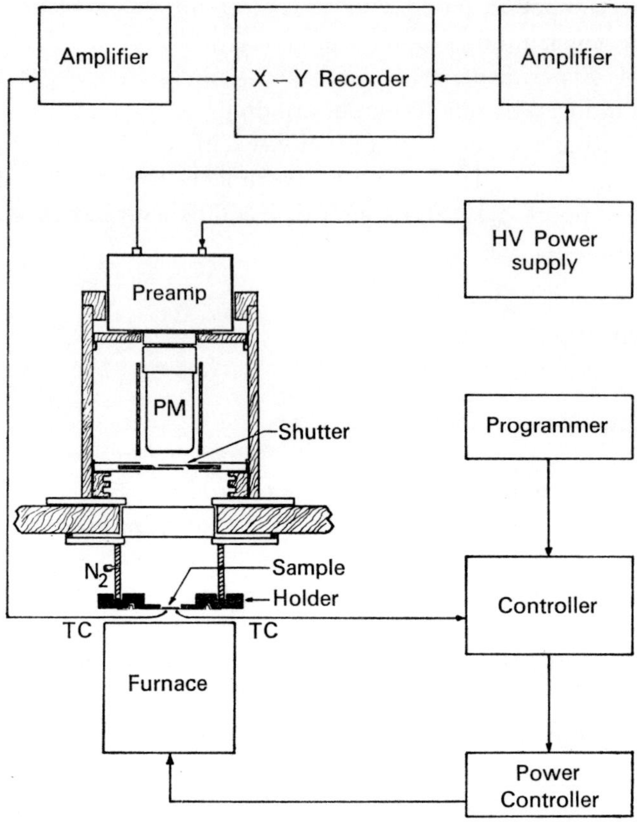

Figure 5 Block diagram of the glow curve apparatus

during this process is detected by the photomultiplier tube. The signal from the photomultiplier and that from one of the thermocouples are fed into two separate amplifiers and are recorded on the X–Y recorder. This produces the so-called 'glow curve' which, in this case, is the natural thermoluminescence (*N-TL*) produced by the potsherd. About 20 replicate measurements are made for each potsherd in order to obtain a more representative result.

We have found that even though replicate samples were taken from a single piece of pottery that had been ground and mixed thoroughly, there were variations (standard statistical deviations) of the order of from ±5 to ±7%. This indicated that the corrections obtained by artificial bombardment should be applied to the identical samples that were measured for natural thermoluminescence. Fortunately, our mounting technique with silicone oil on aluminum foils allows this to be done easily. Therefore, each labelled sample is heated and measured for natural thermoluminescence and it is then bombarded with X-rays (for 60 seconds at 30 kV and 12·7 milliamps). After this the artificial glow curve (*A-TL*) is obtained by reheating the sample. The peak height of this glow curve is used as a correction factor for each individual measurement. (We have found that the peak heights of replicate runs are more consistent than the total areas of the glow curves.) The standard statistical deviation of the ratio is reduced to less than

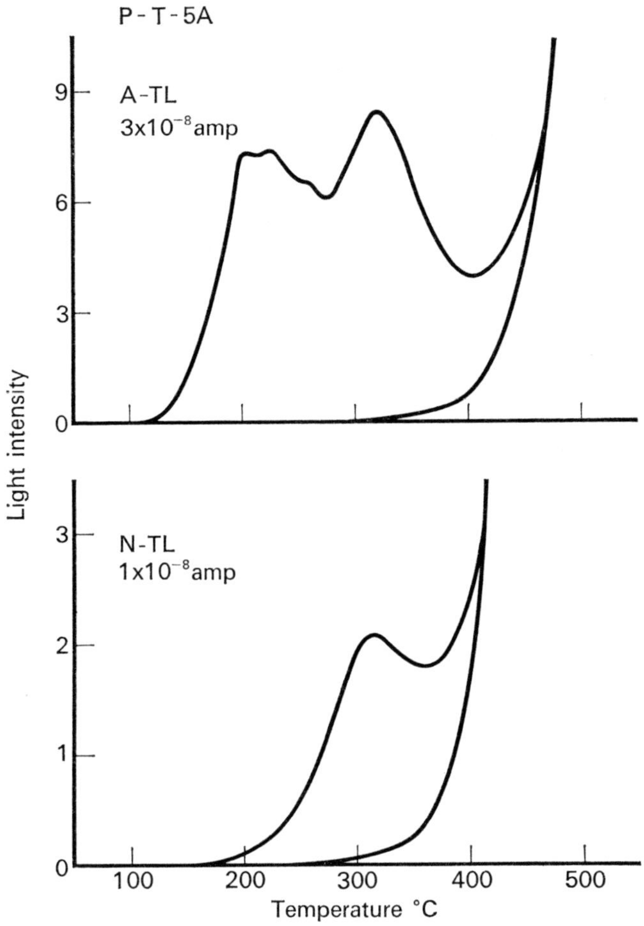

Figure 6 Examples of the *N-TL* and *A-TL* glow curves obtained from measurements of Sample P-T-5A

$\pm 5\%$. Examples of the natural thermoluminescence and artificial thermoluminescence glow curves are shown in fig. 6.

Finally, after the rate of alpha bombardment, the natural thermoluminescence, and the artificial thermoluminescence have been obtained, one may calculate the value of the specific thermoluminescence of the given potsherd as follows:

$$Sp.\ TL = \frac{R}{\alpha} \qquad \text{eq. 2}$$

Where,
Sp. TL = Specific thermoluminescence.
R = The average ratio of (*N-TL*) to (*A-TL*).

4 Results and discussion

For age calibration there are two possible approaches. One is to determine the age directly from the ratio of natural thermoluminescence and natural irradiation multiplied by the inverse ratio of artificial thermoluminescence and irradiation dose as shown below:

$$\text{Age} = \frac{N\text{-}TL}{I_N} \times \frac{I_A}{A\text{-}TL} \qquad \text{eq. 3}$$

Where,
I_N and I_A = Natural and artificial irradiations, respectively.

This might be considered to be an absolute calibration, but there is a serious difficulty – namely, that it is not now possible to measure the inherent radioactivity (plus possibly also the contribution from external surroundings) with precision. There is the problem of evaluating the effectiveness of the different types of radiations, α, β, γ, etc., as well as the actual measurement of all of these extremely low-level radioactivities.

Fortunately, there is another means of age calibration – namely, with samples of known age. This method may be considered an indirect approach, but all factors may be measured with greater precision. The specific thermoluminescence (equation 2) is determined for each sample of known age, and this value is then plotted versus its known age

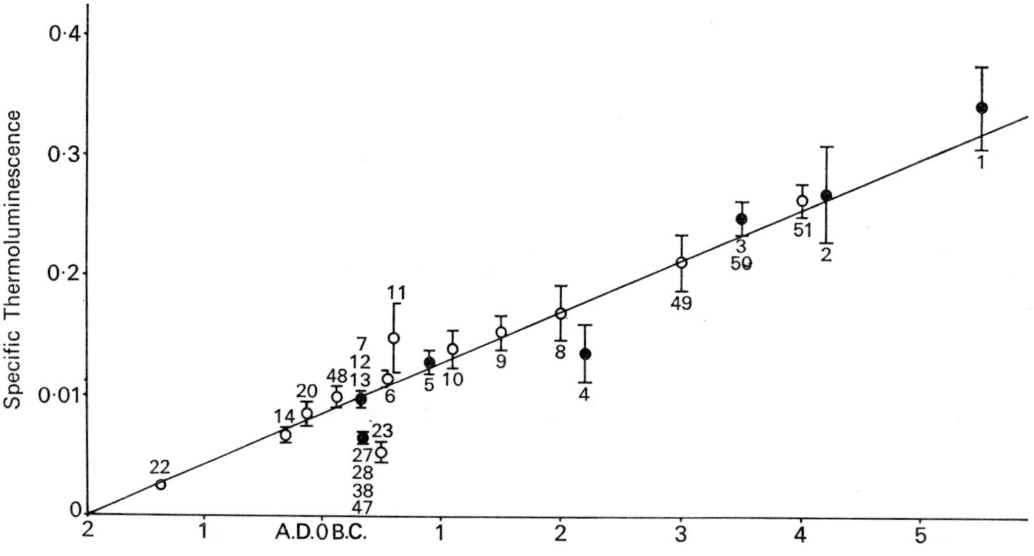

Figure 7 Plot of the specific thermoluminescence versus known-age samples (1966): 1, 2, 3, 4, 5, 9, 10 and 11 from Hasanlu, Iran; 49, 50 and 51 from Susa, Iran; 8 from Baluchistan; 6 and 7 from the Plain of Sybaris, Italy (excavated from four meters below the water table); 12, 13 and 14 from Torre Mordillo, above the Plain of Sybaris, Italy; 20 from Le Muraglie, above the Plain of Sybaris, Italy; 22, Pecos pottery from south-west United States; 23, 27, 28, 38, 47 and 48, Black Glaze sherds from the Agora, Athens

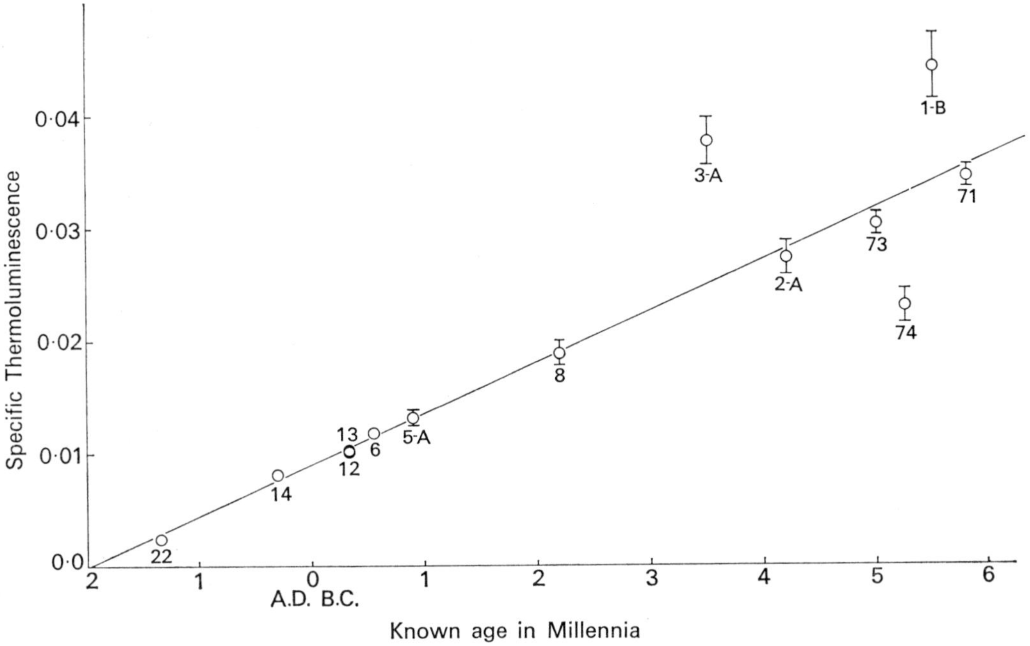

Figure 8 Plot of the specific thermoluminescence versus known-age samples (1967)

as shown in figs 7 and 8. The slope of the line drawn through the average values of these determinations provides the proportionality constant *k* in equation 1, and the ages of samples of unknown age may then be calculated.

In both figs 7 and 8, the age-calibration line is based upon samples from A.D. 300 to 800 B.C. which have been dated firmly by archaeological techniques. The earlier ones are plotted as samples of known age, but the ages of these are dependent upon C^{14} dates of associated samples. In fig. 7, a more complete picture of our measurements of samples of known age is presented than in fig. 8. These were made during 1965–6 (Ralph and Han 1966: 245–7) before the installation of our linear programmed heating system (in March 1967). Even though incomplete, we have shown the data in fig. 8 for purposes of comparison. In both figures, good agreement is noted between specific thermoluminescence and known ages for samples later than 2500 B.C. One exception is the group in fig. 7 (nos 23–47) from the Agora excavations in Athens. These provide an example of loss of metastable electrons due to subsequent heating from continuous occupation at this site. For samples earlier than 2500 B.C. there exist the problems of larger uncertainties as well as some scattering of the so-called known-age samples dated by C^{14} through association only. The scatter appears to be larger in fig. 8, but we should like to point out that not all of the sherds for which the average values were plotted in fig. 7 have yet been remeasured (see, for example, numbers 1, 2, 3). At this time, the important difference that we note between figs 7 and 8 is the significant improvement in the uncertainty of each measurement as shown by the shorter lengths of the lines representative of the standard statistical deviations. The ages of most samples may now be determined with a precision of ±200 years.

Although not shown in the figures, pottery made in the past several centuries can be dated with this method, provided that a sufficient amount of natural thermoluminescence can be detected. A few specific examples are as follows:

(1) Several supposedly Etruscan statuettes were found to be not earlier than A.D. 1850 (Kohler 1967: 16). These figures emitted measurable natural glow curves, but because of their high inherent radioactivities, were proved to be of very young age.

(2) A tile from Rome,[1] purportedly of classical origin, was dated to be approximately A.D. 1700, and therefore, probably, of the Renaissance period. This tile contained normal radioactivity but as revealed in its artificial glow curve, was highly susceptible to radiation damage. It, therefore, was capable of accumulating a sufficient amount of metastable electrons within a relatively short time and it could be dated.

These results indicate that there is a good possibility that thermoluminescence will provide a useful dating method from the period of the Renaissance back to the time of earliest pottery-making.

4.xii.67

University Museum
University of Pennsylvania
Philadelphia

References

Aitken, M. J. 1968. Thermoluminescent Dating in Archaeology. In *Thermoluminescence of Geological Materials*, ed. D. J. McDougall.

Daniels, F., Boyd, C. A. and Saunders, D. F. 1953. Thermoluminescence as a Research Tool. *Science*. 117.

Fleming, S. J. 1966. Study of Thermoluminescence of Crystalline Extracts from Pottery. *Archaeometry*. 9.

Godwin, H. 1962. Half-life of Radiocarbon. *Nature*. 195.

Houtermans, F. G., Jäger, E., Schön, M. and Stauffer, H. 1957. Messungen der Thermolumineszenz als Mittel zur Untersuchung der thermischen und der Strahlungsgeschichte von naturlichen Mineralien und Gesteinen. *Ann. d. Physik*. 20.

Kennedy, G. and Knopff, L. 1960. Dating by Thermoluminescence. *Archaeology*. 13.

Kohler, E. L. 1967. Ultimatum to Terracotta-Forgers. *Expedition*. 9.

Libby, W. F. 1955. *Radiocarbon Dating*. Chicago.

Mazess, R. B. and Zimmerman, D. W. 1966. Pottery Dating from Thermoluminescence. *Science*. 152.

[1] The tile sample was submitted by Mr H. B. VanderPoel, and was found in co-operation with Professor Frank E. Brown of Yale University at an excavation within Paul III's cupola in the Church of S. Maria in Aracoeli upon the Capitoline Hill. It was excavated in 1963 at a depth of 4·20 meters.

Ralph, E. K. and Han, M. C. 1966. Dating of Pottery by Thermoluminescence. *Nature*. 210.

Ralph, E. K. and Han, M. C. 1968. Progress in Thermoluminescent Dating. In *Thermoluminescence of Geological Materials*, ed. D. J. McDougall.

Ralph, E. K., Michael, H. N. and Gruninger, J. Jr. 1965. University of Pennsylvania Dates VII. *Radiocarbon*. 7.

Tite, M. S. 1966. Thermoluminescent Dating of Ancient Ceramics: A Reassessment. *Archaeometry*. 9

Land and freshwater Mollusca in archaeology: chronological aspects

J. G. Evans

This paper discusses aspects of the use of land and freshwater Mollusca in establishing a chronological framework for archaeological deposits. Certain topics will be considered which, while of more theoretical than practical application, will, it is hoped, clarify the background to the use of Mollusca in chronological work. Moreover, as only a limited number of detailed investigations have been made, it is not possible to do more than make one or two general observations and suggest lines for future development of the subject. In case this may sound a despondent note, however, it is clear from work which has been done that the value of molluscan analysis is equivalent to that already established through the use of pollen.

1 Land and freshwater Mollusca

Land and freshwater Mollusca comprise a number of groups of animals of diverse form and habit. The main systematic division is between the bivalves, lamellibranchs or pelecypods (freshwater mussels) and the univalves or gastropods (snails). The bivalves include the large mussels such as *Anodonta* and *Corbicula* and the small, finger-nail or pea clams, *Sphaerium* and *Pisidium.* The gastropods are subdivided into those which are generally gill-breathing and have an operculum or 'door' to close the mouth of the shell (prosobranchs or operculates) and those which are lung-breathing (pulmonates). The former include freshwater species though some have become adapted to life on land. The pulmonates comprise the land snails *par excellence*, such as *Helix*, though there are a number of freshwater families, notably the Lymnaeidae and the Planorbidae. In certain groups of terrestrial pulmonates the shell has become internal or even lost altogether; these are the slugs.

The Mollusca are one of the most successful invertebrate groups and have established themselves in a wide variety of habitats. Non-marine Mollusca, with which this paper is concerned, include those which live on land (terrestrial forms) and those which live in fresh water. In spite of their diversity, however, one feature common to all Mollusca is that they are essentially aquatic animals. Terrestrial molluscs have not evolved efficient structural means for withstanding water loss, so that their habitats and behaviour patterns are largely controlled by the humidity of the environment. Thus the majority of species feed and move around at night when the relative humidity of the air is high; and during the day they confine themselves to moist and sheltered places. Only a few species are able to exist in dry environments, such as grassland plains, bare rocky areas or deserts.

2 Land and freshwater Mollusca in archaeology

Land and freshwater Mollusca are commonly found in archaeological deposits by virtue of their having a mineral shell of calcium carbonate, which is preserved in a wide variety of situations in which the pH is maintained in the neutral or alkaline range. It is under just such conditions, of course, that pollen is least likely to be preserved, and thus Mollusca may be the only chronological indicators available. Typical mollusc-bearing deposits are fluviatile and lacustrine sediments, travertine and a variety of terrestrial sediments, such as cave deposits, wind-blown silt (loess) and sand, calcareous slopewashes and soils. Mollusca are likewise frequently abundant in artificial deposits, such as ditch and pit fills and the occupation debris of mounds, for example, tells and middens. They may also be a component of mud brick.

The study of Mollusca from Pleistocene and archaeological deposits began in the nineteenth century, and the possibility of using Mollusca as climatic, local environmental and chronological indicators of past times has for long been recognized. However, as has recently been pointed out (Ložek 1965), initial investigations were not made on a critical stratigraphical basis, so that only certain principal faunas were determined, such as the loess fauna of Central Europe. Similarly, assemblages from prominent shell layers are well known (the term '*Cyclostoma elegans* zone' was used for one such in the fill of the shafts of Neolithic flint mines in southern England), but these may include a number of distinct faunas, reflecting a succession of different environments, since the stratigraphy of terrestrial deposits, especially soils, is often extremely fine, and requires detailed and close sampling to be of value (Evans 1967). Also, a clear understanding of the origin of a deposit, and of the mechanism whereby shells are incorporated into it, is a prerequisite to any proper interpretation of the ecological significance of subfossil faunas (Sparks 1964a: 89–91). Thus the fauna of a soil which has formed *in situ* is of strictly local origin, whereas that from a slopewash or windblown deposit may be derived from several acres and include faunas from several kinds of micro-habitat. A further deficiency is that many collections have been made by hand-picking shells. While this may be useful in providing adult examples of the larger species, often lacking in bulk samples, it has been shown (Sparks 1961: 72) how drastically this may bias the fauna towards the large, or otherwise readily recognizable, species.

Apart from incomplete stratigraphical information, the ecological significance of ancient faunas has often been misunderstood due to a lack of data about the habitat preferences and environmental factors controlling the range of many of the critical species. Many workers who have been concerned with using Mollusca as climatic and chronological indicators have failed to understand the way in which local environmental factors control the composition of a fauna. This applies particularly to the moisture regime which, as far as it affects land molluscs, may often be governed by local factors such as the thickness and texture of the soil, the character of the subsoil, the topography and the vegetation, and *not* by the overall rainfall value. This means that similarities in molluscan faunas may reflect similarities only in local environmental conditions, not in climate, and may thus be of no chronological significance. For further discussion of this subject, the reader is referred to the papers already quoted by Sparks (1961, 1964a) and Ložek (1965), to a third paper by Sparks (1963) having a specific bearing on archaeology, and to three papers by Kerney (1963, 1968; Kerney *et al.* 1964).

3 Chronological aspects

The distribution and abundance of molluscan species in the world is heterogeneous. This is related in the first instance to the evolution of distinct groups of Mollusca in different parts of the world, the individuality of which is enhanced by major climatic differences over the earth's surface and by geographical barriers to dispersal, mainly the oceans and high mountain ranges. On a lesser scale, variation relates to local habitat diversity, each habitat having its own distinct fauna. In addition, a fauna may reflect the history of environmental change so that similar habitats may yet have different faunas if their history be dissimilar. Finally, man has caused changes in the molluscan fauna of various parts of the world, not only by interference with the environment but by acting as a dispersal agent for certain species. In general, therefore, the pattern of molluscan populations at any one time relates to factors of both a spatial and historical kind. The chronological value of this pattern is limited to those areas of human culture over which faunal changes are synchronous and to those periods when faunal change takes place more rapidly than cultural change. The synchroneity of faunal change will depend on the extent and nature of environmental change and on the rate of dispersal of various species. The rate of faunal change will be controlled by the rate of evolution and the response to environmental change and dispersal by man.

(a) *Evolution*

'The outburst of evolutionary development appears to have taken place at an earlier date among land and freshwater Mollusca than it did among the mammals and already to have slowed down to such an extent that little more than subspecific differentiation occurred during the Pleistocene' (Kimball *in* Zeuner 1959: 329). Sparks, of the British fauna, writes: 'it seems practically impossible to detect evolutionary changes in non-marine Mollusca in the Quaternary period' (1963: 315), and the same would seem to apply to the North American fauna. Exceptions may occur in the genus *Viviparus*, represented by a variety of species in the Tertiary and Quaternary; and perhaps also in *Valvata*. In North America it has been suggested that the freshwater planorbid, *Promenetus exacuous exacuous*, known only from Sangamonian (Last) Interglacial and later times, may have evolved from the Middle Pleistocene species *Promenetus exacuous kansasensis* (Taylor 1965: 601).

There has been a tendency among workers on fossil Mollusca to erect new species on insufficient morphological evidence, without giving due heed to the variation in modern and fossil forms. This has led to the suggestion that certain species have evolved, flourished and then become extinct during set intervals of Pleistocene time; that is, these species are *zone fossils* in the geological sense of the word. The application to these of such subspecific names as *pleistocenica, yarmouthensis* etc. has enhanced this concept. Evolution, almost by definition, must proceed hand in hand with extinction, and, in the absence of environmental pressures, in theory at the same rate, so that the two processes cancel each other out with respect to the number of species living at any one time. However, while the rate of evolution in Mollusca has slowed down by Pleistocene times, the rate of environmental change has dramatically increased, and this has caused the extinction of a number of species, especially in north temperate latitudes where fluctuations of temperature have been most marked. In other words, there has been a net loss of species. But this relates barely, if at all, to evolutionary change and is merely an extension of that aspect of molluscan zoogeography which is discussed below, namely the alteration of the distribution and abundance of certain species in response to environmental change. This is not to deny the possibility of evolution having taken place, but simply to stress that more taxonomic and stratigraphical work is necessary before zone fossils can be established for Pleistocene time. The problem has been discussed by various workers, among them Sparks (1963: 315), Shimek (1930: 40) and, from the archaeological viewpoint, Eiseley (1937).

Evolution need not be confined to morphological changes; the physiology and ecology (biotype) of a species may also change, and this without concomitant changes in shell morphology (West 1968: 124–5). Perhaps the best known example is that of the gastropod *Potamopyrgus jenkinsi* which in Britain has spread from brackish to freshwater habitats during the last hundred years. In the fossil record physiological changes can be detected only if there is detailed and independent evidence of the environment, or if the presence of a particular species is anomalous in terms of its present-day ecology with respect to the rest of the assemblage. Thus the land snail, *Pupilla muscorum*, occurs in the Late-Weichselian of Britain in association with species and in situations which suggest a marsh environment. This is at variance with its present-day ecological requirements which restrict it to dry places. It can never be quite certain, however, that such ecological anomalies have an evolutionary basis, since unknown environmental factors may be involved. This applies particularly to the cold periods of the Pleistocene, when the present-day temperate regions were within the sphere of periglacial climate, and when climatic conditions of a kind unknown at the present date may well have prevailed, enabling xerophile and hygrophile species of Mollusca to coexist.

(b) *Alteration in the distribution and abundance of Mollusca in response to environmental change*

The composition of molluscan populations alters in response to environmental change. The degree of alteration will vary more or less directly with the rate and amplitude of change, and will be influenced also by geographical barriers controlling migrations in and out of an area. Thus in the Tertiary Era, when climatic change was slow, we cannot expect to build a detailed chronology on the pattern of molluscan change. The Pleistocene, however, provides us not only with rapid and intense climatic oscillations but also with large-scale changes in the configuration of geographical barriers, notably the rise and fall of ocean level, causing changes in the distribution pattern of land and sea, and the retreat and advance of continental ice-sheets.

The overriding environmental factors controlling the composition of molluscan populations are climatic (temperature and rainfall), and a change in the value of one of these may be reflected by a change in the distribution and abundance of one or more species in a population. Where a species is at the limit of its range with respect to a particular climatic factor, then it will be most sensitive to, and provide the most critical indication of, a change in the value of that factor; that is, slight climatic changes will be registered. Towards the centre of the range of a species only more intensive changes will be registered.

But before a species can be safely used as a chronological indicator, we must have detailed knowledge of the factors controlling its range. Climatic changes, in that they are generally widespread and synchronous, provide the safest framework on which to base a chronology. Environmental changes other than those of climatic origin may also cause the composition of a molluscan population to alter; for instance, human interference with the soil and vegetation may have a quite drastic effect. But unlike climatic changes, these may not be synchronous, in which case faunal similarities will be a reflection only of habitat similarity and no criterion of age. Even with climatic changes there may be a time-lag before their reflection in the fauna. This is due partly to the slow rate of dispersal of Mollusca into areas which have become ecologically acceptable, and partly to their ability to hang on in locally suitable habitats in areas where the overall environmental regime has

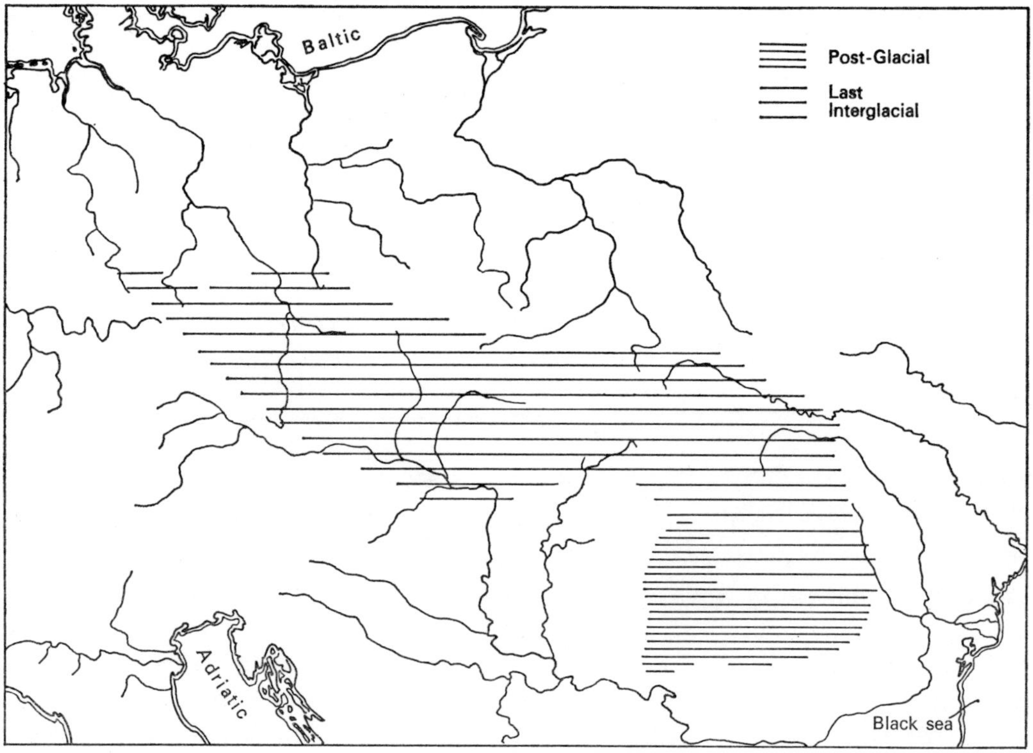

Figure 9 Last Interglacial and Post-glacial distribution of *Helicigona banatica* in Central Europe. (Re-drawn after Ložek 1965.)

become adverse. Thus Sparks, of the Last Interglacial fauna in Britain writes: 'The apparent slowness of arrival of Mollusca in the early part of the Interglacial is contrasted with their apparent survival into intemperate climates in the later part of the Interglacial' (1964b: 23). Finally, we must know the area over which a species can be used as an indicator. In fig. 9 the restriction of the Central European land snail, *Helicigona banatica*, in the Post-glacial, compared with its former widespread distribution in the Last Interglacial, is clearly brought out (Ložek 1965: 213). Only in the area where the species is found outside its Post-glacial distribution can it be used as an interglacial indicator.

(c) *Human introductions*

Due to the presence of geographical or climatological barriers to dispersal, a number of species have been unable to occupy to the full their potential range. For instance, the tropical zone effectively prevents intermixing of species from temperate regions of the northern and southern hemispheres; and the Post-glacial submergence of land bridges has resulted in island faunas being impoverished by comparison with their counterparts on the continental mainland. Through the agency of man, however, such barriers may be overcome, and the spread of certain species of Mollusca, either accidentally in the course of human migrations and trade, or deliberately as food or for other economic reasons, has occurred in several parts of the world. The examples of the Roman snail, *Helix pomatia*, and the common snail, *Helix aspersa*, widely used for food in antiquity and to the present day, are perhaps the most well known and best documented. Quick (1952) discusses the spread of both species from temperate Europe into the New World and the southern hemisphere in the nineteenth and twentieth centuries.

The accidental spread of a number of species has also taken place on a large scale over the last 2,000 years or so. This relates not only to trade movements etc., the active agencies of dispersal, but also to the opening up of suitable habitats through forest clearance and agriculture. For instance, the drying out of the soil has favoured the spread of the Mediterranean xerophile genus, *Helicella*, into western and central Europe.

The basis of a chronology established on the evidence of the molluscan record is thus essentially similar to that used in palynology, but with the important difference that the molluscan record generally reflects local environmental conditions to a marked degree; the pollen record is more representative of changes over a wide area and is thus better suited to the detection of climatic change. This is due to differences in the way in which the two kinds of organism are incorporated into soils and sediments. The pollen content, especially of peat and lake sediments, may derive from a wide area, since it is air-borne in the first place and may be further transported by water. Similarly, the molluscan content of fluviatile sediments may derive from a wide area, and contain not only aquatic but land snails also. But in the case of terrestrial sediments this is not so. Due to the relatively large size of molluscan shells, they are not transported long distances by terrestrial or aerial agencies, with the result that the molluscan content of soils is of strictly local origin, and that of sub-aerial sediments probably derived from not more than a few acres. This is the main limitation of molluscan analysis as a chronological technique, applying to the use of evolutionary changes, environmentally-induced changes and human introductions alike. Each species is not distributed at random over its range but is restricted to a particular habitat, so that absence of a species, or variations in its abundance, may simply reflect local environmental conditions and be no criterion of age. In spite of these difficulties, however, work in two areas, namely central Europe and southern England, has demonstrated that a detailed record of climatic change can be preserved and separated from the effects of local environmental influence, and is thus of chronological value. This we will now discuss.

4 Southern England

Little systematic work has been done in Britain on faunas earlier than those of Hoxnian Interglacial age. West (1968) gives a bibliography of the more recent work. Hoxnian faunas are known from Hoxne (Sparks *in* West 1956) and Swanscombe (Castell *in* Ovey 1964); and Kerney (1959) has investigated a Hoxnian tufa which yielded a rich terrestrial fauna, at least one species of which, *Acicula diluviana*, is not known from later faunas in Britain or Europe. The fauna of the Last (Eemian or Ipswichian) Interglacial is known in some detail (Sparks 1964b) and an attempted correlation with the pollen record has been made. But, apart from the possibility of distinguishing the faunas of the various interglacials one from the other, within individual interglacials little zonation is yet possible. Faunas from the cold phases of the Pleistocene are inadequately known, but are certainly restricted to a limited number of species and will probably turn out to be fairly monotonous. Sparks (1963: 315) has warned against using such 'facies faunas' in chronological work.

Mainly through the work of Kerney (1963, 1968) the sequence of faunal change through the Late-Weichselian and Post-glacial (Flandrian) periods is now well known, and at a number of sites a fairly detailed zonation is possible. Fig. 10 shows a generalized diagram of the faunal changes in south-east England during these periods. The Late-Weichselian (pollen zones I–III) fauna is restricted and of open-country aspect. *Pupilla muscorum* is an important element of the fauna, and *Columella columella*, which does not survive into the Post-glacial, may be considered an index species. During the climatic amelioration of zone II (Allerød Interstadial) a number of thermophile species of more southern affinities than the rest of the fauna come in, notably *Abida secale* and *Helicella itala*. The restricted nature of the fauna is maintained, however, through zone III and it is not until the beginning of the Post-glacial that further diversification sets in.

At first (zones IV to VI) a number of northerly elements appear in strength (fig. 10, *Carychium*, *Acanthinula* etc.), some for the first time, others which were already present in the Late-Weichselian. The period is characterized by two Boreal-Alpine snails, *Vertigo genesii* and *Discus ruderatus*. Later, towards the end of zone VI (i.e. at the beginning of the Post-glacial thermal optimum), species of more southerly affinities such as *Pomatias elegans* and *Discus rotundatus* appear, while *Vertigo genesii* and *Discus ruderatus* become rare and eventually die out altogether. These changes are, in the main, temperature controlled, though the spread of forest over Britain, providing shelter and moisture, was obviously not without effect in favouring a rich fauna; it was certainly responsible for the temporary extinction of the open-country element of the fauna.

During the later part of the Post-glacial from about 3000 B.C., when human interference with the vegetation and soil began, the situation is more complex since it becomes

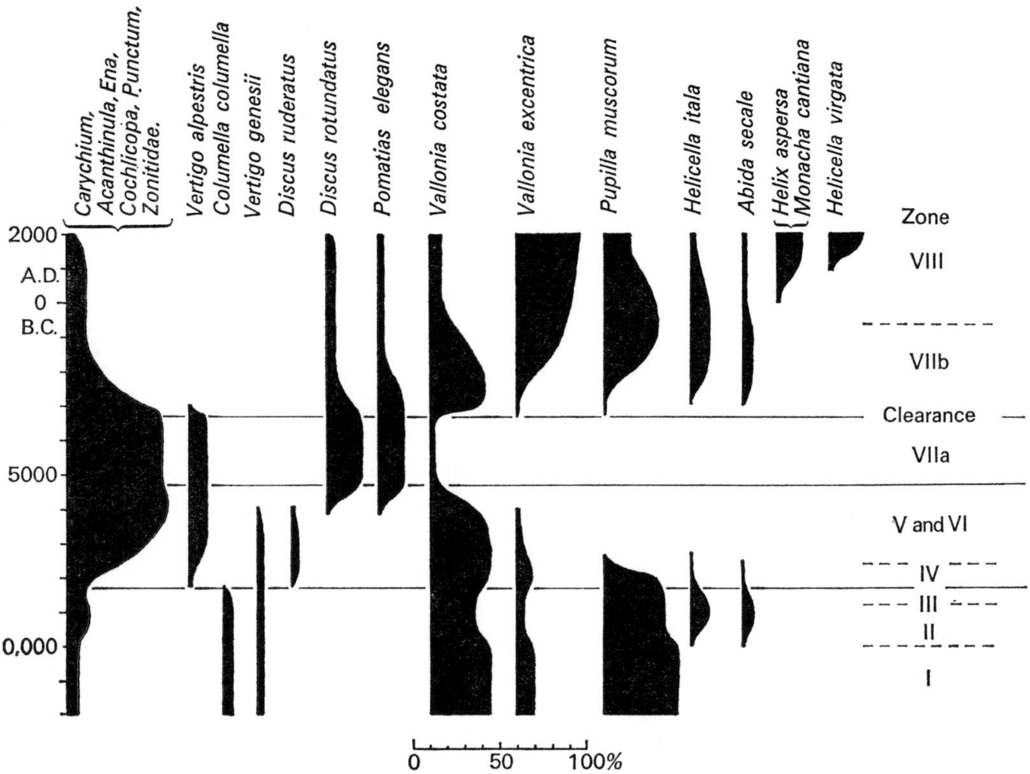

Figure 10 Generalized diagram of the pattern of faunal change in south-east England during the Late-Weichselian and Post-glacial periods in an area which is now open country. To clarify the diagram, only certain species have been shown. *Carychium* etc. includes *Lauria cylindracea, Cepaea, Hygromia* and *Vitrina*; *Vertigo alpestris* includes *Vertigo substriata* and *Acanthinula lamellata*; *Discus rotundatus* includes *Acicula fusca*

increasingly difficult to distinguish between faunal changes which are climatically controlled and those which are caused by man. Man-induced changes mainly result in the fauna assuming a more open aspect; xerophiles and grassland species become a major component, while certain of the extreme conservative species of the Post-glacial woodland fauna become confined to areas of damper climate in the north and west of the country (fig. 10, *Vertigo alpestris* etc.). Other faunal changes, however, such as the restriction of *Pomatias elegans* and *Ena montana*, have been convincingly shown to be, at least in part, the result of a lowering of temperature since the Bronze Age (Post-glacial thermal decline) (Kerney 1968).

Faunal changes caused by human interference with the environment cannot be used as a basis for establishing a chronology unless they are synchronous over a wide area, which is generally not the case. However, in southern England primary forest clearance seems to be associated at first with an increase of *Vallonia costata* among the open-ground species (Evans 1968). This is to be expected as this species forms a minor component of the zone VIIa woodland fauna, never dying out altogether. Perhaps it may not be too rash to suggest that the presence in abundance of *V. costata*, and the absence of other open-ground species, is an indication of Neolithic activity. With increased opening up of the environment, three other species soon become present; they are *Vallonia excentrica*, *Helicella itala* and *Pupilla muscorum*, and together with *Vallonia costata* they come to comprise a major component of the fauna. The later history of these four species depends very much on local patterns of land use, but in general it is *Vallonia excentrica* which eventually becomes most widespread and abundant, the others becoming restricted, though often locally abundant in suitable habitats.

Species introduced by man include *Helix aspersa*, *Monacha cantiana* and possibly *Helix pomatia* in the Roman period; and various species of *Helicella* (fig. 10, e.g. *Helicella virgata*) in medieval times (Kerney 1966).

The possibilities of using such a scheme for dating archaeological deposits can, as yet, only be speculated upon, and the fact remains that the most important use of land Mollusca is as indicators of local environmental conditions (Fowler and Evans 1967: 296–7). On the chronological side, limitations are imposed by the fact that most work has been done on sites later than 3000 B.C., when the effect of man complicates the picture of faunal change. During the 1930s a considerable amount of work was done on land Mollusca from archaeological sites in south-east England, and an attempt was made to set up a sequence of faunal change, the basis of which was said to be climatically controlled. The possibilities of such a system for dating archaeological sites were quickly exploited, for instance by Mrs M. E. Cunnington with her 'Evidence of climate derived from snail shells and its bearing on the date of Stonehenge' (1933). Burchell (1961) also attempted something along similar lines. In the light of recent research (Kerney 1968) such work has become largely discredited. On the other hand, during the earlier part of the Post-glacial, and possibly also during the Late-Weichselian when, as we have seen, certain clear-cut faunal changes took place which are controlled primarily by climate, one feels there may be scope for using Mollusca as chronological indicators. Possible sites are those in which Mesolithic artefacts are stratified in the tufaceous deposits often abundant in the shells of land and freshwater molluscs; for example, Blashenwell (Bury 1950) and Prestatyn (Clark 1938). The faunas of caves may also repay investigation.

5 Central Europe

The Pleistocene mollusc fauna of central and western Europe is known from fluviatile deposits of ancient river terraces, lake marls, travertines, loess and associated soils. Most of our knowledge comes from Czechoslovakia, and mainly through the work of Ložek. A useful English summary is that of Ložek (1965), and the most comprehensive work is Ložek (1964).

The warm phases of the early Pleistocene are characterized by species such as *Helicigona čapeki* and *Gastrocopta serotina*, unknown from later periods. The presence of *Gastrocopta* is of interest. This genus is now extinct in Europe but may be found still in North America, a situation which probably reflects the greater scope for molluscan migrations in North America than in Europe. Index fossils are also present for the later interglacial periods. 'Central Europe in the Last Interglacial (Eemian) contained *Gastro-*

copta theeli . . ., which is known today only from temperate Asia; it also had a number of southern elements, e.g. *Helicigona banatica* . . . which now occur over a relatively small area in the South Carpathians or Alps' (Ložek 1965: 213) (fig. 9). The fauna of the Göttweig Interstadial at the beginning of the Last Glaciation is characterized by climatically tolerant species, and can be distinguished from the fauna of the Last Interglacial. The Göttweig fauna is, however, much richer than associated loess faunas and faunas from more minor Last Glaciation interstadials (Ložek and Kukla 1959).

The cold phases of the Last Glaciation are characterized by the *Columella* fauna, named after the species *Columella columella*, which, although present in earlier glacial periods, is most abundant during the last. This species now lives in Scandinavia, north of 67° latitude, and to the east in Siberia, between 61° and 69° latitude, and its southward spread during the Last Glaciation in Europe may be compared with the eastward spread of *Columella columella alticola* in North America during the same period.

Faunal changes in the Late- and Post-glacial periods compare with the sequence in the British Isles. There is a rather restricted Late-glacial fauna; the early part of the Post-glacial is characterized by *Discus ruderatus* which later, although not becoming extinct, is restricted to the montane zone and certain lowland relict localities; there is a rich Atlantic (thermal optimum) fauna; during the Sub-boreal period human interference causes certain forest elements of the fauna to decline while steppe elements such as *Theba cartusiana* and *Helicella striata* become characteristic; and, in the recent period, a humanly-introduced species of *Helicella*, *H. candicans* appears.

Land Mollusca have been studied in detail from a number of archaeological sites, for instance the Palaeolithic site of Dolní Věstonice (Klima *et al.* 1961) and the Neolithic settlement of Zámeček (Ložek 1951). Unfortunately, however, decalcification of the loess through leaching during the Post-glacial has often resulted in the destruction of land molluscs, as has happened, for instance, at Bylany.

6 North America

Much of the work in North America has been done on Pleistocene faunas from freshwater and loess deposits of the Great Plains. The most comprehensive summary is that of Taylor (1965). Little of value has been done on archaeological deposits.

Two differences from the situation in central and western Europe have an important bearing on the pattern of faunal change. First, the North American ice sheet extended some 10° of latitude further south than that of Scandinavia, causing climatic changes of rainfall to be of some considerable importance. Second, the main mountain ranges run north/south rather than east/west, so that movements of Mollusca in a north/south direction in response to temperature fluctuations will be unhindered, and there will be less chance of species becoming extinct. This means that differences between the faunas of the various interglacials and glacials will be less marked than in Europe.

The faunal changes may be summarized as follows. During the Nebraskan and Kansan Glaciations conditions on the plains appear to have been fairly equable. Molluscan faunas were rich in species and both northern and southern elements were present. More than one-third of Nebraskan species are unknown from later periods (Frye and Leonard

1965). Faunas of Illinoian age are less rich and their affinities are northerly; a number come from loess. The Sangamonian (Last) Interglacial is the only interglacial from which Mollusca have certainly been obtained; the affinities of the fauna are southerly. The Wisconsin was the most severe of all the North American glaciations and molluscan faunas of this age are correspondingly depauperate and characteristic. 'The southward and eastward spread in the Great Plains and Ohio Valley of a cold-steppe fauna during part of Wisconsin glacial times is an event that is unknown previously in the Pleistocene' (Taylor 1965: 606). The period is characterized by the alpine Rocky Mountain snail *Columella columella alticola* and by *Discus shimeki*.

In spite of the amount of analysis of Mollusca from North American Pleistocene deposits, one feels that the data available is not of a sufficiently critical nature to be of chronological value. This is partly because of the insecure stratigraphy of the deposits, but also because a number of faunal differences are almost certainly a reflection of both local environmental conditions and collecting deficiences. Detailed stratigraphical investigations on individual sites would prove rewarding. Clearly there is an abundance of suitable sites, and, in the absence of pollen from many of these, Mollusca would seem to be the best approach to palaeoclimatic and chronological investigations.

7 The Middle East

Work in the Middle East has been confined to archaeological sites. Little systematic collecting has been done, however, most collections having been made by hand-picking shells. One of the difficulties with all archaeological work on Mollusca, and particularly in the Middle East, is the problem of distinguishing between shells derived from animals living on a site and those brought in by man for food. This topic is discussed by Reed (1962) in his classic 'Snails on a Persian Hillside'. An attempt to systematize the use of land snails as climatic indicators in Iraq was made by Harris (1961), based on the present-day ranges of certain species. The theoretical basis of this is sound, but there is a virtual lack of subfossil material, so that comparisons cannot be made.

8 Africa

Little work has been done on the subfossil Mollusca of Africa, though suitable deposits are present. Verdcourt (1963) on the Miocene Mollusca of Rusinga Island, Lake Victoria, found that the fauna was not very different from that which prevails today. Differences can be ascribed to changes of rainfall, resulting, in hilly areas, in a disjunct distribution of certain relatively hygrophilous species. However, interestingly enough, when the opportunity arises, due to geographical isolation, rapid evolution and endemism may result. Thus Fuchs, of the Pleistocene deposits of Lake Albert and Lake Edward, wrote: 'The Mollusca . . . are of interest because of the large numbers of extinct species in an assembly of Pleistocene age, while the known Miocene deposits of Central Africa have been shown to contain a majority of living species' (1936: 93). The Mollusca of the Fayum in Egypt were investigated by Caton-Thompson and Gardner (1934). Here an interesting alternation between Nilotic species and endemic species was detected and equated with periods when the Fayum was linked to the Nile and when it was cut off. Fossil faunas are also known through the work of Sparks and Grove (1961, 1964) from the Central Sahara and north-east Nigeria.

9 Conclusions

It is salutary to recall that the presence of molluscs in archaeological deposits was recognized more than a century ago, and yet their detailed investigation has only recently begun. Contrasted with the rapid development of palynology in the last forty years, and considering the potential of Mollusca in chronological and palaeo-climatic studies, it is perhaps rather surprising that such a state of affairs should have arisen. In this paper I have pointed out some of the reasons for deficiencies in the study of Mollusca in the past, and at the same time have shown something of their potential in chronological and palaeo-climatic research. In conclusion, the need cannot be stressed too much for detailed stratigraphical data, and for information about the way in which environmental factors control the distribution and abundance of molluscan species.

Acknowledgement

This paper was written during the tenure of a Natural Environment Research Council Assistantship.

19.iv.69

Institute of Archaeology
London

References

Burchell, J. P. T. 1961. Land shells and their role in dating deposits of Post-glacial times in south-east England. *Archaeological News Letter.* 7:34–8.

Bury, H. 1950. Blashenwell tufa. *Proc. Bournemouth Nat. Sci. Soc.* 39:48–51.

Caton-Thompson, G. and Gardner, E. W. 1934. *The Desert Fayum.* London.

Clark, J. G. D. 1938. Microlithic industries from tufa deposits at Prestatyn, Flintshire, and Blashenwell, Dorset. *Proc. Prehist. Soc.* 4:330–4.

Cunnington, M. E. 1933. Evidence of climate derived from snail shells and its bearing on the date of Stonehenge. *Wilts. Archaeol. Nat. Hist. Mag.* 46:350–5.

Eiseley, L. C. 1937. Index Mollusca and their bearing on certain problems of prehistory: a critique. *Publs Philad. Anthrop. Soc.* 1:77–93.

Evans, J. G. 1967. *The Stratification of Mollusca in Chalk Soils and their Relevance to Archaeology.* Unpublished Ph.D. thesis, University of London.

Evans, J. G. 1968. Changes in the composition of land molluscan populations in north Wiltshire during the last 5,000 years. *Symp. Zool. Soc. Lond.* 22:293–317.

Fowler, P. J. and Evans, J. G. 1967. Plough-marks, lynchets and early fields. *Antiquity.* 41:289–301.

Frye, J. C. and Leonard, A. B. 1965. Quaternary of the southern Great Plains. In *The Quaternary of the United States*, eds H. E. Wright and D. G. Frey. Princeton. 203–16.

Fuchs, V. E. 1936. Extinct Pleistocene Mollusca from Lake Edward, Uganda, and their bearing on the Tanganyika problem. *J. Linn. Soc.* (Zoology). 40:93–106.

Harris, S. A. 1961. On the land snails of Iraq and their potential use in determining past climatic conditions. *Sumer.* 17:107–13.

Kerney, M. P. 1959. An interglacial tufa near Hitchin, Hertfordshire. *Proc. Geol. Ass.* 70:322–37.

Kerney, M. P. 1963. Late-glacial deposits on the Chalk of south-east England. *Phil. Trans. R. Soc.*, B. 246:203–54.

Kerney, M. P. 1966. Snails and Man in Britain. *J. Conch., Lond.* 26:3–14.

Kerney, M. P. 1968. Britain's fauna of land Mollusca and its relation to the Post-glacial thermal optimum. *Symp. Zool. Soc. Lond.* 22:273–91.

Kerney, M. P., Brown, E. H. and Chandler, T. J. 1964. The Late-glacial and Post-glacial history of the Chalk escarpment near Brook, Kent. *Phil. Trans. R. Soc.*, B. 248: 135–204.

Klima, B., Kukla, J., Ložek, V. and Vries, H. de. 1961. Stratigraphie des Pleistozäns und alter des Paläolithischen rastplatzes in der ziegelei von Dolní Věstonice (Unter-Wisternitz). *Anthropozoikum.* 11:93–145.

Ložek, V. 1951. The Quaternary molluscs of the settlement 'Zámeček' at Nitriansky Hrádok (Extended summary of Czech text). *Anthropozoikum.* 1:37–52.

Ložek, V. 1964. Quartärmollusken der Tschechoslowakei. *Rozpr. Ústred. Úst. Geol.* 31:1–374.

Ložek, V. 1965. Problems of analysis of the Quaternary nonmarine molluscan fauna in Europe. *Geol. Soc. Am.* Special Paper 84:201–18.

Ložek, V. and Kukla, J. 1959. Das lössprofil von Leitmeritz an der Elbe, Nordböhmen. *Eiszeitalter Gegenw.* 10:81–104.

Ovey, C. D. (ed.). 1964. *The Swanscombe Skull. A survey of research on a Pleistocene site.* Royal Anthropological Institute Occasional Memoir No. 20.

Quick, H. E. 1952. Emigrant British Snails. *Proc. Malac. Soc. Lond.* 29:181–9.

Reed, C. A. 1962. Snails on a Persian hillside: ecology – prehistory – gastronomy. *Postilla.* 66:1–20.

Shimek, B. 1930. Pleistocene and Recent mollusks. *Nautilus.* 44:37–41.

Sparks, B. W. 1961. The ecological interpretation of Quaternary non-marine Mollusca. *Proc. Linn. Soc. Lond.* 172: 71–80.

Sparks, B. W. 1963. Non-marine Mollusca and archaeology. In *Science in Archaeology*, eds D. Brothwell and E. Higgs. London. 313–23.

Sparks, B. W. 1964a. Non-marine Mollusca and Quaternary ecology. *J. Anim. Ecol.* 33 (suppl.): 87–98.

Sparks, B. W. 1964b. The distribution of non-marine Mollusca in the Last Interglacial in south-east England. *Proc. Malac. Soc. Lond.* 36:7–25.

Sparks, B. W. and Grove, A. T. 1961. Some Quaternary fossil non-marine Mollusca from the central Sahara. *J. Linn. Soc.* (Zoology). 44:355–64.

Sparks, B. W. and Grove, A. T. 1964. Fossil non-marine Mollusca from Mongonu, north-east Nigeria. *Overseas Geol. Miner. Resour.* 9:190–5.

Taylor, D. W. 1965. The study of Pleistocene nonmarine mollusks in North America. In *The Quaternary of the United States*, eds H. E. Wright and D. G. Frey. Princeton. 597–611.

Verdcourt, B. 1963. The Miocene non-marine Mollusca of Rusinga Island, Lake Victoria, and other localities in Kenya. *Palaeontographica*, A. 121:1–37.

West, R. G. 1956. The Quaternary deposits at Hoxne, Suffolk. *Phil. Trans. R. Soc.*, B. 239:265–356.

West, R. G. 1968. *Pleistocene Geology and Biology with especial reference to the British Isles.* London.

Zeuner, F. E. 1959. *The Pleistocene Period: Its Climate, Chronology and Faunal Successions.* London.

Archaeology with a short, isolated time-scale: New Zealand

Wilfred Shawcross

New Zealand (fig. 11) was probably one of the last fertile, substantial areas of the earth to have been colonized by prehistoric man. It marks the end of migratory movements and its former isolation seems to have ensured little or no cross-play with other societies. Thus, within limits, what took place in New Zealand must have resulted from the inherent powers of its settlers, rather than from cultural and technological 'leapfrogging', found in areas more open to the diffusion of influences from centres of development. Such a situation is most suitable for the study of cultural processes, which, indeed, the archaeology of the country amply shows to have taken place (see Golson and Gathercole 1962 for a useful outline). But any study of cultural processes will require some control over the time dimension, the weak point in the logic of earlier generations in ethnology. The need for this control is taken for granted by archaeologists, who normally divert a considerable amount of effort towards establishing and refining time-scales.

Yet the archaeologist also experiences difficulty over handling time, perhaps more than he suspects. The root of the difficulty seems to lie in the archaeologist wishing to perceive historically exact events, when his methods of time measurement would permit him only to make generalizations. How many cultural sequences throughout the world are there, neatly divided into boxes of time, with exact boundaries, which are quite outside the archaeologist's power to define? They would be harmless enough if so much more was not erected on such spuriously exact foundations. It is not, however, the purpose of this paper to hunt out 'wrong-thinking' in others, though a surprising amount of self-righteousness may be hidden beneath the surface of academic writing; the intention is rather to face up to the fact that there is no known method of time measurement which will yield the precise age of an event. This is well reflected in the misunderstandings of archaeologists over radiocarbon dates. It is not to be wondered at that an exact-seeming figure, although followed by a mathematical recognition of vagueness ($\pm$), may be mistaken for an event. The true situation has been lucidly explained in one of the few available texts on radiocarbon dating for the layman, that by H. A. Polach and J. Golson (1966: 15).

1 Methods of time-measurement applicable to New Zealand prehistory

New Zealand appears to have been totally isolated in ancient times from any civilization with a calendar. Consequently, its prehistory cannot be cross-dated through trade goods

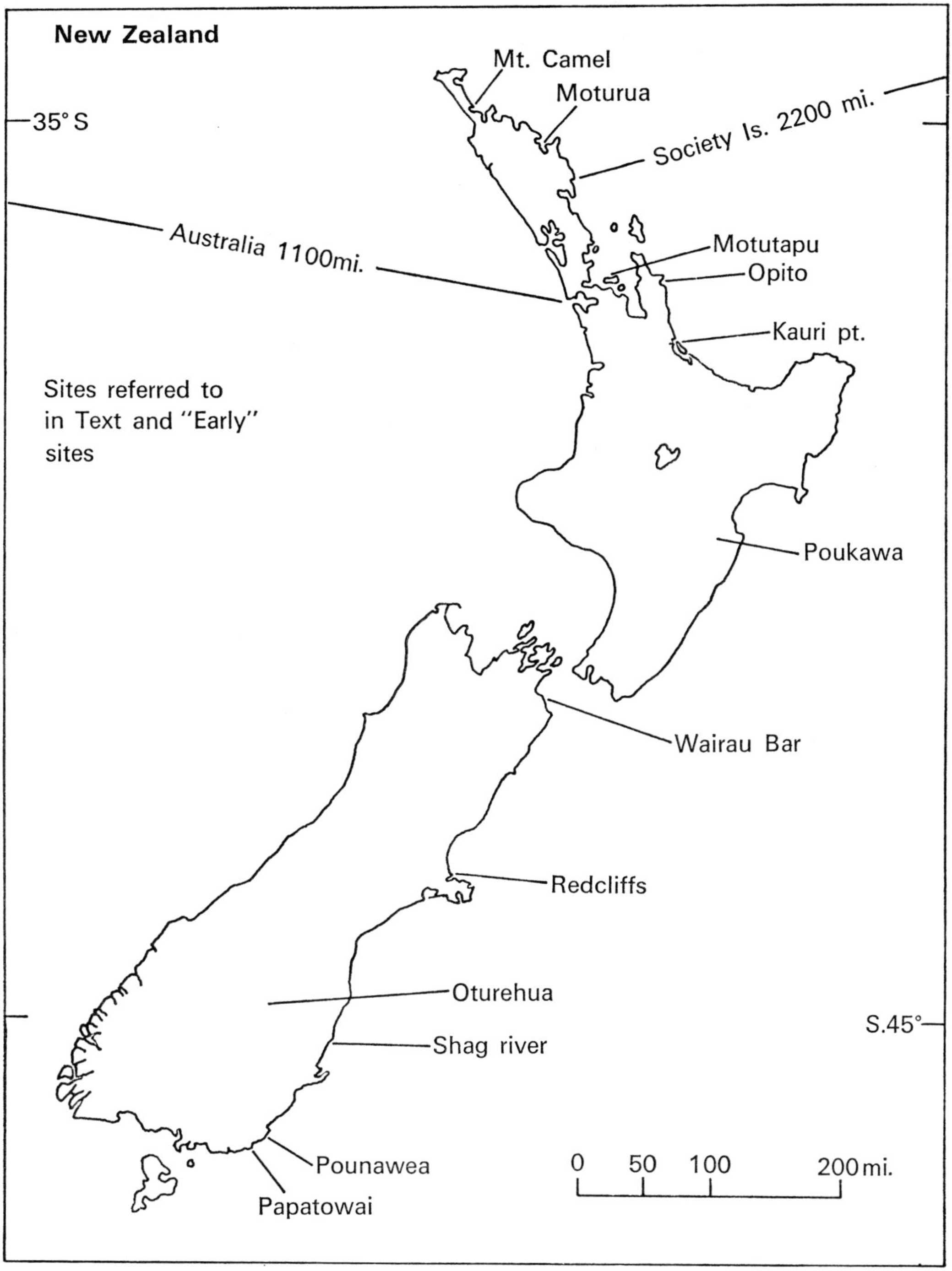

Figure 11 Map of New Zealand showing sites mentioned in the text and the distribution of the majority of early sites along the east coast. It also indicates the position of the country in relation to Australia and the Society Islands.

or diffused traits. Even the era of dispersal of the ancestral Polynesian stock, presumably from South East Asia, is uncertain (see Suggs 1960: 65, who correlates the dispersal with political developments in Shang dynasty China). Therefore, the archaeologist is forced to construct independent time-scales in order to establish a structure for prehistory. The first of such independent scales was introduced in the nineteenth century, when it was recognized that Polynesian genealogical tables showed a high degree of internal consistency and were not, as Europeans may have supposed, poetical fantasies. The scale so constructed will be discussed below. Much more recently investigations have been made into the possibility of applying dendrochronology, but little progress has been made. There are practical obstacles, in particular the irregularity of ring formation in New Zealand timbers (Bell and Bell 1958: 11) and the absence of timber, especially in the form of large, unmodified structural members, from the majority of archaeological sites. Measurement of obsidian hydration has a greater chance of wide application, because obsidian from a number of North Island sources is often represented in flake industries on sites, and the method has been investigated by R. C. Green and W. R. Ambrose. But here, too, there are restrictions imposed by the relatively short period of time and by the fairly extreme range of soil climates involved. Green has published accounts of the results so far obtained, but points out that as yet the method can scarcely supply calendrical age measurements (Green 1964: 136). Ambrose has continued this study and is currently working on control methods for establishing the soil climates of particular sites. Finally, there is radiocarbon dating, which is the most highly developed of any available method of time measurement in the present situation, and has the advantage of employing organic materials which may be confidently expected in most sites worth archaeological investigation.

2 The genealogical time-scale

When the European navigators, Abel Tasman and James Cook, arrived off New Zealand in 1642 and 1769 respectively, they discovered it already inhabited. Travellers and natives each fell back on a body of knowledge to explain the existence of the other. We know little about the Maori explanations, except from snatches of recollections and inferences made from their behaviour that they concluded the visitors must have come from the spirit world. Captain Cook had a Society Islander on board the *Endeavour* who was able to communicate in his own language with the Maori and who recognized many similarities as well as differences between himself and them. On such grounds it was concluded that the inhabitants of both island groups, though isolated by thousands of miles of ocean, had a common origin. Subsequently, it was found that the islanders themselves believed that their ancestors had come from overseas and traced their origins through successive generations back to distant ancestors in a homeland called Hawaiki (not to be confused with Hawaii).

In the 1870s the Hawaiian scholar Abraham Fornander treated these Polynesian traditional genealogical tables as historical documents, and calculated the date of the original settlement of Hawaii on the basis of an average span of thirty years per generation. This idea was taken up by a number of New Zealanders, in particular Percy Smith (1840–

1922), who had recognized that genealogies, employed by the Maori to establish legal claims, showed great consistency (Roberton 1956: 45). Smith and others attempted to derive a history, in the European sense, from Maori traditions and also to articulate it on a time-scale based on genealogies calibrated on a twenty-five year generation (1956: 47). The result of this reconstruction is a historical outline known to most New Zealanders and indeed accepted as a factual account, in which the original discovery of the islands was made by a Hawaiki explorer named Kupe, about A.D. 950. He returned to his homeland with sailing instructions and was followed some generations later by another explorer, Toi, who was supposed to have founded settlements about A.D. 1150. However, the majority of the tribes traced their genealogies back to the arrival in A.D. 1350 of a group of ancestors associated with named canoes, in what has been termed the 'fleet'. The three dates quoted above have become an established part of New Zealand culture.

Unfortunately, more recent studies of these methods and sources of Smith's reconstruction have revealed that the consistency of the canoe traditions does not extend to the two supposedly earlier visits. These have been found to have been interpolated, and a case has been made out by D. Simmons for Kupe and Toi being contemporaries of the 'fleet' (Simmons 1963: 59 and 110). The most recent study of the canoe traditions has been by J. W. Roberton, who has applied methods of critical analysis to the genealogies. He has recognized that some supposed lines would have been physiologically impossible, but that once these discordant specimens are dropped there remains a body of consistent traditions. Roberton followed Smith in calibrating his genealogies, but chose a shorter generation of twenty years as more appropriate for Polynesians; he also applied other criteria based on a realistic assessment of human reproductive powers. On this basis he estimated that the line of descent of the historical figure Te Wherowhero, born about A.D. 1790, could be traced back to the canoe ancestor Hoturoa, supposedly born about A.D. 1230. Now it must be apparent that all such calculations involve a series of variables although they may be expressed for convenience by averaged, precise quantities. In view of the observation earlier in this paper that archaeologists may expect an unrealistic degree of exactness in their time-scales, it is worth expressing Roberton's data in terms of variable quantities, acknowledging that the methods will be crude.

First, it will be found that the Hoturoa–Te Wherowhero genealogy in Roberton's Chart I may be traced through some six lines of 20, 21, two of 22, and two of 26 generations respectively, making an average of $24{\cdot}5 \pm 1{\cdot}5$ generations. The next question is what constitutes a Maori generation? First, it is helpful to recognize a definition of marriage without the implications of its European usage, and for this it is convenient to follow J. Hajnal who expresses it as 'entry into a union which is regarded as appropriate for the bearing and rearing of children' (Hajnal 1965: 105). But at what age this was preferred in Maori society is unknown, as it is, indeed, for any prehistoric society (1965: 106). In Europe, during the past few centuries, the usual intervals between generations may be taken to be between twenty-five and thirty years (Eversley 1965: 30), but this is considered to be significantly longer than in other societies (Hajnal 1965: 104), and would overwhelmingly suggest that the Maori also had short generations. On the other hand, it should be remembered that the genealogies in question are those of a warrior aristocracy and that there would be restrictions on marriage owing to the small size of communities, incest taboos, and rank (Biggs 1960: 19), and that in a society where polygamy was practised young men may tend to remain unmarried for a comparatively long time and then marry much younger women (Hajnal 1965: 129). Against this is the impression, and it cannot be stronger, conveyed by Bruce Biggs in his study *Maori Marriage*, that marriage was youthful (1960: 28), and he cites only a single case, presumably abnormal, of a man marrying at 28 (1960: 35). With these uncertainties in mind, a suggested generation of 23 ± 5 years appears reasonable. Combining this with the previous estimate of $24{\cdot}5 \pm 1{\cdot}5$ generations for the Hoturoa–Te Wherowhero line, there is an elapsed maximum interval of 728 years, averaging round 563·5 and reduced to a minimum of 414, which may be expressed in European calendar dates of A.D. 1062, A.D. 1226, and A.D. 1376. The point which is established here is not the agreement of the average with Roberton's calculation, which necessarily follows from the use of the same data and premises, but the existence of a latitude of 150 years on either side of the mean, obtainable without distorting the evidence and without introducing any other sources of variation.

The first synthesis of New Zealand prehistory on an archaeological foundation was R. S. Duff's *Moa Hunter Period of Maori Culture*, originally published in 1950. The evidence on which the new approach was based was principally the large assemblage of burials, ornaments, adzes and fish hooks associated with the remains of extinct birds (moas) at Wairau Bar (fig. 11). These finds were made in a series of excavations through the 1940s onwards. Although the archaeological methods employed now look unsophisticated, the evidence was interpreted according to archaeological concepts which still operate. What was recognized was that an early period could be identified through its distinctive assemblage, which surpassed any local variations and which developed by unexplained processes into the equally distinctive Maori culture observed by the first European explorers. At the time of the original publication of Wairau Bar the only available method of time measurement was by cross-dating with the genealogical time-scale, and it seemed logical then to put forward the theory that equated Maori Culture with the traditions of the 'fleet', thus making the Moa-Hunters correspond with the supposed earlier arrivals.

3 Radiocarbon dating

Shortly after the first publication of the *Moa-Hunter Period* the development of radiocarbon dating made possible an independent determination of the age of archaeological sites, and, with the refinement introduced by gas-counting, of which the New Zealand laboratory was one of the pioneers (Golson 1955: 130), it became theoretically possible to date archaeological materials throughout the entire prehistoric period. But to appreciate the advantages of the method in such a situation it is necessary to recognize certain problems characteristic of, or exaggerated in, New Zealand.

There is no evidence here for prehistoric pottery, or any artefact of comparable plasticity and typological variability, by which local sequences or links between sites might be established. A further problem is due to the discontinuity of archaeological deposits. There is no site so far known which may be claimed to cover the full span of prehistory, and it is particularly unfortunate that no site hitherto reported seems to demonstrate the process by which the Moa-Hunter assemblage developed into the Classic Maori. Yet this developmental process, possibly accelerated by the introduction of a few significant traits rather than any intrusion of a new culture, has been preferred by archaeologists since the original publication of Duff's scheme. The relevance of this problem to the theme of the present paper is, of course, that change either requires time or must be introduced by transposition from elsewhere. There are two good reasons why the latter process is not preferred in this case. First, derivation from outside only transfers the problem elsewhere, and sufficient is known about the archaeology of the rest of Oceania to be emphatic that Classic Maori culture can be even less readily related to the prehistoric assemblages of other island groups than to that of the Moa-Hunters. Secondly, an intrusive culture would equally be expected to involve transitional sites in which some mixture of assemblages might be found, or at least evidence be preserved for the dispossession of the preceding culture. Living cultures do not evaporate without trace at the appearance of a rival, and it is difficult to see how an established settlement of several hundred years' duration would be numerically inferior to anything but the most massive military invasion, for which there is no evidence. The discontinuity of sites, combined with the absence of any widely distributed artefact which may surely be demonstrated to have passed through typological changes, make it very difficult to order sites and assemblages into more than 'early' or 'late', with a consequent circularity of archaeological interpretation. A vigorous attempt to break away from this effect is to be found in Roger C. Green's *Prehistoric Sequence of the Auckland Province*, in which a series of six phases of development were postulated. The criteria by which each phase was to be recognized were largely drawn from economic, social and architectural evidence, rather than artefactual assemblages, but subsequent work has lent little support to its underlying theories. (See, for example, the criticisms put forward by L. M. Groube 1967: 16.)

It is for these reasons that New Zealand archaeologists are forced back on ordering their evidence first by employing radiocarbon dating. This is not a unique case and here at least structures and assemblages may be correlated with time measurements; but it is only a short step to prehistories constructed entirely from series of radiocarbon dates. Such would literally indicate that there is evidence for human settlement by the date of the oldest measurement and that from then onwards man persisted. This is not a greatly inflated parody, for published examples may easily be found. At the same time, such an approach is not completely invalid, for if the sources of the dates could be selected by some strictly controlled method of sampling, they would be a guide to the population dynamics of a region.

4 Radiocarbon dating for the past millennium, and the need for correction tables

Since the inception of radiocarbon dating there has been continuous and extensive progress in evaluating and improving its basic premises. The late H. L. de Vries discovered that the radiocarbon ages of tree rings, which were known to belong to the late eighteenth century A.D., diverged from their expected ages. This approach was applied and extended by a number of other laboratories, and as a result there are at least four sequences now available which compare the variation between radiocarbon age and 'true age' during the period covered by New Zealand prehistory. These are shown transcribed on to a common scale in the accompanying diagram (fig. 12). It is perhaps characteristic of this field of research, as well as of archaeology, that each laboratory presented its results by a different visual method. In the present instance the figures have been expressed in natural scales, as probably the simplest to follow. The longest of the runs is that of Willis, Tauber and Munnich (1960); the most complete (that is, having the most measurements) is that of Stuiver and Suess (1966). These, together with Dyck's curve (1967), are all taken from samples of North American timber. The fourth is a run obtained by the New Zealand

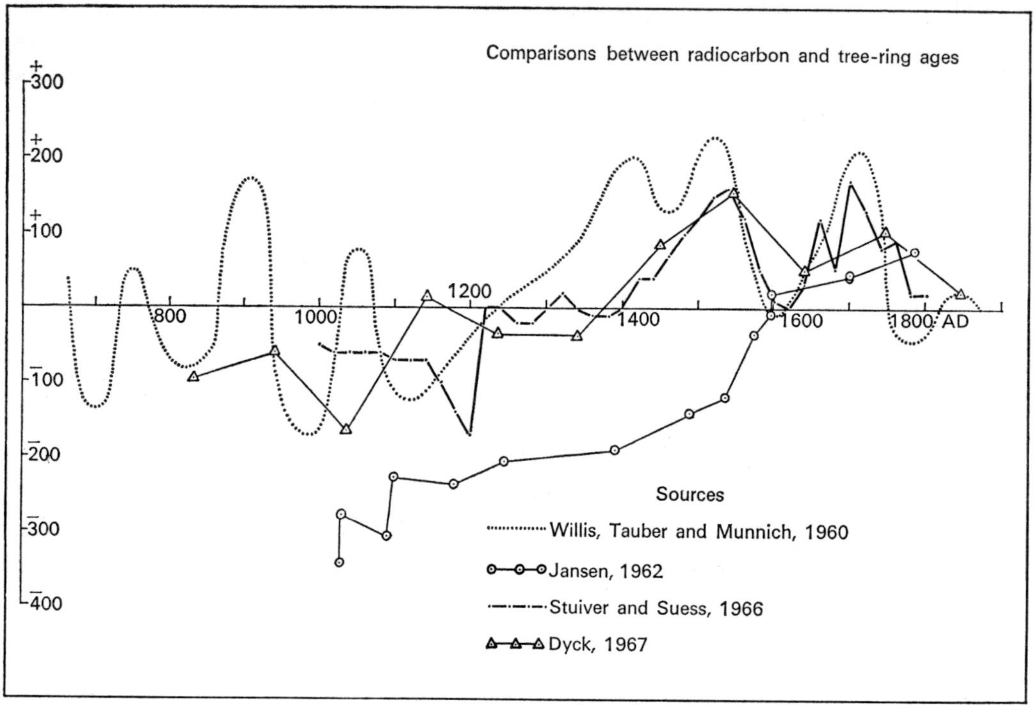

Figure 12 Four curves comparing recent radiocarbon and tree ring ages plotted on a common scale. Note that the lines joining points are primarily a visual guide and that for simplicity the points have been omitted from Willis, Tauber and Munnich's curve.

laboratory, using New Zealand *kauri* timber (Jansen 1962). The three northern hemisphere runs show a fair measure of agreement, as well as illustrating the risks of which every elementary textbook on statistics warns, of joining points on a graph. The danger of joining points too far apart appears when a tighter group of measurements reveals further fluctuations. But even the twenty-year intervals of the Stuiver and Suess run may obscure significant fluctuations. There are only three brief periods during the past thousand years when the three northern runs coincide closely with the calendar scale, namely the second quarter of the thirteenth century, the first quarter of the seventeenth century, and probably the beginning of the nineteenth century. There are two periods when all three are in some measure of agreement about extreme divergence from the calendar scale, these being the second half of the fifteenth century and the first three-quarters of the sixteenth, and then the fifty years on either side of the beginning of the eighteenth century. In each case the radiocarbon ages are too young and may indeed be up to 150 years too young. Prior to about A.D. 1200 the agreement is less clear, but suggests that radiocarbon ages may be too old by again up to about 150 years.

Unfortunately, the New Zealand run reported by Jansen shows serious divergence not only from the calendar scale but also from the results obtained by the northern hemisphere laboratories. All of the runs are in some agreement for the seventeenth and eighteenth centuries, but earlier than that the New Zealand dates tend to exaggerate age by up to 300 years, and, judging by their trend, one might shudder at what prospect would be unfolded by another, older, *kauri* log.

Stuiver and Suess draw attention to the paradox that while there will be a radiocarbon age for each calendar year, though not necessarily the same, the reverse is not true (Stuiver and Suess 1966: 538). In some instances a series of alternative true ages may exist for a radiocarbon date. It may be suspected that Stuiver and Suess, working in North America, looked on this point as academic rather than as a caution to archaeologists, but it applies all too painfully to New Zealand prehistory, for here the archaeologist has no independent means of knowing the calendrical age of his sample and so

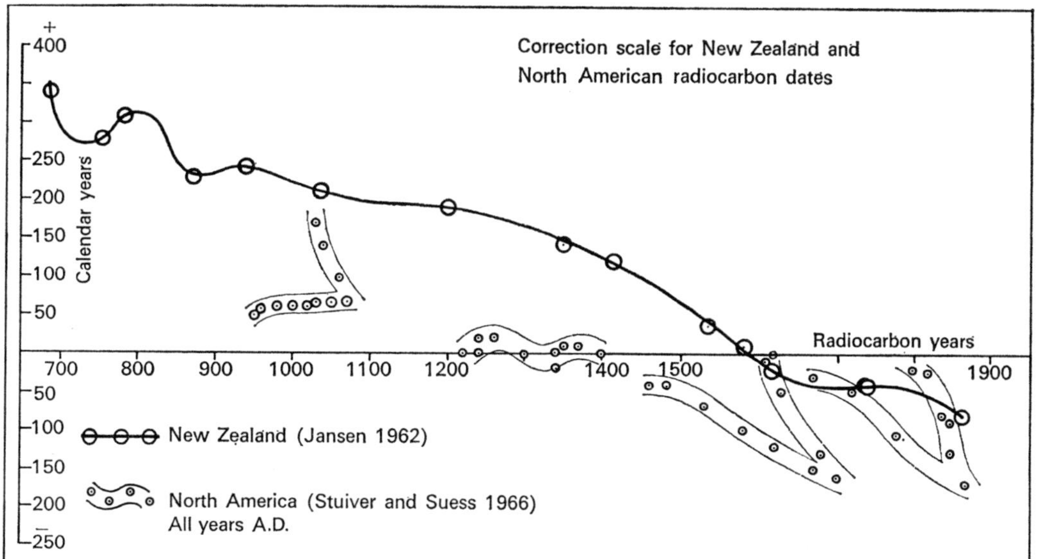

Figure 13 Correction scales plotted for New Zealand and North American radiocarbon dates. The radiocarbon age is read along the horizontal scale and the 'true' age is found at right angles, at the intersection of the curve. This illustrates the paradox noted by Stuiver and Suess that a radiocarbon age may have several true ages. It also implies that certain radiocarbon estimations should not be obtained in North America, for example between 750 and 850 B.P. This is not true for New Zealand, where they are frequent, see fig. 14.

cannot readily determine the necessary correction, unless he is fortunate in obtaining a sequence of dates. This situation is demonstrated in the accompanying correction diagram (fig. 13). If the very complete series of determinations by Stuiver and Suess is transformed into a scale for converting radiocarbon to calendrical measurements, the apparently continuous series disintegrates and exposes breaks and alternative readings. For example, a radiocarbon date of A.D. 1670 might refer to three separate calendrical ages of A.D. 1640, 1550 and 1515 respectively.

A correction scale for the New Zealand series appears as a much simpler, continuous curve, though it too involves several awkward features. Perhaps the most unfortunate is its already noted exaggeration of the northern hemisphere trends. Also the gaps between the points are wide and may obscure significant fluctuations. A third difficulty is that there is evidence for the New Zealand *kauri* developing double annual rings (this has been observed on a tree of known age grown by the D.S.I.R.; information kindly provided by Professor P. Bergquist), the consequences of which might be to shorten the present scale up to a half.

Some explanation for the apparent differences between the northern and southern hemisphere measurements is needed. They cannot be adequately explained away by reference to statistical error, for they show internally consistent trends. Perhaps, indeed, there have been variations in the relative proportions of atmospheric radiocarbon in the two hemispheres and some lag in their achieving equilibrium, or the cause may be more local, such as the extensive volcanic disturbances of the North Island. Certainly, an examination of archaeological samples (from the South Island) has already led M. Trotter to conclude that charcoal samples tend to supply unacceptable results (Trotter 1968: 86). These samples are distinctly recorded as coming from twigs and not from heavier timbers, which are known to have survived in the dry climate of that area long after death. Curiously, the unreliability appears to be associated with samples taken from plants, while organic matter of animal origin such as bone collagen is preferred. It is recognized that fractionation in grasses and seeds may cause variations of up to 200 years, while aquatic plants may derive their CO^2 from water containing dissolved carbonates (Dr V. R. Switsur pers. comm.). But it is not obvious how an animal, subsisting ultimately on plants anyhow, can make a more reliable vehicle for radiocarbon.

With all of these qualifications in mind the New Zealand archaeologist is left with the problem of reconciling his radiocarbon dates. He may ignore the existence of the divergence of radiocarbon from calendrical ages, and perhaps trust that all will be quietly sorted out later. This could well be a policy of some archaeologists who seem to publish dates which coincide with their theories but display a deep reticence over any which are so inconsiderate as not to agree. Alternatively, some attempt might be made either to allow for the very wide margins of error, well beyond the published standard deviations, or, thirdly, to correct the dates. The preferable correction scale is presumably that based on the local series of measurements.

But it must be confessed that some doubt lingers over the adequacy of the New Zealand correction scale. Its exaggeration of some of the divergences in the northern hemisphere, and the risk of error from double annual tree-rings have already been noted. Furthermore, there may be some hint that, even without the correction scale, samples from the eighteenth and early nineteenth centuries may already have been made too old. There is insufficient material to make a case, particularly as few workers are interested in late dates, but taking samples from the author's own field-work, there is a measurement too old by half a century for charcoal from deposits at a site on Lake Ngaroto, associated with European-introduced items, which would be unlikely to be older than 150 years, and were probably closer to 130 years. A radiocarbon age of 196±79 B.P. (R2169/3) is of course well within acceptable limits, yet such an amplification of age is disconcerting. The same tendency to exaggerate may be present in a sample (R1950/4) from the latest deposits of the Kauri Point Swamp site. There is no evidence to suppose that this is post-European, but the decorative style of the artefacts (see Shawcross 1964: 394) is so similar to those collected on Captain Cook's first voyage in 1769, and illustrated by Sydney Parkinson, that an age of A.D. 1661±53 again seems excessively old, though statistically unexceptionable. It would sometimes be helpful if the dates predicted by archaeologists were published alongside their results, for although the prophetic powers of the individual might suffer, it is possible that such trends might be more readily recognized. A further ground for uncertainty about the New Zealand correction scale is the virtually complete absence of archaeological age determinations later than 1700 A.D. (fig. 14). This raises the issue of an expected increase in the number of settlements and corresponding radiocarbon dates as time progresses, and will be examined in detail shortly.

There are roughly a hundred radiocarbon measurements of archaeological samples in New Zealand. In their uncorrected state they have generally been taken to indicate an approximate span of a thousand years of prehistoric settlement (Groube 1968: 145), and as this corresponds quite closely to the formerly accepted, though now discredited, span of the traditional genealogies, it has been tempting for archaeologists and traditionalists to seek support from each other. Outside this span of a thousand years there are several of what might be termed 'wildcat' dates. The site of Oturehua in Otago has supplied dates in the eighth millennium B.C. (Leach 1969: 52) and the site of Poukawa in the North Island has been dated to about 1320±200 B.C. (Pullar 1965: 11). This is not the occasion on which to attempt to resolve these controversial issues, and though it is obvious that they fall well outside the zone of probability created by the rest, experience (as witness Olduvai Gorge) warns that archaeologists cannot afford to be too dogmatic about their cherished time-scales.

If attention is concentrated on the zone in which the majority of dates are clustered, it will be found that almost all of the sites which may be identified as early on artefactual and palaeontological grounds were first occupied during the twelfth century A.D. With the recent availability of determinations for the Mt Camel site, Houhora in the far North, it is now possible to recognize a pattern of a dozen or so 'early' settlements strung throughout the whole length of the country – a length of a thousand miles. Apart from the 'wildcat' sites there are very few radiocarbon dates for cultural materials earlier than these. M. Trotter has recently given grounds for doubting a date of A.D. 780±60 for a site at Redcliffs, which had previously held the position of the earliest site (Trotter 1968: 87). L. M. Groube has mentioned an equally early date of A.D. 800 for a cultivation soil on the island of Moturua, and has also supported this by predicting that earlier sites should have existed before the appearance of the relatively dense settlement (in his opinion) of the twelfth century (Groube 1968: 144).

This raises the issue of population, and therefore site expansion during the prehistoric

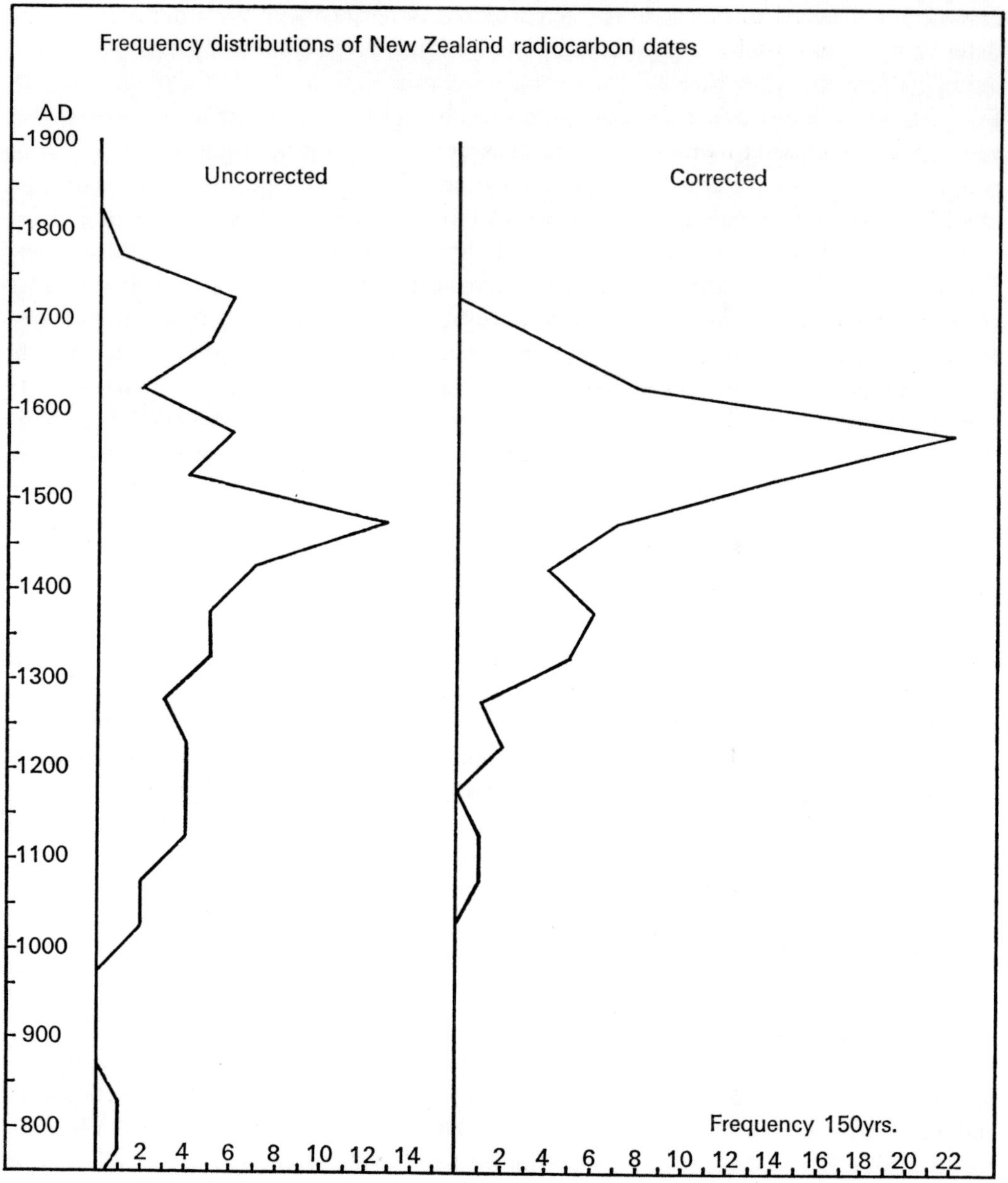

Figure 14 Frequency distribution of New Zealand archaeological radiocarbon dates: total of seventy-five available dates. The uncorrected curve shows the dates as reported, the corrected one adjusts them according to Jansen's evidence.

period. The demographic process of settlement seems first to have been recognized by Andrew Sharp, who has pointed out in his *Ancient Voyagers in the Pacific* that 'One canoe load of people, borne on to one of the islands [of Polynesia] in the early centuries of the Christian era with a rate of increase of 5 per cent to 10 per cent per generation, could account for the total population of the entire grouping in historical times' (1957: 57). As a theoretical proposition it is therefore worth examining the potentials of population growth in prehistoric New Zealand.

The capacity for population increase of even the relatively slow breeding human being is formidable. A crude birth rate of 100 per 1,000 population per year is possible, though the highest observed rate is about 65 per 1,000 (Thomlinson 1965: 147). It is realistic to examine actual rates of population increase, which, for example, is relatively high by world standards in New Zealand, with an average annual percentage increase of 2·1 in 1966 (*New Zealand Official Year Book* 1966: 55). During the same year the specifically Maori part of the population increased at a rate of 3·5% (1966: 72). On the other hand, population growth is not inevitable, or may be exceedingly low: in the order of 0·3% per annum (Eversley 1965: 52).

Population growth curves were calculated with these guides in mind, using annual compound rates of 3%, 1·5% and 0·3% respectively (fig. 15). (I wish to thank Mr B. Bagley for his assistance and the programming of these calculations.) Each of these curves starts with a minimum number of ten persons at A.D. 1000, and it is quite simple to adjust them for a different sized original group or date of settlement. But before discussing the curves, a further comment is necessary in connection with the upper limit of a quarter of a million on the population. The question of the size of the Maori population at the time of Captain Cook's first visit is vigorously debated, and estimates and guesses have put it at between 100,000 and half a million. Some commentators have ensured the impregnability of their own opinions by averaging those of everyone else: a device which, though providing academic security, adds no validity. Others have recourse to an estimate ascribed to Captain Cook, though the writer has been unable to track such an observation down in the explorer's published journals. It seems probable that the figures so frequently quoted for New Zealand are as unreliably based as those revealed by Robert Schmitt for other Polynesian islands (1965: 57), and in the case of New Zealand it seems out of the question that the explorers, spending a few weeks at a few isolated points on the coast, and knowing nothing about the population structure of the Maroi, let alone modern statistics and sampling methods, could have made estimates accurate within the nearest half million! The writer is currently engaged on an independent approach to this question, the results of which so far favour a figure of the order of 100,000, but for the purposes of the present discussion the limits on the curves should be left open.

A growth rate of 3% per annum, starting at A.D. 1000, would have populated New Zealand as fully as the most generous could wish by the fifteenth century, and would have left little standing room for the explorers by the time of their arrival. On the other hand, a rate of 0·3% per annum would have increased an original population of ten to only thirty-three persons in 500 years, and has therefore been omitted from the diagram. At such a rate, the existence of a population within the range of any of the commentator's figures would require an extremely massive original settlement, or lend support to the previously noted 'wildcat' dates for early settlement, but would still seem unrealistic, because it is a

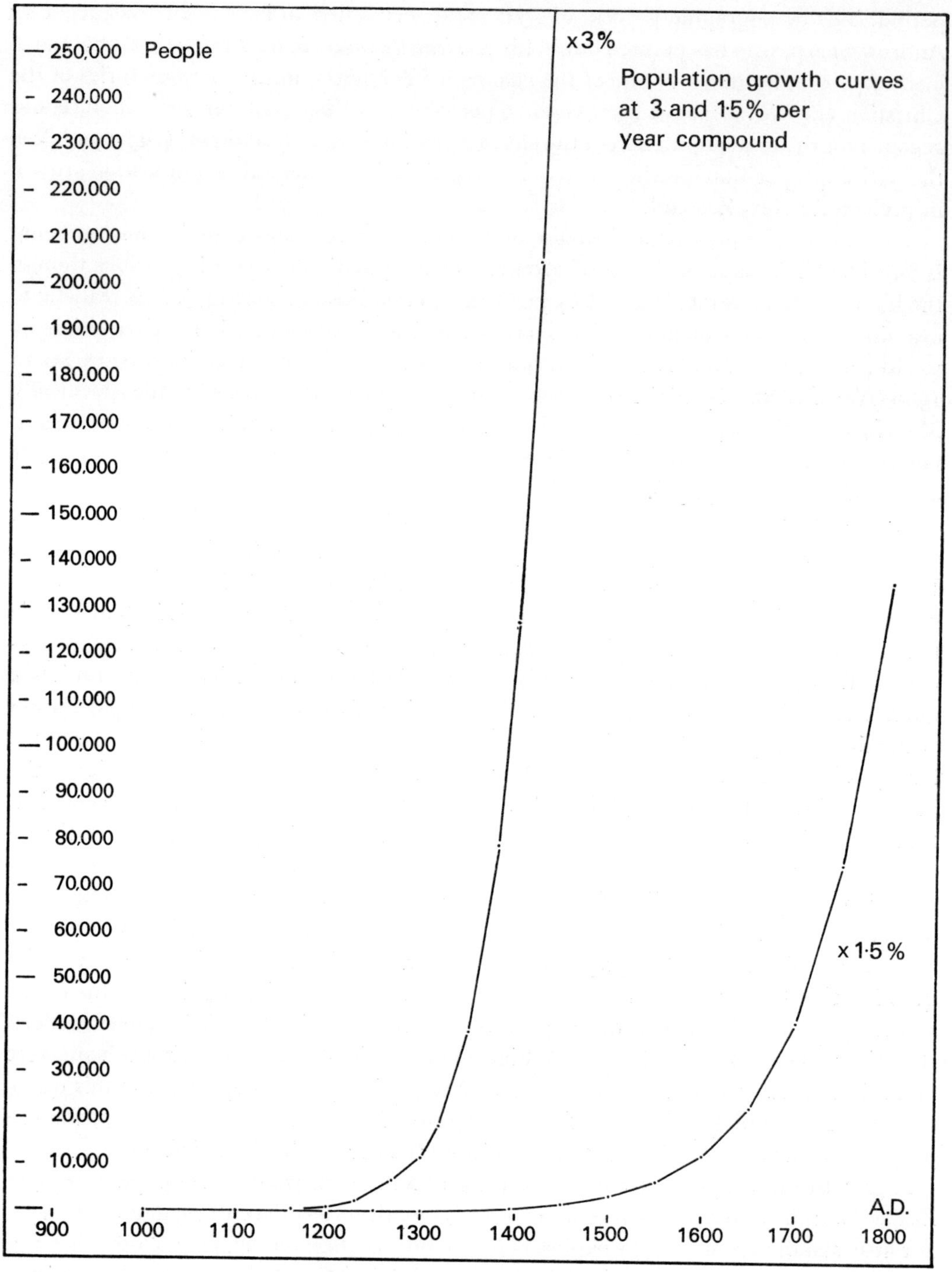

Figure 15 Theoretical population growth curves at 3 and 1·5% per annum rates, starting with ten people each at A.D. 1000. A generous allowance for the 'fleet' traditions would give an initial settlement of 1,500 people. To fit these curves it would be necessary to bring forward the date of arrival to A.D. 1200 and A.D. 1400 for the 3 and 1·5% rates respectively.

rate more likely to be associated with populations in equilibrium with their environment. On other grounds, not to be discussed here, it would seem that New Zealand was far from fully exploited even within the range of prehistoric economics. Having inspected the possible extremes of population growth rates, the intermediate rate of 1·5% appears attractive for an A.D. 1000 origin, though the higher rate would be preferable if the origin was delayed until the fourteenth century. Either of these alternatives would suggest a realistic size of population at the time of European contact.

Anticipating criticism makes it necessary to examine the logic of the argument. There is absolutely no reason to suppose that a population, newly arrived in such a situation, would in reality immediately fix itself on a 1·5% (or any other) rate of growth and steadily maintain it. Rates are not causes, but retrospective simplifications. Rates change and the usual model is in fact a logistic curve, in which there is a progression of low, increased and then reduced rates as equilibrium is achieved (Thomlinson 1965: 67). Equilibrium is itself a generalization, for an inspection of prehistoric economies suggests rather the attainment of a succession of equilibria.

There are thus serious qualifications to the use of the population growth curves, but it is necessary to recall that the issue is the frequency of dated archaeological sites. For such purposes it seems quite justifiable to treat such a rate of expansion as a rough guide to the expected growth of prehistoric population and, consequently, at a further level of generalization, an indicator of increasing frequency of settlements. If archaeological sites could be conveniently restricted to single-phase occupations, if the pattern of settlement were uniform throughout the country, and if archaeological investigations with radiocarbon sample gathering were random, one might predict that the frequency of dates would correspond to population growth.

A comparison between the expected curve and the available evidence (fig. 14) fails to show such a pattern of growth. There is a fairly even distribution of dates throughout the scale back to the twelfth century, but with an unexpected concentration in the late fifteenth century. The pattern of increase becomes a little more obvious if the dates are corrected, using fig. 13, but there is still an abrupt increase in frequency, now delayed to the second half of the fourteenth century, and, less satisfactorily, a sharp decrease in the seventeenth century, leaving an awkward gap in the eighteenth century. In fact, some of the bias of these results must be ascribed to archaeological methods, as the hypotheses implied. The tendency has been not only to try to obtain the earliest date for the commencement of a sequence of deposits, but also to investigate the oldest-looking sites at the expense of the supposedly more recent. Furthermore, a pattern of increasing re-use of sites as time progresses may be expected. Groube has perhaps assumed at least some of the previous hypotheses in arguing that the widespread distribution of early sites along the east coast of the North and South Islands during the eleventh and thirteenth centuries would indicate an initial settlement several centuries before (Groube 1968: 144).

But an alternative interpretation is possible, namely that the cluster of virtually contemporary early sites does represent a significant proportion of the original, major settlement of the country. It seems to be more than a coincidence that several occupation sequences, so widely distributed throughout the country and displaying such strong cultural similarities, should all commence at so close a time. But even allowing that some of these early sites have been destroyed or are not yet found, there would probably have been little more than a dozen of them with early twelfth-century dates, or, if one applies the correction scale, fourteenth-century dates. Such a scheme would coincide reasonably well with the traditional accounts of the major settlement of New Zealand by a number of perhaps contemporary canoe-loads of voyagers, genealogically dated, as has been shown above, to between the eleventh and fourteenth centuries A.D. It has the virtue of economy, for it would associate a consistent group of traditions, hitherto without any material association for their appearance, with an archaeological phenomenon, the origin of a number of occupation sites. As radiocarbon dating and traditional genealogical calculations are both subject to range of variation the most that may be looked for is an overlap, which is indeed found between the twelfth and fourteenth centuries. As a conclusion, it may be observed that when an event, such as the settlement of New Zealand, becomes obscured through the variation inherent in methods of time measurement, it is a warning to archaeologists that they cannot handle time with historical precision. How many prehistories are there sporting falsely exact time-scales?

Acknowledgements

I wish to thank Dr H. Tauber of Copenhagen and Dr V. R. Switsur of Cambridge for generously sparing their time to discuss radiocarbon dating with me. I also wish to thank Mr L. Lockerbie of the Otago Museum, chairman of the N.Z. Archaeological Association Radiocarbon Committee, who has himself done much to establish radiocarbon dating in New Zealand, for his courtesy and assistance. Finally, I think it appropriate to express my gratitude to the New Zealand radiocarbon laboratory and its director, Mr T. A. Rafter, for the outstanding service provided.

18.v.69

Department of Anthropology
Auckland University

References

Bell, V. and Bell, R. E. 1958. Dendrochronological Studies in New Zealand. *Tree Ring Bulletin*. 22, 1–4:7–11.

Biggs, B. 1960. *Maori Marriage*. Wellington.

Duff, R. 1956. *The Moa-Hunter Period of Maori Culture*. Wellington.

Dyck, W. 1967. Recent Developments in Radiocarbon Dating. *Current Anthropology*. 8, 4: 349–51.

Eversley, D. E. C. 1965. Population, Economy and Society. In *Population in History*, eds D. V. Glass and D. E. C. Eversley. London.

Golson, J., 1955. Dating New Zealand's Prehistory. *Journal of the Polynesian Society*. 64, 1: 113–35.

Golson, J. and Gathercole, P. W. 1962. The Last Decade in New Zealand Archaeology. *Antiquity*. 36:168–74, 271–7.

Green, R. C. 1963. *A Review of the Prehistoric Sequence of the Auckland Province*. Auckland.

Green, R. C. 1964. Sources, Ages and Exploitation of New Zealand Obsidian. *Newsletter, N.Z. Archaeological Association*. 7, 3:134–43.

Groube, L. M. 1967. Models in Prehistory: a Consideration of the New Zealand Evidence. *Archaeology and Physical Anthropology in Oceania*. 2, 1:1–27.

Groube, L. M. 1968. Research in New Zealand Prehistory since 1956. In *Prehistoric Culture in Oceania*, eds I. Yawata and Y. H. Sinoto. Bishop Museum, Hawaii.

Hajnal, J. 1965. European Marriage Patterns in Perspective. In *Population in History*, eds D. V. Glass and D. E. C. Eversley. London.

Jansen, H. S. 1962. Comparison between Ring Dates and 14C-Dates in a New Zealand Kauri Tree. *New Zealand Journal of Science*. 5:74–84.

Leach, B. F. 1969. Radiocarbon Dates for the Oturehua Quarry Site, Central Otago (S134/1). *Newsletter, N.Z. Archaeological Association*. 12, 1:52.

Polach, H. A. and Golson, J. 1966. *Collection of Specimens for Radiocarbon Dating and Interpretation of Results*. Australian Institute of Aboriginal Studies, manual no. 2. Canberra.

Pullar, W. A. 1965. Note on Ash Beds at Poukawa, Hawkes Bay. *Newsletter, N.Z. Archaeological Association*. 8, 1:11–13.

Roberton, J. B. W. 1956. Genealogies as a Basis for Maori Chronology. *Journal of the Polynesian Society*. 65, 1:45–54.

Schmitt, R. C. 1965. Garbled Population Estimates of Central Polynesia. *Journal of the Polynesian Society*. 74, 1:57–62.

Sharp, A. 1957. *Ancient Voyagers in the Pacific*. London.

Shawcross, W. 1964. An Archaeological Assemblage of Maori Combs. *Journal of the Polynesian Society*. 73, 4:382–98.

Simmons, D. R. 1963. *The New Zealand Myth*. M.A. thesis, Auckland University.

Stuiver, M. and Suess, H. E. 1966. On the Relationship between Radiocarbon Dates and True Sample Ages. *Radiocarbon*. 8:534–40.

Suggs, R. C. 1960. *The Island Civilizations of Polynesia*. New York.

Thomlinson, R. 1965. *Population Dynamics*. New York.

Trotter, M. M. 1968. On the Reliability of Charcoal for Radiocarbon Dating New Zealand Sites. *Newsletter, N.Z. Archaeological Association*. 11, 2:86–8.

Willis, E. H., Tauber, H. and Munnich, K. O. 1960. Variations in the Atmospheric Radiocarbon Concentrations over the past 1300 years. *American Journal of Science Radiocarbon Supplement*. 2:1–4.

Medieval British and Irish coins as dating evidence for the archaeologist

Michael Dolley

It is probably safe to say that improvements in excavation techniques are in large part responsible for a general tendency over the last few years for more and more medieval coins to be found in the course of archaeological investigations of particular sites. One might instance the very complete series of Anglo-Saxon and later coins which was brought to light by Mr Philip Rahtz at Cheddar, the even more notable and extensive assemblage of Anglo-Saxon, Norman and Plantagenet coins recovered by Mr Martin Biddle in the course of several years of excavations at Winchester, and nearer home and yet more recently a critical group of late Hiberno-Norse and early Anglo-Irish coins unearthed by Mr Breandán Ó Ríordáin at the High Street site in Dublin. To be stressed, though, is the fact that these instances could be multiplied almost indefinitely, and scarcely a week goes by, in summer at least, without some archaeologist somewhere bringing to the numismatist's notice one or more coins recovered from a stratified context. The purpose of this note is to suggest both the potential value and the possibly less obvious limitations of what has become an increasingly important branch of evidence. This increasing importance, incidentally, is one that is qualitative as well as quantitative inasmuch as the numismatist is better placed than ever before to date the new material and so to assess its potential significance. But it is also relative since he has become more and more dependent on coins from archaeological sources now that so much construction work is undertaken by the mechanical earth-digger and the bulldozer instead of being, as formerly, the almost exclusive preserve of the often unexpectedly keen-eyed 'navvy' with his pick and shovel.

The first point that needs to be made is that chance losses need not afford a representative cross-section of coins actually in use at a given period. The really valuable coin is less likely to be lost, and if dropped will normally be sought. Exceptionally, the loss of a gold noble of Henry IV recently recovered from the sump of a medieval privy in London must have been long and loudly bewailed by its unfortunate owner, but if noticed at the time may have been accepted, since a search would have been almost as difficult and certainly much more unpleasant than the proverbial haystack hunt for a needle. In normal circumstances, however, large gold coins only very rarely would have been the victims of such casual loss. Conversely it is the very small coin that is more likely to have been lost, though a rough-and-ready statistical corrective may be thought to be here afforded by the circumstance that the same small coin is less likely to be found even by the most competent excavator. This weighting against recovery in modern times is the more unfortunate because small coins are not normally hoarded, and so are proportionately under-represented in coin-hoards as such where the container, even if disintegrated or shattered, has usually ensured that the totality of the contents will be recovered and brought to the notice of the numismatist charged with publication. For example, a total of sixty-nine coin-hoards from Ireland and Great Britain have thrown up a total of 860 or so Anglo-Irish pence of Edward I, but only 20 of the halfpence and farthings. Yet, there is some documentary evidence still extant which suggests that the numerical proportion of pence to halfpence and farthings actually struck was not as 40 : 1 but rather as 5 : 1. What the discrepancy between the two sets of figures does underline is simply the fact that at this period halfpence and farthings were not normally hoarded. The second point that needs to be made at this point is that in multi-denominational coinages, such as existed over most of these islands after the middle of the fourteenth century, the small coin which was also a small-change coin was not only much more likely to be lost but also to have an inordinately long life. In England, for example, pennies of Edward III, and perhaps of his father and grandfather, even though worn smooth, obsolete and for all practical purposes demonetized, still were circulating when Henry VII came to the throne, while a few have found their way into coin-hoards concealed as late as the latter half of the reign of Henry VIII. It is, indeed, one of the twists of history that such coins, though generally capable of being dated as regards their striking with a very great deal of precision, often are of comparatively little value for dating-purposes where the archaeologist is concerned.

What was the life-span of a typical medieval coin? To this question there is no simple answer. It was only very recently that some of us were privileged to be allowed to sort a massive new Viking-age hoard from the Swedish island of Gotland, with an almost mint penny of Æthelræd II struck *c.* 975 lying beside German bracteates which it is difficult to date earlier than the middle of the twelfth century. Even in these islands there have been coins of which the official currency extended over a century and more. The Confederate Catholics at Kilkenny in 1642 provided for the continued currency of *dominick grotes* (i.e. of pre-1541 coins of Henry VIII), and in process of publication is a little hoard from Galway where groats with the initial of Jane Seymour occur beside a half-crown struck quite late in the reign of Charles I. On the other hand, there are medieval coins of which the official currency cannot have been more than a very few months, the so-called *Benediction Hand* pence of Æthelræd II being a case in point. What it is proposed to essay here is to supply the field-archaeologist in these islands with some indication of the probable life span of those coins which are most likely to occur in medieval levels. To be grasped from the first is a quite fundamental dichotomy. The precision with which the striking of a coin can be determined need not be matched when it comes to an estimate of the period of its currency. In the Norman period, for example, coins appear to have been demonetized pretty efficiently after they had been current only two or three years. Under the Plantagenets, on the other hand, there are numerous coins which might be current for a half-century and more, though the date when they were actually struck can often be established to within a year or so.

English coinage began with a small issue of gold which still is the subject of considerable controversy. Essentially, though, the coins belong to the middle of the seventh century, and this bracket would seem to embrace striking and currency alike. The silver *sceattas* which succeeded them began most probably in the 690s and continued to be struck and to circulate into the second half of the eighth century. As with the gold, however, the circulation area was limited and regional, and a specialist numismatist like Mr Stuart Rigold is really needed even for a provisional evaluation. Not later than early in the last quarter of the eighth century, the *sceatta* was superseded by the penny struck on a wider and thinner flan but apparently to the same standard. No hoard is known which contains both *sceattas* and the new pence, and this suggests that demonetization of the former had been remarkably complete. With the penny for the first time it was normal for an English coin to bear the name of a ruler, be he king or archbishop, and the name of the mint and/or the moneyer, the man responsible to the ruler for its quality. As a result it is usually possible for a trained numismatist to establish the date of striking with a very considerable degree of precision. A coin of the Kentish rebel Eadberht Præn, for example, must have been struck between 796 and 798. A coin of Offa of Mercia struck at Canterbury from a die which was later employed by Eadberht may be presumed to have been struck not all that number of months before Offa's death touched off Eadberht's revolt, a useful indication of date when it is recalled that Offa's reign had lasted very nearly forty years. On the other hand, there are still many coins the striking of which even a specialist like Mr Christopher Blunt would hesitate to date more nearly than to within a decade. About the middle of the ninth century there does seem to have occurred in Southern England a formal and efficient demonetization of all earlier issues, but the proportion in which the oldest coins occur in late coin-hoards may suggest that throughout the period there had been a fairly pronounced tendency for older pieces to find their way to the melting-pot.

In the second half of the ninth century, and over the greater part of the area of Southern England where coin had come into general use, there grew up the concept of periodic coinage. Coins of a uniform design would be issued, and after a number of years they would be withdrawn and replaced by others with some new design. Consequently the numismatist in theory should always be able to date any coin within a matter of at most a decade, with this precision extending to the period of its currency as well as to the bracket within which it may be supposed to have been struck. Unfortunately the system broke down under the pressure of the great Viking attacks during Ælfred's reign, and coin-hoards from the tenth century suggest that a fairly efficient demonetization *c.* 890 or thereabouts was the last systematic withdrawal of the totality of the coinage for not far short of a century. Under the successors of Ælfred, the use of coin was extended to virtually the whole of the English kingdom; while the relative plenty of the surviving coins means that the date of striking of most of the pence and halfpence can be established within quite narrow limits. Again there would seem to have been a tendency for older coins to go out of currency, but the apparent absence of any really effective demonetization before the last years of the reign of Eadgar means that there are many occasions when the numismatist has still to report 'struck between year x and year $x+5$, probably lost before year $x+15$, but conceivably in circulation as late as *c.* 973'. What cannot be stressed too much, though, is the importance of closely recorded stratification. Let us assume that a penny of Eadmund (939–46) is found in a level sealing an earlier level containing a coin of Edward the Elder struck *c.* 920. There begins to be a presumption that both losses occurred within the normal life of each coin, and the excavator would probably be justified who gave to the lower level a provisional dating *c.* 925 and to the upper level a date in the region of 950. In such an evaluation of the evidence numismatist and archaeologist should work together as a team, and the entirety of the evidence must always be made available to all the collaborators. For example, it was an exactly described scatter of a handful of thirteenth-century English and Anglo-Irish pence from the floor of a soon-abandoned crypt at Mellifont which was responsible for the suggestion that the coins represent the whole of a private cache from behind one of the collapsed beams, rather than strays from the house's official treasury which there is some reason to think then occupied an adjoining chamber.

At the end of the reign of Eadgar, and some of those most familiar with the whole of the evidence still think that the most likely date was Michaelmas 973, there occurred a formal and utter demonetization of all coins then in currency. They were replaced by new coins of absolutely uniform type, and even the dies, with a very few exceptions, give the appearance of having been engraved by a single hand. Very soon afterwards Eadgar died, but the new design was continued under his son Edward the Martyr, and into the early part of the reign of Æthelræd II, the only significant development being that cutting of the dies was progressively decentralized. Probably at Michaelmas 979 the type was again changed, and twice again before the end of the century, and the fact that there were almost certainly changes of type in 1003 and 1009 has led to the suggestion that from the first a sexennial type-cycle had been envisaged. It is conveniently overlooked by critics that models for so fundamental a reform existed not just on the Continent but, in the not all that distant past, in England itself. However this may be, a characteristic of the English coinage from *c.* 975 for nearly two centuries was that every so many years, at first usually six, and later three but sometimes two, a new design appeared on English coins, and it will be appreciated that once the relative sequence has been reconstructed, as it has now been thanks to the generosity of the Swedes in making available to students from abroad the evidence of their unrivalled coin-hoards, there is a reasonably dated *terminus post quem* for each and every English coin that the archaeologist is likely to find. Often, too, the date of striking can be given with a precision that at first sight may seem to smack of witchcraft rather than of science. For example, it can be shown that the *Last Small Cross* type of Æthelræd II was introduced in the autumn of 1009, but that the authorities had been toying with an alternative design where the royal portrait and the reverse cross would be replaced by representations of the Lamb of God and the Dove of the Holy Ghost. A very few coins with these revolutionary designs in fact had got into circulation, and it is difficult to see how such pieces could have been struck before the late summer of 1009 or after the early autumn.

Nor is this the end of the story where the archaeologist is concerned. The evidence of coin-hoards and a few hints in the documents of the time suggest that when a new design was introduced there was only a short period of grace, possibly as little as six months, before the type superseded was called in. Thus, in most cases the numismatist is able to suggest not just a *terminus post quem* for the striking, but a likely *terminus ante quem* for the loss. Again, too, it is sometimes possible to suggest this date of loss with what must seem almost magical precision. For example, at the very end of the *Crux* type, probably in the summer of 997, experiments were being made with the portrait on the obverse which anticipate that actually adopted for the succeeding *Long Cross* issue. Hoard-evidence, however, is decisive that the experimental coins went out of circulation when the *Long Type* issue proper was introduced. Should an archaeologist, then, discover one of these pennies in a stratified context, the presumption must be that it had been both struck and lost within a matter of six months. It is a wry thought that such precision is not normally obtainable in the case of modern coins which purport to bear the year of striking – deceptively in many cases as the Royal Mint itself admitted not so many years ago. Recently, too, some of us have begun to make a special study of those issues which had a currency of six years – nine, possibly, in the case of that embracing the calamitous last years of Æthelræd II – and techniques are slowly being evolved which may make it possible to identify individual coins as belonging early or late within an emission. This is specialist work, and the archaeologist should not be surprised, still less dismayed or disappointed, when his chosen numismatic specialist seeks a second opinion from other experts in the particular field, such as Mr F. Elmore Jones. There are in these islands fewer than a dozen numismatists who are generally qualified to advise on finds over the whole medieval period, but not one worth his salt who would pretend to equal competence in each and every series.

From *c.* 1035 until *c.* 1135 the types of the English penny were changed every two or three years, and the sequence does seem at last to be generally agreed even though it is only in the last year or so that the last piece has fitted into place – thanks very largely to Mr T. F. R. Jones's 1962 and 1963 excavations at Llantrithyd which brought to light the scatter from a looted hoard which nearly doubled the number of specimens then known for one extremely rare type of Henry I. Consequently it is usually possible, despite centralized die-production, to date coins from this particular century with a very great degree of precision, and again there is a broad coincidence between currency and period of issue, coins still being demonetized – or so it seems – within a matter of months of a new type's inception. The comparative anarchy of the middle years of Stephen's reign, though inevitably exaggerated by contemporaries, did have quite devastating consequences where the coinage was concerned. Most of his coins can be dated to the early, middle or late part of the reign, but there is no evidence for any systematic demonetization between the king's accession and his final acceptance of Henry of Anjou in 1153, so that his earliest coins may well have been current for fifteen years and more. Four years after his own accession, Henry II threw overboard the whole concept of periodic change of type. His great recoinage of 1158 envisaged a system under which coins would remain legal tender indefinitely, and in theory there was to be no difference between a coin struck in 1160 and 1170. In practice it is often possible for a numismatist to detect stylistic differences, and Mr D. F. Allen's development of L. A. Lawrence's classification means that most of the coins can be reasonably closely dated as regards their striking. Since, however, the earliest were still current a quarter of a century after they had been struck, it is only with the latest that a probable date of loss can be established with anything like the precision possible in the case of their late Saxon and Norman counterparts. Fortunately the demonetization of 1180 does seem to have been accomplished with great efficiency. The new coinage introduced in that year remained current until 1247, and a half-hearted reform in 1204 still left in circulation a high proportion of the original issues. As before it is usually possible to date the striking of a particular coin with some precision – quite recently Mr John Brand has modified somewhat a chronology worked out by

Lawrence – but it is only with the very latest coins, and those far from common, that the numismatist can suggest a date of loss with any greater accuracy than to the nearest decade. Incidentally, under Richard and John there was no change of the royal name, the coins continuing to read HENRICUS REX as they had under Henry II and were to again under Henry III. The year 1247 saw another major recoinage, but this time the new coins were to remain current for only half as long, the next recoinage taking place under Edward I in 1279. Once more, the date of striking of a particular coin is not too difficult to establish, though date of loss remains quite another matter.

Edward I's great reform of 1279 had many elements of novelty. The moneyer's name disappeared from the coins, and there was a realistic proportion of halfpence and farthings – hitherto these denominations had normally been obtained by the private citizen literally dividing pennies when and as the need arose. The types of the penny adopted were novel but remained constant until late in the reign of Henry VII, so that it is not surprising that worn specimens occur as we have seen in fifteenth- and even early sixteenth-century contexts. Theoretically there were recoinages in 1344 and 1351 with downward adjustments of weight, but there was no intentional differentiation of the design, and it needs a numismatist to tell a penny of Edward III from one of his grandfather, or, for that matter, from one of Edward IV. This discrepancy between date of striking and possible date of loss is the more unfortunate because the magnificent work of the Fox brothers more than half a century back means that the different issues between 1279 and 1344 can be dated with quite remarkable precision, while the few loose ends are fast being tied up by present-day researchers such as Mr Elmore Jones and Mr Peter Woodhead.

In the 1340s gold coins were successfully added to the English currency, as in 1351 were two silver denominations larger than the penny, namely the groat and half-groat. Thanks to the work of students such as Lawrence for the fourteenth century, and Mr Blunt and the late C. A. Whitton for the fifteenth, not to mention Mr Herbert Schneider with respect to the gold of the whole period, the date of striking of the great majority of the coins continues to be capable of being established with a very high degree of exactness, but, as usual, date of loss is often another matter. Fortunately for the archaeologist, though, the period was one when the weights of both the gold and the silver coins had periodically to be adjusted downwards to meet inflationary pressures, and it is usually possible to suggest quite reasonable limits within which the gold and larger silver coins are likely to have been lost. But, as already remarked, it is precisely these coins of the higher values which are less likely to come an excavator's way.

This all too brief survey of the potentiality of the English material may be rounded off by a sketch of the position obtaining in Scotland and in Ireland. What use of money there was in Scotland before the twelfth century seems clearly associated with, and confined to, the Vikings who brought in a limited amount of English and foreign coin. In the 1130s the Scottish kings started striking on a very small scale, and at the same time considerable quantities of English coins began to be introduced. By the end of the century a Scottish coinage was firmly established, but always it was supplemented by substantial import of English coin, and it is interesting to see Scotland following suit whenever there was a major development in England. This position continued to obtain until the middle of the fourteenth century, but after that Scotland was unable to keep up with the resources of her more powerful and much richer neighbour, and the weights of Scottish coins soon fell much more steeply than was the case with their English counterparts. A consequence of this was that English coin began to circulate much less freely in Scotland, and fifteenth-century Scottish hoards contain only a proportion of English pieces, while it is only the odd Scottish coin that is now found in an English context. This contrasts with the position before 1356 when Scottish pence were virtually legal tender south of the Border, and when Scottish hoards were composed predominantly of English pence. The pioneer work of Burns at the end of the last century has worn extremely well, and there is particularly happy collaboration between the National Museum of Antiquities, the Hunterian Museum and private individuals such as Mr Ian Stewart, whose special competence Mr Robert Stevenson and Miss Anne Robertson are enabled by their own distinction generously to recognize. The position in Scotland, then, is broadly comparable with that obtaining in England for the Plantagenet and post-Plantagenet periods, virtually all coins being capable of being dated with considerable precision as regards their striking, and rather less exactness as regards their period of currency. Again, inflation in the fourteenth and fifteenth centuries does mean that coins of the major denominations (and Scotland was very prolific in varieties of these) did not normally enjoy a very long life except when subjected to speculative hoarding, while theoretically obsolete small change tended to linger on in general currency.

In Ireland the position is again fortunate in the extreme. The National Museum in Dublin and the Ulster Museum have had, in Dr Liam O'Sullivan and Mr Wilfred Seaby, officials peculiarly at home in the Hiberno-Norse and Anglo-Irish series, and deft in cultivating the happiest of relations with other workers in the field. Before the tenth century virtually no money seems to have been brought into Ireland, but then the Vikings imported increasing quantities of English coin before beginning in *c.* 995 a coinage of their own. Most of these Dublin issues can be dated to the nearest decade, and a falling weight-standard means that it is unlikely that the currency of a given piece was particularly long, especially since some trouble was taken clearly to differentiate the various emissions. Soon after 1125 Ireland relapsed into virtual coinlessness, but surprisingly soon after the Anglo-Norman invasion a local coinage was being produced to meet the needs of the new colonists. In 1204 this was integrated by John into the main stream of English coinage, and for the next century the primary function of the Irish mints was to supplement the issues of those in England, a very high proportion of the coins being shipped overseas without first going into circulation in Ireland. Increasingly, however, quantities of English coin found their way across the water, and in the fourteenth and early fifteenth centuries what coined money there was in Ireland consisted almost entirely of English and Scottish pieces, many of them obsolete and all in a progressively more and more worn condition. It is only very occasionally that an expert will hazard any very close dating for a single find, though formulae are being worked out which should enable hoards to be dated rather more closely, and one thing for which the archaeologist in these islands must always be prepared is the possibility that he himself will bring to light a coin-hoard. In recent years this has actually happened, at Southampton and Winchester as well as at Llantrithyd and Mellifont. During the years from 1460 to *c.* 1505, the Anglo-Irish colony took the bit between its teeth and struck numerous coinages in defiance of the English king. These, during the last few years, have been studied in depth, and the dates of striking are often known almost to the year. Some were demonetized almost at once, but others were more enduring. A number were current through the sixteenth century, and hence dating of loss is often a matter of the very greatest difficulty.

It is to be hoped that the foregoing may have indicated to archaeologists the broad pattern of exactness with which they can hope that their finds of individual coins can be dated when referred to a competent numismatist. Gaps and omissions there are in plenty. Wales provides one obvious example, though there, generally speaking, the pattern follows the English one with perhaps a greater tendency for coin to linger after formal demonetization where the writ of the English king did not run. Equally, due consideration has not been given to the question of foreign coin. At different times, though almost always in technical breach of legislation, quite a number of European and even Islamic coins might enjoy a more or less furtive currency, and again there are very few numismatists who are able to indicate the chronological limits within which such pieces are likely to have been lost. Kufic *dirhams*, Carolingian *oboles*, *rosaries*, *lusshebournes*, *chaises d'or*, *doubles tournois* and *double patards*, all are likely to be met with, and especially when the site under excavation is that of a medieval emporium. Often it will need the expertise of a numismatist not only to date but also to evaluate the significance of the find – for example a Samanīd *dirham* in an early tenth-century context will normally point to Viking contact and not to direct trade with Bokhara and Samarkand. More, too, might have been said about hoards, and especially on the subject of every numismatist's secret hope. This is that he may be granted a hoard still in its container, or at least with the coins extracted from the vessel and laid out in the presumed reverse order of their insertion. By the use of serial-numbered small envelopes the last should be perfectly feasible, and much light might be thrown on the hoarding habits of the owner. In particular we should be able at once to decide whether a particular hoard had been accumulated over a number of years, or whether it was ready money hastily concealed in some crisis, a distinction which at present often cannot be made at all, especially in those cases where corrosion prevents an accurate assessment of wear, a criterion which at the best of times can be as deceptive as subjective.

In conclusion there should be stressed yet again the importance of the closest liaison between the archaeologist and the numismatist. If the latter is to give all the assistance of which he is capable, he must be kept fully in the picture. So much can depend on so little. For example, a coin adhering to masonry may have come into contact with it when the mortar was wet, in which case the *terminus post quem* seems unassailable, or the adhesion may be consequent upon corrosion of the coin, in which case the wall may have been a century old when the coin found its way against it. Nor is stratification always a completely reliable guide. The writer knows of what was demonstrably a late nineteenth-century electrotype of an ancient coin which had found its way under an early nineteenth-century footing, presumably because of a combination of a drought and massive soil-shrinkage with subsequent heavy rain. Given co-operation and mutual confidence, though, the archaeologist and the numismatist should be able to resolve many problems of chronology, especially when neither expects too much of the evidence.

22.i.68

The Queen's University
Belfast

Metres, areas and robbing

Martin Biddle *and* Birthe Kjølbye-Biddle

This paper presents three aspects of excavation method and interpretation which have arisen during the last few years on excavations in Winchester. The first deals with the introduction of metric measurements and the advantages of a co-ordinate system; the second with problems of open-area excavation on deeply stratified sites; the third with the excavation and interpretation of robbed structures.

1 The metric system and co-ordinate planning

The utility of the metric system has long been recognized by archaeologists who are now already beginning to make the change-over that is national policy for the 1970s. Professor R. J. C. Atkinson has already described in *Antiquity* the code of practice adopted by the Department of Archaeology at University College, Cardiff (1965: 299). His article suggests the use of a number of metric scales including 1 cm. to 25 cm. Although this is close to the normal English scale of 1:24 (*i.e.* ½ inch to 1 foot) it is somewhat awkward and unusual. In the metric system it will normally be found best to draw plans at 1:20, sections and details at 1:10. There are, however, very real advantages, apart from conformity, which derive from the adoption of the metric system.

Plans and sections are rarely reproduced at standard scales in British publications. They are not therefore easily comparable, even within one paper, except by using the visual scales normally provided. Using the metric system such drawings can be easily reproduced at standard scales, such as 1:50, 1:100, 1:200 etc. They are then comparable one with another and with drawings in other publications, provided only that the scale of reduction is quoted. Visual scales should, of course, continue to be given. A drawing made at 1:20 can be reproduced for publication at 1:100 merely by instructing the blockmaker to reduce to 1/5 linear.

In practice metric measurements are much simpler to use than the English, and it is only when using metres that a true co-ordinate system can be employed. This makes it possible to refer to any point on a site by a unique reference exactly comparable to a National Grid Reference. There are three main advantages:

(1) The use of cumbersome references, involving Arabic and Roman numerals and letters, with the inherent likelihood of confusion, is eliminated.

(2) Surveying is quick, easy and accurate: a point is fixed by two co-ordinates and not by triangulation with its many possible errors; the use of measuring frames permits the rapid planning of even the most complex features.

(3) Large numbers of individual finds can be quickly and exactly plotted.

A co-ordinate system can be established and used in the following way (fig. 16*a*):

(1) A theoretical point of origin (0/0) is chosen to lie outside any possible extension of the area to be excavated. This point is conventionally to the south-west.

(2) From this point a co-ordinate system is then applied to the site in such a way that the axes run north and east, or parallel to the main axes of the site, whichever is most convenient. In order to eliminate a possible source of confusion in giving references, the values on the axes in the area of the excavation ought to be different, e.g. on one axis in the 200s, on the other in the 100s. In practice, the point of origin (0/0) will thus lie well away from the site and is completely arbitrary.

(3) The next step (fig. 16*b*) is to mark the divisions of each axis by pegging at regular intervals around the perimeter of the excavation as convenient, 10, 5, 2 or 1 m. apart. Further pegging will be adapted to the nature of the excavation. If a grid of trenches is being used, the baulks will be laid out in the normal way, and pegged as necessary. This is not, however, the best use of the co-ordinate system, which is especially suited to open-area excavation (see below). Within such an area-excavation the intersections of the co-ordinates can be marked with nails or by thin steel rods driven into the ground at 1 m. or 2 m. intervals. Each peg or rod is then labelled with its co-ordinate (Eastings before Northings, as in a National Grid Reference).

(4) The result is that any area, any point on the site, likewise the exact location of any find, can be referred to by a single unique reference consisting of two co-ordinates: e.g. 135/237 could refer either to a point or, when appropriately labelled (e.g. by writing M in a square, [M], in front of the number), to a 1 m. square whose south-west corner was defined by these co-ordinates. In the same way 147·51/239·49 would refer to a 1 cm. square, in fact for practical purposes to a point (fig. 16*b*). The addition of the Ordnance Datum (O.D.) level fixes such a point in three dimensions.

(5) The presence of labelled co-ordinate markers on the ground means that in surveying no measurement need be taken longer than half the side of the marked square, i.e. 1 m. or 0·5 m. By using thin steel frames, 1 m. × 0·5 m., divided by cross-wires into 10 cm. squares, laid on the ground in relation to the co-ordinates (plate 1), all detail can be planned without further measurement, since at 1:20 each 10 cm. square on the frame is represented by a 0·5 cm. square on the drawing.

(6) The co-ordinate markers also ensure a high degree of accuracy in planning, since each marker is set out from the pegged axes. Each of the many co-ordinate markers is thus an individually surveyed point. Errors cannot, therefore, build up in the course of planning, since an error in one marker would immediately be discovered by comparison with the next.

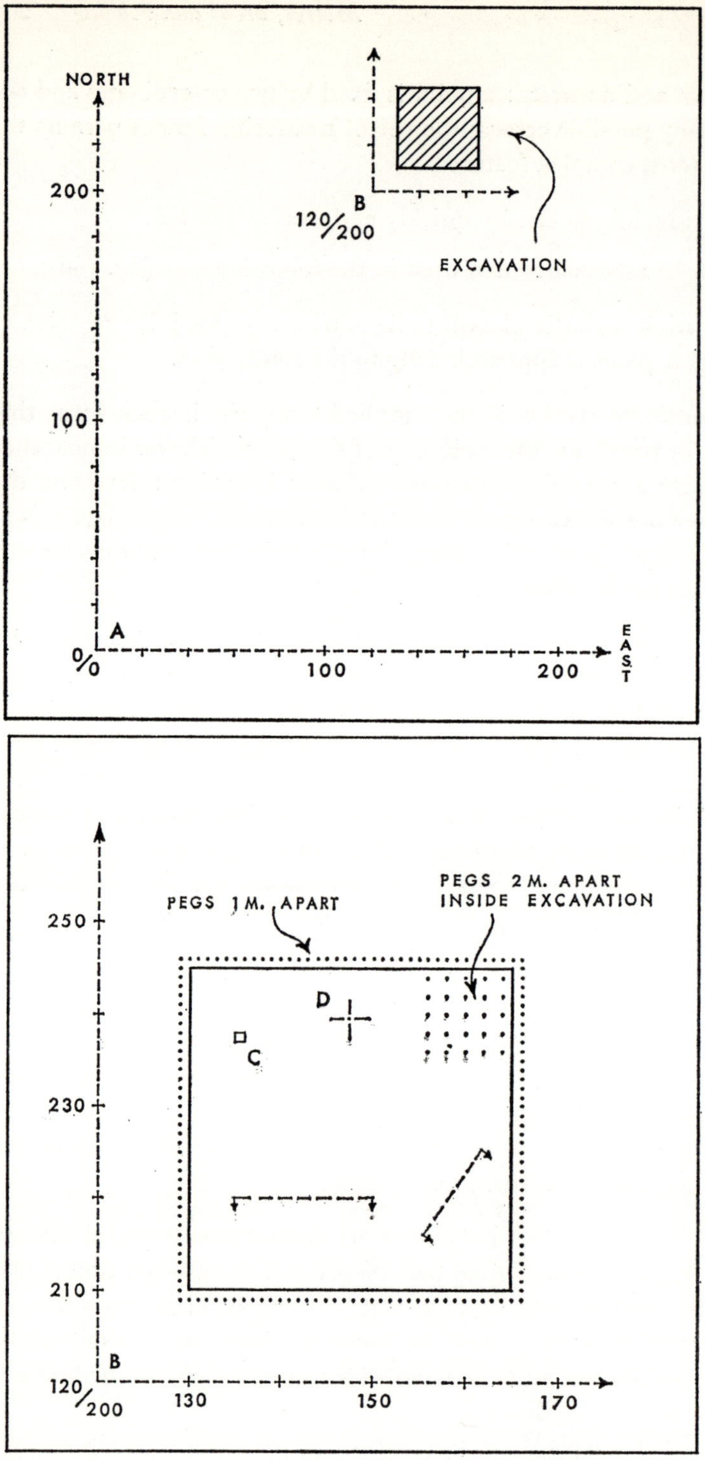

Figure 16 (*a*) The theory of the co-ordinate system (1:4,000), and (*b*) the application of the co-ordinate system (1:1,000). In these figures – A: theoretical point of origin, O/O; B: false point of origin with values suitable for the excavation area. The values of B control the theoretical position of A; C: point in the excavation (or S.W. corner of a [M], i.e. 1 m^2) referred to by two co-ordinates: 135/237; D: a point of which the co-ordinates are 147.51/239.49

Plate 1 The control and planning of an open-area excavation (Lower Brook Street, Winchester, 1968). Note the stringing-out of the baulk/section lines, the white squares of the co-ordinate markers, and the use of the planning grids

Plate 2 The excavation of a robbed building: the foundations of the tenth-century eastern apse of the Old Minster at Winchester were almost totally robbed out in A.D. 1093–4. The plan was recovered, and the sequence of construction established, by excavation of the robber trenches in 1965

Plate 3 Old Minster, Winchester, 1964. This foundation of large stone blocks had been partly removed by stone-robbers, but the bottom edge of the robber-trench still preserved the outline of the missing stones. To the left, a peak of earth is visible between two robber-trenches of foundations of different periods

Plate 4 Old Minster, Winchester, 1963. In this case, a trial trench has run along a totally robbed foundation, the line of which is preserved, even to the detail of individual stones, by the bottom edge of the robber-trench

Plate 5 Hen Domen, Montgomery. Building I from the south-west. Scales in feet

Plate 6 Hen Domen, Montgomery. Typical post-socket. Scale in inches

Plate 7 (below left) Chandraketugarh: the brick temple *Photo. Archaeological Survey of India*

Plate 8 (below right) Nagarjunkonda: ghats on the Krishna *Photo. Archaeological Survey of India*

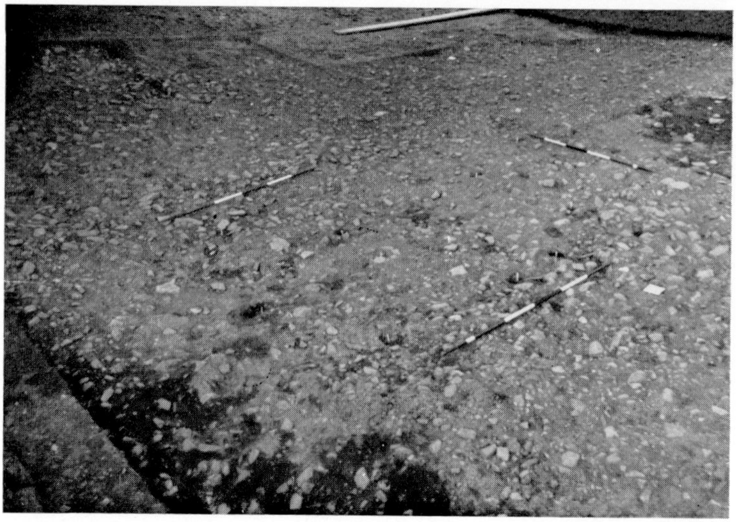

2 A method of open-area excavation

One of the major problems in excavation is the need to combine the conflicting requirements of horizontal and vertical observation and record. This problem is particularly acute in the excavation of large areas. The normal solution, first devised by Sir Mortimer Wheeler at Maiden Castle, has been to excavate a grid of squares divided by baulks. In this way the excavation of a large area can be combined with a permanent record of the vertical stratification. Other advantages of the method include ease of control, subdivision and record, together with ready access to all parts of the site for the removal of spoil; it is clear that the method is sometimes particularly suited to the excavation of stone buildings. There are, however, serious disadvantages: the trench pattern is imposed on the site, often to the detriment of the pattern of structures, and once established the trench pattern is fixed. The deeper the squares go, the more difficult it becomes to view and comprehend the structures as a whole. If the alignment of the structures proves to be oblique to the trenches, serious distortions confuse the vertical record. Furthermore, if 10-ft squares are dug, as much as 36% of the area will be left unexcavated beneath the baulks, even if these are only 2 ft 6 in. wide – hence the well-known cry: 'It's under the baulk.' These baulks must either be dug later in isolation, or left undug, in which case they will for ever obscure much of the plan. On a site with very complex stratification, correlation of layers from one side of a baulk to the other may be impossible.

The disadvantages of the grid excavation method are such that it is impossible to dig deeply stratified timber buildings satisfactorily in this way. Sites like this occur in towns: at Verulamium in 1958 Professor Sheppard Frere abandoned 10-ft squares in favour of long trenches 12 ft wide to excavate superimposed timber buildings with highly complex stratification (1959: 6). In Winchester even this compromise has had to be abandoned in favour of a single large uninterrupted area, 30 m. by 24 m. (Biddle 1965: 245 and 1966: 313–16). Open-area excavation has been used successfully on single period sites, or sites where there is no significant stratification above the general level of the natural soil, such as Yeavering and Cheddar (Webster 1963: 86–8), but it is equally necessary on very deeply stratified sites where it is vitally important to combine a full overall appreciation with a constant vertical record.[1]

After the exact area for excavation has been selected, pegs are put at 1 m. intervals all round the edge of the excavation.[2] The whole of the first level – garden soil, turf etc. – is then stripped off. The exposed surface is very carefully cleaned. If no features appear, the process of stripping and cleaning is repeated in, for example, 5 cm. levels until layers or other features are reached. A full co-ordinate system can then be set out, and co-ordinate markers inserted at 1 m. or 2 m. intervals within the pegged area. It must be emphasized that such horizontal stripping is only to be used in unstratified deposits,

[1] Mr Humphrey Case has told us of his use of this method on a Bronze Age barrow at Poole, Dorset, in 1949 (1952: 154–7), adding that he would always use this method again for deep excavation.

[2] When the axes of the site are unknown, and cannot be discovered before excavation by one of the prospecting techniques, it may be necessary to regard this first pegging as provisional and to re-orientate the grid after the first stripping has revealed the axes of the site. If this difficulty is likely to occur, the initial pegging need be sufficient only to measure-in any finds from the first stripping. These preliminary pegs must, of course, be recorded by their final co-ordinates when the final system is established.

such as the top level of a site. The first level that has been stripped in this way is no loss: it is not sealed and any features in it are more likely to have shown up with very careful horizontal cleaning than in section; if nothing has been found in this way, it is fairly certain that nothing useful would have emerged from trenching in squares. When distinct layers or other features such as buildings appear, they must be very thoroughly cleaned and planned in all their detail (see below). At this stage it is possible to ask questions of the site as it has emerged and to decide on further action, and only now, when the main lines are starting to emerge, is it necessary to decide on the position and direction of sections. Some of these will be major sections which will hopefully illustrate the total history of the site; others will be minor or temporary sections, such as pit or post-hole sections, designed to solve local problems. When the section lines have been decided, they must all be strung out on the ground, allowing no more than 25 cm. for the width of any baulk. The section lines are then planned and given reference numbers. Because of the co-ordinate system, a section line may be described as being, for example, on the 220 line, or, if it is diagonal to the axes, as running from 155.50/216 to 161.75/225.10. The co-ordinates of each end of a section must be recorded, and also the direction of view (fig. 16*b*).

The layers are now removed and recorded, the extent of each being planned in the usual manner. Excavation continues to either side of the baulks (or, if there are no baulks, as in a quadrant, to one side of the section line only) until a major layer appears which seems to extend over a considerable area. The surface of this layer is traced wherever it extends, and, after cleaning, the baulk sections are drawn, particular care being taken to record the top of the lowest surface. The O.D. level of each section datum is recorded. The baulks can now be removed to the exposed surface and an unimpeded view obtained of the entire site. A second basic plan is then made of every detail over the whole site. Any intermediate plans of lesser features lying above the surface now reached can be related to this or any other major plan, since they are keyed to the relevant co-ordinates. It is especially easy to compare plans one to another if they are all drawn on transparent plastic film.

One can now pause again and consider the problems of the excavation with the entire site visible before one, and with a full vertical and horizontal record of the excavation readily available in an easily comparable form. Questions can again be asked of the site, major problems isolated and decisions taken on the way to solve them in further excavation. The major sections already established will continue, others may be added and lesser sections can be placed as required. Excavation will then recommence and continue in this way until complete. Whenever it is necessary to continue the drawing of lower levels in sections already partly drawn, it is only necessary to relate the O.D. level of the new datum to the O.D. level of the old datum already marked on the drawing. If care has been taken in the last part of the drawing to measure the top of the lowest layer (which has in turn become the uppermost layer), damage to the surface of this layer during excavation does not affect the section, as the top of the layer is already recorded.

The main advantage of this method is that the excavation area is open and is never impeded by permanent baulks. The pattern seen in excavation is the actual pattern of the site and not the imposed pattern of trenches. An overall view of the horizontal is always obtainable. At the same time there is a complete vertical record in sections, some of which will record the entire sequence of stratification, while others will have been established to answer problems as they appear. Although none of the baulks are permanent, the sections have been drawn from proper visual observation and not just from levelling, as has been advocated in other suggested methods of open-area excavation. Most important, the method is completely flexible at all stages.

There are, of course, difficulties. It cannot be overemphasized that the method requires exceptional site discipline, cleanliness, care and clarity of thought. If the nature of the site demands open-area excavation, and these requirements cannot be met, then an excavation should not be attempted. It is particularly easy to forget to lay out section lines when digging recommences after a pause. Section lines must be kept strung out at all times (plate 1), except during photography, and the level must be in constant use to ascertain the absolute relationships of one part of a section to another, as well as the overall relief of the site. Since baulks are only preserved vertically for a few levels at a time, and there is no opportunity to return to the evidence when the baulk has been removed, it is necessary to record the minutest changes in colour and texture in section and in plan. In practice, plans should show a picture of the entire excavated surface, no part of which should not be represented by some convention on the plan. Even an apparently featureless clay surface is itself a clay surface, and its extent can, and must, be shown. Every stone, every variation should be drawn, and full use made of colour on the drawing. The plans ought to be as detailed and sensitive a record of the site as the sections normally are.

The use of the co-ordinate system and of measuring frames makes so detailed a record comparatively simple and quick to prepare. Since it is also most useful to relate plans from level to level, it is convenient to draw them on a transparent medium, such as plastic film. This is dimensionally stable and unaffected by rain and mud. It can be preprinted in standard sheets with a grid which ensures exact correlation from plan to plan. Such film – Ilford Azoflex is especially suitable – takes all drawing media, and is so transparent that many plans can be superimposed and read without the need for a tracing box.

A more fundamental problem concerns the actual procedure of the excavation. When one chooses a distinctive and extensive layer as the point at which to pause, record sections and remove baulks, a qualitative decision is taken which may not really reflect an equally important phase in the history of the site. Major floors may have been worn away, so that they are represented in excavation only by minor patches removed and recorded between one (apparently) major layer and the next. This is a problem that can be examined in subsequent interpretation, and the records of such an excavation are designed, especially in the use of transparent film, to permit such a reinterpretation and re-combination of plans. Only the site photographs, recording the major stages of the excavation, cannot avoid the full implications of decisions made in the progress of the excavation.

In conclusion, this suggested method of open-area excavation seems to give exceptional flexibility of approach, while combining the need for horizontal and vertical excavation and record. It requires, however, great site discipline and well-trained workers, a difficulty which can be met by working slowly while people are being trained.

3 The excavation of robbed structures

When buildings are robbed, even the foundations are often removed, leaving only trenches (called robber-trenches) which are usually back-filled with rubble and rubbish that cannot be re-used. If foundations have been robbed in this way, the only method of tracing the plan of the building is by excavating the robber-trenches. All this is now common practice and has been known for some time. W. H. St J. Hope and Harold Brakspear began to understand how to trace monastic plans from robber-trenches in the first decade of this century (e.g. at Stanley Abbey, excavated in 1905–6, Brakspear 1907: 493–516), and much of the plan of Abingdon Abbey was recovered in this way in 1922 (Biddle *et al.* 1968), but it was Sir Mortimer Wheeler in the 1930s at Verulamium who first demonstrated the nature of robber-trenches in an archaeologically modern manner (Wheeler 1936: plate CVIIB, cf. plate LXXXVIIIA). Subsequent comment in many excavation reports and manuals has been limited to the tracing of plans by means of trenching at right-angles to robber trenches. There seems to have been little comment on the possibility of working out the structural sequence of a building, the foundations of which have been very heavily, or entirely, robbed.[1] As a result of the excavation of the Old Minster at Winchester in 1962–8 (plate 2), it appears that, with close observation of the shape and filling of robber-trenches, it is possible to establish the constructional sequence of walls of which only robber-trenches survive, as well as the sequence of robbing, though the latter may not be significant (Biddle 1965: 251–4).

Three factors control the value of robber-trenches as evidence for the structural history of a building:

(1) The activity of the robber. Comment has often been made on the haphazard character of robbing, where walls are left in one place, but completely removed in others. It is necessary to consider how the robber worked. He certainly did no more than was absolutely necessary; he stood on top of the wall, or actually in the robber-trench where the wall had already been removed, and only dug into or along the wall, rarely cutting into the surrounding soil. Having taken the stones he wanted, he threw the debris behind him, filling up the bottom of the trench as he went. The general mess will have been considerable, small pieces of wall would easily be missed, but economy of effort and quick filling ensured that the exact line of the bottom of the foundations was often perfectly preserved in the bottom of the robber-trench. Sometimes even the outline of individual foundation blocks can be seen impressed in the sides and bottom of a robber-trench (plates 3 and 4) (Biddle 1964: plate LIIIA). The upper parts of the sides of robber-trenches may slope steeply outwards, worn by weather and by the trampling of workmen during robbing. Frequent spills of soil in the filling of the robber-trenches are the result of this process. It is, therefore, the outline formed by the bottoms of robber-trenches, rather than the tops, which preserves most closely the plan of the foundations of the robbed building (fig. 17, A1, 2).

(2) Variation in foundations. Foundations of any one period of a building are likely to be similar, made of the same material, to the same width and depth. The main reason for variation within one period would be a change of superstructure; for example, a tower, or monumental entrance, would probably require deeper foundations. On the other hand, there is no reason why foundations of different periods should be similar. They might by chance be similar, but more usually, even if of similar materials, they will be of different

[1] An attempt in this direction was made in 1938 by J. S. P. Bradford and R. G. Goodchild in the excavation of the Roman temple at the Noah's Ark, Frilford (1939: 31 and plate IB).

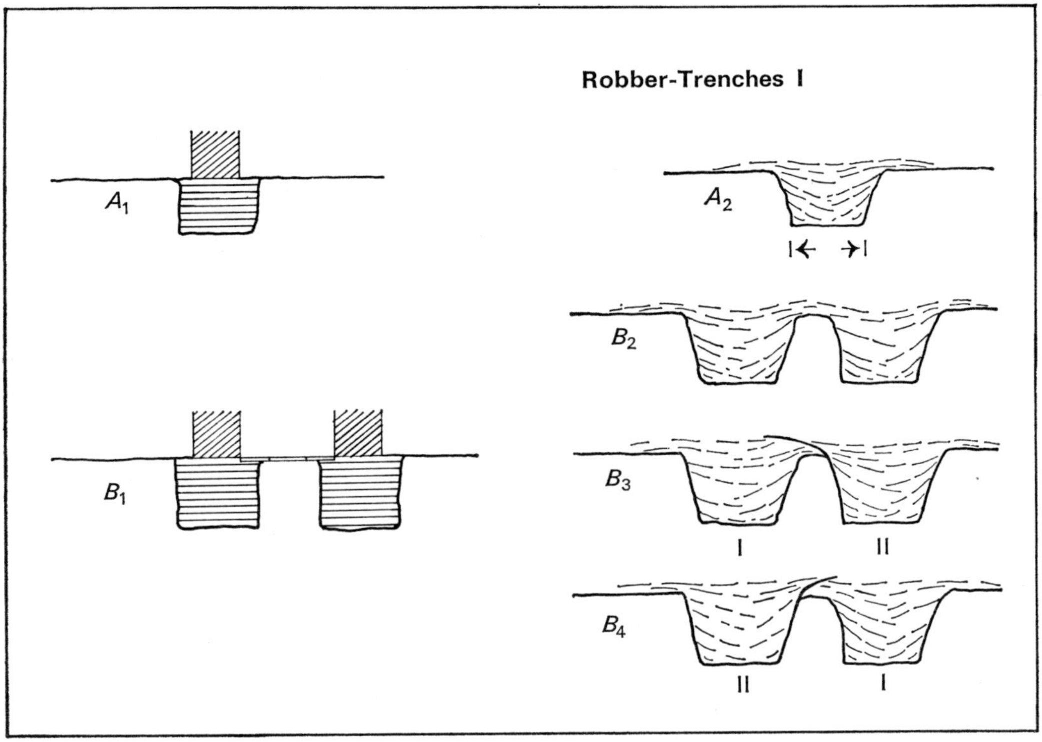

Figure 17

width and depth. Changes in period may therefore be reflected in sudden changes of level in the bottom of a robber-trench, or in its width (fig. 18). Records of the depth to which foundations were actually dug would not be kept, so variation would be bound to occur between the foundations of an original structure and those of alterations and additions to it. Anyone who has looked at surviving foundations of different periods in one building knows that they do vary.

At the point of junction between work of one period and another, foundations were often dug in such a way that they did not bond properly with the older structure. Above ground, this would be reflected in a straight-joint in the stonework. Below ground, a peak of undug soil would be left between the two foundations, because the foundations were narrower at the bottom than at the top (fig. 18, plate 3A). When such a peak of soil is found in the bottom of a robber trench it is an indication, even if the level of the bottom does not change, that the structure was here of two periods. These peaks do survive, even after robbing, and again show how minute details are preserved because of the way in which the robber worked. One must, of course, remember that ancient building-operations might not be strictly logical; foundations of different depth may be of the same period (e.g. additions of the same period to north and south of a standing church would be separate structures, not necessarily of the same character), and peaks of soil could represent the junction of the work of different gangs.

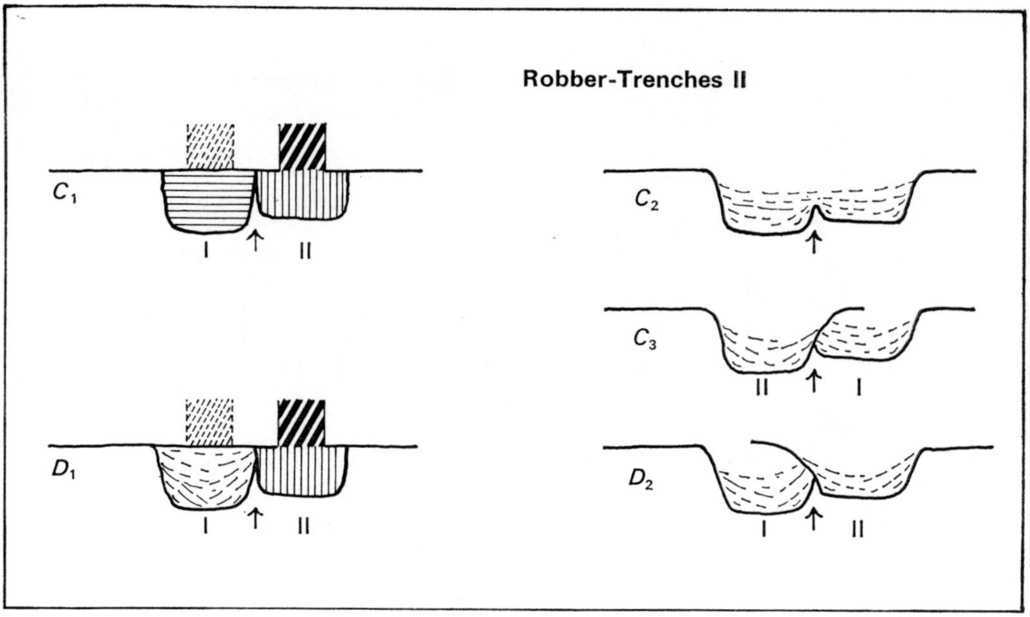

Figure 18

(3) The sequence of robbing. Not every part of a building is necessarily robbed at the same time. Part of a church may be left for ecclesiastical reasons; a wing of a house may serve some purpose long after the rest has gone; a building may be robbed from one end to another, or in fits and starts in no particular pattern. Such a sequence of robbing may, or may not, be of much significance. If, however, part of a building is suppressed in alteration and robbed-out, while the rest of the structure is not robbed until very much later, the sequence of robbing is most important, although the end product of both robbings – the trenches and their filling – may seem almost identical. The sequence of robbing must therefore be considered in the examination of any robbed structure. This sequence will show in the way in which the layers of one robber-trench cut, or merge with, those in another.

Turning to practical problems of excavation, the only way to appreciate the problems of a robbed building, and to decide how to solve them, is to see the plan of the robbed structure over large areas, or in its entirety (plate 2). Here is a clear case for open-area excavation, because only then can the problems be comprehended and the sections placed before any deep disturbance is begun.

The robber-trenches themselves must be excavated by means of transverse and longitudinal sections, so that the sequence of robbing as reflected in the behaviour of the filling may be recorded. Particular care should be given to examining and recording the character and behaviour of the bottom and lower sides of robber-trenches.

As for problems of interpretation, the stratigraphic evidence preserved in the filling of the robber-trenches is evidence only of the sequence of robbing. The sequence of construction is interpretation based on the total behaviour of the robber trenches compared one to another, in plan and in section, both in measurable features and non-metrical characteristics. In arriving at such an interpretation the basic requirement is an overall comprehension of the whole structure during excavation. The following possible situations may occur and must be carefully considered (figs 17–19):

A single foundation of one period (A1) is normally represented by a simple one-period robber-trench (A2).

Two walls of the same period close to one another, for example, the opposite walls of a corridor (B1), will appear as robber-trenches in one of the three following ways: simultaneous robbing and filling will be represented by two contemporary robber-trenches (B2); if one wall is robbed before the other, one or other of the robber-trenches will be the later (B3 or B4), but this sequence refers only to the robbing and not to the relative date of the walls concerned.

When two walls of different periods stand side by side (C1), their difference in date can be established after even the most thorough robbing. If both foundations are robbed at the same time (C2), the fact that two periods of construction are present may still be revealed by the different levels of the bottoms of the robber-trenches, and by the survival of a peak of earth between them. If the later wall and foundation are robbed first, and the earlier foundation second (possibly because, being already reduced to floor level, the earlier work was found only during the robbing of the later wall), then the sequence of robbing (C3) is the reverse of the sequence of construction. It may happen that the earlier wall has already been robbed before the final demolition, for example, at the time of alteration (D1); in this case the robbing of the later foundation will cut the earlier robber-trench (D2), and the sequence of robbing will reflect the sequence of construction.

Other variations can occur when an addition has been made to a building, particularly if this involved the demolition of a wall of the original structure (E1, E2). When Period II is built (fig. 19) Wall *a* of Period I may be robbed out entirely, or be destroyed only to floor level. If the foundation of Wall *a* is left in, the robbing of Wall *b*/*c* in the final demolition will cut Wall *a* (E3). Likewise, if the foundations of Wall *a* were entirely robbed-out during the alterations, leaving only a robber-trench, this robber-trench will be cut at the final demolition by the robber-trench of Wall *b*/*c*. A section taken along the line Z–Y will show that there is no change in the level of the bottoms of robber-trenches *a* and *b*, whatever the date of their respective robbings, and will thus indicate that Walls *a* and *b* were probably built at the same time. By comparison, in section W–X, changes in the bottoms of the robber-trenches, and the presence of a peak of soil, show that Walls *b* and *c* were built at different times, even if robbed at the same moment (E6).

If the foundation of Wall *a* was left in at the time of alteration and only discovered during the robbing of Walls *b* and *c* (these would inevitably be robbed first, because they would be standing and visible at the time of demolition), *a* might be robbed after the robbing of *b* and *c*. This would show in section Z–Y by robber trench *a* cutting robber-trench *b* (E4). It may, of course, happen that foundation *a* was robbed out as soon as it was discovered during the robbing of *b*. In this case section Z–Y will show only one period of robbing (E5). Other variations in the robbing sequence may occur, but the ones discussed are the most likely.

It will be noticed that section Z–Y may show three different robbing sequences, although Walls *a* and *b* were built at the same period. The interpretation of Walls *a* and *b*

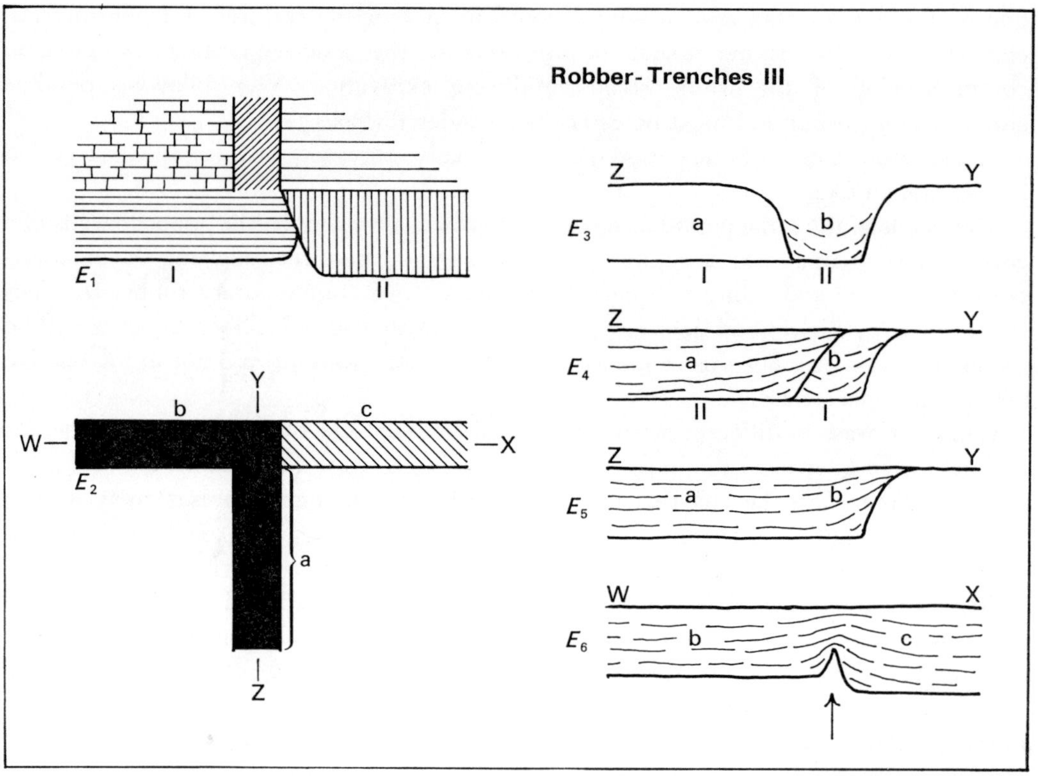

Figure 19

as contemporary can only be based on the similarity of their foundations as shown in the width and depth of the bottoms of their robber-trenches, as compared with the character of robber-trenches in other parts of the building, for example, robber-trench *c* in section W–X (E 6). Such an interpretation can only be confirmed by considering the sense it makes in relation to the whole plan of the robbed structure.

In case it might be thought that this discussion has been purely theoretical, we ought to say that it is based on our experience in the excavation of the Old Minster at Winchester, where all these variations have occurred.

In conclusion we stress that a final interpretation of the structural sequence of a robbed building can only emerge from considering all the factors of variation against an overall understanding of the plan and use of the structure. The result can never be more than an interpretation, but the more factors that are considered and solved, the more reliable this interpretation is likely to be. These considerations take the interpretation of robbed structures much further than seems previously to have been thought possible, and show that the excavation of major stone buildings should never (as sometimes happens with our national monuments) be entrusted to anyone but an experienced excavator with sufficient assistance to make detailed records.

22.iv.69

Winchester Research Unit
Winchester

References

Atkinson, R. J. C. 1965. British Archaeology and the Metric System. *Antiquity*. 39:299.

Biddle, M. 1964. Excavations at Winchester, 1962–3. *The Antiquaries Journal*. xliv:188–219.

Biddle, M. 1965. Excavations at Winchester, 1964. *The Antiquaries Journal*. xlv:230–64.

Biddle, M. 1966. Excavations at Winchester, 1965. *The Antiquaries Journal*. xlvi:308–32.

Biddle, M., Lambrick, H. T. and Myres, J. N. L. 1968. The Early History of Abingdon, Berkshire, and its Abbey. *Medieval Archaeology*. xii.

Bradford, J. S. P. and Goodchild, R. G. 1939. Excavations at Frilford, Berks., 1937–8. *Oxoniensia*. iv:1–70.

Brakspear, H. 1907. The Cistercian Abbey of Stanley, Wiltshire. *Archaeologia*. lx:493–516.

Case, H. 1952. The Excavation of Two Round Barrows at Poole, Dorset. *Proc. of the Prehistoric Society*. N.S. xviii:148–59.

Frere, S. S. 1959. Excavations at Verulamium, 1958. *The Antiquaries Journal*. xxxix:1–18.

Webster, G. 1963. *Practical Archaeology*. London.

Wheeler, R. E. M. and Wheeler, T. 1936. *Verulamium: A Belgic and Two Roman Cities*. Oxford.

Some aspects of the excavation of timber buildings

Philip Barker

It is now almost a platitude that the only way to understand the remains of timber buildings is to strip them horizontally over as wide an area as possible. Since the First World War there have been significant shifts in emphasis in excavation technique, first towards horizontal, then to vertical, and now again towards horizontal methods. The early excavators of our Roman towns, for instance, stripped whole groups of buildings, or even *insulae*, at a time, but paid little attention to the details of stratification. The plan was dominant. In the rigorously disciplined era of the 'thirties, when excavation techniques made enormous strides, principally under the influence of Sir Mortimer Wheeler, the section, the grid and three-dimensional recording became paramount. In the following years the plan receded in importance, often only being completed with a large proportion of interpolated dotted lines, the section seeming to offer a microcosm of the site's history. A glance at excavation reports spanning the Second World War will show how many beautifully-drawn, highly-detailed sections are coupled with summary plans. This emphasis on the section led to hundreds of sites being sampled by trial trenching, and the results were used as the basis for generalized statements about the whole site. A single section, even of a ditch, can be grossly misleading, as anyone who has cut multiple sections will know. At Hen Domen, Montgomery, the timber-castle site on which many of the observations in this paper are based, seven motte-ditch sections drawn within a length of sixty feet were all different, and only careful collation produced a solution which may yet, with further work, prove to be mistaken. It is abundantly clear that only total, or near-total, excavation will yield results which are not misleading. The possible exception, which has led to misapplied methods, is the more formalized, stereotype Roman building which may be dug in small areas, the plan being then extrapolated from them with some confidence. Prehistorians and, latterly, medievalists have found this method quite inadequate for the understanding of complexes of timber buildings, especially as in many cases the layers associated with these buildings are too thin, or more important, too discontinuous, to be seen in the sections, themselves frequently cut on a prearranged grid which takes no account of the underlying structures. Pioneer work, notably by Professor Bersu in Britain (see, for example, Bersu 1949) and Professor Steensberg in Denmark, has shown that the only way to elucidate the intricate patterns of the timber buildings to be found on many prehistoric and medieval sites, is to combine highly detailed observation of the layers in plan with a study of their composition in depth, a fully three-dimensional approach in which, so far as possible, every cubic centimetre of soil is made to yield the maximum information. Research in the 1950s on the peasant houses of deserted medieval villages stimulated the adoption of area techniques in medieval archaeology in England; in particular, the excavation of the classic site at Wharram Percy, begun by Professor Beresford, was continued in 1953 by Mr Hurst and Mr Golson, using techniques developed by Professor Steensberg. That these techniques are equally valid on sites full of stone buildings, even Roman ones, is now increasingly accepted. It is also becoming apparent that if sites, thought to contain only stone buildings, are excavated horizontally and in great detail, the plans of unsuspected timber buildings may emerge, as at Wroxeter (below).

A great many excavations of timber-built settlements are on land which has been under the plough for centuries since the site's desertion. When the topsoil is stripped off, either mechanically or by hand, in many cases a succession of pits, post-holes and timber-slots, often dating from the whole length of the occupation, is revealed at one level, and the chief problem is the unravelling of the tangle of features into a coherent sequence of patterns. This paper is not concerned with this type of excavation, but with sites where the evidence is more deeply stratified and presents itself in a multiplicity of ways. The examples will be drawn from the castle site at Hen Domen, Montgomery, and from a small area close to the site of the public baths at Wroxeter, *Viroconium Cornoviorum*, in Shropshire.

1 Hen Domen

Hen Domen is the site of a small timber castle built soon after the Norman Conquest and abandoned by 1300. It has never been ploughed, and a stone-free turf, some four inches thick, has developed over the underlying archaeological layers. As the writer, who directed the excavation, had no idea what to expect under this turf, the method used was to strip it by hand from an area of approximately 5,000 sq. ft (all that could be dealt with by the labour available), to remove all the topsoil (Layer I), which was easily distinguished by its texture and colour from the underlying layers, and to clean the surfaces of these layers meticulously without removing a single stone (plate 5). It very quickly became apparent that the stones were not randomly distributed but formed patterns. The most striking of these were circles of small stones which varied in diameter from a few inches to a foot or more (plate 6). The stones were sometimes set on edge and often enclosed a shallow saucer-shaped depression, rarely more than an inch deep, which contained dark stone-free soil. These depressions were emptied with great care, and as a check against accidental 'manufacture' of the features, the buckets of spoil were examined to ensure that no stones had been removed. They were clearly not post-holes of the conventional kind, having virtually no depth. The first one or two of these circles to be discovered were thought to be accidental alignments, but when it was seen that they formed rows (fig. 20, IV), it was apparent that they must represent man-made structures, not necessarily flimsy, but not deeply embedded, the sockets or emplacements of posts standing on the ground. When the whole underlying surface was studied, it could be seen that in a number of places the stones were aligned in rows which were often very short but were apparently related to the circles. Examples of these in fig. 20 are features 22/9, 22/13, 21/1, 21/23, 21/5, 13/21 and the line south of features 21/16 and 21/15.

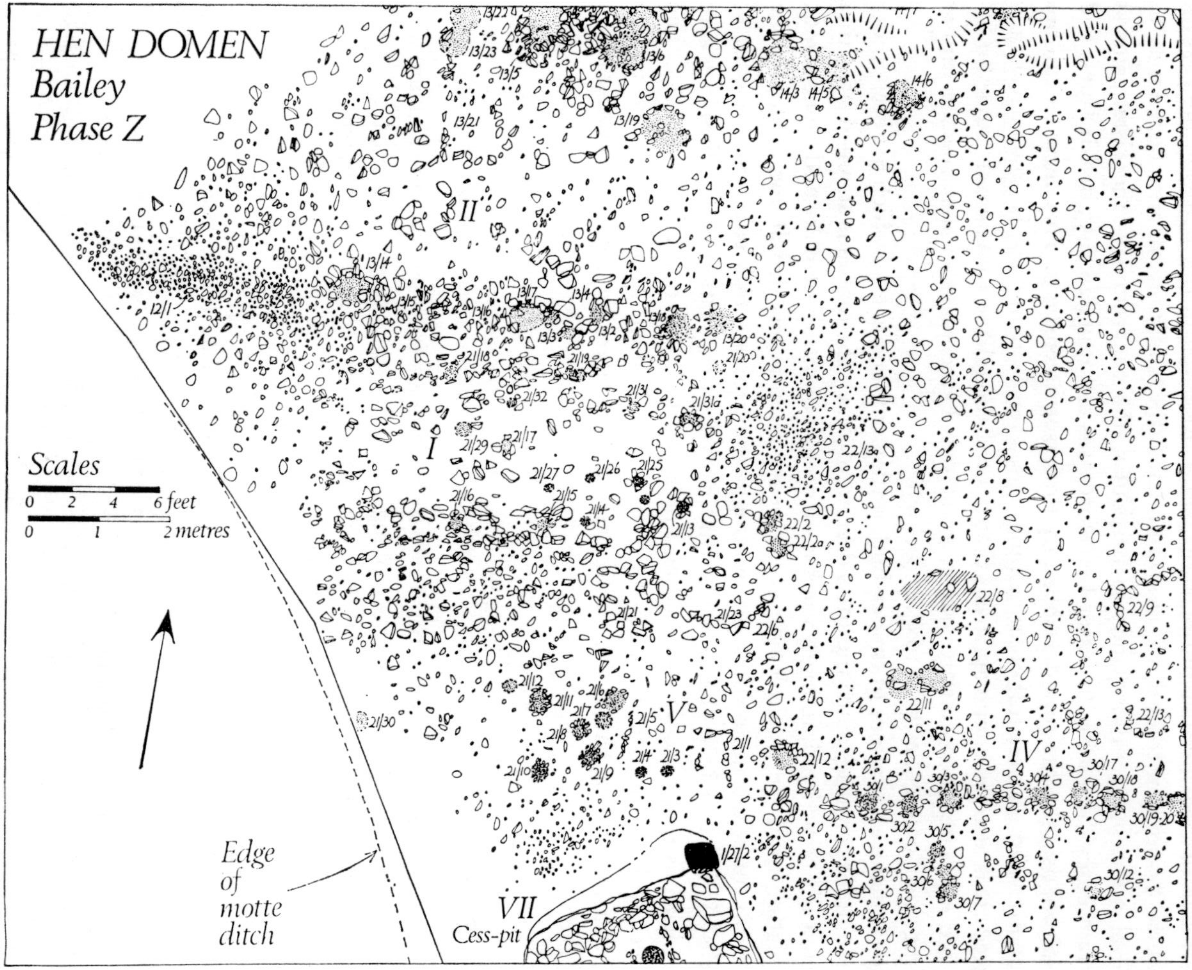
HEN DOMEN
Bailey
Phase Z
Scales
0 2 4 6 feet
0 1 2 metres
Edge of motte ditch
VII
Cess-pit
I
II
IV
V

Figure 20

Two coherent structural plans can be distinguished in the area reproduced in fig. 20. Structure IV appears to be a fence, attached perhaps to the corner of the large cess-pit VII, the stone circles representing post-sockets, though it must have been strutted since it could hardly have stood unsupported. A rectangular building, I (figs 20 and 21), lies to the north of the cess pit. It is bounded on the east by a pebble surface F/22/13a, on the south by a greater accumulation of larger stones, and on the north by a path F/12/1 which passes between it and a row of larger shallow post-sockets, Features 13/14, 13/15, 13/16, 13/17, 13/4, 13/3, 13/2, 13/18. Its side walls are marked by parallel rows of small stones and its doorway appears to lie between post-sockets 21/31a and 21/13, leading to the pebble surface. Stone alignments 21/23 and 22/6, together with sockets 22/2 and 22/2a, may form a small outhouse. A few small post-sockets lie between the parallel rows of stones which form the side walls, and there are also some cross-rows of stones which divide the side-wall rows into partitions or cells. There is an important diagonal stone-row between Features 21/16 and 21/31, which, although its structural relationship with the rectangular building was baffling, was recorded as it appeared. Though there is little doubt that the stone arrangement and the post-sockets represent the site of a building, it is difficult to envisage it in three dimensions. The same difficulties apply, of course, to the other structures adumbrated in fig. 20, as well as those in the excavated area beyond the portion depicted. Discussion of the probable form of construction is outside the scope of this short paper, but it appears to be some sort of transition between post-hole, ground-fast building and true timber-framing. The building almost certainly had a wooden floor, and there was no trace of a hearth.

Up to this point, the technique of excavation had been simple, consisting merely of cleaning everything underlying Layer I, the humus. The question then arose, what to do next? It happened that winter intervened and frost loosened the top inch or two of the surface, together with many of the stones. It was decided merely to remove the loosened earth down to the next recognizable layer, whatever that might prove to be, and to remove all the loose stones, leaving those that were more deeply embedded. In this way a layer between one and two inches thick was removed over the whole surface, except at the tail of the rampart where the layer, called for convenience Master Layer II, was three to four inches thick. It was with surprise and pleasure that we watched a whole new pattern of stone alignments, postholes and other evidence of buildings emerge. Two areas of this penultimate occupation, Y, are reproduced as figs 21 and 22.

The plan of building IX (fig. 21) consists of a stone arrangement, 21/36, which is symmetrical about the long axis of the building, being polygonal in outline but containing symmetrically a double semi-circle of stones. A short line of stones, 21/39, joins 21/36 to two short alignments, 21/38 and 21/37, which lie at right-angles to the building's axis. These proved to be the anomolous diagonal line of stones, noted above, crossing building I, and its significance was now recognized.

Roughly parallel to 21/38 and 21/37 was a slight scarp, of about an inch, down to a clay and earth floor 21/40, which was bounded on the north-west by a mass of stones, the edge of which was more or less at right-angles to the axis of the building. There was one post-hole of ordinary form, 21/41. Indications of the side walls of this building were, as can be seen, almost entirely lacking. They can, however, be interpolated with some confidence from the corners of the polygonal/apsidal end, past the ends of 21/38 and

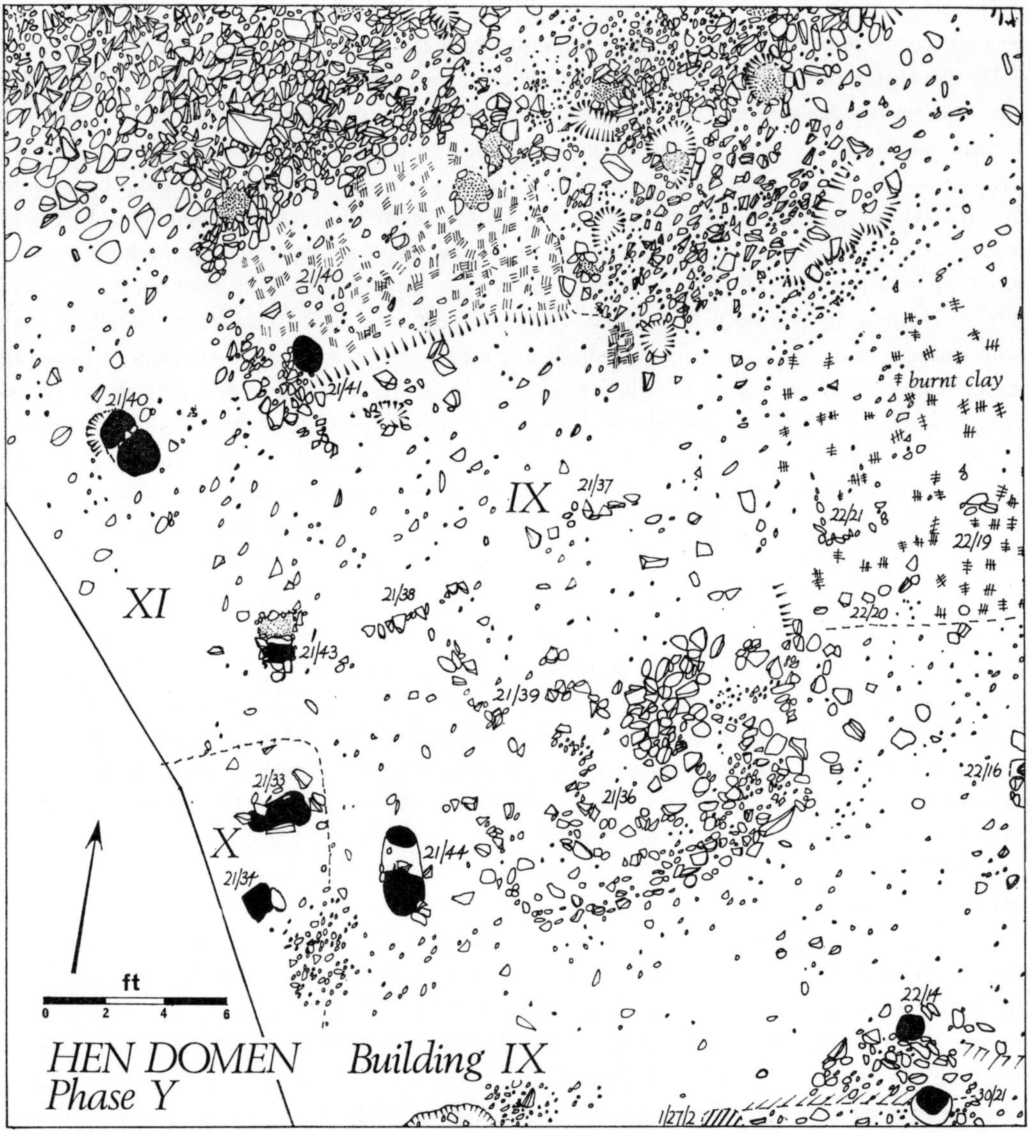

Figure 21

21/37 to join the sides of the clay floor 21/40. If this is done, a three-bay apsidal building, lying north-west/south-east, emerges, with perhaps a small porch in the north-east wall, indicated by alignments 22/21 and 22/20. (Though these may be connected with the as yet incompletely excavated burnt area to the east.)

It is tempting to see this as a chapel of the twelfth century (a date in accordance with the pottery and the stratification beneath), and this assumption is strengthened somewhat by the discovery of a stone holy-water stoup in one of the underlying post-holes of a previous building on the same alignment.

Whatever the truth of this interpretation, it is important to note here that the floor of

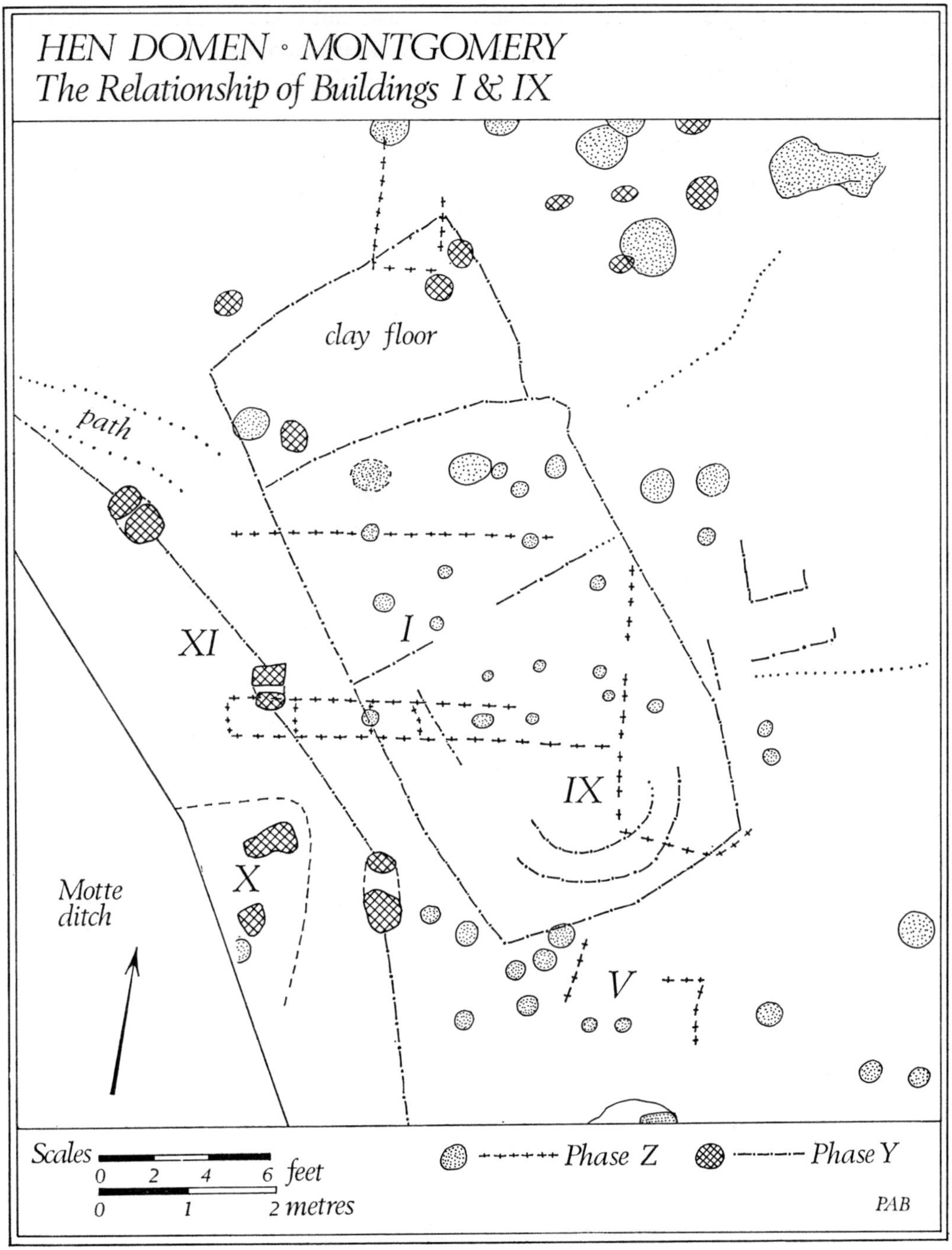
HEN DOMEN · MONTGOMERY
The Relationship of Buildings I & IX
clay floor
path
I
XI
IX
X
Motte
ditch
V
Scales
0 2 4 6 feet
0 1 2 metres
Phase Z
Phase Y
PAB

Figure 22

this building lay only some six inches below the grass, and that an intervening building had been removed from above it. One ploughing of the site may well have removed both the last two periods of buildings, leaving only the conventional post-holes of the buildings lying beneath, which would then have been called the last occupation.

Building IX, whatever its function, must have been fully-framed in order to have stood up, and the stones, which were all that was left, were probably packed against, or under, the horizontal timbers, the ground-sills of the side walls simply lying on the ground. In contrast to building IX, structure XI, which was contemporary, was a palisade with deep double post-holes of normal type, with the exception of 21/43 where the northern one of the pair was only an inch deep and packed round with stones like the post-sockets of phase Z.

On the bulbous end of the bailey rampart (fig. 23), close to the site of the chapel, another building, XIV, revealed itself in a most interesting way. Some small groups of stones lay on the boulder clay of the rampart and a number of post-holes had been cut into it. More striking, however, was an area of reddened clay where burning had outlined a semi-circular or polygonal pattern with an extension eastward along the crest of the rampart. This eastern extension led between two post-holes 5/2 and 5/3, to a pebbled path, 6/21. The post-holes appear to be those of a porch leading into a D-shaped building, probably, from its position on the end of the rampart, a tower. A right-angled stone alignment, 5/6, culminating in post-hole 5/5, lay with remarkable precision parallel to the burning pattern on the north side of the building, and was continued southward by a depression, 5/7, which probably marks the position of a door-sill. Another shallow post-hole, 5/9, lay on the east–west axis of the building. A stone alignment, 5/13, lay east–west at the same distance south of the axis as the edge of the burning lay to the north. This suggests that the two post-holes, 5/10 and 5/11, with a small pebble surface leading to them, do not mark the south wall of the building, but perhaps held the ladder which led to the upper storey, or storeys, of the tower, and that 5/13 represents the south wall. The building seems, therefore, to have imprinted itself on the ground when it was burnt down, air being sucked through the door when the roof collapsed, forming a blast-furnace effect which generated great heat within the building, but much less outside it. This theory was reinforced when a replica Iron-Age hut built on Bredon Hill, Worcestershire, was burnt down by vandals. The roof, which in this case was thatched, collapsed inwards and the roof timbers burnt their image on the floor inside, though there was no burning outside the walls which were of wattle and daub (Reynolds 1967).

If the Hen Domen tower had not been burnt down it would have been very difficult, if not impossible, to reconstruct its plan simply from the post-holes. Once again, a combination of post-hole and ground-sill construction seems to be indicated.

There was no sign of the bailey palisade. This was accounted for by the discovery in the outer ditch of beams, six inches square in section and totalling eight feet in length. A trench, three inches wide, had been cut down the centre of the beam, the trench being stopped at each end. Peg holes, fifteen inches apart, suggest that these were sills carrying vertical planks at least three inches thick and fifteen inches wide, which would have made a very substantial palisade, supported by being framed to its fighting platform and simply standing on the level crest of the rampart.

The layers representing Phases Y and Z have now been removed over the whole

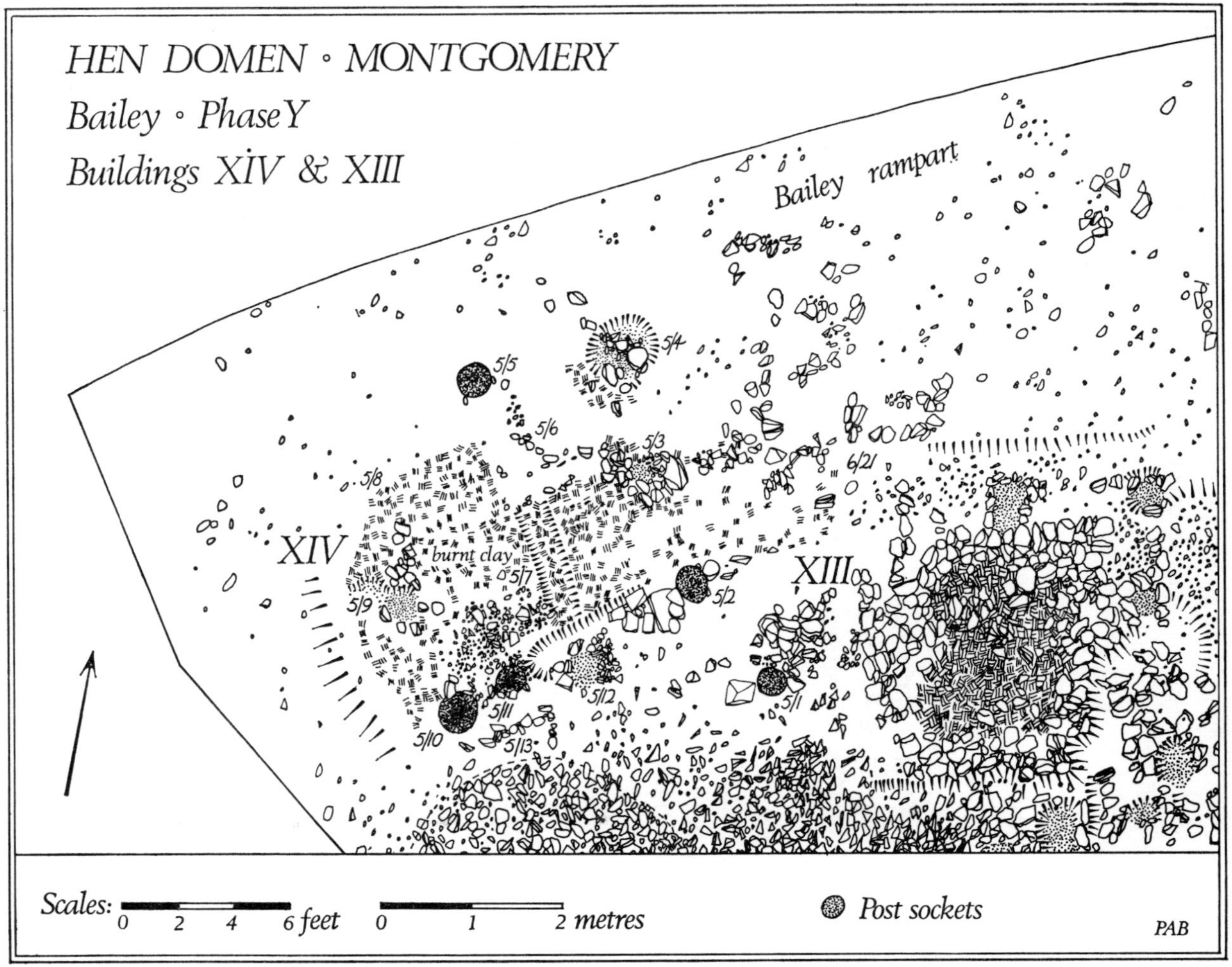
HEN DOMEN · MONTGOMERY
Bailey · Phase Y
Buildings XIV & XIII
Bailey rampart
5/4
5/5
5/6
5/3
6/21
5/8
XIV
burnt clay
5/7
5/9
XIII
5/2
5/12
5/11
5/10
5/13
5/1
Scales: 0 2 4 6 feet 0 1 2 metres
Post sockets
PAB

Figure 23

excavated area, and the underlying structures prove to be stake-hole or post-hole built, though one cannot be sure that evidence such as that for Phases Y and Z was not removed during early rebuilding.

2 Wroxeter, site 68

From 1966 to 1968, during the summer schools run by the University of Birmingham Extra-Mural Department, under the general direction of Dr Graham Webster, exploratory excavations on behalf of the Ministry of Public Building and Works were carried out by the writer on a small area (Site 68) in the north-east corner of the baths insula (5) of the Roman city of *Viroconium Cornoviorum.* The excavated area is within 200 ft of the 'Old Work', the standing wall of the *frigidarium* of the baths, and lies between the street and the baths precinct (plan in Webster and Stanley 1964: fig. 28 & plate XVIII, and Barker 1968: fig. 26).

The field had been ploughed for many years and it was expected that the upper occupation layers would have been lost. Nevertheless, in the light of the experience at Hen Domen, the method used was to strip off the topsoil by hand and to clean the area meticulously, removing only dark earth and leaving all stones, tiles, mortar-fragments and pottery in place. There was very little debris indeed in the topsoil, except at the highest point of the street; this had clearly been struck by the plough which had overturned some of the stones of its surface, but it soon became apparent that elsewhere the latest archaeological layers were undisturbed. Further evidence for this vital conclusion will be adduced below. Only those post-holes and stake-holes which contained dark topsoil were emptied. Other features which had apparently been backfilled with stones, mortar and other debris were left for phase two of the excavation. The plan of the resulting features, drawn as objectively as possible by a group of students each taking adjoining four-foot strips across the area, is reproduced in fig. 24, with a partial interpretation in fig. 26.

The most conspicuous feature was an L-shaped area of roof-tile fragments, b, with some pottery, including large sherds of samian ware, packed in rows on edge with the interstices filled with mortar fragments. This tiled area was bounded by stake-holes, and divided by narrow slots and stake-holes into three compartments. North of it was a hearth, h1, of blocks of sandstone set on edge and burnt red, together with the clay floor, a, into which they were set. This hearth partly overlay another, h2, of hypocaust tiles which had been subjected to heat sufficient to fragment them and turn them grey. The clay floor, with its hearth, was separated from the tiled area by a narrow earthen space bounded by small post- and stake-holes. The northern end of the floor had a distinctly rounded end, and a slot, or slots, containing stake-holes on its western side.

The whole complex appears to be the foundation and floors of a timber and wattle building with curving sides, which had been destroyed at its southern end by two pits, p1 and p2. The tiled area seems to be a carefully-laid hard-standing, separated by an entrance passage from the clay floor with its hearth. The building thus bears a remarkable resemblance to the long-houses, sheltering both men and animals, familiar from the excavations of medieval deserted village sites.

Between this building and the street were a number of very shallow post-sockets like

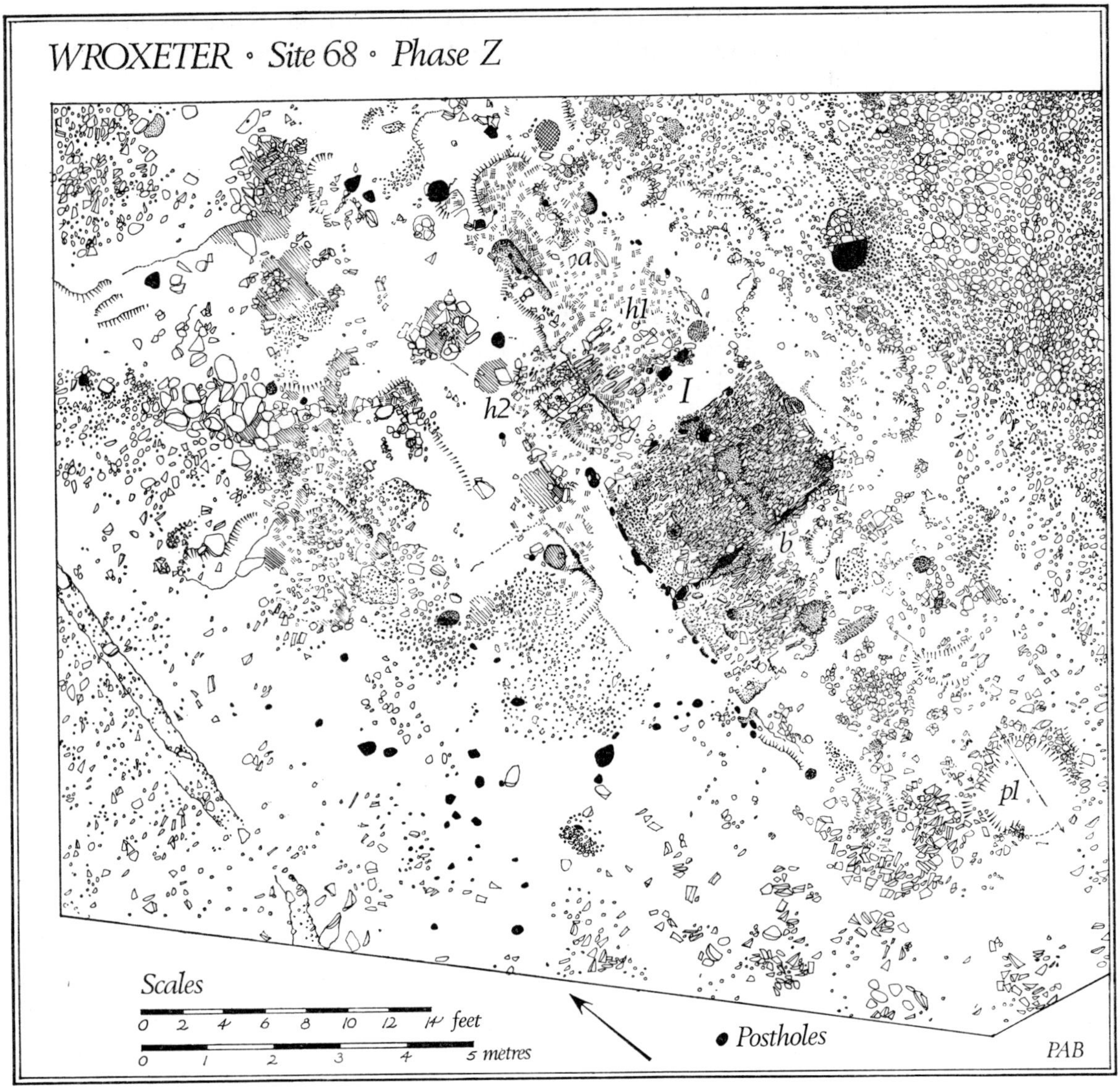
WROXETER • Site 68 • Phase Z
a
h1
h2
I
b
pl
Scales
0 2 4 6 8 10 12 14 feet
0 1 2 3 4 5 metres
Postholes
PAB

Figure 24

those of Phase Z at Hen Domen. It seems likely that hearth h2 belongs to an earlier building (perhaps on a different alignment), since it would have been on the wall line of the latest building. West of the building were a number of very slight rectangular depressions, pebble-paved, which possibly represent the sites of outhouses. There was also an uninterpretable scatter of small post-holes. North of these were a number of back-filled pits and post-holes, presumably belonging to an earlier phase.

It can be demonstrated that this building is the last structure on the site, since the post-holes and stake-holes of the hard-standing were packed round with tile fragments which stood upright, projecting above the surface of the hard-standing. They had been protected during the life of the building by the fact that they were very close to the standing posts, and perhaps later by the stumps left protruding. If the plough had run over them only once, it would have knocked them down, and, in fact, the building gave everywhere the appearance of being undisturbed. None of the post-holes had had rubble pushed into them – they had simply silted-up with top-soil. This is a remarkable circumstance when it is remembered that the site lies in the highest corner of the field, but it gives every reason to hope that the latest levels may be preserved elsewhere, not only in this field but in a large area of the city.

As at Hen Domen, the removal of these latest layers was more difficult than their exposure. In general one could only instruct the trowellers, who started in a line on the northern edge of the site, to trowel down to the next distinguishable archaeological layer, whatever that might prove to be, and at whatever depth. In effect, decisions had to be made every few inches as they moved backward across the site, and the writer assumed Siva-like attributes, using each trowel-hand as if he had multiple arms. Inevitably this kind of excavation is subjective, though one strives as hard as possible towards objectivity by consulting the trowellers on every small decision, to minimize the possibility of inventing layers and features. In the event, as at Hen Domen, the penultimate layers proved to be a matter of an inch or two only under the surface drawn in fig. 24. There was a marked change in character in the surface of what, for convenience, is called Master Layer III (which consists, it will be appreciated, of the surfaces of all the penultimate layers). It may be argued here that some are, as it were, more penultimate than others, and it will be clear from a glance at figs 24 and 25 that both surfaces could be subdivided into a multiplicity of periods. The overlapping and incompatible features in fig. 25 alone suggest at least nine periods, or sub-periods, including repairs. When one considers that this situation probably exists over the whole area of the city, and that evidence from the side walls of pit 1 suggests that on the present site, 68, the uppermost stone building still lies some feet below the present surface, it will be seen that the situation is complicated.

In Phase Y there were, in contrast to Phase Z, very few stones but considerable areas of burning. There was a significant curving line of burnt clay under the eastern wall of Building I, but, as will be seen from fig. 26, it was not coincident with that wall but crossed it at an angle, and probably represents an earlier building, II, on a slightly different alignment. Under the clay floor of Building I (fig. 24, a) was a hearth, h4, which from its position may belong to Building II. Hearth h1 itself overlay an earlier hearth, h3.

West of Building I a curving line of burnt clay, small post-holes and stones enclosed a mass of stake- and post-holes. These appear to be the remains of a third building, III, parallel to I and a little further away from the street. A pad of burnt clay, ?h5, perhaps

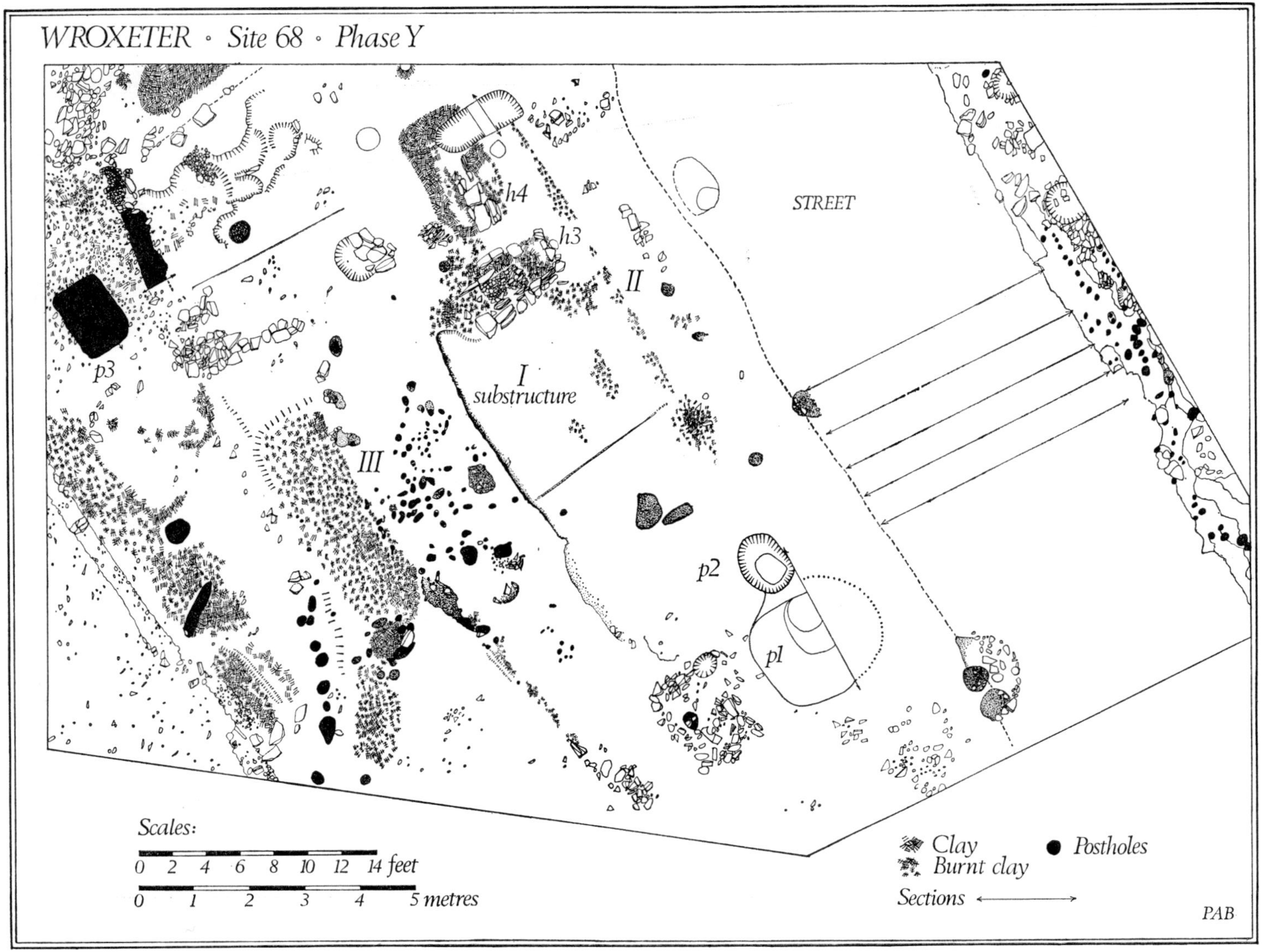
WROXETER · Site 68 · Phase Y
STREET
h4
h3
II
I
substructure
III
p3
p2
p1
Scales:
0 2 4 6 8 10 12 14 feet
0 1 2 3 4 5 metres
Clay
Burnt clay
Postholes
Sections
PAB

Figure 25

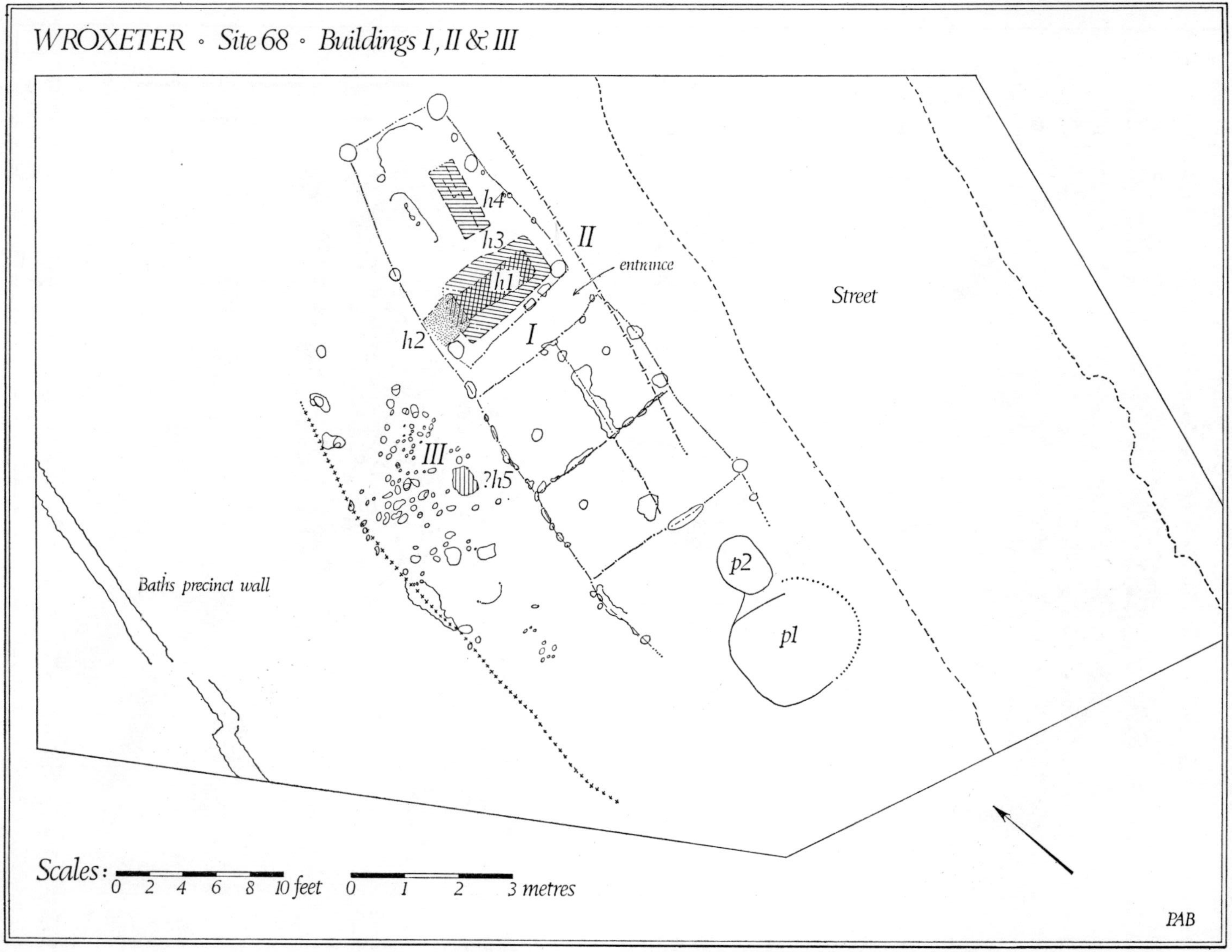
WROXETER · Site 68 · Buildings I, II & III
II
entrance
Street
h4
h3
h1
h2
I
III
?h5
p2
p1
Baths precinct wall
Scales:
0 2 4 6 8 10 feet
0 1 2 3 metres
PAB

Figure 26

marks the site of its hearth, and an adjacent rectangular area of burnt clay, with a circle of post-holes at its southern end, may be the remains of an outshut, or other attached building. The relationship between Buildings II and III cannot be demonstrated. Further structures are certainly represented by the features north and west of Building III, but they will not be understood until the excavation is extended. This is not the place to discuss the date or ancestry of these buildings, except to mention that the floor of Building I is given a *terminus post quem* by sherds of fourth-century pottery embedded in it.

It will be clear from the examples discussed here that trenching or gridding of these sites would have produced only inconsequent patterns of features, some of which might not have seemed worth recording. If the reader doubts this, it is illuminating to mask the drawings to simulate trenches or grids of any desired shape and size and then to attempt interpretations.

Although in this paper the emphasis has been laid very strongly on the importance of the plan, it must not be thought that the section is disparaged. Though buildings such as those described will rarely be visible in section, nevertheless cumulative sections along predetermined lines through the whole depth of the site are invaluable for demonstrating relationships, and can be achieved without loss of the plans of each phase by excavating up to the predetermined line, drawing the exposed face, and proceeding with the removal of the rest of the layer. It goes without saying that pits, post-holes, ditches and the like are sectioned in the normal way, though in the case of large pits, such as the cess-pit at Hen Domen, the cumulative section has proved of great value. There is, of course, no reason why larger features such as whole buildings should not be sectioned cumulatively along lines chosen to demonstrate the most important relationships, and this technique could profitably be extended to the excavation of stone buildings.

The most difficult of all structures to recover by excavation are those which simply stood on the ground, without post-holes or sill-walls. Such buildings might be substantial and semi-permanent, in the sense that they would be expected to last more than a single generation, and conceivably much longer. The excavation of the timber town of Novgorod (Thompson 1967), in which very few of the buildings were sunk into the ground, would have been very interesting (and very difficult) if the timbers had not been preserved, and the plans of these substantial, sometimes three-storeyed, buildings may only have been recovered by plotting the distribution of inorganic finds, and other slight remains.

Many sites, particularly on clay soils, have defied attempts to produce plans of their structures by excavation, and it seems likely that in these cases we are dealing with buildings the timbers of which were laid on the surface. If we are to recover the plans of such buildings, it will be necessary not only to excavate with the utmost sensitivity, but also to record every scrap of evidence in the greatest detail, however unprofitable it may seem at the time. The plotting of every stone, every sherd of pot, every bone, every burnt area or slight change of surface may be the only way to discover patterns which will in turn reveal the plans of buildings. Lines of nails recorded *in situ* may indicate the joists of floors of which no other trace remains, and it has been suggested that medieval peasant houses were kept so clean that they will be found by plotting the distribution of potsherds, the houses being in the empty spaces. In other cases, the edges of cobbled yards, which abutted on to timber buildings, may indicate the lines of walls and the building plan be suggested in negative form. At Hen Domen a large isolated post-socket in the centre of a cobbled area eluded interpretation until it was noticed that the upper surfaces of the cobbles were worn, presumably by the traffic of feet, except in a line leading away from the post-socket towards the abutment of the motte bridge, which suggests the presence of a sill-beam, joined to the base of the upright post and protecting the cobbled surface from wear. It is clear that every scrap of evidence, every hint of former structures must be adduced on these difficult sites. The danger, of course, is that we shall see what is not there, that we shall, even unconsciously, see what we want to see. To safeguard against this self-defeating subjectivity, sites such as these should be excavated by a team, with constant consultation. Photogrammetry will help to produce an objective record, and also should enable the structural surfaces to be examined stereoscopically after they have been destroyed – two-dimensional drawings and even photographs do not present the convincing picture which anyone walking round the site can see. The presentation in published form of the rather elusive evidence for these highly detailed structures of many phases poses a difficult and expensive problem. One would hope for the increasing use of transparent multi-coloured overlays. Such diagrams, and the printing of stereo-pairs, would be worth many thousands of descriptive words.

Increasingly, scientific aids will have to be brought to bear on the type of excavation we are discussing, and perhaps the chief contribution will come from soil science. Most sites of timber buildings now consist almost entirely of superimposed layers of soil, or soil and stones, containing the ghosts of structures which themselves have undergone an earth-change into soil. Many of us who excavate these sites constantly interpret soil layers with little more than our intuition and experience as guides. We say that this feature is a hearth (might it not be a small dump of burnt clay?), this layer was washed down (could it have been wind-blown?), this post-hole filling looks and feels the same as that one (are they therefore contemporary?); does this micropodsol, itself a natural event, reflect a man-made disturbance? – what is the source of this vivianite, and what archaeological significance has it? – and so on. The archaeologist who uncovers great complexes of stone buildings needs to be half architectural historian in order to be able to interpret them, and the excavator who digs timber buildings needs to be half soil scientist if he is to understand fully the medium into which his buildings have been transformed (see L. Biek and I. W. Cornwall *in* Brothwell and Higgs 1963: 108–22).

It should be possible, by comparative analysis of their filling, to sort apparently undifferentiated post-holes into groups, though observation of the fillings of post-holes known to belong to one building often shows that they are filled with different materials, and it may be that dating techniques such as thermoluminescence will eventually prove to be more useful than qualitative analysis. We should like to know the real and subtle differences between a number of what we glibly call 'occupation layers', and whether, for instance, a floor has been used by cattle or for corn storage. Experiments in determining comparative amounts of phosphates, lignite and other residual traces have not been uniformly successful, but a comprehensive analysis of soil composition, presented visually and laid over plans of the excavated areas, may prove to be of the greatest interest.

Infra-red and ultra-violet photography have not yet been fully exploited, though they have been used to enhance skeletal silhouettes and might be used to enhance the patterns of burning or other changes which we have seen to be significant.

If nothing else, it is to be hoped that soil science will bring some order into the description of the layers we dissect – a simple word like 'silt' tends to have one meaning for the archaeologist and another for the soil scientist. This does not imply the imposition of uniformity, but the use of a common terminology which is a first and necessary step towards closer co-operation.

Progress in the excavation and understanding of timber buildings will ultimately depend on increasingly intense and detailed observation and recording, using every means available now and to be developed in the future. Every site, and every part of every site, is unique; our responsibility for the destruction of sites by excavation is very great, and so, therefore, is the necessity to refine our techniques in every possible way, since we are only just beginning to understand how much information might be extracted by really adequate excavation.

11.iv.69

Department of Extra-Mural Studies
University of Birmingham

References

Barker, P. A. 1968. Road widening at Wroxeter. *Trans. Shropshire Archaeological Society.* lviii:117–22.

Bersu, G. 1949. A Promontory Fort on the Shore of Ramsey Bay, Isle of Man. *The Antiquaries Journal.* xxix:62–79.

Brothwell, D. and Higgs, E. eds. 1963. *Science in Archaeology.* London.

Reynolds, P. J. 1967. Iron Age Hut: A Reconstruction. *Vale of Evesham Historical Society Research Papers.* i:5–10.

Thompson, M. W. 1967. *Novgorod the Great.* London.

Webster, G. and Stanley, B. 1964. Viroconium, A Study of Problems. *Trans. Shropshire Archaeological Society.* lvii:112–31.

Building in ancient India

M. S. Mate

Considerable material pertaining to the art of building in antiquity has come to light during the past decade as a result of archaeological investigations in India. A brief review of the new knowledge so obtained, mainly in respect of secular structures, is presented here.

The most widely accepted and the most recent chronology for Indian archaeology would be on the following lines. The Stone Ages are of no consequence to the present discussion. Next to them comes, more or less out of order, the proto-historic urban culture of the Indus Valley (2500–1700 B.C.). This 'intrusion' is succeeded by regional cultures variously described as Chalcolithic-Neolithic, but signifying, in the main, the existence of settled communities of food-producers and cattle-keepers (2200–1000 B.C.). Then follow the Gangetic Valley cultures with dates varying between 1100 B.C. and 200 B.C. By around the eighth century B.C. at least some of them were about to begin their journey towards urbanization (Wheeler 1966: 100). From then onwards the grounds for fixing the chronology are firm, but paradoxically, the material evidence regarding houses and habitations, both above and below the ground, dwindles rapidly. Use of perishable materials is, of course, one of the more important causes of this situation, but lack of interest on the part of the archaeologists must share at least some of the blame. It is only after the sixteenth and seventeenth centuries A.D. that data reappears, mainly in the form of a number of still extant structures.

The eastward and southward expansion of the Harappan or Indus Valley culture is one of the more significant discoveries of the last two decades (fig. 27). From Rupar in the north to Alamgirpur in the east and Bhagatrav in the south, across the now desert lands of north-western Rajasthan, the ruins of a large number of Harappan stations have been discovered. Of these Kalibangan and Lothal easily stand out as pre-eminent. At the former there exist, in the classic Harappan tradition, two mounds, one smaller (citadel) and the other bigger (town) (fig. 28). Both have ramparts around them but the citadel has a redoubtable fortification around it (*I.A.R.* 1967–8: 44). The ramparts of the citadel are four metres in width, and are reinforced by rectangular bastions on the corners and towers flanking the gate. Built of mud-brick in two sizes, both maintaining the standard Harappan ratio 1 : 2 : 4, the citadel overlies a pre-Harappan fortified settlement practically twice as large, although it is too early as yet to say anything about the buildings and structures of which it was composed. The streets of the town were laid out on a grid pattern, dividing the area into so many rectangular blocks. Each of these had a raised mud-brick plat-

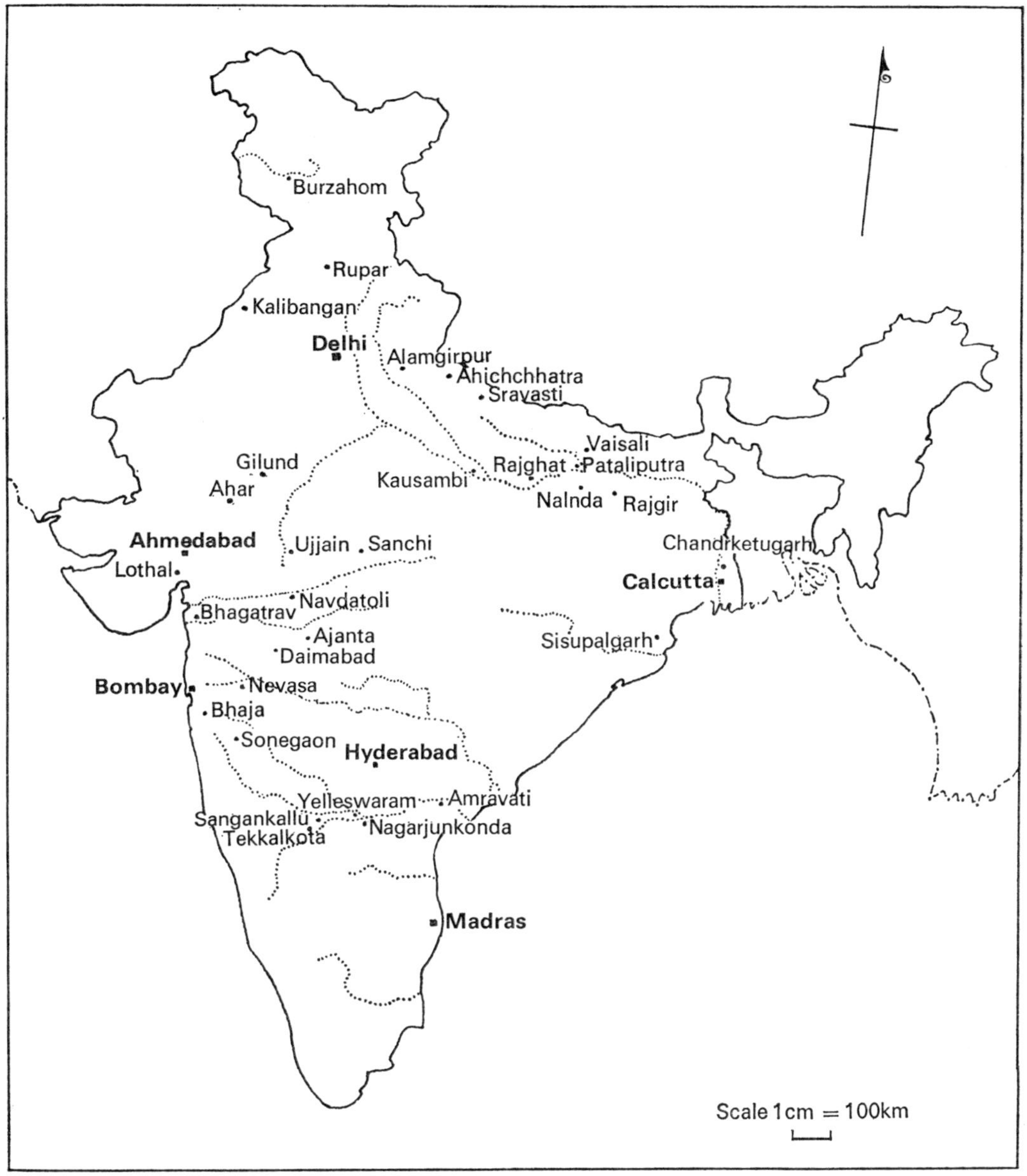

Figure 27

form on which were erected houses on two types of plan: rooms around a courtyard or along a verandah. Rooms were between $1 \times 2{\cdot}50$ m. and 3×4 m. in area. One of the rooms had a tiled floor, showing the typically Indus design of intersecting circles. Unlike the parent cities of Mohenjodaro and Harappa all construction was in mud-brick, kiln-burnt brick being utilized only for drains, baths and, in a few cases, for floorings. Lothal on the western coast adds a further dimension to this study (Rao 1957: 82). Evidence of various sorts had already enabled archaeologists to infer large-scale maritime activity on the part

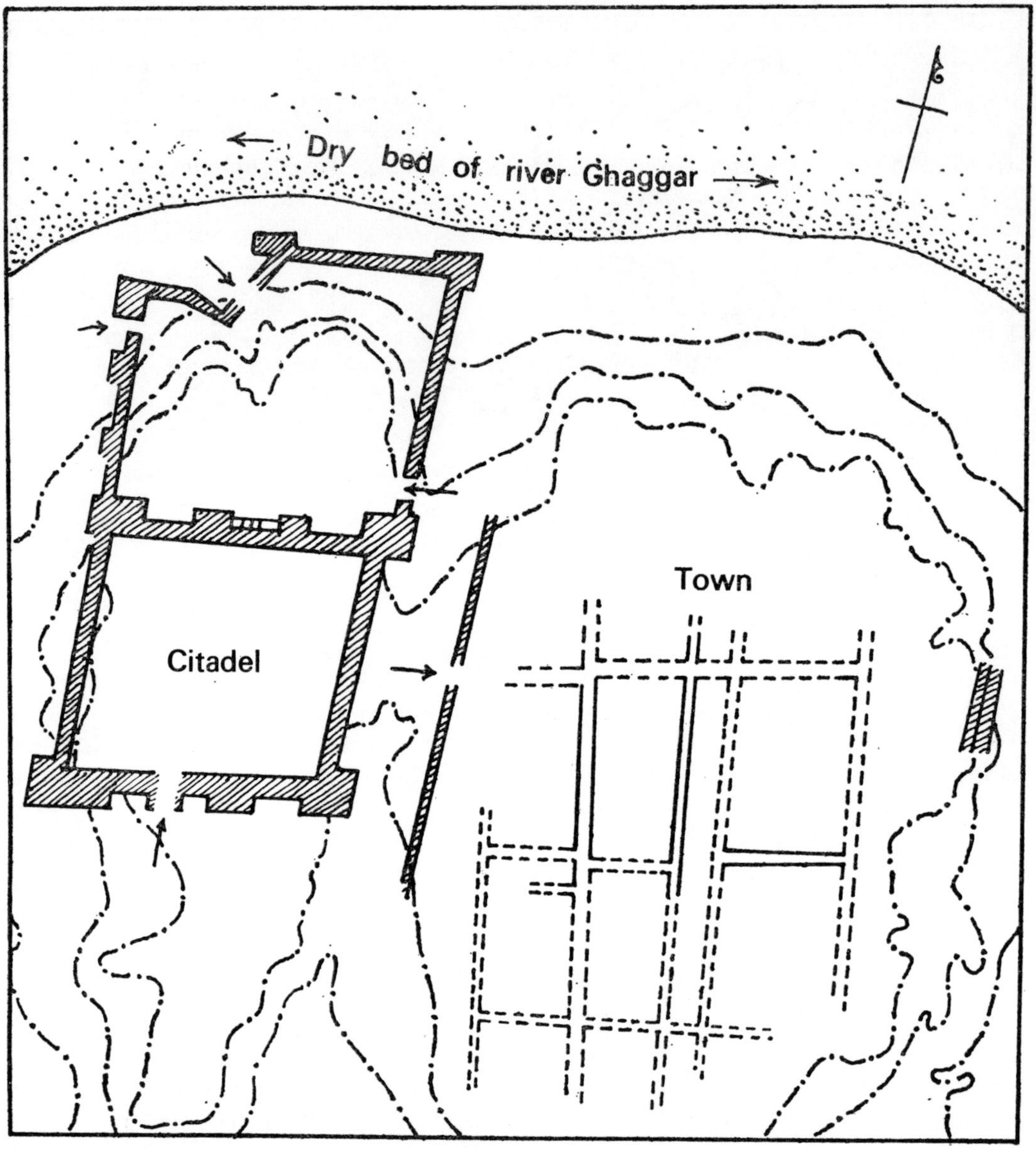

Figure 28 Kalibangan: plan of the citadel and town with ramparts (*I.A.R.* 1967–8) (Courtesy: Archaeological Survey of India)

of the Harappans, but it was only at Lothal that direct and concrete proof of it in the form of a huge dock-yard has come to light. A trapezoidal brick structure with an overall measurement of 205 × 39 m., it speaks of skilled planning and ample experience in navigation. Inlet and outlet channels lined with burnt brick, and wooden gates or partitions fitted in grooves in the walls, controlled the extent and level of water within the dock. As for mud-brick platforms, houses, streets, drains and other facilities of urban life, Lothal followed the standard Harappan practice. Indeed, to our knowledge of the general nature of towns and houses, traffic and drainage systems, very little that is new has been added by recent work; the information obtained being more in the nature of corroboration than fresh discovery. No solutions to existing problems have resulted despite the intensive investigations being carried on. To cite a few, the nature of the roofing, methods of decoration, the relationship of the platforms to the streets, communications between houses on the same platform, the relationship of house foundations to mud-brick platforms, all remain problematic. The views of Marshall (1931: 6), Vats (1940: 12) and Mackay (1948: 20) still prevail.

The Harappan culture, on its decline, was succeeded by small agricultural-pastoral communities mostly along the major river courses of inner India. A very large number of the sites of this period yield only remains of small patches of prepared floorings, mostly of black or yellow clay, rammed over nodules of burnt clay (fallen wall-plaster) or potsherds. A few give indications of post-holes but only rarely do these yield a recognizable plan. Half a dozen sites have, however, produced very good data in this respect. Circular, square or rectangular huts and houses have been uncovered. The Neolithic huts from Sangankallu and Tekkalkota are classic examples of these. The hut from the former had a diameter of 5 m. (*I.A.R.* 1964–5: 1–54; Nagaraj Rao 1965: 480). Square and rectangular houses and houses with more than one room have been reported from Ahar and Navdatoli. At Navdatoli circular huts had a diameter of $2\frac{1}{2}$ to 4 m., whereas the rectangular ones measured up to 3×5 m. (*I.A.R.* 1957–8: 30). At Ahar houses measured on an average 9×5 m., although the existence of larger rooms was suggested by a wall running to a length of 13·70 m. and divided into rooms by mud or mud-brick walls. Methods of construction were simple, direct and effective. Walls were made of bamboo screens supported by timber poles at regular intervals and plastered over on either side with clay. Very little foundation was required. Gilund (*I.A.R.* 1959–60: 43), Ahar (*I.A.R.* 1961–2: 48) and Burzahom in the later Neolithic stage (*I.A.R.* 1960–1: 11) are probably the only sites that have so far yielded mud-bricks, and as such a near-total absence of mud-brick (not to speak of burnt-brick) seems to mark out the Chalcolithic-Neolithic cultures from the Harappan on the one hand and the Gangetic cultures on the other. Openings other than entrances were superfluous. Conclusions as to the nature of the roof have to be drawn from the plans and the nature of the walls of the house. From these it would appear that roofs were made of bamboo and birch, were sloping and were supported directly by vertical posts embedded in the ground. Circular huts generally had central poles, but in a few cases might have rested on the close-knit walls of the hut, as suggested by Nagaraj Rao (1965: 480) (fig. 29). In the case of square or rectangular houses the roofs must have been sloping down from one wall to the other, supported by beams. Trusses, suggesting advanced knowledge of joinery, seem to be absent. The floors were well-prepared. A bed of nodules of burnt clay, stone chips, gravel or potsherds was overlaid with successive layers of clay, very often also of lime. From Gilund, Navdatoli, Nevasa, Sonegaon and a host of sites from North Karnatak and Andhra Pradesh, circular pits have been reported. At Gilund the typical pit had a diameter of 1 m. to $1\frac{1}{2}$ m., whereas its depth varied between 50 cm. and 1 m. The walls and floor were plastered with a thin coat of whitish clay. Obviously these were meant for storage purposes (mostly grain), as is the practice in South India even today. Alternatively, like the ones at Sonegaon, they might have been used as hearths of some sort. At Sonegaon the pits measured between 1·20 m. and 0·75 m.

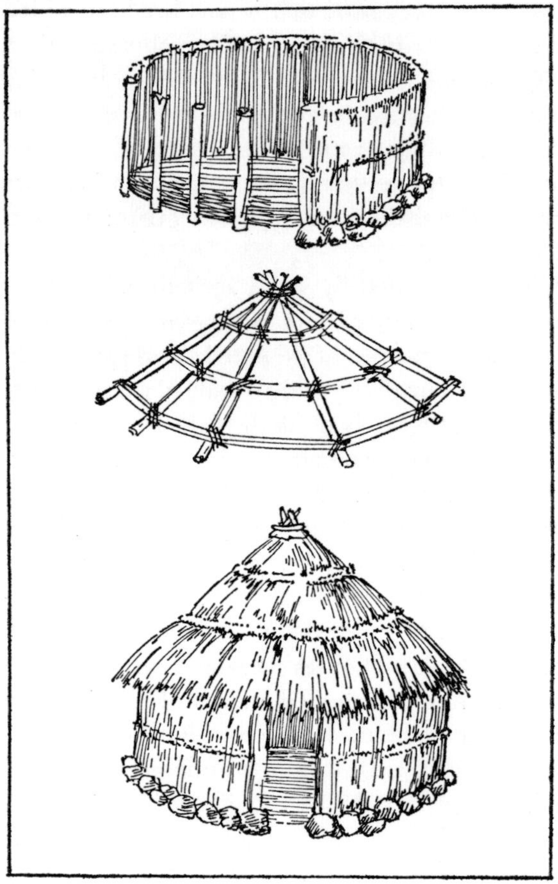

Figure 29 Tekkalkota: circular hut. (The hut, built of bamboo and thatch, has been constructed without a centre-post.)

in diameter, contained burnt earth and ash, and had no linings. Very little of systematic planning is to be found in the distribution of huts in these Chalcolithic settlements. Earthen embankments have been reported from Eran, Nagada and Daimabad, but they seem to be flood-preventive measures and are not features necessarily characteristic of the period.

Easily the most noteworthy discovery of the last decade has been that of the pit-dwellings at Burzahom on the Jhelum. These pits were roughly circular or oval, and were cut in the *karewa* (alluvium) bed (*I.A.R.* 1960–3). Their depth varied between 1·50 m. and 4 m. and the mouth was generally narrower than the bottom, the dimensions in the case of the largest being 2·75 m. at the top and 3·50 m. at the bottom. From the surface level only three or four steps had been cut, which indicates, as the excavators rightly infer, the use of ladders of bamboo or timber. The floor and the walls were plastered with *karewa*. A crescent-shaped ancillary pit, perhaps for storage, and a tunnel connecting two pits, are the more uncommon features. Ash layers on the floors at various levels testify to human occupation. Post-holes have been noted around the mouth of the pit as well as on the floors. These presumably carried timber posts as supports for fig and birch thatching on the roof. The placing of the post-holes in the ground around the mouth of the pit seems to be logical, but the distribution of the post-holes on the flooring as seen in the published photographs is highly puzzling (*I.A.R.* 1961–2: XXXVI A). If there were half the number of posts illustrated, the pits would accommodate only posts and no humans. Even the usual plea of posts of a later habitation having reached down to the lower level cannot be accepted here, for the plan of the pit has remained constant and the post-holes cannot be resolved into any sensible pattern. The pits belonged to the first Neolithic phase at the site (2000 to 1700 B.C.), and fall within the ambit of the Far Eastern Neolithic cultures. The discovery of similar pits has been reported from Paiyampalli (*I.A.R.* 1967–8: 27) in south India, but no precise details are published except their Neolithic associations. It is, therefore, difficult to assess their cultural significance at this stage.

The Gangetic Valley served as the matrix of the so-called 'Early Historic' cultures of India. In due course, possibly within a couple of centuries, other major river valleys of inner India also became the cradles of similarly thriving communities and kingdoms. In the Gangetic Valley, the early phase of the 'Early Historic' is represented by a number of copper hoards. Both the authors of these artefacts and their exact abodes have so far eluded the archaeologists (Wheeler 1966: 94). The next phase is extremely significant. For the first time since the disappearance of the Harappans, diversified requirements, their fulfilment and a greatly sophisticated technology consequent on them now become apparent. After a couple of centuries of teething troubles, patterns and formulae were evolved that continued to influence domestic architecture for the next thousand years or more. The sources of information for this period are more profuse and diverse. In addition to the excavated remains, rock-cut shrines and monasteries, sculptural depictions, as on Barhut or Sanchi stupas, or pictorial representations, as in the Ajanta paintings, offer valuable information. Contemporary literature, too, is an extremely valuable source. Excavated materials give a good idea of the materials and methods used, but it is the latter group of sources, literature, pictures and sculptures that imparts some idea as to the appearance of these structures. They give some idea of the artistic treatment of such parts as the façade or portico, and help interpret the excavated remains. Together they impart the unmistakable impression of a richer, fuller life (Barua 1937: 42; Gupte and Mahajan 1962: xi, xii, xxxix; Zimmer 1955: 20).

It is very rarely indeed that the entire plan of any house has been uncovered in any of the recent excavations. Most of these have been 'vertical' (i.e. limited-area) digs. It is on this account that, as a rule, the excavation-reports delimit a room, mark a door, or a street, or a stair, but only at such wide spacing that they fail to yield complete house-plans. Even when they do, an element of conjecture intrudes where the known facts are put into an order which would otherwise have been meaningless. Evans's restorations of Minoan palaces are a constant reminder, if one be needed, to caution acceptance of conjectural reconstructions at face value.

The plans of all buildings seem to hinge on the square or its multiples. If timber posts and beams were used as profusely as in the medieval times, four pillars with four beams on them would become the basic structural unit. A courtyard, large or small, formed the central part of the theme. Around this were verandahs, rooms and halls. The whole formed a rectangle, the longer arm extending away from the street. The only variation noticed is that of a long verandah with a number of rooms opening into it. The large structural *viharas* (Buddhist monasteries) at places like Sanchi, Nalanda or Nagarjunkonda, or the rock-cut ones as at Bhaja or Ajanta, are more or less enlarged versions of this basic prototype.

The façade or front elevation was in two parts, the upper one probably using timber on a lavish scale. The lower part presented a blank face, except for the entrance, to the street. The upper one had projecting balconies of highly ornate timber work. The curvilinear *chaitya-torana* ('horse-shoe' arch) formed the most frequently recurring motif (Barua 1937: 42).

Roofs of baked clay tiles, fitted on a timber framework with iron nails, were common in the case of better class houses. Such tiles have been recovered in large quantities from almost every excavation of the Early Historic layers. Otherwise, thatching served the purpose. On the analogy of rock-cut *chaitya* halls, it might be mentioned as a probability that ornate structures, especially free standing *mandapas* (pillared halls) had barrel-vaulted timber roofs.

Depictions in Ajanta paintings would indicate that ornamentation of houses depended mainly on colour, painting and ornate wood-work. Walls, ceilings and perhaps even pillars were treated with polychrome designs, while pillars, beams, battens, and bracket-capitals in wood were treated with low-relief carving. Door-frames of timber received the most lavish care from very early times (Agrawala 1967: 83).

It would have been needless to stress that all construction in early India was trabeate but for the discovery of the so-called 'King Udayana's Palace' at Kausambi (*I.A.R.* 1961–2: 51). Built of stone and mortar, this structure uses the true arch almost everywhere, and is dated to any time between A.D. 500 and A.D. 1000. There seem to be two possibilities: one, its construction was carried out by foreign craftsmen well versed in the technique, and two, the structure is late, probably medieval. A close scrutiny of the stratigraphic sequence and of the structural characteristics of the palace is more likely than not to result in confirming the second alternative.

The thick mud-brick and burnt-brick-and-mud walls must have given the Indian of those days, as they do today, a cool and quiet resting place. Not since the palmy days of the Harappans was such fine brickwork executed in the land as in the early centuries of the first millennium A.D. The larger bricks, 58 × 25 × 8 or 53 × 28 × 5 cm., were used by the Indus people, also by a few Early Historic communities like the one at Nevasa. But during the Mauryan period (third to second centuries B.C.) the standard size was 48 × 30 × 10 cm., whereas the Gupta (fourth to seventh centuries A.D.) bricks measured 43 × 23 × 5 cm. These were laid in mud-mortar, the joints were hair-thin and the surface and the joints were rubbed down to a very fine and smooth plane. The excavated remains of an early Gupta temple at Chandraketugarh (plate 7), or the Lakshman temple (*c.* A.D. 800) at Sirpur exhibit this type of brickwork at its best. Within a few centuries moulded bricks of high workmanship appeared all over northern India, from Rajasthan to Bengal. These were used mainly on temples and *chaityas*. Brickwork maintained even then its high standard and perfection, and it is obvious that the detailed rules and regulations to be found in the *silpasastras* were no idle talk (Acharya 1927: 121).

House floors were prepared, as before, by ramming fine clay on a mixture of brick-bats, pebbles, gravel and clay. Lime coating had been used since Chalcolithic times, as shown above. But the Early Historic layers of Nevasa yielded traces of another experiment. Below the clay coating, the floor had a 9 cm. thick layer of hydraulic lime mortar mixed with hemp. It probably helped quick absorption of water.

Some of the more uncommon types of the secular buildings discovered in recent years may now be considered. The remains of the great hall at Pataliputra, described by Megasthenes in the most glowing terms and excavated by Spooner (1916: 53), are now quite well known. Similar free-standing halls, perhaps of later dates, have come to light at Nagarjunkonda (*I.A.R.* 1957–8: 8–9) and Yelleswaram (*I.A.R.* 1960–1: 3). In both cases only stumps of pillars have been found, but they enable one to formulate some idea of their plans, and, more important, testify to a tradition of free-standing *mandapas* or halls. The huge auditorium at Nagarjunkonda is indeed a unique structure (*I.A.R.* 1957–8: 11–12). Its length is 92 m., breadth 77 m., and depth 4·50 m. Flights of steps with treads 60 cm. in width descend from all four sides. All around the ground level (i.e. surrounding the auditorium) is a 3·50 m. wide platform. Six staircases, each 1·80 m. in width, joined this platform to the arena. On the western side there is a pavilion that gradually shrunk in size, 25 × 11·50 m., then 20·60 × 9·80 m., and finally 15 × 13·20 m. This could have been a sort of stage, from which performances were given, or, more likely still, it might have been the 'royal box'. There does not seem to be any parallel to this structure, nor is there any cultural or literary tradition that would explain it. It may not, therefore, be far-fetched to suggest that the Ikshvaku kings (second to fourth centuries A.D.) caused this structure to be erected in imitation of foreign models, both in respect of its form and content. The most likely source seems to be the Roman world, with which this region had close commercial contacts.

The same site has preserved bathing *ghats* (stairs) along the river Krishna (plate 8). Such *ghats* are commonplace today but a *ghat* of such early date and of such magnificence had never been found before. Built of stone it reaches down to the water level in eight stages, with an equal number of sub-stages. This also belongs to the second–third centuries A.D. (*I.A.R.* 1955–6: 25).

The 'Abhishekachi Pushkarani' of Vaisali is a unique structure handed down from the centuries just preceding the Christian era. It is a grand bathing tank, 430 × 201 m., built of burnt-brick of uniform size (37 × 25 × 5 cm.). Two phases were noted in its construction. Today it is known as the 'Kharuna tank' but tradition describes it as a coronation tank of the Lichchhavis, 500 B.C. to A.D. 600 (*I.A.R.* 1957–8: 12). A tank of much smaller dimensions but of a very delightful form, with terraces and treads gradually closing in on the bottom, has been excavated from Nagarjunkonda. It measures roughly 7·10 × 7·10 × 2·60 m., with the bottom approximately 1·80 m. square (*I.A.R.* 1956–7: lv). Incidentally this, being the earliest known example, can be treated as archetypal for the numerous tanks of this kind found everywhere in India during the later centuries. This typical arrangement of small groups of steps, based on terraces along the edge of the tank, is to be seen even in the eighteenth-century tanks all over the country. A smaller tank of irregular shape from the same site is of interest solely as a relic of the sacerdotal practices of the time. Ujjain had a tank, 10 × 8 m., built of brick but quite plain in its appearance. (*A.R.M.M.* I: 69).

These reservoirs and tanks have got to be treated as special-purpose items as well as utilities confined to a small group – perhaps the royal family itself. They do not seem to play any important role in the scheme of water supply as a whole. Nor do the small brick-wells and terracotta ring-wells (usually referred to as 'soak-pits') seem to have much to do with the provision of fresh water. It is very rarely that these reach down even to the old hypothetical water level in the area. Although remains of brick-built channels or terracotta pipelines have been discovered at several places, it seems more probable that they were used for the disposal of refuse water rather than for water distribution (Rajghat, *A.R.M.M.* I: 58; Ujjain *A.R.M.M.* I: 69). Human agency, especially the womenfolk of the house, then as now, served such a purpose admirably, rivers forming the main source.

As indicated above, soak-pits, or wells, channels and pipes were used to dispose of refuse-water. However, all these seem to be arrangements for individual houses or very small, limited localities. Nothing like the town-wide drainage system of the Harappans ever entered these towns and cities.

The same was the case with the streets. Not only were they unpaved, uncared-for and inhospitable, but their narrowness and capricious windings and zigzags are baffling in the extreme. One cannot but wonder at the ingenuity these people showed in ignoring all the sound principles of street-planning their theoreticians had evolved (Acharya 1927: 121).

The most remarkable feature of the building activity of this, the Early Historic, period is, of course, the gigantic ramparts that girdled almost all the major cities. Having learnt the art of erecting comfortable and luxurious houses, early Indians did not take long to realize the value of a physical barrier to protect them. Almost every town that rose to prominence from 400 B.C. to A.D. 400 was encircled with ramparts. To name only a few, Ahichchhatra, Kausambi, Nagarjunkonda, Patna Rajghat, Rajgir, Sisupalgarh, Ujjain, Vaisali (*I.A.R.* 1953–68) all boasted *prakaras* (ramparts). Out of these, a few, Kausambi, Rajghat and Ujjain had, at least in the initial stages, embankments against river floods (fig. 30). Others were defensive structures. The early embankments and ramparts were usually massive walls made of rammed earth. The earth was dug out from the immediate vicinity of the proposed wall, and a continuous ditch or moat was thus obtained. At Ujjain, however, the channel (moat) seems to have been as important as the rampart, because it was mainly a diversion channel for the river. Ramparts were reinforced with stout timber logs and revetted with burnt-brick. The sides of the ditches also were lined with burnt-brick. Gates through these ramparts were provided-for at convenient spots – bastions are not clearly definable yet. At Pataliputra the earthen rampart was raised over a strong timber framework that might have served as a continuous passage as well as the core of the rampart. Soon ramparts of earth, and ditches around them, were found insufficient, and first wooden and then brickwork walls and parapets were erected above the ramparts. Ahichchhatra, Sravasti, and Vaisali all exhibit these advanced features. Utilization of terrain is seen at its best at Rajgir and Nagarjunkonda. At both, the town is situated in a small valley surrounded on all sides by hills (and also a river at Nagarjunkonda). Over the crest of these hills were built stone walls, keeping only a single well-guarded entrance open.

Their gigantic size and the apparent need for constant renewals, as evidenced through successive layers, imply a massive utilization of materials and human effort. One cannot

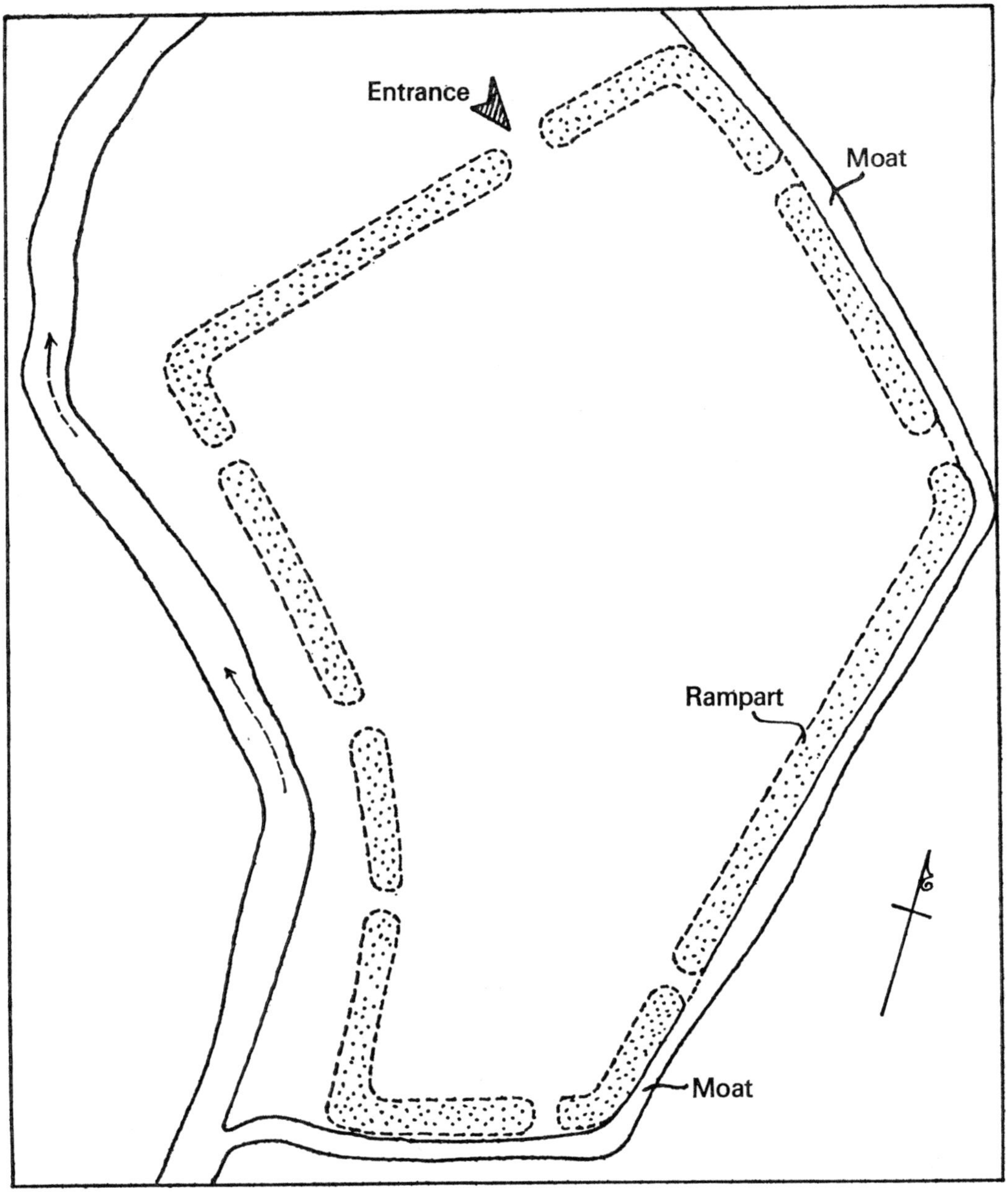

Figure 30 Ujjain: plan of rampart and moat (no scale, after *I.A.R.* 1956–7) (Courtesy: Archaeological Survey of India)

but wonder at the effort involved. This wonder becomes bewilderment when one takes into account the fact that the whole of the historic and quasi-historic literature of ancient India quotes not a single instance of a battle waged around the defence of a city. No account exists of the investment of a city. All battles were fought in the open field. Were these, then, prestige constructions, or were they meant to deter smaller fry – robbers and bandits?

Without being unduly harsh, one might say that houses and secular structures showed little progress on the technological side during a period of nearly one-and-a-half millennia. The buildings of the Early Historic period emphasize, as nothing else does, the great chasm that divided the civilizations of the two rivers – the Indus and the Ganges. Not only was the latter a fresh starter, but, unlike the former, it was immune from any high standard of urban organization and, consequently, civil architecture. Once the making and laying of bricks, and the dressing and joining of wood were mastered, innovation seemed at a discount. Needs were, of course, more diverse than those of the Chalcolithic-Neolithic societies, but once these – the very basic ones – had found appropriate responses, there was no deviation from tradition. The same old materials, methods and modes made life as easy and pleasant as conceivable. No change, therefore, was called for!

7.ii.69

Deccan College
Poona

References

Acharya, P. K. 1927. *Indian architecture according to Manasara Silpasastra.* London.

Agrawala, R. C. 1967. Unpublished Katarmala . . . Problems. *East and West.* 17: nos 1–2.

A.R.M.M. 1964. *Ancient Remains, Monuments and Museums.* New Delhi.

Barua, B. M. 1937. *Barhut, aspects of life and art.* Calcutta.

Gupte, R. S. and Mahajan, B. D. 1962. *Ajanta, Ellora and Aurangabad Caves.* Bombay.

I.A.R. Indian Archaeology – a Review. Archaeological Survey of India, New Delhi.

Mackay, E. 1948. *Early Indus Civilization.* London.

Marshall, Sir John. 1931. *Mohenjodaro and the Indus Civilization.* Calcutta.

Nagaraj Rao, M. S. 1965. Survival of certain Neolithic elements among the Boyas of Tekkalkota. *Anthropos.* 60.

Rao, S. R. 1957. The Excavations at Lothal. *Lalit-kala.* 3–4.

Spooner, D. B. 1916. Mr Ratan Tata's Excavations at Pataliputra. *A.S.I.-A.R. 1912–13.* Calcutta.

Wheeler, Sir Mortimer. 1966. *Civilizations of the Indus Valley and Beyond.* London.

The myth of the mother-goddess

Andrew Fleming

'The great megalithic tomb builders of Western Europe were imbued by a religious faith, were devotees of a goddess whose face glares out from pot and phalange idol and the dark shadows of the tomb walls, whose image is twisted into the geometry of Portuguese schist plaques and the rich carvings of Gavrinis and New Grange.'

These words, written by Daniel (1958: 74), represent one of the most vivid statements of a view which has gained wide acceptance. The most detailed presentation of this idea occurs in O. G. S. Crawford's *The Eye Goddess* (1957). Since the late 'fifties there has been widespread scepticism, much of it unpublished, but the theory has persisted. In 1967 Daniel was still able to link, in a short passage, such diverse sites as Tell Brak, Knockmany and Folkton (1967: 203). It is probable that such statements reveal more about the faith of prehistorians than about that of the megalith builders; there is in fact an urgent need to re-examine the whole hypothesis. We can do this with more confidence now that Ucko has shown (1968: 427–44) that in Egypt, Greece and the Near East the mother-goddess interpretation fits the facts much less well than several other plausible explanations.

The basis for the mother-goddess interpretation appears to be threefold. It is thought that where there are similar burial rites, there should be similarity in religious belief; that the west European megalithic tombs were inspired in some way from the east Mediterranean; and that parietal art and grave furniture present specific evidence for the representation of a female personage who must be considered some kind of deity.

It is agreed that the megalithic tombs of western Europe represent a very widespread and impressive type of burial, requiring not a little skill and hard labour, and presumably inspired by a corresponding intensity of religious belief. But there is no *a priori* reason why a similar burial rite should represent belief in the same deity. Indeed, the megaliths are so widely distributed both in space and in time that one might well expect a complex and changing situation, with fairly local cults normally prevalent. The spread of the worship of a mother-goddess is only one of a number of possible stimuli for the growth of collective burial in large stone tombs. It is equally likely that the rise of this custom is related to the prevalence of a certain type of social structure, and to the availability of certain types of stone. L'Helgouach (1965: 13 ff.) has demonstrated the close relationship between geology and tomb distribution in Brittany, and in Drenthe megaliths occur in areas providing suitable glacial boulders (de Laet 1958: 83). Anyone who has searched for megalithic tombs in the field will know that they often occur in regions where surface formations of similar stone are common; sometimes these are disconcertingly suggestive of the tombs themselves, at any rate at first glance. In some areas the abundance of this stone, or its mode of occurrence, may well have stimulated the development of the earliest tombs. There must also be a relationship between some megalithic tombs and the need for field clearance. This has been suggested by Piggott for Wayland's Smithy (Atkinson 1965: 127), and probably operates in many areas.

In any case, there is less certainty nowadays about the strength of the contacts once thought to be implied by the widespread distribution of these tombs. It is generally agreed that most tombs fall taxonomically into local groups; so do the grave goods as a general rule. Basic, generalized types like the Gallery Grave and the simple chamber have multiple origins, and their widespread distribution is not accorded much significance. At first sight the widespread occurrence of the porthole slab invites our interest. But as Daniel has pointed out (Clifford and Daniel 1940: 162) this is a device which could have arisen independently in several areas, in response to a need to constrict entrances or subdivide passages. And, indeed, if one compares the manufacture and use of the portholes at Los Millares (Leisner and Leisner 1943: tafel 20), in Hérault (Arnal 1963: fig. 12), and in the Paris Basin (Bailloud 1964: 160–1 and plate IV, 4), it is clear that nothing more than a vague idea has been diffused, at most.

The most persistent and convincing candidate for the status of international type is the Passage Grave. But even amongst the Passage Graves there are important local differences. The Leisners' well-known reconstruction of a Millaran tomb (1943: tafel 85) does not bear a close resemblance to L'Helgouach's drawing of Er-Mané-de-Quéric-la-Lande (1965: fig. 6), and neither is very like the picture which has emerged at New Grange (O'Kelly 1968: 41). Yet the Passage Grave *idea*, without insistence on detail, is widespread.

In the cases where diffusion may have occurred, there is little evidence of the nature of the mechanisms involved. Corcoran (1960: 136–7) talks of a generalized megalithic tradition, which is a fair way of describing how, particularly in the Irish Sea area, different and fairly widespread traits could occur in different combinations. It looks as if these ideas were spread by itinerant traders and inter-tribal envoys, and discussed at rural fairs and gatherings of the type which are thought to have taken place in the southern English causewayed camps (Smith 1965: 19). Certainly religious beliefs *might* spread in this fashion; if we are to accept the idea that the spread of megalithic tombs represents the growth of one basic idea, we must also accept that the accompanying architectural details might be spread very casually, and might come under strong local influences from the beginning.

The second assumption which is challenged is the east Mediterranean derivation of these tombs, which allows for the possibility of a religious link with that area. The east Mediterranean prototypes of the megaliths have always been nebulous. Now that there is a good series of early dates from Brittany (Daniel 1963: 143) with some support from Denmark and Britain, there is an almost unanswerable case for a western origin for them. The many areas of northern and western Europe with suitable and suggestive stone could easily have developed their own megalithic traditions, and very probably one or more of these did so without any influence from the east. This does not, of course, rule out the entirely separate introduction of an east Mediterranean fertility goddess; although as

Ucko (1968: 427–44) has so ably shown, the very existence of such a personage there at this early date is questionable.

The mother-goddess hypothesis rests most heavily, however, on the art and ritual equipment found in the tombs themselves. Carvings and relief sculpture on tomb walls, pottery and figurines are generally held to constitute the main evidence. In western Europe, it is clear that anthropomorphic figures of this kind are less easily seen the further north and north-west one goes; this is usually explained by supposing a gradual schematization of the original cult figure as the associated belief spread further from its east Mediterranean source. In the final stages, only an eye here, a breast there, are visible to the believer.

It is now time to turn away from general theory and to see what emerges from a study of the material, fully recognizing the difficulty of saying anything useful about prehistoric beliefs and the probability that several classes of material evidence are lost to us: wooden figures, for instance, of the type suggested by Atkinson at Wayland's Smithy (1965: 131), and perhaps wall hangings.

As was said earlier, if there is a truly international type it is the Passage Grave, and if there is really a single primary idea behind the megaliths, or any kind of initial spiritual unity, it must be searched for first amongst the Passage Graves. Those of Brittany must, on any chronology, stand early in the Passage Grave tradition. Yet the art here is almost totally devoid of anthropomorphic character (Péquart and Le Rouzic 1927: *passim*); the axe is the only clearly recognizable design, amid much whose significance is in doubt. The meaning of the famous 'buckler' figure (fig. 31*f*) is uncertain, but there is no evidence that it represents a deity. There are no face-pots or figurines in the Breton tombs. The Gaignog *stelae* (L'Helgouach 1965: 87) may indeed represent an anthropomorphic concept, but not necessarily a female one. In the end, the strongest possibility is the presence of an axe-cult, which at least would tally with the fine broken axes found in some tombs (Crawford 1957: 76), but not, surely, of a mother-goddess.

The concentric semi-circles at Gavrinis have been linked with both the goddess cult and with the Boyne carvings. However, they are neither anthropomorphic nor feminine, and furthermore stand out clearly from the bulk of Breton Passage Grave art. Indeed, they are distinct stylistically from everything in Brittany, except, perhaps, Conguel pottery. They do not compare closely with the Boyne carvings; the concentric semi-circles are in contrast to the Boyne preference for spirals and concentric circles (see Péquart and Le Rouzic 1927: plates 99–133). At Gavrinis these carvings almost certainly are skeuomorphs of hangings, similar to those at Göhlitzsch (Merseberg) (Clark 1952: fig. 129) or Dolauer Heide (Powell 1960: plate 20), and their uniqueness in Brittany is possibly explained by some theory such as that of L'Helgouach (1965: 89), who is prepared to consider the site as much a temple as a tomb.

In Ireland many of the designs look purely decorative: the pecked triangles and lozenges, the famous threshold stone at New Grange, and the St Andrew's crosses above the entrance there. Convincing representations of eyes are almost non-existent in Ireland; they occur at Knockmany (O'Riordain and Daniel 1964: plate 61) and possibly in the north side-chamber at New Grange (O'Riordain and Daniel 1964: plate 28). But there is no evidence that these eyes are intended to represent female personages. Many of the

Figure 31 Sites and objects mentioned in the text: (*a*) schist crozier, Portugal; (*b*) plaque from Vega del Guadancil, Cáceres, Spain; (*c*) *symbolkeramik* from Monte do Outeiro, Alentejo, Portugal; (*d*) statue-menhir from St Théodorit, Gard; (*e*) carving from Les Pierres Plates, Morbihan; (*f*) carving from Mané Rutual, Morbihan; (*g*) statue-menhir from Ciudad Rodrigo, Cáceres, Spain; (*h*) statue-menhir from l'Isle-sur-Sorge, Vaucluse; (*i*) statue-menhir from St Sernin, Aveyron; (*j*) statue-menhir from Lauris, Vaucluse. (After Arnal and Hugues, Crawford, Gagnière and Granier, and L'Helgouach.) *Not to scale*

designs look as if they have some magical meaning, but the only tentative identification is that of sun symbolism (fig. 33*i*).

Even Crawford, never a sceptic in these matters, realized that the trail was running out in Scandinavia. He cites the face-pots from Danish Middle Neolithic contexts as evidence, but these probably have no more significance than do our Toby jugs. Nor do the Scottish or the Hérault Passage Graves produce convincing mother-goddess symbolism.

This leaves Iberia, and here most of the evidence is to be found in funerary deposits rather than on tomb walls. Most prehistorians would look to the *symbolkeramik* and the evidence of figurines from the south and west to support the mother-goddess hypothesis. The importance of the *symbolkeramik* is debatable. Most of the figures are not specifically female – the fine pot from Monte de Outeiro (Leisner 1965: lieferung 3 (2), tafel 168) (fig. 31*c*) stands out as an exception here – and their divinity has not been established. Are the stags on the *symbolkeramik* also to be considered divine? In any case, pots may have been thought of as female, and perhaps linguistically they were feminine in gender. A possible parallel would be the Cycladic 'female frying-pans' (Childe 1957: fig. 24).

As for the idols, it has been too readily assumed that we know their function and their sex. In the past, anthropomorphic intentions have been inferred for whole groups, largely on the basis of evidence provided by one or two individual members of these groups. This is exemplified in the latest treatment of the baetyls, or short stone pillars (Almagro Gorbea 1968): the important undecorated type A, found in Portuguese Estremadura and Almeria (mostly at Los Millares), has to be related to the decorated Portuguese type B, whose anthropomorphism has in turn to be adduced from baetyls like those from Caisanhos and Folha das Barradas (Leisner 1965: lieferung 3(2), tafel 150). There is no evidence that they are feminine.

Of the phalanges, most have no decoration at all (Leisner and Leisner 1943: tafel 181) and very few are definitely female. Most of the schist plaques, too, are both eyeless and shoulderless. The delightful plaque from Vega del Guadancil (Leisner and Leisner 1959: tafel 55, I) (fig. 31*b*) could be a portrait of a female uncertain of the degree of modesty required of her; but it is equally possible that a loin-cloth, rather than a pubic triangle, is represented here. In any case, this one is exceptional; most of the other plaques give no information about their sex. The same is true of the long-bone idols from Almizaraque and Almagro's cruciform type II, which are certainly anthropomorphic, but not clearly female (Almagro 1966).

While it is probably permissible to use those few idols which are specific as evidence that the plain ones are anthropomorphic in concept, it is much more questionable to claim that they are all female on the basis of one or two. The most female class of all is Almagro's group VIII, clay figurines from Almizaraque and Vila Nova de São Pedro (Savory 1968: fig. 53c) – interestingly enough, from settlement sites. These probably represent cheerful local pornography. These graphic clay figures prompt another reflection; it is strange that a people whose culture was so technically accomplished should not have made any sustained attempt to reproduce the really sensuous aspects of the female form, if a mother-goddess was important to it. There is nothing here of the smoothness of the Ozieri figurines, or of the comfortable curves of the Maltese Fat Ladies.

In any case, the divinity of some of the figurines may be questioned. For instance, what is the status of the schist plaques, some of which may have been worn round the neck, as the perforations indicate? What of the baetyls, in their enclosures outside the tombs? The idols have become articles of faith for those who believe in the mother-goddess hypothesis; but were they such for their makers?

It has been argued that the evidence for mother-goddess worship by the builders of the Passage Graves and other relatively early tombs is really very exiguous. What of later groups?

In southern France and Iberia there are the statue-menhirs, which are only occasionally found in association with megaliths. It is surprising, therefore, to find that they are sometimes supposed to shed some light on megalithic religion. Setting this question aside, it is interesting that on analysis they fall into distinct local groups, which reinforces the initial suggestion that the religious situation in prehistoric Europe was probably fairly complex.

The Iberian examples are distinguished by the fact that they most commonly wear a necklace (Crato), a head-dress (Nuestra Senhora de la Esparança), or both (Ciudad Rodrigo) (fig. 31*g*) (Breuil 1935: vol. 4, plate XLII, 1, 2, 3). The well-known example from Peña Tú (Crawford 1957: fig. 22b) is probably within this group, though not a statue-menhir. No indication of sex is given, and their links with the megaliths are not well established. They are predominantly western in distribution.

In southern France, several groups may be established, as follows:

1. *The Aveyron group* (e.g. fig. 31*i*). This group is stylistically distinct, and occurs '*hors de tout context*' (Arnal 1963: 220). Its dating depends largely on the correct identification of the '*objet*'. The suggestions of Balsan (1952) have been recently confirmed by the finding of the Foumendouyre statue, whose '*objet*' has two lateral holes, bringing it into close relationship with jet and bone objects of the Seveyrac type (Arnal, Hugues and Rodriguez 1966: fig. 4, 4). These objects occur in some Aveyron dolmens, so that in this case it is possible to link the statues with megalithic tombs. A little dating evidence comes from Gard, where a statue-menhir from Colombier, Euzet-les-Bains (Arnal 1963: 220) carries an '*objet*' and was found in association with Chalcolithic pottery. According to Arnal and Hugues (1963) masculine statues, which carry the object, greatly outnumber female ones, distinguishable by their breasts. (In fig. 31*i*, both are marked; the '*objet*' is vertical and gives the appearance of a badly-tied necktie.) The ratio between male and female statues, and the compulsory sex change which was undergone by statues like that from Arribats, are seen as evidence for the late spread of the female form.

2. *The Gard group*. The members of this group are not a closely-knit taxonomic unit. There is the Bouïsset-Bragassargues type, with staring eyes and suggestions of a facial tattoo like that of the Aveyron statues. Arnal (1963: 94) says that these are Neolithic to Chalcolithic in date, and that they are sometimes associated with '*tombes en ruche*'. They are not necessarily female. One of them, Bouïsset no. 2, has a 'crozier' (Arnal 1963: 93). Secondly, there is the Collorgues type (Audibert 1962: 154) (fig. 32*c*), supplied with breasts and usually a crozier. This type is normally assigned to the Chalcolithic, and a link with the Aveyron group is provided by the example from Rosseironne (Arnal and Hugues 1963: plate IV, 3), which has both '*objet*' and crozier. Thirdly, there are less conventional types like St Bénézet, Cazarils (Arnal and Hugues: plate III, 5 and IV, 1) and St Théodorit (fig. 31*d*). Of those whose sex can be determined, more are female than male, taking the group as a whole (Arnal and Hugues 1963: 13).

3. *The Lower Durance group*. These form two stylistic groups; first, the Isle-sur-Sorge type, with two examples (Gagnière and Granier 1963: 52 and fig. 34) (fig. 31*h*). These are not definitely female, and the dating is based on very thin evidence – an alleged association with Chalcolithic flintwork, and a sun-symbol compared with Early Bronze Age carvings at Monte Bego. Secondly, there is the Orgon-Lauris type, T-faced and occasionally with eyes and geometric 'tresses' (fig. 31*j*). Here the dating is based on a possible association with a 'Lagozzian' flint industry and the situation of typical sites in positions liable to flooding, which is a characteristic of these 'Lagozzian' sites. No sex is marked on these small statues, and only one occurs in a funerary context.

The features of some of these southern French statues have sometimes been compared, rather loosely, with those of other groups of art. Many of these comparisons can be dismissed with ease. A T-face, for instance, is a simple way of depicting a face for the unskilled carver; there is no need to compare the lower Durance figures with Moncorvo and Asquerosa. Nor is there any warrant for claiming that the Collorgues 'crozier' (fig. 32*c*) has anything to do with the schist croziers of Iberia (fig. 31*a*), or that facial tattooing, as apparently seen on the Aveyron statues (fig. 31*i*) and the Iberian plaques (fig. 31*b*), was not a common custom in several areas of Europe. The same may be said of the wearing of pendants (Coizard, fig. 32*e*; St Théodorit, fig. 31*d*) and necklaces (Ciudad Rodrigo, fig. 31*g*; St Sernin, fig. 31*i*; Bellahaye, fig. 32*d*). Far from exhibiting wide-ranging links of this type, most of the art under consideration shows a distinctly local pattern – the Gard crozier, the '*objet*' in Aveyron, the head-dress in western Iberia.

Thus for southern France it has been shown that even if the statues can be linked to the tombs – which is frequently not the case – these links are not very strong. Femininity is restricted; female statues occur in the Collorgues group, and sometimes in the Aveyron group.

In Brittany, later megalithic art may be divided into two groups. First, there is the art of the deviant Passage Graves, notably Les Pierres Plates and Luffang (L'Helgouach 1965: fig. 74). The famous face from Luffang (Giot *et al.* 1960: plate 31) is not necessarily female, and the Pierres Plates carvings (fig. 31*e*) are incomprehensible. But the Breton Gallery Graves do carry a female figure. She appears at Prajou-Menhir (fig. 32*b*), at Mougau-Bian and at Tressé (L'Helgouach 1965: fig. 109). On two of these sites she appears in the antechamber. The form of this figure is quite close to the figure with breasts and necklace in the antechambers of five Paris Basin Gallery Graves (Bailloud 1964: 181 and fig. 37) (fig. 32*d*), and these may be compared with the figures guarding the entrances of the rock-cut tombs at Coizard and Courjeonnet (Bailloud 1964: 181 and fig. 37) (fig. 32*e*). These are all linked by tomb typology (including the chamber-with-antechamber idea), by position within the tomb, and by appearance, as well as associated cultural material (SOM pottery and its Breton equivalent). To this group belong the statue-menhirs of Catel in Guernsey (Kendrick 1928: plate V) and Guidel (Morbihan) (fig. 32*a*) (Giot 1959), which are similar to each other and to the larger group mentioned above, and which originate, in the case of Guidel, in an SOM or pre-SOM context.

The SOM associations of this group suggest a date in the first half of the second millennium, or a little earlier. This dating is confirmed by the association at Prajou-Menhir (fig. 32*b*) and Mougau-Bian with carvings of the 'Cypriote' daggers (L'Helgouach

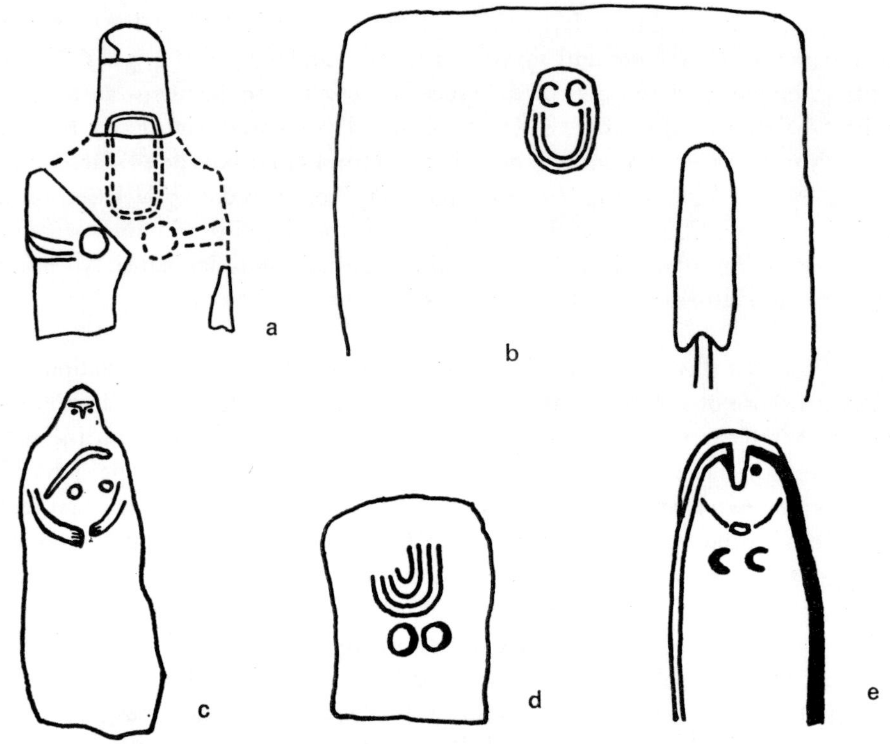

Figure 32 The French mother-goddess province: (*a*) broken statue-menhir from Guidel, Morbihan; (*b*) carving of goddess and 'Cypriote' dagger, Prajou-Menhir, Côtes-du-Nord; (*c*) statue-menhir from Collorgues, Gard; (*d*) carving from Bellahaye, Oise; (*e*) carving in rock-cut tomb, Coizard, Marne. (After Daniel, Giot, Kendrick, and L'Helgouach.) *Not to scale*

1965: fig. 109) which occur in the Plouguerneau hoard (Briard 1965: 60) in association with flat axes.

Thus in France (fig. 32) there is a northern mother-goddess in Brittany, the Channel Islands and the Paris Basin (see map, fig. 34) and a southern one in the Collorgues group of statue-menhirs, perhaps spreading into the Aveyron group somewhat later than the male deity apparently existing there already, if one follows Arnal and Hugues. The chronological relationship between the northern mother-goddess and the southern remains obscure, as does the absolute dating of the southern type. The southern French statues are, as mentioned above, often attributed to the Chalcolithic, which might place them anywhere within the 2500–1500 B.C. bracket. At Lébous (Arnal, Granel and Sangmeister 1964: 195) two statue-menhirs stood in a fort which produced a radiocarbon date of 1920 B.C. ±250. So a chronological overlap between north and south is a distinct possibility, especially since the dates from Les Matignons (Burnez and Case 1966: 193) have demonstrated that flat-based, thick-walled pottery of the SOM general type may start as early as the middle of the third millennium. Whether the two areas can be linked is uncertain, though it should be remembered that this is the time of the Beaker movements, the trade in Grand Pressigny flint (Arnal 1963: 206) and in Breton axes of group A dolerite and group C fibrolite (Giot *et al.* 1960: 81). This provides a context for the spread of a belief in a mother-goddess at this time, though it is difficult to insist on this hypothesis, or to be dogmatic about the direction of movement.

It is possible that both Sardinia and Malta should be included in this late mother-goddess province. Both of these areas probably entertained rather complex religious beliefs, to judge from what has survived, but both include unambiguous female figurines (Guido 1963: plates 5 and 6; Evans 1959: plate 65). Bray has documented quite clearly the links between France and Sardinia at this time, and he has suggested that there were even closer links between the Sardinian Ozieri culture and the Tarxien phase in Malta (1963: 174 ff.). It is possible that one component of the Ozieri culture came from Malta during the Tarxien phase, possibly as a result of deteriorating agricultural conditions in their homeland (Trump 1966: 51). Now, the Maltese Fat Lady is an important element in what is known of Maltese religion; the temples themselves provide evidence that this religion was a compelling one, run by a well-organized priesthood of some kind. If there was emigration from Malta to Sardinia, the best chance of success for the would-be colonists would lie in departure in a strong, well-organized body, accompanied by the appropriate religious advisers. A group of this sort would certainly stand a good chance of establishing its beliefs in its new environment; the tomb at S. Andrea Priu (Guido 1963: fig. 10), which has been so plausibly compared with the Hal Saflieni Hypogeum in Malta, could well be evidence for this. From Sardinia, these beliefs may have spread to France.

This is only a tentative suggestion, and must remain so, especially in the absence of a closer chronology. But I hope that I have shown that firm evidence for a mother-goddess is confined, in Europe, to the province Malta–Sardinia–France; that the mother-goddess is linked more to the idea of collective burial than to megalithic tombs as such (and here one may cite the rock-cut tombs of Malta, Sardinia and the Marne); and that there is no evidence for any mother-goddess worship in most of the cultures associated with the building of megalithic tombs. The mother-goddess is thus both late in date and limited in area of dispersal.

One important group of decorated tombs remains to be considered. In northern Portugal there are around forty painted and engraved tombs (de Albuquerque e Castro 1962). The designs vary considerably in size and content. They mainly comprise wavy lines and elaborate geometric patterns which look very much like skeuomorphic hangings. The designs at Pedralta, Cangas de Onis and Antelas are good examples (Powell and Daniel 1956: figs 11 and 12; Savory 1968: figs 35 and 36). It has been suggested that these designs find their closest parallels in the Irish Passage Graves (Powell and Daniel 1956: 50–1). The comparison is a fair one, though the similarities could result from separate and parallel development if both are thought to develop as tapestry skeuomorphs. However, there are other close links between western Iberia and the British Isles.

A comparison between the illustrations in Sobrino-Buhigas's corpus (1935) and the Scottish carvings illustrated by Simpson (1864–5) indicates some close similarities between Galician and Scottish rock art. It has been suggested that Ireland shares in this community (MacWhite 1946). This similarity is illustrated briefly in figure 33 (*c* and *f*). If it is thought that this kind of parallel, close as it seems, is generalized enough to result from coincidence, it is hard to ignore the evidence of the Tagliatella-type labyrinth. This

Figure 33 The Atlantic art province: (*a*) carving from Knowth, co. Meath; (*b*) Tagliatella-type labyrinth carved on rock, Mogor, Galicia; (*c*) rock-carving from Salcedo, Galicia; (*d*) carving from Casal, Minho, Portugal; (*e*) geometric carving from Barclodiad y Gawres, Anglesey; (*f*) rock-carving from Mevagh, co. Donegal; (*g*) tomb carving of 'anthropomorphic figure' from Chão Redondo no. 2, Aveiro, Portugal; (*h*) carving on slab from Clear Island, co. Cork; (*i*) possible sun symbols from the Irish Passage Graves. (After Breuil, Albuquerque e Castro, Eogan, MacWhite, Piggott, and Powell and Daniel.) *Not to scale*

highly specialized design is found at Mogor, Galicia (fig. 33*b*), at Holywood (Wicklow) and at Tintagel in Cornwall (Lorenzo-Ruza 1956), though the last two examples occur isolated from other art.

It has always been difficult to separate totally the rock art of Ireland and north Britain from, on the one hand, the art which occurs occasionally on cists containing Food Vessel or Beaker burials, and on the other hand the art of the Irish Passage Graves. Recent finds from New Grange have emphasized the links between the rock art and Passage Grave art (O'Kelly 1964: 289); and indeed O'Kelly suggests a re-examination of their relationship. The parallelism between Galicia and Britain suggests that the geometric decoration of the Irish and north Portuguese tombs may also be directly related, and that tapestry skeuomorphs were developed in one area and passed to the other. A third factor in this relationship may be the designs which have been alleged to be anthropomorphic. Peña Tú (Crawford 1957: fig. 22b) may be a representation of the deity with the head-dress mentioned above. But it is possible that the figure from Châo Redondo no 2. (fig. 33*g*), claimed by de Albuquerque e Castro as masculine, may be related to figures of the Barclodiad y Gawres type (Powell and Daniel 1956: fig. 11) (fig. 33*e*). Furthermore, stelae like Pola de Allande (Powell and Daniel 1956: plate 33) may be linked with those from King's Mountain and Clear Island (Powell and Daniel 1956: plate 32 and fig. 11) (fig. 33*h*). It is interesting also how close is the newly-discovered 'anthropomorphic figure' from Knowth (Eogan 1967: plate XLI) (fig. 33*a*) to the long-known stele from Casal (Breuil 1935: vol. 4, plate XLII, 5) (fig. 33*d*). The concentric squares with rounded corners and the two 'eyes', themselves surrounded by concentric grooves, amount to quite a close correlation.

This Atlantic art province, then (fig. 33 and map, fig. 34), includes cup-and-ring markings, Tagliatella-type labyrinths, geometric paintings and engravings inside tombs, and possibly a very schematic human figure, of uncertain sex, in a few tombs and on *stelae* set in isolation. It is difficult to gain a clear impression of the religious concepts represented by these designs, especially since little work has been done on the province as a whole. One possibility is that sun-worship was involved. There are numerous sun-symbols on the Irish Passage Graves (O'Riordain and Daniel 1964: plate 43) (fig. 33*i*) and it is interesting that at Antelas, in Portugal, a clear sun and moon are represented together (de Albuquerque e Castro 1962: tav. CLXIV, 3). Into this picture would fit sites like Granja de Toniñuelo, Badajoz (Breuil 1935: vol. 4, plate XL, 1 and 2), with its possible sun-symbols. The significance of the cup-and-ring markings, the labyrinths, and the anthropomorphic figures – if this is what they are – is unclear, and further work is required here.

How were these motifs and ideas diffused, and in which direction? In the absence of good dating evidence, this remains uncertain. The carbon dates from New Grange (G. E. Daniel, pers. comm.) suggest that the Irish Passage Graves may date from at least the middle of the third millennium. The magnificence of sites like New Grange and Knowth, with its sun-symbols, is in great contrast to the poverty of the Portuguese sites, and is far more appropriate to an area where a cult is strong and important. It must be admitted that the Irish climate of today provides a complete explanation of any prehistoric efforts to placate the sun!

The north English/Scottish cup-and-ring markings are normally referred to the Bronze

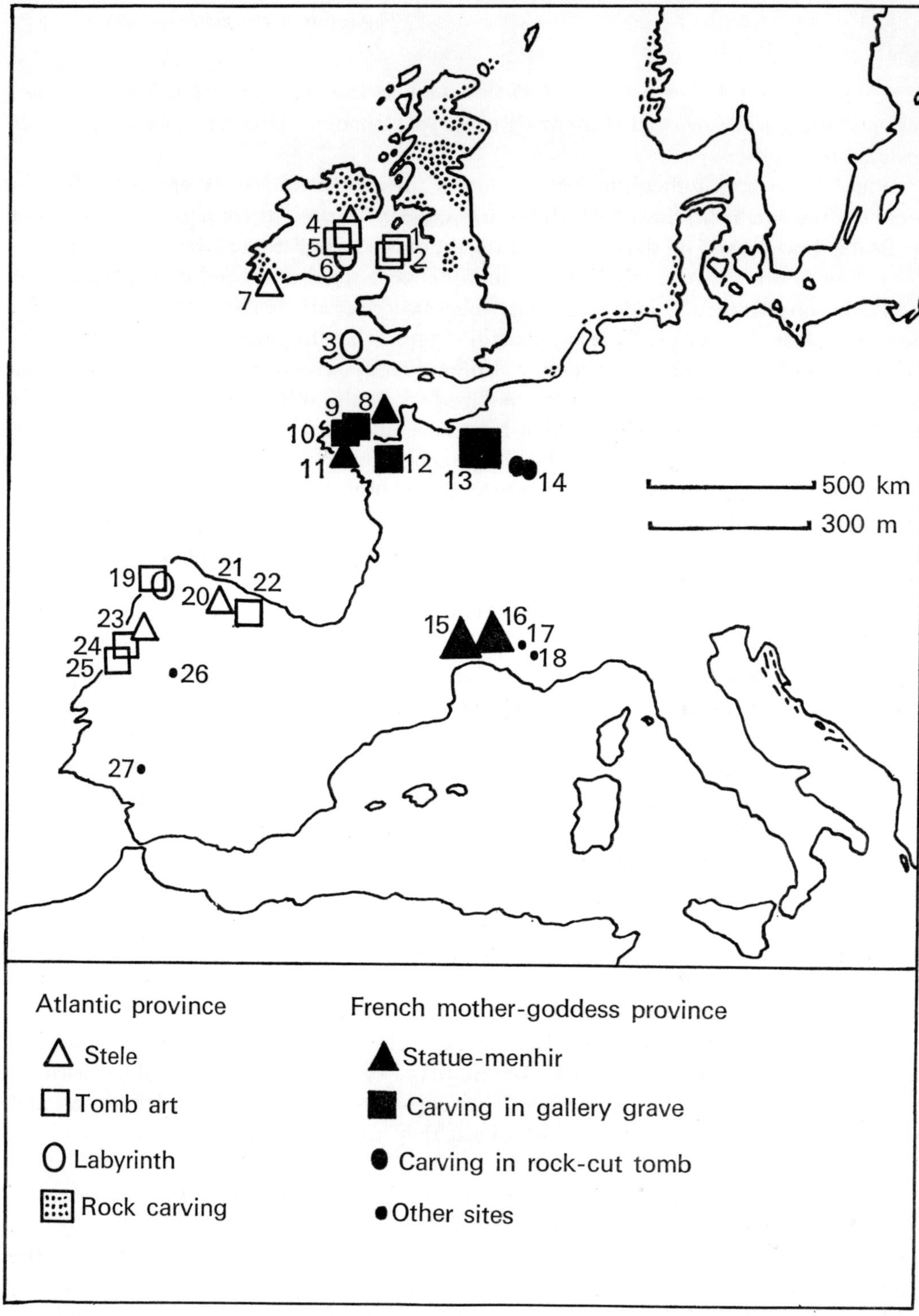

Figure 34 Map of western Europe showing the two main provinces of megalithic and associated art. The numbers refer to sites as follows: 1. Barclodiad y Gawres; 2. Bryn Celli Ddu; 3. Tintagel; 4. King's Mountain; 5. New Grange and Knowth; 6. Holywood; 7. Clear Island; 8. Catel; 9. Prajou-Menhir; 10. Mougau-Bian; 11. Guidel; 12. Tressé; 13. Paris Basin sites; 14. Coizard and Courjeonnet; 15. the Aveyron group; 16. the Gard group; 17. L'Isle-sur-Sorge; 18. Lauris; 19. Pedra Coberta; 20. Mogor; 21. Pola de Allande; 22. Cangas de Onis; 23. Casal; 24. Pedralta; 25. Châo Redondo; 26. Ciudad Rodrigo; 27. Granja de Toniñuelo

Age, and may date from a time when Irish metallurgists were exporting their products, and perhaps their beliefs, across the Irish Sea (Megaw and Hardy 1938). Their activities in the export field are clear by now in Denmark and the Low Countries (Butler 1960: 201) and in north-western France (Briard 1965: 51–77). Whether they worked in Galicia is at present uncertain. At any rate, these highly mobile smiths are obviously possible agents for the diffusion of the putative sun-cult, a full 2,000 years before the missionary activities of their more celebrated descendants.

The two distinct provinces of megalithic art, including related art in rock-cut tombs, on *stelae*, and on open rock surfaces, are indicated on the map (fig. 34). The art of Ireland and western Iberia should be completely separated from that of France. Stylistically, the two provinces could hardly be more different – this seems clear whether or not my tentative ideas on the beliefs of the two areas are accepted.

One point which emerges from this study is that in both provinces the relevant art was only partially connected with megalithic tombs. In the mother-goddess province, for instance, there are numerous isolated statue-menhirs, while in the Atlantic province art may be found on rock surfaces and *stelae*, as well as in tombs. This serves to emphasize what I said at the outset – that the practice of a religion and the choice of a particular burial rite are separable, and in many cases probably were distinct.

These two groups of art are unrelated to the earliest of the European megaliths, and there is no good evidence yet for any date of before 2500 B.C. for either group. So we still know little, far too little, about the genesis of megalithic tombs and the rituals and beliefs which informed the building of the earliest examples. In the past, the acceptance of the simple hypothesis which has come under criticism here has seriously held up study of the rituals implied by grave goods and tomb design. The mother-goddess has detained us for too long; let us disengage ourselves from her embrace.

Acknowledgement

I would like to express my thanks to the administrators of the Sheffield University Research Fund for providing the means for studying in Spain and Portugal, and to Dr Glyn Daniel for useful criticism of this paper.

11.iv.69

Department of Ancient History
University of Sheffield

References

Albuquerque e Castro, L. de. 1962. L'Art mégalithique au Portugal. *Atti del VI Congresso Internazionale delle Scienze Preistoriche e Protostoriche*, III:370–4.

Almagro, M. 1966. *El Idolo del Chillaron y la Tipologia de los Idolos del Bronce I Hispano.* Madrid.

Almagro Gorbea, M. J. 1968. *Los Idolos Betilos del Bronce I Hispano; sus tipos y cronologia.* Madrid.

Arnal, J. 1963. Les Dolmens de l'Hérault. *Préhistoire.* 15:1–239.

Arnal, J., Granel, M. and Sangmeister, E. 1964. Lébous. *Antiquity.* 38:191–200.

Arnal, J. and Hugues, C. 1963. Sur les statues-menhirs du Languedoc-Rouerge. *Archivo de Prehistoria Levantina.* 10:23–8.

Arnal, J., Hugues, C. and Rodriguez, G. 1966. La Statue-menhir de Foumendouyre. *Congrès préhistorique de France.* 18:379–88.

Atkinson, R. J. C. 1965. Wayland's Smithy. *Antiquity.* 39:126–33.

Audibert, J. 1962. *La civilisation chalcolithique du Languedoc oriental.* Montpellier.

Bailloud, G. 1964. *Le Néolithique dans le Bassin Parisien.* Paris.

Balsan, L. 1952. Deux pendeloques inédites des dolmens aveyronnais. *Bulletin de la Société Préhistorique Française.* 49. 171–5.

Bray, W., 1963. The Ozieri Culture of Sardinia. *Rivista di Scienze Preistoriche.* 18:155–90.

Breuil, H. 1935. *Les Peintures Rupestres Schématiques de la Péninsule Iberique.* 4 vols. Lagny.

Briard, J. 1965. *Les Dépots Bretons et l'Age du Bronze Atlantique.* Rennes.

Burnez, C. and Case, H. 1966. Les Camps Néolithiques des Matignons à Juillac-le-Coq (Charente). *Gallia Préhistoire.* 9:131–245.

Butler, J. J. 1960. Bronze Age Connections Across the North Sea. *Palaeohistoria.* 9:1–286.

Childe, V. G. 1957. *The Dawn of European Civilization.* London.

Clark, J. G. D. 1952. *Prehistoric Europe: the economic basis.* London.

Clifford, E. M. and Daniel, G. E. 1940. The Rodmarton and Avening Portholes. *Proceedings of the Prehistoric Society.* 6:133–65.

Corcoran, J. X. W. P. 1960. The Carlingford Culture. *Proceedings of the Prehistoric Society.* 26:98–148.

Crawford, O. G. S. 1957. *The Eye Goddess.* London.

Daniel, G. E. 1958. *The Megalith Builders of Western Europe.* London.

Daniel, G. E. 1963. *The Megalith Builders of Western Europe* (paperback edition). London.

Daniel, G. E. 1967. The Megalith Builders of the SOM. *Palaeohistoria.* 12:199–208.

Eogan, G. 1967. The Knowth (co. Meath) Excavations. *Antiquity.* 41:302-4.

Evans, J. D. 1959. *Malta.* London.

Gagnière, J. and Granier, J. 1963. Les Stèles Anthropomorphes du Musée Calvet d'Avignon. *Gallia Préhistoire.* 6:31–62.

Giot, P.-R. 1959. Le Tumulus de Kermené en Guidel (Morbihan) *Annales de Bretagne.* 66:5–30.

Giot, P.-R. *et al.* 1960. *Brittany.* London.

Grimes, W. F. 1960. *Excavations on Defence Sites, 1939–45*, vol. I. London.

Guido, M. 1963. *Sardinia.* London.

Kendrick, T. D. 1928. *The Archaeology of the Channel Islands.* London.

Laet, S. de. 1958. *The Low Countries.* London.

Leisner, G. and Leisner, V. 1943. *Die Megalithgräber der Iberischen Halbinsel. Der Suden.* Berlin.

Leisner, G. and Leisner, V. 1956. *Ibid. Der Westen.* 1. Berlin.

Leisner, G. and Leisner, V. 1959. *Ibid. Der Westen.* 2. Berlin.

Leisner, V. 1965. *Ibid. Der Westen.* 3 (2 vols). Berlin.

L'Helgouach, J. 1965. *Les sépultures mégalithiques en Armorique.* Rennes.

Lorenzo-Ruza, R. S. 1956. In *Revista de Guimarães.*

MacWhite, E. 1946. A New View on Irish Bronze Age Rock-scribings. *Journal of the Royal Society of Antiquaries of Ireland.* 76:59–80.

Megaw, B. R. S. and Hardy, E. M. 1938. British Decorated Axes and their diffusion during the earlier part of the Bronze Age. *Proceedings of the Prehistoric Society.* 4:272–95.

O'Kelly, M. J. 1964. New Grange, co. Meath. *Antiquity.* 38:288–90.

O'Kelly, M. J. 1968. Excavations at Newgrange, co. Meath. *Antiquity.* 42:40–2.

O'Riordain, S. P. and Daniel, G. E. 1964. *New Grange.* London.

Péquart, M. and Le Rouzic, Z. 1927. *Corpus des signes gravés des monuments mégalithiques du Morbihan.* Paris.

Piggott, S. 1954. *The Neolithic Cultures of the British Isles.* London.

Piggott, S. 1962. *The West Kennet Long Barrow.* London.

Powell, T. G. E. 1960. Megalithic and other Art; Centre and West. *Antiquity.* 34:180–90.

Powell, T. G. E. and Daniel, G. E. 1956. *Barclodiad y Gawres.* Liverpool.

Savory, H. N. 1968. *Spain and Portugal.* London.

Simpson, Y. J. 1864–5. On Ancient Sculpturings of Cups and concentric Rings, etc. *Proceedings of the Society of Antiquaries of Scotland.* 6 (appendix):1–140.

Smith, I. F. (ed.). 1965. *Windmill Hill and Avebury: Excavations by Alexander Keiller (1925–39).* London.

Sobrino-Buhigas, R. 1935. *Corpus Petroglyphorum Gallaeciae.* Santiago de Compostela.

Trump, D. H. 1966. *Skorba.* London.

Ucko, P. J. 1968. *Anthropomorphic Figurines of Predynastic Egypt and Neolithic Crete.* London.

Ethnography and archaeological interpretation of funerary remains[1]

Peter J. Ucko

Professor Childe argued on one occasion (1958a: 4) that the value of the specific ethnographic comparison, for example between the designs of modern Australian and prehistoric Irish carvings, was 'just to show the funny kinds of meanings or purposes that may be attached to the queerer kinds of archaeological data', and such comparison, he argued, was a waste of time. However, in the same article he also stated that: 'It is no more legitimate to impute to Palaeolithic hunters or Neolithic farmers the motives and values of twentieth-century Europeans and Americans than to birds or ants.' It is clear that what is considered funny or queer by one person or culture may be thought normal by another, and there is no reason to think that modern peoples living in remote areas of the world are any more or less peculiar than ourselves, or than any of the groups who lived at various different times and in different areas of the ancient world. The primary use of ethnographic parallels, I have argued several times elsewhere (Ucko and Rosenfeld 1967: 150–8; Ucko 1968: 419–26; Ucko in press), is simple. It is to widen the horizons of the interpreter, as Childe recognized was necessary in his second statement. I have tried to show with cave art (1967), figurines (1968) and rock art (in press) that without a widely orientated approach to archaeological interpretation, the data revealed by the archaeological material itself tends to become swamped by unitary and all-embracing explanation. It is true to say that the careful use of ethnographic data has served to do one major thing – to present the possibility of varied and heterogeneous reasons or causes for a practice. As far as I am concerned, the use of ethnographic parallels can only in very

[1] This paper was delivered as a lecture to the Conference of *The Prehistoric Society* on 'The Interpretation of Funerary Evidence' held in London on 21–3 March 1969. I have left the text and style of this paper essentially unchanged from the lecture delivered on that occasion except for the addition of references; the final section of the paper on 'horizontal stratigraphy' is a short preliminary statement which I hope to expand in the near future. For reasons of time I omitted almost all of the introduction to this paper on the use of ethnographic parallels at the Prehistoric Society conference, but I have reinserted my views on this subject for this publication.

I would like to thank the following people for their comments and interest in this paper, for without them it would have been much more restricted in scope and intention: Dr A. J. Arkell, Mrs M. J. Baldwin, Professor N. A. Barnicot, Dr Maurice Bloch, Mr Stephen Cretney, Dr J. P. Garlick, Dr Jack Goody, Mr Mark Hassall, Mr H. W. M. Hodges, Dr G. W. B. Huntingford, Dr P. Kaberry, Mr Robert Layton, Dr Joan Lewis, Dr Godfrey Lienhardt, Miss Mary-Jane Mountain, Mr Kenneth Painter, Mr John Picton, Dr Vernon Reynolds, Dr Andrée Rosenfeld, Mr Michael Rowlands, Dr Ruth Tringham and especially Dr Peter Morton-Williams. Without the prolonged and merciless pressures exerted by my friends Drs John Alexander and Ian Longworth this paper would probably never have been written, and they would have been spared their 'glimpse into the abyss of original chaos'.

exceptional cases suggest a one-to-one correlation between the acts of tribe A and the remains of culture B, but what they *can* do is to suggest the sorts of possible procedures which may result in the traits characterizing culture B. In Professor Hawkes's words: 'You can use ethnological data obtained from modern primitives to stimulate your imagination by suggesting the sort of religious institutions and spiritual life your prehistoric peoples may or could have had . . .' (1954: 162). Unfortunately, Hawkes continues the sentence, 'but you cannot this way demonstrate what they did have, and you know you cannot even hope to unless you can show some real connection between *this* modern and *that* prehistoric', and he thus highlights a view which may, if taken to its extreme, find itself divorced from anthropological methodology. On the one hand, it has been held that cultural tradition alone can be profitably used to link the known (in this case usually the historic) to the unknown (in this case the prehistoric), and this approach leads to the concentration of attention on the practices over time *within one particular area*. On the other hand, anthropologists have long accepted the use of the comparative method (see, for example, Radcliffe-Brown 1951). Its use directs attention to the variety of cultural responses which have arisen, in different areas and at different times, to cope with problems and situations which are common to human existence. The first approach necessarily relies on the assumption of human cultural continuity (in this case restricted and defined geographically) which in the context of funerary procedures suffers from the practical defect that our knowledge of funerary dicta from early historic civilizations is often meagre in the extreme. In many areas of the Old World there are often hundreds, and even thousands, of years between the earliest written funerary records and the earlier prehistoric activities in the same area (Ucko 1968: 412–13). The second view assumes as proven that no human society is static, whether literate, non-literate or pre-literate, and is therefore concerned with the social situations which may result in similar or different cultural solutions, irrespective of the geographical location or the particular peoples concerned. In the context of funerary practices this is especially important for, as will be shown later in this paper, burial rites are known to change frequently in many situations, and yet, as Adams has recently argued (1968: 203), the various functional possibilities of differential disposal of the dead (especially those which can be found in the archaeological record) are few in number, and may appear in the archaeological record as abrupt changes and therefore as particularly significant.

Just as it is no longer felt necessary today to take up the extreme positions of the 'diffusionists' and 'inventionists', so these two views need not be opposed. Where there is good evidence for continued cultural tradition in a particular area, let it by all means be remembered; where there is textual evidence, let it be produced. But it must be realized that where one particular cultural trait has remained the same over time, it does not necessarily follow that other cultural traits have not changed either – where the same pottery types or funerary practices continue over a space of time, religious beliefs may just as well change as remain static. The real test whether or not any set of material from a particular area is really relevant to the interpretation of earlier material from the same region must again depend on the procedures inherent in the comparative method; it must depend on the closeness of the fit between the facts revealed by the archaeological data and the model which can be constructed from other sources, whether these be from the modern practices of human groups elsewhere in the world or from the ancient practices of people in the same region. If the historic tradition is the important variable, then the fit will be closest with this material; if the common denominator is human experience, then the fit may equally well be with unrelated groups of people.

Normally, when the range of ethnographic activities is considered, the result is a multiplicity of possible explanations of a particular set of archaeological data; to assess the closest fit, or in other words to narrow down the range of possible alternatives, it becomes necessary to focus in detail on the archaeological data which exists. What I am suggesting is that one of the prime results of the use of ethnographic parallels is to take the archaeologist back to his own material – the width of the approach will make the archaeologist re-analyse his own material. In the context of funerary remains, renewed attention will become focused on bone material, on funerary structures and on the context and arrangement of corpses. It may sound as if all archaeologists should also be anthropologists, and to an unfortunate extent this is in many ways true: 'unfortunately, our ethnologist colleagues tend to concern themselves with aspects of culture not directly manifested in archaeological remains, so that the archaeologist is obliged to invade their realm to secure the data he needs' (Campbell 1968: 18).

Evelyn Waugh's mortuary hostess of Whispering Glades asked Mr Barlow 'now what had you in mind? Embalmment of course, and after that incineration or not, according to taste. . . . Normal disposal is by inhumement, entombment, inurnment, immurement, but many people just lately prefer insarcophagusment.' Whatever the complexity or simplicity of the rite, the standard disposal of the dead is a characteristic of man not shared by other vertebrates, even the higher apes. It has commonly been held by the archaeologist that burial practices are synonymous with afterworld beliefs, and almost everyone has accepted the presence of burial offerings and funerary goods as an indication of belief in either the sort of afterworld where the goods may be useful, or in a journey to the afterworld during which the offerings will be needed. Thus, '. . . Neanderthal man certainly displayed signs of spirituality . . . in his treatment of the dead' (Clark and Piggott 1965: 61), and '. . . ritual burial presupposes some recognition of the spiritual nature of man, of the existence of a soul capable of living on after death' (Clark 1960: 232). It is also often argued that formally held religious beliefs imply formal disposal of the dead. Ethnographically, at least, the situation is not always so simple.

The pagan Nupe of Nigeria have a myth of the origin of burial which is much older than Islam in that area and which approaches burial in a quite profane way. Two sons and a daughter were born to the ancestress Adama. 'When they grew up the two young men both desired their sister. They quarrelled and one was killed. It was thus that death and murder first appeared in the world. The remaining couple did not know what to do with the dead body. They carried the corpse on their shoulders for three days, lamenting and crying, but could not get rid of it. At last, god caused the earth to open, and they placed the body inside. Thus the practice of burial and of three days' mourning for the dead began. [It is, incidentally, interesting to note that the Nupe do not, in fact, observe a three days' period of mourning.] The couple now stayed together and begot a male child who became the ancestor of the Nupe people' (Nadel 1954: 9–10). An attitude to burial simply as a means of disposal, even when a specially designated burial area exists, is not uncommon ethnographically.

It is true to say that burial very often does imply some kind of belief in a spiritual being, but the beliefs involved may be of the most general kind. Amongst the south-eastern Bantu, for example, graves are sacred only because it is at the grave that the spirits of the deceased are contacted, but there is no associated belief in a journey to the after-world, and there are no developed ideas about the soul (Gluckman 1937: 127). Amongst the Nuer of the Sudan ordinary burial is a matter of little interest to the community; it amounts to a job of disposal to be performed as quickly as possible by close kin and with as little fuss as possible; sacrifices are only very rarely offered to the dead, and their graves are left unmarked and are almost immediately forgotten (Evans-Pritchard 1951: 209–10; 1956: 144). As will be seen shortly, absence of burial in no way signifies absence of afterworld beliefs.

Surely, then, burial goods must be surer signs of afterworld belief? It is clear that many peoples do indeed place offerings in the tomb, and in some cases these are certainly to provide for the needs of the dead. Among the Nankanse of Ghana, however, it is reported that burial goods are not placed in the tomb to accompany the dead. The archaeologist, however, would find some! These would include the occasional arrow or bangle, and he might well be tempted to identify those few graves with objects in them as those of particularly rich individuals. In fact, however, these objects are included because, during the burial activities, the soul of a *living* person has become trapped in the grave and the sexton has failed to get it out. When this happens the favourite articles of the living person are placed by the sexton in the grave, for while they remain in the grave the person will *not* die. As Rattray says 'such a custom might throw a new interpretation on the reason for such articles being found in graves' (1932: 186). More recent ethnography from the Lugbara of Uganda is both interesting and probably applies to quite a number of primitive tribes. Burial amongst the Lugbara has little or nothing to do with the belief in an afterlife, and the tomb goods have no purpose connected with the afterworld; they are simply the visible expression of part of a person's social personality, the visible expression of his having left the living. A man may be buried with his quiver, representing his activities as a hunter and warrior; with his gourd, representing his mature status as a person who drank with other mature men; with his stool, representing his elderhood; with his oracle objects, representing his status as an operator. A woman may be buried with her beads, representing her status as a girl; with her firestones, representing her status as wife; and with her grinding stones, representing her status as a mother (Middleton 1960: 29, 200). Finally, the poor archaeologist might well be misled by the offerings buried with the pets in Woodlands Private Animal Cemetery in Burwash (Sussex) – these include a teddy bear, coats and blankets, collars, favourite toys and foods in the shape of rubber bones and actual chocolate. In several cases, at least, the pet owners had no thoughts about their animals needing these objects in an afterworld, or on the journey to an afterworld, but simply wished to dispose of objects which had particular emotional connotations (M. J. Baldwin, pers. comm.).

The archaeologist has tackled the opposite situation – the absence or paucity of burial offerings – in two different contexts; first, as a general diachronic phenomenon, and secondly, as evidence to distinguish the poor members of a group from the rich of the same society. On the diachronic cultural level there is little to add ethnographically to the work of Childe, who opposed the commonly reiterated view that the richness of tomb offerings must reflect the general cultural level of wealth or poverty, and who stressed instead that the number and richness of grave goods after the Early Bronze Age, for example, became less and poorer although the cultures were undoubtedly richer than before (Childe 1944: 85, 87–8, 92; 1945: 13–19). As society became richer, so also it became more reluctant to 'waste' its riches; in Ashbee's words, '. . . has the greed of the heirs overcome their religious scruples?' (1960: 173). Childe also opposed the view that there must have been a change in religious beliefs to account for the paucity of grave goods at a time when the culture was certainly rich, and he pointed out that religious ideas need not have changed prior to a change in custom, but that, over time, ideas of the afterworld might well become less individualistic and more spiritual to correspond to burial custom (1944: 88). Ethnographically there is no doubt that paucity of actual grave goods in the tomb does not correlate with particular types or systems of afterworld belief. Offerings may exist but never reach the tomb for two main reasons, either because they are destroyed before burial, or because they are 'symbolically' there, in other words they are thought to be there. Thus the LoDagaa of Ghana are a group of people who have an explicit and well-developed mythology and belief in an afterworld, which includes a journey to the afterworld and a river crossing. The dead are given only a nominal number of offerings in the tomb, for the majority are consumed during the funeral ceremonies (Goody 1959: 137; 1962: 73; and pers. comm.). Amongst the nearby Lober, no goods at all are actually placed in the tomb, for the deceased's weapons had been placed near to him before burial, and by this symbolic action he may take such weapons with him (Rattray 1932: 446).

Ethnographic evidence also suggests that the second archaeological approach, the identification of poor and rich members of the same society from funerary remains, may not always be as simple as it might at first appear. Archaeologists have at different times used very different and various criteria to try to identify and distinguish the rich from the poor within a community; these include paucity or wealth of *all* tomb-goods, paucity or wealth of certain specified *types* of tomb-goods, separate areas of cemeteries and standardization of burial custom, size of funerary constructions, and the indirect evidence of physical remains. This variety of approach to the problem has in itself not always been helpful; for example, most of the literature on Predynastic Egypt suggests that certain tombs were those of particularly rich individuals, and such rich tombs have, in the majority of cases, been so named by the archaeologist because they contained human figurines. However, when the total number of funerary offerings is considered, it is clear that Predynastic human figurines were placed in some tombs with many tomb goods, in many tombs with few tomb goods, and in very many tombs with no tomb goods at all (Ucko 1968: 181). Two important theoretical points have been made on the subject of the social significance of burial goods, but have been little considered in actual analyses. The first, by Professor Piggott, stresses that all tomb offerings are bound to have been socially selected, according to criteria that remain unknown today, and that where offerings were placed in the tomb, these will in no sense represent a random sample (1969: 558). It follows that the richness or poverty of offerings may in no real sense reflect either the actual material conditions of a society or the actual wealth of any individual, for these may both be subordinated to social and ritual sanctions. The second, by Professor Childe, stresses the impossibility of making relative assessments of wealth and poverty without having comparative material (1958a: 3). In other words, it is impossible to assess whether a particular megalithic burial, for example, is really significantly rich unless one also has available for comparison less rich forms of contemporary burial. As will be seen shortly, it is the absence of comparative 'commoner' material which can frequently be inferred from the physical remains. Even when such comparative potentially 'commoner' material is available, as, for example, in the Bronze Age barrow and flat-grave burials of Denmark, the evidence shows that both forms of burial included particularly rich individuals (Broholm 1944: 285).

It is already clear that, on the general cultural level, paucity of burial goods does not necessarily imply a low level of material wealth. High-ranking and wealthy priests of certain cults of the Yoruba of Nigeria are given funeral rites of great splendour, together with a profusion of valuables which are displayed at the funeral. These valuables, which are provided by the kinsmen of the dead person, do not however find their way into the grave, but are taken by the deceased's fellow priests of the same cult association. In other cases, images of wood, brass, clay or ivory may be placed in a Yoruba grave simply because the dead person's heirs are not members of the same cults as he was and do not know how to handle them, or because they were used for sorcery and are therefore too dangerous to keep. Apart from such images, Yoruba grave goods may include items of personal equipment but not valuables. Clearly, in the Yoruba case, individual wealth will not be reflected in either the number or quality of tomb goods (Peter Morton-Williams, pers. comm.). There are, however, several ethnographic echoes of the criteria already selected by the archaeologists. In Dahomey, for instance, the individual's wealth is reflected both in the number of offerings placed in the tomb and the depth of the actual tomb (Herskovits 1938: 359) – the latter trait, incidentally, being one not always considered by the archaeologist and one which at Tiszapolgar-Basatanya was found to be in no way correlated with richness or poverty of offerings (Bognár-Kutzian 1963: 386 ff.). Amongst various tribes of Nigeria we find that chiefs are always accorded a different burial from all others in the society (Meek 1925: 105, 112–13); furthermore, in certain of these tribes particular areas of the funerary hill are reserved for different ranks of chiefs and nobles (Meek 1931a), a practice which may be thought to parallel the selection of definite areas of various cemeteries for rich and poor. In Madagascar, in the recent past, ordinary tombs of the Merina population (excluding their slaves) were built outside village walls, nobles' tombs inside village walls, those of the highest nobles had mortuary houses built on top of the tombs, and kings were placed in model boats inside one of three especially huge tombs (Bloch 1967: 173; and pers. comm.). But these examples do throw some doubt on Childe's simple twofold distinction between chief and king, the former buried in a way similar to commoners but with more pomp and expense, and the king buried in a way significantly different from anyone else in the society (Childe 1958b: 13). Selection of separate sites for the poor is, of course, also known in Christian cemeteries, customarily the northern parts which were not within the sun's 'genial influence within whose rays no imp or fairy, demon of ill, or spectre pale can haunt the silent graves' (Gomme 1887: 205–6), a reservation for the poor sanctioned by Acts of Parliament from the nineteenth century onwards. In ancient Rome, too, the poor had at certain times a special cemetery reserved for them and at other times were exposed to birds of prey, or were thrown down wells or on to rubbish heaps (Nock 1932: 322). In at least one northern Nigerian tribe, it is the poor who receive no burial at all; Hindus who can afford it are cremated and then taken to the Ganges for disposal, whereas the poor are now given to burial. For the pets of Woodlands there is similar discrimination, the rich owners burying in one cemetery with headstones and other paraphernalia, and the poor saving some twenty guineas by burying in a separate cemetery, without permanent markers or upkeep. As is known from Dynastic Egypt, for example, burial areas for poor and rich are not always reserved in this way, for at Thebes poor graves are scattered anywhere between and around the larger and richer tombs (Abdul-Qader 1966: 3–4). For the archaeologist to decide what, if any, differentiation of poor from rich has been adopted at a particular site, and to get reasonable comparative material, it is therefore vital to uncover a large area of a burial ground.

This variety of ethnographic practice leads to the vexed archaeological problem of interpreting the significance of barrows, megaliths, and other large funerary structures in terms of the richness and poverty of the deceased. And this problem in itself leads back to the physical remains, as well as to the significance of absence of burial. Several archaeologists have stressed the size of certain funerary structures, and have maintained that the work of their construction was so great that they must have been made for rulers, chiefs or kings of some sort (e.g. Childe 1958b: 66, 128; Fox 1959: 122; Griffiths 1960: 329–30). But one of the confusing elements in such an interpretation is the number of both primary and secondary burials often associated with such constructions, for they are assumed to be too many to represent anything less than several members of a royal, or chiefly, lineage or family, and yet they are too few to represent more than a very small part of the total population. Many archaeologists have assumed that the burials of commoners are still to be uncovered. It was with this problem in mind that Childe paid especial attention to the distribution of the chambered cairns of Rousay Island in the Orkneys, a small area with relatively well preserved remains, and concluded that 'each tomb . . . belonged to a noble or leader and his or her family, the labour force . . . [being] supplied by his followers' (1942). It is certainly true that in several societies today the size of tombs often reflects status, and from ancient Egypt, interestingly enough, there seems evidence to show that it is the actual power rather than the theoretical ranking of different established titled groups which is reflected in the size of funerary structures (Abdul-Qader 1966: 13). But there are also ethnographic examples which suggest that the large funerary structure may have a very different meaning: the Merina of Madagascar build large tombs of stone, one or more to each village, which represent to them a visible expression of stability and 'belonging somewhere'. This tomb construction is extremely costly, so much so that any individual is forced to choose his own potential tomb fairly early in life, shortly after marriage, in order to contribute to regular maintenance of a tomb, improving its appearance, and refurbishing the concrete. A Merina does this by joining a particular tomb association which looks after such funerary affairs, but before this he has to choose which tomb he wishes to be buried in, for he has the right to opt for either of his parents' tombs, his grandparents' tomb, or even his wife's tomb (Bloch 1967; 1968; and pers. comm.). There is a twofold importance to this example; first, that the size and standardization of such tombs is in no way correlated with particular emphasis of religious belief, for in this society, although there is a general belief in ghosts, there is no regular ancestor worship of any kind, and second, that the expenses connected with funerary construction bear no relation to actual material wealth, for the Merina tombs are by far the best built and most solid structures in their society, and they contrast greatly with the normal poor, impermanent, shabby dwelling houses. They have stone and cement walls with the top packed by a huge stone slab covered with concrete. From a trap-door, an underground staircase leads to a massive stone, acting as the door to an underground burial chamber of about twenty feet square, in which the corpses are laid on shelves. Merina explanation for spending much more on a tomb than a house is that 'one stays much longer in the tomb'. A Merina tomb contains the bones, therefore, not of a royal lineage but of a cross-section of a local population, including males, females and children, some of whom are related by marriage and some by kinship. These bones are in most cases not deposited in the tomb at death but usually after a gap of some years. The more recent corpses are then placed in a more honoured position – the upper shelf on the north side – while the longest dead are moved into new places to make room (Bloch 1967; 1968; and pers. comm.). On the basis of Merina practice, it is perhaps necessary to re-think the assumption that very costly tombs must always imply a ruling family or dynasty. The differently-aged individuals of different sex in several chambered long barrows such as Lanhill and West Kennet, need not all have been either related or sacrificed to accompany a leader (Keiller *et al.* 1938; Piggott 1962). Around the entrances to Merina tombs are 'temporary' burials of children and certain categories of adults, including the very poor who await the reopening of the tomb (Maurice Bloch, pers. comm.). In the Merina case, any interpretation of these 'temporary' burials as satellite burials of wives, slaves or sacrifices would be quite out of place. It is worth noting, at this point, that a lapse of a considerable time, often several years, between funeral and second burial is a very common feature of ethnographic practice. In all cases where there is any data, this long interval is said to be to allow sufficient funds and arrangements to be organized. The lapse in time between death and funeral in many societies, including the Jews who have special experts to guard the body and look for any signs of life (Polsen *et al.* 1962: 229 ff.), may well be correlated with what has been called 'the morbid fear of premature burial' which still causes many people today to order in their wills that their own death must be proved either by surgical incision, the application of heat, or even decapitation before burial (Mant 1968: 18–19). The only sure sign of death until very recent times was the onset of putrefaction.

With the Merina example in mind, the importance of physical remains associated with archaeological material is obvious. In the end it is clear that the number, sex, and age of individuals found in a funerary structure will greatly influence interpretation as to who it was that was selected to be buried in a particular way. In a recent highly ingenious set of calculations, Professor Atkinson has deduced for chambered tombs of Neolithic England that only a selected part of the population received such burial, and he states that 'the bodies of some, and perhaps the majority, of the dead were habitually disposed of in a way which has left no archaeological trace' and that 'the population of the greater part of the British Iron Age does not appear in the funerary record', and he asks 'where, for that matter, are the burials of our Late Bronze Age?' (1968: 92). Atkinson maintains that there is no difficulty in supposing that all this funerary material has no record in the archaeological data (1968: 92). Professor Clarke has also pointed to the combination of frequent human bones on Iron Age A sites and rare burials, and has suggested an explanation in terms of either cannibalism or exposure of the corpses (1962: 169). Nevertheless, it is striking that it has apparently proved difficult for many archaeologists in the past, including Childe (1951: 61), to accept that any adult section of the population was simply left unburied. The archaeologist's apparent feeling that abandonment implies lack of concern with the dead is not supported by ethnographic practice. Abandonment is simply one of the many forms of disposal of the dead among, for example, the Australian aborigines, and is regarded by them in no different way from all their other methods (Howitt 1904). The Nandi of Kenya can serve as an example of concern with an afterworld nevertheless associated with the practice of abandonment; but the same practice and association of ideas is true of several other tribes (Huntingford 1953a). The Nandi believe that, at death, a person's shadow also dies, but his heart continues to live and eventually journeys to spirit land. This journey can take place only through the agency of hyaenas, and for this reason the corpse is laid out for the hyaenas to eat it. Should it remain uneaten for more than four days, appropriate sacrifices are undertaken to ensure that it will be eaten, for a heart which does not go to spirit-land is highly dangerous (Huntingford 1953b; and pers. comm.).

So far I have only briefly mentioned by implication what is perhaps the most important of all the lessons to be drawn from the ethnographic material – the point stressed most strongly by Dr Goody in his 1955 paper to the British Association (Goody 1959) – namely, that in the vast majority of cases known ethnographically, a culture or society is not characterized by one type of burial only, but that, on the contrary, one society will undertake several different forms of burial, and that these forms will often be correlated with the status of the deceased. Ethnographically, differences in place of burial may differentiate the rich from the poor, and there are several archaeological examples of status differentiation also by place of burial. Thus at Olen Island the lack of very small infants leads to the conclusion that they at least were buried, if they were buried at all, in a different place from the rest of the population, possibly within the settlement (Gurina 1956: 47). At Tiszapolgar-Basatanya, Kutzian records (1963: 392 ff.) that in Period I there was a striking disparity in numbers of males and females, an imbalance of 44 females to 100 adult males, and 50 female children to 100 male children, and concludes that there must have been a social reason, as opposed to a natural sexual disparity, for this imbalance. She postulates either sacrifice or infanticide, with subsequent disposal away from the main cemetery. The archaeological picture so far, therefore, is that certain groups were buried in areas away from the rest of the population. Ethnographically, the picture is rather different; burial customs in society after society reflect different categories of people, categories which are sometimes defined on purely social grounds and sometimes on physical characteristics which may, of course, also have an associated social definition. Furthermore, these differences are reflected not only in the use of different places for burial but also in such funerary features as the degree of elaboration of rites, the types of grave construction used, the different forms of orientation of the bodies, different degree of contraction or 'flexure' (Sprague 1968: 481) of the body, the use of cenotaph as opposed to tomb, or the absence of any form of burial.

In many societies babies and children are distinguished in burial custom from adults. In Rome, babies with no teeth received no burial at all (Nock 1932: 322); amongst the Shona, babies and older children were buried near flood water and away from the rest of the population (Ballock 1950: 175 ff.; Peter Fry, pers. comm.); amongst the Murngin, there is further differentiation by age: the newborn received no burial, the young child was buried in the camp, and the older child was buried at the camp edge (Warner 1964: 424–5); amongst several Ghanaian tribes, children were placed at crossroads, a place of dispersal to help scatter the potentially annoying habits of individuals who were, by their age, still only incipient human beings (Goody 1962: 148 ff.); amongst the Ashanti, any infant who dies under the age of eight days is buried in a pot in a latrine, for he was in fact just a ghost child and had no real intention of staying in this world (Rattray 1959: 59–60); amongst several tribes, disposal of babies and young children was characterized by an absence of, or at most perfunctory, burial ritual. There seems little reason not to associate these forms of child disposal with the high infant mortality rate amongst most primitive and prehistoric peoples. It is only necessary to remember the advice in the Middle Ages to a woman who had just produced her sixth child, 'Before they are old enough to bother you, you will have lost half of them, or perhaps all of them' (Yudkin, 1968: 46) to see, first, why so many societies only accept a child as a fully-fledged social human being after a certain age, and second, why British law is so exceptional when it states that any child, even the stillborn should it have 'any sign of life', is subject to the normal adult inhumation and cremation laws of the country (see Polsen *et al.* 1962: 38).

A cursory look at African ethnography shows that in many societies various other categories, apart from children, may be singled out for different burial from the rest of the population. These include lepers, those killed by lightning, those who die in childbirth, those who have died violently in battle, those who have drowned, those who are said to have died of smallpox or dropsy, witches, twins, priests, chiefs, the murderer, the suicide and the very old. It is worth spending just a minute or two with a few specific examples. The Nandi, the tribe who normally dispose of corpses by exposing them to hyaenas, *bury* their very old and those with no first teeth, for both categories can go straight to spirit-land without the hyaena agency, for they are near to the spirits and were in any case just coming or just going (G. W. B. Huntingford, pers. comm.). In many societies the lepers and those who are said to die from dropsy and smallpox receive no burial or are buried in the bush, a fact which makes one wonder whether the physical remains from prehistoric burial grounds really give those who collect incidence of disease in antiquity any sort of reasonable sample. In several societies cenotaphs, with or without replicas of the deceased, are erected for those who die by drowning, or those who died while far away (Herskovits 1938: 394 ff.), a feature tending to reinforce the courage of those who in reports such as the excavation of Crig-a-mennis (Christie 1960: 88–9) have insisted that their particular barrow was empty of any corpse, and have not assumed such factors as particularly bad conditions of preservation to explain the absence of skeletal finds (e.g. Coles *et al.* 1965).

I have already said that many other methods exist, beyond that of placing a body apart or not burying the body at all, to differentiate categories of people. It is quite clear that the more the archaeologist manages to refine his definitions and terminology for describing such factors as body contraction the more likely he is to recognize what may have been socially significant differences in funerary practice. The archaeologist often assumes that the significant features of orientation are the direction of the head and the way the corpse faces; ethnographically, there are many different ways of orientating a body apart from these two more obvious ways. 'Cases occur when the body is placed to lie in a position of definite relationship to its axis and not to the direction in which it is facing.' In another case the dead 'are interred on the south side of the village . . . [and] this position is definitely related to the south point of the compass and . . . the act of placing the body in a definite position relative to the village is really orientation' (Perry 1914: 281). It used to be claimed by ethnographers that the corpse was always orientated in the direction in which the spirit was to travel, a direction which correlated both with the position of the land of the dead and the home of the peoples' forefathers (Perry 1914: 282–6). There is no doubt that there are many examples, such as some groups of the Shona of Rhodesia (Ballock 1950: 176) where this *is* the aim of orientation, but this is by no means invariably true. In the case of the Merina, with their huge stone collective tombs, there are strict rules as to the standardization of both tomb structure and orientation, tomb entrances facing west and the heads of all corpses placed at the east end. This strictness has no relation to the ancestral area, which is in the north-east, which itself has no geographical relation to the hill of the dead (Maurice Bloch, pers. comm.). We must note still one more variation on the theme of the direction of the head; in some tribes, where the head is placed south and the feet north, the deceased is in fact orientated to look north at the land of the dead, for this is the position which he will be facing when he rises up (Perry 1914: 282). This practice is reminiscent of Christian practice where the heads should be placed to the west and feet to the east so that, according to folk lore at least, the rising body faces east at the time of the Last Judgment. And here it is important to note that in Christian practice also, orientation of this kind is used to differentiate certain categories of people, for a Roman Catholic priest and bishop is not only buried in a specially reserved part of the cemetery but is also laid with his feet to the west (Dearmer 1931: 42; and see Polson *et al.* 1962: 229) so that 'in death, as in life, he faces his flock'.

It may not be the direction of the head and feet which is in fact the important feature in orientation. At Egyptian Armant the excavators suggested that the rather erratic orientations of north/south and east/west were due either to the Predynastic Egyptians having tried to orientate to the sun and moon, using the river as a convenient guide 'thinking of it as always running north and getting muddled where it changed direction', or that the burials were 'unrelated to the sun and intended to be parallel to the river, the bodies lying in the direction of the flow of the water' (Mond and Myers 1937: 10). Such relation to a river, up which the spirit will travel to the land of the dead, is a practice known ethnographically from several tribes (e.g. Perry 1914: 282).

There is still one more variable to be considered – the direction which the corpse faces – for in some societies it is this which may be the most important criterion. As is well known from Muslim practice, the corpse may face the direction of a particularly important place, in this case Mecca. Most commonly, but not always, in West African practice at least, the body lies on the left or right side depending on its sex, just as was undoubtedly the case at such sites as Tiszapolgar-Basatanya (Bognár-Kutzian 1963: 354). Ethnographically, in Africa there is usually no religious significance associated with this variable. In Nigeria and Ghana, many different tribes place the male on his right facing east and the female on her left side facing west. The male faces east towards the rising sun so that he knows when to prepare for the hunt or for working on the farm; the female faces west so that she will know when it is time to prepare the food for her husband – 'the sun is setting, I shall not have time to grind; I shall not have time to get my husband's food' (e.g. Meek 1925: 123; Rattray 1932). Such standardization is not in any way general – thus in Dahomey there is no rule at all regarding on which side the corpse should lie (Herskovits 1938: 352).

I fondly imagine that Ashanti practices would contribute to an archaeologist's nightmare, for in Ashanti there is a general rule that the body should *not* face the village; however, there are some Ashanti who say that immediately after burial the body turns itself round to face the village. Some, but not all, Ashanti therefore bury the dead *facing* the village knowing that the body will turn itself round and will therefore eventually conform to the rule of facing the forest (Rattray 1927: 162).

So much variability has been seen to exist both between cultures and within a culture, that it becomes all-important to consider the question whether prehistorians are generally correct in laying so much stress on the usefulness of burial customs to identify different groups of people, and are right in assuming that burial practices are the kind of traits which can be treated as diagnostic of different cultures (and therefore of cultural contact and change). In a sense there is historic archaeological material to suggest that funerary monuments are not always good indicators of different religious beliefs and different ethnic groups. Finley has recently drawn attention to the fact that we know virtually nothing at all about the Jewish community which undoubtedly existed, in significant numbers, during the Empire in Sicily (Finley 1968: 168–9). The reason for this ignorance is that the Jews spoke Greek not Hebrew, they had no specially reserved burial place apart from the rest of the population, and their tombstones were inscribed like those of the non-Jews, except for the occasional seven-branched candelabrum and the very occasional inscription, 'never having broken the commandment'. If funerary procedures and structures do not always distinguish quite different populations, and if one and the same population uses several different modes of burial, is it really possible to agree with Professor Piggott's view that burial is the most conservative of rites (1938: 92–4)? Ethnographically, and there would seem little necessity to assume a different situation in prehistory, one of the features characterizing burial rites is their speed of change and their relative instability. By far the most important study of this problem was carried out by Professor Kroeber as long ago as 1927: 'The distribution of burial and cremation customs [in aboriginal California] failed to conform to the distribution of other culture traits in the area and was irregular in itself. The line separating the two mortuary practices on the map ran across rather than with topographic, climatic and floral boundaries. They departed considerably from the approximately definable culture areas and sub-areas. *And there was no agreement whatever with the distribution of other customs, connected with death* . . . [my italics]. It must be remembered that native California is a region of unusual cultural stability' (1927: 308). Turning to Africa and Australia, Kroeber notes the infinite variety of burial customs and points out that 'several methods co-exist in one tribe, and the same method has different applications in successive tribes. . . . These variations between adjacent peoples, and the numerous instances of co-existence of several practices within one population, constitute a powerful argument for instability' (1927: 313; and see Meek 1925: 104–5). Certainly it is common in Africa to find that different sections of the same tribe have different burial customs, and that some of these have been adopted and adapted from Muslim influence in a remarkably short time. Similarly, the Australian Murngin were quick to adopt a new way of marking graves, in addition to grave posts, by setting up ceremonial masks, a feature adapted from Malay ships (Warner 1964: 458). Adams may be correct when he makes the interesting point that, 'Other factors being equal, it is probable that continuity of tradition depends very largely upon frequency of activity . . . and most primitive communities are small and there may be an interval of months, or occasionally even years, between deaths' (Adams 1968: 203). This view recalls Firth's distinction between social organization and social structure. The social structure provides the precedent and limits the range of alternatives while the social organization is concerned with 'concrete activity' and acts of choice and decision in which the time element is an important variable (Firth 1951: 35–40). Furthermore, there are ethnographic indications that rather mundane matters may radically affect burial customs – a feature which again points to relative instability. Thus, the LoDagaa shorten the set length of time before a corpse should be buried if there is farming to be done, and they choose the position of the funeral stand according to the availability of shade trees (Goody 1962: 79). When the archaeological material is examined with variation and instability in mind, there are many echoes of the ethnographic record. At many provincial Roman sites, cremation and inhumation rites followed each other many times and with great rapidity (Nock 1932: 325–7); in several barrows, such as Arreton Down, inhumation and cremation rites were used within a maximum of two generations and possibly within the same generation (Alexander *et al.* 1960: 271); Adams has recently shown for the Sudan that burial customs reflect neither ethnic stability nor ethnic change (1968: 202–3); there is evidence from ancient Egypt that orientation of offering chambers may change without any alteration in religious belief, and that a feature as mundane as the slope of the ground may change the whole orientation of graves (Reisner 1932: 165, 188); there is also the evidence from many sites that at the same time as inhumation in a cemetery, bodies were also disposed of in the settlement (e.g. Gurina 1956: 47); there is evidence of the contemporaneity of barrow and flat grave burials (e.g. Glasbergen 1956: 141); and so on.

For some time now, Professors Piggott and Clark have made it clear that, in their view, a change from inhumation to cremation, or vice versa, cannot simply, or necessarily, be equated with the arrival of newcomers or a change in religious beliefs (e.g. Piggott 1965: 145; Clark 1960: 232). Ethnographically, there are cases from different parts of the world where cremation is used for one section of the population and inhumation for other sections of the same population (e.g. Macleod 1965: 129 ff.). The weight of evidence for ancient Rome is strongly on the side of the view that there were no changes in religious belief to explain the switch from cremation to inhumation, and furthermore these two practices were in no way distinguished either in funerary regulations or by funerary terminology (e.g. Momigliano 1963: 103; Nock 1932; de Visscher 1963: 3, 18, 32). And, after all, England is a country where burial rites have changed both rapidly and considerably in recent times but without an associated change in religious beliefs; in 1885 only 3 cremations took place, 13 years after the Regular Cremation Act there were 1,400, and in 1960 35% of the population was cremated (see Polson *et. al.* 1962: 149). Even more striking, perhaps, is the fact that within a space of three years a tenth of the Roman Catholic population of some British towns has adopted cremation rites. Despite this wealth of evidence, there are still many prehistorians who assume that cremation reflects some new form of spiritualism as compared to materialistic inhumation (e.g. Broholm 1944: 291), and many who assume that where both inhumations and cremations are found in a single site, these represent either the activities of two groups of different peoples or a recent intermingling and fusion of previously independent communities (e.g. Smith and Simpson 1966: 134).

Ethnographically, the funerary record also warns us against being too negative, for clearly at any given moment burial practices *may* in some way characterize particular societies. Ethnography suggests that the archaeologist may perhaps still have further to define and refine his methods of analysing funerary material. It is clear that certain regions and groups of tribes, for example the so-called southern Nilo-Hamites of East Africa, *are* characterized by particular funerary practices – in this case the exposure of the body to hyaenas, although there are minor variations regarding which section of the population, children and/or the very old, receive inhumation burial. Only the Sandawe stand out from the rest of these East African tribes, for they practise deep inhumation burial inside the cattle pen, but these are the very people who, on totally different grounds, have long been thought possibly not to belong to this Nilo-Hamitic linguistic group (Huntingford 1953a: 13, 139). Similarly the funerary customs of three related tribes on the north-west coast of America do serve to link them together, for they share a common cremation practice and yet all of them inhume their shamans in isolation away from the rest of the population. But it is equally important to note that one of these tribes buries the shaman lying on his side, while the other two place him in a sitting position with knees raised to the chin (Macleod 1925: 128–9). It may therefore be true to say for some groups of tribes that there is one particularly characteristic method of disposal of the dead but at the same time no exclusive burial type. In other areas, such as the Mississippi, it may be that some individual tribes, but not *groups* of tribes, are characterized by a particular method of disposal, although again not by an exclusive burial form (Bushnell 1920: 146). Why this should be so for some areas and tribes but not for others, such as Australia, the ethnographer cannot as yet say. In the majority of cases it would seem that the archaeologist may have, where possible, to switch his attention away from the one exclusive burial form (e.g. cremation versus inhumation) to the exceptional and possibly diagnostic cultural trait such as the crossed legs of inhumed skeletons (S. Sulimirski, pers. comm.), or to the varying *proportions* of different burial practices within a particular group or area, in order to construct any sort of diagnostic typology of funerary customs. In no case will this be easy to do, but in many ways it is an essential procedure, for simple classification alone of burial types, without their relative proportions, offers too many dangers. As I have said already, the range of possibilities of different forms of burial is in any case not very large, and it is especially small when considered from the point of view of what is visible in the archaeological record. Hence non-meaningful similarities between different societies are bound to be found wherever a number of societies practise several different disposal methods at the same time. In many cases, those where both exposure and burial existed, this will again focus attention on the physical remains discovered, for only on the basis of comparison between assumed demography and actual numbers of individuals discovered is it possible to assess the likelihood of a form of disposal having existed which has left no direct traces in the archaeological record. The interpretations of the significance of the physical remains will also have to be refined. For example, it is not generally realized that cremation, even at temperatures between 700-950° C as used in modern England, will leave bone remains of up to 3 in. long (Polson *et al.* 1962: 153), and that ethnographically, for instance on the north-west coast of America, it is the custom for widows to carry around large charred bones for several years while looking after their husband's buried ashes (Macleod 1925: 123). Assessment of the minimum number of individuals represented in cremation remains may have to rely just as much on the total weight of ashes as on large diagnostic bone remains. Similarly, it may not be sufficient simply to assume that incorrect articulation implies that various corpses have been lying around together for some time before burial, for the Ashanti rearranged the skeletons of kings after the flesh had been removed from the bones, and, so it is reported, often rearticulated the skeleton wrongly (Rattray 1959: 59–60).

Several tribes, such as the Nigerian Jukun, dig two different types of grave, one oval with lateral niche and the other rectangular with central niche, and both forms are claimed to be indigenous by the Jukun themselves (Meek 1931b: 218 ff.). It is, of course, possible that they *may* in fact have had different histories, but the important point is that at any given moment a culture may include more than one grave type without the people themselves making any distinction between them. It is possible that, rather than simply recognizing different grave types, the archaeologist may find study of more detailed features more rewarding. Thus the archaeological suggestion that a period of transition may be represented by graves which are large enough for inhumations but in fact contain only cremations (e.g. Proudfoot 1963: 405), may well have much to recommend it. This feature finds an interesting parallel with transitional Jewish practice, for in orthodox terms the instruction 'thou shalt in anywise bury him' rules out the practice of cremation. However, over the last years, more and more rabbis are accepting cremation provided that the ashes are buried in a coffin of the normal size and shape used for inhumation (see Polson *et al.* 1962: 264 ff.).

As I pointed out at the beginning of this paper, the useful ethnographic parallel is almost bound to add variability to archaeological interpretation and to an archaeological approach. Furthermore, although burials and funerary structures, to the archaeologist, are static items uncovered in excavation, they are, of course, the result of various social processes. Several archaeological studies of cemeteries pay close attention to the assumed growth patterns of these burial places, but they focus attention on the chronological implications without considering the possible form of social processes which must have been involved. It is significant that it is standardization which characterizes the archaeologists' concept of 'horizontal stratigraphy', a phenomenon for which there are considerable archaeological claims: '. . . it is the horizontal spread of a cemetery that gives the best clues. Once the original core can be located . . . and the general line of its expansion established . . . , it is possible to obtain a fair idea of the relative age of individual graves, even when provided with no closely datable grave goods' (Clark 1960: 130; and see Hodson 1968: 13). Obviously a cemetery must, over time, grow in some way or another but the rows of graves or the 'logical, if not necessarily regular pattern of growth' (Hodson 1968: 22) assumed in several recent archaeological studies, contrasts greatly with most ethnographic procedures. A particular area may be specified for burial for many different reasons, including hygiene, but in the many ethnographic cases where this occurs there is no more regulation than the occasional division of the area by class or clan. Ethnographic practice varies from the Shona, where it is the dying man himself who, where possible, specifies the exact place of his own tomb and is buried by his sons-in-law (Peter

Fry, pers. comm.), to the LoDagaa, where reciprocal groups act mutually for each other as grave diggers and it is they who choose the particular spot for burial (Goody 1962: 67–8; and pers. comm.). Although these practices may lead to groupings of kin or neighbours on some occasions, in most the graves are placed more or less haphazardly within the designated area and in no case do they result in more or less regular rows of chronologically differentiated graves (Bognár-Kutzian 1963: 229–31). Not even the rich and prosperous of Chinese society were laid in orderly manner in a cemetery, for here 'geomancy was the "cause" of dispersed burial' (Freedman 1968: 78). Amongst the Egbira of Nigeria, where Muslim and Christian influence has resulted in a graveyard under the control of a resident warden, the colonial policy of separating the graveyard into three different parts, for Muslims, Christians and traditionalists, and arranging the graves in neat rows, has failed – the grave diggers are much too concerned to choose sites where land is relatively free of rocks to conform to government wishes or the nearness of kin (John Picton, pers. comm.). It is only with modern Christianity, where we find an incumbent in whom is vested the freehold of a churchyard, who in practice controls what monuments are erected in the churchyard and who can specify where burials are placed, that there is the sort of organization apparently assumed for prehistory in some studies of horizontal stratigraphy. But even in the growth of Christian cemeteries, chronology and order have often been sacrified to personal idiosyncrasy, conflicting pressures, and human error. In the newly-acquired extension to a churchyard in Buckinghamshire, for example, the plan was to have several regular rows of graves. The first grave in this new extension was placed centrally in the area furthest from the old graves; the relatives of the deceased managed to prevail over established custom in having the inscribed headstone placed at the east end of the grave so that the new grave could be seen clearly from the longer-established part of the graveyard. Subsequent burials, with headstones at the west end of the graves, were placed in a row on *either side* of this first burial. One grave plot in the row remains empty, for the ground was then so uneven that the part-time gravedigger concerned assumed that a burial had taken place there on a previous occasion; another grave plot contains only the ashes of a male cremation and is marked only with a small horizontal plaque, and this plot will be used later for the inhumation of the deceased's wife. If this is the sort of irregularity that occurs under even such a strict burial regime, it is vital to ask what sort of social situation must have existed in prehistory which allows the archaeologist to question his own methods of relative dating when he finds a grave which he considers to be out of place (e.g. Hodson 1968: 22). In Allerton cemetery, at least, *grave-goods* would presumably be better guides to the dates of burials than would the horizontal stratigraphy of the graves – a recent advertisement in the *Liverpool Daily Post* read: 'Double-grave for sale; purchased many years ago by well-known Liverpool family in the best part of Allerton cemetery but now surplus to requirements.'

14.iv.69

University College London

References

Abdul-Qader, M. Mohammed. 1966. *The Development of the Funerary Beliefs and Practices displayed in the private tombs of the New Kingdom of Thebes.* Cairo.

Adams, W. Y. 1968. Invasion, Diffusion, Evolution? *Antiquity.* 42:194–215.

Alexander, J. *et al.* 1960. Report on the Investigation of a round barrow on Arreton Down, Isle of Wight. *Proc. Prehist. Soc.* 26:263–302.

Ashbee, P. 1960. *The Bronze Age Round Barrow in Britain.* London.

Atkinson, R. J. C. 1968. Old mortality: some aspects of burial and population in neolithic England. In *Studies in Ancient Europe*, eds J. M. Coles and D. D. A. Simpson. Leicester.

Ballock, C. 1950. *The Mashona and Metabele.* Cape Town.

Bloch, M. E. F. 1967. The significance of tombs and ancestral villages of rural Merina social organisation. Ph.D. thesis.

Bloch, M. E. F. 1968. Tombs and conservatism among the Merina of Madagascar. *Man JRAI.* NS 3 (1):94–104.

Bognár-Kutzian, I. 1963. *The Copper Age Cemetery of Tiszapolgár-Basatanya.* Budapest.

Broholm, H. C. 1944. *Danmarks Bronzealder.* Copenhagen.

Bushnell, D. I. 1920. Native cemeteries and forms of burial east of the Mississippi. *Bureau of Amer. Ethnology.* 71.

Campbell, J. M. 1968. Territoriality among ancient hunters: interpretations from ethnography and nature. In *Anthropological Archaeology in the Americas.* Washington.

Childe, V. G. 1942. The chambered cairns of Rousay. *Antiquaries Journal.* 22:138–42.

Childe, V. G. 1944. *Progress and Archaeology.* London.

Childe, V. G. 1945. Directional changes in funerary practices during 50,000 years. *Man.* 4:13–19.

Childe, V. G. 1951 (revised 1963). *Social Evolution.* London.

Childe, V. G. 1958a. Valediction. *Bull. Inst. of Archaeol.* 1:1 ff.

Childe, V. G. 1958b. *The Prehistory of European Society.* London.

Christie, P. M. 1960. Crig-a-mennis: a Bronze Age barrow at Liskey, Perranzahuloe, Cornwall. *Proc. Prehist. Soc.* 26:76–97.

Clark, G. 1960. *Archaeology and Society.* London.

Clark, G. 1962. *Prehistoric England.* London.

Clark, G. and Piggott, S. 1965. *Prehistoric Societies.* London.

Coles, J. M. *et al.* 1965. The excavation of a neolithic round barrow at Pinacree, Perthshire, Scotland. *Proc. Prehist. Soc.* 31:34–57.

Dearmer, P. 1931 (12th edn). *The Parson's Handbook.* London.

Evans-Pritchard, E. E. 1951. *The Nuer.* London.

Evans-Pritchard, E. E. 1956. *Nuer Religion*. London.

Finley, M. I. 1968. *Ancient Sicily to the Arab Conquest*. London.

Firth, R. 1951. *Elements of Social Organisation*. London.

Fox, C. 1959. *Life and Death in the Bronze Age*. London.

Freedman, M. 1968. *Lineage Organisation in South-eastern China*. London.

Glasbergen, W. 1956. Barrow excavations in the eight beatitudes, I. *Palaeohistoria*. 2–3.

Gluckman, M. 1937. Mortuary customs among the South-eastern Bantu. *Bantu Studies*. 11:117–36.

Gomme, G. L. (ed.) 1887. Popular superstitions and traditions. *The Gentleman's Magazine Library*.

Goody, J. 1959. Death and social control among the LoDagaa. *Man*. 59:134–8.

Goody, J. 1962. *Death, Property and the Ancestors*. London.

Griffiths, W. E. 1960. The excavation of stone circles near Penmaenmawr, North Wales. *Proc. Prehist. Soc.* 26:303–39.

Gurina, N. N. 1956. Olen island cemetery. *Materiali Isledovania Po Archaeologii CCCP*. 47.

Hawkes, C. 1954. Archaeological theory and method; some suggestions from the Old World. *Amer. Anthropol.* 56 (2(1)):155–68.

Herskovits, M. J. 1938. *Dahomey*. I. New York.

Hodson, F. R. 1968. The La Tène Cemetery at Munsingen-Rain. *Acta Bernensia*. 5.

Howitt, A. W. 1904. *The Native Tribes of South-Eastern Australia*. London.

Huntingford, G. W. B. 1953a. *The Southern Nilo-Hamites*. London.

Huntingford, G. W. B. 1953b. *The Nandi of Kenya*. London.

Keiller, A. *et al.* 1938. Excavation of an untouched chamber in the Lanhill long barrow. *Proc. Prehist. Soc.* 4:122–50.

Kroeber, A. L. 1927. Disposal of the dead. *Amer. Anthropol.* 29:308–15.

Macleod, W. C. 1925. Certain mortuary aspects of North-west Coast culture. *Amer. Anthropol.* 27:122–48.

Mant, A. K. 1968. The medical definition of death. In *Man's Concern with Death*. London.

Meek, C. K. 1925. *The Northern Tribes of Nigeria*. London.

Meek, C. K. 1931a. *Tribal Studies in Northern Nigeria*. London.

Meek, C. K. 1931b. *A Sudanese Kingdom*. London.

Middleton, J. 1960. *Lugbara Religion*. Oxford.

Momigliano, A. 1963. An interim report on the origins of Rome. *Roman Studies*. 95–121.

Mond, R. and Myers, O. H. 1937. *Cemeteries of Armant*. I. London.

Nadel, S. F. 1954. *Nupe Religion*. London.

Nock, A. D. 1932. Cremation and burial in the Roman Empire. *Harvard Theological Review.* 25 (4):321–59.

Perry, W. J. 1914. The orientation of the dead in Indonesia. *J. Roy. Anthropol. Inst.* 44:281–93.

Piggott, S. 1938. The Early Bronze Age in Wessex. *Proc. Prehist. Soc.* 4:52–106.

Piggott, S. 1962. *The West Kennet Long Barrow.* London.

Piggott, S. 1965. *Ancient Europe.* Edinburgh.

Piggott, S. 1969. Conclusion. In *The Domestication and Exploitation of Plants and Animals,* eds P. J. Ucko and G. Dimbleby. London.

Polson, C. J. *et al.* 1962 (2nd edn). *The Disposal of the Dead.* London.

Proudfoot, E. V. W. 1963. Excavation of a Bell Barrow in the parish of Edmondstam, Dorset, England. *Proc. Prehist. Soc.* 29:395–425.

Radcliffe-Brown, A. R. 1951. The comparative method in social anthropology. *J. Roy. Anthropol. Inst.* 51:15–22.

Rattray, R. S. 1932. *The Tribes of the Ashanti Hinterland.* I. Oxford.

Rattray, R. S. 1959 (3rd edn). *Religion and Art in Ashanti.* Oxford.

Reisner, G. A. 1932. *A Provincial Cemetery of the Pyramid Age. Nag-ed-Der,* III. Oxford.

Smith, I. F. and Simpson, D. D. A. 1966. Excavation of a round barrow on Overton Hill, North Wiltshire. *Proc. Prehist. Soc.* 32:122–55.

Sprague, R. 1968. A suggested terminology and classification for burial description. *Amer. Antiq.* 33(4):479–85.

Ucko, P. J. 1968. *Anthropomorphic Figurines of Predynastic Egypt and Neolithic Crete.* London.

Ucko, P. J. In press. Some aspects of the interpretation of human representations in early post-Palaeolithic prehistoric art. *Archivi di Centro di Studi Preistorici, Val Camonica.*

Ucko, P. J. and Rosenfeld, A. 1967. *Palaeolithic Cave Art.* London.

Visscher, F. de. 1963. *Le Droit des Tombeaux Romains.* Milan.

Warner, W. L. 1964 (revised edn). *A Black Civilization.* New York.

Yudkin, S. 1968. Death and the young. In *Man's Concern with Death.* London.

Contributors

Homer L. Thomas is Professor of Archaeology at the University of Missouri; **Robert W. Ehrich** teaches Anthropology at Brooklyn College of The City University of New York.

Elizabeth K. Ralph is Associate Director of the Applied Science Center for Archaeology at the University Museum, University of Pennsylvania; **Mark C. Han** is a Research Associate at the Center.

John Evans has recently held a Research Assistantship at the Institute of Archaeology, London University, where he worked on the application of land-snail studies to the archaeology of sites in the British Isles.

Wilfred Shawcross is Senior Lecturer in Prehistory in the Department of Anthropology, Auckland University, New Zealand. He was appointed there in 1961 after graduating in archaeology at Cambridge, where he specialized in the Palaeolithic and Mesolithic fields.

Michael Dolley, whose work has been chiefly in numismatics, is Reader in Modern History at the Queen's University of Belfast.

Martin Biddle is Director of the Winchester Research Unit. He is married to **Birthe Kjølbye-Biddle**, who is Stud. mag. art. of the University of Aarhus and is supervising the excavations of the Anglo-Saxon cathedral at Winchester.

Philip Barker is Lecturer in Archaeology in the Department of Extra-Mural Studies, University of Birmingham.

M. S. Mate teaches at Deccan College, Poona, where he is Reader in Ancient Indian History, Art and Architecture.

Andrew Fleming, whose particular field of interest is the British Early Bronze Age, teaches prehistory in the Department of Ancient History, University of Sheffield.

Peter J. Ucko is Lecturer in Anthropology at University College, London. He is the author of works on prehistoric art, and is currently preparing a book on attitudes to death and disease.

Notes to Contributors

Manuscripts should not normally exceed 5,000 words in length. They should be typed on good quality quarto paper (i.e. approx. 10 in. × 8 in., or 26 cm. × 21 cm.), using double spacing throughout. Two copies of the manuscript should be submitted, the author retaining another. Manuscripts and other correspondence should be addressed to the Executive Editor – Dr Colin Platt, Faculty of Arts, The University, Southampton, England.

Referencing should follow the modern scientific convention. Footnotes, wherever possible, should be avoided. Bibliographical references, to be included in the text, should list the author's last name, date of publication, and number of page, e.g. (Clark 1952: 211). Where an author's name has been cited already in the text, reference need only be made to the date of publication and page, e.g. (1952: 211). Extended references should be listed alphabetically at the end of the paper, e.g.

Bouard, M. de. 1965. La mesure de la résistivité électrique des sols en archéologie. *Annales de Normandie.* 15:461–77.

Clark, J. G. D. 1952. *Prehistoric Europe: the economic basis.* London.

Wace, A. J. B. 1958. Aegean Prehistory: a Review. *Antiquity.* 32:30–4.

Wheeler, R. E. M. 1943. *Maiden Castle.* Oxford.

Text figures, site plans and distribution maps should be drawn on strong paper, white card, or good quality tracing film. They should measure approximately twice the intended final size (i.e. a published full-page illustration may not exceed 8 in. × $5\frac{5}{16}$ in., or 20.5 cm. × 15.5 cm.) Plates should be printed on glossy paper and should be mounted on thin card. Figures, maps and plates should be titled and numbered.

Each contribution should be accompanied by a brief abstract (100–150 words) summarizing its contents. Abstracts of the papers printed are at the end of each issue, together with a short note on individual contributors, which should also be supplied.

It is important that authors should submit accurate, well-prepared copy, ready for the printer. Re-drawing of maps or figures cannot be undertaken by the editors, who may return sub-standard work to contributors for re-presentation in an improved form. Galley proofs of all articles will be sent to authors, who are reminded that these are intended for checking, not re-writing. Failure to return proofs by the required date may lead to the executive editor sending his own corrected proofs to the printer without further reference to the author.

Twenty free offprints will be supplied to authors on publication of a paper. Additional offprints may be purchased at cost price, and should be ordered not later than on the return of corrected proofs.

Abstracts

Thomas, H. L. and Ehrich, R. W.

Some problems in chronology

This paper underlines the necessity for employing a broad and integrated approach to the construction of chronologies. Simple local archaeological sequences are not sufficient by themselves, nor can they be completely satisfactory even when combined with relative chronologies mechanically arrived at by distribution studies of inadequate data. General interregional co-ordination in historical terms is essential to the reconstruction of culture history. Batteries of techniques derived from different disciplines must complement and control each other if an adequate synthesis is to be achieved. Some cautions are raised in regard to the use of radiocarbon determination, now the direct and indirect foundation of most chronometric dating.

Ralph, E. K. and Han, M. C.

Potential of thermoluminescence in supplementing radiocarbon dating

Thermoluminescence in pottery is due to the fact that radiations from the traces of radioactive elements in pottery bombard the other constituents of the clays and raise electrons to metastable levels. The pottery may be thought of as a semi-conductor. Electrons do not have complete freedom of movement as they do in conductors, but with an extra boost such as a push from an alpha particle, they can move into excited or metastable levels. As the name implies, the electrons are not stable in these new positions, so that when the pottery is heated, such as in firing, each electron falls back to a stable position and, as it does so, it emits a photon of light. On being re-heated at a later time (in the laboratory) the amount of thermoluminescence observed is, therefore, representative of the accumulated collection of metastable electrons as a result of radiation damage and hence of the time elapsed since the original firing of the pottery. The amount of light detected (or number of protons emitted) depends upon both the time which has elapsed since the original firing of the pottery (presumably above 400° C) and the rate of bombardment from traces of radioactivity. The work done in thermoluminescence at the Pennsylvania University Museum, Philadelphia, involving pottery of known age, is discussed.

Evans, J. G.

Land and freshwater Mollusca in archaeology: chronological aspects

The theoretical background to the use of land and freshwater Mollusca in establishing a chronological framework for archaeological deposits is discussed. Certain deficiencies in earlier studies

are reviewed. Details of the stratigraphy of a site and of the modern ecological tolerances of Mollusca are two of the most important factors for any proper understanding of the significance of Mollusca for chronological work. Because of the way in which shells are incorporated into deposits, local environmental influences are difficult to separate from those of climatic origin. With careful work, however, this can be done, as is shown by the pattern of faunal change in southern England since the Last Glaciation. Work in four other areas, Central Europe, North America, the Near East and Africa, is briefly reviewed.

Shawcross, F. W.

Archaeology with a short, isolated time-scale: New Zealand

In many respects New Zealand presents an excellent situation for the study of cultural processes in prehistory. However, difficulties are experienced over measuring the age of archaeological evidence, due to absence of precise methods of dating. It must be recognized that available methods are incapable of indicating exact events, but should be treated as variable quantities. This is illustrated for the estimation of the age of settlement from traditional genealogies. When radiocarbon is examined it is found that an additional factor of variation must be taken into account: the divergence of radiocarbon from true ages, observed by a number of laboratories in measurements of tree rings. The New Zealand run appears to diverge from those made in the northern hemisphere. When allowance for the degree of variation between the two methods is made, and after examination of the questions of population and site increase, it is seen that the radiocarbon ages for the beginning of a number of early settlements falls within the range of the most acceptable traditions. This suggests a hypothesis for New Zealand prehistory: that the so-called 'Moa-Hunter' sites, previously associated with 'pre-fleet' (and therefore questionable) traditions, may in fact be the evidence for the first major settlement of the country. At the same time, the mathematical generalizations involved in such calculations make it impossible to treat these separate lines of evidence as conclusively referring to the same event.

Dolley, R. H. M.

Medieval British and Irish coins as dating evidence for the archaeologist

The value of coins as dating evidence to the medieval archaeologist in Great Britain and Ireland has increased with recent discoveries. In assessing the value, for this purpose, of individual coin issues, the author discusses the monetary policies of successive Anglo-Saxon and post-Conquest kings. England, Scotland and Ireland are considered in turn, with comments on current research in each. The need for close liaison between the archaeologist and the numismatist is stressed.

Biddle, M. and Kjølbye-Biddle, B.

Metres, areas and robbing

The use of the metric system on English sites has brought with it advantages in the control and planning of open-area excavations, the applications of which are discussed against the background of experience in Winchester. The same background provides the basis for a discussion of the excavation and interpretation of robbed structures.

Barker, P.

Some aspects of the excavation of timber buildings

At two excavations, Hen Domen (medieval) and Wroxeter (Roman), vestigial remains of final-period timber structures have been identified in the upper layers of the sites. The author

discusses the variety of evidence encountered, the techniques employed to recover the plans of the buildings, and the possible development of such techniques in the future.

Mate, M. S.

Building in ancient India

Archaeological excavations during the last decade have revealed various facets of the art of building as practised in ancient and Early Historic India. Several varieties of structures, hitherto unknown in such contexts, such as huge ramparts and embankments, auditoria and beautifully-designed tanks, have come to light. Very little of town-planning, however, is visible. Investigations in Harappan remains add additional emphasis to the concept of Harappan urban architecture as a rigorously standardized mode. The period that intervenes between the two civilizations is shown to have been characterized by a slow and tedious progress from bamboo-and-mud to mud-brick structures.

Fleming, A.

The myth of the mother-goddess

The megalithic tombs of western Europe have been supposed traditionally to have been connected with the worship of an east Mediterranean mother-goddess, largely on the basis of parietal art, grave goods and some possibly contemporary statue-menhirs. As a result, exaggerated claims have been made for the anthropomorphic and specifically female character of the art, its religious meaning and possible international comparisons. But much megalithic art should be classified on a purely local basis. Positive evidence for a mother-goddess is confined to France, and can be dated at present no earlier than the late third millennium B.C. All French art should be considered separately from the art of Ireland and western Iberia, which is similar enough to allow the identification of an Atlantic art province, possibly connected with sun-worship and also relatively late. The beliefs of the earliest megalith builders remain a subject for future work.

Ucko, P. J.

Ethnography and archaeological interpretation of funerary remains

Archaeological funerary remains are discussed in the light of ethnographic funerary practices. It is argued that only with the widest possible approach to the archaeological material is it possible to appreciate the full significance of excavated remains. Not all burials reflect a deep concern with an afterworld or ancestor cult, and not all burial offerings need have been placed in the grave for the use of the deceased. Different burial practices may be adopted for particular categories of the population within a culture, and it is argued that the relative proportions of different burial forms may be more diagnostic of a culture than one type of funerary practice. Examples are discussed where the number of funerary offerings may not reflect the wealth of the deceased, and where the large and expensive tomb may not be the prerogative of a ruling class, or noble lineage. Variety and variability is a feature of the ethnographic funerary record which contrasts strangely with some of the archaeological assumptions about burial practices.

World Archaeology

Volume 1 No 3
February 1970

This issue: Analysis

Cover

Elephant femur and rib fragment
surrounded and underlain by artefacts

Three issues a year, February, June and October
Single copies £1 5s
Annual subscription £3 3s ($8.00) post free

Orders to the publishers:
Routledge & Kegan Paul Ltd
Reading Road, Henley-on-Thames, Oxon

World Archaeology

Volume 1 No 3 February 1970

Published thrice yearly by the proprietors
Routledge & Kegan Paul Ltd
68–74 Carter Lane, London EC4

Printed in Great Britain by
The Camelot Press Ltd, London and Southampton

Issues of *World Archaeology* now in preparation cover the themes 'Early Man' (June 1970), 'Urban Archaeology' (October 1970), and 'Subsistence' (February 1971). Further issues are planned for the future on the themes 'Technological Innovation', 'Social Structures', 'Art and Design', and 'Cultural Survival'.

The editors welcome suggestions for contributions to any of the projected issues, and would be glad at all times to consider important new work for immediate publication, whether or not it coincides with an announced theme.

Contents

page

289 Systems theory, computer simulations and archaeology
James Doran

299 Cluster analysis and archaeology: some new developments and applications
F. R. Hodson

321 Discrimination of British Lower and Middle Palaeolithic handaxe groups using canonical variates
J. M. Graham, with a note by Derek Roe

343 The production of pottery from a Romano-British kiln site: a statistical investigation
C. R. Orton

359 Socio-political implications of lowland Maya burials: methodology and tentative hypotheses
William L. Rathje

375 The scientific analysis of ancient ceramics: a review
D. P. S. Peacock

390 An elephant butchery site at Mwanganda's Village, Karonga, Malawi, and its relevance for Palaeolithic archaeology
J. Desmond Clark and C. Vance Haynes Jr

Systems theory, computer simulations and archaeology

James Doran

Introduction

Until comparatively recently, say fifteen years ago, interpretive archaeology was a discipline which made virtually no use of mathematical or scientific techniques and concepts. Few suggested that it should. It was hard to see how the complex and ill-structured problems facing archaeologists could be tackled other than by the direct application of their own experience and intelligence.

The outlook has changed somewhat. Scientific techniques such as radiocarbon dating, pollen analysis, and geomagnetic surveying have provided new and valuable sources of information for the archaeologist. Mathematical techniques such as seriation analysis and factor analysis have been used to try to make objective, and more powerful, reasoning previously carried out on a purely intuitive basis. Most of these mathematical techniques are still experimental, and have yet to be established as standard archaeological tools.

The electronic computer has been deeply involved in these developments. Archaeologists collect large quantities of data, and if numerical techniques are to be used at all then a computer is almost certain to be needed to carry through the calculations. Of course, the rapid increase over the last decade in the computing facilities generally available partially explains why these techniques are receiving ever more attention.

Similar trends are apparent in allied subjects such as anthropology and social geography. In particular, location analysis has influenced archaeologists, with its emphasis on the study of all aspects of a population and its environment, and on the use of quantitative methods and models (Haggett 1963).

In the last few years some archaeologists have become aware of another subject which, it seems, they should study. This is systems theory, sometimes equated with cybernetics. Not only does systems theory itself involve abstract ideas a little difficult to grasp for those with a non-scientific background, but it brings in its train other subjects such as information theory and games theory which are highly mathematical in content, and yet which are nevertheless claimed to be of archaeological significance. An archaeologist who is aware of these developments finds himself, apparently, faced with the choice either of losing touch with some of the most interesting and important developments in his subject, or of embarking upon a course of study for which nothing in his training has prepared him.

This paper is an attempt to help such an archaeologist understand what systems theory is, and what it has to offer. It is written from the standpoint of a computer scientist with a good working knowledge of the archaeologist and his problems.

Archaeological systems theory

The term 'general system theory' seems to have been coined by von Bertalanffy (1950). He proposed this 'new basic scientific discipline' and described it as a 'new scientific doctrine of "wholeness" '. By a system he meant any large assemblage of intercommunicating elements which can reasonably be regarded as a unit in itself: components forming a machine, neurones forming the brain, cells forming a living organism, employees forming an organization. He stressed the desirability of finding the general laws which applied directly to systems, rather than attempting to understand their complex and sometimes mysterious behaviour by studying the properties of their constituent elements.

Today systems theory still seems to have much the same very general objectives. These objectives are closely related to those of cybernetics, itself, as we shall see, a rather ill-defined subject. Cybernetics gathered momentum as a subject rather earlier than von Bertalanffy's paper, and is usually associated with Norbert Wiener. In the first part of my discussion, involving descriptions of the thinking of Flannery and Clarke, I shall follow their lead and use the term 'systems theory' although many of the concepts involved were introduced by the cyberneticists.

Important concepts of systems theory are those of *self-regulation* (or *homeostasis*), *positive* and *negative feedback*, *oscillation* and *dynamic equilibrium.* Perhaps the easiest way to convey the meaning of these terms is by an example. Consider a class of schoolchildren left by their teacher to work by themselves, and suppose that we are primarily interested in the overall noise level which the class generates. Initially the noise level will be low but it will soon start to climb as each child, hearing more noise around him, makes more noise himself. This tendency of the noise to amplify itself is an example of *positive feedback.* At length, however, we may assume that the noise level will reach such a pitch that the more responsible, or timid, members of the class will attempt to quieten their fellows. Now the greater the noise, the greater the dampening effect, and we have an example of *negative feedback.* The overall effect is that the class will settle to some particular noise level by a process of *self-regulation.* Of course, there will be a certain amount of *oscillation* in the noise level, both in the initial adjustment period, and even afterwards. When the teacher returns he will find that the class has found its way to a state of *dynamic equilibrium* in that although, of course, the individual components of the system (the children in the class) are far from motionless, the system taken as a whole is unchanging. In fact, the equilibrium is also *stable,* in that any outside intervention which changes the noise level, for example a brief visit from another teacher, will, within limits, have only a temporary effect.

This example gives, of course, only a general impression of the meaning of these forms. It is possible to make them considerably more precise and to construct equivalent mathematical models. These latter, however, will be capable of productive use only in a few of the situations to which the original informal definitions apply.

A recent and illustrative example of the application of these concepts in archaeology is a paper by Flannery (1968) discussing the food-collectors and early food-producers of Mesoamerica between about 8000 B.C. and 200 B.C. He adopts an ecological approach and is concerned to identify the plant and animal species used as food during the period, paying special attention to seasonal and locational variations and to the decisions which the population had to make if they were to exploit their environment efficiently.

Flannery considers each food source, for example cactus fruit, and white-tailed deer, as a subsystem of the total ecosystem and discusses each separately, stressing in each case the regulatory factors which prevent exhaustion of the food source. He also proposes as stabilizing mechanisms, 'seasonality', the availability of certain fruits and animals only at certain seasons, and 'scheduling' the organization by the population of its hunting and collecting activities at times when there is a choice of food sources. Finally Flannery discusses the 'positive feedback network . . . which eventually made maize cultivation the most profitable single subsistence activity in Mesoamerica' (1968:80), but does not exhibit this network very clearly.

Although this brief summary is far from doing justice to Flannery's discussion, it does, I hope, suggest the rather limited role which specifically systems theoretic ideas play in the discussion. Flannery himself stresses the *negative* virtues of his approach: that it avoids over-simple thinking of the type which attributes cultural evolution 'to "discoveries", "inventions", "experiments", or "genius" ' (1968:85). Certainly this is a point to be given considerable weight, but even so one wonders if system theory is not, in this case, simply a neutral vehicle for Flannery's own clear thinking.

Clarke's general systems model for archaeological processes

Clarke (1968), in a recent major book, has discussed a variety of new concepts and techniques of potential value to archaeologists. He tries to clarify both the way in which archaeologists should study their subject, and the nature of the entities which they must define and relate whilst doing so. In particular, he puts forward a general model for archaeological processes, which is intended to serve as a descriptive framework for any of a variety of archaeological entities, such as 'cultures' and 'artefact-types' as they develop through time. This model is based on concepts drawn from systems theory and related subjects, and goes much further than the simple ideas used by Flannery in the paper discussed in the previous section.

Clarke's presentation of his model is long and sometimes involved. Given the complexity of the topics he is dealing with, this is not surprising. Here I shall first list the model's main features, and then explain and discuss each. Although my discussion is bound to be incomplete, it will suffice for our purpose, which is to weigh up the value of such ideas for archaeologists, and it may also serve as a useful introduction to Clarke's own discussion and the sources which lie behind it.

The main features of Clarke's model are as follows:

(1) There is a *system* (e.g. a 'culture') which passes with time through a succession of distinct *states*. The sequence of states exhibited, called the *trajectory*, depends upon the history of the system and on the influence of the *environment* (which may itself be physical or cultural) with which it interacts.

(2) There are *regulatory mechanisms*, including *feedback*, which strive to keep the system in one of a set of possible *equilibrium states*.

(3) The system is typically very *complex*, and only *partially observable*.

(4) If we are dealing with a cultural system, then at least some of the regulatory mechanisms involved can usefully be described in terms of *information theory* concepts such as *variety*, *equivocation* and *redundancy*.

Let us now look at each of these aspects of the model in turn. The concept of a system following a trajectory is quite well exemplified by reference to the work of Murdock, quoted by Clarke (1968:107–9). Murdock studied the structure of several hundred primitive societies, and defined forty-seven types of society. He estimated, for each of these types, which of the others might have been its immediate evolutionary ancestor. There were, on average, four or five possibilities some much more likely than others.

Clarke suggests that this enables us to reconstruct possible system trajectories, meaning the sequence of types which might follow one another by a process of evolution. Thus it appears that a Neo-Yuman type of society might well evolve into a Matri-Hawaiian type, then into a Patri-Eskimo type, then into a Normal-Eskimo type and so on. However, a Neo-Yuman society might also become Bi-Yuman or one of several other alternatives. As Clarke points out, which way the cat will jump in practice will be influenced both by the previous trajectory of the system, and by the environment in which the system exists.

Mathematicians have studied the abstract properties of processes such as this under the general heading of Markov processes, and Clarke suggests that the corresponding notation and theory should be incorporated into his model. Unfortunately the abstract theory does not exactly match the archaeological case (Clarke recognizes this by defining 'Semi-Markov processes'), and in any case it is hard to see how the type of mathematical theorem proved in the abstract theory could ever have real archaeological significance.

The second of the important features of the model is the existence of regulatory mechanisms. Since these involve broadly the same concepts as these explained at the beginning of the previous section (feedback, dynamic equilibrium etc.) no further explanation is necessary, except to say that, in the model, the effects of these regulating mechanisms or subsystems is to keep important variables of the system within acceptable limits in spite of major fluctuations in the environment. For example, the regulatory mechanisms might operate to keep food supplies adequate in spite of a very cold winter.

The third characteristic of the model is that the system is supposed complex and impossible to observe in its entirety. Obviously, this problem is as fundamental as the air we breathe. Clarke attempts to consider it in terms of the Black Box problems discussed by Ashby (1956: chapter 6). A Black Box problem is, loosely, the task of finding the general relation between what goes into some mechanism or system, and what comes out of it, from external observation alone. For simple problems of this type one can present reasonable heuristic strategies for their solution. However, a Black Box of the complexity of the kind of archaeological system which Clarke is considering is so far beyond these simple strategies that they apply to it, at best, only as guide lines for clear thinking on the part of the investigator.

Finally, Clarke works into his model a number of concepts drawn from information theory. In doing so he uses several technical terms well outside their normal sphere of reference, admittedly making clear that this is a dangerous thing to do.

Information theory, or communication theory, is a highly mathematical subject, and no non-mathematical introduction to it can avoid being at least partially misleading. The well-known little book by Shannon and Weaver (1949) is both sound and not too difficult to follow. Having given this warning, I shall now try to give a glimpse of the content of the subject or, at least, of that part of the subject which is relevant here.

The theory is concerned with the transmission of messages via a communication channel which has a limited transmission capability, and a tendency to garble the messages entrusted to it. Suppose you wish to give someone's christian name to a person at the other end of a bad telephone line, and you decide to spell it out letter by letter. Then the message is the sequence of letters. The *information* contained in the message is the number of alternative messages that might have been sent, in this case the size of the set of possible christian names one of which the recipient expected to be given. This is a rather unexpected definition of information content. It rests on the idea that it is the choice of a particular message from a set of possible messages that conveys information, not the form of the message itself. The word *variety* is sometimes used to indicate the amount of choice available in some set of possible messages. Returning to our example, the word *equivocation* refers to the fact that when the recipient hears a letter he is still not quite sure which letter was actually spoken at the other end, because of the garbling effect. This residual uncertainty is the equivocation. Finally, the *redundancy* in a message is the extent to which it can be recovered even after garbling. For example, the message DEVID is obviously a garbled form of DAVID.

I must stress that the above definitions are merely my own attempt to convey the spirit of the rigorous mathematical definitions which form the basis of the abstract theory.

Clarke uses these terms to help him add two new ideas to his model. Firstly, he points out that the self-regulating capacity of a culture system, its ability to remain stable when its environment fluctuates, depends upon the amount of variety it shows; that is, upon the amount of information it contains or can transmit in some sense. This is an extrapolation of a theorem in information theory. The second addition to the model is that an equilibrium state for a culture system is to be regarded as one in which 'the rate of destruction of information variety is minimized' (Clarke 1968:96), the destructive agent being interaction between subsystems involving 'equivocation'. On the other hand, 'redundancy is the vital factor which makes for consistency and continuity, preserving the system in its present general format' (1968:91). A non-technical way of putting this might be: a high measure of cultural agreement between sub-sections of a society makes for overall stability.

Although Clarke's use of technical terms in this way possibly does help some readers understand the useful insights he has to offer, there is an obvious danger of misleading or baffling at least as many others. Clarke does not attempt to apply his model as a whole to any specific archaeological process. He uses it rather as a conceptual framework within which to discuss the various archaeological entities which he considers. He does, however, occasionally give a concrete example of a particular aspect of the model such as feedback or oscillation.

How useful is systems theory?

We have now considered two important attempts to make use of systems theoretic and related ideas in an archaeological context. Just how useful are these new ideas? Both

Flannery and Clarke are careful not to claim too much, but equally both clearly believe in their respective approaches.

It can reasonably be argued that the value of any innovation depends both upon its own merits, and on the merits of the regime which it replaces. What is systems theory intended to replace in archaeology? Clarke seems to feel that it should, to at least some extent, replace 'the murky exhalation which passes for "interpretive thinking" in British Archaeology' (Clarke 1969: opening paragraph). And it is surely true that interpretative archaeology in this country is largely a case of individual archaeologists grappling with complex, ill-defined, and often, one suspects, insoluble problems each with his own approach and intellectual attitude. In spite of the experience and expertise at work it is inevitable that mistakes are made, that theories are put forward and accepted without adequate supporting evidence, and that as much effort is spent in correcting the errors of the past as is spent in gaining new understanding.

Thus, although this inefficient state of affairs is certainly not peculiar to archaeology, nor indeed to non-scientific subjects, it is surely true that archaeological thinking can only benefit from being better organized, more objective, and able to call upon more agreed general principles. And, of course systems theory appears to offer just the conceptual framework which is needed. We can say with confidence that systems theory *does* provide a new way of looking at old problems, and therefore it will almost certainly lead to important new insights. Old too simple ways of thinking will often come under attack and be replaced by arguments and models which, though often hesitant and wrong, may at least match the problems in complexity.

But to be fully effective a conceptual framework of this nature must enable actual archaeological evidence to be unambiguously and objectively expressed within it, and meaningful and productive conclusions to be drawn from the evidence, again unambiguously and objectively. These much more demanding criteria do not seem to be met by systems theory. The terminology and concept framework within which facts and ideas are to be expressed seems dangerously vague. Although concepts such as dynamic equilibrium, positive feedback, Markov process, redundancy are all capable of mathematical definition, it is not these definitions which the proponents of systems theory have used, but rather the imprecise ideas which give rise to the definitions. Without the rigorous definitions there is no mathematical theory, and without the mathematical theory there is no way of drawing objective conclusions from the evidence beyond what there has always been, the archaeologists own reasoning ability. At best some degree of standardization of argument might be achieved.

Flannery can, for example, point to an example of positive feedback in the ecosystem of Mesoamerica in the period he considers. But there is little he can do to quantify that observation. And if he could, by some miracle, attach meaningful figures to the various food-procurement systems he studies, what would happen then? Although there certainly is a solid body of mathematical theory and techniques labelled 'system theory', it forms a branch of control engineering and is most unlikely to be of practical use in such a context.

But, the reader may say, surely systems theory is more or less the same as cybernetics, and cybernetics has a great deal to offer? Let us see.

Cybernetics

What is the current state of cybernetics? It is *not* a well-defined, coherent subject with a solid body of practical and theoretical results to its credit. Indeed, it is reported that during a recent German conference on cybernetics someone remarked: 'While this conference is in progress everyone in this room is a cyberneticist. But when the conference is over, each person is once again a biologist, a chemist, an engineer . . . anything else but a cyberneticist' (Aischutz 1968: 111). One can add that the conference participant might just as well have been a specialist in information theory, a computer scientist, a psychologist, or one of a variety of types of mathematician. Nevertheless, there *are* conferences on cybernetics, so there must be something to discuss.

One definition of the subject is that it is the study of communication and control in animals and machines. This is a very wide definition which can be held, and usually is held, to cover the study of the relationship between all human behaviour, including reasoning and cognition generally, and self-organizing and reasoning machines. Two consequences follow from this objective. First, just about everyone has some reason to be interested in cybernetics, even if the interest is only a purely speculative one. Secondly, the subject does not itself make much progress. In fact, a cybernetician seems to have the choice either of pursuing fascinating, ambitious, but always imprecise and inconclusive trains of thought or of becoming a more conventional research worker in one of the fields related to cybernetics such as those mentioned above.

Thus in 1956 Ross Ashby published a very useful book entitled *Introduction to Cybernetics*. But if one seeks the advanced theory corresponding to the introductory ideas which he presents, one must go to information theory, to the formal theory of automata, and to certain branches of probability theory – all three technical subjects with nothing like the range of application claimed for cybernetics.

A more recent book, also entitled *Introduction to Cybernetics* is by Glushkov (1966) a leading Russian scientist. The topics he discusses are even more mathematical and remote from general application. They include the abstract theory of algorithms, the propositional and predicate calculus, and mathematical results concerning abstract self-organizing systems. There is also a chapter on electronic digital computers and programming.

Within the last twelve months Young (1969) has published a useful little book, entitled simply *Cybernetics*, which concentrates on what we know about the brain and its functioning, and on the means by which various capabilities of the brain have been matched by machines, usually the programmed digital computer. This is the hard core, in so far as there is a hard core of cybernetics today.

A reader who wishes to obtain a more panoramic view of current work in this whole general area might browse through the *Encyclopaedia of Linguistics, Information and Control* edited by Meetham and Hudson (1969).

Thus the idea that cybernetics can provide archaeologists with powerful new concepts and techniques is also somewhat misconceived. Insofar as cybernetics exists as a subject in its own right it has only rather vague concepts and no techniques. It seems more realistic to suggest, as many others have done, that digital computer methods, and the concepts associated with them, can offer the help which the archaeologist needs.

Computer simulations and archaeology

There has now been a wide variety of experiments involving computer processing of archaeological data. Clarke (1968) describes many of them, and another valuable source is Cowgill (1967). I do not propose to discuss these experiments here, important though they are. In most of them the machine carries out a set of extensive and rather dull calculations, the algorithm involved being drawn from the more or less standard mathematical repertoire. In this final section I shall briefly present the computer in what seems to me to be a much more promising and interesting role, which has as yet received rather little attention from archaeologists, even though in some ways it can be regarded as the practical equivalent of systems theory. I mean the use of a computer to construct and test a 'simulation' of some complex system evolving in time.

An important point for the reader to grasp at the outset is that this does *not* mean that the system concerned must fit some mathematical model. Indeed, one of the great advantages of using a computer program to simulate evolving systems is that a much wider range of possibilities can be accommodated than can be expressed mathematically. Valuable discussions of this and other relevant points are contained in the papers by Fleisher (1965) and Gullahorn and Gullahorn (1965).

Let us consider a very artificial but hopefully illuminating archaeological example. Suppose that a certain large island has been extensively excavated and has produced a considerable amount of archaeological evidence. From this evidence it is clear that at one time the population of the island was small but with a distinctive culture involving primitive farming. Then, over a period of hundreds of years, the island was settled and finally dominated by rather more advanced invaders with a quite different cultural background. The indigenous population was totally absorbed except for certain cultural elements adopted by the newcomers. This is the outline picture. The task is to fill in the details.

The following are some of the general factors which seem relevant to this task:

(1) the numbers and skeletal characteristics of the invaders compared with the indigenous population, and the way in which the two populations merge,

(2) the topography of the island including good landing and settlement points and trade routes etc.,

(3) the artefacts, burials and settlements characteristic of each population and their evolution and interaction with time,

(4) the food resources of each population and the extent to which these are seasonal or localized,

(5) the extent to which material remains survive to be excavated, and the actual locations of the excavated sites.

No doubt the reader can easily improve and extend this list.

Any comprehensive theory of what happened on the island during the period in question must make precise the details of all the relevant factors, and suitably integrate them. The 'best' theory is that which best fits the observed excavation evidence, the dictates of general archaeological knowledge, and common sense.

What the computer offers is the possibility of writing a computer program which embodies, at some level of abstraction, precise specifications of all the relevant factors and of their interactions. These specifications need not embody any general laws, nor need they be mathematical in form, but each must be operationally complete so that together they enable the machine to generate a possible 'history' of the island for the period. In addition, the program will generate an estimate of what the consequential archaeological record would be. Given such a program, the task of the archaeologist would be to vary the factor specifications, using his own experience and insight, until the events and deposits predicted by the machine best matched the actual excavation evidence. It would, in fact, be very much a case of 'reconstructing the events at the scene of the crime' with the machine doing the tedious task of moving the 'actors' and 'scenery'.

For our specific example, the simulation might have as its main components:

(a) a fixed 'map' of the island including information about climate, vegetation and fauna, together with

(b) a specification of the type of settlement characteristic of each population, including information about its size, material products and demand upon the natural environment, and

(c) rules specifying the dynamics of the system – the rules which determine where and when settlements are founded, when a settlement is abandoned, what forms of trade and conflict there are between settlements, and in what ways the material cultures of the populations evolve.

The machine would simulate the passage of time by repeatedly updating the map and the settlements 'attached' to it by reference to the rules and specifications given – and the 'history' so generated might well be both surprising and illuminating.

The reader may object that the factors listed above would, in any real situation, involve an enormous amount of detail, far more than any computer could possibly cope with. This is true but not entirely relevant. No archaeologist can cope with such enormous amounts of detail either. The computer simulation would be just the type of simplified and abstract representation of the true situation which the archaeologist is now forced to use by his own limitations. Co-operation between archaeologist and machine might enable rather more evidence to be considered, rather more systematically, than would otherwise be the case.

A different possible objection is that only very rarely is there anything like enough evidence available to make a comprehensive simulation of this type even remotely feasible. Probably most archaeologists are concerned with problems of a far more limited nature. Comprehensive models are built, if at all, by many hands over many decades. Fortunately, computer simulation techniques are useful for simple as well as complex systems – I have merely chosen a rather complicated example.

There is nothing new about computer simulation of dynamic systems (see, for example, McLeod 1968). Simulations of transport systems, commercial organizations and no doubt, battlefields are commonplace. Some programming languages are specifically designed to make simulation easy. How useful such modelling will actually be in archaeology is, of course, a matter for experimentation, but if nothing else the attempt to create computer simulations will certainly encourage that clarity, precision, and objectivity of thought which so many are seeking.

Acknowledgements

I am very grateful to Dr F. R. Hodson of the Institute of Archaeology, London, for his suggestion that I should write this paper. It has been written during my tenure of an SRC research fellowship.

15.viii.69

S.R.C. Atlas Computer Laboratory
Chilton, Didcot, Berkshire

References

Anschutz, H. 1968. Prospects for the development of the psychocybernetics of intelligent behavior. In *Purposive Systems*, eds H. von Foerster *et al.* Washington. 111–23.

Ashby, W. Ross. 1965. *An Introduction to Cybernetics.* London.

Bertalanffy, L. von. 1950. An outline of general system theory. *British Journal of the Philosophy of Science.* 1:134–65.

Clarke, D. L. 1968. *Analytical Archaeology.* London.

Clarke, D. L. 1969. Towards analytical archaeology: new directions in the interpretive thinking of British archaeologists. Paper presented to the *C.N.R.S. International Symposium on the Use of Electronic Computers in Archaeology.* Marseilles, April 1969. (Proceedings to be published.)

Cowgill, G. L. 1967. Computer applications in archaeology. *AFIPS Conference Proceedings, Volume 31* (1967 Fall Joint Computer Conference) Washington. 331–7.

Flannery, K. V. 1968. Archaeological systems theory and early Mesoamerica. In *Anthropological Archaeology in the Americas*, ed. Meggers. Washington. 67–87.

Fleisher, A. 1965. The uses of simulation. In *Computer Methods in the Analysis of Large-Scale Social Systems*, ed. J. M. Beshers. Joint Center for Urban Studies of the Massachusetts Institute of Technology and Harvard University. 144–6.

Glushkov, V. M. 1966. *Introduction to Cybernetics.* New York.

Gullahorn, J. T. and Gullahorn, J. E. 1965. The computer as a tool for theory development. In *The Use of Computers in Anthropology*, ed. D. Hymes. The Hague. 427–48.

Haggett, P. 1965. *Location Analysis in Human Geography.* London.

McLeod, J. ed. 1968. *Simulation.* New York.

Meetham, A. R. and Hudson, R. A. eds. 1969. *Encyclopaedia of Linguistics, Information and Control.* Oxford.

Shannon, C. E. and Weaver, W. 1949. *The Mathematical Theory of Communication.* Urbana.

Young, J. F. 1969. *Cybernetics.* London.

Cluster analysis and archaeology: some new developments and applications

F. R. Hodson

1 Introduction

Although numerical techniques for seriation have received a good deal of attention from archaeologists, techniques of cluster analysis, which may prove to be of much wider relevance, have not. It is also unfortunate that some of the few best known excursions into this field by archaeologists have been confused in both aim and method. During the last few years, great advances have been made in the theory and practice of cluster analysis, but this work tends to be reported in periodicals and research reports that an interested archaeologist may well miss. The purpose of this paper is to draw attention to some of this recent work and to demonstrate and assess on archaeological data some currently favoured methods. Special attention will be paid to the newly developed and promising k-means approach.

Cluster analysis makes use of numerical procedures to divide a given group of units into homogeneous sub-groups. For an archaeologist, this kind of compression or classification is perhaps the most basic and important of all the tasks that he has to perform. Whether an intuitive or a numerical approach is followed, and whether the resulting clusters ('types', 'complexes') are regarded primarily as an arbitrary summary of data, or as a direct reflection of significant patterns of human behaviour, it is clear that no interpretation of archaeological finds can be attempted until this initial stage of organization has been completed. If it is considered that this critical stage should be carried out as explicitly and objectively as possible, numerical procedures will be of immediate interest because of the precision that they exact in specific cases, and because of the light that they throw on the classification process in general. An additional bonus would be that once developed, a suitable numerical procedure should be able to deal rapidly and thoroughly with very large amounts of material.

The need for suitable methods of cluster analysis has been felt for some time in a number of different disciplines (including anthropology), but because of the number of tedious, if simple, calculations involved, it was not until high-speed computers were developed that real, practical advances could be made. Sokal and Sneath's fundamental book of 1963 on 'numerical taxonomy' reflects the surge of experimentation and achievement that followed computer developments of the 'fifties. Since 1963 interest in cluster analysis has, if anything, increased still further. Significantly, theoreticians have at last begun to establish a formal background to cluster analysis which may test empirically generated procedures and suggest new procedures for the practising taxonomist to use. In the following sections an attempt will be made to discuss cluster analysis from a practical, archaeological point of view.

2 General considerations

1 Preliminaries and the basic strategy of clustering versus ordering

In a practical situation the archaeologist as classifier starts from what he considers a relevant body of material and organizes it into an order or grouping of some sort. Implicit for this process, although rarely explicit, is, first, a decision about what is in fact relevant, and, second, a strategy of classification (a definite aim for the classification and a method for achieving it). The same stages are involved in a numerical classification, but they must be explicit. The 'relevant body of material' is specified as a descriptive list, which is then translated into quantitative terms (e.g. presence or absence, or relative proportions of various features) as in table 1. Then a general strategy is chosen and a suitable numerical procedure is applied. This is almost certain to involve estimates of relationship – 'coefficients' of some kind or another as a preliminary to, or as part of, the sorting strategy. Any numerical classification, then, must depend largely on how well the data list has been compiled and on the suitability of the coefficient chosen, but these are problems common to many different aspects of numerical presentation and analysis and will only be mentioned here in passing.

The major choice of strategy for an archaeologist at a given stage of his study will be between 'ordering' and 'clustering'. An ordering strategy will accept each separate unit as such and will study overall relationships between these units – major dimensions and trends. The end result will give the position of each unit in relation to the overall configuration that has been worked out. Two well attested procedures of this kind are Principal Components Analysis, which exploits only linear relationships but which is economical with computer time (Hodson 1969) and Multi-dimensional Scaling, which makes less assumptions but is rather more greedy of computation. Seriation, probably the most familiar ordering process to archaeologists, may be considered as a special, one-dimensional case of this general approach and is most suitably tackled by one of these two methods, preferably the latter (Doran and Hodson 1966; Gowgill 1968; Kendall 1969) rather than by developments of the rather restrictive matrix ordering techniques of Brainerd and Robinson (1951). A clustering strategy on the other hand serves a different purpose: to reduce the number of units of study by combining similar units into classes which will then form a new basis for interpretation. Here the results will be presented diagrammatically as either a hierarchical tree or 'dendrogram' showing the progressive fusion of units into larger clusters, or a Venn diagram with clusters separated from each other and enclosed within boundaries.

Of course it is possible to use both strategies in studying the same material, and to combine results from both strategies in the same diagram. For example, figure 8 presents the results of an ordering procedure where units are projected on to co-ordinates defined by a principal components analysis. This gives ordering of the units in two dimensions (the 1st dimension in fact representing a rough chronological seriation). At the same time six discrete clusters are indicated from the results of a k-means cluster analysis. Figure 10 by contrast shows the results of using the average values for these six clusters as a new set of 'units' which have then been ordered by multidimensional scaling.

In some rare cases an ordering technique may give a rough indication of discrete clusters but the two strategies are conceptually and computationally quite distinct.

2 *Q and R modes of analysis*

Another preliminary consideration is to decide which aspect of the data is being investigated in any specific analysis. A data list consists of a set of units described by a set of properties: for example, in psychology this could be a list of individuals described by their performance on a set of intelligence tests, in ecology a list of stands or areas described by the floral species represented, in archaeology a set of tools described by elements of shape and decoration. In each case the analyst must decide whether he is seeking clusters of units (a q-type analysis) or properties (an r-type or 'inverse' analysis). That is to say that in the psychological example the analyst may be interested in either clusters of intelligence tests (that presumably assess the same basic qualities) – an r-type analysis, or in clusters of individuals classified into 'types' over a wide range of performance – a q-type analysis. The first analysis may help him to perform the second: it may enable him, for example, to reduce the number of tests given, but it will not generally cluster the individuals into types. In archaeology too the choice is open but must be made. For example, if the archaeologist is investigating the technology behind tools – the way that styles of retouch are related to types of raw material, shapes of blanks and so forth, it seems appropriate to perform an r-analysis and search for clusters (or 'dimensions' or 'factors') of related properties. As in the psychological example this may assist in defining properties for a subsequent q-mode cluster analysis in the search for 'types' of tool. However, the r-analysis will not itself divide the tools into groups.

Several numerical studies published by archaeologists appear to have sought a taxonomy of artefacts by an r-mode procedure. Matthews (1963) pointed out this confusion but it still seems to persist in some of the studies that deal with 'attribute cluster analysis'. If an 'attribute analysis' like this is claimed to indicate a taxonomy, the claimant should make clear (1) exactly what procedure of clustering has been used, (2) exactly which clusters of attributes have in fact been discovered, (3) exactly how clusters of artefacts have been derived from the clusters of attributes.

The examples of cluster analysis described in this paper are in the q-mode.

These preliminary comments on clustering versus ordering and q- versus r-modes of analysis may seem to have been unduly laboured, but these rather fundamental aspects have not been emphasized in some of the general accounts of numerical techniques given by archaeologists (e.g., Clarke 1968).

3 *The choice of a specific clustering procedure*

One by-product of the recent interest in cluster analysis has been a bewildering proliferation of techniques (cf. Ball 1965; Lance and Williams 1967). It might be expected that these differing techniques would represent different ways of reaching the same result.

This is unfortunately far from true and, as the following examples will show, different techniques will produce quite different results from the same material even when the same coding and measure of similarity have been used. In fact, the different approaches reflect different ways of defining the deceptively straightforward concept of 'homogeneous clusters'. The non-numerical taxonomist is faced with the same problem, but if numerical techniques are used it cannot be evaded. This need for the precise description of a classificatory process is perhaps the single most important aspect of the numerical approach.

In practice, the specific method of cluster analysis chosen by an archaeologist may be dictated by what is available at the local computing centre. However, if, as would be hoped, a choice exists, any available technique will have to be considered from three points of view: given a specific set of data to be analysed, is the procedure:

(1) practically feasible
(2) practically suitable
(3) theoretically sound?

Only the first of these considerations is in any way straightforward. Despite differences in the size and speed of individual computers, and despite the different accomplishments of programmers, it is possible to set rough limits to the size of problem that can be reasonably tackled by different types of cluster analysis. For example, a logical approach to clustering would be to define all possible groupings of the units concerned and to pick out the grouping that best satisfied a stipulated criterion. However, this approach is automatically ruled out by the enormous number of possible partitions for even a small data set.

In practice, most standard approaches to clustering have a built-in limit to the number of units that they can treat. Often this limit is set by the need to refer to a record of relationships between all pairs of units in the study (a similarity matrix). With n objects such a matrix requires $\frac{1}{2}n(n-1)$ entries. For 100 units this means 4,950 storage locations – no great demand on a standard research computer. However, 1,000 units would require 499,500 entries, which is really impracticable. Procedures that store and operate on the original data matrix escape this dilemma, but will have their own limit set by the intricacy of the similarity measure used. Demands on the computer made by a wide range of different approaches are given by Ball (1965).

Questions of practical and theoretical suitability are far less straightforward but an attempt will be made to assess the techniques described from both points of view.

3 Examples

In this section four approaches to cluster analysis will be demonstrated on the same set of archaeological material. The order in which they are presented is partly historical and partly logical.

1 The data

The units to be clustered are a set of thirty Iron Age fibulae, mainly from the La Tène cemetery of Münsingen near Berne. They have already been used to compare some classification techniques and their archaeological context has been described in detail (Hodson, Sneath and Doran 1966; Hodson 1968).

For this exercise, which concentrates solely on a comparison between clustering techniques, and which does not attempt to achieve optimal descriptions and similarity estimations, thirteen measured variables only have been used (figure 1 and table 1). These

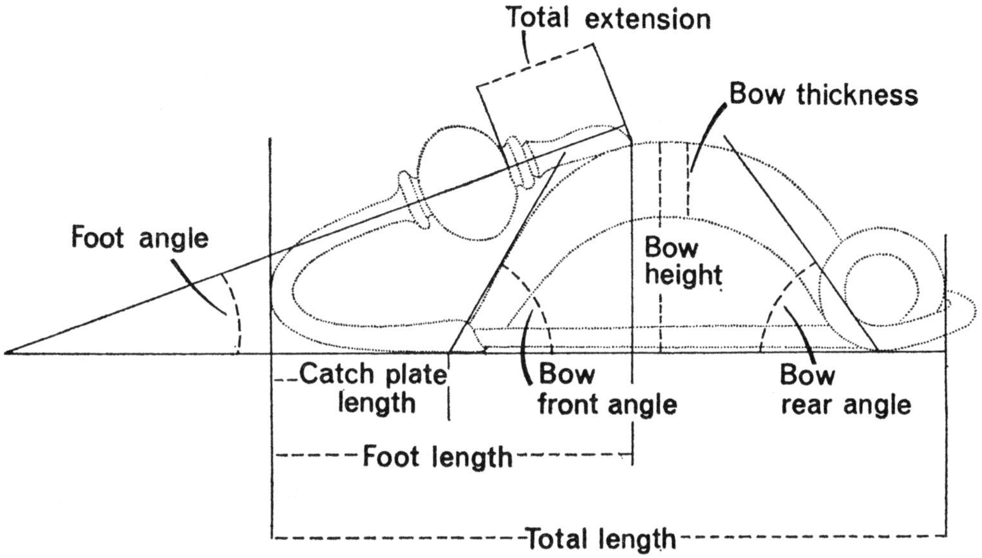

Figure 1 Attributes used to 'describe' La Tène brooches for the analyses. As well as the variables indicated, the width of the bow, the width of the foot-extension, the diameter of the coils and the number of coils were also used (see table 1)

ignore decoration and attempt to describe only the overall shape of the objects. Three angles and ten dimensions are involved, the latter expressed as a proportion of total length so that shape and not size is being considered. These proportional values were logarithmically transformed (0·1 being added to the raw score to accommodate zero values); all values were then divided by the standard deviation of the relevant variable. The estimate of similarity or rather difference on which all these analyses depend is Euclidean distance (Sokal and Sneath 1963: 143). This is calculated for any two objects by taking the difference between their scores for each variable in turn and squaring it. The sum of these squares gives squared Euclidean distance between the two objects. A matrix of these distances between each pair of fibulae is stored in the computer for use in the first three of the analyses.

External criteria for judging clusters are included in the diagrams in two forms: by reproducing the profiles of fibulae, archaeologists may be able to judge to their satisfaction whether clusters are reasonable or not; an indication of 'best estimated date' is also given (Hodson 1968), since it is to be expected that fibulae clustered together should be of similar date. Five phases are represented by the symbols from light = early to dark = late,

The following results may also be compared with a Multi-dimensional Scaling Analysis and with 'intuitive' analyses of the same fibulae previously published by Hodson, Sneath and Doran (1966).

TABLE I

Details of thirty fibulae which make up the sample of test data. Asterisks indicate that the extension of the foot is clipped over on to the bow. Measurements are given in millimetres, angles in intervals of ten degrees

	Grave	Museum no.	Foot length	Bow height	Bow front angle	Foot angle	Coil diam.	Bow rear angle	Element diam.	Foot ext. length	Catchplate	Bow width	Bow thickness	Foot ext. width	No of coils	Total length
1	149	389	93	24	7	10	16	1	13	31	47	3·5	3·5	*	4	114
2	190	615	21	7	6	9	6	5	2	11	10	3·5	1·7	*	12	35
3	161	125	33	15	2	8	7	3	8	10	20	3·9	3·2	*	4	60
4	31	812	23	26	4	7	9	5	12	1	16	6·2	7·7	2·8	4	74
5	49	798	20	23	2	8	7	1	8	5	16	7·7	5·2	2·6	6	68
6	6	673	27	15	6	8	7	5	3	11	11	3·7	3·5	1·8	4	55
7	THAMES		10	16	1	10	9	1	7	0	11	6·1	4·1	0·0	4	45
8	23	643	15	18	1	10	10	1	5	0	15	3·5	3·5	0·0	4	40
9	149	391	31	13	4	9	7	4	5	11	18	17·6	1·4	3·6	6	54
10	149	398	19	17	2	7	6	2	6	10	12	9·2	6·6	3·9	6	39
11	101	491	41	23	3	8	11	3	14	15	24	7·3	5·8	8·6	6	71
12	171	149	47	17	5	9	10	4	8	14	26	5·8	4·7	6·0	6	78
13	130	545	29	15	3	8	6	3	6	10	17	11·7	3·9	6·4	6	47
14	157	085	23	13	3	8	6	2	10	7	15	5·2	2·7	5·4	12	41
15	97	478	20	15	1	7	5	1	12	4	12	4·7	4·8	3·5	6	38
16	85	436	17	16	1	7	7	1	8	3	11	5·1	3·5	2·2	6	44
17	91	464	20	15	2	7	7	3	6	10	12	5·5	3·8	3·9	6	50
18	61	821	20	13	5	8	5	2	10	5	10	4·4	4·4	5·1	6	36
19	94	474	21	18	2	9	9	1	5	6	15	8·1	2·3	1·9	4	49
20	121	348	28	17	1	10	10	2	8	6	20	2·5	2·6	2·2	4	53
21	181	212	94	15	7	10	12	5	11	31	50	4·3	4·3	*	6	128
22	68	587	22	18	1	8	7	1	5	8	17	8·8	3·0	2·4	6	59
23	61	830	20	14	1	8	6	1	3	4	14	14·3	1·4	1·7	6	44
24	130	549	22	15	3	8	7	3	13	1	17	5·0	4·6	2·5	10	47
25	80	529	12	22	1	6	9	1	9	0	11	6·8	6·4	0·0	4	45
26	149	399	27	15	1	8	10	2	9	11	19	8·2	4·0	7·6	4	53
27	48	788	15	19	2	8	7	3	3	4	12	3·7	3·5	1·9	4	56
28	44	752	10	10	2	10	6	2	2	—	9	2·0	2·3	2·2	3	26
29	HALLSTATT		9	13	3	10	4	4	9	0	8	9·6	5·0	0·0	22	28
30	193	611	68	18	7	9	9	7	3	50	18	9·3	6·5	*	4	110

2 *A digression: the dubious technique of matrix ordering and contouring*

Several archaeological studies have claimed to discern clusters or 'homostats' from the positioning of 'high' values in an 'ordered' similarity matrix. It is difficult to accept this as a serious approach to cluster analysis. In these cases, a matrix has been ordered to recover one-dimensional seriation in the manner suggested by Brainerd and Robinson (1951) before Multi-dimensional Scaling had been developed. It is possible to conceive of some rather unlikely situations where satisfactory clusters could be indicated by such ordering (where high values would cluster exclusively and regularly along the diagonal). Sokal (1966) does give a biological example, but such situations are unlikely in archaeology, and do not occur in the relevant published experiments (Clarke 1962: fig. 4; 1968: fig. 127b; Johnson 1968: fig. 14). To attempt at this stage to divine clusters visually from the partly ordered matrix would seem misguided, especially since more standard clustering techniques are expected to deal with this kind of situation directly, without any preliminary, laborious matrix ordering and contouring. Although Sokal and Sneath (1963:176) and Sokal (1966:113) mention and illustrate shaded matrices, they make it clear that they do not regard matrix ordering as a precise method of cluster analysis.

3 *Single-link cluster analysis*

This approach (sometimes referred to as 'nearest neighbour' sorting) was used for some of the earliest computer classifications (e.g., Sneath 1957) and has remained of great interest and importance since (Sokal and Sneath 1963:180). An archaeological application has already been reported by Hodson, Sneath and Doran (1966).

The actual clustering procedure may most easily be followed from the dendrogram in figure 2. The two most similar units (11 and 18) are joined first. The next highest similarity is then taken and so on. As the procedure continues, if one of the linked units is already in a group the whole of the group is involved in the fusion; if both units belong to groups, both groups fuse. The process continues until all units are linked into one group. This procedure may be carried out by hand on quite a large similarity matrix if such a matrix can itself be calculated.

The clusters suggested by this method are like chains with ends that may be very distinct, and this kind of structure has not been found generally useful by some practising taxonomists (Williams, Lambert and Lance 1966; Hodson, Sneath and Doran 1966). Recently, however, this method was shown to be the only directly hierarchical procedure regularly in use that possessed the formal properties required by a comprehensive theory of clustering (Jardine and Sibson 1968), and interest has revived in the method (e.g., Holloway and Jardine 1968).

In this example (fig. 2), as with a larger sample of fibulae previously analysed, the chaining effect is evident and about one-third of the brooches are linked on singly as outliers of a larger group. It would seem difficult to derive a very comprehensive taxonomy for the brooches at any level in this hierarchy. Groups that are suggested seem reasonable, but relatively few groups are suggested.

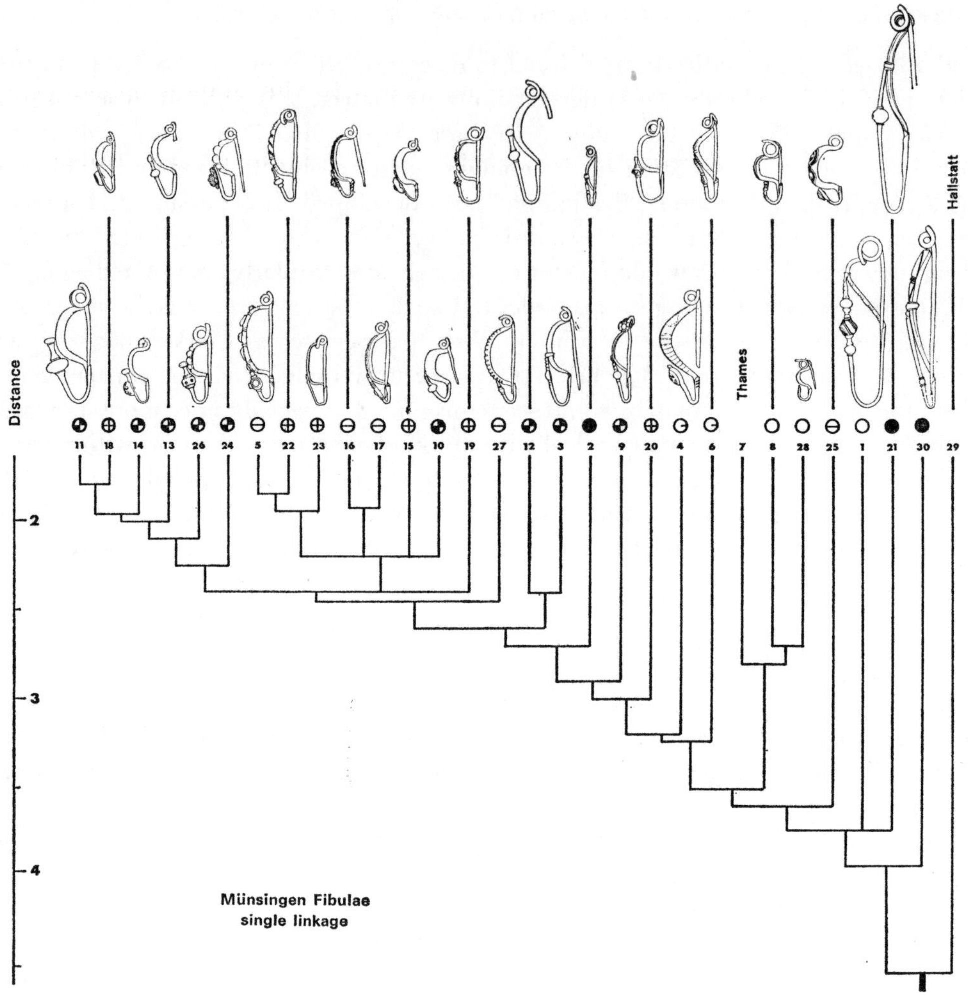

Figure 2 Single Link Cluster Analysis of thirty fibulae. Symbols represent 'best estimated' date from early (open circles) to late (filled circles). The fibulae from Hallstatt and the Thames cannot be dated in this sequence, but the former should be the earliest fibula of the series. From the dendrogram clusters could be defined at any level of the hierarchy by a horizontal line at the required distance level: each stem crossed would then represent a cluster. Working downwards, a main group soon forms (at distance 2·5) and units then chain on to this singly or in small groups, making it difficult to define a working taxonomy for the group

4 *Average link cluster analysis*

Various methods of clustering have been devised empirically to avoid the chaining characteristics of Single Linkage, notably Average-Linkage (weighted and unweighted versions) and Complete Linkage (or 'furthest neighbour' sorting). These are discussed in detail by Sokal and Sneath (1963: 181) and extensive comparisons of results have been given by Sokal and Michener (1967). Lance and Williams (1967) have shown that these methods (together with Single-Linkage) are in fact closely related and that for many similarity coefficients a single procedure is able to produce any of these options (or intermediate effects) by varying the parameters of a simple linear equation that is used to calculate the relationship between groups during clustering. One of these options (Unweighted Group-Average) has seemed promising with archaeological data (Hodson, Sneath and Doran 1966; Johnson 1968; Hodson 1969) and is demonstrated again here (fig. 3). With this procedure units (or clusters) are only allowed to join existing clusters if

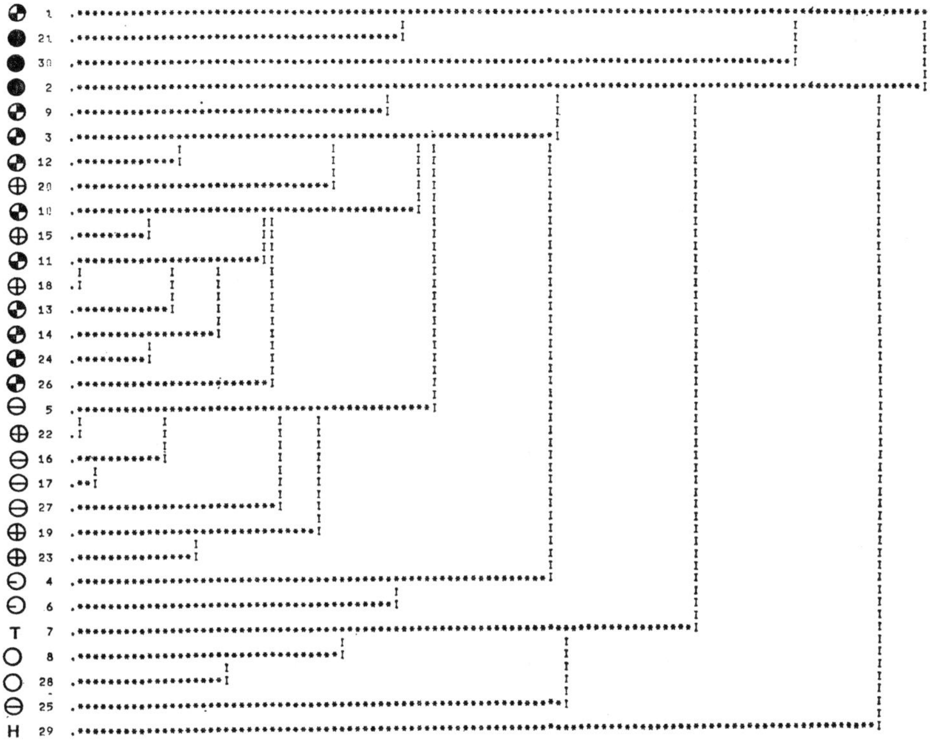

Figure 3 Average-Link Cluster Analysis of thirty fibulae (Unweighted Pair-Group variant). This dendrogram was provided directly by the lineprinter of the computer. Symbols of date have been added as for figure 2. Again, at any horizontal level in the hierarchy each stem would be treated as a cluster. This method prevents the formation of chain-clusters and provides the kind of structure that is useful for taxonomy. However, in doing so, it may force the units into an over-arbitrary framework

the average similarity between all the relevant units reaches the stipulated level. However, although favoured by practising taxonomists, all of these methods have been shown to have undesirable mathematical properties (Jardine and Sibson 1968). These authors point out, for example, that very slight differences in the original data, in the way that it has been scaled and in the way that similarity has been estimated may have major effects on the resulting clusters. It is also very easy for units to become trapped in clusters at an early stage of the analysis from which they cannot later escape. An instance of the arbitrary nature of the procedure may be cited from fig. 3: nos 22 and 23 are calculated as relatively similar (distance 1·95), but because 22 is marginally closer to 5 than to 23 (1·85) and because 23 is relatively unlike 5 (3·5), 22 and 23 are in fact kept apart by this method until several other fusions have taken place. From some points of view (for example, if judged by the clustering of date symbols) this dendrogram represents a reasonable taxonomy – perhaps the best of any presented. A practising taxonomist may feel that he expects distortion and that the results from Average-Linkage justify the means. However, it is difficult to be satisfied with methods where the distortion is as hidden and unpredictable as it is with Average Linkage, and the value of all the methods discussed in this section must at present be considered in extreme doubt.

5 *Double-link cluster analysis*

A possible alternative escape from the Single-Linkage difficulties, but one that is theoretically acceptable, has been suggested by Jardine and Sibson (1968). Their procedure allows clusters that would be immediately fused in Single Linkage to overlap by a certain number of units before fusing. Described rather loosely, the double-link stage requires two similarity links between one unit, pair or cluster and another pair or cluster (i.e. allows one overlap) before fusing, triple-link would require three links (allowing two overlaps) before fusion and so on. This is a hierarchical approach to cluster formation like the others so far discussed, but the results of higher degrees of overlapping would necessarily be difficult to represent by a dendrogram and these authors suggest the use of Venn diagrams which would allow links and overlaps to be represented at a specific level of similarity (e.g., fig. 6). Jardine and Sibson further suggest a relevant computing algorithm that should be feasible for up to twenty-five units. Little practical work with this system seems yet to have been attempted.

Experiments with archaeological data suggest that degrees of overlapping higher than triple-linkage are of theoretical interest only, defying representation. For these fibulae even the triple-linkage stage resulted in such complex overlapping that interpretation would be quite impossible. However, the dendrogram(fig. 4) represents the double-link stage for these data (single links between pairs of units being ignored so that the dendrogram could be drawn). A rather worrying feature is that the chaining effect of Single-Linkage is still apparent. The reasonable grouping of 1 with 21 and 12 is recovered in this version in contrast with Single-Linkage, but on the other hand the grouping 7, 8, 28, which is recovered by the other three methods of clustering, is lost as a definite cluster by double-linkage. This particular example, where the data are clearly difficult to separate into discrete groups, seems to suggest that the additional complication of overlapping clusters is hardly worth while. It would still be impossible to define a comprehensive taxonomy from this analysis for any level of similarity.

Because of the lack of comparative results with this method, results from two other sets of archaeological data analysed by a provisional double-linkage-only program will be mentioned briefly. These are the samples of fifty Upper Palaeolithic sites and one hundred bronze analyses already investigated by Average Linkage (Hodson 1969).

The fifty Palaeolithic sites do seem to represent a simpler basic structure than the fibulae, with a fairly discrete division into two large clusters and a small third cluster. Figure 5 represents a double-linkage dendrogram for these data, that may be compared

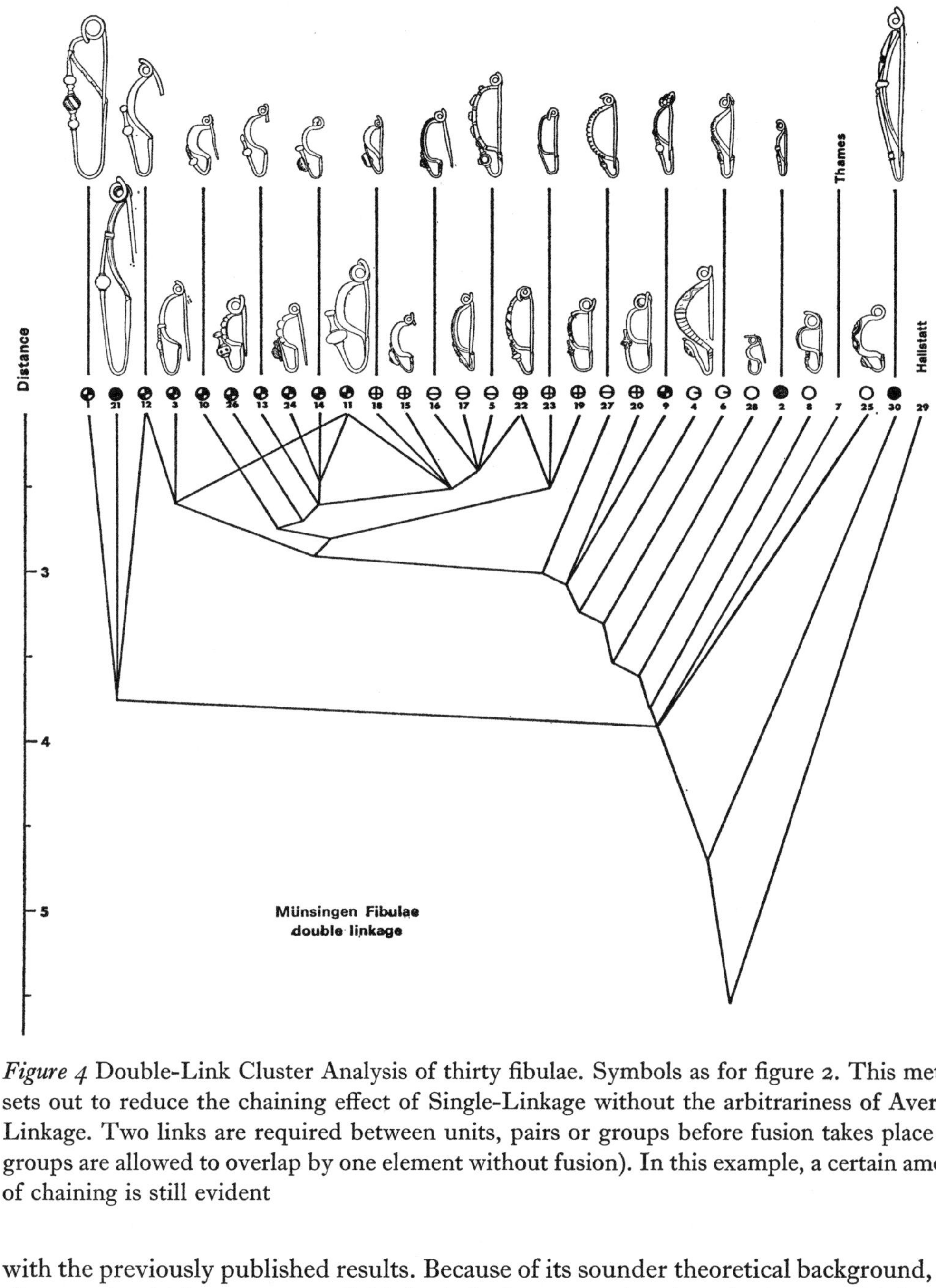

Figure 4 Double-Link Cluster Analysis of thirty fibulae. Symbols as for figure 2. This method sets out to reduce the chaining effect of Single-Linkage without the arbitrariness of Average-Linkage. Two links are required between units, pairs or groups before fusion takes place (i.e. groups are allowed to overlap by one element without fusion). In this example, a certain amount of chaining is still evident

with the previously published results. Because of its sounder theoretical background, this diagram should form a more reliable basis for interpretation than the Average-Link result (Hodson 1969: fig. 22). It would be out of place to expand on this result here, but the structure of the Aurignacian cycle with a nucleus of 'typical Aurignacian' and less obviously clustered variants (once again including the three later Ferrassie Aurignacian levels as a distinct cluster) is of interest and more in accordance with informed archaeological opinion than the bipartite division suggested by Average Linkage. Here the

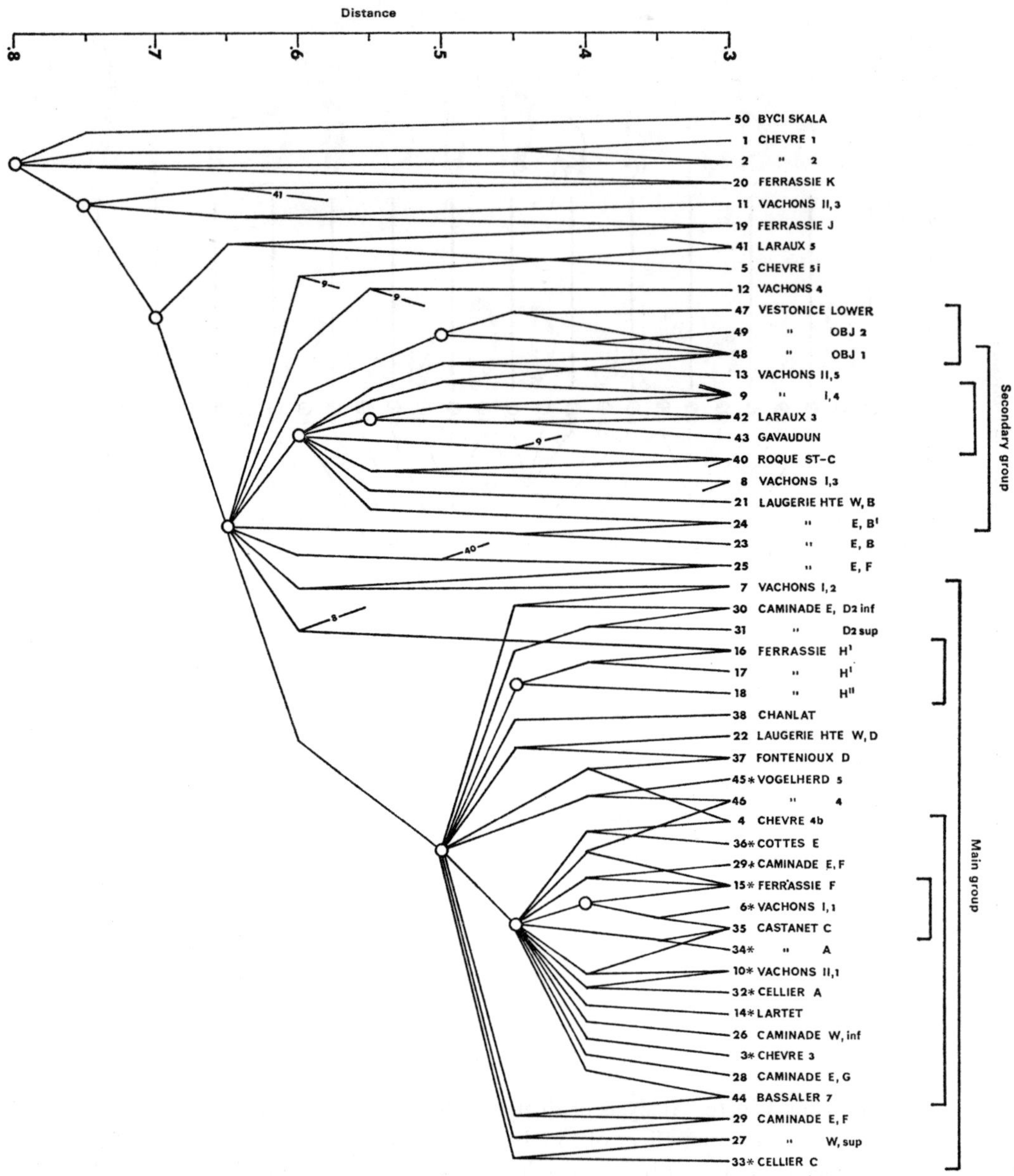

Figure 5 Double-Link Cluster Analysis of fifty Upper Palaeolithic assemblages that have been described by their content of flint tools. Single links between assemblages are shown as well as double-link clusters (marked by circles at nodes in the dendrogram). Asterisks mark levels with split-based bone points. An analysis like this may be expected to suggest a broad taxonomy for these sites based on their total range and relative proportions of flint tool types. The 'main group' corresponds with Aurignacian, the 'secondary group' with Gravettian of conventional taxonomies. More details of these data and analyses by Average Linkage and Principal Components have been published previously (Hodson 1969)

double-linkage result would seem to suggest a possible basis for interpretation.

The third set of trial data, the metal analyses, tended to produce one major group with few smaller clusters and many linked pairs (cf. fig. 6). As for the fibulae, this is not a result that could easily be made the basis for interpretation.

On this very limited investigation, it would seem that in some situations Double-Linkage may provide a valuable result, but that in others the chaining effect will still be too strong for a useful taxonomy to be indicated.

6 *The k-means approach*

The approaches to clustering illustrated so far required a similarity matrix between all units to be calculated and stored for reference. As mentioned in the introduction, this sets an automatic limit to the number of units that can be readily analysed (any more than, say, 150–200 units immediately begin to present problems). A whole range of procedures have been under development for some years that, instead, store and operate on the original data list and a series of hypothetical cluster centres or averages (hence *k-means*). Individual units are repeatedly compared with these centres, which are progressively modified as a result, but at no stage does a complete set of pair-relationships have to be estimated, still less stored. This immediately makes it possible to contemplate analysing a thousand or more units at a time.

The direct aim of most relevant procedures is to achieve a partition of the units into k clusters so that some overall measure of dispersion-within-clusters is minimized. In practice this often involves minimizing the total sum of distances between all the units and the cluster centres to which they are allocated. This approach is basically not hierarchical, but by varying the value of k it is possible to construct a hierarchy of partitions if this is desired (fig. 7).

Three fundamental difficulties are how to calculate 'distances', how to look for a 'best' partition and how to know that a 'best' partition has been achieved or at least approximated. The most rigorous approach to these problems is probably that described by Friedman and Rubin (1967). The result presented here is based on ideas published by Ball (1965, 1967) and Ball and Hall (1965).

The measure of homogeneity of clusters used is the sum of squared Euclidean distances between each unit and the centre of the cluster to which it is allocated – the Sum-Squared Error (SSE). It is convenient to express this 'error of fit' as a percentage of 'Total Error' (the sum of distances between each unit and the overall average for the whole sample). The logarithmic value of this error plotted against the number of clusters should help to reveal the clustering characteristics of the whole sample (fig. 9). The main operations carried out by the experimental program are:

(*1*) *Initialization:* after calculating various statistics and standardizing the data a first set of cluster centres is created: the overall sample mean forms the first, and then units are considered successively. As soon as one is found to be sufficiently distant from this mean (as set at the start of the analysis) it initiates a second cluster centre; the next unit sufficiently distant from both initiates a third and so on until all units have been considered or a maximum number of clusters has been reached.

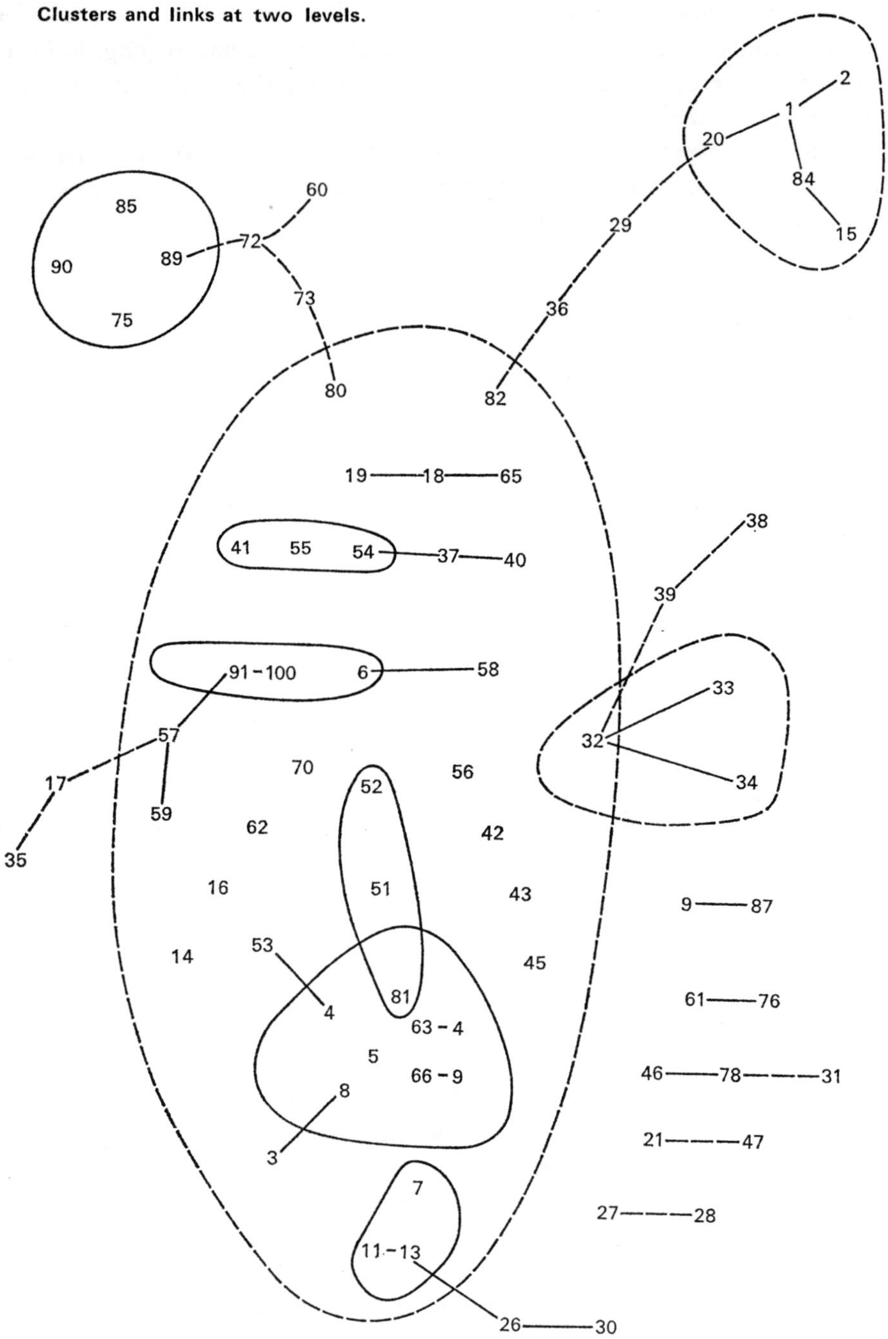

Figure 6 Double-Link Cluster Analysis of one hundred metal tools, described by their content of eight trace elements. Distance is Euclidean distance calculated from standardized, log-transformed percentage values of trace-elements. Clusters and single links are represented at two stages in the analysis. The tendency of Single Linkage to form a single main group and chains is to a certain extent discernible in this Double-Linkage result. Details of the data and an Average-Link analysis have been given elsewhere (Hodson 1969)

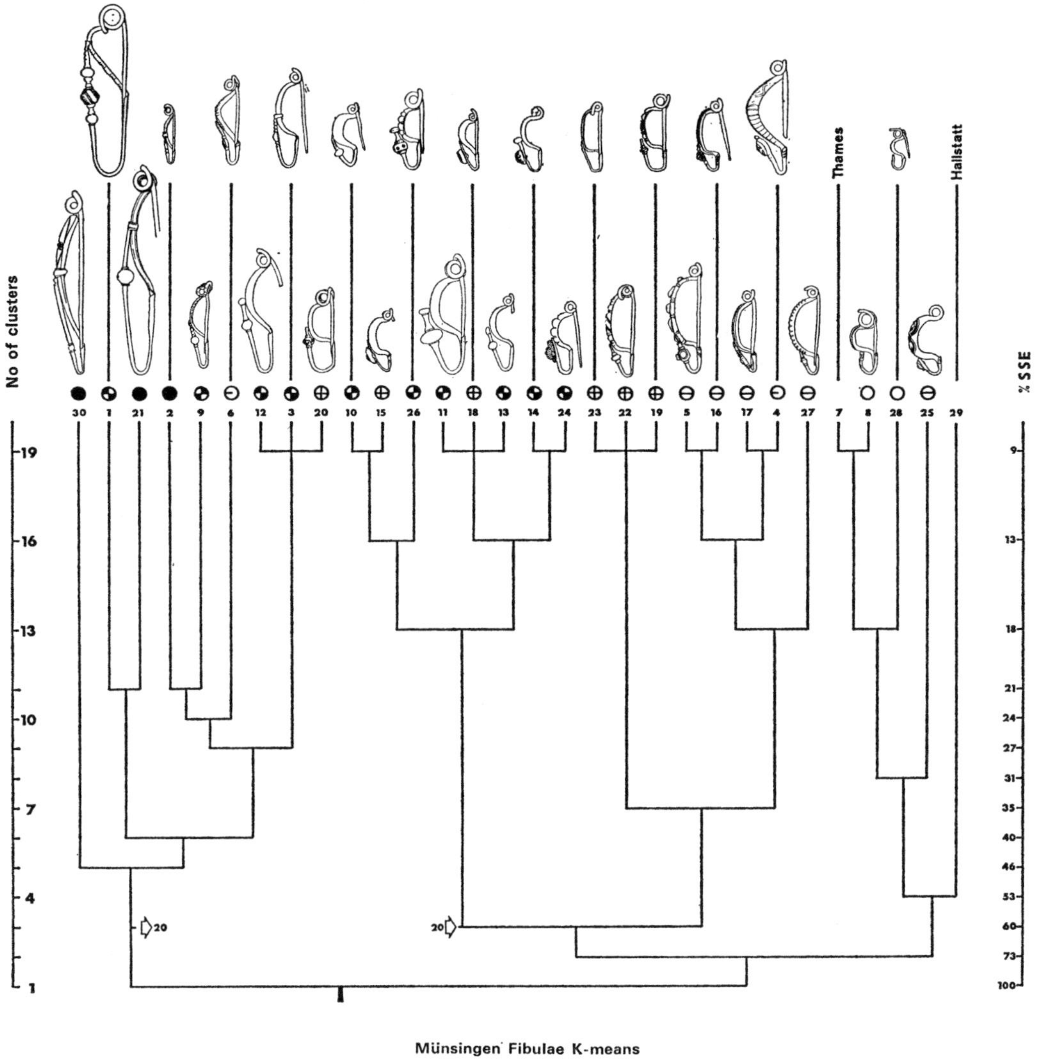

Figure 7 K-means Cluster Analysis of thirty fibulae. Symbols as for figure 2. The dendrogram results from partitioning the sample into various numbers of clusters (from two to nineteen). At each partition an attempt is made to minimize an 'error of fit' shown at the right (see also figure 9). Although represented as a hierarchy, the formation of clusters is not a single continuous process, and so fibula 20 is able to 'migrate' at the three-cluster partition

(2) *Main cycle:* (a) each unit is assigned to the current cluster centre to which it is closest (by Euclidean distance).

(b) new averages or centres are calculated for each current cluster.

(c) information about the clusters is printed out.

(3) *Splitting:* the cluster or clusters with the highest SSE are split by finding the variable with the greatest standard deviation in the cluster and dividing units into two groups according to their score on this variable.

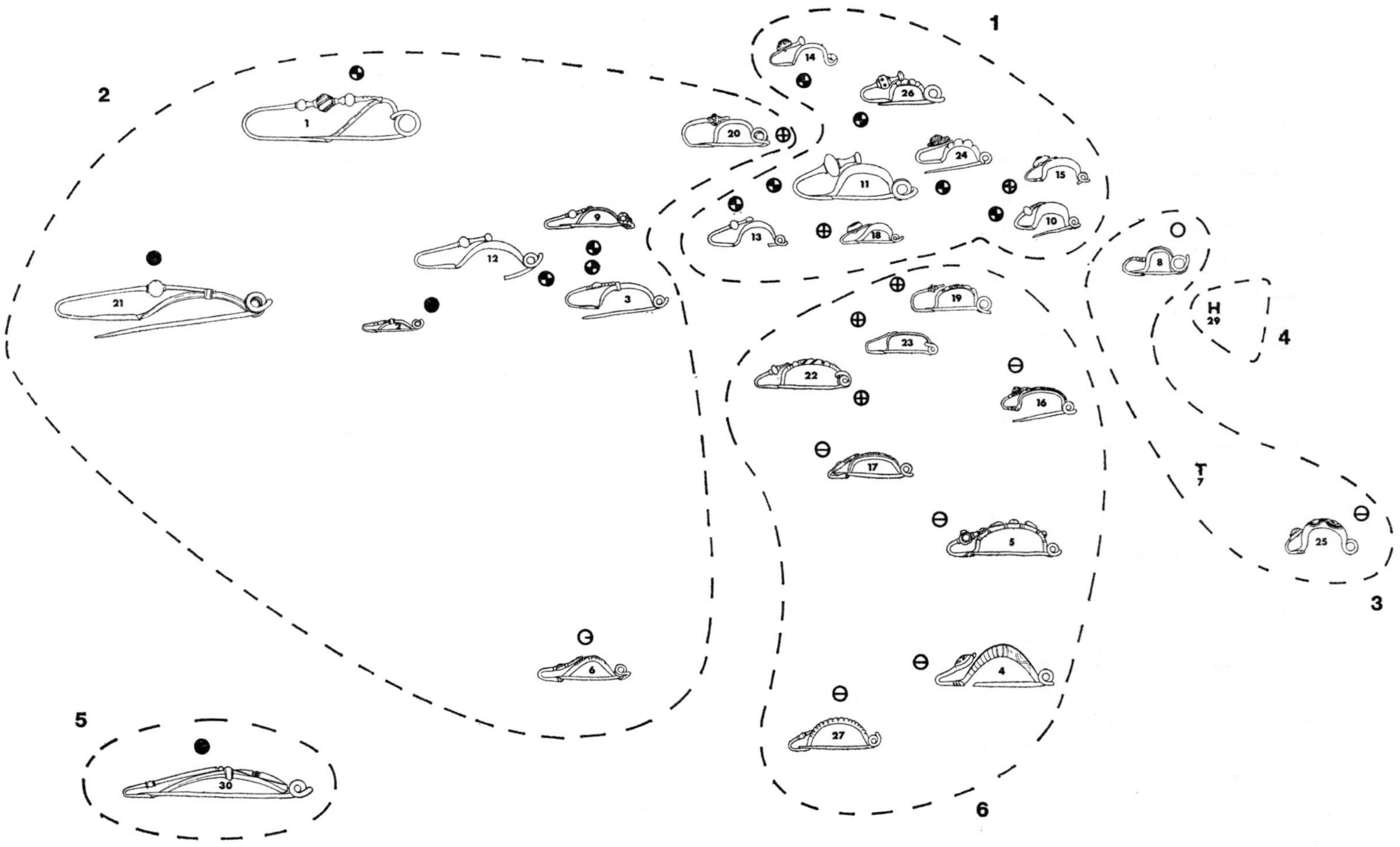

Münsingen Fibulae six clusters (K-means method) plotted against two principal components.

(4) *Lumping:* the pair or pairs of clusters that when joined minimally increase the SSE are joined.

Stage 3 or 4 is automatically followed by Stage 2.

In this form, the program is rapid and would be intended to break up a large sample into reasonable, smaller groups for more detailed study. However, the result for the small trial sample of fibulae is of some interest (fig. 7). The dendrogram is drawn up from a series of 'best' partitions for different k so that the hierarchy does not represent a continuous division or agglomeration of groups (for example, fibula 20 is able to 'migrate' at the three-cluster level). The graph of per cent SSE against number of clusters (fig. 9) shows a gradual drop in the 'error' and suggests no obvious level of significant clustering. For contrast a graph of values calculated by the same program for a standard set of Iris data (Fisher 1936) is included. Three species of Iris are involved setosa, versicolor and virginica; four measurements were taken on fifty plants of each species. Here the graph shows a marked drop at the two clusters level (where in fact the fifty setosa were separated from the rest) and a further steep drop at the three, four and five cluster levels (where this program only approximately separated the three species). This comparison between the two SSE curves highlights the lack of clear structure that must often be expected with archaeological data. In practice, in circumstances like this the archaeologist would usually be able to call on some outside evidence to help him pick a suitable level of clustering within a continuous hierarchy.

Considering that this program is intended to deal quickly with large samples, the suggested clusters of fibulae are remarkably encouraging if judged by the grouping of 'best date' symbols.

Since this type of program operates directly on a data matrix it is possible to print out a great deal of useful information about clusters during the analysis. The cluster centre itself is, of course, of great interest, representing the average score for the units it includes. The average distance of units from this centre indicates the homogeneity of the cluster. Other useful information simply calculated is a matrix of distances between cluster centres – a similarity matrix in fact that may itself be 'seriated' if desired. As an example

---

Figure 8 Clustering and ordering ('seriation'). The fibulae are 'seriated' in the first two dimensions defined by a principal components analysis. The components are calculated from a matrix of correlation coefficients between thirteen measured attributes (see figure 1). The first, horizontal component accounts for 41% of variation in the correlation matrix and is best summarized by the height of fibulae relative to total length. The second, vertical component accounts for 16·5% of the variation and is largely defined by length of catch plate. The fibulae are located in this plane by their 'score' on these components. (Thus fibula 30, with short catch plate and low bow, is located at the extremes of each component.) The rough progression of date symbols from light (right) to dark (left), i.e. from early to late, shows that the ordering on the first component is related to time. Boundaries have been added to the diagram to indicate the partition into six *clusters* given by the k-means analysis (fig. 7). Thus results from the two separate strategies (ordering and clustering) are represented together. (Fibula 28 was omitted from the P.C. analysis because of a missing value, see table 1) of this, figure 10 represents a scaling analysis of the six cluster centres suggested by the fibula analysis. This gives a seriation of *clusters.* This diagram may be compared with figure 8 where cluster boundaries for the same six clusters are shown on an ordering of the separate units (derived from a principal components analysis). The relative configuration of clusters is similar in each case.

This is a trivial example but indicates how for a very large problem a seriation of clusters (like figure 10) might be practicable where a seriation of separate units (like figure 8) might not.

Because of its versatility and its ability to tackle really large problems, the general k-means approach seems to promise much for the future.

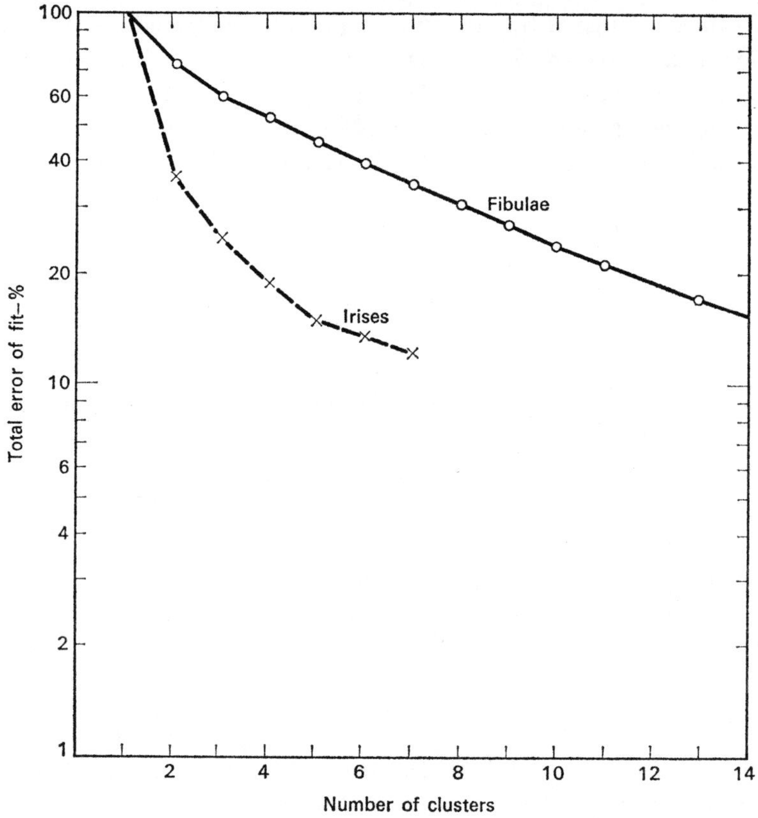

Figure 9 Clustering characteristics for two contrasting sets of data after k-means analysis, as indicated by their 'error of fit'. The 'error' for any partition is calculated in this k-means variant as the sum of squared Euclidean distances between each unit and the cluster centre to which it is closest. This value is represented here as a percentage of the 'total error' (the sum of squared distances between each unit and the total sample mean). The upper graph represents the fibula results shown on figure 7. The error of fit shows a gradual decrease as the number of clusters is increased. The lower graph shows the corresponding result for Fisher's Iris data: four measurements taken on fifty each of three species of Iris. The curve shows a rapid drop for the 2–5 cluster range which corresponds roughly with the number of species. For the fibulae, no correspondingly clear level of clustering is suggested

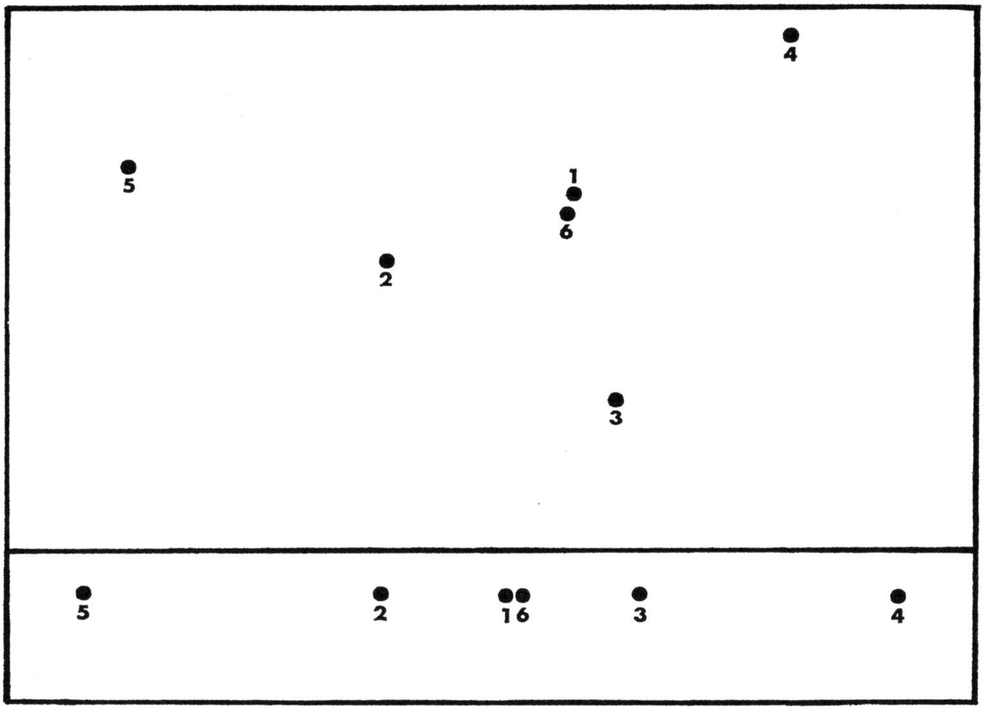

Figure 10 A seriation of clusters. The cluster centres or average values for the six clusters shown on figure 8 have been ordered in one and two dimensions by a multidimensional scaling procedure. Here, the results from one strategy (clustering) have been taken as the starting point for another (seriation). The overall position of clusters is similar to that on figure 8

4 Summary and conclusions

Although techniques of cluster analysis have developed a great deal in the last few years and although some encouraging results have been obtained with archaeological material it would seem quite premature to claim that any single method of cluster analysis had yet really proved itself as a completely satisfactory archaeological tool. It would also be unwise to play down the difficulties facing any objective attempt at archaeological taxonomy whether by numerical or any other means.

In this review four possible approaches have been demonstrated and discussed. The first three are agglomerative hierarchical techniques that attempt to define a continuous structure through the data starting with single units and amalgamating them progressively into larger and larger groups. The most simple and direct approach and one that is theoretically acceptable is Single Linkage (fig. 2), but despite attempts to reinstate this as a working technique in some fields, it is difficult to believe at the moment that Single-Linking will ever be very useful to archaeologists because of the lack of structure that it can reveal in material where intermediate, transitional units are the rule rather than the exception. From the few Double-Linkage results so far available (figs 4–6) it also seems unlikely that this theoretically attractive extension of Single Linkage will be able to deal much better with many regular archaeological situations. Average-Linkage (fig. 3) is able to suggest a useful kind of taxonomic structure with standard archaeological data, but it incorporates a tendency to make hidden, arbitrary assignments and so loses its value as a clearly controlled procedure. Although agglomerative hierarchical techniques have until recently held the field in numerical taxonomy, their future perhaps begins to look a little bleak.

A major alternative, the k-means approach, may well be more promising (figs 7–9). Here, an iterative technique attempts to find a 'best' partition into the number of groups demanded. One great attraction of this approach is that it operates directly on a data list of objects and properties and not on a stored similarity matrix. This means that information about the nature of clusters in terms of properties is always available, and also that large numbers of units can conceivably be dealt with. This is an important consideration in archaeology where many outstanding taxonomic problems do involve a very large number of units: the adequate definition of flint or pottery types, for example, or the definition of trace element groupings in metal artefacts. These are just a few very obvious examples where several thousand units are involved and where small random samples would seem inappropriate. However, the more rigorously a criterion of homogeneity for clusters is defined, the more computation time will be needed, so that even here an upper limit of units may be relatively low.

At the present time one possible approach might perhaps be to have a k-means program based on Euclidean distance (like the program described earlier) that could break down a large data set into reasonably homogeneous groups. These could then be dealt with separately by a more rigorous technique. Just what this would be for archaeological material is not clear at the moment, but a further k-means procedure could well be one answer.

Acknowledgements

The multi-dimensional scaling program was written by J. E. Doran, the Average-Linkage program by G. Shadaksharrapa. The other programs were written or adapted by the author, some during tenure of an SRC Senior Research Fellowship (1966–7). The provisional k-means program is based on the published work of G. H. Ball. All the programs were written in Atlas Algol and run on the London University Atlas Computer. I would especially like to thank Dr J. Howlett of the SRC Atlas Computer Laboratory, Chilton, Professor D. G. Kendall of the Cambridge University Department of Pure Mathematics and Mathematical Statistics and Professor I. Olkin of the Stanford University Department of Statistics for great help and encouragement in this work.

28. viii. 69

Institute of Archaeology
London

References

Ball, G. H. 1965. Data Analysis in the social sciences. *Proc. Fall Joint Computer Conference 27.* Pt I:533.

Ball, G. H. 1967. *A comparison of two techniques for finding the minimum sum-squared error partition.* Stanford Research Institute, California.

Ball, G. H. and Hall, D. J. 1965. *ISODATA, a novel technique for data analysis and pattern classification.* Stanford Research Institute, California.

Ball, G. H. and Hall, D. J. 1967. A clustering technique for summarizing multivariate data. *Behavioural Science.* 12:153.

Brainerd, G. W. 1951. The place of chronological ordering in archaeological analysis. *American Antiquity.* 16:303.

Clarke, D. L. 1962. Matrix analysis and archaeology with special reference to British beaker pottery. *Proc. Prehist. Soc.* 28:371.

Clarke, D. L. 1968. *Analytical Archaeology.* London.

Cowgill, G. L. 1968. Archaeological applications of factor, cluster and proximity analysis. *American Antiquity.* 33:367.

Doran, J. E. and Hodson, F. R. 1966. A digital computer analysis of palaeolithic flint assemblages. *Nature.* 210:688.

Fisher, R. A. 1936. Multiple measurements in taxonomic problems. *Annals of Eugenics.* 7:179.

Friedman, H. P. and Rubin, J. 1967. On some invariant criteria for grouping data. *Journal of the American Statistical Association.* 62:1159.

Gower, J. C. 1967. A comparison of some methods of cluster analysis. *Biometrics.* 23:623.

Hodson, F. R. 1968. *The La Tène cemetery of Münsingen-Rain.* Berne.

Hodson, F. R. 1969. Searching for structure within multivariate archaeological data. *World Archaeology.* 1:90.

Hodson, F. R., Sneath, P. H. A. and Doran, J. E. 1966. Some experiments in the numerical analysis of archaeological data. *Biometrika.* 53:311.

Holloway, J. D. and Jardine, N. 1968. Two approaches to zoogeography. *Proc. Linn. Soc. Lond.* 179:153.

Jardine, N. and Sibson, R. 1968. The construction of hierarchic and non-hierarchic classifications. *Computer Journal.* 11:177.

Johnson, L. 1968. *Item seriation as an aid for elementary scale and cluster analysis.* Bulletin No. 15. Museum of Natural History, University of Oregon.

Kendall, D. G. 1969. Some problems in statistical archaeology. *World Archaeology.* 1:68.

Lance, G. N. and Williams, W. T. 1967. A general theory of classificatory sorting strategies. I. Hierarchical systems. *Computer Journal.* 9:373.

Lance, G. N. and Williams, W. T. 1967. A general theory of classificatory sorting strategies. II. Clustering systems. *Computer Journal.* 10:271.

Matthews, J. 1963. Applications of matrix analysis to archaeological problems. *Nature.* 198:930.

Robinson, W. S. 1951. A method for chronologically ordering archaeological deposits. *American Antiquity.* 16:293.

Sneath, P. H. A. 1957. The application of computers to taxonomy. *J. Gen. Microbiol.* 17:201.

Sneath, P. H. A. 1966. A comparison of different clustering methods as applied to randomly-spaced points. *Classification Society Bulletin.* 1, 2:2.

Sokal, R. R. 1966. Numerical Taxonomy. *Scientific American.* 215, 6:106.

Sokal, R. R. and Michener, C. D. 1967. The effects of different numerical techniques on the phenetic classification of bees of the *Hoplitis* complex (Megachilidae). *Proc. Linn. Soc. Lond.* 178:59.

Sokal, R. R. and Sneath, P. H. A. 1963. *Principles of numerical taxonomy.* San Francisco and London.

Williams, W. T., Lambert, J. M. and Lance, G. N. 1966. Multivariate methods in plant ecology. V. Similarity analysis and information-analysis. *J. Ecol.* 54:427.

Discrimination of British Lower and Middle Palaeolithic handaxe groups using canonical variates

J. M. Graham, *with a note by* Derek Roe

The British handaxe material discussed in this paper has been assiduously collected by Derek Roe and a gazetteer of the British Lower and Middle Palaeolithic sites has been published by the Council for British Archaeology as their research report number 8 (Roe 1968a). Further publications cover the metrical approach that Roe has adopted in dealing with the handaxes, a preliminary report (1964), and a more comprehensive coverage later (1968b). In the preliminary paper Roe argues cogently for the primary study of 38 sites that 'all provide a substantial number of implements of which it can be stated with fair or clear certainty that they all belong together, that is, that they occur together within very close limits indeed of time and space' (1964: 249 and 1968b: 2). It is these 38 groups of implements (listed in table 1) that have been analysed. Archaeological details of the sites and a distribution map are given by Roe (1968b: 3, fig. 1) and are not repeated here. From table 1 it will be seen that the 38 groups give a grand total of some 4,800 axes, yet despite Roe's initial hope that all sites would provide a substantial number of implements site 4 Round Green, site 21 Holybourne and site 30 Swanscombe Upper, have only 14, 19 and 18 examples respectively. None the less, taken as a whole, the 8 measures that have been determined for each of nearly 5,000 axes provides a highly satisfactory set of data for analysis. Such a large sample is all too rare in archaeology. While Roe explains in full (1964 and 1968b) how he derived his measures, the vast body of raw data is not published but has been punched on paper tape suitable for computer input. It is this body of data which has been used in the canonical analysis.

Before examining the handaxe data in any more detail, it will be as well to have clearly in mind the questions that we are hoping to answer by its further study. The problem is not the usual one in archaeology of trying to divide artefacts into like groups or types, for the axes are already grouped according to their find-site. Instead we wish to see if the 38 assemblages can be satisfactorily distinguished purely by the 8 measured variables. It is to solve this multivariate problem of discriminating between assemblages that canonical analysis has been developed (Bartlett 1965, with references). A canonical variate is a combination of the simple measures in certain proportions, known technically as a linear combination. That is to say, it is a sum of terms of the form:

(weighting factor) × (simple measure).

The purpose of canonical analysis is to determine the weighting factors to give the best possible discrimination between groups. The canonical variates will be better discriminators between groups than any of the simple measures in isolation.

TABLE I

Identification of the British Middle and Lower Palaeolithic handaxe groups submitted to analysis

	Site name	Number of handaxes		Site name	Number of handaxes
1	Gaddesden Row (Hertfordshire)	45	21	Holybourne (Hampshire)	19
2	Bowman's Lodge (Kent)	30	22	Hoxne (Suffolk)	111
3	Stoke Newington (London)	63	23	Foxhall Road (Suffolk)	74
4	Round Green (Bedfordshire)	14	24	High Lodge (Suffolk)	68
5	Caddington (Bedfordshire)	35	25	Warren Hill *worn series* (Suffolk)	116
6	Barton Cliff (Hampshire)	110	26	Oldbury Rockshelters (Kent)	31
7	Allington Hill (Cambridgeshire)	54	27	Santon Downham (Suffolk)	100
8	Broom (Dorset/Devon)	172	28	Shide, Pan Farm (Isle of Wight)	44
9	Caversham Channel (Berkshire)	157	29	Swanscombe Middle Gravels (Kent)	164
10	Chadwell St Mary (Essex)	99	30	Swanscombe Upper Loam (Kent)	18
11	Corfe Mullen (Dorset)	45	31	Tilehurst (Berkshire)	97
12	Croxley Green (Hertfordshire)	37	32	Twydall (Kent)	55
13	Cuxton (Kent)	184	33	Wallingford Fan Gravels (Berkshire)	100
14	Dovercourt (Essex)	165	34	Whitlingham (Norfolk)	143
15	Elveden (Suffolk)	74	35	Wolvercote Channel (Oxfordshire)	47
16	Farnham Terrace A (Surrey)	40	36	Furze Platt (Berkshire)	474
17	Baker's Farm (Buckinghamshire)	239	37	Warren Hill *fresh series* (Suffolk)	641
18	Fordwich (Kent)	194	38	Knowle Farm (Wiltshire)	461
19	Highlands Farm (Oxfordshire)	200			
20	Hitchin (Hertfordshire)	80			

Handaxe data collection and previous analysis

These topics are exhaustively covered by Roe (1964 and 1968b); reference will here be confined to certain points which seem of special relevance.

The 8 variables for each of the 4,800 axes were kindly supplied by Derek Roe on 8-hole paper tape originally punched for input to the Oxford University KDF 9 computer. They were the following, given for each axe:

1	Weight in ounces	(Wt)
2	Length in millimetres	(L)
3	Breadth/Length	(B/L)
4	Thickness/Breadth	(Th/B)
5	B_1/B_2	
6	L_1/L	
7	T_1/L	
8	Thickness/Breadth	(Th/B)

Variables 1 and 2 are simple measurements taken directly from the handaxes (Roe 1968b: 23). The remaining measures have been justified in some detail by Roe (1964: 251–61), who argues convincingly that each one is vital in the discrimination of one shape of handaxe from another. These are summarized visually on figure 11 and for some a description is given below:

5 B_1/B_2 — B_1 is the breadth of the object at $\frac{1}{5}$ of its length from the point. B_2 is the breadth of the object at $\frac{1}{5}$ of its length from the butt end. The ratio is particularly sensitive to the pointedness or bluntness of the axe.

6 L_1/L — L_1 is the distance from the butt end of the widest point of the object. L is the overall length. Once more the ratio reflects the overall shape showing whether the axe is widest at butt, mid-point or tip.

7 T_1/L — T_1 is the thickness of the object at $\frac{1}{5}$ of its length from the tip. L is the overall length. The ratio gives a measure of the 'refinement' or index of the fineness of finish.

These have been calculated without the aid of a computer, and while it would be possible to check ratio 3 (B/L) for human error, ratios 5, 6 and 7 would have to go unchecked unless someone is prepared to punch the remainder of the original data on paper-tape. There is no special reason for suggesting that the ratios are wrong, but it is worth stressing the point that a computer is extremely quick and reliable when it comes to the simple matter of dividing one number by another. A human being when faced by over 25,000 divisions could be forgiven for hesitating to begin; an average modern electronic computer would complete the task in about 2 seconds.

Of these measurements T_1 was unfortunately taken only for pointed axes – that is those with a L_1/L ratio less than 0·35. Hence for ovate axes variable 7 would be zero, while variable 8 (zero for pointed axes) would repeat variable 4 Th/B. This is clearly not satisfactory as far as logical correlation of the variables is concerned, but until T_1 has been measured for the ovate axes no direct remedy is possible, other than the total omission of variable 7 and consequently of variable 8 from the analysis. This course has not been followed on this occasion, but might be in the future.

It has been shown that the data collection and selection is entirely dependent on the prior work of Derek Roe and it will be as well to complete the explanation of this by reference to his attempts to make use of the data. He made it clear that he thought of his objects as being simple and wished to 'devise effective methods of study which are correspondingly simple, and can be used and understood by anyone without special equipment or special mathematical knowledge' (1964: 251). To this end he pursued an approach

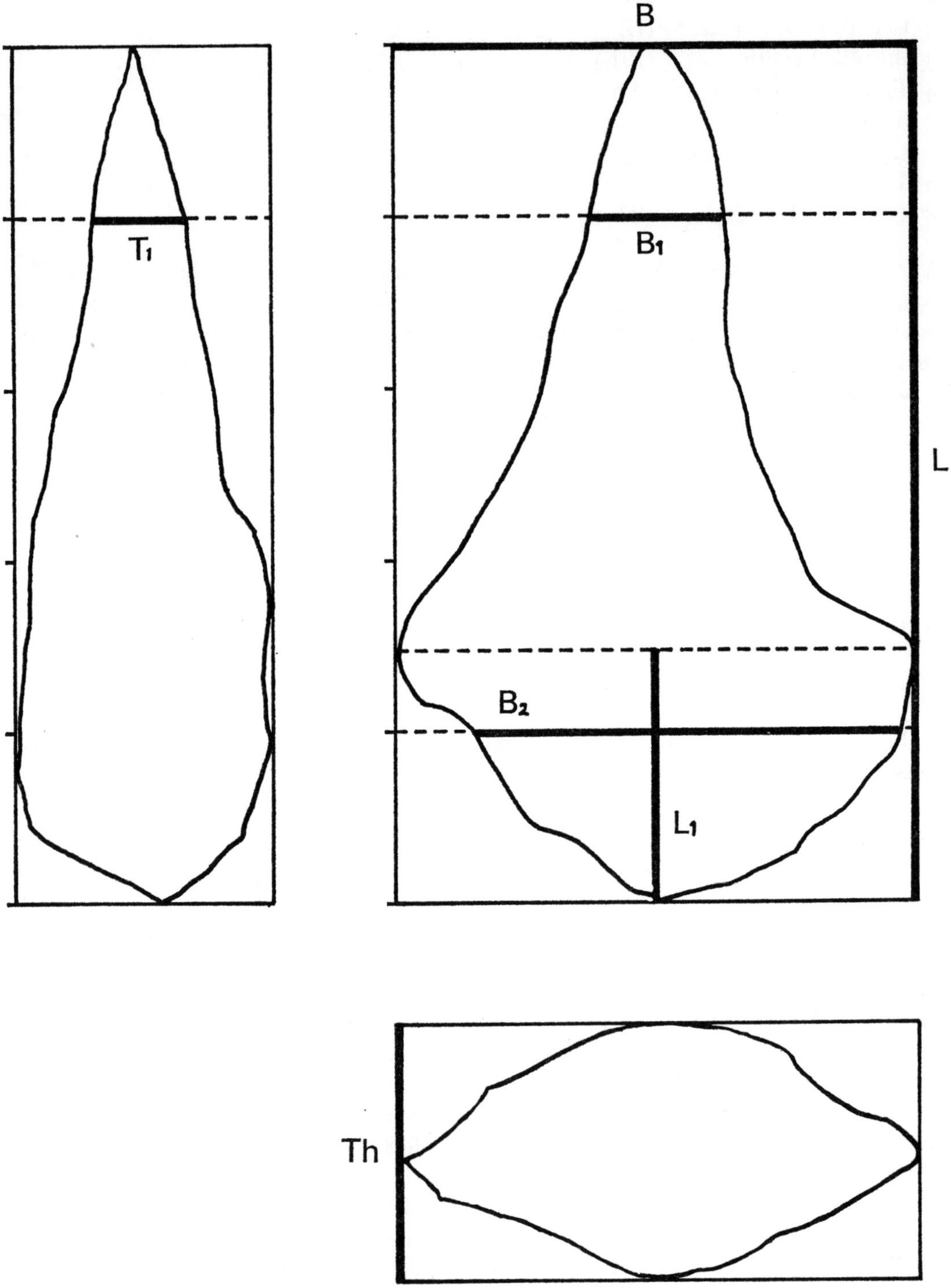

Figure 11 The original linear measurements taken from the 4,800 handaxes

where his simple measurements or ratios could be plotted, thus allowing direct visual inspection of the extent to which a measure discriminated between one shape of axe and another. In this way he selected three ratios B/L, B_1/B_2 and L_1/L to construct what he termed a tripartite shape diagram to show the complete range of outline shapes present in any group of handaxes (see Roe 1968b: fig. 4). The final result of this is a series of three B_1/B_2 against B/L plots to cover each group of axes: one for axes with high values of L_1/L (maximum width towards the point), the second for middle values of L_1/L (maximum width in the middle) and the third for low values of L_1/L (maximum width towards the butt end). These have been produced by Roe (1968b: figs 5–46) for all the 38 sites and form a major element of consideration in his later classification scheme.

Apart from a visual representation of the data Roe has also calculated the mean and standard deviation of each of the 8 variables for every group. He has then used them in a *t*-test comparing each site with each other, 'space does not permit the resulting 5,624 values of *t* to be quoted here, but they have been taken into consideration throughout the process of sorting the handaxe groups' (Roe 1968b: 26). Hence while the original measurements that Roe made were essentially simple the combination of them all into some final summary scheme is by no means so obvious. It is here in particular that it is worth seeing the data as a problem in multivariate statistics. This done, canonical analysis can be suggested as a method of considering all 8 variables from the 38 sites at once, and producing a linear combination of the variables that best distinguishes between all the groups. Having made the suggestion, which for reasons of time and tediousness is best carried out by computer, it is not meant in any way to detract from the value of the work that Roe has carried out. Indeed his explicit metrical approach might be regarded by some as revolutionary in Palaeolithic studies, which in certain quarters has not yet even accustomed itself to the legitimate use of the histogram.

Canonical analysis

This account of the method known as canonical analysis has been written for those unfamiliar with multivariate statistics. For an elementary mathematical account of the statistical calculations Seal's *Multivariate Statistical Analysis for Biologists* (1964) can be recommended. A relevant example of the application, though in the field of anthropology, is Ashton, Healey and Lipton (1957). For mathematicians a general introduction to multivariate statistics is given by Anderson (1958), while Bartlett (1965) includes a brief non-technical account of discrimination written for biologists. When canonical analysis is applied to the 38 groups of handaxes it will find a linear combination of the simple variables or measures that best distinguish between the groups. As a partial explanation it may be suggested that if a single variable were selected from two groups of objects it would be a reasonable hypothesis to expect both the means and perhaps the variances to be different for the two groups. Such a hypothetical situation is shown in figure 12*a*. Here D will be a measure of the difference between the two groups. As an example of this applied to the handaxe groups, figure 13 shows Th/B plotted as a percentage for three sites. Here both the mean values and the standard deviation for the sites are different:

		Mean	*S.D.*
31	Tilehurst	0·428	0·061
9	Caversham	0·535	0·118
36	Furze Platt	0·568	0·103

Hence the analogy with the hypothetical variable on figure 12*a* is not very close, but is sufficient to show that while it may be possible to compare a single variable for three sites by direct graphical techniques, it would be very cumbersome to attempt this for

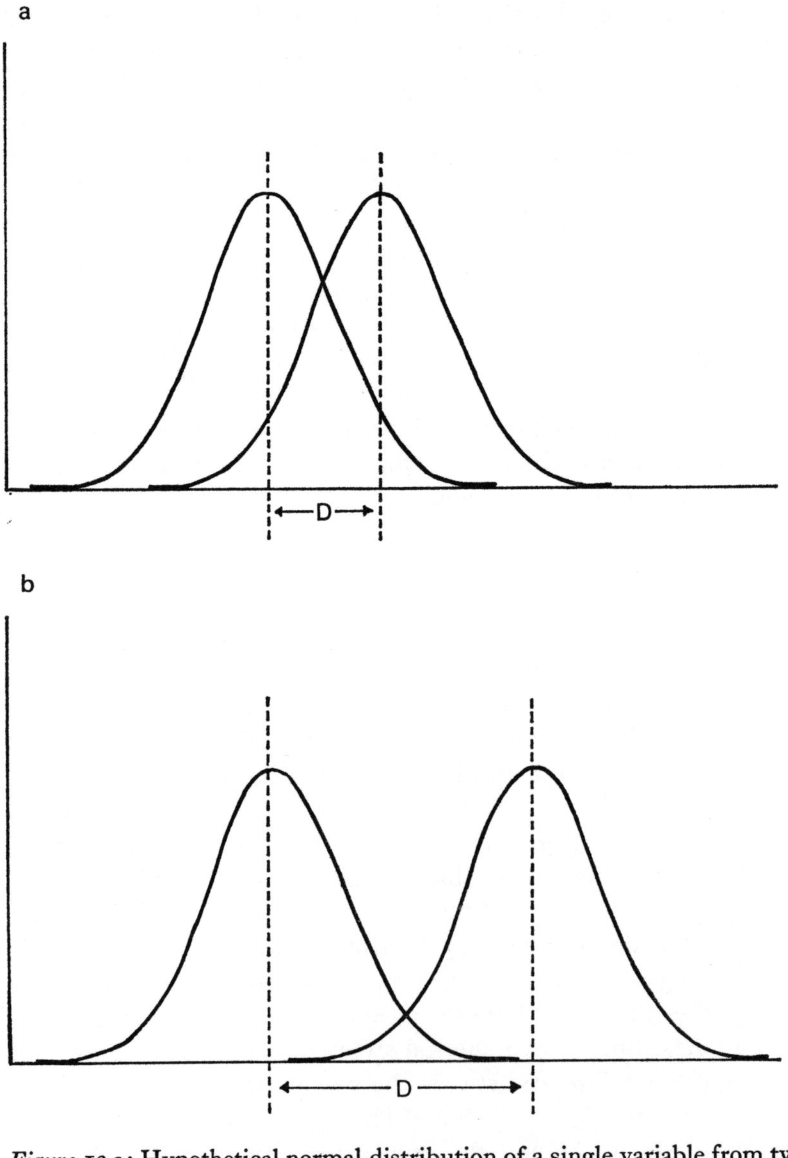

Figure 12 a: Hypothetical normal distribution of a single variable from two groups. b: Result of a combination of simple variables discriminating between groups

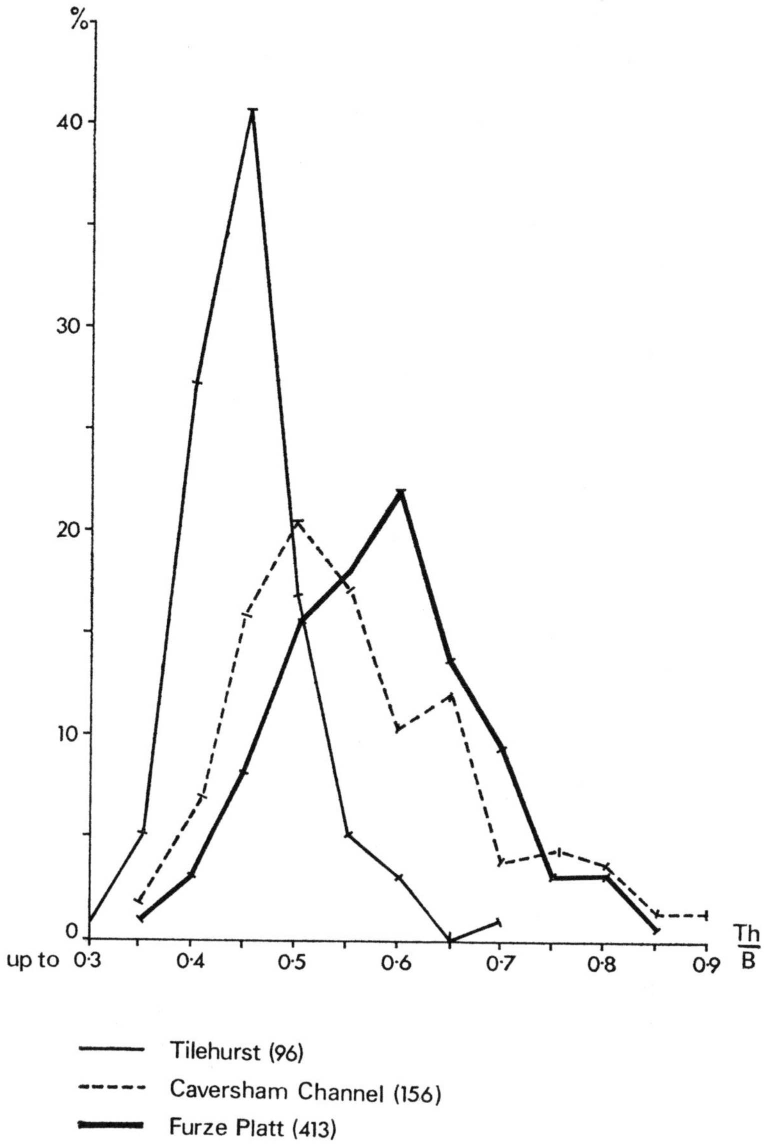

Figure 13 Percentage histogram of the ratio Th/B for three handaxe assemblages

38; the task is even more uninviting when there are 8 separate variables to consider for each site. A first step towards simplification would be to try to combine the variables in some way. This could produce the same results as shown in figure 12*a*, but if, for example, two variables were added together something closer to figure 12*b* might be seen. In other words a much bigger value for D or better discrimination. Canonical analysis extends this idea to finding a weighted sum of all the variables that gives the best possible discrimination. In the simplest case shown in figure 12*a* with a single variable and only two groups normally distributed, it is clear that the best geometric division of the two populations will be given by a point on the variable axis situated mid-way between the two means. For all

8 variables this point becomes a plane boundary in 8-dimensional space. This considerably complicates the geometric model and the type of calculations that have to be carried out.

However, the computations carried out still produce a discriminant function which is as effective as possible in separating the group means while minimizing the within group variance (that is, while minimizing the spread of values for each group; this dual objective ensures that the region where the two distributions overlap is as small as possible [fig. 12*b*.]). From the discriminant function a canonical variate, that is a weighted combination of the original variables, is produced that can be used to give a mean value that locates a particular group. The adequacy of each canonical variate can then be assessed by seeing how much of the variation it accounts for. For more than two groups several canonical variates may account for maximum variation subject to being uncorrelated with each other. Some of these will, of course, represent nothing more than random error. Hence a chi-squared test of significance has been developed to determine how many are representative of significant variation in the data.

There is no space to develop the account of canonical analysis here: for details of the theoretical statistics and some of the calculations involved, the work of M. S. Bartlett (1965) is suggested as a starting point. However, it is vital to have in mind the assumptions which the method makes for the results to be valid. For a linear discriminator to be optimal, the covariance matrices for each group should be the same – within the limits of the sampling error. There are tests for this which were applied in this case. If they are not the same then an optimal discrimination function would need quadratic terms, but a linear one will still be quite good. It is often possible, as has been carried out in this case, to make them the same with a suitable transformation. Taking logs is nearly always effective with physical measurements such as these. The tests of significance assume an underlying normal distribution, but the calculations do not, so that even if the data was to some extent non-normal the discriminant function would still be perfectly in order, but too fine an interpretation of the tests of significance would be inadvisable.

Results of the canonical variate analysis

In order to apply canonical analysis to the handaxe groups, the 8-hole paper tapes punched in KDF 9 code with the data were read into the Atlas computer and the numbers stored on magnetic tape in Atlas internal code. As a preliminary step the variables were transformed to a normal distribution by taking logs. The Discriminant Function (Canonical Variate) Analysis program (reference PS49 SSP10) written by M. R. B. Clarke of the University of London Institute of Computer Science, could then be applied to the data. The run on which the results presented here are based took only 3 minutes of computer time on the Science Research Council Atlas computer at Chilton.

In applying canonical analysis to the data in the first place it was postulated (see above) that the canonical variates would discriminate between the groups far better than a simple variable. This is confirmed by applying the statistical test known as chi-squared to the eigenvalues – one of the mathematical quantities that arises during the analysis which is directly related to the variance accounted for by that canonical variate.

Variate Number	*Eigenvalue*	*Degrees of Freedom*	*Chi-squared*
1	0·62	44	2304·7
2	0·26	42	1109·1
3	0·21	40	928·7
4	0·12	38	540·3
5	0·04	36	208·7
6	0·03	34	149·5
7	0·01	32	62·4
8	0·01	30	60·5

All the variates are significant, that is, they are better discriminators than would be expected by chance, and the first three are very highly significant. Variate 2 has about half the significance of variate 1, while variate 3 is only slightly less significant than variate 2. In other words while the first variate is very much more significant than the rest it is still wise to consider variates 2 and 3 as well.

The discriminant function is used to produce a series of weightings of the original variables, which is given below for the first three canonical variates:

Original Variable	*Variate Number 1*	*Variate Number 2*	*Variate Number 3*
1	0·74	−0·78	−0·03
2	−0·67	0·69	0·25
3	−0·89	1·37	0·18
4	1·31	1·19	1·35
5	−1·19	−0·48	1·34
6	−0·25	−0·15	−0·35
7	0·12	0·26	0·17
8	1·01	0·74	0·10

These show that the first variate is weighted to use variables 4 and 8 very heavily, both of them the ratio Th/B. This seems to be very satisfactory from the point of view of the logical duplication of the two variables that was noted in the section on data collection. Variate 2 puts more stress on variable 3, the ratio B/L, though Th/B is still very much in evidence. Finally variate 3 returns the emphasis to Th/B. Hence the analysis must at least be seen to stress the discriminatory power of the ratio Th/B.

Figure 14 has the 38 groups positioned by plotting the computed value of canonical variate 1 against canonical variate 2 (for site identification see table 1). The centres of the circles mark the group mean values; the extreme members have been very well discriminated, but can at the same time be arranged in small clusters. Figures 15 and 16 also show the groups positioned by canonical variates 1 and 2. However, this time, before the sites were plotted, the group mean was divided by the square root of the eigenvalue of the appropriate canonical variate. This correction allows a circle to be drawn centred on the group mean whose area covers 90% of the handaxe population of the group. The

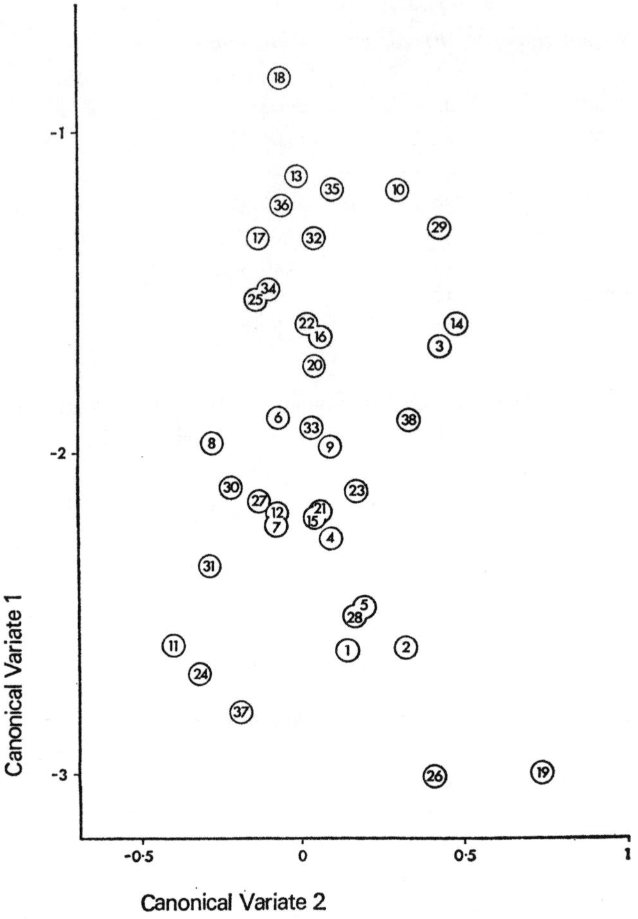

Figure 14 Handaxe groups positioned by the first and second canonical variates as calculated. For site identification see table 1

result of doing this appears as figure 16, where if two site circles do not overlap it can be safely concluded that the handaxe assemblages are significantly different from one another. Site 18, Fordwich, immediately springs to attention as it is very highly distinct from all other sites. At the same time Highlands Farm (19) and Oldbury Rockshelters (26) both stand alone but far closer to the main concentration of sites. Apart from these big contrasts it is also very easy to compare any two sites and see how closely they resemble one another in terms of the measurements of the handaxes supplied for the analysis.

However, while this may answer certain specific questions very precisely, it is difficult to carry this two dimensional picture of the handaxe assemblages in the head for reference. Instead it is most convenient to simplify this by putting them into a few discrete classes. This will also facilitate comparison with other classification schemes and correlation with other sources of evidence about the sites. It would be possible to submit some form of the canonical variates as distance measures to a further computer program which would attempt to recognize clumps or clusters in the data and so produce a classification scheme.

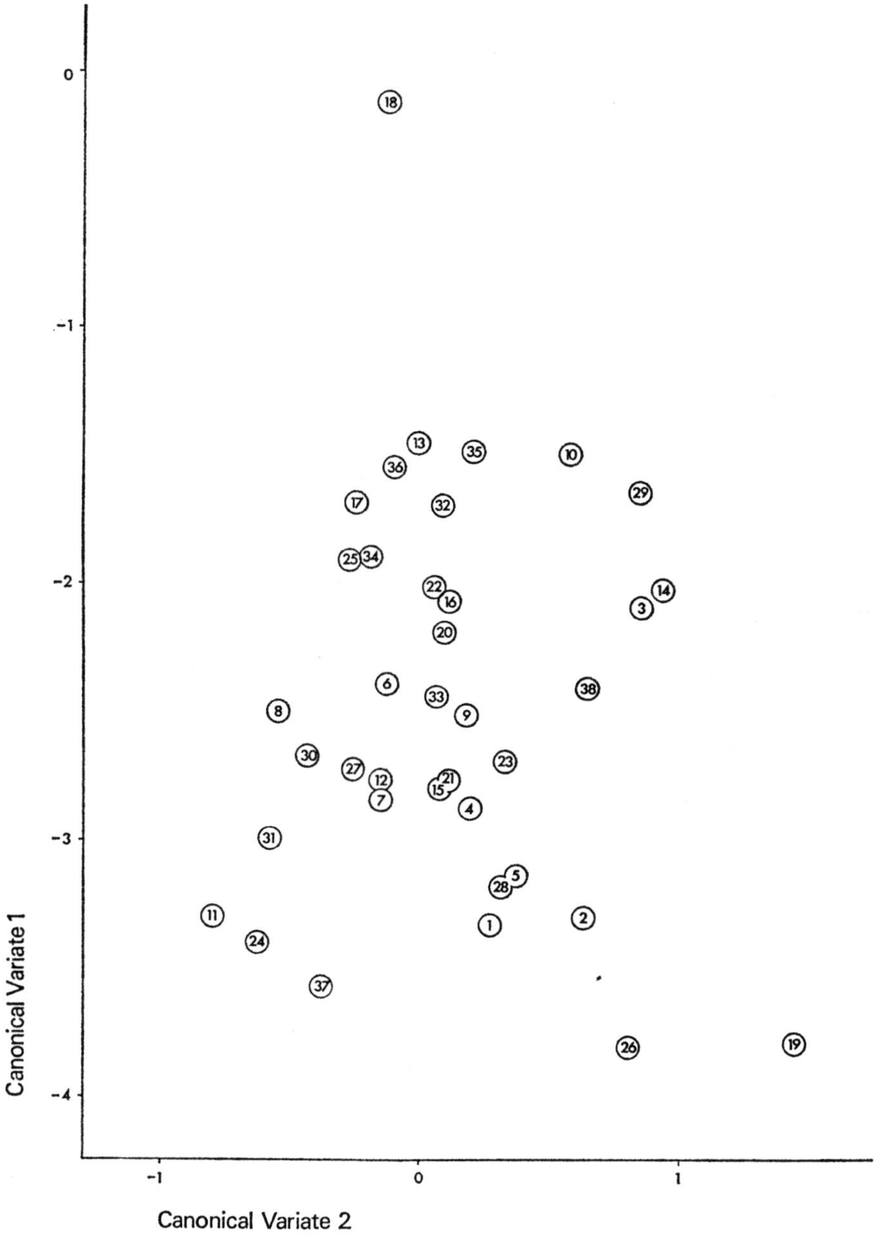

Figure 15 Handaxe groups positioned by the first and second canonical variates corrected in preparation for drawing circles that include 90% of the group population. For site identification see table 1

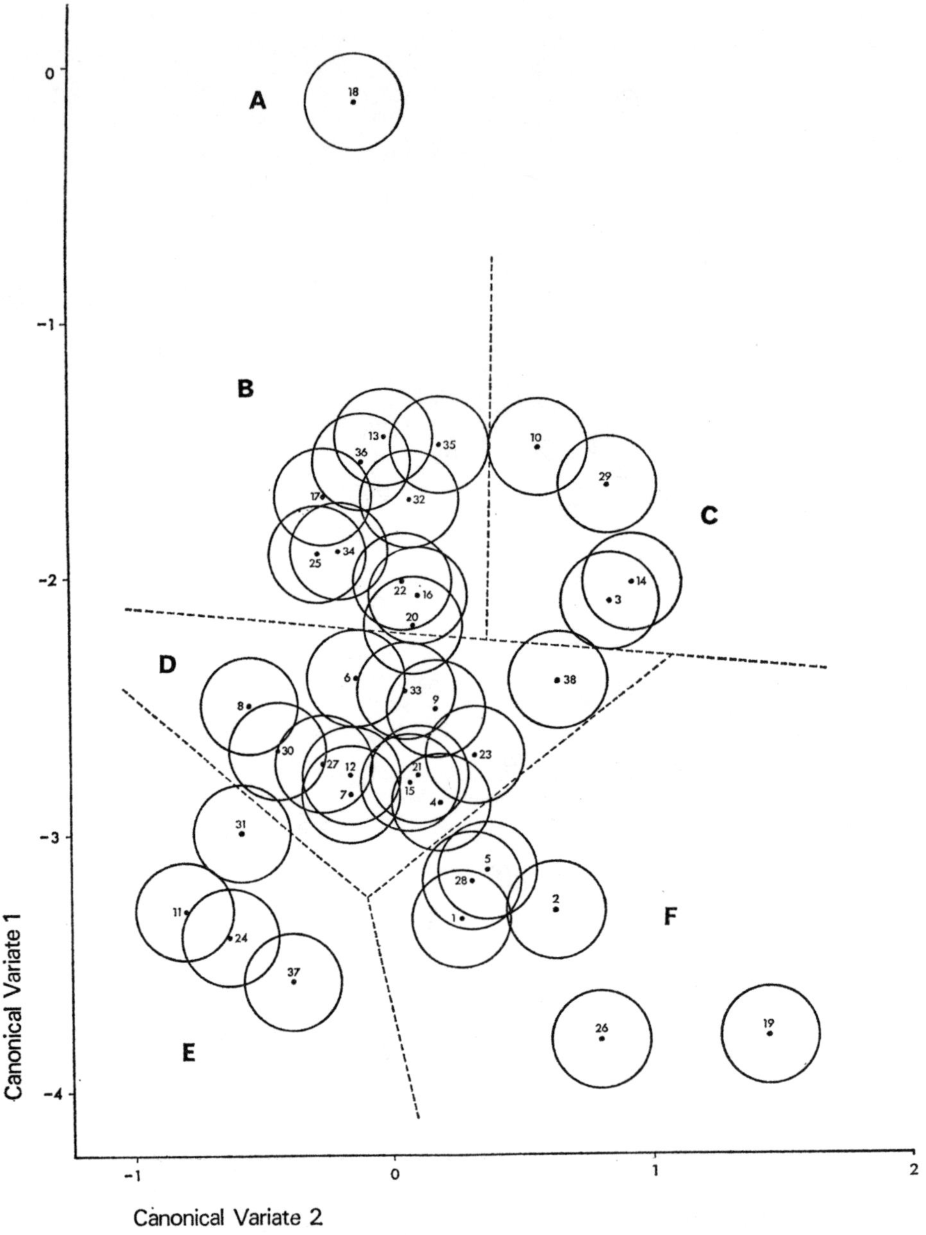

Figure 16 Handaxe groups positioned by the first and second corrected canonical variates with circles drawn to include 90% of the group population. A personal intuitive division into classes A–F is indicated with dashed lines. For site identification see Table 1

But this would not be very appropriate on this occasion as the canonical variates are essentially irreducible measures of distance. In any case our own pattern recognition abilities are far in advance of any computer program once the data has been reduced to the manageable proportions of a single two dimensional diagram which was, of course, the whole point of undertaking the canonical analysis in the first place. Hence the dashed lines of figure 16 which demarcate the bounds of a sixfold classification are not positioned by computer calculation, but by an intuitive personal attempt to make lines of demarcation follow blank areas to minimize the likelihood of misclassification. At the same time this has the effect of keeping dense areas of overlapping sites together. As a further consideration the classification was applied to the corrected plot of canonical variate 1 against canonical variate 3 (figure 17) and some sites were reclassified to fit better with this further source of evidence.

Hence a non-statistical heuristic classification, using the precise information supplied by the computer and plotted for visual inspection in figures 14–17, is given in table 2. It will be recalled that the chi-squared value for canonical variate 1 was 2304·7 while for the second variate it was 1109·1. Table 2 reflects this disparity in significant discrimination with a twofold division based on high and low values of canonical variate 1; this can be correlated with high and low values of the simple ratio Th/B (see below). The division is also convenient as canonical variates 2 and 3 do not always keep the same clusters of groups together (compare figures 16 and 17). Class A (figure 16) may seem a little anomalous with only one member, but it seems commensurate with the separation shown by Fordwich (18). The group of classes B and C are more distinct from the rest of the groups than they are from themselves. Classes B and D include two series of sites that very closely resemble one another, while class F includes two sites which stand alone. It will be recalled that reservations were expressed in the data section about Round Green (4), Holybourne (21) and Swanscombe Upper (30) because of the small number of axes from them, but from their allocation to class D it may be provisionally concluded that the small numbers have left them undifferentiated rather than producing highly anomalous results.

Finally it is as well to recall rather more precise statistics to give more meaning to the classes that have been suggested in terms of the simple variables and thus the shape of the handaxes. The most direct way of seeing this is by examining the correlation between the original variables and the canonical variates:

Number of Original Variable	*Canonical Variate Number 1*	*Canonical Variate Number 2*	*Canonical Variate Number 3*
1	0·49	−0·73	0·22
2	0·25	−0·29	0·14
3	−0·52	0·12	−0·23
4	0·66	0·38	0·58
5	−0·48	−0·29	0·75
6	−0·39	−0·17	0·48
7	−0·50	−0·12	0·56
8	0·70	0·32	−0·16

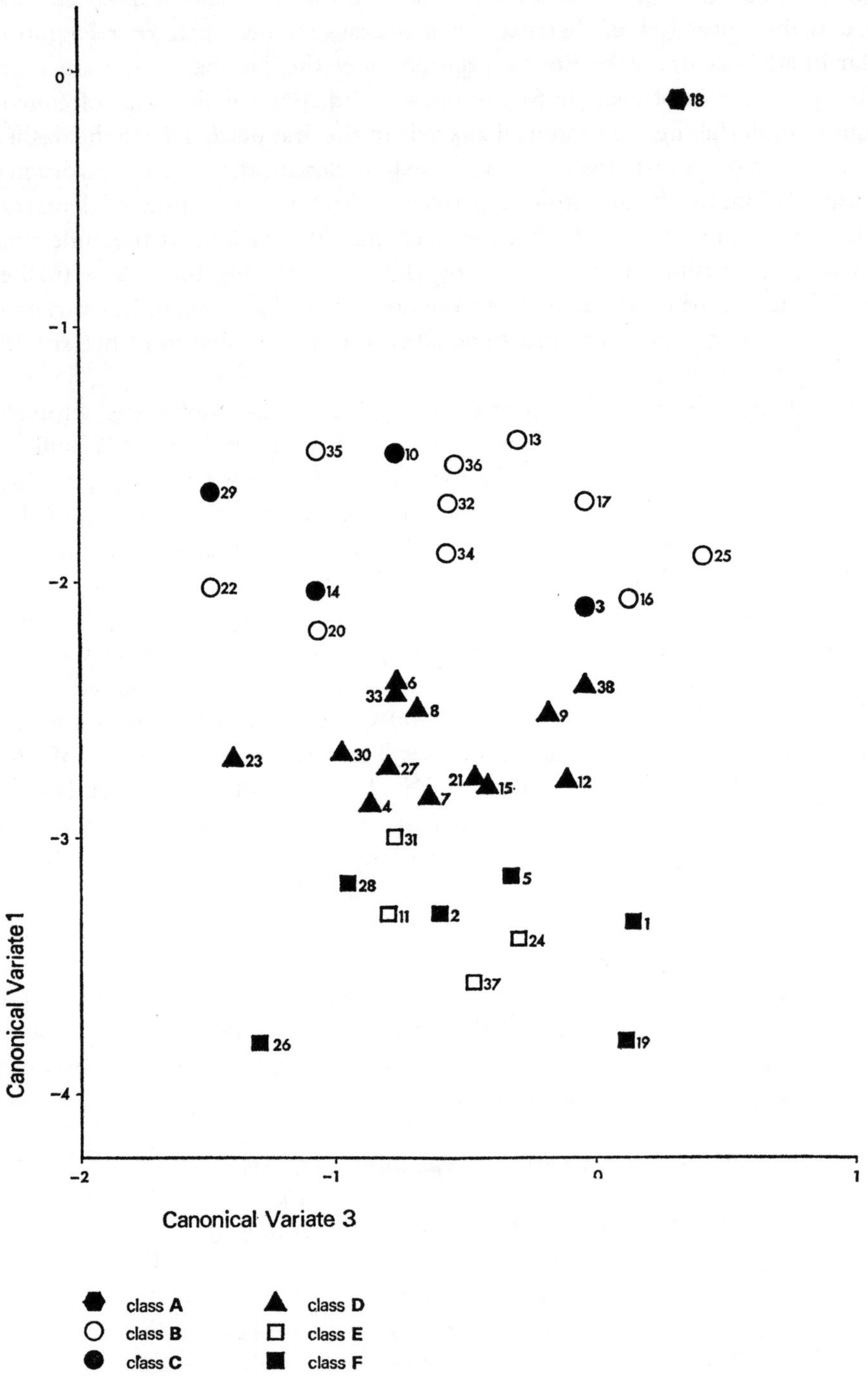

Figure 17 Handaxe groups positioned by the first and third corrected canonical variates with symbols representing classes A–F. For site identification see table 1

TABLE 2

Classification of the British Middle and Lower Palaeolithic handaxe groups by intuitive examination of the first three canonical variates

CLASS A	CLASS B	CLASS C	CLASS D	CLASS E	CLASS F
18. Fordwich	13. Cuxton	10. Chadwell St Mary	38. Knowle Farm	31. Tilehurst	5. Caddington
	35. Wolvercote Channel	29. Swanscombe Middle Gravels	6. Barton Cliff	11. Corfe Mullen	28. Shide Pan Farm
	36. Furze Platt	14. Dovercourt	33. Wallingford Fan Gravels	24. High Lodge	2. Bowman's Lodge
	17. Baker's Farm	3. Stoke Newington	9. Caversham Channel	37. Warren Hill (*fresh series*)	1. Gaddesden Row
	32. Twydall		8. Broom		26. Oldbury Rock-shelters
	25. Warren Hill (*worn series*)		30. Swanscombe Upper Loam		19. Highlands Farm
	34. Whitlingham		23. Foxhall Road		
	22. Hoxne		27. Santon Downham		
	10. Farnham Terrace A		12. Croxley Green		
	20. Hitchin		7. Allington Hill		
			21. Holybourne		
			15. Elveden		
			4. Round Green		

The first canonical variate is most positively correlated with variables 8 and 4, both the ratio Th/B. This means that the high values at the top of figures 14–17 position groups whose handaxes tend to have high values of Th/B – that is, they are thick and, if it is safe to conclude this, crude. Because of the negative correlation with variable 3 they also tend to have small values of B/L which should mean they are also relatively narrow axes. Canonical variate 2 is also most highly correlated at the positive end with variables 4 and 8 showing again the power of the ratio Th/B. The third variate on the other hand is most highly correlated with the ratio B_1/B_2 which is best thought of as representative of the blunt-endedness or pointedness of an axe, which Roe also in part expresses by the ratio L_1/L.

If a check is made of the ratio Th/B (Roe 1968b: table 11), Fordwich (18), as would be expected, has the highest mean value of 0·691. And in general there is a close correlation between the scores on canonical variate 1 and Th/B. However, Highlands Farm (19), thrown to the extreme small values on canonical variate 1 (figure 14) with Oldbury Rockshelters (26), has a mean value for Th/B of 0·515 while Oldbury has the smallest mean value of all the sites at 0·408. We do not expect an exact fit between simple variable and canonical variate, but this does seem anomalous particularly when a non-normalized data run did not place Highlands Farm with Oldbury, but between Bowman's Lodge (2), Caddington (5) and Tilehurst (31) (Graham 1968: figure 1). This may relate to the high positive weighting on variable 8 with the normalized data run, which, as was observed in the data description, is unsatisfactory both because it repeats variable 4 and also because of the zero values that occur when a measurement for variable 8 has been produced. Light may be shed on this when further runs with selected variables have been completed.

The correlations then again suggest that the simple ratio Th/B is most important as a discriminatory factor. It is noteworthy that Roe selected to use the ratios B/L, B_1/B_2 and L_1/L in his tripartite shape diagrams. Once more it would be possible to re-run the discriminant function program using these three variables only, and see how this would change the picture. It is worth stressing finally that the scores of the groups on the canonical variates shown on figures 14–17 are the results of precise calculation by computer involving over 38,000 handaxe variables; the classification summarized in table 2, and also shown on figure 16, is a personal intuitive construction constrained particularly by the desire to avoid mis-classification of assemblages rather than to distinguish many small classes.

Acknowledgements

For the material on which this study has been carried out I am much indebted to Derek Roe who has furnished me with every help when his assistance has been sought. I am very pleased to be able to append his comments on the results, which he has produced at very short notice.

The work was undertaken in the first place as part of an M.Sc. project at the London University Institute of Computer Science where I was financed by a Science Research Council Advanced Course Studentship. I have always received kindly advice from all members of staff there, and am particularly indebted to Michael Clarke who wrote the canonical analysis program and has read some of the sections of this paper. For the cultivation of my interest in archaeology I remain much in debt to all the members of the Department of Archaeology, University College, Cardiff, and particularly to Professor Richard Atkinson who first made me aware of the value of applying statistics to archaeology.

24.viii.1969

Computer Unit
University of Reading

References

Anderson, J. W. 1958. *An Introduction to Multivariate Statistical Analysis*. New York.

Ashton, E. H., Healey, M. J. R. and Lipton, S. 1957. The descriptive use of discriminant functions in physical anthropology. *Proceedings of the Royal Society*. B, 146:552–72.

Bartlett, M. S. 1965. Multivariate statistics. In *Theoretical and Mathematical Biology*, eds T. H. Waterman and H. J. Morowitz. New York. 201–23.

Graham, J. M. 1968. *Experiments in Numerical Taxonomy*. M.Sc. thesis, London University.

Roe, D. A. 1964. The British Lower and Middle Palaeolithic: some problems, methods of study and preliminary results. *Proceedings of the Prehistoric Society*. 30:245–67.

Roe, D. A. 1968a. *A Gazetteer of British Lower and Middle Palaeolithic Sites*. Council for British Archaeology Research Report 8.

Roe, D. A. 1968b. British Lower and Middle Palaeolithic handaxe groups. *Proceedings of the Prehistoric Society*. 34:1–82.

Seal, H. L. 1964. *Multivariate Statistical Analysis for Biologists*. London.

Comments on the results obtained by J. M. Graham

Derek Roe

At the close of a lecture to the Prehistoric Society in October 1967, in which I first gave the results of six years' research on the handaxe groups of the British Lower and Middle Palaeolithic, I offered to make my data available to anyone who cared to study it using more sophisticated statistical techniques than I had employed. I was delighted when John Graham accepted this offer, and I am grateful to him for the careful study he has made, using a canonical variate analysis.

The publication schedule for his paper has unfortunately left me only a very short time in which to consider the results he has obtained, so that these notes must count as a preliminary comment rather than a careful interpretation. They are mainly confined to the question of what groupings can be discerned among the 38 handaxe assemblages.

Table 3 reproduces the structure of groups and subgroups suggested in my own analysis of the 38 assemblages (Roe 1968b: 54–70). It is worth remarking at the outset that Graham's work was based solely on the metrical data, while I was able also to take into account various non-metrical criteria, notably the frequency in each assemblage of certain technological features of handaxe manufacture, especially 'S-twist profiles', deliberately twisted tips, and the use of 'tranchet finish' (1968b: 64–8). I also found the presence or absence of certain distinctive handaxe types, such as the large transverse cleavers and the '*bout coupé*' handaxes, to be important.

Graham's results are summarized in his figures 14–17, and in table 2 he has gone further, with an intuitive attempt to draw up, from the evidence of his scatter distributions, a summarizing table showing clusters of handaxe assemblages. Neither his scheme, nor my counterpart one in table 3, is really intended to be used in total isolation from the evidence and the previous stages of each argument, and each is to some extent a personal and partially intuitive summary, but they still make an interesting comparison.

Graham's scheme appears to me neither precisely similar to my own, nor drastically different. While I proposed two main handaxe shape-traditions, subdivisible into Groups, he discerns a series of Classes, some of which are inclined to overlap while others remain wholly distinct. His Classes A, B and C seem to form one constellation and Classses D, E and F another.

The ratios which most affect handaxe shape (that is, the outline shape of an implement seen in the plan view) have not played the main part in Graham's analysis, but it is interesting to find that the whole of my 'Pointed Tradition' except a single site, Foxhall Road, is included in his Classes A, B and C, together with only three of my 'Ovate Tradition' sites. The three are Fordwich, Farnham Terrace A, and Warren Hill (worn

Final sorting of handaxe assemblages by D. A. Roe (1968)

- POINTED TRADITION
  - Group I — Pointed handaxes with cleavers
    - Furze Platt
    - Baker's Farm
    - Cuxton
    - Whitlingham
    - Twydall
    - Stoke Newington
  - Group II — Pointed handaxes with ovates
    - Sub-Group A
      - Swanscombe Middle Gravels
      - Chadwell St Mary
    - Sub-Group B
      - Hoxne
      - Dovercourt
      - Hitchin
    - Attributed to Group II
      - Foxhall Road
  - Group III — Pointed handaxes (plano-convex technique)
    - Wolvercote
- (INTERMEDIATE)
  - Group IV — No clear shape preference
    - Broom
    - Santon Downham
    - Barton Cliff
    - Wallingford
- OVATE TRADITION
  - Group V — Coarse, narrow, irregular handaxes
    - Fordwich
    - Farnham Terrace A
    - Warren Hill (*worn series*)
  - Group VI — Ovates, tending to more pointed shapes
    - Sub-Group A
      - Knowle Farm
    - Sub-Group B
      - Elveden
      - Allington Hill
    - Sub-Group C
      - Bowman's Lodge
      - Tilehurst
    - Sub-Group D
      - Oldbury
      - Shide (Pan Farm)
    - Attributed to Group VI
      - Holybourne
      - Round Green
      - Swanscombe Upper Loam
      - (Caversham)
  - Group VII — Ovates, tending to rather blunt-ended shapes
    - Gaddesden Row
    - High Lodge
    - Warren Hill (*fresh series*)
    - Highlands Farm
    - Croxley Green
    - Corfe Mullen
    - ?Caddington

series), which comprised my Group V; they can all be argued geologically as 'early' sites, perhaps pre-Hoxnian. I found these three industries to be somewhat generalized, as opposed to the very strong preference for specific handaxe shapes seen at, for example, Swanscombe (Middle Gravels) or Gaddesden Row, although 'ovate types', as I defined them metrically, were in the majority in all three cases. I wrote that 'While these three sites all belong to the Ovate Tradition, their industries (especially that of Fordwich) incorporate plenty of archaic-looking handaxes which are specifically pointed types' (1968b: 71).

Graham separates Fordwich, in his Class A, from the other two, which both fall in his Class B. There is no doubt that Fordwich is the most striking handaxe assemblage of classically archaic appearance in Britain (heavy, thick, narrow handaxes, lacking all technological refinement). It is also the largest and best sample amongst those three sites. I considered that the other two approached it in morphology, and placed them in the same Group; it would be quite satisfactory from the archaeological point of view to pick Fordwich out from among them, but perhaps less so for Farnham Terrace A and the Warren Hill worn series to occur in the same cluster as Hoxne, Whitlingham, the Wolvercote Channel and the rest of Graham's Class B. It is worth remembering here, and in all cases where our groupings differ, that I chose as my starting point for sorting the assemblages handaxe outline shape (based on a combination of B/L, B_1/B_2 and L_1/L), whereas Graham's statistical methods suggested in the course of his work that emphasis should be placed on some of the other original variables, notably Th/B.

The whole of my Pointed Tradition Groups I and II, except Foxhall Road, are included in Graham's Classes B and C. As regards Foxhall Road, I had only attributed it to my Group II after hesitation (1968b: 61–9, 74), being aware that it had a certain 'intermediate' character. Graham's placing of it in his Class D, and its location on his figures 16 and 17 are therefore of considerable interest. The rest of my Groups I and II reappear somewhat in disarray, though I see that in figures 16 and 17 some of the sites which I placed close together remain so (e.g., Swanscombe Middle Gravels (29) and Chadwell St Mary (10); Cuxton (13), Baker's Farm (17), Furze Platt (36), Whitlingham (34) and Twydall (32)). The Wolvercote Channel (35) assemblage (the single site forming my Group III) does not stand out as something separate, not surprisingly, since Graham was not concerned with the technological (non-metrical) evidence. The Wolvercote industry specialized in pointed handaxes made by a distinctive 'plano-convex' technique, and had no proper cleavers or ovates. I have suggested that it is likely to be of relatively late date (1968b: 73), and if this is correct it could even conceivably be separated from Farnham Terrace A and/or the Warren Hill worn series by a couple of hundred thousand years.

My uncertain 'Intermediate Group' (Group IV), and the whole of my Ovate Tradition, except the three Group V sites already discussed, fall within Graham's Classes D, E and F. It is interesting to see that the Intermediate Group sites remain fairly close to each other in figures 16 and 17, and that the Group has survived intact in Graham's Class D. These four sites were 'intermediate' in the sense that they showed no clear preference for ovate or pointed handaxe shapes, such as is usually found, but they were also the four sites in which the evidence for the unmixed nature of the sample was weakest. Also in Class D fall the three numerically weak but otherwise pure assemblages, Round Green

(4), Swanscombe Upper Loam (30) and Holybourne (21), of which I could make little owing to the small sample size. Here too is to be found the Caversham Channel (9) sample, which was deliberately drawn from several different gravel pits, and was included only to test certain specific archaeological hypotheses (Roe 1968b: 11–12). In fact, all the dubious or intermediate assemblages have gravitated to Graham's Class D in table 2; their individual positions should also be studied on figures 16 and 17. There is little more that can be said of them, except to make the point that none of them really seems to be redirected by Graham's analysis towards any of the more satisfactory Groups I proposed, and also to note that Foxhall Road (23), where the unity of the assemblage and hence the validity of the sample do not seem to be in doubt, has joined them.

Within my Ovate Tradition, apart from the 'early' sites of Group V already discussed, I discerned two other groups, though I thought that the distinction between them was somewhat fine: Group VI, where the ovate handaxes had a tendency to be of rather more pointed shape, and Group VII, where they were rather more blunt-ended. Some independent support for this division was also forthcoming from the non-metrical evidence I studied. Graham's analyses have tended to redistribute the sites of my Groups VI and VII, and in table 2 they fall variously in his Classes D, E and F. I see again that some of the assemblages which seemed to me most like each other have remained close together in some of the diagrams at least – for example, Allington Hill (7) and Elveden (15), or Corfe Mullen (11), High Lodge (24) and the fresh series from Warren Hill (37). Others, however, have not, such as Bowman's Lodge (12) and Tilehurst (31). I am glad to see that Shide Pan Farm (28) and Oldbury Rockshelters (26) remain reasonably close together, since I regarded both of these as Mousterian industries, linked, apart from the morphology of their handaxes, by the presence of the '*bout coupé*' handaxe type, of well made flake tools and of Levalloisian technique. The other thirty-six sites are all Acheulian.

Caddington (5) seemed to me to fall somewhat between my Groups VI and VII, and I could only place it tentatively in Group VII after discussion (1968b: 59, 67). The redistribution of the Group VI and VII sites in Graham's diagrams does not cast much further light on this situation, and in his summary table he has placed Caddington in his Class F; of the other five sites in that Class, three belonged to my Group VI and two to my Group VII.

The most puzzling feature to me of Graham's results, as regards my Ovate Tradition sites, is the way in which the Highlands Farm (19) assemblage has been pushed out to an extreme position in most of the diagrams, e.g., figure 16. I myself did not find the morphology of the Highlands Farm handaxes to be of an 'extreme' character in any direction. It seems perfectly reasonable to me that Fordwich (18) should be similarly pushed out from the main concentration of assemblages (figs 14–17), since the industry there did have several extreme features, especially its high mean for the Th/B ratio. Oldbury (26) is also an outlying site on most of Graham's scatter diagrams; the Oldbury handaxes were the smallest, broadest and flattest of all the 38 assemblages – that is to say, the Oldbury mean values for Length and Weight were the lowest of all, and those for B/L and Th/B were the highest and lowest respectively. But the Highlands Farm industry offered no such extremes, and I would be glad to have its position on Graham's diagrams more satisfactorily explained.

Various further comments could doubtless be made, after further study, on Graham's and my respective placing of individual sites, and the reader will doubtless pick out other points of interest by studying the various diagrams and comparing the two tables. Space unfortunately does not permit me to recapitulate here the archaeology of the 38 sites, or such facts as are known about their relative chronology; these subjects are dealt with in my recent account of the British handaxe groups (1968b).

In general, the results which Graham and I have obtained in our different ways from the same body of data seem to be in reasonably good agreement. But ultimately, if there is to be a real understanding of which handaxe industries lie closest to each other in the British sequence, such metrical and statistical studies as these cannot be regarded as a complete substitute for the filling of the appalling gaps in our knowledge of the relative chronology of the assemblages under discussion. To propose a pattern of morphological likes and unlikes is not necessarily to solve problems of chronological and cultural relationships. The need for more information about the Pleistocene geology of the British Palaeolithic sites is only too obvious, and there are many other problems. For example, may some handaxe industries, which do not resemble each other morphologically, be contemporary activity-variants made by the same people? Part of the answer to this might be forthcoming in specific cases from precise geological dating, which would demonstrate the contemporaneity or otherwise of the assemblages, but another useful approach might be to cast light on the actual uses of the different handaxe types by microscopic study of the utilization and wear traces on perfectly fresh examples. This kind of study is still in its infancy in Britain. These and other approaches to the outstanding problems of the earlier Palaeolithic should have at least as much to contribute in the coming years as simple or sophisticated statistical studies like the two examples to which these comments relate.

20.viii.69

Department of Ethnology & Prehistory
University of Oxford

The production of pottery from a Romano-British kiln site: a statistical investigation

C. R. Orton

1 This paper describes some statistical analyses of archaeological material (waster sherds) from a late first- and early second-century Romano-British kiln site. The assumptions underlying the use of statistical techniques are discussed, and a particularly useful test for comparing frequency distributions (the Kolmogorov-Smirnov test) is described. This test could be of much wider application than that described in this paper; for example, it could be of use in dealing with measurements of flint flake and blade assemblages. Higham (1968) mentions its use in a study of the bones of prehistoric European domestic fauna.

During the 1967 and 1968 seasons some two tons of pottery were excavated from the kiln site in London's Highgate Wood (Brown and Sheldon 1969a), consisting of wasters found under the following circumstances:

(a) on a pottery waster dump,

(b) in pits, probably originally dug to provide clay, and later filled with rubbish,

(c) associated with the kilns,

(d) as a scatter, seemingly disturbed and probably derived from the dump.

So far, some 14% of this material has been examined by students in archaeology classes at the City Literary Institute and Camden Adult Institute, priority being given to finds from those areas which appeared to have been least disturbed. For purposes of this analysis six groups are considered:

(a) from the base levels of three parts of the dump,
(i) trench 2, level 3,
(ii) trench 3, level 3,
(iii) trench 6, level 3,
(b) from two of the pits, (iv) trench 8, feature 3,
(v) trench 33, feature 1.
(c) from the furnace area of one of the kilns, (vi) trench 24, kiln 3.

For ease of reference these lots will be referred to as L2, L3, L6, etc. Finds from other levels were examined but not included in the analysis because the amount of pottery in them was too small to be useful. L24 was almost as poor, and was omitted from part of the analysis.

The rim sherds could readily be divided into five categories (plus those too worn to be identified), each of which was closely correlated with a particular form of vessel. As the identification of bases or body sherds with form of vessel is far more problematical, this analysis is restricted to rim sherds.

Category	*Rim shape*	*Form of vessel*
1	lipped everted	shouldered jars with pronounced necks
2	unlipped everted	beakers (and jars with beaker-like rims)
3	beaded	shouldered jars with restricted necks
4	horizontal, grooved	bowls and dishes with internal lid grooves
5	horizontal, without grooves	bowls and dishes without lid grooves

Some drawings of representative pots of the various categories are shown in figure 18.

2 Work already done on this material has been described by Brown and Sheldon (1969b). The statistical work is based on the distribution of diameters of each shape of rim in each lot. Allowance has been made where possible so that vessels represented by more than one rim sherd are only counted once. Table 1 shows the numbers of rims of each shape in each lot (Appendix 1).

The distributions of each shape by diameter are given in tables 2(i)–2(iv). The distribution of category 3 is not given as no analysis of these rims was attempted. Diameters are expressed in one-inch groupings, e.g. 5″–6″, 6″–7″ and so on. The distributions can be illustrated by histograms (Brown and Sheldon 1969b) or by cumulative distributions (see graphs 1, 3, 5 and 6) (Appendix 2). These graphs can be read by taking a particular diameter (e.g., 7″) and finding the height at which the graph crosses the 7″ line (e.g., 80%). Then 80% of the rims of that shape have a diameter of less than 7″. The proportion of rims with diameters between, for example, 6″ and 7″ can be found by reading off the proportions for 'less than 6″' and 'less than 7″' and subtracting.

Although cumulative distributions give a less immediate visual impression than histograms, they have two useful analytical advantages. First, the median diameter (that exceeded by 50% of the rims) can be read off instantly, and second, a statistical test for comparing distributions (the Kolmogorov-Smirnov test) can be applied to them. It will be described in a later section.

3 The first stage of any statistical analysis is the construction of a model, or set of assumptions, which will provide a framework in which the analysis takes place. Very often this is not done formally, or even consciously, but in this case a discussion of possible assumptions is needed to show why certain techniques can be used, and how different assumptions lead to different treatments.

Since we are interested in the actual production of pottery, rather than the wasters resulting from it, the first assumptions must be about waster rates, that is, the relationship between the surviving waster rims and the original production. In mathematical terms, we can represent this relationship by means of a survivor function S, which would equal the number of surviving waster rims divided by the number of pots actually produced. S will depend first on the form (f) of the vessel, and within each form it will

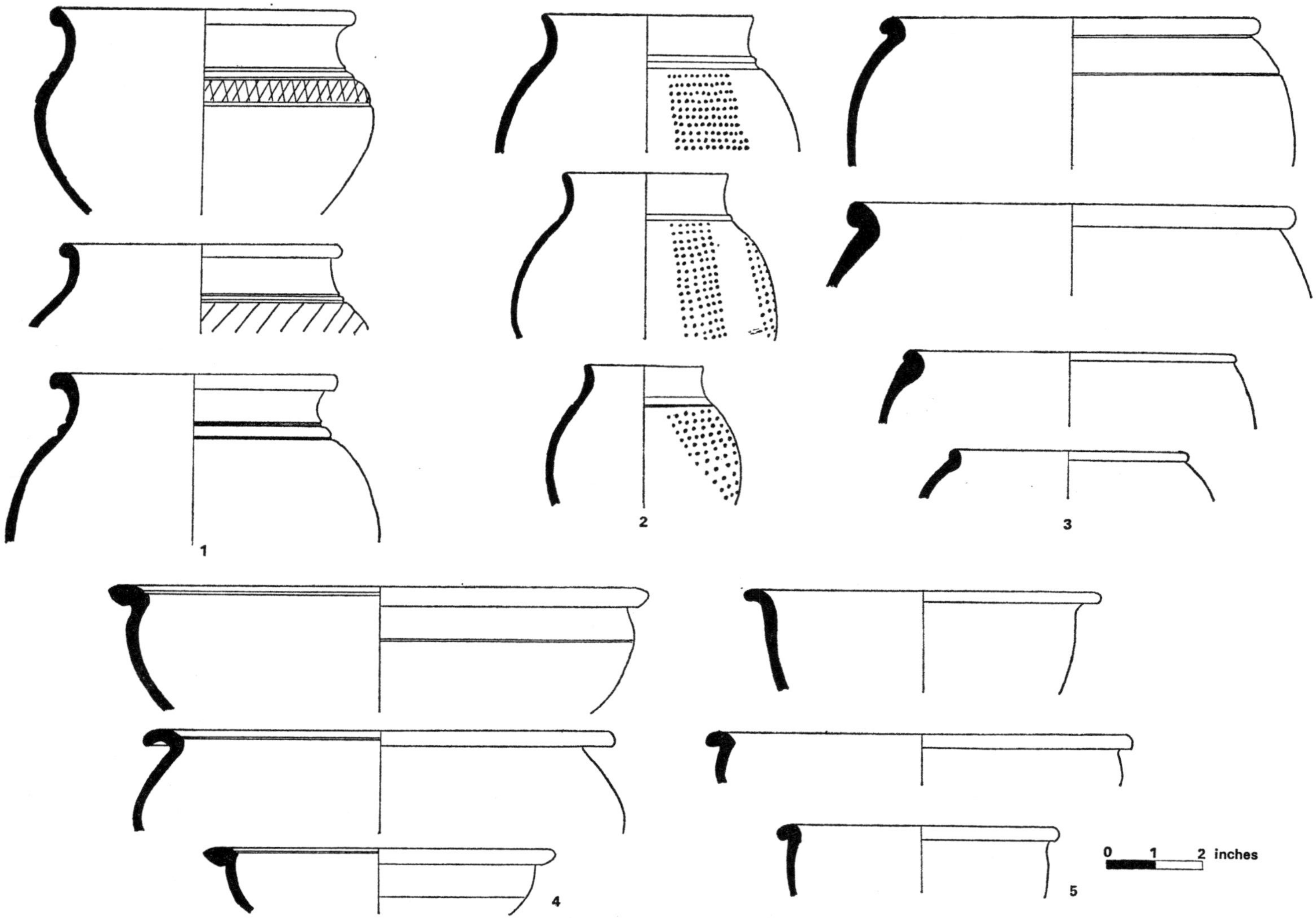

Figure 18 Some examples of the Highgate pottery. Scale in inches

depend on the rim diameter (d); it will quite possibly depend on time (in a fairly long-term sense: technical improvements over a period of years might lead to a lower waster rate, for instance). It will also be subject to random fluctuations, due to variations in the raw material, firing conditions and accidents. We can express all this neatly in the equation $s = S(f, d, t) + e$, where e expresses the random element, and s is the rate for one firing; over a large number of firings the random terms would have an average of zero.

Different assumptions about the nature of S – which cannot be observed directly – enable us to draw different sorts of conclusions about the pottery produced. For example, if we assume that S does not depend on the form of the vessel, then production of equal quantities of jars and beakers would result in the discovery of equal quantities of jar and beaker rim sherds, and by working backwards from our discovered rims we could make statements like '40% of the total production consisted of jars'. Further, if we assume that S is independent of rim diameter, we are able to say '50% of the jars produced had a rim diameter of 8″ or less', or the like. And if we assume the independence of S from time, statements like 'beakers become progressively less important in the production' are possible.

These are called 'first-order assumptions' because they concern only one of the variables: form, diameter or time, 'second-order assumptions', concern changes in S due to two variables. An example is the assumption that the relationship between S and the diameter does not depend on the form – in statistical terms there is no diameter × form interaction.

This statistical analysis is based on the second-order assumptions that there are no form × time or diameter × time interactions (i.e. in the former case this means that if the waster rate of jars decreased as time passed, the waster rate of other kinds of pottery would decrease similarly). In fact, it is doubtful that the site was in operation for long enough for any time-effects to have become apparent, other than short-term random fluctuations.

4 The second part of the model concerns the stratigraphy, or lack of it, of the site. We cannot assume that we are dealing with sealed layers, and chronological considerations are of less immediate importance than usual. In general, at Highgate and probably at other similar kiln sites, a level, instead of being an independent entity, 'given' in the nature of the site, becomes an arbitrary unit of excavation, particulary in the areas where a large horizontal spread of rubbish is cut by several trenches. A dump area may have been built up over a period of time by the throwing out of wasters to no set pattern; one here, another there, a lot from a firing accident next to them, the whole lot shovelled back to keep a path clear, and so on. It would be dangerous to look for sequences or trends in such a jumble.

It is just possible that the disorganizing process at work in the gradual accumulation of a rubbish dump would so mix the material that it became homogeneous, and subject only to random variation. Before attempting any analysis it was necessary to test statistically that this was not so – a chi-squared test on table 1 showed significant differences from homogeneity, both in the dump and between it and the pits.

Finally, we must tie together these two sets of ideas, about the unit of production (the firing) and the unit of excavation (the layer). After each firing, the wasters (a proportion of the production represented by our survivor function *S*) are thrown together onto a dump, not necessarily near to the previous dumping. The sort of effect postulated can be seen in the dumping of wheelbarrows full of different soils on a spoil heap. As the dump is cut, shovelled and variously disturbed, the sherds of a particular firing will tend to become more dispersed, but not so much as to become randomly distributed throughout the dump. The experience of beating a cake demonstrates that very vigorous mixing is required before homogeneity of the ingredients in the mixture is achieved. When the dump is excavated, any chosen area will probably contain the 'dense' parts of a number of dumpings, plus odd sherds and intermediate amounts from other nearby dumpings. Nearness in space does not imply nearness in time. While there will not in general be time differences, in the accepted sense, between the levels, such differences as exist are due to time, in the sense that they are the product of short-term variations in production and waster rates.

5 Within this framework, we can begin to examine our data (tables 1 and 2, graphs 1, 3, 5 and 6). We have already seen that the differences in table 1 are significant, and we must now ask two questions about the cumulative distributions:

(i) are these distributions of waster sizes meaningful in terms of the actual production?

(ii) could the differences between the distributions of different lots have arisen simply by chance?

(i) A single distribution curve means little in terms of the production, because the survivor rate *S* may well vary with diameter, and the curve will not represent the distribution curve of the pots produced. However, if we have two such curves, for the same rim-form from different lots, the relationship between the two will correspond to the relationship between the hypothetical curves for the production, because any differences in *S* at one diameter will necessitate similar changes in *S* at the other diameters, under the 'no diameter × time interaction' assumption. We cannot compare distribution curves for different forms from the same lot (because there may be a form × diameter interaction), but we can, by comparing two sets of distribution curves (like graphs 1 and 3) which relate to different forms, come to conclusions about the production as a whole.

(ii) We wish to test whether our cumulative distributions for any one category could all have arisen by chance from the same 'parent' distribution of rims, or whether the differences between them reflect differences in the manufacture of pottery. A similar question arises frequently in other fields of archaeology, for example in dealing with the dimensions of flakes and tools from different Palaeolithic assemblages. A simple test of the hypothesis that the parent distributions of two of our sample distributions are the same is the Kolmogorov-Smirnov test. The two sample distributions are plotted on a graph, with the vertical scale adjusted to read '1' at the 100% line (see fig. 19), and the maximum vertical distance D between the two graphs is measured. There are tables of 'critical values' of *D* for various sample sizes (Massey 1952) and if the measured *D* exceeds the critical value the hypothesis is rejected.

In figure 19, for example, about 80% of sample (a) but only 40% of sample (b) have a diameter of 7″ or less. The maximum value *D* occurs just below the 8″ diameter, and is about 0·45. If the numbers of rims in the samples (n and m, say) are large (over 30) the critical value for D is equal to:

$1{\cdot}36\sqrt{(n+m)/nm}$ for the difference to be significant at 95% confidence level
or $1{\cdot}63\sqrt{(n+m)/nm}$ for the difference to be significant at the 99% confidence level (Smirnov 1948).

Suppose in our example $n=m=100$, these citical values are about 0·19 and 0·24 respectively, so we would reject the hypothesis.

The data as recorded are 'grouped'; that is, instead of recording individual measurements we put them into groups – 6″ to 7″ etc. This modifies the test but the method remains the same. The only paper on the effect of using grouped data appears to be by Gihman (1952).

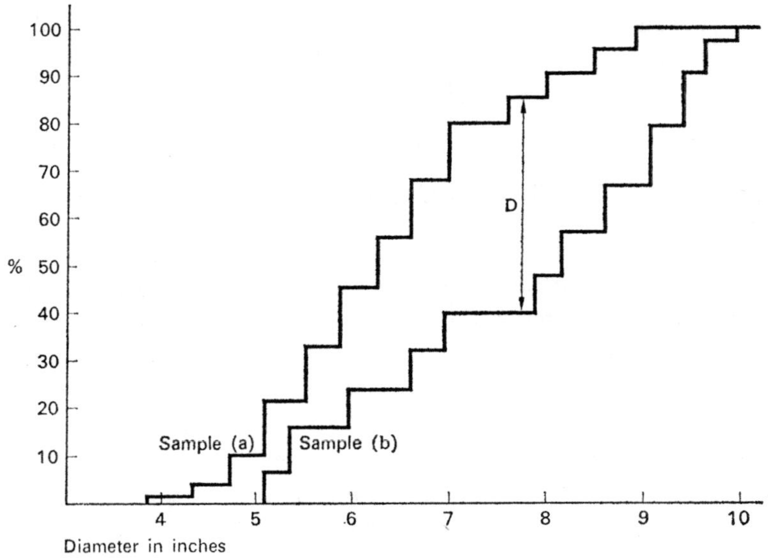

Figure 19

6 It is convenient to rewrite table 1, expressing the number of rims of each category as a percentage of the total in each lot, and omitting L24, which has a smaller number of rims than the other lots and is rather a special case, being associated with one of the kilns. This gives us table 1*a*.

The first distributions to be examined are those of category 2 (see table 2 (i) and graph 1). From the graph we see that the two lots with the highest proportion of category 2 rims (L2 and L6, with 33% and 29% – see table 1*a*) have the greatest median diameters (5·9″ and 6·2″) and the lot with the lowest proportion of category 2 rims (L33, with 13%) also has the smallest median diameter (4·2″). L3 and L8 are intermediate in both proportion and median diameter.

Graph 2 shows the explanation. Here the cumulative distributions are drawn so that they show the number of category 2 rims of less than a given diameter as a proportion of all rims in each lot, not just of the category 2's. For example, the proportion of category 2 rims of less than 7″ diameter in L8 is 16%. All five distribution curves are very similar up to 6″ diameters, where they read from 13% to 17%, but from there they diverge widely. The L33 rims stop at that point, the L3 and L8 curves rise slowly and the L2 and L6 curves continue to rise sharply. In other words, the differences between the lots in both proportions and median diameters are due to the rims over 6″ diameter: below that diameter the differences are not significant. There are in fact two different vessel forms in category 2: genuine beakers with rim-diameters of less than 6″, and jars with beaker-like rims 6″ or more in diameter. It is possible that a few of the rims of less than 6″ diameter are from beaker-like jars.

The genuine beakers (category 2a) form a remarkably stable element of the production, comprising around 15% of the rims in each lot. The proportion of beaker-like jars (2b) fluctuates wildly, from none in L33 to 16% in L2 and L6. The category 2 line of table 1a can be split between these two categories (2a and 2b), as shown in table 1*b* (q.v.).

A possible explanation for these fluctuations is that beakers were a stock item of production, in more or less steady demand, while the beaker-like jars were in the nature of 'special orders', made from time to time to meet the demand of a particular market. If we add together the proportions of categories 2b and 3 (bead-rimmed jars) we see that the total proportion is almost constant (within sampling variation) in the lots from the dump, and again in the lots from the pits. The difference between the proportions from the dump and the pits is accounted for by the difference in the proportion of category 1 jars (see table 1*c*). In general, there seems to be some interchangeability between categories 2b and 3; both are partly supplanted by category 1 in the lots from the pits.

7 We next turn our attention to the category 1 rims (table 2(ii) and graph 3). There is a strong similarity between the structures of tables 2(i) and 2(ii). The diameters follow a distinct pattern: in both cases the L33 median is significantly less than the other medians, while the differences between L8 and L3, and between L2 and L6, are not significant (see table 3). The Kolmogorov-Smirnov test shows just the same pattern in the distributions as a whole, which pattern can be simply illustrated as below. Here lots whose distributions are not significantly different are joined by a horizontal line, either above or below the letters. All other differences are significant:

category 1 L33 $\underline{\text{L3 L8}}$ $\underline{\text{L6 L2}}$ (with $\overline{\text{L8 L6}}$ joined above)

category 2 L33 $\underline{\text{L3 L8}}$ $\underline{\text{L6 L2}}$

The only difference between category 1 and category 2 is the relationship between L8 and L6. A visual comparison of graphs 1 and 3 illustrates the point.

We have already seen that the pattern of the category 2 cumulative distributions is due to the varying proportions of category 2b rims present. The category 1 pattern is due to a different cause – the individual distributions are all very similar in shape, but differ in location. To demonstrate this, the distributions of graph 3 are re-plotted on graph 4, with the individual curves scaled up or scaled down to have a median of about 6·5″. For example, the median diameter from L33 is 5·7″, so the diameter at each plotted point is increased by $(6{\cdot}5-5{\cdot}7)/5{\cdot}7=14\%$ to bring the median up to 6·5″. Similarly the curve for L2 and L6 are scaled down by about 12% and 6% respectively. The graph shows that when the curves are adjusted in this way, the differences between the resulting distributions are not significant.

We can infer from this that the jars (category 1) were manufactured to a basic range of sizes (from about 4″ to 10″ diameters, with 6″ to 7″ being most popular), but that the dimensions of all sizes of jar in the range could vary by up to 28% from the basic scale.

Thus the patterns of cumulative distributions for categories 1 and 2, although very similar, are caused by two distinct mechanisms. The similarity could be explained by supposing that one worker made both categories, to a standard range of sizes in each case (graphs 2 and 4). At times when he was also making special batches of large category 2b vessels, the standard sizes of the category 1 vessels tended to 'drift' a little larger – his idea of what was standard being influenced by the unusually large category 2's he had recently made. Taking L33 as standard, L3 and L8 have a few large category 2's and slightly larger category 1's, and L2 and L6 have more large category 2's and rather larger category 1's.

For the effects of this piece of 'quality control' to have carried through to the excavated material, it would be necessary to assume that both beakers and jars were produced at the same firing.

8 The remaining jars (category 3, bead rims) are dealt with briefly in this section. Brown and Sheldon (1969b) note the presence of 'pygmy' jars of this form, and an apparently bimodal distribution. There is more variety in both size and fabric in this category than in any other. Because of this, and the small size of the sample, no statistical analyses have been undertaken.

9 The last two remaining categories are bowls, with and without internal grooves for lids (categories 4 and 5). Their distributions are shown in tables 2(iii) and 2(iv), and in graphs 5 and 6.

Applying the Kolmogorov-Smirnov test to graph 5, the category 4 vessels fall into two groups: those from L2 and L33, and those from L3, L6 and L8, which are significantly larger in diameter. If we reduce all diameters to a common median, as in section 7, the distributions again follow a common pattern (see graph 7). The vessels from L8 have an odd distribution, with a gap in the centre of the range, but as there are only thirteen rims in all, this is not as unusual as it appears.

The common pattern could again reflect a standard range of sizes, with shifts of the whole range from lot to lot. A similar pattern is followed by category 5, except that the L3 distribution differs from those of L6 and L8 (see graph 6). However, the sample sizes are smaller than for other categories.

The relationship between these two categories is similar to, but less marked than, that between categories 1 and 2, which we have already noted. It is therefore tempting to suppose that the same mechanism underlies both relationships, so that one worker made jars and beakers (categories 1 and 2, and perhaps 3), while a second made bowls and dishes (categories 4 and 5). However, the evidence is indicative rather than conclusive.

10 Early conclusions on the post-excavation work are summarized by Brown and Sheldon (1969b). We can further conclude that the proportion of jars and beakers in the whole production was fairly steady (the proportion of wasters varied from about 68% to about 80%, but this might not be the same as the proportion of vessels actually made).

Each type of pot seems to have been made to a standard range of sizes, the whole range being subject to variations due to causes which in modern terms would be thought of as 'demand' or 'statistical control' (or the lack of it). Relationships between these variations suggest that there were two workers (or groups of workers) throwing the pottery, one making jars and beakers and the other making bowls and dishes.

Further work will continue in three directions:

(i) the counting and measuring of sherds from more levels,

(ii) an attempt to discover whether chronological relationships can be established. For example, since part of the dump overlies the kilns so far discovered, any pit containing wasters from those kilns would be earlier than at least part of the dump,

(iii) it should be possible to break down the five broad categories of pottery into smaller, but still natural, groupings, which might explain some of the variations observed.

Eventually, progress on these three points, and of course more excavation, will lead to a clearer understanding of the industrial organization of a Roman pottery factory.

Acknowledgements

Thanks are due to A. E. Brown and H. L. Sheldon for allowing use of the data, to the latter for providing the drawings in figure 18, and to the students at the City Literary Institute and the Camden Adult Institute who sorted and measured the pottery.

15.viii.69 *London*

Appendix 1

TABLE 1

Numbers of rims of each category in each lot

	Lot						
Category	L2	L3	L6	L8	L24	L33	Total
1	201	321	161	84	19	181	967
2	159	136	111	33	4	45	488
3	31	129	16	2	4	29	211
4	59	194	47	13	38	69	420
5	35	75	42	35	15	10	212
Total	485	855	377	167	80	334	2298

TABLE 1a

Numbers of rims of each category in each lot, as percentages of all rims in the lot

	Lot				
Category	L2	L3	L6	L8	L33
1	41·4	37·5	42·7	50·3	54·3
2	32·8	15·9	29·4	19·7	13·5
3	6·4	15·1	4·2	1·2	8·7
4	12·2	22·7	12·5	7·8	20·6
5	7·2	8·8	11·2	21·0	3·0

TABLE 1b

Numbers of rims of categories 2a and 2b in each lot, as percentages of all rims in the lot

	Lot				
Category	L2	L3	L6	L8	L33
2a	16·7	13·1	14·0	15·5	13·5
2b	16·1	2·8	15·4	4·2	—

TABLE 1c

Numbers of jar rims of categories 1, 2b and 3 in each lot, as percentages of all rims in the lot

	Lot				
Category	L2	L3	L6	L8	L33
2b	16·1	2·8	15·4	4·2	—
3	6·4	15·1	4·2	1·2	8·7
Total	22·5	17·9	19·6	5·4	8·7
1	41·4	37·5	42·7	50·3	54·3
Total jars	63·9	55·4	62·3	55·7	63·0

TABLE 2

Rim diameters (numbers of rims in each size range)

2(i) *Category 2 pots*

Lot	2–3″	3–4″	4–5″	5–6″	6–7″	7–8″	8–9″	9–10″	Over 10″	Total
L2	1	10	28	42	34	22	15	2	5	159
L3	3	29	41	39	18	6	—	—	—	136
L6	4	14	13	18	21	18	12	4	3	107
L8	4	5	10	7	1	2	2	1	1	33
L33	2	16	22	5	—	—	—	—	—	45
(L24)	—	—	—	3	—	—	1	—	—	4
Total	14	74	114	114	74	48	30	7	9	484

2(ii) *Category 1 pots*

Lot	2–3″	3–4″	4–5″	5–6″	6–7″	7–8″	8–9″	9–10″	Over 10″	Total
L2	—	2	5	32	42	56	34	20	10	210
L3	—	5	31	91	97	46	27	15	9	321
L6	—	3	7	31	45	39	15	9	12	161
L8	—	2	13	15	25	13	6	6	4	84
L33	—	3	36	69	53	17	2	1	—	181
(L24)	—	—	1	4	6	4	3	—	1	19
Total	—	15	93	242	326	175	87	51	36	967

2(iii) *Category 4 pots*

Lot	Under 4″	4–5″	5–6″	6–7″	7–8″	8–9″	9–10″	10–11″	11–12″	Over 12″	Total
L2	—	—	1	3	10	14	14	12	5	—	59
L3	—	—	3	15	15	21	35	33	23	49	194
L6	—	1	1	1	4	3	8	15	11	3	47
L8	—	—	—	—	2	2	2	—	7	—	13
L33	—	2	3	6	9	16	17	.........16*.........			69
(L24)	—	—	—	—	8	14	9	2	2	3	38
Total	—	3	8	25	48	70	85	62	48	55	420
								........+16*........			

* In Lot 33, category 4 pots over 10″ were grouped together.

2(iv) *Category 5 pots*

L2	1	3	6	10	2	8	2	1	1	1	35
L3	1	1	3	10	26	18	7	5	1	3	75
L6	1	—	2	3	3	6	3	6	15	3	42
L8	1	5	2	2	1	5	2	4	13	—	35
L33	—	—	2	4	3	—	—	—	—	—	9
(L24)	—	—	1	1	4	6	2	1	—	—	15
Total	4	9	16	30	39	43	16	17	30	7	211

TABLE 3

Median diameters of category 1 and category 2 rims from each lot

Category	L33	L3	L8	L6	L2
1	5·7″	6·3″	6·5″	6·9″	7·3″
2	4·2″	4·9″	4·7″	6·2″	5·9″

Note: the discrepancies between some totals in table 2 and the corresponding entries of table 1 are due to sherds which could be identified, but which were too worn or too fragmented to be measured accurately.

Appendix 2

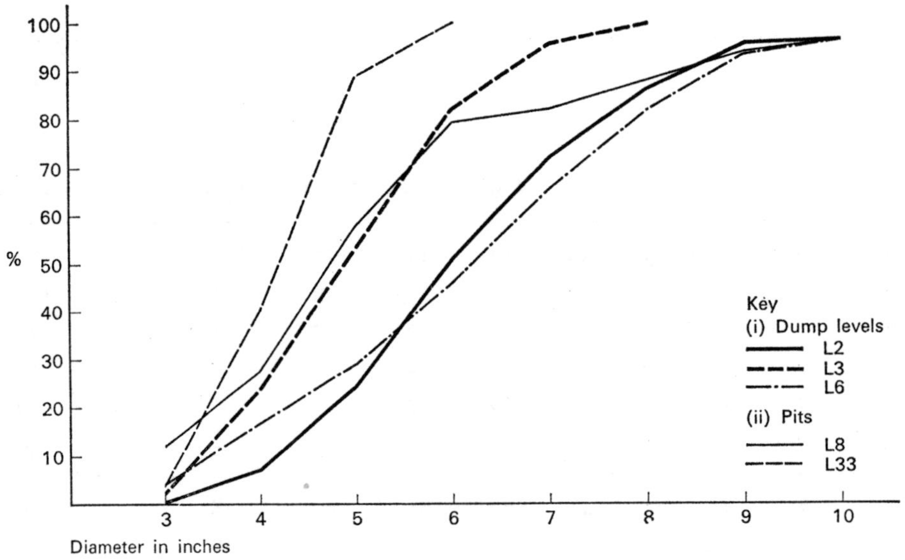

Graph 1 Category 2 rims in each lot

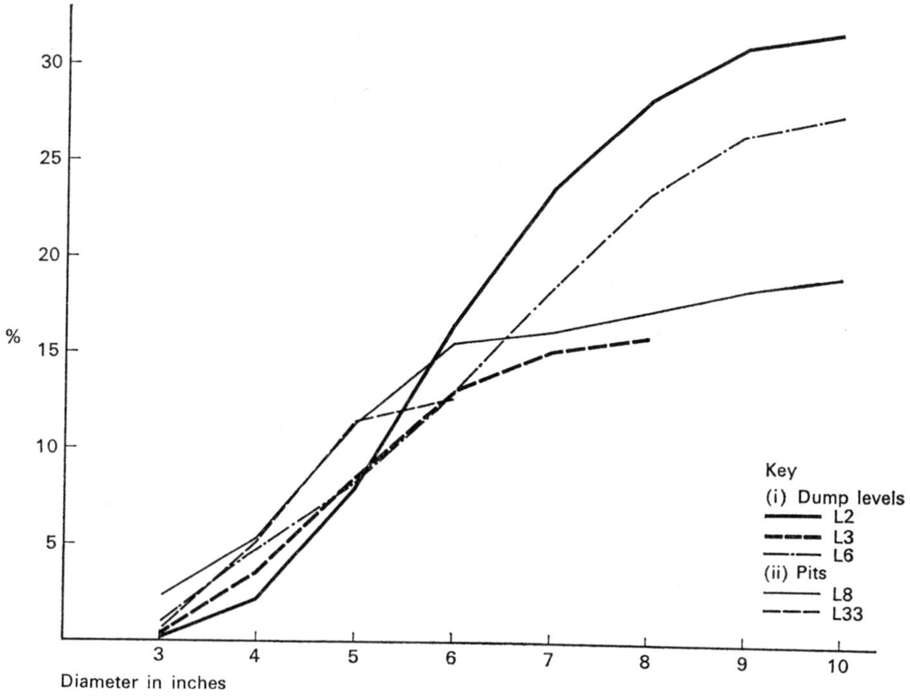

Graph 2 Category 2 rims in each lot, as percentages of all rims in the lot

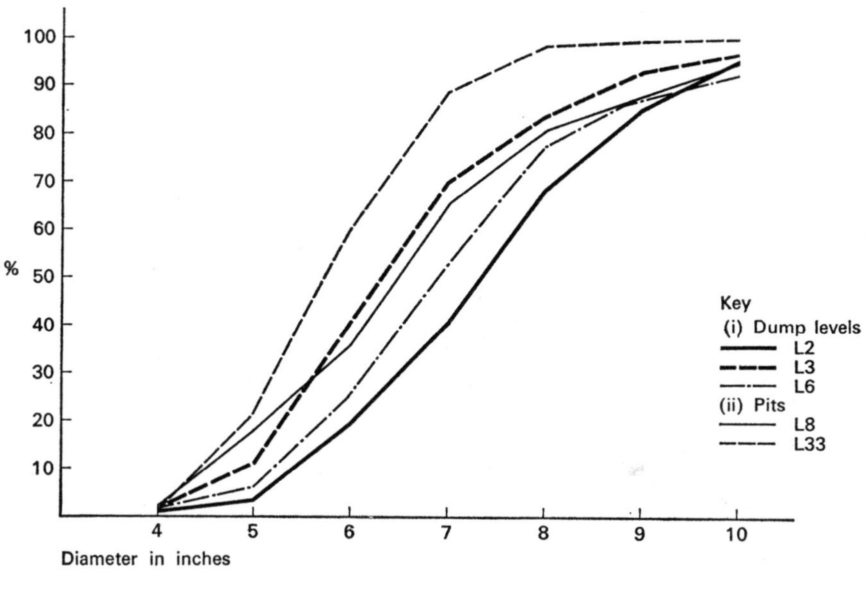

Graph 3 Category 1 rims in each lot

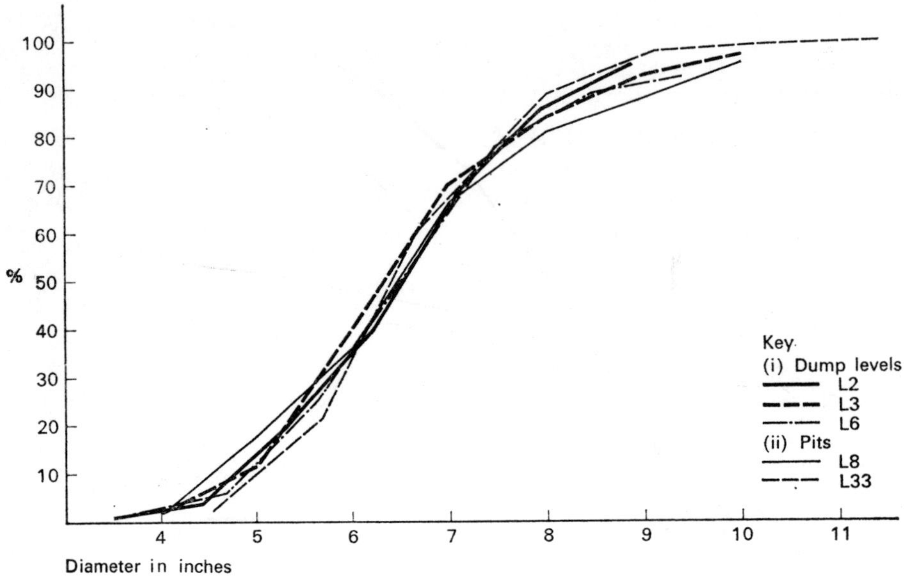

Graph 4 Category 1 rims in each lot re-drawn to a common median

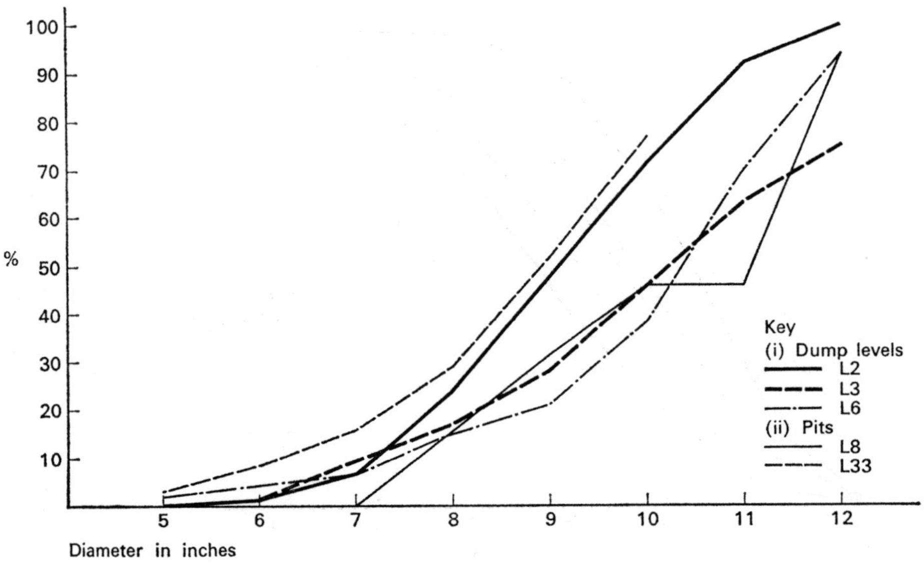

Graph 5 Category 4 rims in each lot

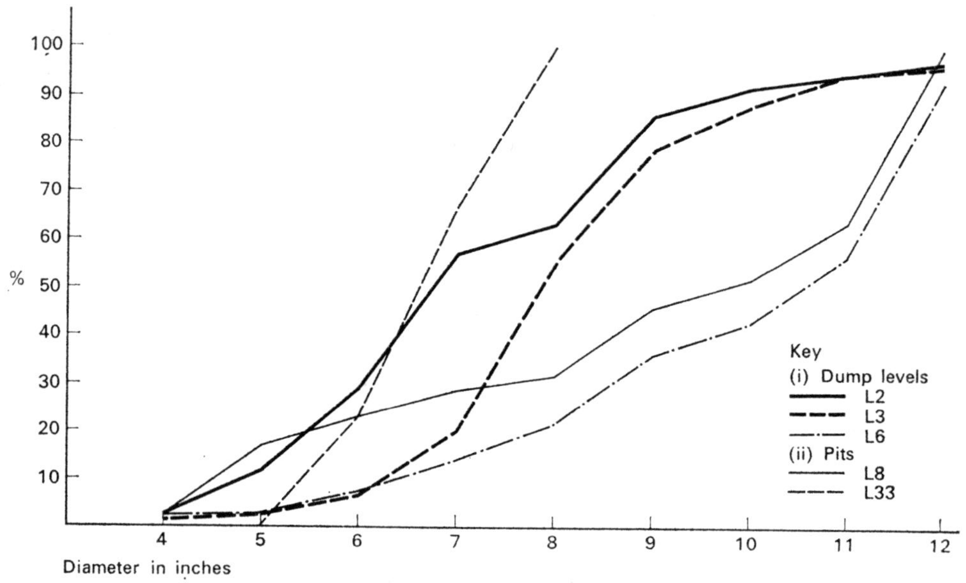

Graph 6 Category 5 rims in each lot

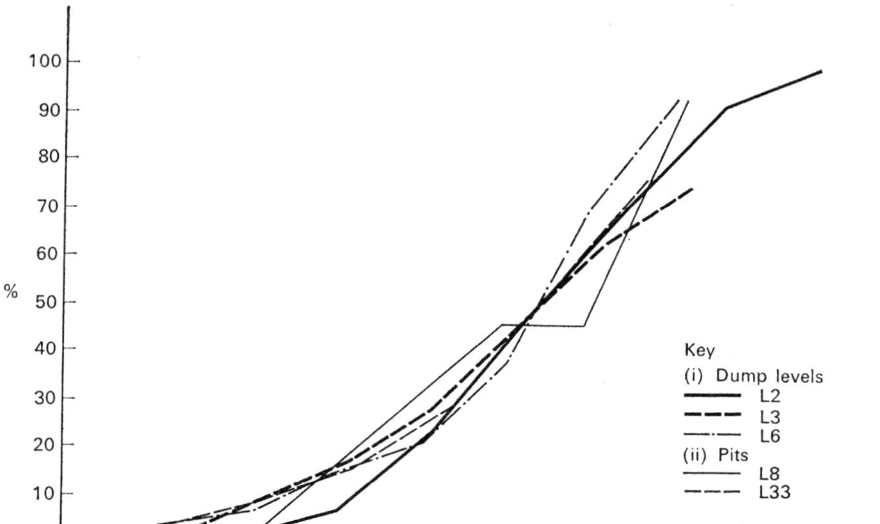

Graph 7 Category 4 rims in each lot, re-drawn to a common median

FA

References

Brown, A. E. and Sheldon, H. L. 1969 a and b. Excavations in Highgate Wood 1966–68, parts 1 and 2. *The London Archaeologist*. 1.

Gihman, I. I. 1952. On the empirical distribution function in the case of grouped data. *Doklady Akad. Nauk S.S.S.R.* (NS). 82. (In Russian.)

Higham, C. 1968. Size trends in Prehistoric European Domestic Fauna, and the problem of local domestication. *Acta Zoologica Fennica*. 120.

Massey, F. J. Jnr. 1952. Distribution table for the deviation between two sample cumulatives. *Annals of Mathematical Statistics*. 23.

Smirnov, N. 1948. Tables for estimating the goodness of fit of empirical distributions. *Annals of Mathematical Statistics*. 19.

Socio-political implications of lowland Maya burials: methodology and tentative hypotheses[1]

William L. Rathje

Ever since the first modern explorers trudged through the tropical rainforest of the Petén, the remnants of Classic Maya civilization have fascinated scholars and laymen. What kind of society spawned the houses, palaces, and temples which are now only ruins? Perhaps the best informants are the builders themselves, who have been in their graves for over a millennium. Excavated burial data indicate a change in emphasis within Classic Maya society (A.D. 300–900) from recruitment of political and religious functionaries from the whole Maya population to the recruitment of officials from small ascribed segments of the population. These and other data suggest that one of the factors underlying this change was Classic Maya economic organization and a system involving wealth as a prerequisite for achieving office. Burial data, in addition to providing evidence of metamorphosis in the structure of Classic Maya society, furnishes a means for testing hypotheses to explain how and why socio-political mobility developed into socio-political stratification.

Many other models of the socio-political organization of Classic Maya society have been proposed. Although they often present diametrically opposed views, most models share three features: they are usually synchronic, they are often constructed from ethnographic data, and they have not been systematically tested by the archaeological record (Haviland (1967) is one exception). In contrast, it is proposed in this paper to use archaeological data primarily, with ethnographic data as a supplement, to construct and to test a diachronic model of Classic Maya socio-political organization.

The interrelationships between those who have access to community resources in terms of goods and services and where that wealth is concentrated and distributed are crucial to any study of socio-political organization. During the Maya Classic a great deal of energy was consumed in individual expenditures to produce food and shelter; however, some of the products of individual and collective energies were not *directly* utilized toward this goal. They were invested in two forms of what in this paper is called 'wealth': (1) items only indirectly relevant to subsistence: temple and palace structures, carved stone monuments, decorated pottery, obsidian eccentrics and 'ceremonial' tools, musical instruments, jade and shell ornaments, and all items placed in burials; and (2) the community resources in terms of labor and products needed to obtain these items. For the purposes of this paper, the primary interest is in the patterns of distribution of 'wealth' in the form of grave goods.

[1] This paper was read at the Conference of *The Prehistoric Society* on 'The Interpretation of Funerary Evidence' held in London on 21–3 March 1969.

The archaeological data in this study are derived from burials. The whole paper rests on one postulate supported in the Maya area by ethnographic (Ruz L. 1968: 15–32; Pope 1969), ethnohistoric (Ruz L. 1968: 63–78), and archaeological data (Haviland 1967; and sample test 2): burials and associated artefacts were not randomly distributed, but varied in direct relation to other aspects of Classic Maya society.

Before the burial data can be utilized, their interrelations in time and space must be defined. Archaeologically established time units containing similar burials and burial distributions were lumped together. The interments found at each site quoted in this paper were divided into two chronologically significant types of burial patterns, one early and one late. Due to local variations, the transition between burial configurations did not occur at each site at the same point in time. Therefore, to make early and late burial data more easily comparable between sites, time will be considered relative to burial patterns. The time range of early and late burial patterns at each site will be called the Early and Late Period respectively.

In addition to these chronological relationships, spatial relationships are important variables. Burials were interred into the temples and palaces, which together form ceremonial centers, and into the small houses scattered throughout the outlying areas surrounding ceremonial centers (figs 20*b* and 20*c*). Temples are square clusters of a few rooms on high, pyramidal platforms. Palaces are structures of multiple rooms in parallel rows on low, rectangular platforms. Houses are small platforms which once supported perishable superstructures of probable domestic use. Only burials in thoroughly excavated structures, where their space and time associations are understood, were utilized in this paper.

The ideal study would involve burial populations from temples, palaces, and house platforms in and around a single ceremonial center. The available data, however, are incomplete from any one site (Tikal may prove to be an exception). In this paper a selection has had to be made of one component of temple and palace burials from the Petén and one component of house mound burials from British Honduras (fig. 20). Therefore, an assumption must be made: that the populace of the Southern Lowlands during the Maya Classic shared common patterns of socio-political organization, just as it shared common patterns in architecture, ceremonial parphernalia, calendrics and epigraphy, and burial customs. This assumption will be implicitly tested when the model proposed by this paper is tested site by site (cf. sample test 1).

The burial patterns from two sites will serve to illustrate the techniques involved in isolating patterns in terms of wealth and the important aspects of the model developed. The first burials to be studied came from a group of small house platforms at the rural site of Barton Ramie in British Honduras (Willey *et al.* 1965; and figure 20*c*). Sixty-five structures were tested and two were completely excavated. A total of 117 burials of known data were recovered. Of these, 43 were attributed to the Early Period (pre-A.D. 700 phases: Jenny Creek through the Tiger Run–Spanish Lookout transition), and the remaining 74 to the Late Period (post-A.D. 700 phases: Spanish Lookout and New Town).

The age distribution patterns of the Early and Late Periods proved to be significantly distinct. The remains of 19 mature adults and a total of 24 adolescents, young adults, and old adults were recorded from the Early Period platforms. In contrast, Late Period structures yielded 44 mature adults but only 30 individuals of other age groups. Thus, the

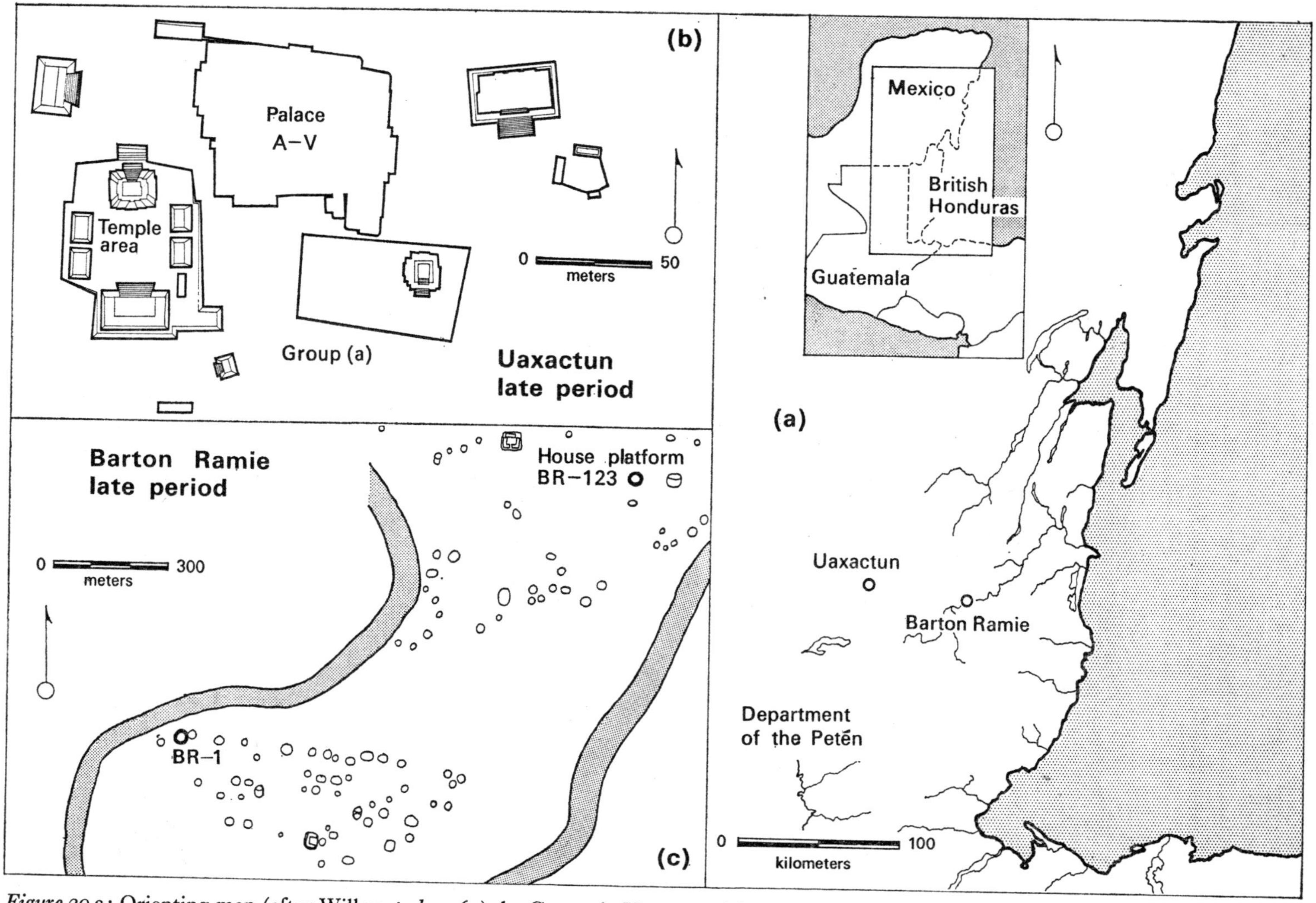

Figure 20 a: Orienting map (after Willey *et al.* 1965). b: Group A, Uaxactun (after Smith 1937). c: The south-east portion of Barton Ramie (after Willey *et al.* 1965)

proportion of mature adults in the house platform burial population increased from 44% in the Early Period to 59% in the Late Period (fig. 21*a*).

One explanation for this change is that individuals often died young during the Early Period. There is, however, no evidence for any shift in the environment or subsistence which could account for an increased lifespan in the Late Period. In fact, Barton Ramie skeletal studies suggest just the opposite effect – the development of a poorer level of nutrition in the Late Period (Willey *et al.* 1965: 535–44, 570). Therefore, the small proportion of Early Period mature adult burials must be ascribed to some other cultural mechanism.

Other shifts in burial patterns were discovered by comparison of age and artefact distributions. Although young adults represented only 22% of the Early Period population, they were buried with more than 50% of the Early Period grave goods. Adults were associated with the remainder. The Late Period distribution pattern was a direct reversal of the Early Period trend. Young adults, 18% of the population, were associated with less than 10% of the grave goods, while mature adults were accompanied to the grave with almost 80% of the Late Period burial artefacts. Thus, although the proportion of young adults in the population decreased only 4%, the proportion of grave goods associated with young adults dropped 40% (fig. 21*b*).

Based on these data, Early Period (fig. 22: 1–23) and Late Period (fig. 23: 30–56) patterns are clearly discernible. During the Early Period young adult interments were the wealthiest burials placed in house platforms (fig. 22: 7–13). From other ethnographic and archaeological data it might be logically expected that adult burials would

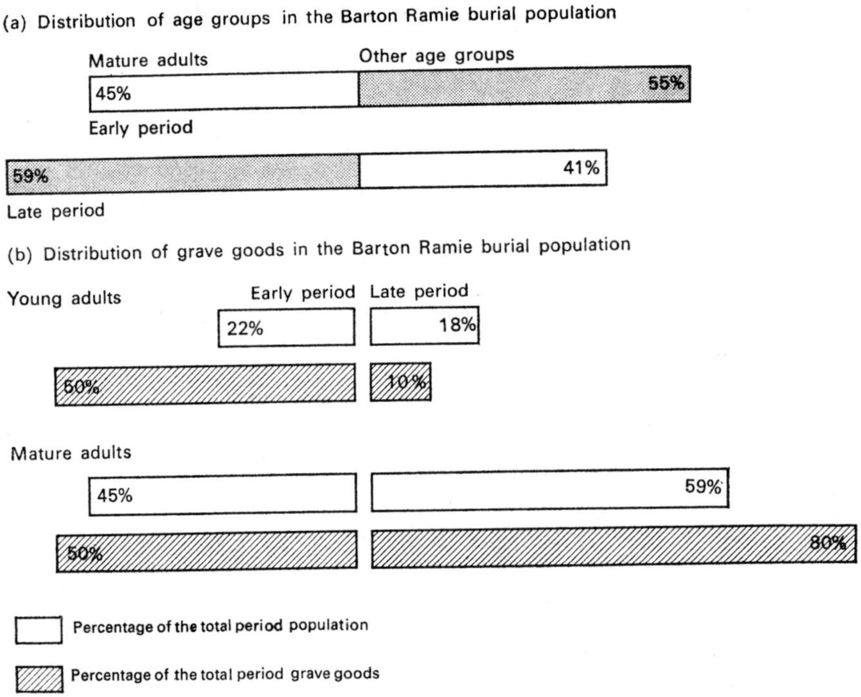

Figure 21 Age and wealth interrelationships in the Early and Late Periods at Barton Ramie

Early period burial pattern

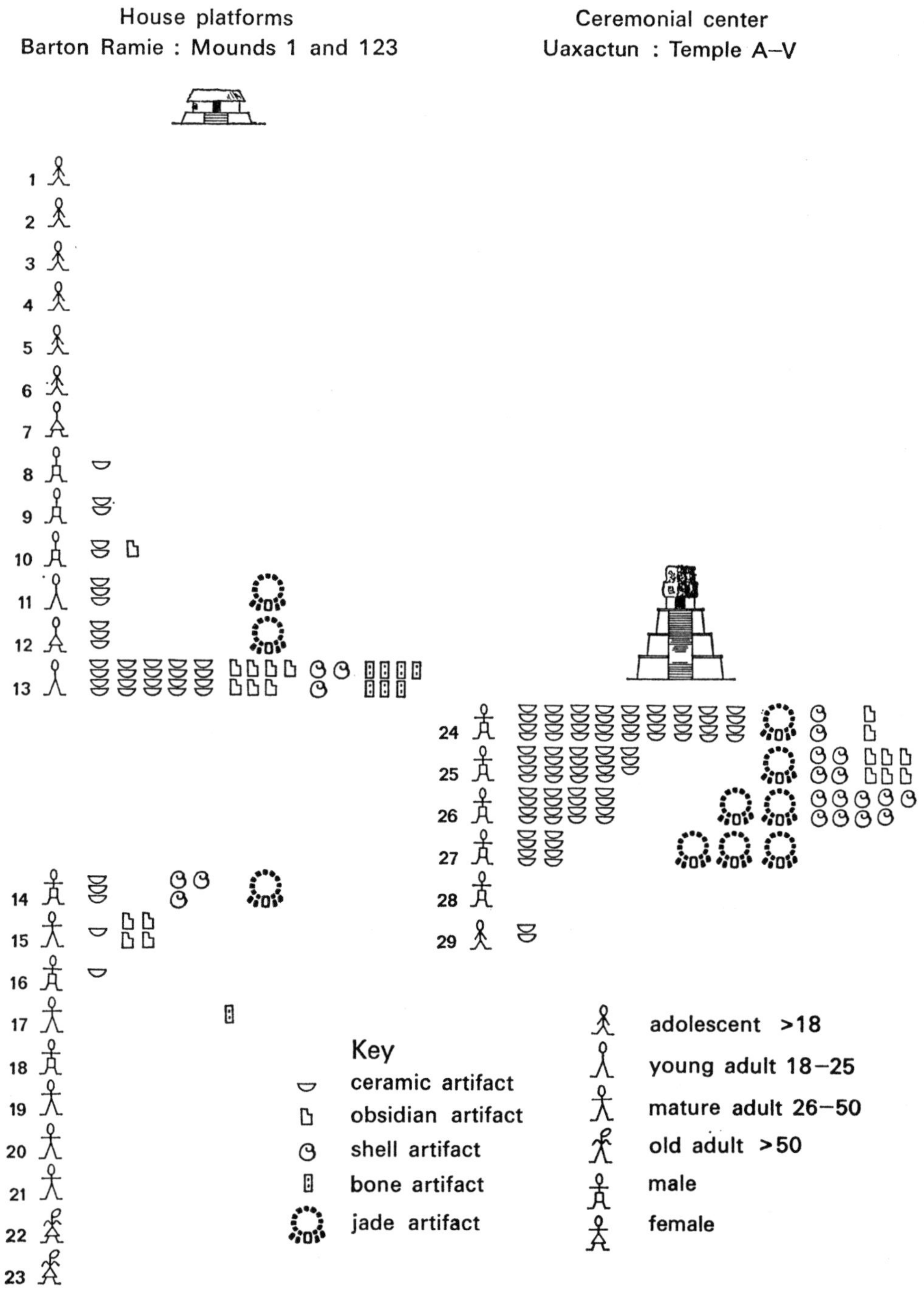

Figure 22 Hypothesized Early Period age and grave goods burial distributions (cf. appendix)

also contain a large number of grave goods; yet a surprisingly small number of adults, associated with a meagre assortment of grave artefacts, were buried in Early Period house platforms. Therefore, both a proportion of adults and also expected distributions of wealth among adults were missing. This suggests that the wealthy adults living in the outlying areas surrounding ceremonial centers were not interred in the platforms on which they resided. During the Late Period, a larger proportion of adults were buried in house platforms. Few individuals living in rural houses were wealthy, and most artefacts were placed in the graves of mature adults. In contrast to wealthy young adult Early Period burials, young adult interments were the poorest found in Late Period houses.

In order to explain these changes in house platform interment patterns, burial data from ceremonial centers were examined. The excellent excavation report of Structure A–V at Uaxactun in the heart of the Petén provided an ideal opportunity for study of the patterns of ceremonial center burials (Smith 1950; and fig. 20*b*). During the Uaxactun Early Period (pre-A.D. 600 phases: Tzakol 1–3), Structure A–V supported three small temples on an elevated plaza. Excavation revealed six Early Period interments, four of which were laid to rest in carefully constructed tombs containing numerous pots, carved jades, whole and carved shells, bone tubes, obsidian lancelets, and jaguar pelts (fig. 22: 24–7). Such artefacts are often associated with Maya functionaries pictured on pottery, stelae, and wall murals. These data indicate that the four burials were important functionaries engaged intimately enough in the ceremonial center's activities to be interred there at death with a degree of pomp. All of these burials were male adults!

Two other Early Period burials were interred in the plaza with much less attention. One may have been a lower class helper of the important functionaries (fig. 22: 28); his grave contained no artefacts. The other burial (fig. 22: 29), that of an infant placed under a stairway, may have been a dedicatory offering to some aspect of construction. This pattern of wealthy adult tomb burials and a few dedicatory offerings and poor interments is found in the temple areas of most Classic Maya sites during both the Early and Late Periods.

Temple areas continued to be used and constructed in other areas of Uaxactun during the Late Period (post-A.D. 600 phases: Tepeu 1–3), but at this time Structure A–V was converted into a maze of palace buildings and terraces (fig. 24). In direct correlation with this change, the burial population of A–V increased sixfold. Instead of only one adolescent, there were fourteen; instead of five male adults, there were twenty-four adults, half of whom were male and half female. Late Period A–V palace burials also differed from Early Period A–V temple interments in terms of the distribution of artefacts. Instead of only the extremes of wealth, there was a continuum ranging from rich to poor (fig. 23: 57–77).

Palaces were associated with age, sex, and artefact distributions similar, except in degree of wealth, to those found in Late Period Barton Ramie house platforms (fig. 23). Perhaps the palace was a residential unit or associated with a nearby house platform population. In addition, rich burials and their distribution indicate that palaces served a function in the administrative business of ceremonial centers (cf. sample test 2 and fig. 24). It is worth noting that in most Classic sites the richest burials in the Late Period, as in the Early Period, were placed in temple areas.

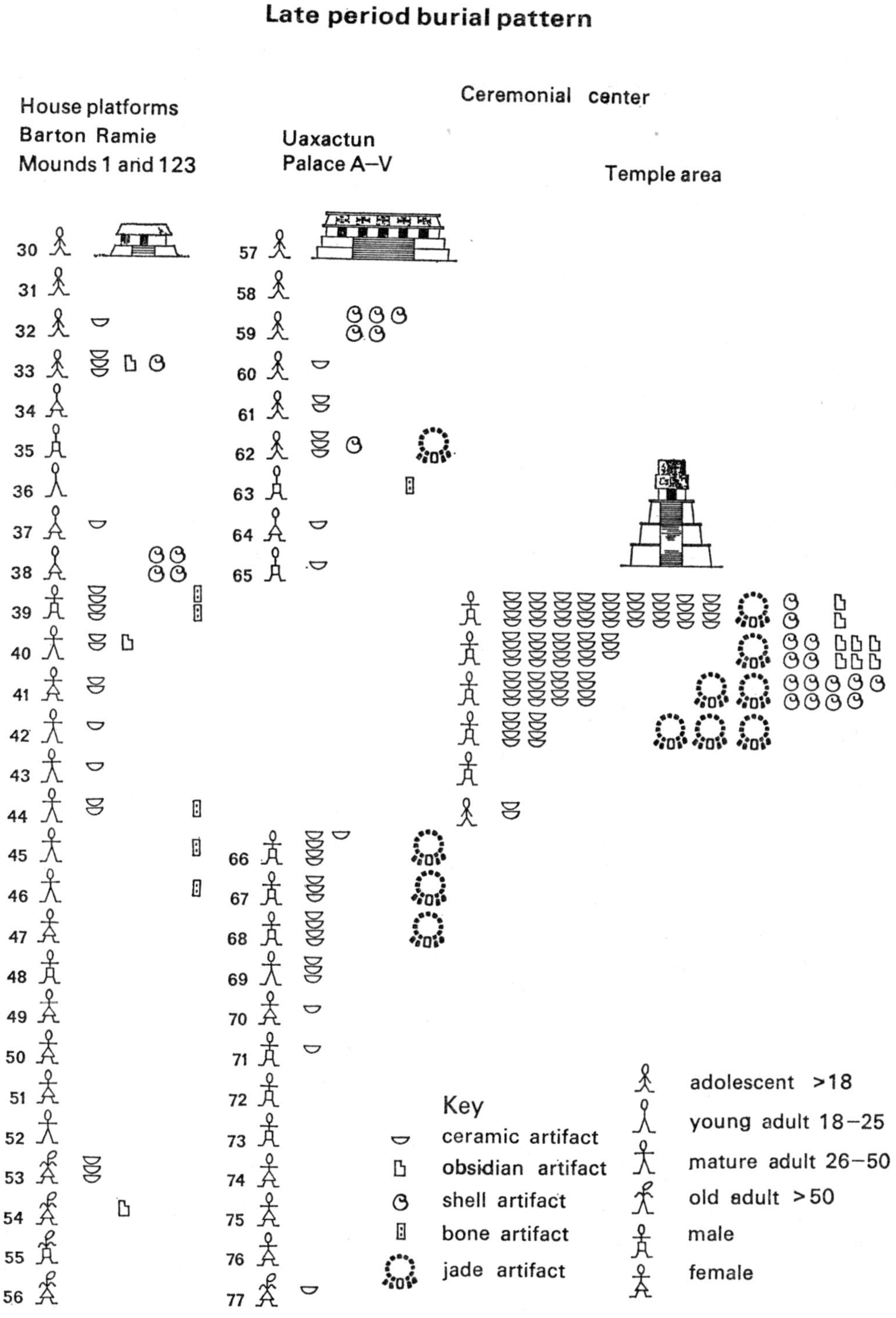

Figure 23 Hypothesized Late Period age and grave goods burial distributions (cf. appendix)

A diachronic, archaeologically testable model of Classic Maya socio-political organization was constructed from these data by two processes. The first was a careful study of the burial patterns just described. The second process included exposure to Maya ethnographic and ethnohistoric data and general anthropological theory to suggest the types of mechanism by which the archaeological patterns were formed. The role of ethnography as a supplement to archaeology is best illustrated by the use of data collected and interpreted by Dr Vogt (1961, 1969) and Dr Cancian (1965, 1967) at Zinacantan, a modern Maya community in highland Chiapas, and by Dr Bunzel (1952) at Chichicastenango, a modern Maya community in Guatemala. The ethnohistoric reconstructions by Dr Calnek (1962) and Dr Carrasco (1961) were also valuable. These studies all demonstrated that wealth was a prerequisite for attaining positions of political and/or religious authority in late pre-Conquest and in post-Conquest Mexico. Based on the preceding archaeological burial patterns, it is proposed in this paper that the above system was also a Classic Maya pattern and that it led to the changes in burial patterns between the Early and Late Periods.

The basic postulates upon which this hypothesis rests are: (1) population grew (Willey *et al.* 1965: 561–81), (2) ceremonial centers functioned as foci of administration (Tourtellot 1969) and concentration of resources (compare figs 20*b* and 20*c*; fig. 22: 1–23 and 24–9; fig. 23: 30–56 and 57–77), (3) persons in positions of authority had access to wealth in terms of community resources (Ruz L. 1968; Landa 1941; Calnek 1962). The resulting Early Period model is clearly drawn by the burial data (fig. 22).

House platforms were missing mature adult burials; temples were full of them. The wealthiest Early Period burials were those of mature adults in temple areas and young adults in small houses. It is here proposed that the Early Period Maya population lived on house platforms and farmed nearby lands. As the Maya successfully exploited their chosen ecological niche, wealth accumulated within house platform populations. Due to the environment and the state of Maya technology, population was widely dispersed. Redistribution and trade centers played an important part in the economic and ceremonial integration of Maya communities. Clusters of temples and plazas functioned as foci of wealth concentrations in terms of intra-Petén and foreign trade, ceremonialism, and building construction. Wealth to support these activities was a prerequisite for initiation into ceremonial center activities and power positions. Thus the Early Period Maya invested his surplus toward increasing personal and community prestige, through the expansion of ceremonial centers in the form of temple construction, trade, and ceremonialism. Young adults collected wealth in the form of food resources and ceremonial objects with which to sponsor the specialists, ceremonies, and the community works involved in filling an office. The death of such individuals while accumulating wealth accounts for the rich young adult interments in Early Period house platforms. Especially significant to this model is burial 6 from mound BR-1 (fig. 22: 13) which included 18 pots 'arranged one over the other as though they contained food and drink' (Willey *et al.* 1965: 566), 2 pottery drums, 1 bone needle case, 2 bone needles, 6 projectile points, 3 'ceremonial' bladelets, 1 obsidian blade, 1 obsidian 'eccentric', 4 carved bone tubes, 2 shells, 1 composite shell ear ornament, and a turtle carapace.

Those who lived to attain office achieved a privileged position. Ceremonial center officials functioned at the hub of wealth mobilization and labor organization systems. Thus

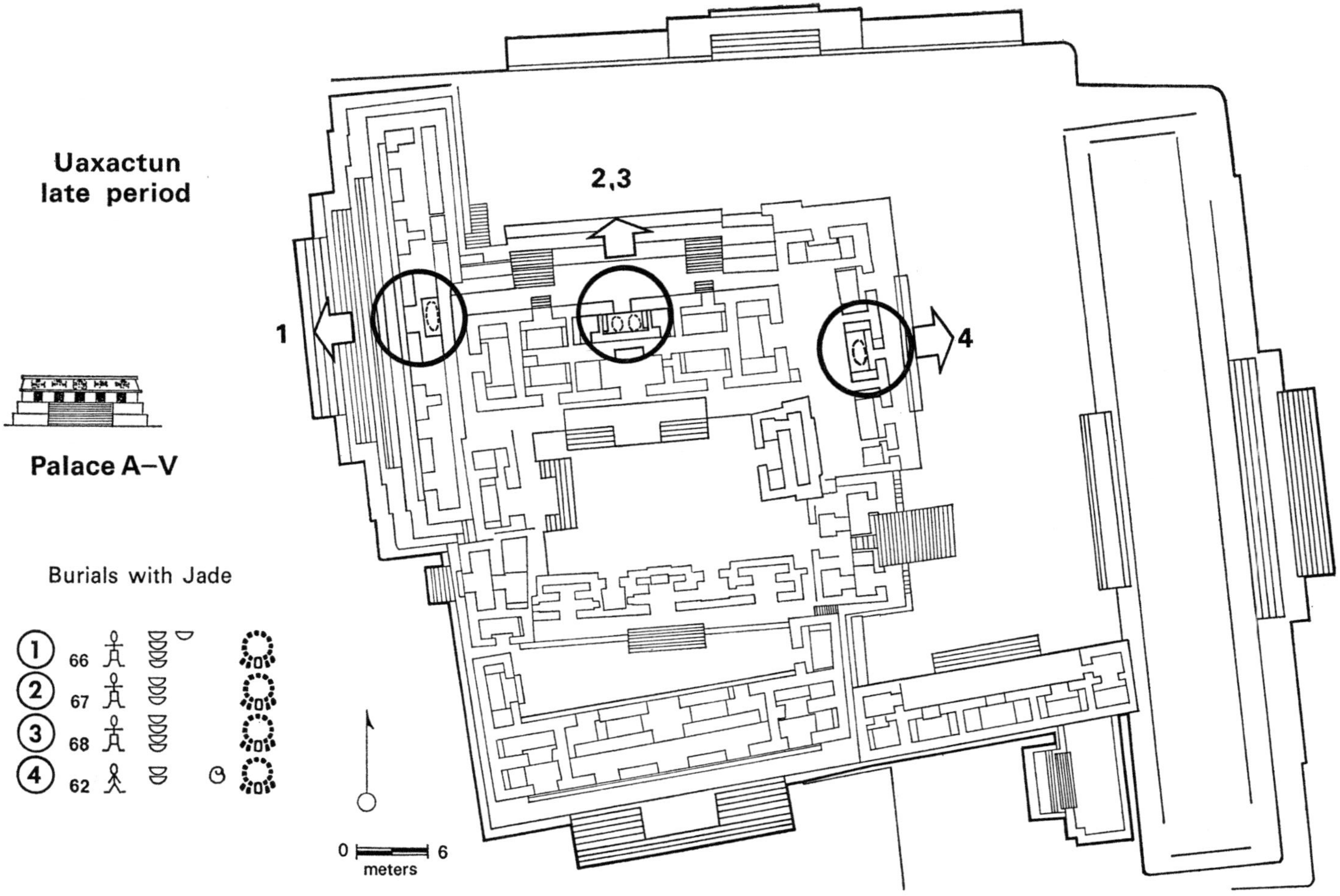

Figure 24 Illustration of sample test 2

these functionaries had access to wealth involved in running the center and no doubt used some of it to attain higher offices. A constant influx of wealth into the ceremonial center was maintained by the system of wealth as a prerequisite for achieving office. In addition, wealth flowed out from the center along family lines to outlying areas as adults who had attained positions of authority helped related young adults obtain goods for their initiation into office. At death office holders were buried in the ceremonial center with which they had been associated; thus the rich adults buried in temple areas account for the adults missing from outlying houses. Those who had not been initiated in ceremonial center activities were interred in their house platforms. Both wealthy and poor individuals resided on widely scattered house platforms, but after death they were separated by differential burial. Thus Early Period socio-political structure emphasized mobility in terms of individuals living on outlying house platforms attaining ceremonial offices and authority positions. This organization provided a solid economic, ceremonial, and socio-political integration between house platform and ceremonial center populations.

The appearance of palaces marks the end of the Early Period and the beginning of the Late Period. It is suggested here that the Early Period temple-house platform relationship was displaced in the Late Period by a temple-palace relationship (fig. 23). Ceremonial center functionaries, were no longer drawn from dispersed house platform populations but were recruited from small population segments living in, or associated with, palaces. The sex, age, and wealth distributions of Late Period burials are strikingly similar to house platform distributions. Thus ceremonial centers held groups which could perpetuate themselves without drawing upon outside house platform populations. Individuals living on house platforms no longer held office and were no longer buried in ceremonial centers. In the Late Period Barton Ramie house platforms the proportion of adults increased, young adults no longer held a special position, and burial goods were distributed with expected skews toward mature adults. Socio-political mobility between rural populations and ceremonial center populations had ended.

What were the mechanisms of change between the Early and Late Periods? Outside influence, especially that from Teotihuacán, cannot be discounted; however, the nature of the economic structure of the Southern Lowland Maya is another important factor. Ethnographic, ethnohistoric, and archaeological data can be put together to define the Classic Maya economy as 'mobilizing' (cf. Smelser 1959). In Nash's words,

> 'A system of mobilization for exchange collects goods and services into the hands of an elite for the broad purposes of the society. It has the social correlates of centricity and stratification needed to make redistributive exchange a viable mode, but it differs functionally from redistribution in two senses. Mobilization exchange promotes and underlines the power and prestige differences between the economic and political elite and the rest of society; the expenditure of the collected goods and commandeered services goes to implement ends defined by the elite' (1966:32–3).

It is suggested here that an important factor in implementing the concentration of wealth for community goals was (especially during the Early Period) the system of wealth as a prerequisite for holding office. This mechanism was adaptively advantageous because (1) it continued to insure reinvestment of wealth in terms of personal resources for community good (this system was constantly reinforced as wealth was continually drained off in the form of grave goods, caches, carved monuments, and monumental architecture, all of which yielded little direct economic return), and (2) it selected office holders from individuals who had wealth in terms of those who also possessed administrative competence. This system in correlation with the other postulates of this paper explains the socio-political changes through time isolated in burial and grave wealth distribution patterns.

Population growth during the Maya Classic is well documented by excavations and settlement pattern surveys. Thus during the Early Period more and more people were competing for high status positions, and a smaller percentage of them attained these offices. As competition intensified and the number of competitors increased, the prerequisite wealth was harder to collect. Only those who had access to ceremonial center power and wealth could afford to provide the goods necessary to obtain office; it is likely that such wealth distributions followed family lines. Thus the accretion and redistribution of wealth became a circular movement within proportionately fewer and fewer families. This introduced an incipient hereditary mechanism. Authority positions had to be achieved, but accident of birth determined, to a greater and greater extent, those who had a chance of attaining it.

As wealth and authority positions localized in proportionately fewer and fewer families, those who attained office undoubtedly became an easily distinguished class with many common goals and interests which were implemented in ceremonial centers and not in cornfields. Using their special access to ceremonial center resources, segments of house platform populations began to construct buildings for residential and bureaucratic use. The move to ceremonial centers was no doubt slow; but the economic and ideological gap between the elite and the average farmer widened until it was finally embodied in a physical gap between palaces and house platforms. Populations living in palaces provided a solidified bureaucracy which choked off recruitment of functionaries from outlying areas. Attainment of positions was always attributable in some degree to inherited wealth; it was always achieved in terms of the results of the investment of that wealth. Socio-political mobility had not ended. It had merely been confined, in large measure, to populations within ceremonial centers who had family tie-ins to community goods and services.

The same factors that developed a ceremonial center elite within the whole Maya population developed an elite within the ceremonial center population. Status changes emphasized hereditary mechanisms. Wealth buried with children (fig. 24: 62) was not earned by the child's actions, but by the niche the child filled in relation to the position of its relatives. The existence of hereditary ruling lineages has been proposed through the use of burial data (Haviland 1967) and deciphered glyphs (Proskouriakoff 1960, 1961, 1963–4; Kelley 1962).

It has been hypothesized here that the nature of access to political and religious authority positions changed through time along a continuum between varying degrees of achievement and ascription. It has been proposed that one mechanism involved in this change was the prerequisite of wealth for attaining office. Thus burial data and suggestions from ethnography have provided a model of the socio-political organization of the Classic Maya and the processes that brought about some of the obvious changes between Early and Late Period material culture patterns. But a model is not an end in itself; it must be validated by systematic testing of all possible archaeological data. To test the model a computer project was designed. The data relevant to the model from over 1,000 burials representing excavations from twelve sites are now being coded on to punch cards.

The proposed testing project will involve two procedures. First, the burial patterns upon which the model is based must be substantiated from every site producing usable data.

Sample test 1

Is it statistically significant that young adults buried in Early Period house platforms were associated with more grave goods than young adults buried in Late Period house platforms? A chi square test run on a preliminary sample yielded a significance level of 0·001, indicating a consistently high degree of association between cultural period, age at death, and amount of burial wealth. It is therefore significant that the nature of the relationship between age and wealth reversed itself between the Early and Late Periods. This test confirms the model. If similar results are obtained from all sites yielding relevant data, the assumption of the uniformity of Southern Lowland Classic Maya socio-political organization will gain support.

Once the model is refined by the first testing procedure, a second battery of tests will be run. If culture is an integrated system and changes in burial patterns are related to changes in socio-political organization, then shifts in socio-political organization also affected other aspects of Maya culture. The model can be used to predict these changes and can be tested by how accurately such predictions fit the archaeological record. For example:

Sample test 2

One isolated cluster of features in the Late Period Uaxactun palace was especially significant: the four burials, three adult males and one child, with the most grave goods, including the only Late Period A–V jade (fig. 23: 62 and 66–8). If wealth in terms of grave goods is correlated with holding power, then the position of these burials within A–V should be indicative of such a function in relation to the structure.

Results. All four were buried in 'throne' benches in centrally located palace rooms (fig. 24). These rooms were positioned at the head of stairways and face plazas; they were constructed and used consecutively, not concurrently. In a study of palace architecture, Clemency Coggins (1967) proposed that such palace rooms were audience chambers where high status officials held court. The audience chamber burials provide a neat correlation between wealth and positions of administrative authority in ceremonial centers.

Sample test 3

A complex of items associated (in varying degrees) with authority positions and ceremonialism can be defined using temple and palace burials (polychrome pottery, carved bone objects, eccentric flints and obsidians, jade ornaments, shell ornaments). If access to such offices was open to house platform populations in the Early Period, but restricted to ceremonial center populations in the Late Period, such items will be significantly fewer in number in Late Period house platform burials than in Early Period house platform burials.

Results. The Early and Late Period burials at Barton Ramie yielded 113 and 111 associated artefacts respectively. The quantity of monochrome ceramics remained constant (41 Early, 39 Late); however, the total number of polychrome ceramics, ceremonial blades, carved bone tubes, and jadeite and shell ornaments decreased from 45 to 21. A chi square test run on these data yielded a 0·025 significance level. Thus it is significant that there are fewer items of the ceremonial center authority and ritual complex found in the Late Period Barton Ramie house platforms.

Sample test 4

If, in the Late Period, specific house platform populations used palaces for residential and administrative functions, then palace burials will contain a domestic tool complex similar to those found in house platforms (utilitarian obsidian and bone tools, spindle whorls) and items similar to those found in temple area burials (jade and shell ornaments, stingray spines, eccentric and ceremonial obsidians).

Results. A preliminary computer sorting of the artefacts from 427 burials indicates that this prediction is confirmed by the archaeological data.

Only time and money limit the number of such tests that can be devised and run by computer with the 1,000 burial sample.

The basic elements of the model proposed in this paper are not new; however, certain aspects of its generation and future use differ from most of the existing Classic Maya models. The model was purposely diachronic, was generated directly by archaeological data and indirectly by suggestions adopted from ethnographic data, and is testable by systematic use of further archaeological data. As it now stands, the model is not fully substantiated. It has been proposed not so much to prove its own validity as to find valid answers to questions about Classic Maya Society. Therefore, whether further testing confirms or refutes the model, knowledge of Classic Maya burial patterns and socio-political organization will have been increased.

Appendix to figures 22 and 23

Burials 1–23 Representative Early Period Burials from Barton Ramie Mounds 1 and 123

Burials 24–9 Early Period Burials from Structure A-V at Uaxactun

Burials 30–56 Representative Late Period Burials from Barton Ramie House Mounds 1 and 123

Burials 57–78 Representative Late Period Burials from Structure A-V at Uaxactun

1 BR-123-13
2 BR-1-14
3 BR-1-15
4 BR-1-19
5 BR-1-20
6 BR-123-26
7 BR-1-25
8 BR-1-21
9 BR-123-20
10 BR-123-19
11 BR-123-13
12 BR-123-31
13 BR-1-6
14 BR-123-30
15 BR-1-16
16 BR-123-32
17 BR-1-23
18 BR-123-35
19 BR-123-21
20 BR-123-24
21 BR-1-21
22 BR-1-17
23 BR-123-14

24 A22
25 A31
26 A29
27 A20
28 A39
29 A66

30 BR-1-5
31 BR-123-2
32 BR-1-24
33 BR-123-22
34 BR-123-28
35 BR-123-23
36 BR-123-9
37 BR-123-24
38 BR-1-10
39 BR-123-18
40 BR-1-1
41 BR-123-5
42 BR-1-3
43 BR-123-36
44 BR-1-4
45 BR-123-6
46 BR-123-7
47 BR-123-3
48 BR-123-17
49 BR-123-26
50 BR-123-25
51 BR-123-12
52 BR-123-33
53 BR-123-10
54 BR-123-4
55 BR-123-29
56 BR-1-7
57 A25
58 A44
59 A55
60 A8
61 A57
62 A48
63 A24
64 A64
65 A47
66 A43
67 A34
68 A40
69 A38
70 A51
71 A46
72 A23
73 A52
74 A30
75 A67
76 A33
77 A68
78 A32

Unnumbered burials in figure 23

These burials are a construct of Late Period temple area burials using data from Tikal, Palenque, and Altun Ha. In order to simplify the point of the patterns illustrated – that Late Period temple area burials followed essentially the same pattern as Early Period temple area burials – the burials from Early Period Uaxactun were used as representative of Late Period temple area burial patterns. Uaxactun itself may not have continued the complex temple area burial pattern to the same degree as the above sites.

Acknowledgements

I am deeply indebted to Drs Gordon R. Willey and Evon Z. Vogt for their helpful suggestions, patience, and encouragement, and to Dr G. L. Gowgill, Dr J. Ladd, A. L. Smith, K. Day, W. Fitzhugh, J. Humphries, T. Layton, R. Meadow, P. Shankman, and E. Sisson for their willing assistance and constructive criticisms. Many of the aspects of this paper were developed in discussions with Dr Jeremy A. Sabloff and Gair Tourtellot. For their generous and stimulating comments I am very grateful.

21.iii.69 *Harvard University*

References

Bunzel, R. 1952. *Chichicastenango: A Guatemalan Village.* American Ethnological Society. Publication 22.

Calnek, E. A. 1962. *Highland Chiapas before the Spanish Conquest.* Ms. University of Chicago.

Cancian, F. 1965. *Economics and Prestige in a Maya Community: the Religious Cargo System in Zinacantan.* Stanford.

Cancian, F. 1967. Political and religious organization. *Handbook of Middle American Indians.* 6. Austin.

Carrasco, P. 1951. The civil-religious hierarchy in Mesoamerican communities: pre-Spanish background and colonial development. *American Anthropologist.* 63:483–97.

Coggins, C. 1967. *Palaces and the Planning of Ceremonial Centers in the Southern Maya Lowlands.* Ms. Peabody Museum, Harvard University.

Haviland, W. A. 1967. Stature at Tikal, Guatemala: implications for Ancient Maya demography and social organization. *American Antiquity.* 32, 3:316–325.

Kelley, D. H. 1962. Glyphic evidence for a dynastic sequence at Quirigua, Guatemala. *American Antiquity.* 27, 3:323–35.

Landa, D. de. 1941. *Landa's Relacion de las Cosas de Yucatan.* Trans. and ed. with notes by A. M. Tozzer. Papers of the Peabody Museum of Archaeology and Ethnology, Harvard University. 18.

Nash, M. 1966. *Primitive and Peasant Economic Systems.* San Francisco.

Pope, C. 1969. *The Funeral Ceremony in Zinacantan.* Ms. Harvard University.

Proskouriakoff, T. 1960. Historical implications of a pattern of dates at Piedras Negras, Guatemala. *American Antiquity.* 25, 4:454–75.

Proskouriakoff, T. 1961. The Lords of the Maya Realm. *Expedition.* 4, 1:14–21.

Proskouriakoff, T. 1963–4. Historical data in the Inscriptions of Yaxachilan. *Estudios de Cultura Maya.* 3:149–67, 4:177–201.

Ruz L. A. 1968. *Costumbres Funerarias de los Antiguos Mayas.* Seminario de Cultura Maya. Mexico.

Smelser, N. J. 1959. A comparative view of exchange systems. *Economic Development and Cultural Change*. 7, 2:173–82.

Smith, A. L. 1937. *Structure A-XVIII, Uaxactun*. Carnegie Institution of Washington. Publication 483, contribution 20.

Smith, A. L. 1950. *Uaxactun, Guatemala: Excavations of 1931–1937*. Carnegie Institution of Washington. Publication 588.

Tourtellot, G. 1969. *Itzán, the Río Pasión Region and Classic Maya Site Planning*. Ms. prepared for presentation at the April Northeastern Anthropological Association, annual meeting, Providence, R.I.

Vogt, E. Z. 1961. Some aspects of Zinacantan settlement patterns and ceremonial organization. *Estudios de Cultura Maya*. 1:131–51.

Vogt, E. Z. 1969. *Zinacantan: A Maya Community in the Highlands of Chiapas*. Cambridge.

Willey, G. R., Bullard, W. R. Jr, Glass, J. B. and Gifford, J. C. 1965. *Prehistoric Maya Settlements in the Belize Valley*. Papers of the Peabody Museum of Archaeology and Ethnology, Harvard University. 54.

The scientific analysis of ancient ceramics: a review

D. P. S. Peacock

1 Introduction

Although the scientific analysis of pottery fabrics began in the nineteenth century (e.g., Richards 1895) it is only in the last decade that work of this type has been widely undertaken. Pottery has always been of prime importance to the archaeologist, but due perhaps to archaeology having roots in classical history or in eighteenth-century antiquarianism and subsequently developing as an humanity, the emphasis has been largely upon morphology and decoration. Typological evidence has, of course, been subjected to detailed scientific analysis (e.g., Clarke 1962) but here we shall be concerned solely with the much neglected study of *fabrics*: the material of which ceramics are made.

The object of this paper is to draw the attention of archaeologists to the way in which studies of this type can provide information which is valuable and often essential to the correct interpretation of pottery evidence. Our museums contain vast and ever growing collections of ceramics of all types and it is high time that this store of potential information was more effectively utilized.

2 Preliminary considerations

The aims of the scientific study of ceramics can be conveniently considered under two principal headings: (1) technology, and (2) characterization. The elucidation of technology, the methods by which clays were prepared, shaped, finished and fired, has been the principal objective of many analysts (e.g., Grazhdankina 1965; Hodges 1966; Kociszewski and Kruppê 1968; Sayko 1965; Wirska 1967). This is hardly surprising since the history of technology is an important and interesting field in its own right. However, the results of such studies deserve to be more fully integrated with the findings of conventional typological examination since technological data can contribute to the interpretation of ceramic evidence. In primitive pottery, it is reasonable to suppose, for example, that the way in which the paste was mixed would be dictated by tradition in just the same way as the subsequent processes of forming and decoration. Perhaps in some cases it may be an even more reliable index of the heritage of the potter: for whereas typology may be influenced by relatively ephemeral contacts (e.g., by copying of traded articles), a rather more drastic influence may be needed to change basic technological processes such as clay preparation or firing, though the social mechanisms by which such innovations can be effected have yet to be fully assessed (cf. Shepard 1964).

We can see such a change if we compare the fabrics of the British primary series of Bronze Age Collared Urns with those of the preceding Neolithic Fengate and Mortlake pottery from which the main formative element is thought to stem (Longworth 1961). Study under a hand lens of many hundred Collared Urns from sites throughout lowland Britain shows that they are practically invariably tempered with grog (crushed pottery), but while the Fengate style sometimes contains grog, the bulk of the Neolithic pottery is tempered with crushed calcined flint. Clearly a widespread technological change has taken place and the source of the innovation would seem to be the Beaker invaders, for Hodges (1966) has shown that Beaker pottery is practically invariably grog tempered. What this technological break in the evolution of Collared Urns may mean in terms of changes in social structure is an interesting question difficult to assess at present. The new evidence need not alter Longworth's main conclusions but it does suggest that there may have been a rather stronger Beaker element than has hitherto been allowed.

It is, however, the scientific *characterization* of pottery that has produced the most spectacular results and it is here that the main emphasis of this review will lie. Characterization involves the examination of the properties of ceramics with a view to isolating materials of different origin and ultimately establishing their source where possible. To do this effectively and objectively recourse to scientific techniques is normally essential.

However, with the resources at present available to archaeology it is usually impossible to analyse more than a very small proportion of the vessels of any one type. If the results of scientific analysis are to be extrapolated effectively, it is essential that a system be devised for the accurate description of the macroscopic features of pottery fabrics, so that visual comparison can be facilitated. It is of course already customary for notes on fabrics to be included in pottery reports, but, whereas typology is often described in minute detail the fabric usually receives scant notice. Furthermore in the writer's experience (which is restricted to Europe in general and Britain in particular) the majority of published descriptions are of little value. Inclusions are often misidentified (e.g., felspar recorded as shell) and the terminology is vague and imprecise. The term 'gritty', for example, may be used to cover anything from sand to large inclusions of perhaps crushed flint, while the much abused term 'calcite gritted' can cover anything from pottery containing shell, through calcite (*sensu stricto*) to limestone fragments. Clearly a standardized terminology is urgently needed and since pottery is essentially a modified sedimentary rock it would seem reasonable to adopt the terminology long ago established by sedimentary petrologists (see, e.g., Shepard 1968). However, herein lies a difficulty for although we might reasonably expect sediments to be described by trained personnel, most of the macroscopic descriptions of pottery will have to be made by people unfamiliar with the appropriate discipline. The need therefore is for a simple system which can be rapidly and unambiguously applied. At least a partial answer may lie in the adoption of simple tests for recognizing the commoner tempering materials and the use of visual comparative charts, such as that published by Matson (1963: pl. XXIV), for determining the approximate size and quantity of inclusions. The introduction of colour-charts (e.g., by De Laet and Thoen 1969) is a useful step along these lines.

3 Scientific methods

There are many scientific techniques which can be applied to the study of ceramics and the more important ones are outlined in this section, together with a discussion of certain facets of their application which directly concern the archaeologist.

(*a*) *Chemical methods*

Chemical analysis has found considerable application in the study of ceramics, particularly in problems of characterization, for different clay deposits can be distinguished by their chemical composition. In theory at least, any analytical technique can be used. The now classical gravimetric method of silicate analysis is of little use as it is excessively laborious, but it was applied, for example, by Jenkins (1908) to show that briquetage from Iron Age saltworking on the Essex coast was made from local raw materials. It is usual, however, to restrict the work to partial analysis for minor and/or trace elements and the method normally used is optical emission spectrometry. This involves taking a very small sample of pottery (usually by drilling in an unobtrusive place), which is burnt between carbon electrodes. The light emitted is split by a system of prisms and the resulting spectrum photographed. The presence of different chemical elements is represented by lines at specific places on the photographic plate and their intensity is proportional to the percentage of the element. Thus if a sample of unknown composition is run and the intensity of different lines compared with that of a sample of known composition, the chemical composition of the unknown can be quantitatively estimated. As might be anticipated this process is not very accurate but an error of 10–30% is unimportant when considering elements present in the order of 1–2% or less.

The choice of which elements to measure tends to be somewhat arbitrary. Aluminium, magnesium, iron, titanium, manganese, chromium, calcium, sodium and nickel have been most commonly studied in this country (e.g., Richards 1959; Catling, Richards and Blin-Stoyle 1963; Hartley and Richards 1965), though Freeth (1967) has drawn attention to the dangers attendant on the postdepositional migration of such mobile elements as calcium, manganese and iron. Although this can be taken as a useful warning against placing too much emphasis on too few analyses or even on those from a single site where such changes may be taking place, in fairness it must be stated that groupings using these elements often seem to make archaeological sense.

Bouchard (1966) has made a contribution to the problem of choice of elements, based on a study of vessels taken from sites spread throughout Europe and North Africa. She suggests that iron, manganese, copper, chromium, nickel and cobalt will be most generally useful in characterizing wares made from different clays, while titanium, lead, tin and silver are of little value, but unfortunately elements other than these were not considered. Mitrichev (1965), on the other hand, lists the following elements in order of their usefulness: manganese, nickel, sodium, copper, magnesium, silicon, calcium, iron, barium and aluminium. Thus, although the method is useful, there is no general agreement about the best elements to study and resolution of this problem might help to enhance the technique's powers of archaeological differentiation. The writer is inclined to think that the optimum elements will vary from one geological province to another, and before attempting a major ceramic study it might be advisable to analyse a selection of clays from the region in order to determine which chemical elements are likely to give optimum ceramic differentiation.

Another method of chemical analysis which is coming to the fore, is X-ray fluorescence spectrometry. When a specimen is irradiated with X-rays it emits secondary or fluorescent X-rays characteristic of the different chemical elements present in the sample. By analysing the spectrum of fluorescent X-rays it is possible to determine both qualitatively and quantitatively the elements present (see Hall 1960). Since the technique can be non-destructive it is not surprising that it found an archaeological application early in its career, when Young and Whitmore (1957) used it to distinguish oriental ceramics from different centres of production. However, the method suffers from the drawback that it only analyses the material to a depth of about 0·01 to 0·1 mm. and thus if the surface has been treated in any way or if surface enrichment in chemical elements has taken place during burial, the analysis may not be representative of the sample as a whole. This difficulty can be overcome by crushing about 2–5 g. of pot to a fine powder after removal of the outer layers. This is then made up into an artificial 'pellet' the surface of which can be analysed to give a true picture of the chemical composition. Although the quantity of material required is large by comparison with samples for spectrographic analysis, it is usually possible to remove this amount without unduly affecting the archaeological value of sherded material, and the sacrifice is admirably compensated by the increased accuracy and by the fact that it is possible to analyse major as well as minor and trace elements with comparative ease. Furthermore, the pellets are not destroyed by analysis and can be stored for future reference. Although this technique has been little used to date, it is now becoming standard equipment in university geochemical laboratories and we can look forward to its increased application by archaeologists. The writer, for example, has used it in the study of prehistoric pottery in south-western Britain.

Neutron activation analysis is another non-destructive method which is receiving attention at present. The sample is bombarded with neutrons in a nuclear reactor, inducing weak radioactivity. Study of the gamma-ray spectrum from this enables qualitative and quantitative determination of the constituent elements. Preliminary work has been carried out on various groups of Mediterranean pottery (Sayre and Dodson 1957), on Samian ware (Emeleus 1960; Emeleus and Simpson 1960) and on pottery from a number of sites in America (Sayre, Murenhoff and Weick 1958; Bennyhoff and Heizer 1964). As Shepard (1968, 1966b) has pointed out, a drawback with this work is that only the concentrations of sodium and manganese have been studied, and although the results show promise it is difficult to put much weight on characterization based on two elements.

Aspinall, Slater and Mayes (1968) have recently begun to examine pottery from some eighty British medieval kiln sites using the neutron activation analysis to determine trace elements. In preliminary work on material from two kilns, ten elements were studied and satisfactory differentiation was obtained. Perlman and Asaro (1969) have studied an even more comprehensive range of elements, but their paper is concerned mainly with methodology, and it is difficult to assess the full archaeological value of their work from the few illustrative results quoted.

(*b*) *Petrological methods*

A particularly valuable method of studying ancient ceramics is by examination in thin section under the petrological microscope. This involves removal of a small fragment of pottery (*c.* 10 mm. × 10 mm.) which is fixed to a glass microscope slide and ground with a diamond lap or with abrasive powder until it is exactly 0·03 mm. thick (see, e.g., Cornwall 1958 for method). Most of the minerals are then transparent, and can be studied under the petrological microscope, an instrument equipped with optical refinements which enable the precise determination of mineral and rock inclusions. Clay minerals are too fine-grained to be identified in this way and so the study is limited to coarse inclusions, either naturally occurring in the clay or added as temper.

Thin sections are invaluable in research into ancient technology for it is usually possible to determine the way the paste was mixed (from the types and distribution of inclusions), whether the vessel was wheel or hand-made (since wheel-turning will tend to orientate long inclusions parallel to the pot walls) and the firing temperature (by observing changes in certain key minerals).

The method is, however, equally valuable in characterization, for pots made in a similar way from the same materials will appear alike under the microscope. Furthermore, when rock inclusions are present it is frequently possible to determine the source of raw materials from the types present, if the geology of the area under consideration is known. The precision that is possible will depend upon the extent of the natural outcrops of the parent rock of the inclusions. Thus if the parent rock is, for example, a limestone or sandstone which outcrops over a wide area, the provenance of the pottery will be defined only within broad limits, whereas the presence of an unusual igneous rock may enable the source to be defined within very close limits.

Unfortunately a great deal of pottery contains inclusions of quartz sand and little else. In thin section all that can be seen are grains of quartz embedded in a matrix of baked clay and it is usually impossible to say much about the provenance of such commonplace materials. Heavy mineral analysis is a useful approach in such cases (Peacock 1967). About 20–30 g. of pot are crushed and floated on a liquid with a specific gravity of 2·9. The quartz and clay float while the heavy minerals (e.g., zircon, garnet, tourmaline etc.) sink enabling them to be separated and mounted on a microscope slide. Since sands of differing geological origins can be distinguished by their heavy mineral assemblages, pots of different origin can likewise be characterized. In some parts of the world, such as Britain, a considerable amount of work has been done on the distribution of heavy minerals throughout the geological systems and in such cases it may be possible to refer to the geological literature and to discover the system with which the mineral assemblage in the pot is most closely related. From the distribution of rocks of this type it may be possible to limit the source area of the pottery. The main drawbacks are that the method involves destruction of a considerable quantity of pottery, and it is excessively laborious. It is not surprising therefore to find that it has been little used in archaeology: Peacock (1967) has reviewed some of its applications, to which should be added Wallis and Evens's (1934) study of pottery from Pant-y-Saer, Anglesey. Although not suitable as a technique for routine examination it has considerable potential in answering specific questions.

(*c*) *Other techniques*

Although the principal methods for the study of ceramics have been outlined above, a number of other techniques have been used on occasion, some of which have produced interesting results.

One of the drawbacks of thin section examination is that it does not permit study of the clay mineralogy of the pottery. Clay is not a homogeneous material but is made up of submicroscopic grains of various clay minerals of which common examples are kaolinite, illite and montmorillonite. Since clay mineralogy varies in different deposits, this can, theoretically, be used to characterize pottery. However, in practice, most clay minerals are destroyed by heating above about 500° C and hence it is applicable only to very low fired wares.

The writer has studied the clay mineralogy of certain Iron Age pots from Cornwall showing that they contain a predominance of montmorillonite. This information is useful from several points of view. Firstly, the clays, suspected as the source on other grounds, are also montmorillonitic, and secondly, the fact that this mineral is preserved at all indicates a firing temperature of less than 300° C since at this temperature the structure undergoes changes (Grim 1968: 314).

Clay mineralogy is studied by X-ray diffraction. The sample is bombarded with monochromatic X-rays, which are diffracted at different angles depending on the crystals present. Hence by studying the angles at which maximum diffraction occurs it is possible to identify the crystalline components. The sample required for this work is very small indeed.

The method is also of value in the study of wares fired at a very high temperature where new artificial minerals have developed in the fabric. Thus Bimson (1969) discusses its use in the identification of porcelain and stoneware where it is of value in distinguishing products of different centres and in detecting forgeries.

X-ray diffraction need not be limited to clay minerals and their high temperature alteration products. Since any crystalline substance can be identified in this way, the overall mineralogical composition of all types of pottery can be examined, and Young and Whitmore (1957) suggest that diffraction patterns may be an ideal way of 'finger-printing' pottery of different origins. However, the method cannot be regarded as a substitute for thin sectioning, for it gives no information about the way the minerals are distributed in the paste and this is often of considerable importance. On the other hand, since the technique can be non-destructive, it is a useful source of mineralogical information when sampling is not possible.

The organic matter present in many types of pottery has received little attention. However, an interesting advance in this field has recently been made by Duma and Lengyel (1969). They investigated the causes of the black appearance of pre-Scythian pottery from Mezöcsát on the northern edge of the Great Hungarian Plain and showed that it was due to an admixture of blood in the clay. Using a method of fluorescence analysis they were able to assess this quantitatively. Their discovery is of considerable interest as it opens up a new field of study, and from an archaeological point of view it would be valuable to know more of the geographical and chronological distribution of the technique of adding blood.

Sauter (1967) has recently investigated coatings on Hallstatt ceramics by infra-red spectrometry and shown them to be lacquer-like coatings of resin.

(*d*) *Selection of methods*

It will be clear from the above survey, which is by no means exhaustive, that the archaeologist is today confronted with an impressive array of techniques with which to examine his pottery fabrics and hence the question of choice of method arises. Ideally, the methodology should be tailored to fit the case under study, though in practice it is likely to be determined by what is readily available. On the broad question of whether to analyse chemically or petrologically, the obvious answer is that both should ideally be employed, since as Shepard (1968: xi) has pointed out, interplay between the two disciplines may be valuable in assessing the results from each. When, however, selection has to be made, it is important to consider the nature of the problem, since both approaches have limitations; though if technology is to be studied, thin sectioning is essential, for much of the required information can only be obtained in this way.

The optimum method for characterization will depend largely upon the texture of the ware. Petrology has the advantage that it may be possible to pinpoint sources of raw materials, but if distinctive rock fragments are absent this may be difficult. Wares of different origin would have to be characterized on granulometric considerations (e.g., grain size, sorting, ratio of quartz grains to clay matrix etc.) and the source of the individual groups would then have to be investigated by heavy mineral analysis.

This is not practicable with the very fine-grained well levigated wares and chemical analysis is ideally suited to such cases. Although this approach is useful in grouping wares of different origin, the actual source is not easy to ascertain, and it is usual to investigate this by considering distributional evidence. However, if a study is also made of the geochemistry of the principal clay deposits in the distribution area of the pottery, there is no reason why the sources should not be limited on chemical grounds. Catling, Blin-Stoyle and Richards (1963) claim that correspondence between pots and clay is not to be expected if the clays have been refined, and that dehydration on firing will alter the composition. However, Freeth (1967) has demonstrated by practical experiment and analysis that there is no reason why clays and pots should not be directly compared. For such comparisons to be valid it is, of course essential to ascertain that no extraneous matter has been added to temper the clay, and examination under the petrological microscope is a vital prerequisite.

Even if chemical analysis is ultimately adopted as the optimum method of investigation, it would be preferable to preface such work with a limited petrological investigation, in order to enhance understanding of how chemical elements are distributed in the paste: thus it may be possible to understand *why* a group of pots shows a particularly high concentration of a certain element or elements, e.g., a high calcium value might prove to be a result of the addition of limestone or shell to the clay (cf. Shepard 1968: vi).

In summary, the writer would advocate the adoption of the petrological microscope for the routine investigation of ceramics to be supplemented by chemical analysis where possible, rather than vice-versa.

4 Applications

Since not all archaeologists are equally enthusiastic about the encroachment of science into a field that was once a preserve of the arts (e.g., Hawkes 1968) it is perhaps as well to follow the above methodological outline with a discussion of the archaeological aspects of this work. In this section the writer proposes to review a few of the more important contributions that have been made to archaeology by the scientific study of ceramic fabrics.

It is appropriate that a survey of this type should begin with consideration of Anna Shepard's now classical work on the Rio Grande Glaze-Paint pottery (1942, 1966). Although not the earliest work of its kind, it was one of the first to bring home to the archaeological world the full value of the petrographical approach. Shepard studied the pottery from sites in the Upper Rio Grande Valley of New Mexico with particular reference to the sequence obtained from Kidder's excavation at Pecos, a site continuously occupied from about A.D. 1300 to A.D. 1838. Archaeological thought on the area had for many years proceeded on the assumption that the pottery at each site was locally made, hence it was supposed that although there were artistic stimuli from outside, the ceramic development of each site was essentially a local matter. As a result of a thorough and painstaking study of numerous thin sections Shepard revolutionized this by showing that there was a large-scale movement of pottery suggesting the existence of a hitherto unsuspected trade. Shepard was indeed fortunate in her choice of study area, for the varied geology made it possible to distinguish the products of different regions on the basis of rock temper. Materials such as andesite, basalt, tuff or sandstone had been added to the clay according to their local availability and these became the key to the classification of the pottery. It was possible to show the way in which the ceramic sequence at Pecos was related to innovations at specific localities and to changes in trade patterns.

In view of the remarkable success of this investigation conducted over thirty years ago, it is perhaps surprising that extensive studies of this kind have been few and far between until recent years, though the situation is rapidly changing. In Britain, the pioneer work of Cornwall and Hodges (1964) on Neolithic pottery has been followed by an extensive study of pre-Roman Iron Age pottery from western England (Peacock 1968, 1969b). Study of the pottery from the Severn Valley and Welsh Borderlands, comprising vessels ornamented with stamped impressed or linear tooled decoration, points to the Malvern Hills as the abode of specialist potters serving the region (Peacock 1968). The pots do not contain rock fragments local to the find-sites, but are instead tempered with igneous and metamorphic rocks which can only be matched in the Pre-Cambrian Malvernian, or with limestone or sandstone, for which there are good grounds to postulate a source in the Malvern region. The transportation of raw materials rather than pots cannot be substantiated in view of the typological homogeneity between sites and the use of iron repair rivets on some sites, suggesting that the community did not possess people competent to make replacement vessels.

A similar conclusion resulted from the study of ornate 'Glastonbury' ware found on many Iron Age sites throughout south-western England (Peacock 1969b). Six centres of production in Cornwall, Devon and Somerset were postulated and doubtless others will come to light when more material is available for study. The products were transported over distances up to 150 miles.

The centralized production of Iron Age pottery is a new concept, and its implications go far beyond the light it throws on the social organization of the time. For the past forty years thought on the British Iron Age has proceeded within Hawkes's ABC framework (Hawkes 1931, 1959). In the scheme put forward in 1959 Hawkes sought to explain the Iron Age in terms of a series of regional immigrations, the intrusive peoples ultimately merging with the indigenous population to produce new distinctive insular cultures. However, this scheme is based largely on a consideration of pottery since this is the only find common to the majority of Iron Age sites. Underlying the use of pottery evidence in this way is the assumption that it is made in the home so that the distribution of differently ornamented styles will represent the areas of settlement and influence of peoples of different cultural background (see Brailsford 1960). In the west of England, pottery studied can now be seen as a traded product, and the distribution of different styles may represent nothing more than the marketing areas of different groups of potters. Whether these correspond to the homes of different groups of people remains to be demonstrated. The evidence available so far does not favour this, for the pottery distributions cut across zones based, for example, on hill-fort architecture (e.g. Fox 1964: fig. 37). Thus in this case petrological study provides information which appears to cut at the basis of the accepted structure of the British Iron Age, and it is clearly desirable that pottery from the rest of lowland Britain should be investigated. Here the problems are greater, mainly because of lack of variation in the geology, a factor which greatly facilitated study in the west and south-west.

Most of the early work in Britain concerned with Neolithic pottery has recently been reviewed with a reassessment of the problem of the fine 'Hembury' ware, which was distributed through south-western and southern Britain in about 3300–3000 B.C. (Peacock 1969a). It was suggested that the fabric of this can be matched petrologically with the clay which is found above the gabbro outcrop on the Lizard peninsula in south Cornwall. Since the distribution of this pottery corresponds broadly with that of Cornish stone axes it was postulated that it may have been a trade ware. The movement of Neolithic pottery was, of course, demonstrated long ago when Obenauer (1936) isolated petrologically five imported groups from the settlement at Köln-Lindenthal. In one case, (Import II), the presence of basaltic hornblende, augite, plagioclase and biotite led him to postulate a source in the volcanic areas to the south of Cologne. It has been customary (Clark 1952: 251) to equate these imports with occasional visits of people from another area, but if a trade hypothesis is accepted for the fine Hembury ware, it might also apply to the Cologne material.

It would, however, be wrong to give the impression that petrological study is only of value when the long-distance movement of pottery can be demonstrated. It is always valuable to have scientific confirmation of a local source and this at least puts subsequent ceramic discussion on a sound basis. Krug (1965), for example, has studied the ceramics from the kingdom of the Cimmerian Bosphorus (between the sea of Azov and the Black Sea) demonstrating production at Panticapaeum, Phanagoria and Hermonassa. The local origin was confirmed by careful comparison with clays from the Kerch and Taman peninsulas involving separation and study of heavy and light fractions and differential thermal analysis. The latter was used in comparison of clay from Phanagoria with pottery. On applying heat at a steady increasing rate, clays display endothermic and exothermic reactions at different temperatures depending upon their composition, and the Phanagorian clays and pottery displayed similar characteristics.

Krug (1965) also made an extensive study of the pottery of the Cherniakov culture, produced over wide areas of the Ukraine in second to fourth centuries A.D. The coarse wares varied petrologically from site to site, and sometimes within a single site, as a result of the use of different local raw materials. However, the contemporary fine black polished ware with inclusions principally of quartz, 0·1–0·03 mm. across, displayed a remarkable homogeneity in microtexture throughout the area studied. It appears that potters, working at different centres, were producing a remarkably consistent paste regardless of variations in the local clay available, and Krug suggests there must have been a single widely used technological recipe in circulation throughout the area.

Space does not permit further discussion of the application of petrology to ceramics but other examples are the works of De Angelis (1960), Farnsworth (1964), Felts (1942), Gladwin (1937), Guerreschi (1966), Reyman (1959), Sundius (1955) and Williams (1967), while more references to the Russian literature are to be found in papers by Krug (1965) and Petrun (1966).

Spectrographic analysis has produced much valuable information about the movement of ancient pottery. An important study of Mycenaean and Minoan pottery, involving the analysis of over 500 sherds, has been published by Catling, Richards and Blin-Stoyle (1963), but this will not be discussed here as it has already been criticized in detail by Shepard (1968: iv) who suggests that the results might have been clarified by study of thin sections. This deficiency has now apparently been rectified (Millett and Catling 1967) but the results have not yet been published. The spectrographic work has continued since 1965 when Shepard wrote her review (Catling and Millett 1965 a and b, 1966, 1969) and more data are awaiting publication. This study which now involves more than a thousand samples from over fifty sites is of considerable importance and interest.

Another useful spectrographic investigation is the study by Hartley and Richards (1965) of 270 sherds of Romano-British mortaria. These, trituration grits apart, are often fine-grained and may not be so amenable to microscopic examination. The study was largely restricted to kiln finds with the objective of setting up reference standards to facilitate the recognition of the products of different centres. Although extreme differentiation was exceptional, the results clearly demonstrate the feasibility of chemical characterization of mortaria. Used in conjuction with archaeological evidence, the results are of particular value in, for example, tracing the movements of potters such as G. ATTIVS MARINVS who appears to have worked at three widely separated places – Colchester, Radlett (Hertfordshire) and Hartshill (Warwickshire).

As further examples of the application of spectrographic analysis we may cite papers by Musty and Thomas (1962) and Payne (1966).

5 Conclusions

Although the above survey is of necessity brief and by no means comprehensive, it should be evident that the scientific analysis of pottery fabrics has an important role in archaeological research. It is perhaps not too much of an exaggeration to claim that studies which consider typology alone are based on about half of the available data. Admittedly, the two classes of information are not always of equal importance: in some cases study of fabric may add little to what can be deduced on typological grounds, but frequently knowledge of the composition is essential if the evidence is to be correctly assessed. This applies particularly to primitive ceramics, which often have an exaggerated place in archaeological thought because of the lack of other evidence. We can no longer assume that hand-made pottery is of necessity home made, nor can we deduce the organization of pottery production by analogy with the activities of present-day primitive potters. Objective scientific methods are available for assessing such questions and the need is for their application.

However, this is not to claim that the technique is perfect. The chemical approach would benefit from more work on the selection of elements for study, while in petrology one of the most pressing needs is for the adoption and application of suitable granulometric methods for characterizing the ubiquitous sandy wares in thin section. At present the comparison of such sherds tends to be somewhat subjective, the petrologist pronouncing whether the fabrics 'look' alike under the microscope. In practice these comparisons have limited value, for the texture of a sandy potsherd is an extremely complex matter, depending on factors such as the proportion of sand to clay, roundness of the grains, their sphericity and the properties of the size distribution. If each of these were isolated, measured, and expressed in terms of mathematical parameters as is customary with sedimentary rocks, it would put the study of such wares on a much more objective basis. The writer is engaged in research into this question and a report will be published in due course.

The last decade has seen impressive advances in instrumentation and doubtless this trend will continue. A particularly interesting and very recent development is the use of a portable X-ray fluorescent spectrometer for on-site analysis of ceramics (Frierman *et al.* 1969). The advantage of this approach is that it enables problems thrown up by the analysis to be investigated on the site, and could prove of considerable importance, particularly on sites of difficult access.

In general, the most successful analyses appear to be those carried out on a large scale, drawing on contemporary pottery from sites throughout a wide geographical region. By contrast the writer knows of a number of references, which need not be cited, where geologists of repute have come to the wrong conclusion about the source of a sherd simply because they were asked to pronounce upon a single piece which they were unable to see in its true distributional perspective.

If we are to see an increase in the scope of analyses in the future as seems desirable, it will soon be necessary to introduce objective methods to sort and classify the mass of scientific data obtained. The computer has already been used in typological work (Clarke 1962) and there is every reason for applying it to fabric studies. The problem of grouping chemical analyses of ceramics is analogous to that of metal analyses and the methods discussed by, for example, Hodson (1969) could apply to this field also. Furthermore, petrological data can easily be coded in a manner suitable for computer analysis and Krug and Krug (1965) have already pioneered a statistical method for classifying pottery on the basis of thin sections. The development of such approaches may well be the most important aspect of ceramic analysis in the next few years.

15.viii.69

Department of Archaeology
University of Southampton

References

Angelis, A. M. de. 1960. Ricerche mineralogiche su ceramiche preistoriche italiano. *Sibrium.* 5:178–205.

Aspinall, A., Slater, D. N. and Mayes, P. 1968. Neutron activation analysis of medieval ceramics. *Nature.* 217:388.

Bennyhoff, J. A. and Heizer, R. F. 1964. Neutron activation analysis of some Cuicuilo and Teotihuacan pottery: archaeological interpretation of results. *Amer. Ant.* 30:348–9.

Bimson, M. 1969. The examination of ceramics by X-ray powder diffraction. *Studies in Conservation.* 14:85–9.

Bouchard, A. 1966. De l'emploi des méthodes chimique et spectrographique pour l'étude des poteries antique. *Geol. Rundschau.* 55:113–18.

Brailsford, J. W. 1960. Problems of Iron Age pottery: an introduction to a discussion. In *Problems of the Iron Age in Southern Britain*, ed. S. S. Frere. London. 95–6.

Catling, H. W., Blin-Stoyle, A. E. and Richards, E. E. 1961. Spectrographic analysis of Mycenaean and Minoan pottery. *Archaeometry.* 4:31–8.

Catling, H. W. and Millett, A. 1965a. A study of the Inscribed Stirrup Jars from Thebes. *Archaeometry.* 8:5–83.

Catling, H. W. and Millett, A. 1965b. A study of the composition patterns of Mycenaean pictorial pottery from Cyprus. *Ann. Brit. School Arch. Athens.* 60:212–24.

Catling, H. W. and Millett, A. 1966. Composition & provenance: a challenge. *Archaeometry.* 9:92–7.

Catling, H. W. and Millett, A. 1969. Theban Stirrup Jars: questions and answers. *Archaeometry.* 11:3–20.

Catling, H. W., Richards, E. E. and Blin-Stoyle, A. E. 1963. Correlations between composition and provenance of Mycenaean and Minoan pottery. *Ann. Brit. School Arch. Athens.* 58:94–115.

Clark, J. G. D. 1952. *Prehistoric Europe, The Economic Basis.* London.

Clarke, D. 1962. Matrix analysis and archaeology with particular reference to British Beaker pottery. *Proc. Prehist. Soc.* 28:371–82.

Cornwall, I. W. 1958. *Soils for the Archaeologist.* London.

Cornwall, I. W. and Hodges, H. W. M. 1964. Thin sections of British Neolithic pottery: Windmill Hill – a test site. *Bull. Inst. Arch. London Univ.* 4:29–33.

Duma, Gy. and Lengyel, I. 1969. Fluoreszenzanalytische Untersuchungen aus bluthaltigem Ton hergestellten urzeitlichen Gefässe. *Arch. Austriaca.* 45:1–16.

Emeleus, V. M. 1960. Neutron activation analysis of Samian Ware sherds. *Archaeometry.* 3:16–24.

Emeleus, V. M. and Simpson, G. 1960. Neutron activation analysis of ancient Roman potsherds. *Nature.* 185:196.

Farnsworth, M. 1964. Greek pottery: a mineralogical study. *Am. J. Arch.* 68:221–8.

Felts, W. M. 1942. A petrographic examination of potsherds from Ancient Troy. *Am. J. Arch.* 46:237–44.

Fox, A. 1964. *South-West England.* London.

Freeth, S. J. 1967. A chemical study of some Bronze Age pottery sherds. *Archaeometry.* 10:104–19.

Frierman, J. D., Bowman, H. R., Perlman, I. and York, C. M. 1969. X-ray fluorescence spectrography: use in field archaeology. *Science.* 164:588.

Gladwin, N. 1937. Petrography of Snaketown pottery. In H. S. Gladwin *et al.*, *Excavations at Snaketown.* Medallion papers, Gila Pueblo, Arizona, No. 25. Chap. 17.

Grazhdankina, N. S. 1965. Metodika Chimiko-technologichogo issledovaniya drevney keramiki. In *Arkheologiya i Yestestvennye Nauki*, ed. B. A. Kolchina. Moscow. 152–60.

Grim, R. E. 1968 (2nd edn). *Clay Mineralogy.* New York.

Guerreschi, G. 1966. Ceramica preistorica al microscopio. *Sibrium.* 8:151–60.

Hall, E. T. 1960. X-ray fluorescent analysis applied to archaeology. *Archaeometry.* 3:29–35.

Hartley, K. E. and Richards, E. E. 1965. Spectrographic analysis of some Romano-British mortaria. *Bull. Inst. Arch. London Univ.* 5:25–43.

Hawkes, C. F. C. 1931. Hill-Forts. *Antiquity.* 5:60–148.

Hawkes, C. F. C. 1959. The ABC of the British Iron Age. *Antiquity.* 33:170–82.

Hawkes, J. 1968. The proper study of mankind. *Antiquity.* 42: 255–62.

Hodges, H. W. M. 1966. Aspects of pottery in temperate Europe before the Roman Empire. In *Ceramics and Man*, ed. F. T. Matson. London.

Hodson, F. R. 1969. Searching for structure within multivariate archaeological data. *World Arch.* 1:90–105.

Jenkins, J. H. B. 1908. The chemical examination of some substances from the Red Hills of Essex. *Proc. Soc. Ant. London.* 2nd Ser. 22:182–6.

Kociszewski, L. and Kruppê, J. 1968. A method of physico-chemical investigation prompting the study of technology in the history of pottery production. *Arch. Polona.* 6:161–84.

Krug, G. K. and Krug, O. Yu. 1965. Matematicheskiy metod klassifikatsii drevney keramiki. In *Arkheologiya i Yestestvennye nauki*, ed. B. A. Kolchina. Moscow. 318–25.

Krug, O. Yu. 1965. Primeneniye petrografii v arkheologii. In *Arkheologiya i Yestestvennye nauki*, ed. B. A. Kolchina. Moscow. 146–52.

Laet, S. J. de and Thoen, H. 1969. Etudes sur la céramique de la nécropole gallo-romaine de Blicquy (Hainaut), IV: La céramique 'à enduit rouge-pompéien' *Helinium*. 9:28–38.

Longworth, I. 1961. The origins and development of the primary series in the Collared Urn tradition in England and Wales. *Proc. Prehist. Soc.* 27:263–306.

Matson, F. T. 1963. Some aspects of ceramic technology. In *Science in Archaeology*, ed. D. Brothwell and E. S. Higgs. London.

Millett, A. and Catling, H. W. 1967. Composition patterns of Minoan and Mycenaean pottery: survey and prospects. *Archaeometry*. 10:70–7.

Mitrichev, V. S. 1965. Spektral'nyy analiz keramiki. In *Arkheologiya i Yestestvennye nauki*, ed. B. A. Kolchina. Moscow. 171–4.

Musty, J. W. G. and Thomas, L. C. 1962. The spectrographic examination of English and Continental medieval glazed pottery. *Archaeometry*. 5:38–52.

Obenauer, K. 1936. Petrographische Untersuchung der Keramik. In W. Butler and W. Haberey, *Die Bandkeramische Ansiedlung bei Köln Lindenthal*. Leipzig. 123–9.

Payne, J. C. 1966. Spectrographic analysis of some Egyptian pottery in the eighteenth dynasty. *J. Egypt Archaeol.* 52:176–8.

Peacock, D. P. S. 1967. The heavy mineral analysis of pottery: a preliminary report. *Archaeometry*. 10:97–100.

Peacock, D. P. S. 1968. A petrological study of certain Iron Age pottery from Western England. *Proc. Prehist. Soc.* 34:414–27.

Peacock, D. P. S. 1969a. Neolithic pottery production in Cornwall. *Antiquity*. 43:145–9.

Peacock, D. P. S. 1969b. A contribution to the study of Glastonbury ware from South-western Britain. *Ant. J.* 49:41–61.

Perlman, I. and Asaro, F. 1969. Pottery analysis by neutron activation. *Archaeometry*. 11:21–52.

Petrun, V. F. 1966. O mineralogo-petrograficheskikh issledovaniyak v arkheologii. *Zap. Vses, mineral. Obshchest.* 95:627–32.

Reyman, T. 1959. Metoda stosowania szlifów przezroczystych w badaniach nad ceramiką starozytna. *Archaeologia Polski*. 3:166–76.

Richards, E. E. 1959. Preliminary spectrographic investigation of some Romano-British mortaria. *Archaeometry*. 2:23–31.

Richards, T. W. 1895. The composition of Athenian pottery. *Amer. Chem. J.* 17:152–4.

Sauter, F. 1967. Chemische Untersuchung von 'Harzüberzügen' auf hallstatt-zeitlichen Keramik. *Arch. Austr.* 41:23–36.

Sayko, E. V. 1965. Tekhnologiya keramiki srednevekovykh masterov. In *Arkheologiya i Yestestvennye nauki*, ed. B. A. Kolchina. Moscow. 161–7.

Sayre, E. V. and Dodson, R. W. 1957. Neutron activation study of Mediterranean potsherds. *Am. J. Arch.* 61:35–41.

Sayre, E. V., Murenhoff, A. and Weick, C. F. 1958. The nondestructive analysis of ancient potsherds through neutron activation. *Brookhaven Nat. Lab. Pub.* 508.

Shepard, A. O. 1942. *Rio Grande Glaze Paint Ware, a Study Illustrating the Place of Ceramic Technological Analysis in Archaeological Research.* Carnegie Inst. Washington.

Shepard, A. O. 1964. Temper identification: 'Technological sherd-splitting' or an unanswered challenge. *Amer. Ant.* 29:518–20.

Shepard, A. O. 1966a. Rio-Grande glaze-paint pottery: a test of petrographic analysis. In *Ceramics and Man*, ed. F. T. Matson. London. 62–87.

Shepard, A. O. 1966b. Problems in pottery analysis. *Amer. Ant.* 31:870–1.

Shepard, A. O. 1968 (fifth printing). *Ceramics for the Archaeologist.* Carnegie Inst. Washington.

Sundius, N. 1955. Mikroskopische Untersuchung von Keramik – Scherben aus der Wikingerzeit und den frühen Mittelalten. In D. Selling, *Wikingzeitliche und Fruhmittelalterliche Keramik in Schweden.* Stockholm. 244–9.

Wallis, F. S. and Evens, E. D. 1934. Report on the heavy minerals contained in the coarse Pant-y-Saer pottery. *Arch. Camb.* 89: 29–32.

Williams, J. L. W. 1967. *A Petrological Study of the Prehistoric Pottery of the Aeolian Islands with Special Reference to the Stratigraphical sequence.* Ph.D. thesis, London University.

Wirska, M. 1967. Metoda mikroskopowej analizy cienkich szlifow w badaniach zabytkow ceramicznych. *Ochrono zabytkow.* 20:39–45.

Young, W. J. and Whitmore, F. E. 1957. Analysis of oriental ceramic wares by non-destructive X-ray methods. *Far East Ceramic Bull.* 9:1–27.

An elephant butchery site at Mwanganda's Village, Karonga, Malawi, and its relevance for Palaeolithic archaeology

J. Desmond Clark *and* C. Vance Haynes, Jr

Introduction

The site to be described in this paper was found and excavated in the course of the geological, palaeontological and archaeological field programme carried out in 1965 and 1966 in the Lake Malawi Rift, the Rungwe volcanic massif and the southern Rukwa basin by a team under the sponsorship of the University of California at Berkeley and financed by the National Science Foundation, Washington. A general summary of the results was presented at the Dakar meeting of the VIth Pan-African Congress on Prehistory and Quaternary Studies in December 1967 (Clark *et al.*, in press) so that the Quaternary succession is summarized only briefly here as a basis for a preliminary discussion of the oldest and one of the most interesting archaeological sites in the Malawi Rift.

The floor of the Malawi Rift trough (formerly known as the Nyasa Rift), with the lake, is sunk approximately 4,000 feet below the central African plateau at an elevation of 1,500 feet above sea-level. Numerous normal faults have divided the area into a series of ridges and troughs elongated in a north-westerly direction paralleling the lake shore. A succession of sediments dating from the Mesozoic upwards is preserved here. The Pleistocene sediments are preserved in graben in an area *c.* 12 × 60 miles in extent and are moderately tilted eastwards so that stratified exposures are best observed on eroded, west-facing scarps.

The major Quaternary deposits are divided into three sedimentary units, informally designated the Chiwondo, Chitimwe and Karonga formations. The Chiwondo formation, consisting mainly of lacustrine mudstones, marls and tuffs, contains vertebrate remains of Plio-Pleistocene to Middle Pleistocene age and is unconformably overlain by red, clayey gravels, grits and sands of the Middle Pleistocene to Holocene Chitimwe formation that contains 'Middle Stone Age' to Iron Age artefacts. The Karonga formation consists of Holocene alluvium making up four terraces along major drainages and the alluvial-lacustrine flats adjacent to Lake Malawi.

In spite of intensive search, no artefacts were found in the Chiwondo formation and the earliest human occupation belongs to the end of the Middle or earlier part of the Upper Pleistocene.

Stratigraphy and dating

The Mwanganda site was exposed by recent erosion on a north-west-facing slope of a small gully close to the village of that name about five miles west of Karonga. In this area (fig. 25*a*) the Chiwondo formation is overlain by ten to fifteen feet of Chitimwe sand and gravel. From the stratigraphy at the site (fig. 25*b* and table 1) it is readily apparent that the artefacts and bones occurred on the contact between the two units and within a truncated soil (Qco 1c) at the top of the Chiwondo formation (plate 1).

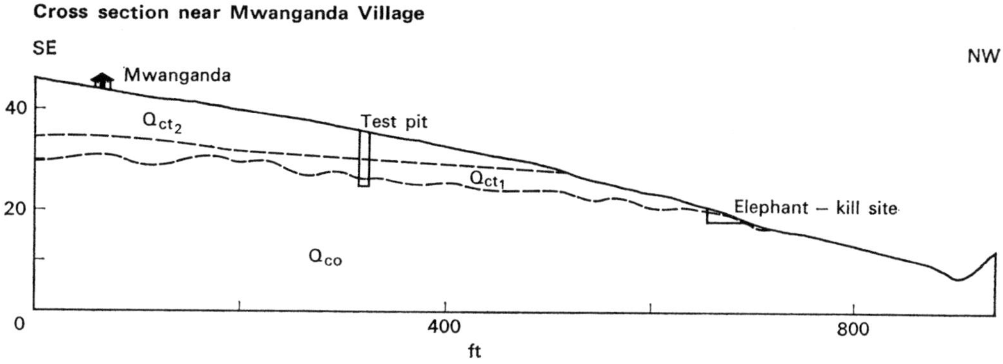

Figure 25a Geologic cross section near Mwanganda Village, Malawi, showing the Mwanganda elephant kill site and stratigraphic test pit in the Chiwondo (Qco) and Chitimwe (Qct) formations

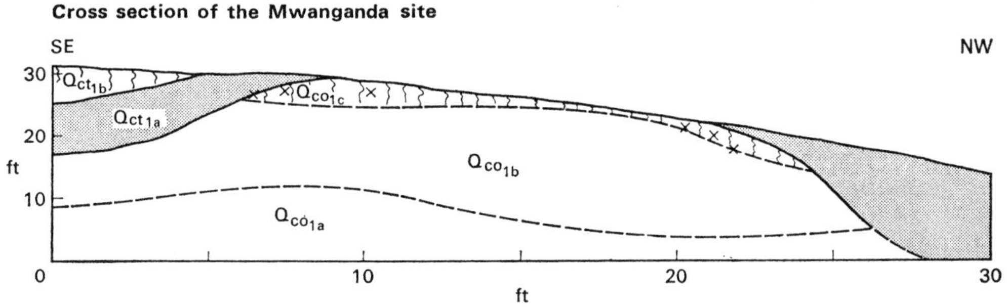

Figure 25b Geologic cross section of the south-west wall of the Mwanganda site showing the position of artefacts and bones (x) with respect to the contact between the Chiwondo (Qco) and Chitimwe (Qct) formations. Vertical wavey lines indicate palaeosols

The stratigraphic sequence exposed by excavation here in 1966 showed, at the top, a foot of sand and slopewash alluvium (Karonga formation), five feet of coarse, red sand and one foot of sandy, pebbly gravel (Upper Chitimwe formation). Under this the Lower Chitimwe deposits consist of two feet of dark brown sand (Qct 1b); a clayey, coarse sand with strong, medium, blocky soil structure; and overlying moderately rounded pebble gravel composed largely of derived calcite concretions and with a mottled white/grey matrix of sandy clay (Qct 1a).

TABLE I

Stratigraphic Units

Symbol	*Description*	*Max. Thick.*
	Karonga Formation	
Qk	Sand – light brownish-grey, laminated, loose, silty sand slope wash alluvium	1·0 ft
	Upper Chitimwe Formation	
Qct_{2b}	Sand – light red, massive, slightly clayey, coarse sand with dispersed insect burrows and tree roots in upper half. Upper 6 in. is pale brownish-grey, slightly hard sand with weak laminations and sharp upper contact.	5·0 ft
Qct_{2a}	Gravel – pale greenish-grey, sandy pebble gravel of rounded quartz, quartzite, feldspar and gneiss. Sharp contacts.	1·0 ft
	Lower Chitimwe Formation	
Qct_{1b}	Sand – dark brown (7·5YR4/2 dry, 3/2 wet), clayey, coarse sand with strong, medium blocky structure breaking to platey at the Mwanganda excavations. Mottled pale greenish-grey and brownish-red in the test pit.	2·0 ft
Qct_{1a}	Gravel – mottled white and greenish grey, sandy, clayey, moderately rounded, caliche-pebble gravel.	2·0 ft
	Erosional Hiatus	
	Chiwondo Formation	
Qco_{1c}	Sand – dark greyish-brown (2·5Y4/2 dry, 3/2 wet), silty, clayey sand with moderate to strong, medium, blocky structure breaking to angular, and dispersed carbonate nodules (*c.* $\frac{1}{2}$ in. diam.). Gradational lower contact. Artefacts and bones (X) are concentrated in and along the upper contact of this unit. A few fragments occurred below. Sharp upper contact.	0·5 ft
Qco_{1b}	Sand – greenish-grey, clayey sand with dispersed, irregular, carbonate nodules (*c.* $\frac{3}{4}$ in. diam.).	3·0 + ft
Qco_{1a}	Clay – greenish-grey, sandy clay with numerous dispersed, irregular carbonate nodules (*c.* 1 in. diam.). Gradational upper contact.	2·0 + ft

An erosional unconformity separates the Chitimwe formation from the underlying Chiwondo formation, at the top of which are some six inches of dark, greyish-brown, silty, clayey sand with moderate to strong medium blocky structure breaking to angular, and dispersed carbonate nodules (Qco 1c). This grades down into the greenish-grey sand of the Chiwondo proper.

Artefacts and bones are concentrated in and along the upper contact of the palaeosol formed on the Chiwondo and show irregular masses of calcium carbonate adhering to them. If this material is pedogenic, as the soil structure (table 1) suggests, then the occupation took place on top of the Chiwondo formation before the development of the soil had been completed. Erosion and soil formation are both presumably subsequent to the tectonism which elevated the formation. The Chitimwe formation was deposited during and after a period of widespread erosion that truncated the palaeosol and the artefact horizon. Carbonate nodules (table 1) in the earliest channel phase of the Chitimwe are obviously derived from the Chiwondo formation which contains numerous nodules, presumably of lacustrine origin.

As previously reported (Clark *et al.*, in press) the Lower Chitimwe contains rolled artefacts suggestive of Middle to early Upper Pleistocene age, so that the Mwanganda artefacts are of this age or probably older. The sequence of geologic events may have been as follows:

(1) lacustrine Chiwondo deposition in the Malawi Rift during Early and Middle Pleistocene time;

(2) extensive faulting during Middle Pleistocene time[1];

(3) occupation of the Chiwondo surface during a period of weathering followed by more weathering;

(4) extensive erosion; and

(5) deposition of the Lower Chitimwe sediments during Middle or early Upper Pleistocene time.

Carbonates were collected from the pertinent units at Mwanganda and it is hoped that in the near future these will prove useful for geochronometric dating by thermo-luminescent dosimetry techniques (Johnson and Blanchard 1967).

The archaeological occurrence

Most of the bones belong to a single elephant. They occurred dispersed on the edge of a small gully in three concentrations – at least ten ribs, two cervical and five or six thoracic vertebrae, fragments of tusk and mandible and, perhaps, of skull, the proximal end and shaft of a femur and of a humerus and the distal end and shaft of a radius. The artefacts are scattered around and under the bones which, in the course of burial and re-exposure, had suffered further weathering and fracture (plates 2 and 3). Also associated were a heavily worn upper molar, a complete scapula and tusk fragments of hippopotamus and a heavily worn upper molar of giraffe.

In Area 2, immediately upslope to the south, was a further light scatter of artefacts, a lower molar of *Equus*, some fragments of turtle carapace and vertebrae and one or two scraps of the bone of smaller animals. No more elephant bones were found here. Associated with these bones in Area 2 were six or seven bone splinters and flakes from what is

[1] Defined as the period of development and termination of the Acheulian Industrial Complex (Bishop 1963:252).

probably a large bovid. From the morphology of the specimens and their juxtaposition with the artefacts they provide clear evidence of intentional bone breaking by man.

The association of the stone artefacts with the dismembered, broken and dispersed remains leaves no doubt that this is a site where an elephant was butchered by man, the implements for this being made on the spot and discarded when the work was over. Area 2 material, moreover, suggests that it was a site visited by hunting groups on other occasions also.

The artefacts cluster round the three main concentrations of elephant bones, suggesting that three individuals or groups of hunters were involved. Artefacts were found among the rib bones in the north-east corner of the area and, when the femur was lifted (fig. 27, upper left), a further concentration of artefacts was found lying under this bone. The artefact assemblage is, therefore, of particular interest since it can be taken as representative of the butchery tool-kit of that time in south central Africa.

There are 314 artefacts from Area 1 associated with the bones. Analysis of the aggregate (fig. 26) shows that quartz and quartzite cobbles provided most of the raw material and that 99% of the specimens are fresh and unabraded. There are very few large tools

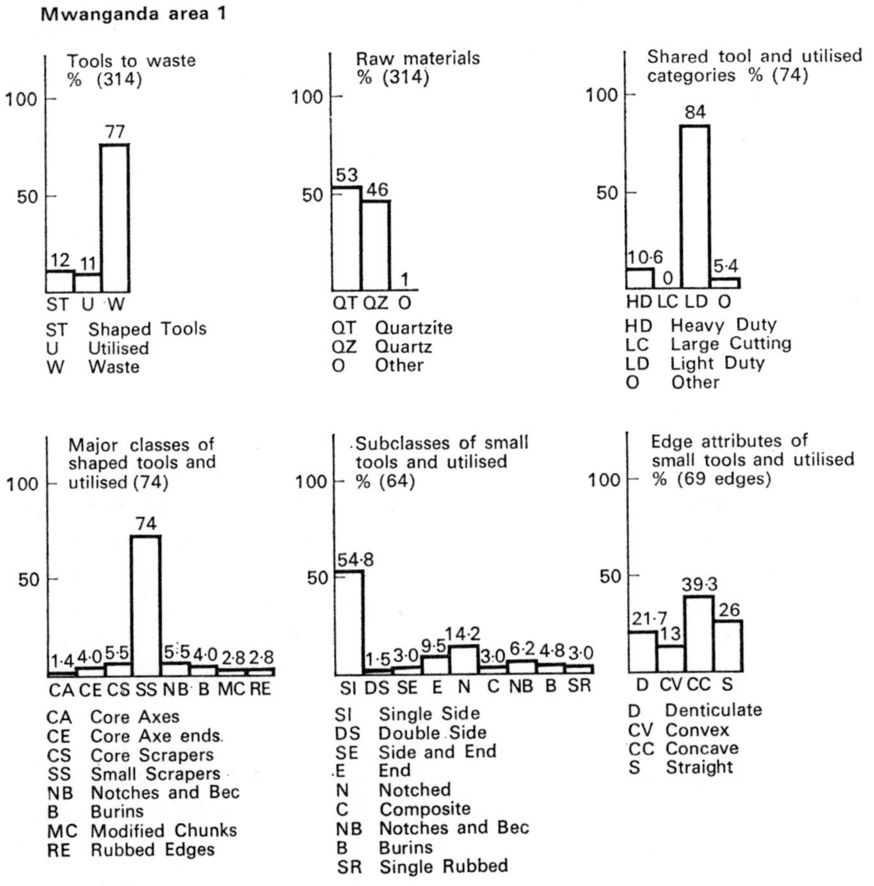

Figure 26 Analysis of artefact component with butchered elephant: Mwanganda, Area 1

present and this may come as a surprise in view of the frequently stated belief that the large cutting tools (handaxes and cleavers) may have been associated with the butchering of large animals. However, from this and other similar archaeological occurrences it would seem that this view is no longer tenable. The only Heavy Duty tools (8) are core scrapers with steep retouch from the flat, ventral face (fig. 28: 2 and 3; fig. 30: 3) and a crude, minimally worked, bifacial core-axe (fig. 28: 1). What are believed to be two tip ends of core-axes were found with the bones (fig. 30: 1 and 2) and a complete example (fig. 28: 1) was picked up at the east side of the site where it had been exposed by erosion in a small gully.

Most of the sixty-two shaped tools (fig. 29) consist of small scrapers which usually show minimal retouch or use of one (fig. 29: 2–9 and 12–13), sometimes of both (fig. 29: 1 and 14) side edges and, more rarely, of the end (fig. 29: 10 and 11) of a flake, fragment or chunk. A significant feature is the number that show concave and denticulate retouch (fig. 26).

Artefacts showing modification and utilization are illustrated at figure 30: 4–11. Four examples were found of an interesting tool formed by two opposing notches that make a *bec* or beak where they converge (fig. 30: 4–6). The other utilized artefacts are flakes showing minimal but unquestionable use of a cutting edge (fig. 30: 7–11).

The breakdown of the unmodified waste – flakes and cores – is shown at figures 31, 32 and 33. Fifty-four of the flakes are irregular, end-struck, and twenty-four irregular, side-struck. Mostly they show one- or two-directional flaking on the dorsal face; the striking platform is plain and is often composed of cortex. There are no large flakes, the upper limit being controlled by the size of the raw material; but some quite small ones occur.

From a comparison of the cores and flakes (fig. 34) it is apparent that suitable cores were brought to the site, broken into two or more pieces and the fragments flaked either from one (fig. 33: 1 and 4), or two (fig. 33: 2 and 3) platforms or radially (fig. 33: 6–8), to remove a number of small flakes, generally with thick cross section. On one such radially flaked core the scars rose steeply to an apex to give it an approximately pyramidal section (fig. 33: 5). None of the cores shows evidence of the Levallois technique and they are comparable to the high or cortex backed disc cores and biconical cores found with Acheulian and Sangoan aggregates.

The composition and main attributes of the Mwanganda aggregate (fig. 26) show that – comparing trimmed pieces to waste – there is, perhaps, a greater percentage of retouched and utilized artefacts than might be expected. Quartz and quartzite are about equally used. The preponderance of Light Duty equipment is very apparent. The tools rarely show any extensive retouch, this being marginal and only sufficient to modify the specimen for use. Signs of utilization are very extensive in the form of minute scarring of the edges, crushing and rubbing. This is entirely in keeping with the inferred nature of the tool-kit – made for a single occasion only. Some 55% of the classes of Light Duty tools are single side scrapers and the breakdown of the edge forms shows that in 39% the working edges are concave; in 26% they are straight and in 22% they are denticulate.

The breakdown of the flakes (fig. 31) shows that there are a little over 50% more irregular end-struck than side-struck flakes. The platform analysis shows that the cobble cortex was more often used than not, with no prior preparation, flakes being removed

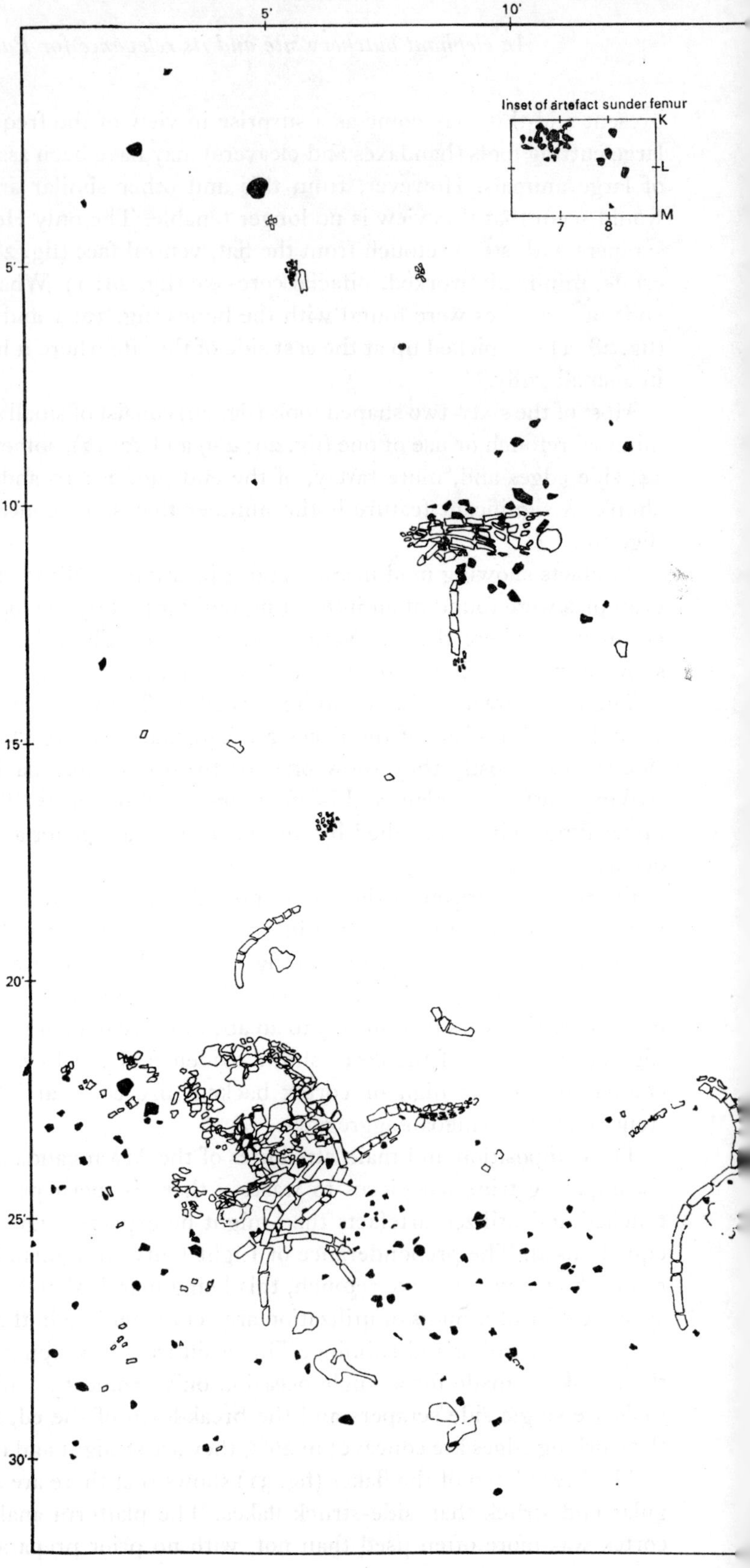

Figure 27 Mwanganda butchery site showing the dispersal of bones and artefacts in Area 1

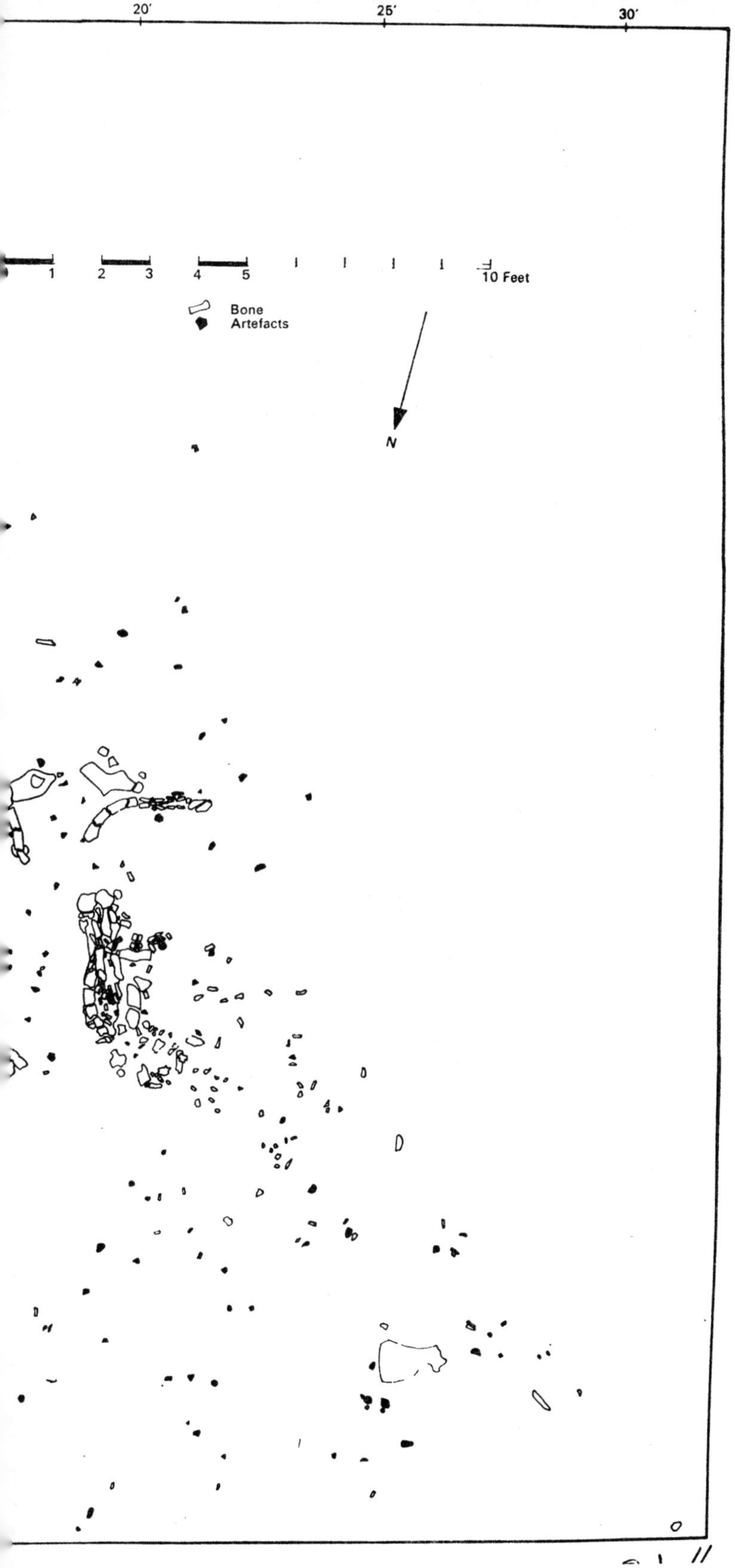

20′
25′
30′
1
2
3
4
5
10 Feet
Bone
Artefacts
N

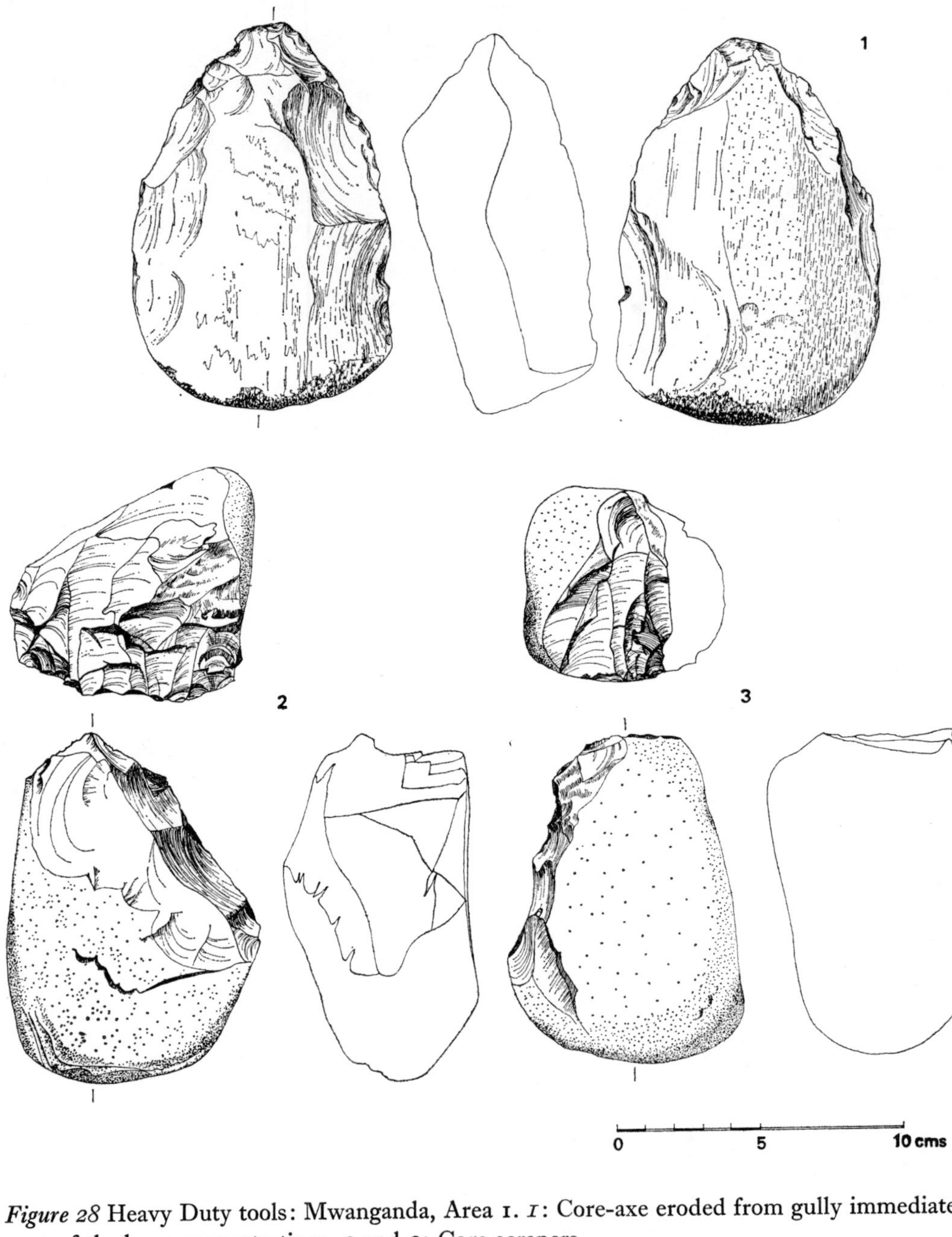

Figure 28 Heavy Duty tools: Mwanganda, Area 1. *1*: Core-axe eroded from gully immediately west of the bone concentrations. *2* and *3*: Core scrapers

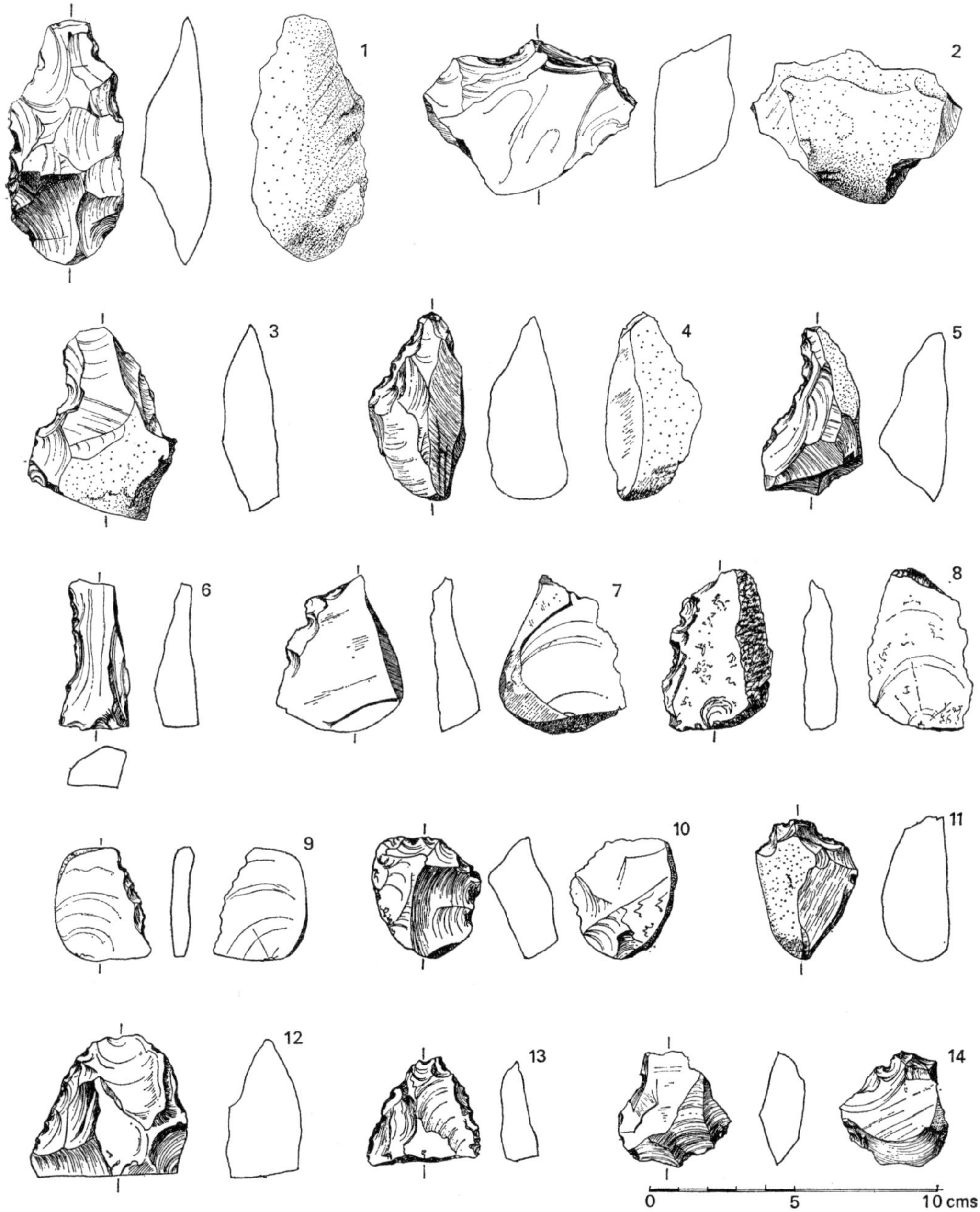

Figure 29 Light Duty tools: Mwanganda, Area 1. *1* and *14*: Side scrapers – double. *2–9*, *12* and *13*: Side scrapers – single. *10* and *11*: End scrapers

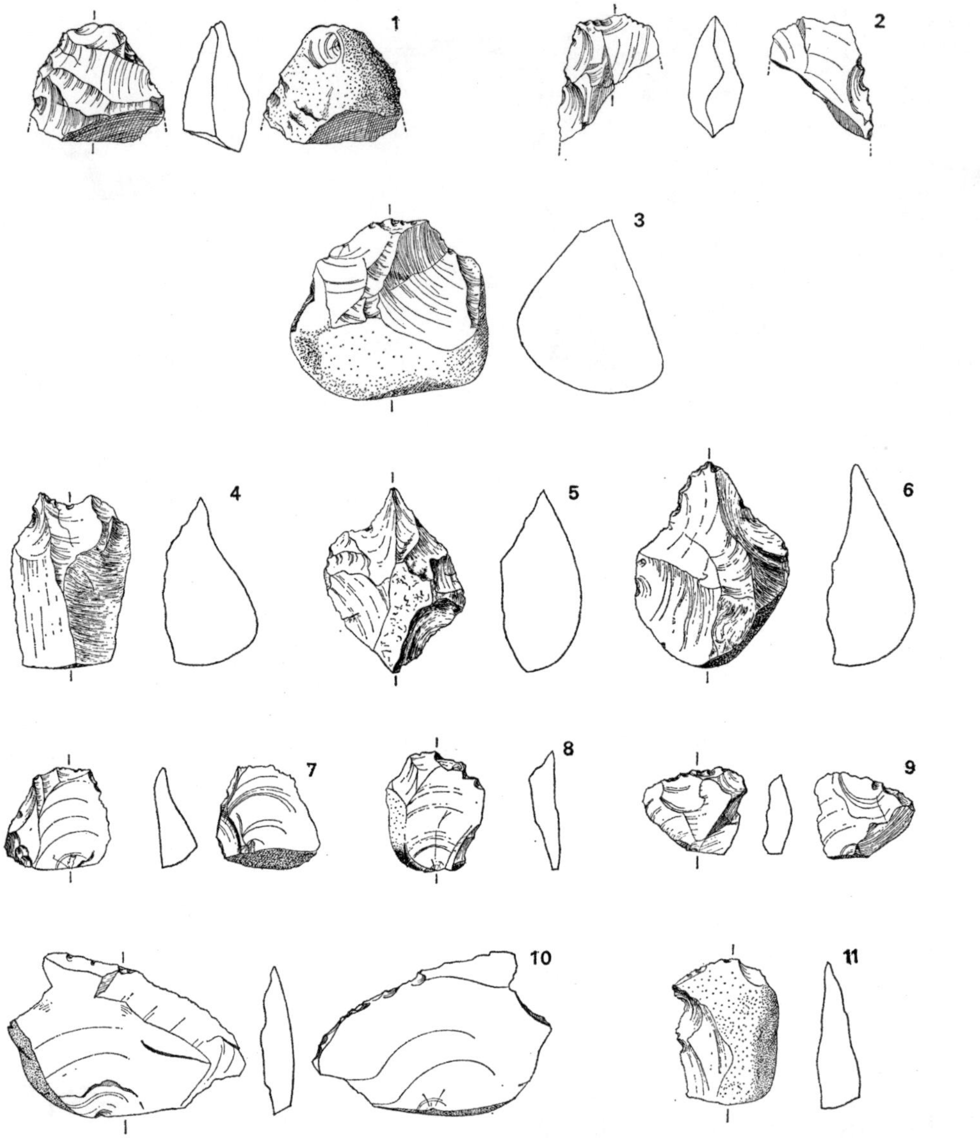

Figure 30 Retouched and utilized artefacts: Mwanganda, Area 1. *1* and *2*: ?Tip ends of core-axes, removed accidentally or for resharpening. *3*: Core scraper. *4–6*: *Becs* or beaked tools formed by two opposing notches. *7–11*: Utilized flakes

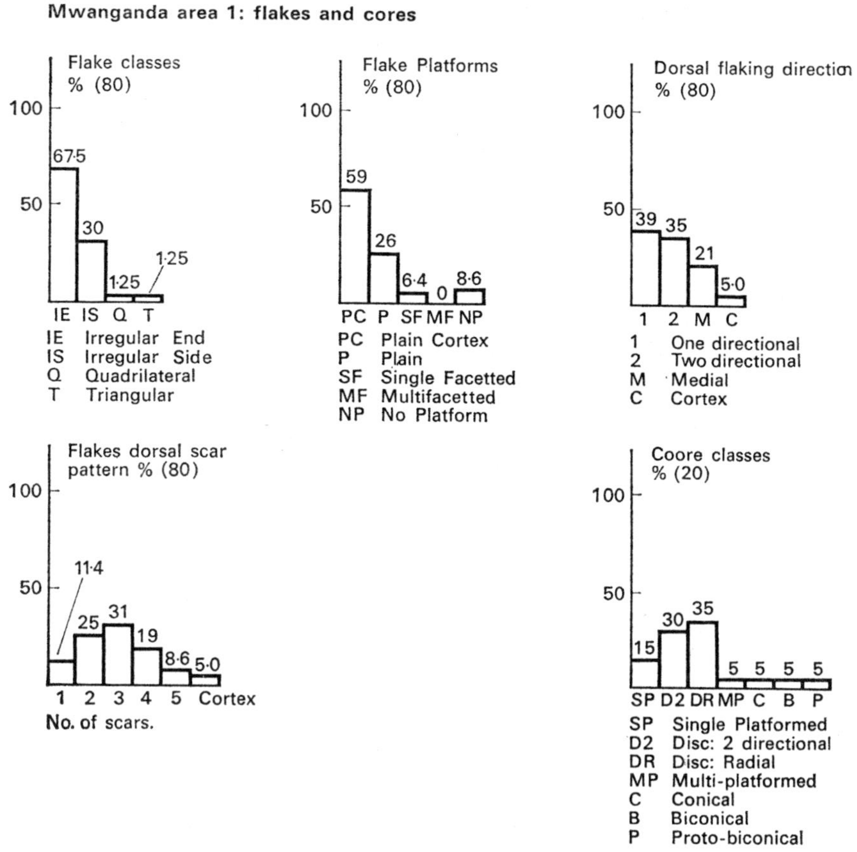

Figure 31 Analysis of flake and core forms: Mwanganda, Area 1

from the fracture surface of the fragment by striking at one or more points on the circumference. Depending on how many flakes are removed, the core (fig. 31) will show a one or two directional, or radial scar pattern – the majority show between two and four scars.

The flake/core dimensions are well seen in figure 34 which demonstrates that there are no flakes in the collection that could not have been struck from the cores at the site. This is in marked distinction to the situation for the later 'Middle Stone Age' aggregates from the Malawi Rift where the cores are quite significantly smaller than the majority of the flakes, indicating re-use of the cores, which were generally prepared by the Levallois or disc core techniques.

That the affinities of the aggregate are not purely Acheulian is suggested by the following characteristics: absence of large cutting tools (handaxes and cleavers), the high

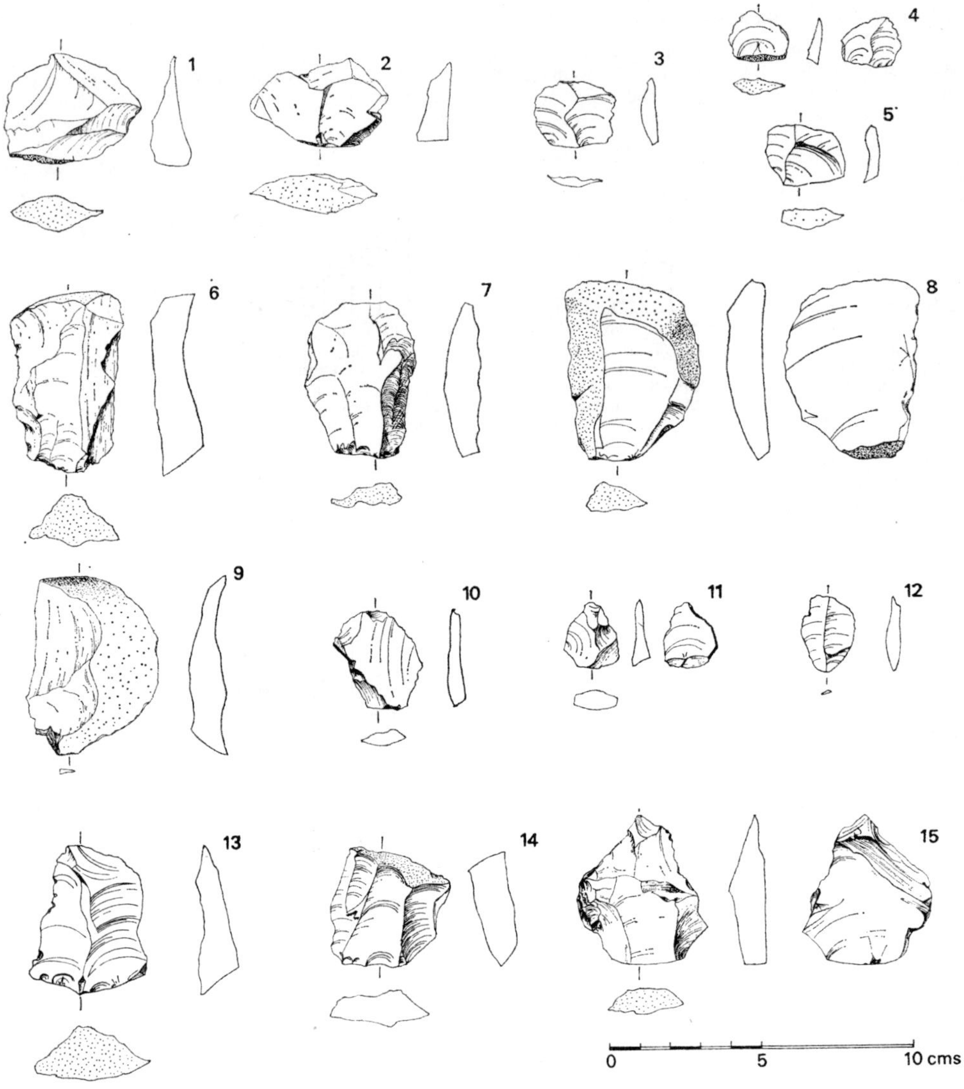

Figure 32 Unmodified side- and end-struck flakes: Mwanganda, Area 1

(2 : 1) end- to side-struck flake ratio (Isaac and Keller 1967) and the relatively flat dorsal faces of some cores. Affinities with the regional 'Middle Stone Age' (or Sangoan) may be indicated by the presence of crude core-axes and the high frequency of concave, notched and denticulate tools. That the assemblage antedates the full development of the regional 'Middle Stone Age' may be indicated by the predominance of the use of the block-on-block and Clacton technique and by the absence of the Levallois or disc core techniques. However, the assessment of the cultural affinities is complicated by the fact that the aggregate may be a distinctive activity facies of whatever industry the Mwanganda Archaeological Occurrence partially represents. It is hoped that geochronometric dates will be forthcoming from the associated carbonates.

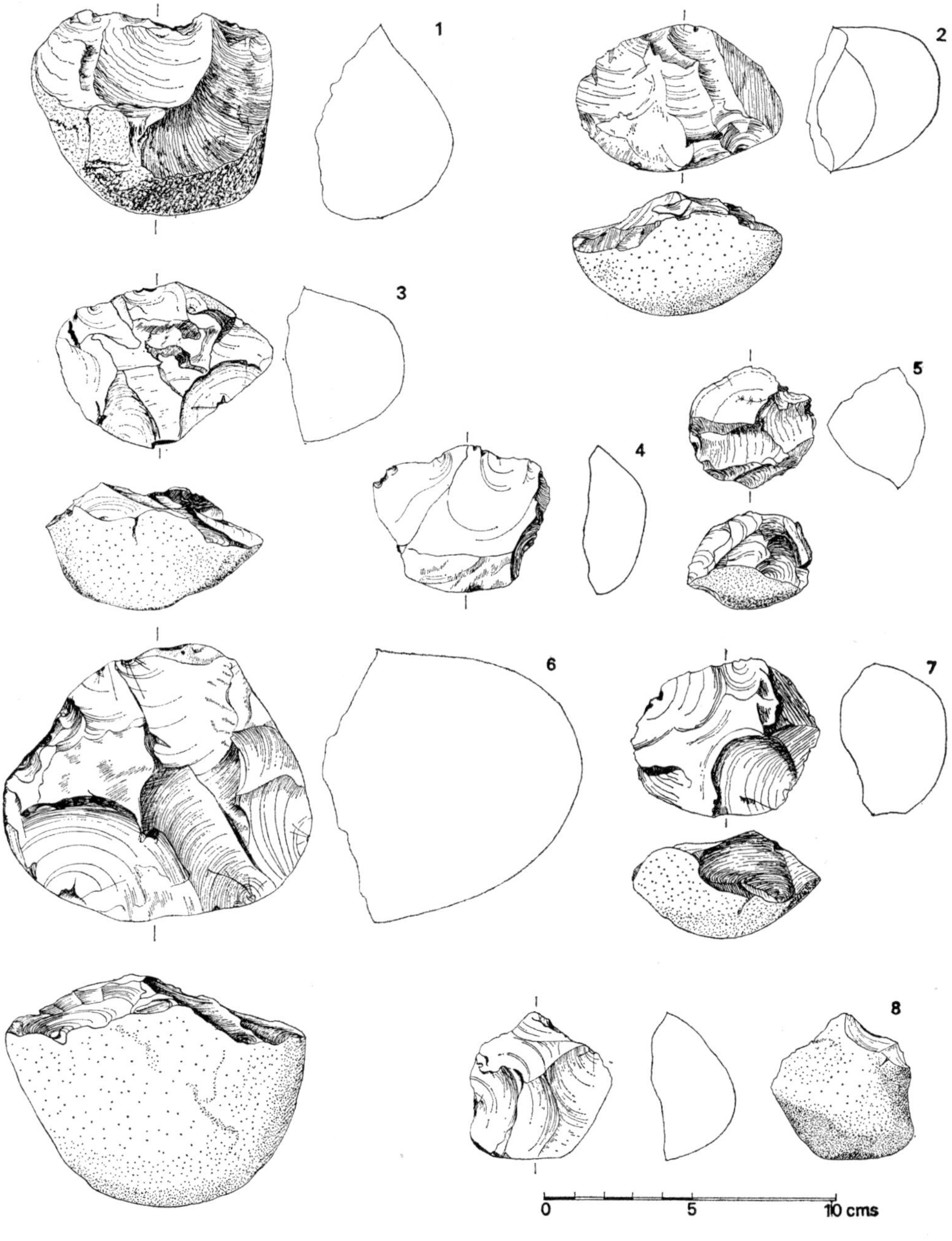

Figure 33 Core forms: Mwanganda, Area 1. *1* and *4*: One directional, single platform. *2* and *3*: Two directional, double platform. *5*: Pseudo-pyramidal. *6–8*: Radially flaked cores

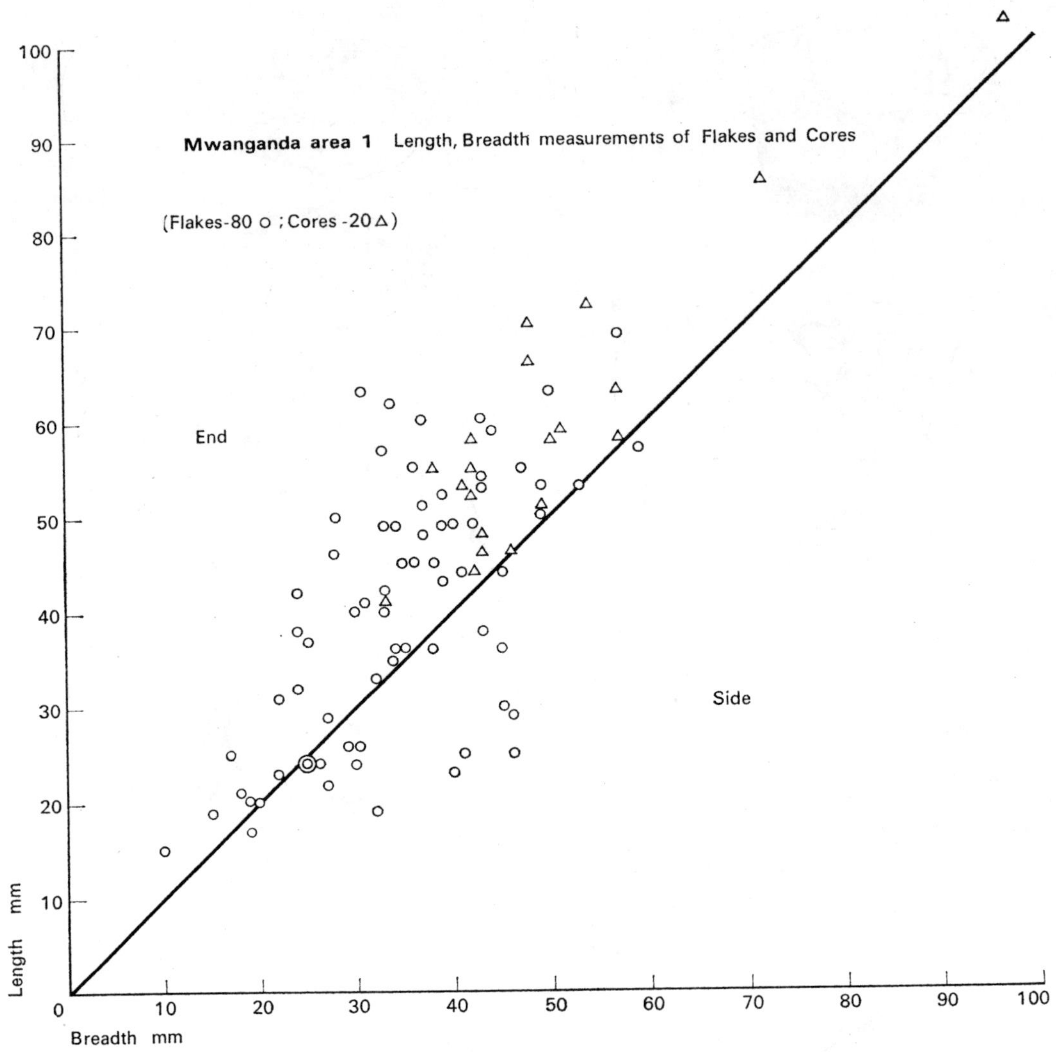

Figure 34 Length/Breadth measurements of flakes and cores: Mwanganda, Area 1

Conclusions

It is pertinent to look for comparable data to those from Mwanganda on the large animal butchery equipment of Pleistocene man. Very little information is yet published. The best comes from the Middle Pleistocene elephant kill sites of Torralba and Ambrona in Spain. In one area at Torralba, Howell found only four flake tools in association with the semi-articulated and unbroken remains of the left side of a large elephant. In another area other broken and unbroken bones of the individual were preserved with charcoal, wood, two cleavers and retouched and waste flakes. Another area produced more extensively broken-up elephant bones from different individuals with a few flake tools (especially side scrapers) and a single cleaver (Howell 1966: 123).

Plate 1 General view of the excavations at Mwanganda's Village, looking south-east. Area 1, where the butchered elephant was found, is the large excavated area in which the men are working. Area 2 lies upslope in the top right-hand corner of the photograph. The deposits of the Lower Chitimwe formation (caliche pebble gravel (Qct 1a)), overlain by the Upper Chitimwe gravel with 'Middle Stone Age' artefacts (Qct 2a) are seen in section filling the gully exposed in the foreground

Plate 2 View looking north over Area 1 showing the easterly part of the disarticulated elephant bone and artefact concentration. The femur is nearest the camera and beyond are the ribs, vertebrae and the skull and mandible fragments

Plate 3 The elephant femur (Area 2) and rib fragment surrounded and underlain by artefacts

Plate 4 Concentration of ribs, thoracic and cervical vertebrae of a hippopotamus excavated in 1968 in the upper part of the Chiwondo formation at Mwimbi, approximately eighteen miles south-south-west of the Mwanganda site. The bones show minimal disturbance prior to burial, though the limbs and head are missing

At Ambrona as many as thirty to thirty-five elephants, and other mammals, are represented and the same kind of artefact and bone occurrences are seen: disarticulated skeletal parts, smashed and complete bones and a low artefact ratio. A bone concentration in the easternmost part of the site, for example, was associated with some half-dozen waste flakes, four flake tools (denticulates, borer, side scraper) and two handaxes (1966: 125). Only 10% of the tools from the 1962 and 1963 excavations at Torralba were large cutting tools and this class comprised only 7·7 % of the lithic equipment on the lower occupation surface at Ambrona (1966: 132–3).

The Upper Acheulian kill site at Lehringen, near Bremen in Germany, yielded, besides the famous wooden spear, only two dozen flint flakes scattered among the bones of the straight-tusked *Hesperoloxodon antiquus*. None of these flakes had been retouched and only a few showed superficial trimming at the butt end (Movius 1950).

On the outskirts of Tomsk in western Siberia at the Upper Pleistocene butchery and kill site of a young mammoth in the loess (Movius 1950: 141, footnote), the broken and splintered bones covered an area 8 × 4 m. and were associated with a single hearth. Many of the bones showed superficial cuts and scraped surfaces but the only artefacts found at the site and made of local material, were nearly 200 blades, flakes and cores, less than 25% of which showed any evidence of use. Again, the absence of retouched forms is significant even though a new assessment of the artefacts in the light of recent studies of edge damage and use patterns might indicate that evidence of utilization is more common than was apparent at the time the discovery was made.

Unretouched artefacts again greatly exceed shaped tools with the single mammoth mandible on the East Gravettian site at Mt Henye in northern Hungary. The mandible was lying in a shallow pit and was associated with seven retouched tools, twenty-two blades and thirty flakes, all unretouched, and three heavier stone fragments (Vértes 1966: 13).

Records of butchery and kill sites from Africa are not so well documented but it would seem that a similar dearth of retouched artefacts exists here also. The earliest are two late Lower/early Middle Pleistocene sites at the Olduvai Gorge. At the top of Bed I in level 6 of the FLK NI site, the nearly complete skeleton of an *Elephas recki* was associated with 123 artefacts consisting of five retouched tools (four choppers and a proto-biface); twenty-three utilized artefacts and ninety-five flakes, fragments and chunks. The skeleton of a nearly complete *Deinotherium* in the base of Bed II at FLK site had with it thirty-nine artefacts consisting of seven flakes, two hammer stones, two choppers, one polyhedron, one discoid, two heavy duty scrapers, one subspheroid, one anvil, six utilized pieces and sixteen manuports (M. D. Leakey, pers. comm.).

The two butchery and living sites at BKII and SHKII from near the top of Bed II at Olduvai have both yielded large numbers of artefacts together with a wide range of Middle Pleistocene genera and species, often represented in large numbers (Leakey 1958). Since, however, there are represented here the results of a number of kills and the artefact assemblage indicates that these sites were both workshops as well as special activity areas, it is not possible to use these data for the present purposes.

Another Upper Acheulian Archaeological Occurrence in the upper part of Bed IV at the HK locality in the main gorge at Olduvai has been interpreted by its discoverer as either a camp or butchery site. In a layer of fine-grained beach sand was found a number of large cutting tools (handaxes and cleavers) together with many unmodified waste flakes, three large cores, spheroids and hammer stones. These were associated with the disarticulated remains of a hippopotamus 'as well as with the bones of a number of other animals'. Only part of the site was excavated but this yielded 459 handaxes and cleavers *in situ* and 93 more eroded on the scree slope. One handaxe was lying adjacent to the hippo jaw (Leakey 1951: 140–2). However, the number of animals represented by the associated fauna suggests that the HK occurrence is a site that was either occupied on several different occasions or on a single occasion for sufficient length of time for it to have served as a home base for more general hunting activities than the butchery of a single hippo. The amount of unmodified waste, as also the large number of handaxes and cleavers would be in keeping with such an interpretation, on the basis of the other evidence to which reference is made in this paper. Here again, therefore, it is unfortunately not possible to isolate the equipment associated with an individual kill.

On one of the lower sand horizons (Sands 4) at the Upper Acheulian site of Isimila in the Southern Highlands Province of Tanzania, a partial skeleton of a hippopotamus, consisting of the ribs and vertebrae, part of the mandible and an incisor, was uncovered. The bones were not greatly dispersed but the skull and limb bones were absent. With the bones were some half a dozen unretouched flakes of quartz and two larger, unworked fragments of mylonite. It is thought that this may represent a kill the missing parts of which were moved away by the hunters (Howell *et al.* 1962: 67, and pers. comm.).

On one of the surfaces (Basal Bed A: Locality I.3) at the Olorgesailie Upper Acheulian site in the Gregory Rift Valley south of Nairobi, part of a disarticulated hippopotamus carcase was found in an area of *c.* 10 × 5 m. The bones comprised parts of the fore and hind limbs, some vertebrae, teeth and skull fragments, and with them, forming part of a single unit, were associated less than one hundred flakes and fragments of artefacts in lava, a few small tools and less than five handaxes (Isaac 1968: 259 and pers. comm.). It seems probable that this is a further instance of butchery practices by Palaeolithic man.

Part of an Upper Acheulian occupation surface, approximately four miles square, excavated by Chavaillon at Garba (Melka Kontoure) fifty miles south of Addis Ababa in Ethiopia (Chavaillon 1967: 60–1) yielded, on the basis of the distribution plot, approximately 296 artefacts. These were mostly large cutting tools (handaxes and cleavers) and spheroids associated with sixty-four fragments of bone – only two of which are of any size, the remainder being small splinters. Many of the cleavers, which are made in obsidian, show use damage of the cleaver edge. This aggregate is associated with a quantity of natural rubble and three large stone blocks. The paucity of bone suggests, at least on this part of the Garba 'floor', that the large cutting tools are not directly related to butchering since, if they were, we would expect considerably more bone to have been preserved.

One enigmatic concentration of bones approximately fifteen feet in diameter was found at the Elandsfontein site north of Cape Town and is presumed to be contemporary with the Upper Acheulian (Fauresmith) horizons. The concentration contained parts of twenty-five antelopes, a zebra and thirteen carnivores (Inskeep and Hendy 1966). No artefacts were present but two or three groups of limb bones were articulated and most of the bones appear to have been complete, though further apart after burial and re-exposure (1966: 113). Clearly, selective agencies had been at work as the percentages of the parts preserved shows, but it is not necessary to invoke human activity to explain this, as Brain's study of Hottentot food middens in South West Africa has recently demonstrated (Brain 1967). The absence of large percentages of deliberately fractured marrow bones, the articulation of some together with the absence of artefacts suggests a 'natural' rather than a human origin for this concentration. The agent may have been a carnivore, although the authors reject this as unlikely and suggest as an alternative the intentional poisoning of a waterhole by man.

The 'pile' of bones, within a six feet diameter, at the waterside site of Kalkbank in the northern Transvaal was associated with a later Pietersburg industry. Here some thirteen different species of animal are represented by 3,619 bone fragments and teeth, and again this site is clearly a living site and not the butchery place of a single animal. The stone artefacts comprise three scrapers, six utilized fragments (irregulars), six unretouched flakes, nineteen cuboids (? hammers), two grindstones and thirty-eight waste fragments (Mason *et al.* 1958: 86).

The only other comparable occurrence we have been able to find from Africa dates probably to the Holocene, although the associated diatoms examined by Cholnoky suggested a lowered evaporation rate and so a late Pleistocene or earliest Holocene age (H. R. MacCalman 1967, and pers. comm.). In the Zoo Park gardens in Windhoek, South West Africa, a butchery site was found in 1961 in which the remains of two disarticulated elephants were associated with a number of Heavy Duty core scrapers, choppers and much Light Duty scraper and flake equipment. I briefly examined the site and the artefacts in 1964 but, as yet, no detailed account has been published or the aggregate analysed. The bones occurred on the edge of, and within, what had once been a small stream course within a marsh resulting from the springs on the ridge above the site. The first elephant was represented by the skull, one tusk, the pelvis and two of the long bones and one isolated limb bone thirty feet lower down the slope. The second animal was found fifty yards lower down the slope again and the parts preserved were a tusk, part of the skull, a femur, vertebrae and, sixteen feet away from these, the mandible and a number more vertebrae and ribs. All these remains were associated with quartz artefacts. Although a radiocarbon date of 5,200 ± 140 years B.P. was obtained from tusk (Robins and Swart 1964: 35) this should be treated with reserve and the assemblage could be older.

From the examples cited above it is apparent that several different patterns can be differentiated among the concentrations of large animal bone and stone artefacts from the Lower Palaeolithic onwards. These may be summarized as follows:

(1) Finds of semi-articulated skeletons where there is minimal evidence of disturbance by either man or animals. A good example of this type of site occurs at Mwimbi, south and west of the Mwanganda site, where, in 1968, the ribcase and vertebrae of a hippopotamus were excavated in the Chiwondo formation (plate 4). Another is, perhaps, the occurrence already referred to from Elandsfontein (Hopefield). The first of these antedates all evidence of human occupation in the Malawi Rift; at the second, conclusive evidence that man was the accumulating agent is lacking.

(2) Partly broken up skeletons of a single animal with only a small degree of bone dispersal and associated with comparatively few stone artefacts. Instances of this kind

are the *Elephas recki* and the Deinotherium remains from the late Lower/early Middle Pleistocene sites of FLK NI and II at Olduvai Gorge; the early Acheulian butchery site at Torralba; the Lehringen elephant and the hippopotamus from the Upper Acheulian horizon at Isimila.

(3) Extensive disarticulation and dispersal of the bones of one, sometimes more than one large animal. These are usually, but not always, found with a comparatively small number of stone artefacts, predominantly Light Duty forms. The Mwanganda Archaeological Occurrence, the Ambrona examples cited, the Olorgesailie hippopotamus and the Windhoek Zoo Park elephants are instances of this kind of site. The Kalkbank butchery site can also probably be included in this category on the basis of the paucity of artefacts, though, since there are thirteen different species of animal represented, it is, in this respect, more typical of the fourth category below.

(4) Multiple kill or 'occupation' sites at which diverse activities were carried on as reflected by the overall area covered by the concentration, the considerable quantities of Large Cutting, Heavy Duty and Light Duty tools and waste which occur in very varying proportions on sites of this kind. Generally bones are broken up and dispersed and a number of different genera, species and individuals, both large and small, are represented. This is, perhaps, the commonest type of site for both Palaeolithic and later times and a number of examples are known. Among those cited are the BKII and SHKII sites at the top of Bed II and the HKIV site in Bed IV at the Olduvai Gorge. Others that may be mentioned here are the DE/89 Horizon B 'occupation' floor at Olorgesailie where numerous Large Cutting tools are found associated with fragmentary remains of horses, bovids, hippos and elephant but mostly with bones of the giant baboon *Sinopithecus*. Preliminary counts of the baboon remains suggest that at least fifty adults and thirteen juveniles are represented (Isaac 1968: 259). The early Acheulian site at Ternifine on the Algerian plateau (Arambourg and Hofstetter 1963; Balout *et al.* 1967) and the STIC quarry at Sidi Abderrahman, Casablanca, Morocco (Biberson 1961: 156–85) are other examples that can probably be included in this category, as can also the Cave of Hearths sequence in the Makapan Valley in the northern Transvaal (Mason 1962: 159–230, 447–53 (appendix by H. B. S. Cooke)). Notable about this category is the diversity of the toolkit, the quantity of waste and the large number of tools that are generally found. Particularly is this so with regard to handaxes and cleavers on the Acheulian sites of this kind.

One further category, or subcategory, may, perhaps, be included, at least in regard to the Acheulian:

(5) 'Occupation' sites with numerous Large Cutting tools together with some Heavy and Light Duty equipment, but very little bone. Of course, it is only possible to take into consideration in this connection those sites where the conditions are such that bone would have been preserved had it been present. Such a site is that at Garba, Melka Kontoure, in Ethiopia. The early Acheulian Archaeological Occurrence at Latamne in northern Syria is another example of this type of site (Clark 1966: 94–6) where the small scraps of bone and isolated teeth that do occur are, perhaps, indicators that the Large Cutting tools are not directly related to butchering practices which included the 'jugging' of a carcase. Again, if these tools were a necessary adjunct to removing the meat from the

carcase of a large animal such as an elephant where the bones are not usually or necessarily broken and the meat may be carried away, it might be expected that they would occur in larger numbers on the sites described as categories two and three above.

The evidence from Mwanganda and the other sites mentioned here, where a single or a minimal number of carcases are present, slight as it is, suggests first, that human butchering practices generally resulted in the disarticulation, dispersal and differential fracture of the bones of the large food animals. It would seem also that they were butchered at the place where they were killed or where the carcase was found.

Secondly, the evidence suggests that Palaeolithic butchering and meat processing equipment consisted predominantly of small numbers of Light Duty tools and cutting flakes and small scraping tools with a few only of larger elements. This large tool element appears to be supplementary rather than primary to the main purpose of the equipment.

Thirdly, it would seem also that little change can be observed in the basic pattern of these occurrences from the Lower Pleistocene right through to Holocene times. Obviously, when more butchery sites and kills of single large animals are excavated and the associated artefact component is precisely known, the degree of variablility through time and between contemporary occurrences will become not only more apparent but more meaningful. Such sites are, however, only one of a number of different activity patterns that are beginning to become manifest in studies of prehistoric hunters and gatherers and it is to be hoped that the future will show increasing attention being paid by African investigators to the recovery of distribution plots and patterning of Archaeological Occurrences from sealed primary context sites in the open.

Acknowledgements

The authors wish to express their grateful thanks to Mr Forward Musukwa, then of Mwanganda Village, the discoverer of the site. They also wish to thank Mrs Barbara Isaac for her drawings of the stone implements and other text figures; Mrs M. D. Leakey for the information concerning the FLK I elephant and the FLK II Deinotherium and for permission to quote this; Miss Rona MacCalman for the information on the Windhoek elephants and for the opportunity to visit the site and examine the artefacts; Professor F. Clark Howell for the details of the Isimila hippo and Professor G. Ll. Isaac for the particulars of the Olorgesailie concentration, for reading the manuscript and for his helpful and valued comments and criticism: this help is most gratefully acknowledged.

6.v.1969

Department of Anthropology
University of California, Berkeley
and
Department of Geological Sciences
Southern Methodist University, Dallas

References

Arambourg, C. and Hoffstetter, R. 1963. Le gisement de Ternifine, I. *Archives de l'Institut de Paléontologie humaine*. Mem. 32.

Balout, L., Biberson, P. and Tixier, J. 1967. L'Acheuléen de Ternifine (Algérie) Gisement de l'Atlanthrope. *L'Anthropologie*. 71, 3–4:217–38.

Biberson, P. 1961. Le Paléolithique inférieur du Maroc atlantique. *Pub. Serv. des Antiquités du Maroc*. 17.

Bishop, W. W. 1963. The later Tertiary and Pleistocene in eastern equatorial Africa. In *African ecology and human evolution*, eds F. C. Howell and F. Bourlière. Chicago. 246–75.

Brain, C. K. 1967. Hottentot food remains and their bearing on the interpretation of fossil bone assemblages. *Scientific papers of the Namib Desert Research Station, Pretoria*. 6, 32:1–7.

Chavaillon, J. 1967. La préhistoire Ethiopienne à Melka Kontoure. *Arqueologia*. Nov./Dec.:56–63.

Clark, J. D. 1966. Further excavations (1965) at the Middle Acheulian occupation site at Latamne, northern Syria: general results, definitions and interpretations. *Annales Archéologiques Arabes Syriennes*. 16, 2:75–113.

Clark, J. D., Haynes, C. V. and Mawby, J. E. In press. Interim report on palaeo-anthropological investigations in the Lake Malawi Rift. *Actes du VIe Congrès pan-africain de Préhistoire et de l'Etude du Quaternaire, Dakar, 1967*.

Howell, F. C. 1966. Observations on the earlier phases of the European Lower Palaeolithic. In *Recent studies in Palaeoanthropology*. eds J. D. Clark and F. C. Howell. *American Anthropologist*. 68.2, pt 2:88–201.

Howell, F. C., Cole, G. H. and Kleindienst, M. R. 1962. Isimila, an Acheulian occupation site in the Iringa Highlands, Southern Highlands Province, Tanganyika. In *Actes du IVe Congrès Panafricain de Préhistoire et de l'étude du Quaternaire*. eds G. Mortelmans and J. Nenquin. *Annales – Series IN – 8° – Sciences Humaines*. Musée Royale de l'Afrique Centrale. Tervuren. 40:43–80.

Inskeep, R. R. and Hendy, B. Q. 1966. An interesting association of bones from the Elandsfontein fossil site. In *Actas del V congreso panafricano de Prehistoria y de Estudio del Cuaternario*, ed. L. D. Cuscoy. II:109–24. Santa Cruz de Tenerife.

Isaac, G. Ll. 1968. Traces of Pleistocene hunters: An East African example. In *Man the Hunter*. eds R. D. Lee and I. DeVore. Chicago. 253–61.

Isaac, G. Ll. and Keller, C. M. 1967. Note on the proportional frequency of side- and end-struck flakes. *South African Archaeological Bulletin*. 23:17–19.

Johnson, N. M. and Blanchard, R. L. 1967. Radiation dosimetry from the natural thermoluminescence of fossil shells. *Am. Mineralogist*. 52:1297–310.

Leakey, L. S. B. 1951. *Olduvai Gorge: a report on the evolution of the handaxe culture in Beds I-IV*. Cambridge.

Leakey, L. S. B. 1958. Recent discoveries at Olduvai Gorge, Tanganyika. *Nature*. 181:1099–1103.

MacCalman, H. R. 1967. The Zoo Park Elephant site, Windhoek. (*1964–5*), ed. E. M. von Zinderen Bakker. In *Palaeoecology of Africa*, Cape Town. 2:102–3.

Mason, R. J. 1962. *The prehistory of the Transvaal.* Johannesburg.

Mason, R. J., Dart, R. A. and Kitching, J. W. 1958. Bone tools at the Kalkbank Middle Stone Age site and the Makapansgat Australopithecine locality, central Transvaal. *South African Archaeological Bulletin.* 13, 51:85–116.

Movius, H. L. 1950. A wooden spear of Third Interglacial age from Lower Saxony. *Southwestern Journal of Anthropology.* 6, 2:139–42.

Robins, P. A. and Swart, E. R. 1964. Southern Rhodesia radiocarbon measurements – I. *Radiocarbon.* 6:31–6.

Vértes, L. 1966. The Upper Palaeolithic site on Mt Henye at Bodrogkereszúr. *Acta Arch. Acad. Sci. Hungaricae.* 18:3–15.

Contributors

James Doran, after five years as a member of a computer research group at Edinburgh University, has recently taken up a research post at the Atlas Computer Laboratory in Berkshire.

F. R. Hodson lectures in prehistory at the Institute of Archaeology, London. His special interest is the Western European Iron Age.

John Graham, an archaeology graduate of University College, Cardiff, is currently a lecturer in the Computer Unit, University of Reading.

Derek Roe is University Lecturer in Prehistoric Archaeology at Oxford University.

C. R. Orton took a degree in mathematics and a diploma in mathematical statistics at Cambridge University. He now works in the Statistical Division of the Ministry of Agriculture, Fisheries and Food.

William L. Rathje took a degree in anthropology at the University of Arizona in 1967. He is now working towards a Ph.D. at Harvard University.

David Peacock is a Research Fellow in the Department of Archaeology at Southampton University.

J. Desmond Clark is Professor of Anthropology at the University of California, Berkeley; **C. Vance Haynes** teaches at the Southern Methodist University, Dallas, Texas.

Notes to Contributors

Manuscripts should not normally exceed 5,000 words in length. They should be typed on good quality quarto paper (i.e. approx. 10 in. × 8 in., or 26 cm. × 21 cm.), using double spacing throughout. Two copies of the manuscript should be submitted, the author retaining another. Manuscripts and other correspondence should be addressed to the Executive Editor – Dr Colin Platt, Faculty of Arts, The University, Southampton, England.

Referencing should follow the modern scientific convention. Footnotes, wherever possible, should be avoided. Bibliographical references, to be included in the text, should list the author's last name, date of publication, and number of page, e.g. (Clark 1952: 211). Where an author's name has been cited already in the text, reference need only be made to the date of publication and page, e.g. (1952: 211). Extended references should be listed alphabetically at the end of the paper, e.g.

Bouard, M. de 1965. La mesure de la résistivité électrique des sols en archéologie. *Annales de Normandie*. 15:461–77.

Clark, J. G. D. 1952. *Prehistoric Europe: the economic basis*. London.

Wace, A. J. B. 1958. Aegean Prehistory: a Review. *Antiquity*. 32:30–4.

Wheeler, R. E. M. 1943. *Maiden Castle*. Oxford.

Text figures, site plans and distribution maps should be drawn on strong paper, white card, or good quality tracing film. The lettering on diagrams should be in the type face Univers (medium weight). This is obtainable on transfer sheets (e.g. 'Letraset') They should measure approximately twice the intended final size (i.e. a published full-page illustration may not exceed 8 in. × $5\frac{5}{16}$ in., or 20·5 cm. × 15·5 cm.) Plates should be printed on glossy paper and should be mounted on thin card. Figures, maps and plates should be titled and numbered.

Each contribution should be accompanied by a brief abstract (100–150 words) summarizing its contents. A short note on individual contributors should also be supplied.

It is important that authors should submit accurate, well-prepared copy ready for the printer. Re-drawing of maps or figures cannot be undertaken by the editors, who may return sub-standard work to contributors for re-presentation in an improved form. Galley proofs of all articles will be sent to authors, who are reminded that these are intended for checking, not re-writing. Failure to return proofs by the required date may lead to the executive editor sending his own corrected proofs to the printer without further reference to the author.

Twenty free offprints will be supplied to authors on publication of a paper. Additional offprints may be purchased at cost price, and should be ordered not later than on the return of corrected proofs.

Abstracts

Doran, J.

Systems theory, computer simulations and archaeology

This paper describes and evaluates recent attempts by archaeologists to make use of concepts drawn from systems theory and cybernetics. It is suggested that these subjects may have less to offer than at first appears, and that the use of computer programs to simulate dynamic systems may be more promising.

Hodson, F. R.

Cluster analysis and archaeology: some new developments and applications

Cluster analysis uses numerical methods to divide a group of units into homogeneous subgroups. Various methods of Cluster Analysis – Single Linkage, Average Linkage, Double Linkage and the k-means approach are demonstrated on a small set of archaeological data and an attempt is made to assess their potential value for archaeologists. The general strategy of clustering is discussed and compared with seriation.

Graham, J. M. and Roe, D. A.

Discrimination of British Lower and Middle Palaeolithic handaxe groups using canonical variates

The problem of discriminating, or distinguishing, between 38 handaxe assemblages is tackled by applying a multivariate statistical method known as canonical analysis. The total of 4,800 handaxes is described by eight variables; these are a combination of direct measurements and ratios developed by Derek Roe for his own study and supplied by him. Three highly significant linear combinations of the original variables, known as canonical variates, were produced by canonical analysis. The scores of the assemblages on two variates were then used to plot them on a single diagram, where distance between sites was representative of the degree of similarity. For ease of reference, a six-fold classification of assemblages is suggested on the basis of the computed statistical results. This intuitive guide agrees well overall with the classification given by Roe.

Orton, C. R.

The production of pottery from a Romano-British kiln site: a statistical investigation

A common way of summarizing archaeological data is to present it as frequency distributions, that is, as tables or graphs classifying the objects concerned according to the magnitude of some common dimension. In this paper some methods of handling such frequency distributions are examined, and a particularly useful statistical test for comparing them (the Kolmogorov-Smirnov test) is described. The assumptions underlying a statistical approach are discussed, together with the nature of the conclusions to be drawn. The whole is illustrated by reference to a study of waster rim sherds from a Romano-British kiln site in Highgate Wood, London.

Rathje, W. L.

Socio-political implications of lowland Maya burials: methodology and tentative hypotheses

This paper employs archaeological data primarily, with ethnographic data as a supplement, to construct and test a diachronic model of Classic Maya socio-political organization. Excavated burial data indicate a change in emphasis within Classic Maya society (A.D. 300–900) from recruitment of political and religious functionaries from the whole Maya population to the recruitment of officials from small ascribed segments of the population. These and other data suggest that one of the factors underlying this change was Classic Maya economic organization and a system involving wealth as a prerequisite for attaining office. Burial data, in addition to providing evidence of this change, furnish a means for testing hypotheses to explain how and why socio-political mobility developed into socio-political stratification.

Peacock, D. P. S.

The scientific analysis of ancient ceramics: a review

Recent scientific work on ceramic fabrics is surveyed in this paper, with particular reference to problems of characterization. All the principal experimental methods are briefly discussed in a non-technical outline, and the archaeological value of petrological and chemical approaches is illustrated with examples drawn from the U.S.A., Western Europe and the USSR. The paper concludes with a consideration of some present problems and possible future developments.

Clark, J. D. and Haynes, C. V.

An elephant butchery site at Mwanganda's Village, Karonga, Malawi, and its relevance for Palaeolithic archaeology

This paper describes a find of associated animal bones and stone artefacts near Karonga in the Malawi Rift. The principal occurrence, Area 1, involved the butchery of a single elephant carcase in late Middle or early Upper Pleistocene times, with some traces in Area 2 of other hunting activities, presumably on different occasions. The elephant bones had been broken and dispersed into three main concentrations.

The geology and archaeology of the site are discussed and the Area 1 assemblage of 314 artefacts analysed. The data from comparable kill sites in Spain, Germany, Siberia, Hungary and various parts of Africa are briefly reviewed. Different activity patterns are distinguishable among them, but they show little basic change from Lower Pleistocene right through to Holocene times.

Index to World Archaeology
Volume One

Index

Index of Contributors

Allen, Harry, *see* Bowler, J. M. *et al.*

Barker, Philip, Some aspects of the excavation of timber buildings Vol. 1, p. 220

Biddle, Martin, and Biddle, Birthe Kjølbye-, Metres, areas and robbing Vol. 1, p. 208

Biddle, Birthe Kjølbye-, *see* Biddle, Martin

Bouard, Michel de, The Centre for Medieval Archaeological Research, University of Caen Vol. 1, p. 61

Boureux, Michel, *see* Rowlett, Ralph M. *et al.*

Clark, J. Desmond, and Haynes, Jr, C. Vance, An elephant butchery site at Mwanganda's Village, Karonga, Malawi, and its relevance for Palaeolithic archaeology Vol. 1, p. 390

Dolley, Michael, Medieval British and Irish coins as dating evidence for the archaeologist Vol. 1, p. 200

Doran, James, Systems theory, computer simulations and archaeology Vol. 1, p. 289

Ehrich, Robert W., *see* Thomas, Homer L.

Evans, J. G., Land and freshwater Mollusca in archaeology: chronological aspects Vol. 1. p. 170

Fagg, Bernard, Recent work in West Africa: new light on the Nok Culture Vol. 1, p. 41

Fleming, Andrew, The myth of the mother-goddess Vol. 1, p. 247

Graham, J. M. (*with a note* by Derek Roe), Discrimination of British Lower and Middle Palaeolithic handaxe groups using canonical variates Vol. 1, p. 321

Han, Mark C., *see* Ralph, Elizabeth K.

Haynes, Jr, C. Vance, *see* Clark, J. Desmond

Hensel, Witold, The origins of western and eastern Slav towns Vol. 1, p. 51

Hodson, F. R., Searching for structure within multivariate archaeological data Vol. 1, p. 90

Hodson, F. R., Cluster analysis and archaeology: some new developments and applications Vol. 1, p. 299

Isaac, Glynn Ll., Studies of early culture in East Africa Vol. 1, p. 1

Kendall, David G., Some problems and methods in statistical archaeology Vol. 1, p. 68

Mate, M. S., Building in ancient India Vol. 1, p. 236

Orton, C. R., The production of pottery from a Romano-British kiln site: a statistical investigation Vol. 1, p. 343

Peacock, D. P. S., The scientific analysis of ancient ceramics: a review Vol. 1, p. 375

Ralph, Elizabeth K., and Han, Mark C., Potential of thermoluminescence in supplementing radiocarbon dating Vol. 1, p. 157

Rathje, William L., Socio-political implications of lowland Maya burials: methodology and tentative hypotheses Vol. 1, p. 359

Roe, Derek, *see* Graham, J. M.

Rowlett, Ralph M., Rowlett, Elsebet S.-J. and Boureux, Michel, A rectangular Early La Tène Marnian House at Chassemy (Aisne) Vol. 1, p. 106

Rowlett, Elsebet S.-J., *see* Rowlett, Ralph M. *et al.*

Sankalia, H. D., Problems in Indian archaeology, and methods and techniques adopted to tackle them Vol. 1, p. 29

Scollar, Irwin, Some techniques for the evaluation of archaeological magnetometer surveys Vol. 1, p. 77

Shawcross, Wilfred, Archaeology with a short, isolated time-scale: New Zealand Vol. 1, p. 184

Thomas, Homer L. and Ehrich, Robert W., Some problems in chronology Vol. 1, p. 143

Ucko, Peter J., Ethnography and archaeological interpretation of funerary remains Vol. 1, p. 262

Index of Subjects

Archaeology with a short, isolated time-scale: New Zealand, Wilfred Shawcross Vol. 1, p. 184

Some aspects of the excavation of timber buildings, Philip Barker Vol. 1, p. 220

Building in ancient India, M. S. Mate Vol. 1, p. 236

The Centre for Medieval Archaeological Research, University of Caen, Michel de Bouard Vol. 1, p. 61

Some problems in chronology, Homer L. Thomas and Robert W. Ehrich Vol. 1, p. 143

Cluster analysis and archaeology: some new developments and applications, F. R. Hodson Vol. 1, p. 299

Discrimination of British Lower and Middle Palaeolithic handaxe groups using canonical variates, J. M. Graham (*with a note* by Derek Roe) Vol. 1, p. 321

An elephant butchery site at Mwanganda's Village, Karonga, Malawi, and its relevance for Palaeolithic archaeology, J. Desmond Clark and C. Vance Haynes, Jr Vol. 1, p. 390

Ethnography and archaeological interpretation of funerary remains, Peter J. Ucko Vol. 1, p. 262

Land and freshwater Mollusca in archaeology: chronological aspects, J. G. Evans Vol. 1, p. 170

Medieval British and Irish coins as dating evidence for the archaeologist, Michael Dolley Vol. 1, p. 200

Metres, areas and robbing, Martin Biddle and Birthe Kjølbye-Biddle Vol. 1, p. 208

The myth of the mother-goddess, Andrew Fleming Vol. 1, p. 247

The origins of western and eastern Slav towns, Witold Hensel Vol. 1, p. 51

Potential of thermoluminescence in supplementing radiocarbon dating, Elizabeth K. Ralph and Mark C. Han Vol. 1, p. 157

Problems in Indian archaeology, and methods and techniques adopted to tackle them, H. D. Sankalia Vol. 1, p. 29

Some problems and methods in statistical archaeology, David G. Kendall Vol. 1, p. 68

The production of pottery from a Romano-British kiln site: a statistical investigation, C. R. Orton Vol. 1, p. 343

Recent work in West Africa: new light on the Nok Culture, Bernard Fagg Vol. 1, p. 41

A rectangular Early La Tène Marnian House at Chassemy (Aisne), Ralph M. Rowlett, Elsebet S.-J. Rowlett and Michel Boureux Vol. 1, p. 106

The scientific analysis of ancient ceramics: a review, D. P. S. Peacock Vol. 1, p. 375

Searching for structure within multivariate archaeological data, F. R. Hodson Vol. 1, p. 90

Socio-political implications of lowland Maya burials: methodology and tentative hypotheses, William L. Rathje Vol. 1, p. 359

Studies of early culture in East Africa, Glynn Ll. Isaac Vol. 1, p. 1

Systems theory, computer simulations and archaeology, James Doran Vol. 1, p. 289

Some techniques for the evaluation of archaeological magnetometer surveys, Irwin Scollar Vol. 1, p. 77